THE PANKHURSTS

Martin Pugh was Professor of Modern British History at Newcastle University until 1999, Research Professor in History at Liverpool John Moores University from 1999 to 2002 and is a fellow of the Royal Historical Society. He has written twelve books on aspects of nineteenth and twentieth century history and is on the board of BBC History Magazine.

ALSO BY MARTIN PUGH

Hurrah for the Blackshirts! Fascists and Fascism in Britain Between the Wars

We Danced All Night: A Social History of Britain Between the Wars

MARTIN PUGH

The Pankhursts

The History of One Radical Family

VINTAGE BOOKS
London

Published by Vintage 2008

8 10 9 7

Copyright © Martin Pugh 2001

Martin Pugh has asserted his right under the Copyright, Designs
and Patents Act 1988 to be identified as the author of this work

First published in Great Britain in hardback in 2001 by
Allen Lane
First published in paperback in 2002 by
Penguin Books

Vintage
Random House, 20 Vauxhall Bridge Road,
London SW1V 2SA

www.vintage-books.co.uk

Addresses for companies within The Random House Group Limited
can be found at: www.randomhouse.co.uk/offices.htm

The Random House Group Limited Reg. No. 954009

A CIP catalogue record for this book
is available from the British Library

ISBN 9780099520436

The Random House Group Limited supports The Forest Stewardship
Council® (FSC®), the leading international forest-certification organisation.
Our books carrying the FSC label are printed on FSC®-certified paper.
FSC is the only forest-certification scheme supported by the leading
environmental organisations, including Greenpeace. Our
paper procurement policy can be found at
www.randomhouse.co.uk/environment

MIX
Paper from
responsible sources
FSC® C016897

Printed and bound in Great Britain by Clays Ltd, St Ives plc

For
Fran, Hannah and Alastair

'It is not right for women, any more than for men, to have characters of tepid milk and water, to be incapable of a divine rage and to be impotent to resist oppression'

Christabel Pankhurst, *The Suffragette*, 10 January 1913

Contents

Illustrations

Acknowledgements

I would like to express my thanks to all those who have helped me in various ways with this book, notably Diane Atkinson; Miss Eveline Bennett; Dr Eugenio Biagini; Gail Cameron (Museum of London); Tish Collins (Marx Memorial Library); Elizabeth Crawfurd; David Doughan, along with his colleagues Sue Gardner, Penny Martin, Christine Wise and Anna Greening at the Fawcett Library; Michael Foot; Sheila Gopaulen (Public Record Office); Professor Brian Harrison; John Humble; Richard Kelly (Manchester Grammar School); Alec Marsh; David Mitchell; Lindsey Muir (Pankhurst Centre, Manchester); Roger Oliver and Mrs Gladys Oliver; and Richard Price (British Library).

I am especially indebted to Julie Gottlieb, Robert Baldock and Duncan Tanner for taking time from their own work to read the chapters for me. John D. Holme very kindly talked to me about his great-aunt, Vera Holme. Dr Piers Brendon generously allowed me to see his notes on some Smyth–Pankhurst correspondence. I owe special thanks to Robert Baldock for the excellent advice which set me on the path leading to this book, to my literary agent, Andrew Lownie, and to Ellah Allfrey and Simon Winder at Penguin. The British Academy's Small Grants in the Humanities also supported my research in the early stages.

I am also grateful to the staff of the following institutions whose papers I have used: Camellia plc, Manchester Local Studies Library, Gateshead Local Studies Library, Leeds University Library, the Mitchell Library Glasgow, the National Library of Scotland, the National Trust (Dyrham Park), John Rylands Library, the British Library Newspaper Library at Colindale, the Family Records Centre, the National Library of Australia, North West Sound Archives, the Scottish Record

Office, the Sydney Jones Library at Liverpool University, the House of Lords Record Office, Edinburgh University Library, and the Newcastle University Inter-Library Loans department, the Museum of London, the Marx Memorial Library, the British Library, the Fawcett Library and the Public Record Office.

I am grateful for permission to reproduce photographs from the Museum of London and the International Institute for Social History, Amsterdam. Every attempt has been made to contact copyright holders. The author and publisher would like to apologize in advance for any inadvertent use of copyright material, and thank the following individuals and organizations who kindly gave permission to make quotations: The National Library of Australia, the *Guardian*, Pearson Education, The British Library, Camellia plc, The House of Lords Record Office, John E. Holme, David Mitchell, The Women's Library, Mrs Christian Quale.

The Pankhurst Family

Richard Marsden Pankhurst m. 1878 Emmeline Goulden
1834–1898   1858–1928

| Christabel Harriette 1880–1958 | Estelle Sylvia 1882–1960 | (unmarried) Silvio Corio | Francis Henry ('Frank') 1884–88 | Adela Constantia Mary 1885–1961 | m. Tom Walsh | Henry Francis ('Harry') 1889–1910 |

| Richard Keir Pethick 1927– | Richard 1918– | Sylvia 1920– | Christian 1922– | Nancy Ursula 1924– | Faith Hope 1926– |

Introduction

The Pankhursts are at one and the same time very familiar and yet rather elusive. Emmeline Pankhurst invariably emerged as the leading woman of the Millennium from the many surveys conducted during the late 1990s. In her role as an Edwardian hunger-striker in the fight for women's votes she gave us one of the enduring images of the twentieth century. In spite of this, one looks in vain for a serious biography of her. Even the names of her family members are frequently confused; the press often refers to an entirely non-existent 'Emily Pankhurst', for example.

For many readers, the Pankhursts come as a shock on close inspection, for the explosive mixture of idealism, self-sacrifice and strategic insight that enabled its members to contribute so notably to national life also made them ruthless, high-handed and self-righteous. They formed what we would nowadays recognize as a rather dysfunctional family. Yet for some years now we have been encouraged by pundits, prime ministers and large sections of the press to believe in the superiority of 'Victorian Values', in the notion of the big, happy Victorian–Edwardian family, and in the decline of parenting skills during the last three generations. To examine Victorian families in any depth is to be thoroughly disabused of such simplistic notions. The consequences of Victorian family life in the shape of the emotional scars borne by the children of the era are too extensive to miss. We must recognize, therefore, that Richard and Emmeline Pankhurst cannot be separated from the era in which they lived. Though Radicals and rebels in some respects, they reflected more of the conventional thinking of middle-class Victorians than they would have cared to admit. This meant, among other things, regarding children somewhat narrowly as potential adults; it also meant breaking up families with an abandon which we would regard as callous. To this must be added a further element. It is a platitude that even routine political careers are detrimental to family life. How much more damaging, then, is the pursuit of a great, all-consuming crusade? Even the most saintly figures have, often unconsciously, forced their immediate relations to suffer for their principles and ambitions; consider, for example, the impact of Gandhi's protracted struggle to free Indians from the grip of the British Raj upon his wife and eldest son. 'It is just and right that women should honour [Emmeline]', wrote Adela in the 1930s, 'for if we lost her as a mother, they gained her as a political leader.' We need to temper the understandable bitterness expressed by Adela and Sylvia with some understanding of the context of Emmeline's life and with sympathy for her plight in the long years of widowhood after 1898 spent coping with four children and financial insecurity. Emmeline's family was disrupted by the untimely deaths of Richard, of four-year-old Frank and of twenty-year-old Harry. Her *second* family of four girls, whom she adopted in a fit of patriotism in the First World War, also broke up in the 1920s. In 1914 she ruthlessly engineered a rupture with Sylvia, who became an unmarried mother, and with Adela, who lost all direct contact once she had been expelled to Australia. As a result Emmeline never saw her grandchildren and she died in comparative poverty in 1928. Thus her life was a mounting personal tragedy played out against the background of her achievements in the public sphere.

But the question remains why such a famous family has been so neglected by biographers. Emmeline herself produced the unrevealing, ghost-written *The Story of My Life* in 1914, and Sylvia published *The Life of Emmeline Pankhurst* in 1935, which added little to what was already known. After that, nothing. In the course of my own work I have been assured by several publishers, keen to publish Pankhurst biographies, that female authors have recoiled from the politics and personalities of both Emmeline and Christabel, a claim corroborated by the fact that the books which have appeared have been notably hostile. Part of the problem consists in the difficulty in explaining exactly where the Pankhursts stand in relation to the modern women's movement. This might seem obvious because of the lasting inspiration they gave to women (and men) to fight gender inequality and injustice. However, Emmeline, Christabel and Sylvia all became both disappointed with the results of winning the vote and detached from the women's movement. Christabel even went so far as to repudiate the whole suffrage cause after 1920. Inevitably there has been some reaction to the Pankhursts' dramatic ideological shifts, especially the pronounced move to the right by Emmeline and Christabel, which appears eccentric from the perspective of the modern women's movement. This helps to explain why Sylvia has received much more attention in recent years; not only her feminism and her consistently left-wing views, but her opposition to racism, remarkable for someone born in 1882, marks her out as a much more recognizably modern figure than other members of her family.

In addition, writing on the Pankhursts has been inhibited by straightforward empirical obstacles. Though huge quantities of material exist relating to the public side of their lives, their private lives are less well documented. Pankhurst correspondence is scattered in small pockets across many collections, but there is no large single archive. Their peripatetic lives and lack of a secure home base militated against the survival of private letters. Moreover, what does survive often deals with political activities and arrangements rather than with their private thoughts and emotions. With their genius for tactics, leadership and decisive action, the Pankhursts were not particularly reflective or introspective people; they did not commit their thoughts to intimate diaries, and Emmeline detested writing in any shape or form. Though this book has drawn usefully on lengthy interviews with former suffragettes, it must be borne in mind that close associates, such as Grace Roe, who saw it as her duty to defend the reputation of Christabel against both hostile writers and other family members, learned their lines backwards and were reluctant to reveal anything beyond a certain point.

The proximate origins of the controversy over the Pankhurst family, which remains lively even today, lie in the publication of Sylvia's monumental account in 1931. Though the book has rightly influenced many subsequent writers, *The Suffragette Movement* suffered from a three-fold bias: it distorted the long-term picture by minimizing the role of the earlier suffrage movement to the benefit of the militants; it exaggerated the role of the Pankhurst family and neglected those who disagreed with them; and above all it antagonized the followers of Emmeline and Christabel by what they saw as excessively critical treatment of them – which was interpreted as Sylvia's revenge for the slights she had suffered from her family. Despite pressure to offer an 'official' version, Christabel published nothing, but after her death a volume of memoirs was discovered. However, *Unshackled* (1959) proved to be a rather wooden account which stuck closely to a propagandist view of the suffragette campaign as an unbroken series of triumphs over malign and dim-witted opponents. No one entered the minefield until David Mitchell produced *The Fighting Pankhursts* in 1967 and *Queen Christabel* in 1977. All subsequent writers stand in his debt for the immense amount of work he did in recovering material from people who knew the Pankhursts, especially during the post-1920 period. However, Mitchell's biography of Christabel has been universally regarded as far too hostile and as insufficiently grounded in the historical background. He also became caught in the crossfire generated by earlier publications, leading to an acrimonious correspondence with Miss Grace Roe whom he accused, along with Enid Goulden Bach (Emmeline's sister), of obstructing his work and that of other writers. He believed that the surviving suffragettes wanted an account of the cause which would effectively displace Sylvia's by offering a sympathetic view of Emmeline and Christabel, and that to this end they co-operated with Antonia Raeburn over her book, *The Militant Suffragettes* (1973), and hoped that the late Jill Craigie, who also adopted a pro-Christabel view and to whom some of her letters were given, would publish a further account on these lines. Fresh controversy broke out following the publication of the first biography of Sylvia Pankhurst by Patricia Romero in 1987. This provoked an academic article by Sylvia's daughter-in-law, Rita Pankhurst, who argued that the book 'bore little resemblance to the person to whom Richard [Sylvia's son] had been close for thirty-four years and whose house I had shared for the last four years of her life'('Sylvia Pankhurst in Perspective', *Women's Studies International Forum*, 11, 3, 1988). The burden of the charge was the large number of inaccuracies in the book, the general hostility which led Romero to disparage Sylvia's work, and the lack of familiarity with the political context in which she operated. Subsequently Dr Richard Pankhurst published *Sylvia Pankhurst: Artist and Crusader* (1979) which relied heavily on his mother's writings, but presented a valuable portrait of her as more than a one-dimensional political figure. Barbara Winslow's *Sylvia Pankhurst: Sexual Politics and Political Action* (1996) was essentially a study of her public work rather than a biography and stopped short of her famous anti-Fascist campaigns in the 1930s. And in 1999 Mary Davis published *E. Sylvia Pankhurst: A Life in Radical Politics*, intended very much as a discussion of her ideas, not as a biography.

The present biography differs from its predecessors by taking account of the perspective of the forgotten Pankhurst daughter – Adela – whose papers are now available at the National Library of Australia and who has been the subject of a short biography by Verna Coleman, *Adela Pankhurst: The Wayward Suffragette 1885–1961* (1996). Emmeline's second, adopted family also gains a fresh perspective as a result of my correspondence with Miss Eveline Bennett.

Though well documented, the suffragette campaign has hitherto been seen through a fairly narrow range of sources. This biography makes full use of the papers in the Public Record Office and the Scottish Record Office, closed until the 1980s and still surprisingly little used, to show the extent to which the state suppressed the movement before 1914. One by-product of official suppression is the Pankhursts' reliance on North America, both as a refuge from British authority and as a source of funds. The book also reveals the extraordinary talent of the Pankhursts as fund-raisers and their close links with commercial interests. It has not previously been recognized that, despite its reputation for making a frontal assault on the British Establishment, in practice the suffragette campaign was well integrated into the Establishment on which it depended for its resources, notably money and personnel. I have also drawn attention to the importance of the network of personal friendships in sustaining the Edwardian suffragettes and the women's movement in general – something which has usually been avoided because of a reluctance to recognize lesbian relationships in a sympathetic way.

However, there was much more to the Pankhursts than the campaign to enfranchise women. They demonstrated a remarkable talent for reinventing themselves, as indeed they had to after 1918. For the first time this biography shows the extent of their role as representatives of the British Government during the First World War, notably through Emmeline's visit to Russia in 1917, which is documented in the largely unknown eye-witness account by Jessie Kenney. I have endeavoured to explain the bewildering ideological twists and turns of their lives, in particular Emmeline and Christabel's move from left to right, Christabel's subsequent repudiation of politics in favour of Second Adventism in the 1920s, and Adela's dramatic shift from Socialism to her flirtation with Fascism in inter-war Australia. By comparison, Sylvia's evolution from suffragism and Socialism to Communism and anti-Fascism, culminating in her fight to save Ethiopia from Mussolini's invasion after 1935, seems to represent a rare strand of consistency with the Victorian Radicalism of Richard Pankhurst.

I

Radical Manchester (1858–78)

'The very stones of Manchester might have cried out to [Christabel] how political reforms were gained, for the blood of the Chartists and Irish Rebels had flowed over them in days not long gone by.'
Adela Pankhurst, 'The Philosophy of the Suffragette Movement', 1934

On the evening of 19 February 1904, Manchester's Radicals packed the Free Trade Hall to witness history in the making. The historic venue, the issue under discussion, the striking personalities involved – all combined to ensure a memorable event. Built in 1856, the Free Trade Hall was a confident political statement, ornately expressed in the Lombard-Venetian style of architecture, by the city's commercial classes. The Hall symbolized their triumph over the landed aristocracy on securing the repeal of the Corn Laws in 1846, finally opening the way to free trade and to the prosperity of mid-Victorian Britain. For decades thereafter any political party or cause that wished to be taken seriously tried to fill the Free Trade Hall. On this particular evening the stage was held for an hour and a half by a pink-faced, slightly stooping, 30-year-old politician notable for his grandiloquent turn of phrase and distinct lisp. Winston Churchill, lately notorious for his escape from a Boer gaol during the war in South Africa, was relaunching his political career with an attack on the Tory advocates of tariff reform and a resolution tailored to his Liberal audience, affirming the meeting's 'unshakeable belief in the principles of Free Trade'. Churchill was in the process of ditching the Conservative Party as it lurched to the right during the Edwardian years; and where better to do this than in the citadel of free trade? Before long the Liberals of North West Manchester, in which constituency the Free Trade Hall stood, were to adopt him as their candidate.[1]

The February rally offered a perfect means of smoothing Churchill's transition from one party to another. *Almost* perfect. For at the conclusion of the speech a 24-year-old woman, as pink and moon-faced as the prospective candidate, rose from her seat on Churchill's platform to propose an amendment to the resolution on free trade by the addition of a sentence about votes for women. The chairman, irritated and flustered, declined to accept it, and, amid loud cries of 'Chair', the woman eventually withdrew. Subsequently Christabel Pankhurst felt she had given way too easily, but there would be many more opportunities to perfect her technique. At least she had proved equal to the occasion; and she had demonstrated a precocity, a sense of timing and an awareness of the value of publicity equal to Churchill's own. Christabel even shared with her victim a disinclination to allow loyalty to party to override her belief in a cause. At this point in 1904, as Churchill was abandoning his Tory allegiance for the sake of free trade, Christabel was in the throes of repudiating the left-wing traditions in which her parents had brought her up.

Manchester was the shock city of mid-nineteenth-century Britain.[2] Sustained by the spread of cotton manufacture and the commercial wealth it generated, the town had steadily sucked in migrant communities from its rural hinterland as well as Irish, Jewish and Welsh people throughout the late eighteenth and early nineteenth centuries. In 1831, its population had stood at 142,000; by 1852, it reached a quarter of a million. Despite this, Manchester was by no means the biggest industrial town at the time. Yet it was not simply size that seemed to contemporaries to make Manchester a phenomenon, but the combination of economic change, social tension and political innovation that it represented. While the cotton trade boasted previously unheard-of rates of growth, it also remained subject to sharp fluctuations as exuberant manufacturers flooded the markets with more goods than they could sell. The city's crucial dependence on the export trade for its output and on imports for its raw materials also exposed Manchester's economy to the vicissitudes of international events. Perhaps the most dramatic example came during the early 1860s when the outbreak of civil war in the United States interrupted supplies of cotton and effectively threw the whole region into unemployment and depression. Even in steadier periods the town presented the alarming spectacle of a population crowded into hastily constructed houses in unplanned streets, notorious for violent disturbances and challenges to the forces of law and order. Intrigued by the heady mixture of political and social change, novelists, pundits and polemicists succumbed to the town's attraction during the 1830s and 1840s, convinced that to understand Manchester was to see what the future held for industrial society. Here Benjamin Disraeli found material for his graphic picture of Britain as a society split into 'Two Nations' and dangerously adrift from the sense of duty and loyalty that kept rich and poor united. For Alexis de Tocqueville, Manchester offered some indications as to the success of the pioneering English attempt to reconcile rapid economic growth with political stability. Friedrich Engels predicted that the increasing immiseration of the workers would generate greater class consciousness and end in social revolution. Even Elizabeth Gaskell, author of *North and South* and *Mary Barton*, earned a reprimand from the *Manchester Guardian* for displaying a 'morbid sensitivity to the condition of the operatives'.

Yet what gave Victorian Manchester its cutting edge was not simply the living conditions of its workers but rather the pretensions of its confident, expanding middle class. In the early decades of the century this middle class had felt just as excluded from influence in national life as working men and women. In the years following the end of the wars with Napoleon in 1815, the manufacturers bitterly resented aristocratic control of government in London as symbolized by the imposition of the Corn Laws – duties levied on imported grain. These punitive taxes were blamed for keeping the price of bread artificially high and, by extension, raising employers' own costs by generating pressure for higher wages. In the view of many employers, the Corn Laws represented rule by an effete landed aristocracy defending its vested interests at the expense of thrusting entrepreneurs such as themselves who were ultimately the architects of Britain's national prosperity. In due course these men developed a programme and a political creed which Disraeli famously dubbed 'The Manchester

School'.[3] No other English town gave its name to a political tradition in this way. Nor did any other local journal, apart from the *Manchester Guardian*, manage to make the transition to the status of a national newspaper. These were symptoms of the importance attached to the city's politics and of the pretensions of Manchester Radicalism during the Victorian and Edwardian periods. Its leaders were inclined to disregard London as a mere seat of pomp and privilege hampered by the deference and apathy of its working population. In the sphere of politics and ideas, so contemporaries had it, Manchester set the agenda.

Certainly from 1815 onwards Manchester found itself at the centre of political controversy and political change. Before 1832, most middle-class men had been excluded from the electorate as much as working men, and in the aftermath of the defeat of the French the two classes made common cause by forming radical societies and by petitioning Parliament to extend the vote.[4] But their activities were often interpreted by the authorities, still shaken by the revolutionary period, as subversive rather than reformist. At a rally held in August 1819 at St Peter's Fields in Manchester, where 60,000 people gathered to demand the vote, the local magistrates panicked and called out the volunteers to disperse the crowds. The volunteers, however, had to be rescued by professional cavalrymen, who killed eleven of the demonstrators and injured hundreds more in their heavy-handed attempts to restore order. This incident, dubbed the 'Peterloo Massacre' in an ironic reference to the Battle of Waterloo, passed into Radical history as a symbol of the oppressive methods of the traditional political elite.

As a result of the passage of the Great Reform Act of 1832, employers and professional men won the Parliamentary vote. This, however, only served to accentuate the politicization of the northern towns. Workers felt betrayed by the middle classes and often campaigned for further reforms under the auspices of the Chartist Movement during the 1840s. Moreover, the 1832 reform led to the introduction of elected municipal authorities for the first time, and in 1838 Manchester became incorporated under the 1835 Act. This led to regular competition in the elections for the new council, intensifying political organization among the middle class and fostering local pride in schemes of improvement for the town. Some of the Manchester Radicals, however, had their eye on the wider scene. In 1838 they established a new pressure group, the Anti-Corn Law League, whose object was to sweep away the import duties and all the restrictions which still hampered the expansion of British manufacturing. The League was very much the product of Manchester, deriving 90 per cent of its funds from the town and surrounding district in the initial years. In its day the League was the most innovative and formidable political machine in the country. Its leaders, Richard Cobden and John Bright, became members of Parliament for neighbouring Stockport and Manchester respectively. Their success in repealing the Corn Laws in 1846, though by no means simply the result of the influence of the League, gave them an enduring prestige and was widely interpreted as a signal triumph for the Manchester School in British national politics; for much of the remainder of the century their ideas set the course for Victorian Liberalism. The construction of the Free Trade Hall at a cost of £40,000 in 1856 gave concrete expression to this northern pride and northern Radicalism.

Ultimately the years between 1846 and 1867 proved to be the peak of Manchester's influence. Those contemporaries who had expected Manchester Radicalism to pioneer a further revolution proved to have been mistaken. This was partly because many of the wealthy and individualistic businessmen who had sustained earlier campaigns gradually became part of the political and social status quo and began to take pride in what had been achieved rather than to demand further change. In 1853 Manchester achieved the status of a city. When Queen Victoria visited in 1851 she noted with pleasure that the immense and enthusiastic crowds were sufficiently well-behaved to require no barriers to restrain them. Yet if Manchester Radicalism came to terms with the values and institutions of the national system, it retained for many years its political status and pretensions. Right up to Edwardian times it was regarded as the cockpit of British politics. Senior and ambitious politicians were attracted to the city to spearhead their parties' campaigns and in the process to promote their own careers. This was why Winston Churchill had seized so eagerly his chance to represent North West Manchester from 1906 to 1908. The Conservative leader and prime minister, Arthur Balfour, sat for East Manchester until his defeat in 1906; and his successor, Andrew Bonar Law, found it worthwhile to tackle a constituency in the city in 1910. In these years, just as in the 1840s, the great controversies over tariffs and free trade were being fought out on the platforms and street corners of Manchester.

It was from this exuberant, Radical and self-confident milieu that the Gouldens and the Pankhursts emerged on to the national stage. The Goulden family epitomized the combination of self-made entrepreneurialism with Radical politics that was so characteristic of mid-Victorian Manchester. Emmeline's father, Robert Goulden, had started life as an errand boy in a local factory, worked his way up to become a junior partner, and eventually managed a calico printing and bleaching works of his own. Little is known of Robert's parents except through the stories passed down to their great-grandchildren.[5] They were both humble cotton operatives of Irish origin. According to Sylvia Pankhurst's account, her great-grandfather had spent some years at sea after becoming a victim of the press gang. He had taken part in the famous meeting at St Peter's Fields in 1819, where he had fled from the cavalry and narrowly escaped with his life by hiding in a cellar. These experiences evidently fed Goulden's appetite for politics, for he and his wife, Mary, subsequently joined the Anti-Corn Law League; their membership cards were proudly preserved in the family.[6]

Robert, their only son, married Sophia Jane Quine, the daughter of a farmer from the Isle of Man, who bore him five sons and five daughters. They maintained the Manx connection with regular holidays at a house in Douglas Bay. After an early struggle Robert Goulden prospered and managed to maintain his large family in some style. During the 1850s he became a partner and set up his home and business at Seedley, a scattered rural settlement on the edge of Pendleton, itself no more than a village on the western side of Salford. The modest-sounding 'Seedley Cottage' was, in fact, a substantial white house set in large gardens with Robert's printing works and several reservoirs immediately adjacent to it. All around stretched a landscape of fields and farms punctuated by a few large properties including Seedley House, Buile Hall and Clay Hall. One surmises that Robert Goulden took some pleasure in intruding his noisome business into the midst of the landed gentry whose politics he opposed so strongly.

Life at Seedley was a fine blend of industrial innovation and traditional country comforts. Jane Goulden presided over a large, and almost self-sufficient, mid-Victorian household. She grew vegetables and fruit, churned butter, bottled jam and pickles and baked bread and cakes. By the 1880s rows of terraced houses had appeared on three sides of Seedley Cottage, but even then the place retained something of its rural outlook. Sylvia recalled a happy, lively household, the large gardens, spacious rooms and an abundance of relatives. For her generation Christmas at Seedley was a wonderful time, especially as the four aunts and five uncles of the young Pankhursts evidently threw themselves into games and theatricals. In one performance of *Cinderella*, Christabel played the prince and Sylvia Cinderella, while two uncles arranged themselves as an elephant for her to ride upon.[7] Even allowing for the warm glow cast on Seedley by Sylvia's later, more troubled life, it must have been a happy, secure and comfortable enclave of Victorian domesticity.

The theatrical talent with which the Goulden uncles were endowed evidently passed down through several generations and was to be an asset to Emmeline and her daughters in their public careers. Robert Goulden himself proved to be an enthusiastic amateur actor, so much so that he acquired his own theatre, the Prince of Wales, in Salford where he played leading parts in Shakespearian plays. He was clearly a versatile and talented individual, a successful entrepreneur but also an idealistic politician and apostle of self-improvement who took advantage of the library and lectures of the Athenaeum Society. Few of the classic Liberal causes passed him by. He supported Parliamentary reform and free trade, and opposed slavery and imperialistic wars. One result was that his family keenly espoused the cause of the North during the American Civil War in the 1860s even though, in view of Robert's reliance on imported cotton, his business interests pointed to support for the Confederacy.

As a child, Emmeline Goulden's outlook was shaped by her grandparents' Radical past and by both Robert and Jane's participation in current controversies. Born on 14 July 1858, she was their second child and eldest daughter. With her shining black hair, violet-blue eyes, high cheekbones and beautiful skin which had 'a kind of velvety bloom', Emmeline impressed contemporaries as a loveable and very feminine girl.[8] How far her mature attitudes and characteristics were moulded by her early upbringing is a matter for speculation. Later, there were suggestions that her feminism had been kindled by her resentment of the favouritism supposedly shown to her brothers. But this is almost certainly a misreading of her upbringing. From an early age Emmeline had been set an example of female leadership. Her mother, according to Adela Pankhurst's account, was 'a handsome, imperious woman whose word was law to her husband and her sons. She had her own opinions about everything she understood and expressed them freely.'[9] She was even reported to have interfered in her husband's business to prevent the practice of searching the women employed in his mills. As for Emmeline's brothers, they were 'the most sweet-natured men it is possible to imagine and in their households the women certainly struck the dominant note'.

As the eldest girl in a large family Emmeline inevitably took on responsibilities for her younger siblings, though this almost certainly had the effect of accentuating her own status as a near-adult in the family. Robert reportedly once remarked 'What a pity she wasn't a lad', a comment which reflected Victorian assumptions and yet revealed how highly he rated his daughter's abilities and how proud he was of her.[10] Emmeline seems to have stood out among her large family from an early age. It was claimed that she learnt to read at the age of three, which probably accounts for her excellent spelling; she read the classic improving works, including John Bunyan's *Pilgrim's Progress* and Carlyle's *The French Revolution*, but preferred French novels, and though she played the piano she refused to practise regularly. In short, Emmeline was a talented and beautiful girl to whom things came easily, but she was also a little wayward and inclined to get her own way. To explain her later feminism as a reaction to the severity of her Victorian parents would be a caricature of them and a misrepresentation. The Gouldens took the trouble to send their daughter to a school in France well-known for teaching sciences and book-keeping to girls. In fact, they allowed her to spend much of her time between the ages of fourteen and nineteen in France pursuing her own interests rather than studying. It would probably be nearer the truth to say that Emmeline was slightly indulged by her parents; she was certainly the apple of her father's eye, and not surprisingly she soon acquired the characteristics of an eldest child in being fully aware of her own importance in the family. Throughout her life Emmeline sought love and attention, and on the whole felt confident about receiving it. Inevitably there was another side to the coin; as a favourite child slightly elevated above her large family, she never knew what it was to be teased and brought down to earth by her brothers and sisters. As a result Emmeline was apt to be rather careless of the feelings of her own children later in life.

It would, therefore, be implausible to argue that she was driven towards feminism by a deep personal sense of grievance or inequality. Indeed, wider analysis of the late-Victorian generation of feminist activists has gone a long way to undermining the idea that they reacted negatively to their family circumstances. On the contrary, many women were led towards active work for women's causes by the positive influence of their fathers, in particular, recognizing their daughters' abilities and potential.[11] This certainly seems to have been the case with Emmeline. Though the Gouldens were by no means advocates of female emancipation, they were alive to her talents, willing to support her, and ready to involve her in matters that more conventional couples would have regarded as falling within the male and adult sphere. It is relevant that Jane set her daughter an example of involvement in political activity and emerged as a personality in her own right in the Goulden household, not merely as Robert's housekeeper.

Three political issues particularly impressed the young Emmeline. As her father sat on the Manchester Committee set up to welcome Henry Ward Beecher, one of the leading advocates of negro emancipation, she acquired an early sympathy for the former slaves of North America. *Uncle Tom's Cabin*, the famous novel by Harriet Beecher Stowe, was read and discussed by Jane Goulden and her children. One of Emmeline's tasks was to collect pennies in a 'lucky bag' to help the newly freed slaves. She also became acutely aware of the struggle for national liberation in Ireland, a cause which was to exercise a major influence on her own tactics in the women's suffrage campaign after 1903. In 1867, when she was nine, two Fenian leaders, arrested in Manchester, were rescued from a prison van in a desperate attack that resulted in the death of a policeman. The three men responsible, who became known as the 'Manchester Martyrs', were publicly hanged in the prison which Emmeline and her elder brother, Walter, passed each day on their way to school. So popular were the executions that part of the prison wall had to be knocked down to allow people to crowd in for the spectacle. Afterwards Emmeline shuddered in horror every time she walked past the rebuilt wall. During the late 1860s Manchester also became the scene of one of the earliest campaigns for women's suffrage, and at fourteen Emmeline returned home from school one day to find her mother preparing to attend a suffrage meeting addressed by Lydia Becker in the city.[12] Jane had no hesitation in agreeing to Emmeline, satchel in hand, accompanying her to hear the arguments.

It was at this stage in his daughter's life that Robert Goulden made what was in many ways the most lasting contribution to Emmeline's outlook on life. He visited France on business from time to time, and, in 1872, when Emmeline was just fourteen, he decided to take her to Paris in order to study at the École Normale in Neuilly, a pleasant suburb of the French capital. While a gentle introduction to the culture and language of France often formed part of the 'finishing' process for upper-class girls, it was less usual for the daughters of self-made provincial manufacturers, and suggests an element of social ambition on Robert's part, as well as a recognition of Emmeline's precocity. As a result she spent several lengthy periods between the ages of fourteen and nineteen in France. Exposure to a foreign country at this stage in life is invariably a major, formative influence and, as an imaginative, romantically inclined teenager, Emmeline responded enthusiastically to the history, culture and language of the new country. Indeed, she found it so liberating by comparison with her life back in Manchester that she did her best to prolong the experience indefinitely. Not that Emmeline's formal education advanced noticeably in Paris, despite the school's very progressive approach to the education of girls. Her health was pronounced too poor to permit sustained school work, though there seems to have been nothing wrong with her – it was wholly characteristic of nineteenth-century medical opinion that education placed too much strain on girls – and as a result she was permitted to spend much of her time exploring Paris and reading French novels in a desultory way. In fact, Emmeline never acquired systematic working habits, nor did she place much importance on formal education for girls, as was to become evident later when her own daughters grew up.

However, France left its enduring mark upon her. Emmeline became fluent in French, a skill which was certainly to prove an asset to her later in life. Her youthful imagination may well have been aroused by the discovery that her birthday, 14 July, fell on the anniversary of the fall of the Bastille in the French Revolution. Far from being lonely in this unknown country, she immediately made a close friend of a girl called Noemi, the daughter of Henri Rochefort, properly known as the Marquis de Rochefort-Lucay, though as a Communist he refused to use his title. In the shape of the Rochefort family the personal and the political now became delightfully entwined. For Emmeline had chanced to arrive only a year after the Franco-Prussian War, which had culminated in a humiliating French defeat and the loss of the provinces of Alsace and Lorraine. Paris itself bore the marks of its recent occupation by the Prussian army. In acquiring her new friend, Emmeline also adopted the French desire for revenge. Indeed, she became violently anti-German, a trait which helps to account for her readiness to suspend the suffragette campaign in order to back the Allied cause in August 1914. More immediately, the defeat of France had destroyed the regime of Napoleon III and triggered the establishment of the Paris Commune in March 1871, a losing cause in which Henri Rochefort had played a central role. As a man who fought duels, suffered imprisonment following the overthrow of the Commune, and escaped into exile, Rochefort offered a heroic and romantic model of manhood with the added attraction of a sophisticated, upper-class style. Emmeline was captivated by this, as indeed she was by most things French, especially the dress, cuisine, literature and radicalism of the country. She returned to Manchester full of youthful pride over her sophisticated Continental clothes.

In later years Emmeline's contemporaries often commented on her love of clothes, her elegant dress sense, and indeed the pleasure she took in shopping in Paris, a penchant fully shared with Christabel. Grace Roe, who became a close associate during the Edwardian period, recalled how much Emmeline disliked the wearing of sweaters by women and that, whenever she disapproved of a person's dress, she would turn away from them and deliberately praise someone else.[13] Moreover, Emmeline adopted pronounced views on the importance of dress for a woman in public life. She believed that a suffragette should always be the best-dressed woman in the room and consciously used her own femininity as a way of disarming critics of the suffragette movement.

Inconveniently for Emmeline, the end of her schooling interrupted this love affair with France. But she managed to extend the experience by returning in 1878 with her sister, Mary, who was also to be enrolled at the École Normale. This time she enjoyed even more freedom, especially as Noemi was able to open the door to the political and literary circles of the French capital. Inevitably the contrast between this independent, adult life in Paris and her position in the family back in Manchester now began to seem unbearable. By this time Noemi had become married to a Swiss painter, Frederick Dufaux. Before long the two girls had hatched a plan for Emmeline to find a husband so that she could remain indefinitely in France. The whole episode is revealing of the young Emmeline: conventional in some ways, immensely enthusiastic, a little impulsive and, above all, fairly confident about her ability to get her own way. Nor was she altogether unrealistic. As a vital, attractive twenty-year-old, Emmeline evidently had no difficulty in finding a suitably educated man keen to marry her. Indeed, according to Sylvia's account, she and Noemi actually took the initiative in approaching the prospective groom.[14] One can well imagine the delight of the two friends as their scheme took shape so readily. Although the gentleman made it clear that he expected to receive a dowry, Emmeline took it for granted that her father would pay up without complaint. Unhappily Mr Goulden, like many a parent confronted with the unexpected consequences of his children's education, showed himself unenthusiastic; indeed, he professed to be outraged at the very idea of 'selling' his daughter in this way. High words were spoken, but to no avail. Consequently the prospective husband withdrew indignantly while Emmeline returned to Manchester, her French sojourn at an end, for the time being at least.

It is tempting to read more into this episode than one should. Despite the arguments with her father, Emmeline let her suitor go quite easily with no sign of remorse. The relationship had presumably been too hastily concocted for her emotions to be seriously engaged. She had been in love with an idea rather than with an individual.Her chief reaction was one of anger with her father for thwarting her and, perhaps, for making her look foolish. Are there, then, grounds for discerning the makings of a feminist in the young girl's frustration at the obvious power exercised by a man? Perhaps, but it seems implausible to portray her as a feminist at this stage in her life; the naïve and romantic fashion in which she sought the marriage seems rather to underline her conventional aspirations. After all, by the 1880s many middle-class Victorian women had become increasingly alive to the drawbacks of early marriage and so were postponing it while they weighed up the choice between a life involving a career and independence on the one hand and a life of domesticity and dependence on the other. Evidently things did not present themselves in this way to Emmeline, no doubt partly because she had not pursued her education sufficiently seriously to envisage taking up a career.

On the other hand, Sylvia, writing from the perspective of the 1930s, put a more political complexion on the experience, suggesting that Robert Goulden's refusal to give a dowry was all of a piece with the breakfast-table arguments he had had with his wife over the household bills.[15] She claimed that this had given Emmeline the desire to have her own income on marriage. The fact that legislation permitting married women to retain their own income was going through Parliament in stages between 1870 and 1882 no doubt kept the thought in Emmeline's mind, and financial matters certainly continued to generate some friction in the family. A few years later, after Emmeline had married, she again called upon her father to endow her with some property, and his refusal led to a lasting rupture between them. This was explained by Rebecca West in a famous essay discussing Emmeline's psychological make-up:

It is an indication that in her there was an element of sex-antagonism, that neurosis which revolts against the difference of the sexes, which calls on the one to which the neurotic does not belong to sacrifice its special advantage so that the one to which the neurotic does belong may show superior . . . Mrs Pankhurst sublimated her sex-antagonism. She was in no way a man-hater.[16]

This may, however, be an unnecessarily elaborate explanation to construct around the young Emmeline. It is far from certain that her reactions were simply influenced by gender, for throughout her life she responded to *women* who crossed her in much the same way. What is unmistakeable is the element of ruthlessness she could display in personal relationships. She also fell out with her brother, Herbert, during the 1890s, and they were not reconciled until 1898. The truth is that Emmeline was the product of a family of talented, high-spirited individualists; but these qualities also made the Gouldens proud, opinionated and high-handed. It was inevitable that from time to time strong words would be spoken and rash decisions made which a sense of pride and stubbornness made it difficult to retract. A similar pattern emerged in due course in Emmeline's own lively but quarrelsome family, and it left its mark on her work for women's emancipation.

After the excitements and attractions of Paris, Emmeline must have found her return to Manchester in March 1878 a distinct anti-climax. She may well have been irritated when Jane took the younger children off to the seaside for the summer, leaving her to keep house for her father and to take her bearings. At least Emmeline had returned at what was, politically, an exciting time. For the last year Radical Liberals all over the country had been aroused by a new moral cause: the oppression of the Christian Slav peoples of the Balkans by their Turkish rulers. This was no remote issue but one which closely affected domestic British politics because the Conservative government under Benjamin Disraeli judged it to be in the national interest to support Turkey; her empire blocked the spread of Russian influence in the Eastern Mediterranean where Britain had vital trade routes, and the Russians were tempted to exploit Slav nationalism as a cover for their own imperial expansion. However, the former Liberal Leader, W. E . Gladstone, who had been in retirement since the 1874 election, had recently returned to politics to champion the rights of the Bulgarians and others to self-determination and to expose the immorality of Disraeli's policy. In common with thousands of other Radical Liberals in the northern towns the Gouldens were enthused by Gladstone's campaign against the 'Bulgarian Atrocities', as they came to be known. Emmeline inevitably became caught up in the demonstrations held in Manchester to support what was now virtually a leadership bid by the former prime minister.

However, on the personal level she found herself in an awkward position. France had widened her horizons, changed her appearance and given her more maturity and, in a vague way, ambition. Yet in the absence of a systematic education and the inclination for further study she had no prospects of a career. In this situation, domestic life in the Seedley household became supremely irritating. On the one hand Emmeline was conscious of the gulf between herself and her brothers, sisters and contemporaries. Yet Herbert was being prepared to join the family firm; and in due course Walter would become an accountant, Harold an actor and Robert a painter. Meanwhile Jane Goulden expected the girls who remained at home to help with what seemed trivial domestic tasks. In effect, the Gouldens had encouraged their daughter to take a wider view of life by living abroad and by participation in politics, but they had stopped short of abandoning the expectations of marriage and motherhood entertained by most Victorian parents.

Emmeline's dilemma reflected her own personality as much as the influence of her upbringing. The maturity that expressed itself in her elegant dress and coiffure and in her readiness to discuss political topics with adults was only half the story, for in personal and emotional terms she remained shy and naïve. It would have been only too easy for her to have acquired a circle of male admirers. But she professed to have no opinion of her brothers' male friends because she did not feel comfortable with or drawn to boys of her own age. This may explain why she eventually chose to skip a generation by finding what she called 'an important man' for her husband, a telling phrase reflecting the pretensions of a precocious but still insecure adolescent. Though in some ways a very courageous and even obstinate person, throughout her life Emmeline looked for a stronger personality to depend upon, first Richard, then, after his death, Christabel.[17] France had left Emmeline strongly attracted to marriage, but in a way that combined the expedient with the idealistic. For her, marriage was to be both an escape route from the family home and a means to the wider public role for which her talents and interests equipped her. It was in this frame of mind that Emmeline first encountered Dr Richard Pankhurst.

2

'Every Struggling Cause' (1879–84)

'My mother certainly knew nothing about male dominance.'
Adela Pankhurst, 'The Philosophy of the
Suffragette Movement', 1934

'Life is nothing without enthusiasms.' The author of these benevolent
if self-indulgent sentiments, Richard Marsden Pankhurst, was born in
May 1834 at Stoke-on-Trent, the third child of Henry Francis Pankhurst and Margaret Marsden; he had two sisters, Bess and Harriette,
and a brother, John.[1] The Pankhurst family name, which is variously
thought to have originated as Pentecost or as Pinkhurst, is associated
with the counties of Sussex and Surrey. Richard entertained the belief
– rather surprisingly, in view of his Radical views – that his family tree
descended from a Norman ancestor, de Pencestre. His grandparents
had migrated from Kent to Staffordshire where his grandfather, Francis
J. Pankhurst, who was a schoolmaster, died in 1857, aged seventy-one.
His father was originally an auctioneer and valuer but had become a
stockbroker by the time they moved to Manchester. In the process
Henry Pankhurst abandoned his inherited loyalty to the Church of
England and the Conservative Party in favour of the Baptist Church
and Liberalism. This was to be Richard's political inheritance. In his
youth he taught in a Baptist Sunday School, though he became so
disillusioned by the poverty of the children he saw there that he lost
his faith and became an agnostic.

An intelligent and studious boy, Richard benefited greatly from his
family's migration to Manchester where, in 1847 at the age of thirteen,
he was enrolled at Manchester Grammar School. Although excluded

from the older universities by his Nonconformity, he attended Owen's College, a forerunner of the Victoria University of Manchester, and received his BA, as an external degree of the University of London, in 1858. He went on to obtain his LLB with honours in the Principles of Legislation in 1859 and his LLD with the Gold Medal of the University in 1863. As these qualifications accumulated Richard seemed to be heading for an outstanding legal career. He was eventually called to the Bar at Lincoln's Inn in 1867, aged thirty-three, and subsequently practised on the Northern Circuit and in the Chancery Court of the County Palatinate of Lancashire. Yet during this period he seems to have been absorbed by a variety of social and political causes as much as by the law. In 1858, freshly graduated, he helped to inaugurate a programme of evening classes for working men at Owen's College, and even became an unpaid lecturer himself. From 1863 to 1876 he served as honorary secretary of the Lancashire and Cheshire Union of Institutes which offered secondary education and technical training to working men.

Richard was also a budding politician with advanced Radical views including free secular education, reduction of the powers of the House of Lords, reform of the labour laws and the enfranchisement of women. An indefatigable author of articles and tracts on legal and consti-tutional issues, Richard also became a familiar sight on Manchester's platforms, distinguished by his pointed, reddish beard and a rather high-pitched voice. For the local Liberals 'The Doctor', as he became known, was just the kind of enthusiastic volunteer needed to keep the party machine running; but from an early stage the cautious party big-wigs regarded him with apprehension for his tendency to go over the top in his determination to set the world to rights.

Writing from the perspective of the 1930s, Sylvia and Christabel Pankhurst created an appealing myth of their father as a noble and idealistic crusader whose promising career had been wrecked by nar-row-minded party politicians and by his devotion to women's suffrage which had damaged him in the eyes of the party leader, W. E. Glad-stone. Although there are undoubtedly elements of truth in this picture, it is none the less a considerable misrepresentation. In spite of his energy, dedication and talents, Richard Pankhurst was something of a failure both professionally and politically. On the face of it this seems surprising. Large and growing numbers of barristers became members of Parliament during the late Victorian and Edwardian period, and it ought to have been possible for Richard to have combined the two careers satisfactorily. However, a Parliamentary career was an expensive luxury at this time. MPs received no salaries until 1911; their election campaigns and constituency agents had usually to be financed from their own resources. Consequently middle-class men invariably spent some time putting their business or profession on to a secure and profitable footing before going into Parliament. But Richard lived a protracted undergraduate life, tilting at every windmill that came into sight, and neglecting his work as a barrister in the process. As he had failed to establish his legal career properly in his thirties, he faced an increasingly precarious existence in his later years just when he was acquiring new responsibilities as a family man.

In addition, there was a personal element to his failure: as an aspiring politician, Richard suffered from the drawbacks of being a political enthusiast. Full of compassion for the poor and disadvantaged, he often found it difficult to get on to the same wavelength as those he wanted to help; so full of information and opinions was he that he appealed to the committed, but did not always reach ordinary voters who failed to share his assumptions and principles. Even in the courts his impatience with and sarcasm towards his opponents sometimes antagonized those he needed to influence and, in the process, disadvantaged his clients. The impression of Richard as an intellectual and a zealot was compounded by his untidy dress, his squeaky voice and his small, penetrating eyes.

Consequently one cannot explain the frustration of Richard's aspirations to a Parliamentary career simply in terms of the fears of narrow-minded rivals; one must recognize the extent to which he handicapped himself by his own impatience and his tactlessness in his dealings with his party. Not that his success was impossible. The Victorian Liberal Party, Britain's governing party from 1846 to 1886, provided a natural home for large numbers of independent-minded Radicals of Richard's type. During the 1860s Richard Pankhurst became, in fact, part of a collection of high-minded Liberals that included John Stuart Mill, Henry Fawcett, Peter Taylor, Professor Thorold Rodgers and James Bryce. Spanning the world of politics, academia, journalism and the law, these men promoted Parliamentary reform, secularism, republicanism, international peace and female emancipation. Yet although their independence and their habit of consulting their consciences on each and every issue made them awkward customers for the Parliamentary managers, they all managed to sit as MPs and even became ministers in some cases. Advocacy of votes for women was no bar to success and promotion, despite Gladstone's personal opposition to the cause. Indeed, he allowed men such as Charles Dilke, Henry Fawcett and James Stansfeld to defy the cabinet's agreed line on women's legislation without forfeiting their posts. The honoured tradition of the independent member, though under pressure from the growing polarization of the parties and the expansion of the electoral machine, was by no means dead in the 1860s and 1870s.

Nothing deterred Richard Pankhurst from lending his support to women's causes. In 1867, when Manchester took the lead in forming a Society for Women's Suffrage, he sat on the executive committee, and for eight years he was to act as an unpaid legal adviser to its leading figure, Lydia Becker, who consulted him closely on the tactics and the arguments to be used in Parliament. In an article written in 1867, Richard adopted a classic individualist rationale for the enfranchisement of women. The basis of political freedom, he argued, lay in the equality of all men and women before the law; for him each individual had a *prima facie* entitlement to all the freedoms and franchises in the constitution. The Reform Act of 1867 used the term 'man' when extending the vote, rather than 'male persons' as in the 1832 Act, and this, he suggested, was used generically in English law to include women.[2] This was fairly typical of his style of argument; for those who accepted his premises about the importance of freedom the case was made, but suffragists soon found that they had to address more down-to-earth considerations in order to convince those who feared the consequences of giving women the vote.

However, for a new campaign Richard's loyal support was indispensable, and he was one of the chief speakers at the first public meeting for women's suffrage held at the Free Trade Hall on 14 April 1868. He also played a key role behind the scenes in the Parliamentary work of the women's movement; he drafted an amendment to the Municipal Corporations Bill in 1869 which successfully enfranchised female ratepayers, as well as the first bill to give women the Parliamentary vote in 1870, and the bills of 1870 and 1882 which allowed married women to retain their own property and income.

In this period the Manchester suffragists considered their colleagues in London to be rather cautious in their tactics and too respectful of Parliament. One of their alternative campaigning methods in the early days was an attempt to force the issue by mounting a legal challenge to women's exclusion from the Parliamentary registers. The reformers sought to demonstrate, on the basis of statutes and usage, that in past centuries female property owners had often been registered and had actually cast their votes. This enabled them to claim that women's suffrage involved the restoration of a long-established practice rather than an innovation. Since most people took the view that the women's vote represented a fundamental change rather than a marginal adjustment or a restoration of rights, this was politically unrealistic. However, the legal-historical case certainly looked respectable, and in any case it kept the cause in the news and offered an excellent rallying point for supporters of the movement. In Manchester a large majority of female ratepayers came forward demanding to be registered on the same basis as the men who paid rates. In the resulting legal case (*Chorlton* v. *Lings* (1869)) Richard Pankhurst acted as junior counsel with Sir John Coleridge. They lost, but they had made the point that, contrary to politicians' claims, many women really did want the vote.

Generous as he was with his support for women's suffrage, Richard also found time for other issues, notably education. Up to this time Britain had relied upon a haphazard pattern of elementary schools funded largely by voluntary, religious organizations. Richard denounced this system as an educational failure on the grounds that many children received no schooling, and as indefensible and unjust because of the religious indoctrination it involved. In 1870 Gladstone's Government attempted to improve the provision of elementary schooling by an act which permitted locally elected school boards to levy a special rate with which to build and fund schools that would be free of denominational teaching. But the board schools were seen as a threat by Anglicans and Catholics, who denounced them as godless institutions. Secular reformers like Richard, on the other hand, saw the legislation as a missed opportunity to purge religious influence from the educational system. Consequently, when Manchester held its first elections for the new school board in 1873, Pankhurst stood as a candidate. Though a Baptist by upbringing, he fought as an Independent. This meant being squeezed between Anglican–Catholic interests on the one hand and the Nonconformists on the other. As a result he came twentieth out of twenty-one candidates. Only the first fifteen were elected.

Unfortunately this initial electoral foray encouraged Richard to give full expression to his opinions about all kinds of institutions and vested interests. In May of 1873 he delivered an address to the Manchester Republican Club, which stirred up a good deal of correspondence in the *Manchester Guardian*.[3] The early 1870s had seen a dramatic upsurge of republicanism in Britain, owing largely to the prolonged withdrawal of Queen Victoria from public life after the death of Prince Albert in 1861. Critics had begun to ask whether the mounting costs of the monarchy were justified when she contributed so little to the life of the country. However, the republican bubble burst quite quickly, failing to attract more than a handful of Parliamentarians. Even a Radical like John Bright declined to take up the cause in spite of his general hostility to privilege and aristocracy. Thus, in adopting a republican stance in 1873, the young Pankhurst was taking a risk and arguably making a tactical mistake. By 1874 Manchester Liberals were becoming severely provoked by his views. The Reverend Philip Harris, who declared himself embarrassed at having to sit on a platform with Richard, denounced him in the local press as one who was:

passing through a phase of Red Republicanism . . . such a torrent of abuse, expressed in the most shrieking tones against every cherished institution in this country. You are at liberty to advocate no Queen, no Lords, no Church, no taxes, but there is no question as to the suicidal policy of the Liberal Party lending their platforms to afford such calumnious spouters an opportunity of uttering their ribald sedition . . . It is one thing to be a Liberal; multitudes of loyal Churchmen are. It is quite another to be a Red Republican, a Communist, and a reviler of all creeds.[4]

In this attack it is tempting to see the origins of Richard's withdrawal from the Liberal Party. However, this was by no means inevitable.

Other Radical Liberals flirted with republicanism for a time but still went on to become MPs and even ministers. The Victorian Liberal Party was a house of many mansions, and for a time it appeared likely that Richard would be able to pursue his ambitions within its walls. This prospect was greatly enhanced after 1876 when British politics became polarized by the campaign over the 'Bulgarian Atrocities', for on this issue Richard energetically adopted the orthodox Gladstonian line. It is difficult at this remove to appreciate the depth of feeling aroused by the Eastern Question during the 1870s. From the perspective of many Victorian Radicals and Christians it involved much more than an issue of foreign policy: it was a great *moral* cause. A British prime minister was prepared to support the Ottoman Turks, whose empire was regarded by Victorian reformers as a survivor from a barbarous age, offensive in an era of progress and improvement. The fact that Gladstone had chosen this issue to make his return to politics after a brief retirement added a personal element to the campaign; for, in effect, he posed a challenge to the aristocratic figures, Lords Granville and Hartington, who had assumed the Liberal Leadership during his absence.

In Manchester, Robert Goulden eagerly turned up to hear Richard Pankhurst denounce Disraelian imperialism and to champion Gladstone's cause, and was impressed by his passion and his erudition. Emmeline, fretting at Seedley during the summer of 1878, quickly succumbed: 'I was charmed with him; he was so eloquent.'[5] In 'The Doctor' she doubtless discerned an English version of Henri Rochefort, an idealistic, heroic figure ready to sacrifice his own interests for the sake of good causes. The twenty-year-old girl was awed and excited by his knowledge, wisdom, boldness and eloquence. With the idea of marriage to an important man already on her mind, Emmeline quickly recognized Richard as a fast-rising public figure, and she longed to be his partner in the inevitable triumph. Though this appears paradoxical from a twentieth-century perspective, Emmeline undoubtedly regarded an early marriage as a means to achieving a public and political role for herself, not as a one-way ticket into domesticity. The fact that he was forty-four and she only twenty was of no particular importance, for such disparities of age were far from unusual among middle-class Victorian couples. Indeed, one may surmise that Richard's age and status gave him an added attraction in Emmeline's eyes. She felt irritated with her father and trapped in the domesticity of Seedley Cottage. Robert would find it difficult to put obstacles in the way of her marriage to so accomplished and educated a figure whom he himself evidently admired.

However, by 1878 Richard Pankhurst had, to all intents and purposes, become a confirmed bachelor who believed that marriage would merely be a handicap to him in his public work. Living comfortably in the parental home for over forty years had left him at liberty to indulge his political interests while enjoying the advantages of family life without the responsibilities it involved. On the other hand, he could not but be flattered by the evident attentions of the vital and beautiful Emmeline. When she artfully sought Richard's help in educating herself, he willingly prepared a programme of improving reading for her. As it happened her return to England coincided with a turning-point in his life, for the recent death of his father heralded the break-up of the family home. His anxiety to find an alternative was further accentuated by the death of his mother in 1879.

In these circumstances their relationship developed rapidly during the autumn of 1878. In a high-minded letter addressed to 'Dear Miss Goulden' on 8 September, Richard outlined his scheme for promoting higher education for women. But by the twenty-third of the month he was writing to 'Dear Treasure' in warmer tones:

I received with greatest joy your charming likeness ... The Carte itself has honestly tried to express you as you are, but of course it could not. The fire and soul of the original can never consent to enter a copy. Still, when the original is absent, the copy consoles and animates.[6]

For an inexperienced lover Richard was learning fast. The letter faithfully expressed his approach to Emmeline – essentially courtly but with a hint of a more basic emotion. During their married life he appeared to the children to treat Emmeline almost as a queen; Adela felt that he deferred to her continually and never cared to go anywhere without her. 'Where's my lady?' was his invariable question on returning home; he almost always addressed her by some term of endearment rather than by her Christian name.

In short, the affair that blossomed during the autumn of 1878 was both a pleasure and a surprise to Richard, while being an enormously flattering experience for Emmeline. This was especially so since Richard clearly envisaged that their marriage would be above all a political *partnership*. 'Every struggling cause shall be ours', he told her, 'herein is the strength – with bliss added – of two lives made one by that love which seeks more the other than self. How I long and yearn to have all this shared to the full between us in equal measure.'[7]

It was only Jane Goulden, who clearly thought Emmeline was being rather forward, who endeavoured to slow down the progress of this whirlwind romance. Not that she disapproved of Richard, but simply of the unseemly haste; she herself had demurred and delayed before agreeing to marry Robert. But Emmeline, one suspects mischievously, went even further in shocking her parents by proposing to dispense altogether with the formalities of marriage by entering into a free union. This was by no means unknown in suffragist circles. One of the oldest suffragist campaigners, Elizabeth Wolstenholme, lived for many years with Ben Elmy, much to the embarrassment of her colleagues. Emmeline was also aware that the Rocheforts had remained unmarried until the wife was on her deathbed, when they went through the ceremony for the sake of their children. However, a free union was a bridge too far even for the radical Richard. And the Gouldens, faced with such an embarrassing prospect, no doubt thought it best to settle for a conventional marriage for fear of what their daughter might come up with next. In fact, despite Richard and Emmeline's impatience, their wedding did not take place until the end of the year. The timing was probably determined partly by the death of Richard's mother, an event which left him so depressed and lonely that he wished to dispense with the elaborate preparations necessary for a white wedding. Much to her disappointment, Emmeline was married in a brown velvet dress in a ceremony held at St Luke's Church in Eccles on 18 December 1879.

In this way began what appears to have been a very happy nineteen-year marriage. Despite some setbacks and sadnesses, no harsh words passed between Richard and Emmeline, or if they did their children remained quite unaware of it. The partnership was founded on a strong mutual appreciation and admiration, and on a common dedication to certain ideals and ambitions. Their domestic life was sustained and strengthened by their network of friends and the causes they pursued outside the marriage. Yet in a sense Richard and Emmeline were almost too compatible for their own good. Up to 1879 Richard had lived a somewhat self-indulgent life, happily diverting himself from his legal work for the sake of his campaigns, and giving his professional services free where his sympathies were engaged. As a result he was not as well placed as he should have been to combine a new family with a Parliamentary career. His life stood in need of some order and realism if his ambitions were to be attained. With the perception of an elder sister, Bess Pankhurst had urged Emmeline to steer Richard away from politics in order to concentrate on the law with a view to becoming a judge.[8] On the contrary, Emmeline's unqualified support for his political ambitions only exacerbated the situation. Convinced of his political greatness, she encouraged him to extend his public work beyond their capacity to sustain it. While relying on his parents Richard had never got to grips with the practicalities of life, and after his marriage he simply handed over responsibility for the household to Emmeline, who had neither the interest in nor the inclination for domestic duties. She in turn passed the housekeeping on to their Welsh nanny, Susannah Jones, who was better at managing. Above all, neither Richard nor Emmeline showed any facility for managing money competently, and the result was a series of expensive miscalculations at a time when Richard had begun to lose legal briefs because of his growing reputation for political extremism.

If Emmeline contemplated with enthusiasm plunging into her husband's public work, she was less well prepared for the conventional side of married life. By the late 1870s some middle-class couples had begun to practise birth control, sometimes for financial reasons and also because childbirth was an extremely dangerous experience even for women in the higher social classes. Repeated pregnancies and miscarriages severely undermined the health of thousands of women, leaving them prematurely aged and vulnerable to illnesses later in life. However, the Pankhursts' sophistication did not extend to matters sexual. In her account, Sylvia gave a strong hint that on the eve of the wedding Jane Goulden had belatedly attempted to offer some advice about sex and pregnancy, only to be brushed aside by her daughter.[9] It seems almost certain that Richard and Emmeline were both virgins at the start of their marriage and embarked upon parenthood as uninformed about sex and reproduction as most Victorians. Certainly Emmeline began to produce children in fairly quick succession, beginning with Christabel, who was born in 1880 only nine months after the wedding, followed by Sylvia in 1882, Francis Henry ('Frank') in 1884, Adela in 1885 and Henry Francis ('Harry') in 1889. According to Adela, Emmeline admitted to a doctor later in life that she had undermined her health by rushing away to help Richard in an election in London only a few weeks after the birth of her third daughter in 1885.[10] She also became seriously ill after the fifth pregnancy in 1889, and her frailty in later life was probably due almost as much to this earlier experience as to her suffering in gaol between 1908 and 1914. Since Emmeline was never particularly keen on mothering small children she came to rely heavily on the assistance of her sister Mary in coping with them, as well as on Susannah. During these early years the family lived in Drayton Gardens in Old Trafford but also spent a good deal of time at Seedley Cottage.

Although Richard showed himself very fond of his rapidly expanding brood, nothing was allowed to impede his political ambitions. Now well into his forties, he could not delay making his bid for Parliament, not least because Emmeline expected him to do so. The question was, how? Between 1883 and 1895 Richard fought three unsuccessful Parliamentary contests. The first of these, a Manchester by-election in September 1883, appeared, at first sight, a natural step for him to take in view of his local connections. In practice, of course, things proved to be far more complicated. By the 1880s Radical Manchester had passed its peak. In the shock election of 1874 the city actually returned two Conservatives amongst its three members. This was partly an immediate reaction to the reforms of the Gladstone government. But it also reflected long-term concerns among Liberal Anglicans as the party became linked with Church Disestablishment, hostility towards the Irish whose concentration in Lancashire undermined Liberal support, and a tendency for many of the successful businessmen who regarded themselves as part of the establishment to see Richard Pankhurst's brand of Radicalism as more of a threat than an ideal. Consequently, though Manchester remained attractive to Radicals like Richard Pankhurst for historic reasons, it was increasingly difficult for them to unite a working-class and middle-class vote in such places. His misfortune was to seek election just in the period when the hey-day of Victorian Liberalism had passed, but slightly before Labour had emerged as a really popular force in the country.

Yet, if the long-term trends were unfavourable, no inexorable logic barred Richard from the House of Commons. Unhappily tactics was not the Doctor's forte. In Manchester he faced a particularly awkward situation because, although the Liberals usually commanded a majority of the votes in the city, they could not count on carrying every seat. Matters had been complicated by the reforms of 1867 in which Disraeli artfully gave Manchester three MPs, but in a single undivided constituency in which each elector had only *two* votes. This meant that the Liberals could expect to take two seats only if their supporters cast their votes fairly equally for two candidates; to nominate too many candidates risked spreading the Liberal vote too thinly and letting the Conservatives gain a majority of the representation.

This was the situation into which Richard blundered in 1883. Gladstone's campaign over the Bulgarian Atrocities had culminated in victory at the general election of 1880 when Manchester Liberals won two of the three seats. But in July 1883 Richard, disappointed by the lack of domestic reforms, declared his intention of standing as an Independent candidate on a programme that included universal adult suffrage, the disestablishment and disendowment of the Church of England, a secular system of education, the abolition of hereditary elements in government and the nationalization of the land. For the 1880s this was a formidable platform, though not impossibly radical. The leading Birmingham Liberal, Joseph Chamberlain, planned to launch a similar programme at the 1885 election in the hope of harvesting the votes of the new working-class electors. The flaw lay less in Richard's views than in his timing and tactics. When the death of Manchester's Tory member threatened to precipitate a by-election in 1883, the local Liberals felt inclined to avoid the expense and trouble of a contest. After all, if a third Liberal were to be elected at the by-election, this would only complicate the general election by pitting three incumbent Liberals against one another. When Richard proceeded to hold an adoption meeting in September, therefore, he was seen as threatening to split the Liberal vote at the next general election.[11]

Consequently the election went ahead with Richard standing as an Independent against a Conservative opponent. Though he had withdrawn from the Manchester Liberal Association, declaring that it failed to represent the views of Liberals, he obviously needed the votes and the co-operation of the local Liberals to win. For this reason he claimed to enjoy the support of John Bright, who was still a hero to Radicals and had sat as a Manchester MP until 1857. Unfortunately, this backfired when Bright allowed a letter to be read out in which he declared that he had neither said nor written a word in favour of Richard Pankhurst. Another setback came when Emmeline sought the help of Lydia Becker, quite reasonably in view of Richard's loyal support for the Women's Suffrage Society. Becker, however, professed to regard him as a 'firebrand', and declined to lend support on the grounds that the Conservative candidate was also pro-suffragist. The explanation for her ingratitude lay partly in the fact that by this time, like many suffragists, Becker had become disillusioned with the national Liberal leaders over votes for women, and they wanted their campaign to remain a strictly non-party affair, especially as the Conservatives were increasingly showing sympathy for the cause. However, this rejection began the gradual process of undermining Emmeline's confidence in the methods and tactics of the constitutional movement for women's suffrage. Richard also had a strong claim on the Irish Nationalist vote, and he appears to have enjoyed the backing of its leading figures, Charles Stewart Parnell and Michael Davitt. Unfortunately, when Parnell visited Manchester he was deterred by the opposition expressed by the Catholic Church because of Richard's views on education and religion in general; as a result he left without giving the endorsement Richard needed. In effect, Richard lost support at both ends over Ireland – moderate English voters were alienated by his pro-Home Rule policy while the Irish themselves were put off by his reputation as an enemy of Catholicism.

The by-election proved to be a quiet one by Manchester's robust standards. Though Richard delivered countless speeches and drove about in a carriage decked out in yellow and green, he lacked the organization, the paid canvassers and the means of conveying poorer voters to the poll on which candidates relied in this period. Ironically, Gladstone's government had recently passed legislation restricting election expenditure and imposing penalties on candidates for the bribery and corruption which were traditionally regarded as a necessary aid to success. Although this reform was not yet in force, Richard chose to abide by its terms, unlike his opponent. He spent £541 on his campaign, a substantial sum in itself, but hardly a tenth of the Conservatives' expenditure.[12]

To lose in these circumstances would not necessarily have been a disaster. If he had polled a large vote, Richard would probably have forced the Liberal Association to take him seriously and include him on the ticket in the future, for it was common in this period to run one Liberal with Radical views with another who advocated more conservative policies in the same constituency. In the event, however, he lost by a humiliatingly wide margin, polling only 6,216 votes to the Conservative's 18,188.[13] Since around 24,000 people had voted for the Liberals at the previous election, it appeared that Richard had been repudiated by three-quarters of the party.

The 1883 by-election had profound ramifications for the Pankhurst family. It effectively scotched Richard's chances of becoming a Manchester MP. He would now have to look further afield, something Emmeline was keen to do. The defeat also accelerated the family's shift towards Socialism during the later 1880s. Christabel was profoundly affected by the election for, although very young at the time, she grew up with the belief that her father had been denied his just deserts by party politicians, and the anti-Liberal bias which characterized her strategy in the Women's Social and Political Union after 1906 sprang from this belief. Indeed, taken together, the early electoral experiences accentuated a temperamental inability on the part of Emmeline, Christabel and Sylvia to co-operate with political parties; none of the Pankhursts remained content for long in a political organization which they did not control themselves.

More immediately the by-election created fresh complications in the domestic life of the Pankhurst family. Robert Goulden had acted as his son-in-law's agent during the campaign, but subsequently felt he had been damaged by the association. He lost money and retired from business, blaming Richard's 'Socialism'. On Richard's part, though his expenditure had been relatively modest, the election had exacerbated his financial situation, and by alienating many local

Liberals he seems to have lost more clients. As a result, despite the ill-feeling in the family, the Pankhursts left their home in Old Trafford and moved back into Seedley Cottage where their third child, 'Frank', was born on 27 February 1884. Emmeline, perhaps rather tactlessly, chose this time to raise the question of the dowry which she claimed her father had promised her at the time of her marriage. It is impossible to know the truth of this argument. Her father may well have given her a promise back in 1878 when turning down the French marriage in order to placate his daughter, or merely have told her to wait and see. If he had given a firm undertaking, Robert had clearly changed his mind, feeling, no doubt, that his son-in-law had cost him enough already. As a result the family quit Seedley Cottage for good early in 1885, taking Mary Goulden with them. Emmeline, who was now pregnant with her fourth child, reputedly never spoke to her father again.

3

Upwardly Mobile (1885–92)

'We lived too much together and within ourselves to be healthy minded.'

Adela Pankhurst, 'My Mother: An Explanation
and A Vindication', 1933

Initially the rift with Robert Goulden did not take the Pankhursts very far. A short cab ride brought the young family to Green Hayes in Old Trafford, one of a succession of rented houses that they were to occupy over the next twenty years until, in 1904, the family ceased to have a permanent home altogether. Richard's failure to buy a house was by no means unusual at this time. In the 1880s the English had not yet developed their obsession with home-ownership, and most middle-class people regarded renting as a perfectly sensible option. By renting, the family could acquire a larger house as the number of children and servants multiplied without the trouble and expense of purchase, and then retreat to something more modest as the family diminished or as financial circumstances deteriorated. The Pankhursts' many moves were to reflect just such exigencies, especially during the 1890s and 1900s.

The years spent at Green Hayes and in Russell Square in London from the mid-1880s to 1892 were an important formative phase, especially for the three daughters, Christabel, Sylvia and Adela. The relationships and the personality traits developed at this stage went far to determining their behaviour as adults. However, the traditional account of the family during the 1880s and 1890s reflected the perspective adopted by Sylvia and the sense of grievance and neglect which she took forward from childhood to maturity. An equally biassed picture emerged later in the accounts of the leading associates of Christabel who, by contrast, disparaged Sylvia as a weepy and emotional child who grew up resentful of her brilliant mother and unable to share her with the world. Both views became exaggerated as a result of the political controversies between Emmeline and Christabel on one side and Sylvia on the other during the Edwardian period and the First World War. More recently an alternative, if no less tangled, perspective has been offered in the account of the *third* daughter, Adela, who has traditionally been overlooked in the writing about the Pankhurst family.[1] In some ways she corroborated Sylvia's critical view of relationships within the family, for she, too, grew up feeling neglected and undervalued by her parents. On the other hand, Adela believed that Sylvia had painted her father as faultless and heaped the blame on her mother, when much of the difficulty lay with Richard for condemning his family to a treadmill of political causes and principles that offered the only way to win praise and attention. It is, of course, easy to exaggerate the grievances and rivalries of childhood which in most families tend to be forgotten later in life; but in the case of the Pankhursts the family squabbles loomed so large and lasted so long, especially when they became mixed up with political differences, that they cannot be explained away. Though the Pankhursts were a vital, brilliant collection of individuals, they were in some ways slightly dysfunctional as a *family*. The tragic breakdown that occurred in relations, arising out of both personal and political issues, between 1913 and 1927 was clearly foreshadowed in childhood and adolescence during the 1880s and 1890s.

The truth is that the Pankhursts developed into a busy, lively, theatrical and argumentative family, but lacked anyone who might have served as a foil to their talents; there was no calm centre in the storm of domestic life. To some extent, it is true, the children's nurse, Susannah, and Emmeline's sister Mary, whom Christabel described as deputy-mother, helped to fill this need. But Emmeline herself was never particularly maternal, preferring to see her children, as so many Victorians did, as *adults* rather than as dependants requiring her support. She nursed none of the children except Christabel, which perhaps explains in part the very close lifelong relationship between them. Emmeline's failings were compounded by Richard who, though fond of his children, could see them only as potential adults. As a result he encouraged the two elder girls to behave as grown-ups, encouraging in them a sense of their own importance and building a gulf between them and the younger children, Adela and Harry. This had the most marked effect on Sylvia, caught between Christabel, who was seen to be more attractive and talented, and the little ones, who could best win attention by being silly or naughty. While Sylvia fought desperately for her mother's affection, Adela regarded Sylvia not as a victim but as a persecutor who told tales on the young ones and went out of her way to belittle them. 'Sylvia with her long face and in the sharp shrill voice peculiar to her, would revive all the humiliations', she wrote.[2]

Even so, one must beware of accepting at face value criticisms made later in life by Emmeline's younger daughters. Adela, for example, dwelt heavily on an episode in 1891, when she was only six, when Richard and Emmeline sent the children off to a boarding house at Clacton-on-Sea for some months under the care of Susannah.[3] The parents only visited them occasionally; Sylvia thought the place squalid and Adela felt neglected. It is tempting to see this as proof that Richard and Emmeline's absorption with one another and their public work allowed a barrier to grow between them and the children. But getting one's children out of the way for lengthy periods was quite typical behaviour among middle-class Victorian parents. Adela and Sylvia, who lived to become mothers in a more indulgent and child-centred age, inevitably remembered this period in a rather hostile light. Any balanced view of Emmeline must take some account of the enormous energy she showed in dealing with her household, her large family and a multitude of public causes and social functions. In addition Richard, while he lived, played an active role in the family, though this was recognized as a positive contribution more by his older children than by the young ones; Harry and Adela were rather frightened of their father. Moreover, as he became increasingly distracted by his work and deteriorating health, Richard was inevitably less involved.

Emmeline imposed a regime that was strict, though not unusual by Victorian standards. Significantly, Christabel found the discipline easiest to bear, whereas the younger children resented it. As was usual at the time, the children did not eat with their parents except on

Sundays, when a more elaborate meal was prepared. They enjoyed a plain diet including breakfasts of porridge, with bread, butter and milk on Sundays, though Sylvia often refused to eat it. Clothes comprised navy blue serge dresses and knickers with green serge coats which were cheap and hard-wearing but much disliked by the girls. Emmeline also had some pronounced and eccentric ideas. Ignoring the evidence that both Sylvia and Harry suffered from poor eyesight, she refused for years to allow them to wear spectacles, resulting in Sylvia enduring migraines for years. This was but one early sign of her reluctance to accept weakness in any shape or form in the Pankhurst family. Emmeline also took a disparaging view of schools, which she considered likely to destroy children's originality; she claimed that her own children were in any case too highly strung to attend.[4] This may simply have been a rationalization of Emmeline's own experience in largely avoiding prolonged and systematic education. Richard, by contrast, believed that all children should attend state schools, but he evidently failed to get his way, not least in the early years. When they lived in London he wanted to send the children to what Adela described as an international school run by Marxists for refugee and destitute children. Though one of the board schools created under the 1870 Act was available in Marchmont Street near their home in Russell Square, the children were told that attendance would not be a good idea for they would 'catch things in our heads'. Consequently, during the years up to 1892, Emmeline seems to have relied on governesses who read to the children from the standard volumes of Victorian literature – Dickens, Thackeray, Scott and George Eliot – and took them to visit the British Museum and the National Gallery. Only after their return to Lancashire in 1893 did the children attend school regularly. But before that time, as Adela put it, 'we lived too much together and within ourselves to be healthy-minded and brooded over troubles that other children in more healthy surroundings would have forgotten in five minutes'.[5]

On the other hand, Richard encouraged the girls to pursue their education in whatever form they chose. On his return from the office in the evenings he would engage the girls in serious conversation and frequently pulled books from his shelves for them to read. He liked to read to them from Walter Crane's *Book of Fairy Tales*, and Hans

Christian Andersen as well as from Dickens and Jules Verne and encouraged them to produce a handwritten family newspaper, 'The Home News and Universal Mirror', which was illustrated by Sylvia. Significantly, the children used their newspaper to report on their parents' speeches and political activities, with the result that it became very much a means of integrating the children into adult life rather than an entertainment or a way of developing their own childish interests. Indeed, Richard's approach to his children, though in some ways indulgent, was at least as serious-minded as Emmeline's. Whereas friends of the family chose dolls as presents for the girls, their parents invariably gave them books. From an early age Victorian notions of personal improvement and doing good were strongly instilled in all the young Pankhursts. 'If you do not work for others', Richard repeatedly told them, 'you will not have been worth the upbringing.' Christabel and Sylvia certainly absorbed this philosophy – but at a price. Keir Hardie, a sympathetic friend, once commented to Sylvia: 'So that's what's the matter with you, too much serious talk.'[6] Moreover, while the two elder children happily conformed to Richard's ideas and saw him as a lovable father, Harry and Adela found him rather intimidating, distant and often absent altogether. This is readily understandable. As the eldest child Christabel, in particular, wanted adult approval, but Adela and Harry – each one, for a time, the youngest in the family – were less co-operative. In any case, the younger ones saw Richard becoming increasingly worried about money, his career and his poor health, a more remote figure whom they did not really understand. Whereas his older children had been a novelty and a delight, the younger ones naturally appeared more of a burden.

In this situation Christabel grew up as a classic example of a clever eldest child: fully aware of her importance in the family, confident, rather adult and essentially conformist. 'She was her mother's favourite', wrote Sylvia, 'we all knew it, and I for one never resented the fact.'[7] A pretty, round-faced girl with chestnut curls and rosy cheeks, Christabel was poised and graceful from an early age. Emmeline, who regarded her as the most attractive of her children, hoped for a time that she would become a ballerina. As a result, Christabel passed through childhood more serenely than her younger siblings, showing far less jealousy or insecurity. Since her parents clearly treated her as an adult in many ways, they accentuated the age gap between her and the others. When the children were perplexed at not being sent to school, it was Christabel who decided they should teach each other at home. When they became worried about Richard's reputation as an atheist it was Christabel, accompanied by Sylvia, who went to ask him for an explanation. Moreover, in each case she accepted the adults' opinions and respected authority; despite her later reputation she was by no means a natural rebel.

However, there was another side to the coin. Like her mother Christabel began to read at a very early age, but showed herself reluctant to undertake systematic study. She enjoyed novels, but otherwise gave the impression of being rather self-indulgent, even lazy. An American friend, Harriet Blatch, once advised Emmeline that what her daughter needed was a stiff course of mathematics and less time spent with novels. It was as though her secure and privileged position left her disinclined to struggle. In spite of her undoubted talents and her prominence, Christabel never quite achieved all that she was capable of during her adult life.

Sylvia, on the other hand, occupied what is often an awkward position as the second child out of four. She enjoyed neither the status of the oldest nor the licence and attention of the younger children. Such children sometimes cope either by becoming highly competitive as a means of winning attention, or alternatively by sulking and retreating more into a private world of their own. Since Sylvia was the least aggressive and most fragile personality within a family of strong characters, she tended towards the latter course and nourished her resentment quietly. Almost all photographs of Sylvia throughout her life seem to emphasize her large, doleful eyes, her long, heavy face and air of gloom. Contemporaries thought of her as emotional, ready to burst into tears at the slightest opportunity. This cannot be ascribed simply to jealousy towards her elder sister, for Sylvia herself conceded that during childhood they were close companions and that she accepted Christabel's leading role. Her resentment was focussed more on her mother who, she felt, minimized her abilities and failed to appreciate her feelings. On the occasion of Richard's final election defeat in 1895, Sylvia burst into tears when the result was declared. But instead of comforting her, Emmeline reprimanded her for letting the family down with this embarrassing display of weakness.[8] As a result Sylvia developed a tendency to sulk and often turned to her aunt Mary for sympathy. During the 1890s Sylvia acquired a fresh cause for resentment when her talents as an artist still failed to arouse much appreciation, while Christabel, unfocussed and indolent, continued to win a disproportionate share of attention without demonstrating any conspicuous abilities. As she advanced towards adulthood Sylvia continued to seek appreciation from her family, but this struggle steadily took its toll; it drove her, for example, to focus on politics rather than simply following her talents as an artist. Political differences eventually caused a huge rift between Sylvia and Christabel as well as with her mother; but this only compounded the poor personal relations between Sylvia and Emmeline. It is telling that when the two daughters wrote their memoirs later in life, Christabel referred to Emmeline as 'Mother', but Sylvia wrote coldly of 'Mrs Pankhurst', and from the First World War onwards she seems to have had hardly any direct contact with her. The rivalry and resentment of childhood ran like a poison through the lives of the three women.

Almost inevitably these complications in her relations with her mother led Sylvia to see her father through a golden aura; after his death she would attempt to settle any family dispute by invoking Richard's views on the subject. In adulthood she remained loyal to his politics and principles especially when, in her view, Christabel and Emmeline had betrayed them. It was symbolic that her first name, Estelle, which had been chosen by Emmeline, was dropped because Sylvia refused to answer to it, whereas Richard's choice was always used. She recalled fondly how he liked to call her 'Miss Woody Way', making a learned little joke of the Latin words *sylvanus* and *via*, and how he sang 'Who Is Sylvia' from Shakespeare's *Two Gentlemen of Verona* to her. Such attention was naturally flattering and reassuring; but by the same token, Richard's death when she was only sixteen came as a devastating blow to this vulnerable personality.

Sylvia at least enjoyed the love and attention of her father, whereas her younger sister, who had been rather grandly named Adela Constantia Mary, believed that she had been largely denied the affection of both parents. It rankled with Adela later in life that in her autobiography Emmeline failed even to mention her by name and never acknowledged her contribution to the suffragette campaign. No doubt Adela's bitterness deepened after the rift of 1914 when she was, in effect, banished to Australia for her troublesomeness. But how did things come to such a pass?

Adela was a very small and a rather sickly child who suffered from bronchitis and weak legs. In fact, for the first six years of her life she walked with the aid of iron splints attached to her legs. Naturally this made her slow and she was often being told to hurry up. Gradually Adela became rather isolated and retreated into a world of her own. Born in 1885, she occupied, for her first four years, the favoured position of youngest child and behaved much as one would expect. Petted by the adults, Adela was inclined to be naughty and became good at attracting attention. Since Christabel was so much more adult she did not impinge strongly on Adela, who saw Sylvia as a rival and a threat. The birth of a new baby in 1889 – all the more acclaimed because he was a boy – deprived Adela of her privileged position. She did not adjust well to being the third out of four children, and in this situation one sees the origins of the unhappy picture she presented later of neglect and loneliness. By the 1890s she was less likely to be petted as a baby and more likely to be scolded for naughtiness. But Adela possessed quite enough of the spirit of both the Gouldens and the Pankhursts to resent this rather than to attempt to compromise. Increasingly she escaped from her dominant sisters and unsympathetic parents to spend time in the kitchen alone with her thoughts; she took to composing imaginative stories and enacted little plays by herself.[9]

As Adela grew up her distinctive personality set her increasingly apart from her more famous sisters. Although the children usually became involved with their parents' causes and activities, they could hardly help noticing that they failed in some ways to conform to the values of their middle-class contemporaries. Like most children they found this embarrassing. Above all Richard and Emmeline never brought the children up to be religious, an omission which inevitably became the subject of gossip among the servants. One of the cooks, Ellen, made clear her disapproval of Richard for his irreligion and his failure to teach the children to say their prayers. On hearing this the children naturally became a little worried, and so Christabel, accompanied by Sylvia, tackled her father on the subject. Richard characteristically treated them to an explanation of the Biblical view of the life of Christ and Christian doctrines, as well as his own scepticism about supernatural interpretations and his conviction that the historical Jesus was a persecuted reformer rather than a figure of legend. He pointed out the books they should read and allowed them to reach their own conclusions, but left them in no doubt that he would be disappointed if they did adopt Christianity.[10] The revealing aspect of this episode is that Christabel accepted her father's views. As the eldest she had a strong instinct to conform, to respect authority and to use it. This became evident much later in life in her association with the political Establishment during the First World War, but perhaps more surprisingly, it also influenced her strategy in the suffragette movement when she deliberately sought to win allies and backing from within the social and political elite that was ostensibly the target of her attack. In contrast, Adela rejected Richard's belief that there was no God: 'I knew inside me that he was wrong.' Later on this generated controversy when Adela taught in a Socialist Sunday School, and Emmeline and Sylvia even objected to her attending church.[11] Here was an early indication that Adela was the most natural rebel in the Pankhurst family.

Amid the turbulence of family life, Emmeline and Richard never lost sight of the wider interests and ambitions that had brought them together in the first place. Fortunately the humiliation of the Manchester election could easily be put aside in the excitement of the two succeeding years. By 1885 Gladstone had enacted the Third Parliamentary Reform Act, which created two and a half million new working-class voters, provoked a campaign by Liberals in the country designed to strip the hereditary peers of their powers and split up most of the old constituencies into single-member seats, thereby producing the modern pattern of representation. Since, by tradition, major extensions of the electorate were closely followed by a general election, 1885 saw an upsurge of political campaigning and controversy, of which the most notorious example was the so-called 'Unauthorized Programme' propagated by Joseph Chamberlain. As Chamberlain was widely expected to inherit the leadership of the Liberal Party before long, and, moreover, advocated many of the policies he himself already espoused, Richard must have felt some confidence that politics was moving in his direction. There seemed every reason to take another shot at winning a seat in Parliament when the general election took place.

However, as Richard had damaged his reputation in Manchester, he shifted his attentions to the constituency of Rotherhithe in south-east London. In many ways this was a wise move. To represent a London seat would be convenient and would avoid the need to maintain two homes. Moreover, with their tradition of Radical clubs and republican societies, many of the working-class districts of the capital enjoyed a brand of politics similar to Richard's. Additionally, Rotherhithe offered the advantage of a compact, newly created constituency of only eight and a half thousand electors requiring less expenditure than a large traditional seat like Manchester. In July 1885 Richard was adopted by the Liberal and Radical Association and, with Emmeline at his side, he commenced his usual energetic campaign of speeches leading up to the poll in November. His chances seemed good not least because he now had an official party nomination in an election which the Liberals won, if not by a landslide. This time Emmeline succeeded in enlisting the help of women's suffragists in his campaign.[12] Not that Richard allowed the prospect of success to influence him too much. True, he went some way to endorsing official Liberalism, in particular its opposition to colonial aggrandizement in the Sudan.[13] On the other hand, when his opponent attacked Gladstone for failing to fulfil his promises in terms of domestic reform, Richard offered little defence, no doubt because he privately agreed. In effect, he declined to endorse the full Gladstonian programme, which he thought lacked appeal to the new voters, choosing instead to emphasize land reform and to attack the hereditary element in British government.[14]

Richard's speeches attracted large audiences and overflow meetings where he aroused enormous enthusiasm. This seemed to augur well for the poll. However, since public meetings were a popular form of free entertainment at this time, they were by no means a reliable indication of a candidate's support, not least because many of those who attended were not themselves entitled to vote. Colonel Hamilton, the Conservative candidate in Rotherhithe, made up in tactical skill what he lacked in eloquence. He quickly dubbed Richard a 'slum politician' for his habit of speaking at street corners, portrayed him as a reject from Manchester, and accused him of trying to leave his atheistical views behind. Soon posters and handbills appeared in the constituency, containing an alleged quotation from Richard's Manchester speeches: 'If there is a God, I deny God.' Several local clergymen displayed this material in or outside their churches.[15] This was standard Conservative propaganda, but in view of Richard's personal and publicly stated convictions on these issues he was bound to be vulnerable to attack. Though quite capable of defending himself by explaining his views – 'I had found for myself that God, the soul and immortality . . . were things unknown and unknowable by the human intellect' – his comments probably went over the heads of the Rotherhithe electors. Emmeline, initially rather shocked at the vulgarity of the campaign rhetoric, became dismayed about this particular issue. She demonstrated a shrewd tactical sense in recognizing that considered explanations of Richard's religious views cut little ice in the rough and tumble of an election. She insisted that he must put in an appearance at church with her in order to demonstrate that he respected Christian principles even if he could not share Christian views. 'I understand these people, I know what to do', she remarked, 'you have always got your head in the clouds!'[16] Here was an interesting sign of her growing political maturity and tactical perception.

Unfortunately, the religious issue was not the only indication of Richard's vulnerability to charges of extremism and eccentricity. When the Radical Association in the neighbouring constituency of Camberwell attempted to nominate a female candidate, Helen Taylor, who was the stepdaughter of John Stuart Mill, Richard could not resist going to speak in her support. But Helen Taylor did not enjoy even the backing of the women's suffrage organizations, partly because she was such a divisive figure and because they felt reluctant to complicate the cause at this stage by urging that women should be members of Parliament as well as voters. As an exponent of 'Rational Dress' for women, Taylor also insisted on wearing trousers in public, thereby focussing attention on her personal eccentricity rather than on the right of women to stand for Parliament. Even Emmeline, who was horrified as much by Helen Taylor's dress sense as by her politics, considered Richard foolish in associating himself with her.

It remains doubtful, however, whether these diverting controversies were really responsible for turning the election against Richard. For all its poverty the constituency was regarded locally as a stronghold of Conservatism. Much of the explanation for this lay in the dominance of the river trades in the local economy, which generated a marked hostility towards foreigners, who were seen as cheap labour, and a liking for patriotic foreign policies. By contrast, Liberal free trade was associated with the freedom of the shipowners to employ foreign labour at lower rates of pay.[17] Since trade was rather depressed in 1885 Colonel Hamilton exploited the constituents' feelings by arguing that free trade had failed to attract business to the Thames. He made a more material and concrete appeal, assisted by the traditional reliance on the local public houses as his committee rooms during the campaign. By comparison, Richard's florid appeals for institutional reform and moral principles enjoyed less credibility amongst poor voters.

On top of this came the Irish factor. Like most poor urban districts Rotherhithe had an Irish community whose vote was efficiently organized by the United Irish League, usually for the benefit of the Liberals who had already conceded land reforms and disestablishment of the Church in Ireland. Since Richard had advocated Home Rule before it became official party policy, he had a stronger claim to Irish support than most. However, Gladstone had not yet adopted Home Rule and, in 1885, the Nationalist leader, Parnell, judged it prudent to increase the pressure on him by withholding the Irish vote from Liberals in the English constituencies at this election. This almost certainly cost Richard crucial votes in a close contest. It also intensified Emmeline's obsession with the Irish, which was later to influence her own tactics in the suffragette movement: it made sense to punish the governing party by splitting its vote even if this meant antagonizing one's friends.

In spite of his difficulties, Richard was clearly considered by the local press to have fought an effective campaign, and the result was expected to be close. In the event he lost by 527, polling 2,800 votes to Hamilton's 3,327, a keen disappointment as much for Emmeline as for him. However, the repercussions proved more troublesome. Choosing to believe that he had lost as a result of his opponent's attempt to condemn him as an atheist, Richard proceeded to sue for slander and libel, seeking damages of £10,000.[18] He had, however, a wider motive than personal grievance: he wanted to test the new libel law for the benefit of other Radical candidates, many of whom had become victims of Tory smears in recent elections.

Legal redress was, however, complicated for it involved four separate cases: against Hamilton, his printer, the *Manchester Courier* from which quotations had been taken, and one Chesters Thompson, a Manchester councillor who had been quoted. When the first case came to court Judge Grantham, who had been an unsuccessful Conservative candidate at the election, took it upon himself to argue that newspapers could not be responsible for what they printed and ought to be protected from libel charges. For good measure he suggested that it was understandable if people felt disinclined to vote for someone with Richard Pankhurst's views. The jury followed his advice to acquit. Emmeline felt so outraged by all this that she took it upon herself to write to Judge Grantham, describing his judgement and summing up as 'the concluding acts of a conspiracy to crush the public life of an honourable man', and accused him of lending 'his aid to a disreputable section of the Tory Party in doing their dirty work . . . for what other reason were you ever placed where you are?'[19] Such remarks put her in imminent danger of a charge for contempt of court. 'Let him send me to prison,' she reportedly cried in her anger. Fortunately for her, the higher authorities took a similarly dim view of the judge's conduct and no action was taken. Richard appealed and, when his case was heard on 11 December 1886, the Court of Queen's Bench granted a new trial and strongly rebuked Judge Grantham. However, as the jury found itself unable to reach agreement in the case against the *Courier*, all Richard extracted was an admission that the libel had been false and an apology. In March Colonel Hamilton came before the Court of Queen's Bench where Richard's case was conducted by Sir Charles Russell. Since the evidence here was fairly clear and difficult to dispute, the jury found in his favour in a quarter of an hour, but unfortunately asked to be directed as to damages. As a result Richard was awarded damages for slander of £405 and for libel of £62 and did not get his costs.

In this way a defeat was turned into a disaster. The election had cost about £500 mostly paid by Richard, who could ill afford it so soon after his Manchester campaign. Now he found himself burdened with the legal costs of his libel cases. It is significant that, though none of this diminished his appetite for political work, he failed to contest the two following elections in 1886 and 1892. Interestingly, the outcome of his second election began to crystallize an underlying difference between Emmeline and Richard in their approach to public affairs. Whereas the insults handed out by the Liberal Party, the suffragists, the Irish and the Tories in 1883 and 1885 had left her shocked and angry, Richard, by contrast, seemed to react with philosophical understanding of his rebuffs. He explained how logical it was from the Irish point of view to make the most of their limited influence in England by voting as they had done in 1885. It was as though he regarded his various causes as more important than his personal advancement, seeing the election campaigns essentially as a means of furthering his principles. Though not elected, he could derive satisfaction from the knowledge that his ideas were rapidly advancing; by 1886, for example, Gladstone himself had taken up Home Rule for Ireland. But Emmeline, lacking Richard's historical perspective on reform movements and his mid-Victorian belief in the inevitability of progress, found herself unable to see things in the same way. For her the point of standing in an election was to *win*.

With the congratulations of the Rotherhithe Liberals ringing in her ears Emmeline concluded that they had been unlucky and must persevere in their efforts to get Richard into Parliament. In the aftermath of the election the attractions of London now loomed so large that Emmeline quickly persuaded herself that it offered the best means of promoting Richard's career. As a result the family had moved south within three months. However, this made the question of the Pankhursts' finances more acute. Initially they moved into some rather grim lodgings while Richard got down to his legal work. He found it necessary to maintain his practice in the north where most of his clients were and was consequently absent from home a good deal. Meanwhile Emmeline determined to boost the family's finances by opening a shop. Since she undoubtedly loved shops and shopping this must have seemed a congenial solution to their dilemma. Throughout her life she was to return to this expedient in times of financial difficulty – and always with disastrous results. For, despite her father's success, Emmeline had little or no notion about running a business, and her pride almost certainly prevented her from seeking his advice. Even Christabel, who wrote that her mother 'moved in a radiant daydream', considered her to be naïve in business and ignorant about basic distinctions between gross profit and net profit.[20]

But if she was aware of her family's misgivings, Emmeline pushed ahead undeterred; she proposed to sell 'fancy goods' – that is, a variety of interior furnishings, prints, furniture and *objets d'art*. She was probably influenced by the fashionable movement associated with William Morris for introducing art and beauty into the practical items which filled Victorian homes. Supplies of milking stools were enthusiastically bought to be painted and enamelled by Emmeline and her sister Mary, whose support was essential to the project. On the advice of an estate agent who told her that the Hampstead Road in St Pancras was a rising neighbourhood, she rented a shop at Number 165, which had living accommodation above. There she opened 'Emerson and Company'. Unhappily, Emmeline's end of the Hampstead Road was still dominated by market stalls and vendors selling meat, vegetables and other perishables. The shoppers, desperately stretching their money to feed their families until the next pay day, lacked the surplus cash to indulge in the goods displayed in Emerson's window. Little of the shrewdness Emmeline showed in political affairs surfaced in her commercial activities. One of her more bizarre decisions was to buy up a large supply of fish hooks. The vendor had taken the trouble to send several of his representatives, posing as ordinary customers, into the shop to enquire about hooks, thereby apparently convincing Emmeline that an unsatisfied demand existed among the fishermen of riverless St Pancras.[21] The sad but inevitable result was that Emerson and Co. lost money rather than earning it.

Meanwhile husband and wife rapidly became drawn into a multitude of radical and feminist causes among the London intelligentsia. The late 1880s was an exhilarating time for anyone with advanced ideas about social and political issues. Novelists and journalists had begun to propagate the notion of the 'New Woman' who was widely thought to be poised to break out of the conventions of Victorian society. In 1888 a series of articles written by Mona Caird in the *Daily Telegraph* – still betraying its original pedigree as a Liberal newspaper – posed the question: 'Is Marriage A Failure?' Richard gave his support to the controversial campaign by the journalist, W. T. Stead, who exposed the trade in young girls by proving that they could be bought for sexual purposes in Britain. At the same time Richard's sympathies with working men were strengthened by their protests over unemployment during the economic depression of 1886–7. John Burns, one of the strike leaders, was prosecuted for sedition and incitement, along with Henry Hyndman and H. H. Champion, and Sir Charles Warren, the Chief of the Metropolitan Police, prohibited all meetings in Trafalgar Square. This repressive policy culminated in the notorious events of 'Bloody Sunday' on 13 November 1887 when attempts by police and troops to disperse the crowds who had gathered to hear speeches by the labour leaders led to two deaths. Both Pankhursts had attended the Trafalgar Square demonstration and Richard subsequently argued that the prohibition on meetings had been illegal and that there was a common-law right to meet in Trafalgar Square. Going further, he claimed that when faced with unlawful violence the citizen enjoyed the right to repel it by force himself as his action was essentially private and a matter of self-defence. At the time most lawyers and politicians were too nervous about organizations of working men and the spread of Socialist societies to entertain such a view, but Richard's readiness to put the case made him an attractive figure among working men and Socialists, some of whom formed the Independent Labour Party a few years later. The Pankhursts' stay in London coincided with several years of acute industrial militancy which reached a peak around 1889. In that year Emmeline helped with the famous strike by the match girls at Bryant and May's factory under the leadership of Annie Besant. Husband and wife were now moving towards the left, though they had not yet abandoned their Manchester Liberalism entirely.

None the less, Emmeline felt uncertain how best to promote Richard's career, though in the event her next initiative was effectively triggered by a tragedy in the family. During September 1888, both parents were away in Manchester in connection with Richard's legal work, leaving the children in the care of their nurse. While out walking the four-year-old Frank appeared to develop a cold and a hoarse cough. During the evening he grew worse, doctors were summoned and Emmeline returned home. At first the doctors treated him for croup, but they realized too late that he had diphtheria. He was buried at Highgate Cemetery on 15 September.

Even among well-to-do Victorian families, child mortality rates, especially for boys, were still very high. But such an unexpected and devastating event inevitably left its mark on all members of the family. In her anguish Emmeline found it impossible to conceal her regret that it was her only son rather than one of the three girls who had been lost, and she dwelt so heavily on Frank's good points that she made Sylvia, for one, feel guilty: 'I longed to have died instead of Frank', she wrote, 'for years that thought would recur with a deep anguish.'[22] Adela, only three years of age, was too young to have suffered the same sense of remorse, though she was obviously aware of the sadness in the family. Sylvia, however, received some help in coming to terms with her grief. It was Susannah, not her mother, who thoughtfully took her to say goodbye to her brother; and though Emmeline refused to hear him spoken of again, Richard told her 'We must not forget Frank'. Sylvia coped in the way that came naturally to her by drawing Frank's picture. She felt unhappy with her sketch, but she took some comfort when her father praised her effort by saying he could see Frank clearly in the drawing.

From her behaviour it certainly appears that Emmeline was the worst affected by the tragedy. She kept the portraits of the boy locked away out of view and refused to talk about him. Her solution lay in pretending that he had not really died at all. She quickly became pregnant for the fifth time and soon started to speak of 'Frank coming again'.[23] On 7 July 1889 she gave birth – mercifully, for her state of mind, to another boy – just under ten months after Frank's death. The new son was given the same names, Henry Francis, as his brother, and he was known in the family as 'Harry'. Even now a fresh tragedy was only narrowly averted. Though attended by a maternity nurse who pronounced her condition to be perfectly satisfactory, Emmeline suddenly turned very white and began to suffer a serious haemorrhage. Susannah had literally to run from the house to find a doctor, which took some time since she was refused by several who lived in the vicinity. Some doctors were reluctant to handle maternity cases, while many were so commercially minded that they would not interfere with someone else's patient. But eventually one came and Emmeline recovered.

In the circumstances it was probably inevitable that the new baby boy would become the centre of attraction, and his health, which was less than perfect, came to be of great concern in the family.

More immediately, Frank's death inspired a new series of moves. As the bad drains in Hampstead Road were diagnosed as the cause of his illness, Emmeline seized the opportunity to shift both home and business to more salubrious surroundings. New premises for the shop were acquired in Berners Street and, when they were demolished, she set up in Regent Street, a more appropriate site but too costly to be viable. At the same time Emmeline took a larger and more elegant house at Number 8 Russell Square, on the corner of Bernard Street. As the house seemed too large and expensive she suggested that some of the rooms could be let to a doctor. In fact, she was so much in love with Russell Square that she could never bear to part with any of it. The first floor comprised two large interconnected drawing rooms which Emmeline's ambitious eye rightly saw as perfect for 'At Homes' and even for small conferences. For she now intended to launch her own salon as a means of capitalizing on their London connections and thus promoting Richard's career.

She proceeded to decorate the first-floor room in yellow, her favourite colour, with a frieze of purple irises, and to fill the house with stylish furniture, Turkish rugs, Japanese embroidery, William Morris prints and Chinese and Persian china cheerfully drawn from the copious unsold stocks of Emerson and Co. Richard, seemingly oblivious to this whirlwind of activity but content for Emmeline to enjoy herself, plugged away at his work until the arrangements were complete. For the children, life in Russell Square proved to be enjoyable in many ways. They had a stream of interesting visitors and adult activities in which they were required to play a part. The large house enabled them to keep out of the way when it suited them, and Sylvia found particular pleasure in the Square's gardens, where she discovered secret places in which to play for hours free from the adults. As her eyesight was poor she was discouraged from reading and instead pursued her interest in nature, drawing and painting. Her father encouraged her by bringing home books such as *The Yellow Dwarf* by Walter Crane, a Socialist artist, and showing her the William Morris illustration 'When Adam Delved and Eve Span, Who was Then the Gentleman?' in *A Dream of John Ball*. In this way Sylvia's sympathy with radical causes developed hand in hand with her interest in becoming a painter and draughts-woman. She devoted hours to sketching and to watercolours, though this remained an essentially private pleasure, and she showed her work only to her aunt Mary, no doubt anxious for a sympathetic response.

During the four years between 1889 and 1892, a cosmopolitan and slightly Bohemian succession of men and women from political and literary circles passed through the Russell Square salon. Emmeline took particular delight in the frequent visits of Henri Rochefort who talked at length with Richard, who was fluent in French, and refused to speak 'the barbarous English language' in case it spoiled his accent. Grant Allen, the novelist later to be famous as the author of *The Woman Who Did*, was another guest. The Pankhursts entertained Enrico Malatesta, the exiled Italian anarchist, and Dadabhai Naoroji, an Indian nationalist who sat as a Liberal MP from 1892 to 1895. Among the many American guests were William Lloyd Garrison, a leading advocate of emancipation for negroes, and the women's suffragist leader, Elizabeth Cady Stanton, and her daughter Harriet Stanton Blatch. Not that Emmeline was always bowled over by her visitors. After attending several seances with the fashionable Theoso-phist, Madame Blavatsky, she pronounced her an impostor. From the ranks of the party politicians came several leading Liberal members, including Richard Haldane, Sir Edward Grey, James Bryce and Sir Charles Dilke. Above all, the Pankhursts increasingly attracted key figures in the Labour and Socialist movements such as Keir Hardie, whom they first met in 1888, Annie Besant, Tom Mann and William Morris. On Sundays, when large 'At Homes' took place, the whole family played a part. The girls dressed in white crêpe dresses, distrib-uted food and took collections for good causes. Sylvia's skills were in demand for writing notices: 'To The Tea Room'. Above all, Emmeline was in her element on these occasions. Elegantly dressed, she proved to be a sparkling hostess always ready to sing at the piano for her guests. Harriet Blatch described her at Russell Square as 'a living flame, as active as a bit of quicksilver, as glistening, as enticing . . . she looked like the model of Burne-Jones' pictures – slender, willowy, with the exquisite features of one of the saints of the great impressionists'.[24] At this stage, however, Emmeline confined herself to a supporting role for Richard's benefit; opportunities to deliver speeches, for example, were firmly declined. But as she gained confidence and became familiar with the famous figures of left-wing politics, she began to emerge as a public figure in her own right.

On the other hand, for all the pleasure the Pankhursts' 'At Homes' gave, it is by no means clear that they really served the purpose of advancing Richard's career. Late-Victorian political hostesses such as Lady Londonderry, Lady Jersey and Lady Waldegrave were widely believed to be capable of influencing the fortunes of both their parties and their own relations and protégés. But Russell Square boasted only the modest social cachet of Bloomsbury – it was a long way from the magnificence of an Osterley Park or a Stafford House where the great hostesses held sway. Rebecca West disparaged Emmeline's salon as 'a naïve and ludicrous parody . . . of the real social functions of power'.[25] At most the Russell Square entertainments made Richard a more familiar figure amongst Socialists and, to that extent, may have accelerated his move away from the Liberal Party. Yet his failure to contest the election of 1892 underlines the limitations of the strategy.

Emmeline's role as political hostess also revealed an underlying ambiguity in her political make-up. Ostensibly an advanced Radical in social and political matters, and indifferent to convention or tradition, she was, in effect, aping the style and techniques of a higher social class, albeit with inadequate resources. Not surprisingly she sometimes found Radicals and Socialists uncomfortable associates. She reacted against Annie Besant for her ugly short hair and her unfashionable dresses. According to Sylvia Emmeline herself never left the house without wearing her veil.[26] Conversely, William Morris disapproved of Emmeline because of her affectation for smart Parisian clothes. Sylvia recalled her mother's experience in 1890 at a Socialist meeting addressed by Henry Hyndman in a dingy hall in a back street at which she rose to leave before the chairman had even completed his opening remarks; it transpired that the appearance of a louse on her glove had been too much to endure![27] It seems clear that from an early stage in life style and social class mattered a great deal to Emmeline; she was an upwardly mobile Socialist thirty years before Ramsay MacDonald made it fashionable. This peculiar personal configuration expressed itself most strikingly after 1906 when she proceeded to lead the militant suffragette movement away from its original working-class constituency and to establish it within the upper-class drawing rooms of Kensington and Chelsea.

In the long run the contacts acquired during the years at Russell Square contributed less to Richard's Parliamentary career and more to the development of Emmeline's feminism. The traditional view of the movement for women's enfranchisement, which originated with the writings of Sylvia and other suffragettes, portrayed the 1880s and 1890s as a period of decline in the campaign for the vote. The leaders of the movement which had begun in the late 1860s were depicted by Sylvia as too respectable, cautious and patient to make any real impact upon the politicians. But of course this perception reflected the suffragettes' need to establish a clear justification for embarking upon militant tactics after 1905. Sylvia's view was essentially a propagandist one, though it has remained very influential ever since. In fact, the late-Victorian period saw major advances for the women's movement. Several long-standing grievances, including the right of married women to their own property and income and the repeal of the Contagious Diseases Acts, which enabled the Army to run brothels for its men in garrison towns, were rectified by the 1880s. More significantly, women's suffragists began to advance their case for the vote in crucial *indirect* ways, particularly by establishing themselves as both voters and as elected councillors in local government. The creation of elected county councils in 1888 gave a further boost to this process. In the first London County Council elections in January 1889 Jane Cobden and Lady Margaret Sandhurst were returned while Emma Cons was nominated as an Alderman by the Liberal majority on the council. When the right of the three women to sit on the L.C.C. was challenged in the courts the Pankhursts were among those who took up the issue. Apart from proving their skills in local government women were also demonstrating a distinct aptitude in the supposedly male sphere by participating in the running of election campaigns. This was achieved through joining the new party organizations, notably the Primrose League founded by Conservatives in 1883 and the Women's Liberal Federation from 1887 onwards. Far from being diversions from the suffrage movement these bodies attracted more women into a public role, and the Women's Liberal Federation in particular had been formed with a feminist agenda by women who frankly intended to use it to promote the Parliamentary vote more effectively from within the party.

Sylvia's account of this period also misrepresented the role of the Pankhurst family itself. For example, Emmeline apparently *endorsed* the Parliamentary strategy, for she joined the Women's Liberal Federation even though she and Richard were leaning towards Socialism, and she even became a candidate for its executive committee in 1891.[28] Her link with the WFL is a reminder that for many years Emmeline participated in the constitutional movement for female emancipation which she and her daughters later disparaged as ineffective and impassive. She and Richard sat on the Committee of the Manchester National Society for Women's Suffrage between 1882 and 1885 even if they did not always agree with its methods. Indeed, they usually sided with Lydia Becker, the leading moderate suffragist, despite her lack of support for Richard's 1883 election.

On the other hand, even in the 1880s Richard and Emmeline felt increasingly impatient with what they regarded as a lack of progress in winning the vote for women. It was during their time at Russell Square that they helped to form a new pressure group, the Women's Franchise League. This initiative grew out of a major tactical dispute within the suffrage movement: what *exactly* were women to demand from Parliament? This was a far more complex question than it appeared to be. Ever since 1870 most of the legislation drawn up to enfranchise women, including Richard's original draft, had been cautious measures designed to give a vote to *unmarried* women and widows. To contemporaries this appeared to make good sense particularly from a tactical point of view. Suffragists assumed that proposals for a modest female electorate were best calculated to reassure politicians fearful of the implications if women suddenly became a majority of voters. It is worth remembering that even in the late-1880s when the British electorate stood at 5,700,000, four out of every ten *men* still remained without a vote. Consequently almost all advocates of votes for women assumed that it would be impractical to demand a vote for all women in the first instance. It was not certain how many women would have been enfranchised by the proposals made in the 1870s but 400,000 is the likely figure. An approximate guide is offered by female municipal voters who comprised single women and widows who paid rates. By the 1890s they numbered over 700,000 or about 14 per cent of the local government electorate.

But the claim for a limited vote for women was based on more than tactics. Many contemporaries felt that the case for enfranchising single women seemed unanswerable in the context of British political thought which held that taxation without representation was unjust. Those who sustained the state by their ownership of property and by contributing to taxation had traditionally been regarded as citizens in the full sense. The repeated extension of votes to women who were local government ratepayers clearly reflected this view. Consequently the bills introduced into the House of Commons by sympathetic MPs invariably omitted to mention married women or, if they did, they explicitly excluded them.

However, these tactics actually played into the hands of the opponents of women's suffrage. Speaking in a debate in 1875 one backbencher complained: 'Under this Bill, elderly virgins, widows, a large class of the demi-monde and kept women . . . [will] be admitted to the franchise, while the married women of England – mothers who [form] the mainstay of the nation – [are] rigidly excluded.'[29] An enormous reservoir of prejudice against and fear of single women stood behind such remarks. But the issue also aroused serious underlying concerns about British society. During the latter decades of the century politicians became increasingly alarmed at the evidence that middle-class birth rates were falling and that young women were postponing marriage; they genuinely believed that wives were more deserving of a vote and felt loath to be seen to reward the unmarried for avoiding matrimony. Many of the Liberal allies of the women's suffrage movement, including Sir Charles Dilke and Jacob Bright, had always felt unhappy about putting forward bills that excluded wives, and by the 1880s they believed this restriction was hampering the cause in Parliament. However, the suffrage organization outside Parliament remained in the control of Lydia Becker, Millicent Fawcett and others who believed that a limited first instalment offered the only realistic hope of success; indeed, they strongly suspected, and with some reason, that anti-suffragists were urging the more democratic proposal precisely because this would ensure its defeat.

By the 1880s the Pankhursts, who had always been close to Dilke and Bright, inclined to the view that the time had come to push for votes for married women. With this aim in mind the Women's Franchise League was formed in July 1889 with Mrs Wolstenholme Elmy as secretary and a committee that included Richard, Emmeline, Ursula and Jacob Bright, Alice Scatcherd, Harriet Blatch, Jane Cobden and Lady Sandhurst. At its first public meeting at the Westminster Palace Hotel on 7 November the League adopted the 1870 bill drawn up by Richard with the proviso that no one should be disqualified from voting by marriage. Although time was to prove the wisdom of this approach, the Women's Franchise League itself did not enjoy much success. Almost from the start it suffered from internal splits and lost sight of its original purpose.[30] Mrs Elmy suspected that the Pankhursts wanted to use the League as a means of restoring the career of Sir Charles Dilke. Once the most brilliant of the Radical Parliamentarians, Dilke's prospects were ruined when he had been cited in a divorce case.[31] This, however, did not deter the Pankhursts who envisaged Dilke as the ideal leader for both the women's movement *and* the independent representation of labour. This was an ambitious programme but a very attractive one in the late 1880s and early 1890s as a result of the revival of Socialist organizations, the upsurge of industrial militancy and the emergence of working men like Keir Hardie who were actively seeking seats in Parliament. It was tempting to see the two causes as natural allies on the grounds that feminism was as fundamentally opposed to the capitalist system as was the labour movement. In this spirit the Women's Franchise League sent its speakers out to labour and Socialist organizations to harness their support. This experience clearly left its mark on Emmeline who later adopted the same approach during the early years of the Women's Social and Political Union.

However, in the early 1890s it proved beyond the powers of the League to unite feminism and the labour movement. Fabian Socialists for example were not usually keen on votes for women which they regarded as a minor reform which would come *after* the achievement of a Socialist society, not before. More immediately Mrs Elmy judged it a tactical mistake to mix women's suffrage with so many other issues. In this she was almost certainly correct, for the Pankhursts were spreading their efforts far too thinly. The League adopted a programme including co-education, the abolition of the House of Lords, trade union reform and a multitude of women's issues. Mrs Elmy resigned as secretary in 1891 to be replaced by Ursula Bright, but still the League did not flourish. It recruited only a few hundred members mostly in London, Leeds and Lancashire. Its income for 1890–91 was only £350. But above all the League wasted its effort on internal faction fighting with the other suffragists. This came to a head in 1892 when the women's suffrage bill was being introduced again in the House of Commons by Sir Alfred Rollit, a Conservative member. The Brights, Pankhursts and others denounced Rollit's bill as 'class legislation aimed to enfranchise only wealthy women and women lodgers'. Ironically, Emmeline's opinion on this point fluctuated wildly, for during the Edwardian period it was this same bill that she attempted to force upon successive governments regardless of the exclusion of wives. In fact, after 1906 she insisted that *any* women's suffrage bill was acceptable however few women it included, but by then she had moved sharply away from her original Radical-Socialist views. Thus in an ideological sense the Women's Franchise League was not a precursor of the Women's Social and Political Union, though its methods did prepare the way for militancy. For example, the League often closed its meetings with a decision to constitute itself as a 'lobbying committee' which then set off to the House of Commons to interview MPs. In 1892 Richard and Emmeline were particularly irritated to find that many of their Liberal allies such as Richard Haldane seemed to assume that since victory could not be expected for some years the precise details in the bill hardly mattered. 'Why are women so patient?' demanded Richard, 'Why don't you force us to give you the vote?'[32] For Emmeline these dealings with sympathetic politicians were all part of the process of disillusionment with parties in general and the Liberals in particular. However, the Women's Franchise League could not expect to make a major impact on the MPs as long as it failed to represent the majority of suffragists in the country; with inadequate funds and membership the League struggled on for several years but the Pankhursts played little further part in it.

By 1892 the bright hopes Emmeline had entertained about the move to London had begun to dim. From 1890 onwards Richard had been suffering from gastric ulcers and was obliged to take long periods of rest. This may help to explain why he missed the chance to contest the election in 1892. However, the underlying problem lay in his semi-detached political stance. In September 1890 he and Emmeline had joined the Fabian Society. Though this was not by any means incompatible with being a Liberal, Richard had effectively broken with his old party by this time. Yet the Fabians had no pretensions to become a popular movement and there was no Socialist organization capable of fighting Parliamentary elections effectively. Richard disapproved of the only alternative Socialist organization, the Social Democratic Federation, whose leaders were rather anti-feminist. The prospect of another expensive election fought as an independent clearly held few attractions. But in this case what remained of the rationale for residing in London?

Eventually finance tipped the balance against London. In their haste to move into Russell Square neither Emmeline nor Richard had appreciated that they had taken the house at the end of a 99-year lease. When this expired in 1892 they found themselves liable for 'dilapidations' – in effect, accumulated repairs and redecoration. They had already had to replace the inadequate brick drains at the insistence of the sanitary authority. Richard duly paid the bill only to find that the owner had no intention of carrying out the improvements. He proceeded to demolish the house, replacing it with the Hotel Russell which still stands on the site. Combined with continued losses on the shop this depressing turn of events undermined Richard's spirits still further. He spent some time at a hydro at Matlock in Derbyshire to improve his health but still suffered bouts of severe pain. Since the bulk of his legal work continued to be in the north it now seemed sensible to withdraw from London and return to Lancashire.

4

The Making of a Political Leader
(1893–8)

'The law is not made to protect the people but to oppress them.'
Richard Pankhurst, John Bruce Glasier Diary, 30 November 1896

As their return to the north-west early in 1893 did nothing to heal the
Pankhursts' breach with the Gouldens, the family spent the first year
moving in and out of three different homes. However, the disruption
of the pattern of life they had enjoyed in Russell Square proved beneficial for the children in several ways. Initially the family took an
apartment – in effect, lodgings – in Southport, probably because the sea
air was thought likely to be good for Richard. Suddenly they found
themselves without servants or a governess, and even Aunt Mary left
them to get married. In this situation Emmeline's reservations about
sending the children to school quickly collapsed. During the spring term
the girls attended Southport High School for Girls run by a Mr and Mrs
Ross, despite Emmeline's feeling that Adela, at seven, was too young. In
fact, the experience of being separated from one another proved a
healthy one. For the first time Adela enjoyed friends of her own age to
play with and she discovered teachers who were willing to provide a
sympathetic ear for her stories. As Adela became conscious of her ability
to entertain and to hold an audience her adult persona as a skilful platform performer and an attentive parent-teacher began to take shape.
Her only embarrassment at Southport arose from her father's stipu-
lation that the girls were to be excused from Scripture lessons. Even
Sylvia, who was told to read a history book while her peers had Scripture,
admitted that she listened with great interest to the Old Testament
stories which formed the staple of religious instruction.

Like her younger sister, Sylvia made many new friends at the school. After the long confinement in the hot-house, adult-dominated world of Russell Square, Southport brought a welcome element of normality into their lives. Sylvia flourished there both because of her willingness to apply herself to work and because she received more encouragement than she had at home. She also enjoyed the advantage of being one of a class of only seven. Her report for the spring term of 1893 put her first in French, English grammar, history, geography, spelling, reading and writing. Since she was ten and three-quarters by comparison with the average age of nine this was not remarkable, but as Sylvia was not accustomed to being first in her family the encouragement was undoubtedly beneficial for her. Under 'Industry' her form teacher commented 'all that could be desired', and the headmistress summed up: 'A most promising pupil.'[1] In these comments one sees the beginnings of the prolific author and indefatigable researcher Sylvia was to become during the 1920s and 1930s.

Significantly, Christabel took relatively little pleasure in the social and academic resources of the new school. Though her work was described as 'Good' or 'Very good' in a number of subjects, being placed in a larger group immediately revealed her limitations. Amongst fourteen pupils she was placed thirteenth in French, fifth in grammar, seventh in history, sixth in geography, thirteenth in arithmetic where the teacher rated her 'Weak', and eleventh in writing where she was described as 'Very Poor'. Overall she was placed ninth out of fourteen girls. This was a disconcerting experience. As the eldest child in the home she had enjoyed a dominant position without effort, whereas in school her teachers quickly concluded that she would do well only if she *tried*. Though only thirteen years old, Christabel had already been firmly cast in a mould from which she was never really to escape. She had been turned into a little adult too early in life.

Unfortunately the Southport experience was interrupted in the summer of 1893 by another move, this time to Disley some sixteen miles south-east of Manchester where once again the children's education was put in the hands of a governess. On the other hand Disley proved to be an enjoyable interlude. For some months it isolated the family from the perpetual round of politicking and threw Emmeline and the two younger children together to a much greater extent than previously. They took a hill-top farm house for the summer and, while Richard travelled by train into Manchester, Emmeline enthusiastically rediscovered her own rural childhood. She hired a pony and trap, purchased a donkey for the children and took part in hay-making and blackberrying. Sylvia happily roamed the fields alone, painting, drawing and writing poetry. However, after a while the pleasures of the countryside inevitably began to pall, especially for Emmeline who found Disley inconvenient for the kind of life to which she aspired. By the autumn she had found a much more suitable home at Number 4 Buckingham Crescent – later renamed Daisy Bank Road – in Victoria Park on the southern edge of Manchester but within easy reach of the city centre. This was a large property, at that time one of only four in the street, set well back from the road in a garden full of lilac, laburnum and hawthorn trees. This third move also involved a return to formal education in the shape of Manchester Girls High School, founded in 1871 with the aim of offering girls an education equal to that commonly enjoyed by boys. However, none of the sisters derived the full benefit from this opportunity. As a much larger institution than they were accustomed to – between five and six hundred pupils – the school left Adela in particular feeling slightly lost. All three disliked the discipline imposed upon them, and found the nine-to-four day and the homework a tiresome burden. However, the Pankhurst girls were generally regarded as quiet and well-behaved despite occasional infringements of the rules. From Emmeline's point of view the emphasis placed on turning the girls into young ladies and on eradicating their Lancashire accents was very welcome. Yet, despite her daughters' abilities, she continued to show little or no interest in encouraging their formal education, preferring simply to let them cultivate their artistic interests. As at Southport Sylvia's talent as an artist quickly attracted attention and praise, though she grew bored with the rigidity of a timetable that required her to study arithmetic, French, history and geography. In the absence of parental encouragement none of the girls responded well to the academic tone of the school; indeed, as time passed Emmeline increasingly undermined its efforts by conducting disputes with the headmistress and by encouraging the girls to take days off at any opportunity. When Richard suggested that Christabel ought to have coaching in order to help her prepare for university matriculation Emmeline actually wept in anger, fearful that her girls would be turned into mere school teachers![2]

The three girls also had to cope with a certain amount of friction between their parents and the school arising out of the Pankhursts' political opinions. The headmistress, the formidable Miss Elizabeth Day, anticipating difficulties, had apparently asked the governors to refuse to admit the Pankhursts on the grounds of Richard's atheistic and republican sympathies. Sylvia became embarrassed when the other girls asked why she did not attend Scripture lessons and whether this meant she was a Jew.[3] Characteristically she responded to the teasing by becoming aloof and taking refuge in her drawing and painting. Christabel, however, found a different way of coping with the situation. She quickly acquired a good reputation with her form teacher who appointed her a class monitor. Unfortunately Miss Day intervened more than once to deny her such distinctions because of minor infringements of the rules, provoking Emmeline to further scorn and increasing Christabel's alienation from the system. The gulf between home and school was deepened when Emmeline employed a private dancing master for the girls. As usual Christabel soon displayed evidence of ability and before long was giving performances at Independent Labour Party meetings and even teaching dancing to the members' daughters. At this Emmeline's imagination took flight and, before long, she had developed an ambition for Christabel to become a professional ballerina. She envisaged travelling around with her to give performances in all the capital cities of Europe. This, she insisted, was far more valuable than the teaching provided by the Girls High School. Although Richard did not regard this as a serious prospect, for several years it was accepted in the family that Christabel would become a dancer. However, she grew a little tall for a ballerina and soon lost interest in the idea. 'People will say my brains are in my feet', she declared.[4] Whether she really had the temperament necessary for the prolonged training of a ballerina seems doubtful. Though extremely upset by this, Emmeline evidently accepted the decisive rejection of her idea by Christabel – an early indication of her readiness to defer to her eldest daughter.

Her new base in Victoria Park enabled Emmeline to resume her public work, albeit without the style and pretension of the Russell

Square salon. In fact, the five years from 1893 to 1898 witnessed her emergence from Richard's shadow as a political figure in her own right. She soon joined the Lancashire and Cheshire Union of the Women's Liberal Federation, which may seem surprising since both Pankhursts had become Fabian Society members in 1890. However, during the 1890s the Women's Liberal Federation had a very feminist agenda including not only votes for women but equal pay, higher education, and the repeal of the protective legislation which excluded women from several industrial occupations. Emmeline's membership was therefore indicative of her continuing zeal for women's emancipation rather than of a return to the Liberal Party itself. In any case, in this period many middle-class Radicals like the Pankhursts belonged to both Liberal and Socialist organizations simply because they shared a common agenda and a similar recognition that in the face of growing urban poverty and economic decline, the old *laissez-faire* philosophy would have to give way to some form of interventionism. What was not yet clear was which political strategy would be most efficacious for achieving a new social policy and for promoting the direct representation of working-class communities in Parliament. In the 1890s the Pankhursts were naturally attracted by the emergence of an entirely fresh organization in the shape of the Independent Labour Party which was founded in 1893. Soon the house in Buckingham Crescent resounded to the talk of leading figures in the ILP and other Socialist movements including Keir Hardie, John and Katharine Bruce Glasier, Tom Mann, Robert Blatchford and Pete Curran, in addition to the veteran German Socialists, Wilhelm Liebknecht and Eleanor Marx. From 1893 the Pankhursts were effectively Socialists and Emmeline finally resigned from the W.L.F. in September 1894. Ursula Bright remonstrated with her over this by pointing out the electoral weakness of the new party: 'You see how badly the Labour Party [.L.P.] were beaten at Attercliffe', she wrote after the I.L.P's first by-election, 'they have not the sympathy of their own class.'[5] She had a valid point. In their impatience with the Liberal Party the Pankhursts failed to recognize how long it would take before the new party became credible among working-class voters. Nor had Emmeline yet adjusted to the *social* implications of association with the Labour Movement. She characteristically complained that after joining the ILP she and

Richard had ceased to receive their usual invitations to functions at Manchester Town Hall!

They also remained oblivious to the extent to which the children suffered from their rigid political views and their involvement with public causes. Adela especially felt herself cut off from normal contacts. For example, when she made friends with a girl called Katie whose father happened to be a Conservative councillor, Richard and Emmeline, egged on by Sylvia, intervened to put an end to it. One of Adela's friends took her side by telling the interfering sister: 'Your face would frighten a crow off its nest.' At this Sylvia almost fainted but promptly reported the incident to her parents.[6] Conversely, Christabel, already showing signs of tiring with her parents' political rigidity, declared that there was no need to cut themselves off from people simply because they themselves were Socialists. This controversy over Katie underlined the fact that the Pankhursts took no part in the social life of their fellow middle-class professionals in Manchester. As a result the children were expected to join working-class children on expeditions of the Clarion Cycling Club and to attend parties organized for slum children. Their reactions to these forced social occasions varied according to age and temperament. As the youngest Adela was simply horrified by the experience because she could not understand the point behind it. Sylvia evidently acquired a lifelong sympathy for the poor and oppressed. But Christabel seemed less moved. When her parents purchased a brand new bicycle she enjoyed the leading role this gave her in the Clarion Club, and, like so many adolescent girls in the 1890s, she revelled in the sense of freedom which cycling brought. However, the forced intimacy with the conditions of working-class life failed to engender much sympathy in the impressionable teenage girl, and it is hard not to see the seeds of her later repudiation of the Labour Movement in the experiences of the 1890s.

Richard and Emmeline had first met Keir Hardie in 1888 at the International Labour Conference in London. At that time his politics, like theirs, were in the process of evolving from his original Gladstonianism towards Socialism. After winning election as an independent Socialist member for West Ham in 1892 Hardie became the leading inspiration for the Labour Movement in Britain. But for the Pankhursts he was a close family friend for many years as well as a staunch political ally. It was in 1893 that Sylvia came home from school one day to find him ensconced in an armchair beside the fire. To the impressionable eleven-year-old he seemed not only a heroic figure, but a very lovable person:

There he was; his majestic head surrounded by ample curls going grey and shining with glints of silver and golden brown; his great forehead deeply lined; his eyes two deep wells of kindness, like mountain pools with the sunlight distilled they always seemed to me . . . I felt that I could have rushed into his arms.[7]

As her florid language suggests, the encounter with Hardie was to be the start of something more than just a political alliance in Sylvia's life.

Although the Pankhursts' growing involvement with the ILP undermined still further Richard's ability to attract clients, it had positive implications for Emmeline's political career. With all her vitality and courage she had, up to this point, played an essentially supporting role for Richard. After the 1885 election the illuminated Address presented to Richard by the Rotherhithe Liberals praised her for 'the noble spirit of wifely devotion and self-denying patriotism she has shown'.[8] Even in the years at Russell Square she had felt too nervous to deliver a speech when the opportunity to do so had presented itself. Yet though she never ceased to promote her husband's claims, a subtle but decisive change in their relationship occurred between 1894 and 1896 as Emmeline raised her own political profile while Richard's career passed its peak. It was chiefly under the auspices of the ILP that she made the transition. The new party proved to be far more congenial towards women's role than the older Socialist organizations at this time. Trapped in its rigid Marxist perspective, the Social Democratic Federation viewed female aspirations essentially as an expression of bourgeois individualism. And although the Fabian Society allowed female participation it remained indifferent towards votes for women; its most prominent female member, Beatrice Webb, actually signed an anti-suffrage petition in 1889.[9] In contrast the ILP both advocated reforms for women and encouraged them to participate in its propaganda. As a result many female politicians first learned to handle audiences by practising their street-corner oratory on ILP soap-boxes. For Emmeline the opportunity to do so arose in connection with local government, a sphere in which the ILP enjoyed its main successes.

Local elections in the late Victorian period were not the furtive and apathetic affairs they became during the twentieth century. Candidates were expected to present themselves on public platforms to address large and often boisterous meetings. The limited concession to enfranchise female ratepayers in 1869 proved to be the thin end of a wedge, for it was soon taken for granted that the right to vote also implied the right to stand for election. As elective local government steadily expanded owing to the creation of School Boards, County Councils, and Parish, Urban and Rural District Councils, a wide field of opportunity opened up for women. Since politicians of all kinds regarded local government as essentially an extension of women's conventional domestic responsibilities and as an appropriate use of their skills and knowledge as household managers and mothers, it seemed to women suffragists absurd to exclude married women from the local electorate. Consequently, during 1893 and 1894 when the Liberal government was enacting legislation to create elective local authorities for parishes and Urban and Rural Districts, several backbenchers, led by Walter McLaren, successfully urged the inclusion of wives. The reforms of 1894 also widened female participation in another crucial way. Of all the local authorities the Poor Law Boards of Guardians, which levied a poor rate to finance assistance for children, the elderly, the sick, unemployed working men, single mothers and indeed anyone suffering from poverty, had long been seen as a suitable forum for women's participation. In spite of this the first female Guardian had been elected as recently as 1875, and up to 1890 the total for England and Wales stood at only eighty. Many potential female Guardians were ineligible because they failed to meet the property qualifications required of all candidates, regardless of gender. These qualifications were abolished by the Liberals in 1894 with dramatic effect on the number of women elected – the number rising to 893 by 1895. Emmeline was one of those who benefited from this reform.

In July 1894 the ILP had nominated Emmeline as one of its candidates for the Manchester School Board. Nineteen candidates were put forward for fifteen places, with Emmeline coming in seventeenth, closely followed by the two other Labour candidates.[10] Though unsuccessful in this first attempt, she stood in December 1894 in the elections for the Chorlton-upon-Medlock Board of Guardians in Manchester and was comfortably returned as one of the two representatives for the Openshaw ward:

Mrs Pankhurst	1,276
Mrs Massey	1,020
A. Stansfield	290
F. J. Burke	190

She retained her seat until August 1898 when she resigned.

Victorian Poor Law Boards were highly influential authorities. The Chorlton Board covered six townships stretching from central Manchester to the east and south-east of the city incorporating a population of 299,000 including 24,000 in Emmeline's Openshaw ward. In a fairly typical winter week in 1894 the Board provided outdoor relief to 3,573 persons and supported another 2,063 inside the workhouse. Its expenditure for the year reached £35,000.[11] Relief was dispensed by paid officers and other staff, presided over by the twenty-four elected Guardians who included five women during Emmeline's term. They held weekly meetings, though much work was also done in the sub-committees. In her first year Emmeline sat on sub-committees for Schools, Female Cases, House Female Side Including Lunatic Wards, and Relief Committee Number Five.[12] In her account Sylvia Pankhurst painted a classic picture of the Poor Law Board as a nest of reactionaries heroically put to flight by her mother's arrival. The local reports certainly confirm that she was frequently at the centre of lively arguments. Many of the Guardians were small businessmen closely attuned to the ratepayers' demand for strict economy. One boot and shoe merchant, Mr Mainwaring, was regularly seen to write 'Keep Your Temper' on his blotting paper whenever one of Emmeline's proposals came up for discussion![13] However, Sylvia exaggerated both the Board's conservatism and her mother's influence on it. Newspaper reports show that Emmeline frequently found herself in a small minority when votes were taken. Sylvia also incorrectly attributed to Emmeline credit for introducing the system of building cottage houses in the countryside so as to remove the children from the workhouse. Back in the 1830s when the New Poor Law system had been introduced, it had never been intended that all categories of paupers should be kept in a single building, but lack of resources usually meant that the boards had nothing beyond a single workhouse and a hospital in the case of the larger authorities. Before Emmeline's election Chorlton had already decided to construct cottage homes for 120 boys and 160 girls and infants as well as schools for the younger ones, workshops, bakehouses, isolation wards, hospital accommodation and a swimming bath.[14] The new programme was implemented during Emmeline's term of office.

On the other hand, her experience on the Chorlton Board greatly accelerated Emmeline's politicization. She found her first close look at the spartan conditions, dreary diet and regimentation inside the workhouse rather a shock. Inmates were obliged to wear a uniform, they had nowhere to keep their letters and personal possessions, and husbands and wives were usually separated. Consequently the day-to-day operation of the workhouse offered great scope for improvement to a newly elected Guardian, especially a female Guardian. Emmeline tried to reduce the hours worked by elderly women from six and a half each day to four, but was voted down by 11 to 5. She pressed successfully for the provision of lockers in which the inmates might store their personal belongings and for proper chairs with backs for the elderly to sit on rather than the usual benches.[15] She also discovered that the girls lacked adequate underwear, nightdresses and warm clothing. These were precisely the kinds of issues about which the male Guardians were ignorant or which they failed to raise because they were thought an improper subject for discussion. The matron confessed that she could not speak to the male Guardians about knickers for the girls: 'It's different for you Ma'm', she told Emmeline.[16]

Emmeline also devoted much effort to cajoling the Board into introducing a more varied diet into the workhouse. Naturally much of the argument turned on cost. Having ascertained the weekly expenditure per head she insisted:

Two and two pence three farthings was surely small enough to suit anybody. What was wanted . . . was less in bulk, but more variety and better quality.

The proportions at present seemed to be wrong. Each inmate had a certain amount of bread allowed to him whether he wanted it or not.[17]

As the price of bread had fallen by half since the 1870s it was tempting to feed the inmates little except bread. But they evidently received it in large dry chunks and as a result a good deal of it was wasted and ended up being fed to the pigs. The revelation that existing practice was wasteful helped Emmeline to press for a series of innovations; bread was to be spread with margarine – a recent and cheap substitute for butter – and made into puddings. It was also agreed to grow more vegetables and to place a weekly order for bacon for the workhouse. In view of the complaints about the poor quality of meat supplied, Emmeline inquired what price was paid for it. When informed it was four pence per pound she commented that six pence was not an extravagant price to pay.[18] This was indeed true, for as a result of the huge imports of beef and lamb from Australia and South America since the 1880s, the average price in Britain had fallen from around one shilling to six pence a pound.

The Chorlton Guardians also found themselves on the sharp end of a major national issue – unemployment – which reached serious levels during the winter of 1894-5. During the months prior to Emmeline's election she and Richard had taken part in a Committee for the Relief of the Unemployed operating from an office in Deansgate in Manchester. Each day she toured the city's markets seeking donations of food from merchants and shopkeepers and then assisted in the distribution of soup and bread in Stevenson Square, Ancoats, Gorton and Openshaw where the distress was great. But the Pankhursts never deceived themselves that these measures were any more than palliatives. Unemployment put the Poor Law system under acute strain both from an immediate financial point of view and from a moral-political point of view. In principle the Guardians were supposed to insist that able-bodied men who applied for assistance should be offered 'indoor relief', that is, to enter the workhouse. To give them outdoor relief was considered likely to undermine their will to work and to become, in effect, a subsidy to low wages. However, these bracing principles had always been regarded as inappropriate throughout the north of England where cyclical unemployment created temporary unemployment for thousands of respectable, hard-working men. When the rules were strictly applied many of those in need refused to apply to the Guardians for fear of entering the workhouse, though many sympathetic Boards gave the men outdoor relief. However, by the 1890s it was increasingly recognized that the resources generated by the rates simply failed to measure up to the scale of the problem. As President of the Local Government Board in the 1870s Joseph Chamberlain had urged local authorities to organize special schemes to provide temporary employment in periods of economic depression. Though many did so, they faced criticism from ratepayers over the costs, as well as from local employers, who considered the work inherently uneconomic, and often from trade unions who regarded the rates paid to the men as too low.

The issue surfaced in Chorlton in January 1895 when the Board had to decide how to respond to enquiries from the Local Government Board in London as to whether applications for relief had increased, whether exceptional arrangements were contemplated, and whether some of the men in distress were failing to apply for assistance.[19] Emmeline persistently urged her fellow Guardians to consider providing more employment:

She noticed there was a tendency to put the present state of affairs down to the depraved character of the people themselves. It should be remembered that these poor people could not make employment. It was another class, amongst whom were most of the members of that Board, who provided employment. Surely it was their duty to devote serious attention to the present unsatisfactory state of affairs which did not guarantee work to men and women willing to work.[20]

However, her opponents pointed out that the Guardians' function was to relieve the unemployed and that they had no powers to employ men for wages. In spite of this it was subsequently reported that the Chorlton Union had employed some of the local unemployed at its stone works.[21] At the end of February 1895 a demonstration by a thousand unemployed men took place in Stevenson Square in Manchester where demands were made that the Government should help local boards to grant relief without loss of voting rights and provide work paid at trade union rates for skilled men and at six pence per hour for the unskilled. Afterwards the men arranged to march to the various Poor Law Boards in Manchester, Salford and Chorlton. Richard Pankhurst introduced a deputation to the Manchester Board urging it to pool resources with the City Council, but the chairman replied that they had no power to provide employment. The deputation then proceeded to wait upon Emmeline and her colleagues: 'Lively Scenes At Chorlton Guardians' reported one local newspaper. After a heated debate Emmeline persuaded the reluctant board to appease the men by agreeing to receive the deputation. When Richard had explained the marchers' case a second rather confused discussion took place. One lady Guardian accused the deputation of bribing the men to attend the march by threatening to withhold soup tickets if they refused. At this a member of the deputation indicated he would inform the crowd outside of her name.[22] Emmeline herself threatened to publicize the fact that only two Guardians had joined her in accepting the marchers' demands. Whether intimidated by all this or persuaded by the arguments, the Guardians agreed that they would send a deputation to the City Council to urge it to take steps to implement a public works scheme for the city. They also adopted the men's view that those who received relief in time of distress ought not to be disenfranchised. Amid considerable excitement the chairman then declared the proceedings closed. Meanwhile, Richard and Leonard Hall of the ILP addressed the waiting crowd outside which was now accompanied by a large force of police. Although unhappy about the announcement that the Guardians refused to do anything substantial, the men eventually agreed to march back to Stevenson Square where they were served with soup before dispersing.

These controversies rapidly projected Emmeline into a position of prominence. In September 1895 she delivered a paper, written by Richard, to the North West Poor Law Conference meeting at Ulverston in which she argued that ever since Elizabethan times the Guardians had enjoyed powers to employ workless people. The ILP's favoured variation on this theme was that Boards should acquire land in order to start farm colonies with a view to drawing off the surplus labour from congested urban areas, though, despite Emmeline's paper, it was far from clear that the boards had the legal power to do so. Though

Emmeline shared these interventionist views, like many of the middle-class women elected to local authorities she also entertained a rather critical attitude towards working-class parents, and, on the basis of the evidence she had seen in the workhouse, she believed that many children would be better removed from their homes to institutional care. In 1897 she delivered another paper at the Northern Poor Law Conference which proposed in somewhat chilling words 'increased powers of detention for children of degraded parents'. Whenever parents were judged to be incapable either financially or morally the Board would acquire 'direct Guardianship'. Such zeal for breaking up families was quite typical of Victorian thinking and Emmeline should not therefore be seen as unduly ruthless or autocratic in her determination to deal with child poverty.

Her experience with the Chorlton Board between 1894 and 1898 not only boosted Emmeline's self-confidence, it also accentuated her natural impatience with those who placed practical obstacles in the way of her ideas, and it gave her a fine appreciation of the absurdity of elected male representatives. The alteration in the relative status of Emmeline and Richard became apparent in May 1895 when he was invited to fight a third Parliamentary election in Gorton. Emmeline pointed out that as the constituency included her Openshaw seat on the Chorlton Board he would derive an advantage from her growing reputation there. His return as the MP would have brought their political partnership to a triumphant conclusion. Gorton was an almost entirely industrial constituency stretching from the east of Manchester to Gorton itself, once a separate township which had railway rolling stock works, and took in Denton with its hat-making factories and Haughton where there were coal mines. Not surprisingly the voters had returned a Liberal member comfortably in 1885 with the support of the local Irish. However, even in such a district the growth of working-class Conservatism had sharply reduced the Liberal majority in 1886 and 1892 when William Mather had only narrowly retained the seat. In 1895 when Mather decided not to stand again, the local Liberals hesitated over finding a new candidate, and it was this which led Richard to declare himself ready to stand on behalf of the ILP.

The account left by Sylvia Pankhurst, and repeated by others, which blamed Liberal opposition for Richard's defeat at Gorton was a complete travesty of the 1895 election. On the contrary the Liberals allowed him an unopposed run against a Conservative in what was, after all, a Liberal seat. William Mather actually urged the voters to support him and even made a contribution to his expenses. But if he were to win Richard needed a shrewdly balanced appeal designed to catch two opinion groups. The former member admitted that his own opposition to the eight-hour working day for coal miners had cost him around four hundred votes in 1892 and as a result he had changed his opinion on the issue.[23] As an ILP-er Richard had no problems here. He advocated the eight-hour day, old age pensions and the nationalization of land, the mines and the railways. But he also made a bid for the orthodox Liberal vote on the basis of his known advocacy of Irish Home Rule, Church Disestablishment, the local veto on licensed premises and the abolition of the House of Lords.[24] Throughout the summer Christabel and Sylvia, carrying Richard's colours, which were yellow and black this time, loyally accompanied Emmeline as she spoke from street corners and canvassed on his behalf.[25] In view of the closeness of the previous election it was crucial for Richard to retain the Irish vote. To this end Emmeline journeyed to Liverpool to enlist the backing of T. P. O'Connor the Home Ruler who represented a local constituency. But despite his sympathy for Richard, O'Connor proved unwilling to offer the Irish vote in view of 'the people he is mixed up with', a reflection of Catholic disapproval of the ILP's Socialism, and a calculation that by splitting the Liberal vote the new party would merely hamper attempts to achieve Home Rule.

Quite apart from the Irish factor, the circumstances of the election in July 1895 were not propitious. The sudden dissolution of Parliament following the collapse of Lord Rosebery's discredited Liberal Government deprived reformers of all sorts of their credibility. In these circumstances Richard's defeat was probably inevitable. But the margin was large: 5,865 votes for Hatch to 4,261 for the ILP. In Gorton the Conservatives achieved a substantially larger swing in their favour than in any of the other Manchester and Salford constituencies. Understandably bitter, Richard berated the Liberals as Tories in disguise in his speech at the declaration of poll and complained that they had let him down. But amid the Conservative landslide an ILP victory there would have been a miracle. In truth he refused to recognize that many working men found the ILP's brand of Socialism unconvincing and were simply alienated by reforms designed to impose moral improvements upon them. This habit of blaming a political party for personal setbacks, which obviously rubbed off on Emmeline and Christabel, had become a convenient alternative to coming to terms with an awkward reality – that their opinions were not as popular as the Pankhursts believed. On the other hand Richard's last defeat did have a more positive aspect. After his intervention in 1895 the Liberals failed to run a candidate in Gorton again. As a result, when the political tide turned against the Conservatives in 1906 the Labour Party was in a position to sweep to victory in the constituency. As so often in his career, Richard's own efforts had sown the seed from which others were to reap the benefits.

Of course, it was not clear in 1895 that this would be Richard's last attempt to get into Parliament. 'There's life in the old bird yet', he told the tearful Sylvia on the night of the election.[26] He remained a valuable acquisition for the ILP and was elected to its National Administrative Council in 1896–7. However, the three-year-old party faced a lengthy period of consolidation before it could hope to pose a serious challenge to the older parties on a national scale. Throughout its life the ILP remained handicapped by a lack of financial resources, especially during the 1890s when most trade unions retained a healthy scepticism about Socialism and were reluctant to allow their funds to be diverted into political propaganda. By way of compensation ILP branches relied heavily on spreading the message at no cost by chalking the pavements and stump oratory at street corners.

In Manchester the local Socialists had for several years held open-air meetings in the Boggart Hole Clough, a sixty-three acre site at Blackley to the north of the city centre. But in 1896 these activities provoked a major controversy when the Clough was acquired by Manchester City Council. Before long the Council's Parks Committee, led by Councillor Needham, determined to put a stop to its use by the ILP. As a result, in May a Trades Council member, John Harker, was brought before the magistrates and fined ten shillings for speaking in the Boggart Hole Clough. As Harker's defence counsel Richard argued that there was no legal authority in the shape of a by-law for banning meetings in the Clough, and he therefore proposed to appeal. The council's heavy-handedness now began to play into the hands of the ILP. A succession of speakers took to the platform to address not the usual few hundred, but audiences running into tens of thousands who had been attracted by the controversy. Since the speakers refused to pay their fines, they began to earn prison sentences for exercising their rights of free speech. In June 1896 two members of the ILP, Fred Brocklehurst and Leonard Hall, were sent to gaol for speaking in the Clough. Emmeline regularly joined them on the platform each Sunday where her pink straw bonnet made her a conspicuous feminine focus in the sea of drab male faces. She planted her open umbrella in the ground in order to collect contributions from the crowd which was by now eager to see how the authorities would respond to the defiance. One of the ILP leaders, John Bruce Glasier, recorded in his diary: 'The scene at the Clough a magnificent sight. Not daring to go too near . . . I could not hear Mrs Pankhurst's speech but her words rang clearly thro' the dell . . . she passed out of the gates with an enthusiastic crowd in her train.'[27] After this meeting summonses were granted against Emmeline, John Bruce Glasier, and three other ladies for causing an annoyance. Their trial at the Central Police Court in Manchester on 3 July was attended by hundreds of people inside and out. Afterwards Glasier was exultant: 'Mrs Pankhurst cross examines splendidly. Delivers a defiant speech. No judgement given.'[28] In fact, Emmeline's case was dismissed though she had made plain her determination to continue to speak in the Clough. On the following Sunday Richard drove to Strangeways prison to greet Leonard Hall on his release and he took the opportunity to warn the Governor that Brocklehurst was being detained illegally and that he would be held accountable if any harm befell him. The Governor took it with some amusement and offered to pass on any complaints.[29] Meanwhile Emmeline continued to appear in the Clough on Sundays, usually acting as chairman for meetings which were now addressed by national figures including Keir Hardie and Ben Tillett and attracted crowds of between 20,000 and 30,000 people.

However, by this time the city council and the magistrates had begun to suffer serious embarrassment from the notoriety their policy had attracted. Richard advertised for witnesses to testify to the good conduct of the crowds and even threatened to subpoena unwilling witnesses including the Town Clerk, the Lord Mayor and the Chairman of the Parks Committee who had injudiciously visited the Clough. In July Keir Hardie announced in court that 431 witnesses were now ready to give evidence! In this way the judicial process simply ground to a halt.[30] Meanwhile two local Liberal MPs, Charles Schwann and Frederick Cawley, questioned the Home Secretary, Sir Matthew White Ridley, about the legal basis of the prosecutions and on why those convicted had been placed in the third category of prisoners rather than being treated as political offenders in the first category. Ridley initially claimed that they had breached a by-law, but subsequently conceded that no such by-law or other authority existed.[31] Belatedly the council enacted a new by-law designed to prohibit public meetings except by authorization of the Parks Committee. The council then withdrew its earlier summonses and re-issued them on the basis of its new authority. At this stage they had made themselves ridiculous by revealing the extent to which they had been motivated by purely partisan objectives. Meanwhile the prosecutions had been brought to a standstill by the long list of witnesses waiting to be heard. Eventually the Home Secretary intervened, imposing a new by-law which bound the Committee to approve any reasonable request to hold public meetings in its parks.

This outcome gave the ILP a propaganda triumph which brought tangible gains when Harker and Brocklehurst were elected to the council in the autumn, in the process defeating Councillor Needham who had inspired the prosecutions in the first place. The ease with which the petty bias of elected politicians had been exposed and the majesty of the legal process had been punctured also made an enduring impression upon Emmeline. The magistrates had been noticeably reluctant to enforce the law against respectable middle-class women; and by posing a direct physical challenge to the authorities the ILP had succeeded in attracting publicity, sympathy and funds far more effectively than by its usual methods. It is not too much of an exaggeration to see in the skirmishes at the Boggart Hole Clough an early blue-print for the suffragette campaigns. However, the comparatively easy triumph they had won in 1896 may well have led Emmeline to underestimate her opponents in the struggle to enfranchise women. Votes for women raised far deeper fears and more complex political issues than the question of free speech in public parks. Moreover, in Manchester the radicals had managed to invoke one level of authority to over-rule another; by confronting the central government they were to take on a far more formidable opponent.

All this, however, remained far into the future. In the short term the controversy helped to turn Emmeline into a political leader in her own right; she increasingly received invitations to address ILP meetings in towns all over the north of England. When Keir Hardie fought a by-election in Bradford in October 1896 she gave him her support. Bruce Glasier met her there and noted: 'Mrs Pankhurst as lively as a cricket [,] full of clever comment, criticism, scandal. [Fred] Jowett and I [sat] quite diverted.'[32]

For Richard, on the other hand, the Boggart Hole Clough proved to be a more mixed triumph. Bruce Glasier consulted him at his chambers in November and reported: 'Dr. does not look in very cheery spirits. His practice must have suffered extremely from his recent prominence in the Clough agitation and ILP movement.' Richard advised Glasier that it was unlikely they would be able to win damages for the imprisonment of Leonard Hall and Fred Brocklehurst. 'The law', he exclaimed 'is not made to protect the people but to oppress them.' If they pursued a claim for damages: 'All the glow of martyrdom would be taken away from our struggle by the glow of gold.'[33] Yet if he felt depressed Richard continued to tackle local and national causes with apparently undiminished enthusiasm. During 1896 he became involved in campaigns for the purchase of the Trafford Park estate by the city council and for the construction of houses for rent to working-class families. During the six-month lock-out of engineering workers in 1897 he spoke regularly in support of the demand for an eight-hour day. 1897 also brought him two new victories. Richard had acted as honorary counsel to the Peak and District Preservation Committee which had waged a three-year struggle to secure a public footpath over Kinder Scout. The Pankhursts joined expeditions to walk the route which was regularly obstructed by the Duke of Devonshire and other landowners. In May 1897 the walkers succeeded in establishing a legal right to make use of the path.

Nearer to home Richard plunged into a controversy over the

disposal of sewage effluent into the Manchester Ship Canal from the works at Davyhulme. As a result the corporation was prosecuted, leading the Rivers Committee to propose to abandon its sewage works and to cut a new culvert to take Manchester's effluent further down river into the Mersey between Warrington and Liverpool where they would be free from prosecution. Richard produced financial, practical and environmental arguments against this scheme, and in September he called a Town Meeting of ratepayers which voted overwhelmingly against the council's idea. A referendum vindicated his view by 49,000 votes to 20,000. Richard's role in this was all the more creditable since the council had offered to appoint him as its legal representative for a fee running into thousands of pounds if he agreed to appear on behalf of the culvert scheme.[34]

Unhappily Richard suffered increasingly from spasms of pain from his ulcers during this period. In a vain attempt to restore his health the family spent much of the summer and autumn of 1897 at a farmhouse at Mobberley in Cheshire. For the children this second rural retreat meant another happy escape from regular schooling. However, their parents' unrelenting involvement in public work continued to take its toll especially on the younger ones. Though the only boy in a family dominated by women, the eight-year-old Harry was not mothered very much by anyone, and the four-year gap separating him from Adela was too great for them to become close playmates. Amid the whirlwind of adult activities which he could not really understand, Harry grew into a lonely child who from an early age took to wandering away from home in search of people willing to take an interest in him. According to Adela's account Harry was not only nervous but also rather backward; this was to cause difficulties as he grew to adulthood because he was neither suited to an academic training nor sufficiently robust for physical labour.

It was, however, Adela who displayed the most alarming symptoms of distress in this period. At the age of eleven she ran away from school and was discovered by the gardener in a neighbouring house in the process of changing out of her school uniform. When the headmistress arrived to collect her in a cab, she recognized that this was more than a childish prank, for Adela's unhappiness had led her to the verge of a nervous breakdown.[35] It was arranged for her to take a year away from school, spending the winter of 1896 at home followed by a holiday with Emmeline's sister, Bess, in Aberdeen. On her return Adela responded well to the encouragement and sympathy of her new teacher, Isobel Rhys, and showed new enthusiasm for her work especially in history and music. Although she had refused to explain why she had run away, Adela spoke to her cousins in Scotland about her unhappiness at home; her story probably got back to Richard because he subsequently took a stricter line with Christabel and Sylvia about teasing their younger sister. The episode demonstrated that beneath the rebellious surface Adela remained a vulnerable and emotional girl who continued to be liable to breakdown under stress throughout her life.

In many ways Sylvia coped best during these years. Now aged sixteen, she often accompanied her father on Sunday mornings on his visits to Ancoats, Gorton and Hulme where, perched on a box or a chair, he addressed audiences of working men and women. Though moved deeply by the poverty of these districts Sylvia was also flattered by the reception Richard enjoyed. But for some years it seemed that Sylvia's own future lay not in politics but in her art. In the summer of 1898 she began to have lessons with Elias Bancroft, a well-known Manchester artist who happened to live in Buckingham Crescent. His advice helped to improve her technique: 'I felt a sense of power in seeing the rounded shapes stand forth from my blank paper', she wrote.[36] When some of her work was sent to the Manchester School of Art she was awarded a free scholarship, the first step on the road to a career as a professional painter and illustrator.

By contrast, Christabel, now aged eighteen, lacked any real focus or ambition. Though on the surface she continued to conform to the ideas and priorities of her parents, even she drew unflattering comparisons, on occasion, between them and the parents of her contemporaries. She spoke revealingly about a friend called Edith whose home life involved a light-hearted round of social activities, visits and entertainments, whereas the Pankhurst home was filled with 'nothing but politics and silly old women's suffrage'.[37] By 1897 Christabel had left school, but she travelled into Manchester for lessons in French, logic and dressmaking, an ill-assorted collection of subjects apparently chosen by her mother. But in 1898 Emmeline rediscovered her own youthful love for Paris which she clearly hoped to share with Christabel. She and Noemi Rochefort had promised each other that when they had married and had daughters they would exchange visits to each other's homes in order to encourage them to learn the two languages. In June Emmeline decided to accompany Christabel to Geneva where her friend now lived, but she made a point of stopping in Paris en route. After a nineteen-year absence she felt elated at revisiting the scenes of her youthful adventures, though evidently disappointed that her daughter was less moved: 'Christabel takes it all with her usual calm', she wrote to Richard.[38] At Geneva Christabel became more appreciative and enjoyed a relaxing holiday sitting in the sun, bathing, taking boat trips on the lake, and going for excursions by motor car. Richard must have felt that Emmeline needed a rest after the pressures and disappointments of their life in England. 'When you return', he wrote, 'we will have a new honeymoon and reconsecrate each to the other in unity of heart. Be happy.'[39] Sadly this carefree interlude was abruptly interrupted by the arrival of a telegram: 'I am not well. Please come home.' Emmeline boarded the first train for Paris.

Back at Buckingham Crescent Richard had returned a little more tired than usual after a Saturday morning spent in his chambers. He suddenly left the mid-day meal, and Sylvia later found him sitting in Emmeline's bedroom evidently in some pain. Refusing to call the doctor he went to bed with a hot water bottle. But the following morning Sylvia was so shocked by his appearance that she ran out to find a doctor who brought oxygen cylinders to help Richard breathe. Sylvia sat with her father holding the tube and the doctor returned at intervals all through Sunday. Alone in the house with thirteen-year-old Adela, nine-year-old Harry and the servants, Sylvia naturally found this a traumatic experience. Although the doctor refused to explain to her what exactly was wrong, she drew her own conclusions on the Monday morning when he insisted that a telegram be sent to Emmeline. After sitting with her father during Monday, she was eventually sent to bed and awoke on 5 July to find him dead. Richard was sixty-four. The ulcer that had caused him so much pain over several years had perforated his stomach. Sylvia's grief was greatly exacerbated by the feeling that she might have done more to save her father by calling the doctor and her mother sooner. Meanwhile Emmeline had boarded her train in London only to catch sight of a fellow passenger's newspaper bearing the news of Richard's death. By the time she reached Manchester Mary and her brother Herbert had arrived to console the grieving children.

The funeral on 16 July was a moving and very public spectacle. In full sunshine Richard's coffin, brilliant with red carnations and geraniums, lay on an open carriage attended by cyclists of the Clarion Club and thousands of mourners, almost exclusively working-class men and women, who walked the route from Buckingham Crescent to Brookwood Cemetary. There his body was lowered into the grave without a burial service of any kind. After a few moments of profound silence John Bruce Glasier delivered an address, and other colleagues paid their tributes.[40] Later a headstone was erected bearing the words 'Faithful and true and my loving comrade', chosen by Emmeline from Walt Whitman.

5

The Emergence of Christabel
(1898–1903)

'Christabel is not like other women. She will never be led away by
her affections.'

Emmeline Pankhurst, quoted in E. Sylvia Pankhurst,
The Life of Emmeline Pankhurst (1935), p. 47

Richard's death left Emmeline so distracted and numbed with grief
that for several months she showed none of her usual vitality and sense
of purpose. Emmeline always found death difficult to handle, and it is
arguable that she never recovered completely from the blow. For the
remainder of her life acquaintances saw in her face 'the same sweet
smile touched by sadness'.[1] But in the immediate circumstances adjust-
ments had to be made. At the end of August she resigned her position
on the Chorlton Board of Guardians and stepped back from public
affairs.

At least the tragedy brought Emmeline and Sylvia closer together
for a time; they, after all, felt Richard's loss most deeply. To Adela it
appeared that Sylvia was determined to make the most of her grief by
accusing other members of the family of being too cheerful; she
believed that her mother would have recovered more quickly 'had
Sylvia's white face and eyes, always red with secret, bitter weeping,
not kept her widowhood always before her'. Emmeline herself now
seemed very much alone, not least because Christabel remained in
Geneva until the autumn of 1898. For a time Sylvia slept in her
mother's bed, and they tried to console each other during the long
empty nights. As Emmeline seemed unable to get a grip on day-to-day
affairs, Sylvia temporarily took over the housekeeping, and before

long she had concluded that as the other children grew up and left home, it would be her role to look after her mother.[2]

An ability to stretch the housekeeping money as far as possible now assumed greater than usual importance, for Richard, who, surprisingly for a lawyer of mature years, had failed to made a will, had left the family in a precarious financial state. The Administration issued by his solicitors within a month of his death put his gross estate at an estimated £500, but after deducting tax, costs and presumably some of his debts, a sum of just £40 16s 11d was left to Emmeline. This, however, did not include all Richard's assets, for a number of his share certificates to the value of approximately £800 remained amongst Sylvia's papers; that these were not sold despite the family's financial difficulties, suggests that by 1898 they were worth very little.[3] Unfortunately, since there were still outstanding debts, some of the paintings, books and furniture were sold, and the family moved to a more modest house at Number 62 Nelson Street. Though once referred to as a 'slum' by Adela, the property was, in fact, an attractive double-fronted, semi-detached residence, built of brick and boasting a pediment at roof level. It enjoyed small gardens at front and back.[4] However, the rooms were undoubtedly smaller than those the children had been used to, and in 1898 the house stood in a much more built-up area closer to the centre of Manchester. At the time the short half mile that separated Buckingham Crescent from Nelson Street looked like a yawning social gulf between the comfortable bourgeoisie on the one hand and the precarious lower middle classes on the other. This perception that she had become downwardly mobile for the first time introduced an unwelcome element of insecurity into Emmeline's life, and one which remained with her. After leaving Nelson Street she spent virtually her whole life occupying temporary homes, in hotels, or as a guest in houses belonging to other people. This is why the lengthy periods enjoyed in the gracious establishments of wealthy suffragette supporters after 1905 gave Emmeline much more than merely the chance of physical recuperation; they offered the vicarious pleasures of a style of life that had slipped from her grasp for ever in 1898.

None the less, like many Victorian families coping with the death of the chief breadwinner, the Pankhursts clung tenaciously to their middle-class status by retaining the services of their servant, Ellen. In addition, Emmeline's sister, Mary, whose marriage had failed by this time, came to live with them, as, for a time, did her brother Herbert. Herbert's presence lightened the atmosphere – according to Adela, he and Emmeline 'were the best of friends and there was more laughter in our house than before my father's death'.[5] However, with the four children these additions to the household no doubt made Nelson Street rather crowded and thus seem smaller than it really was. But at least Mary lifted the unwelcome burden of household management from the shoulders of Sylvia and Emmeline. Other forms of assistance proved less acceptable. When Robert Blatchford proposed to launch a financial appeal on the family's behalf in the pages of the *Clarion* the offer was refused, though Emmeline did agree that a testimonial fund might be raised in memory of Richard to be used to help the ILP. In any case she accepted an offer of paid employment as a Registrar of Births and Deaths for the Rusholme District, a post she retained until 1907. Part of the attraction of this position lay in the fact that it required her presence only for a few hours, usually in the early morning or at the end of the day, thus leaving her free to pursue other interests. Unfortunately Emmeline, who had been in no way chastened by her experience in London, soon resurrected Emerson and Co. at Number 40–42 King Street in Manchester. Writing from Geneva Christabel warned her mother: 'I think you could do something better than that!'[6] In spite of the fact that she used Mary and Christabel to help run the business, thereby minimizing her costs, and also gained the free services of another brother, Walter, who was an accountant, in keeping the books, the enterprise proved to be another financial liability.

If the family's financial problems were resolved after a fashion, the emotional consequences of Richard's death proved to be more problematical, not least because the children were left even more to their own devices. It was Adela's feelings of neglect and resentment immediately after 1898 that coloured her view of her family for the rest of her life. At thirteen she was sent to the 'dirty and noisy' Board School in Ducie Street where, having lost her former friends, she felt lonely and unhappy. Moreover, Ducie Street was in Ancoats, one of the poorest parts of Manchester. Sylvia told her not to be snobbish about it, but for Adela the discovery that she had an infestation of lice in her hair, supposedly acquired from her new schoolmates, acutely underlined the family's fall in the social scale and suggested how little importance they attached to her needs and interests.

During these years Harry, now nine, suffered a succession of ailments including chicken-pox, measles, broken teeth owing to a fall, and poor eyesight. Since he was obliged to struggle on without glasses, he began to experience pain whenever he read. At the small private school run by a Mr Lupton, which Harry attended, he found it impossible to read in the dim light. As a result he began to absent himself and find solitary amusements until he, too, was placed at the Board School with Adela. On discovering that his class mistress was a candidate for the Board of Guardians elections, Harry decided to go canvassing for her, but he requested Adela to accompany him as some voters told him he was too young to know anything about the election! Whether this was Harry's attempt to gain attention and praise from a family which otherwise seemed too busy to notice him but which clearly respected public work, must be a matter for conjecture; but Harry certainly repeated these tactics in 1906 when he stood as a candidate in a mock election at school. For a time Emmeline sent him away to King's School, a small private institution in Hampstead, a move hardly calculated to remedy his sense of isolation in the family. However, Harry was happier there, though Emmeline eventually brought him back to Manchester when she could not afford the fees. Consequently, from 1905 Harry attended Manchester Grammar School. He was popular there, though often teased about his Socialism, and he continued to suffer from nervous depression.

For Adela the clouds lifted briefly when she transferred to the Girls High School. By this time the hated Miss Day had retired and been replaced by a younger and more progressive woman, Sarah Burstall, who was a graduate of Girton College, Cambridge. Burstall, who wanted to raise the ambitions of the girls, encouraged Adela to try for a history scholarship at one of the women's colleges at Oxford or Cambridge. Unfortunately Emmeline remained implacably opposed to this idea, egged on by Sylvia who pointed out that it would be against her father's principles.[7] Adela characteristically ignored her and focused on her work despite suffering from migraines and loneliness. Perhaps as a result of the strain, she succumbed to an epidemic of scarlet fever which badly affected her lungs and forced her to recuperate with her grandmother at Douglas in the Isle of Man. This effectively put an end to Adela's academic hopes; she did not return to school. Emmeline insisted that the family's scarce resources must be concentrated on Sylvia and Christabel who were so clever. This was doubly unfair since neither girl actually cost much apart from her keep, and, to judge from the teachers' opinions, Adela gave every indication of being academically superior to both of them. But at a time when most girls had left school by the age of fifteen, it was very difficult for Adela to argue. None the less, the perception that she had been discriminated against continued to rankle, and understandably so. Even if an Oxford College was considered too expensive an option or an inappropriate one for a daughter of Richard Pankhurst, who had certainly disapproved of the university as a privileged and reactionary institution, there was no obvious reason why Adela should not have attended Owen's College which was almost literally on the doorstep. In 1903 she eventually became a pupil-teacher. This was, at least, a career, albeit a poorly paid one. Meanwhile, Adela found herself dragooned into taking her place at Emerson's while her sisters pursued their studies in art and the law.

By chance, when Charles Rowley came to Nelson Street to advise on the value of certain paintings which were to be sold, he examined some of Sylvia's drawings with great approval. As a result, her still life work was dispatched to the Manchester School of Art which subsequently awarded her a free scholarship. Though she greatly enjoyed her experience at the School of Art, Sylvia spent much of her time at home suffering from neuralgia in her head and arms. She also found it exhausting to have to stand up for long periods when drawing or modelling. Worse, her chilblains were greatly exacerbated by the time spent in the life-room which was obviously well heated; at intervals she escaped from the room and relieved her pain by pouring methylated spirits over her feet. These absences made Sylvia feel characteristically guilty about holding a studentship; in her second year she suggested that she should pay the lower fees for part-time attendance. This would have freed her to devote some time to working in the shop, giving some relief to Christabel. In 1901, Sylvia became a full-time student once again after being awarded the Lady Whitworth

Scholarship as the best female student of the year, a prize worth fees plus thirty pounds.

Meanwhile Emmeline had gradually recovered her appetite for politics, stimulated by the controversy following the outbreak of the Boer War in the autumn of 1899. The early stages of the conflict, which saw British forces defeated and humiliatingly besieged at Ladysmith, Kimberley and Mafeking, generated an excitable mood of jingoism at home. Not for the first time the Pankhursts found themselves in a minority. Richard had always criticized what he regarded as British aggression towards the small Boer republics. Emmeline's younger brother, Harold, who had been touring South Africa as an actor, now returned to denounce the war. In 1900 Emmeline herself resigned from the Fabian Society because of the pro-imperialist attitude of its leading members. This was all very well, but, as always, Pankhurst principles brought retribution upon the younger members of the family. After speaking out in favour of peace at school, Harry was knocked down in the street where his teacher found him, apparently unconscious, and carried him home. At the Girls High School one of Adela's teachers stood silently by while another pupil threw a book which hit her in the face. One of Sylvia's fellow students threatened to follow her home and break her windows because of her opposition to the war!

On the other hand, Emmeline derived great pleasure from the news that Keir Hardie had defied the trend by gaining a Parliamentary seat at Merthyr Tydfil in the general election of October 1900 following the decision by the Conservative prime minister, Lord Salisbury, to take advantage of the patriotic fervour by seeking another term of office. However, despite giving the Government a short-term advantage, the South African war eventually proved to be decisive in undermining the Conservative dominance of British politics that had lasted since the Home Rule split of 1886. As the full costs of the conflict became apparent imperial expansionism lost popularity, and the mood in the country returned to domestic social reform once again. In the process the morale of the left-wing parties and the radical pressure groups rapidly revived, preparing the ground for a fresh phase of campaigning by the advocates of women's suffrage.

As yet, however, the Pankhursts were still endeavouring to pick up the threads of their personal lives and restore some semblance of normality. Emmeline had begun her return to public life by becoming a member of the ILP's National Administrative Council in 1898–9, and in November 1900 she won election as a candidate to the Manchester School Board on which she served until March 1903. In that year the elected school boards were abolished under Balfour's 1902 Education Act, but the education committees of the county councils and county boroughs, which took over their functions, were required to include female representation. As a result, though women were not eligible for election to county councils until an Act of 1907, Emmeline was co-opted on to the education committee from April 1903 until October 1904. It was during this period that she met Teresa Billington, who later became an influential early member of the Women's Social and Political Union. As a schoolteacher who had no religious faith, Billington had become anxious to be relieved of scripture classes. The School Inspector, who was unwilling to grant her request, sent her to talk to Emmeline in her capacity as a member of the education committee. They sat down in a corner of her shop in King Street 'among the green-stained oak and the Poole pottery that graced the simple-life homes of those days'. Emmeline was gracious and lovely, but brushed Billington aside imperiously; her request was 'unthinkable . . . a conscience clause for the teacher was utterly impracticable . . . out of the question'.[8] They parted on friendly terms but only because Billington had not attempted to argue with her. Later, in the Women's Social and Political Union, she was not to accept Emmeline's dictation so readily.

After a two-year absence, Emmeline attended the annual conference of the ILP in Leicester at Easter 1901, accompanied by both Sylvia and Christabel. Even at this stage in the party's history Emmeline and Sylvia found a good deal to criticize in its policy and leadership, though Christabel, interestingly, insisted that it behoved her mother to follow the line taken by the NAC.[9] One issue threw an intriguing light on her political outlook at this time. The Conservative Government's educational reforms aroused immense controversy at this time, particularly amongst Nonconformists who greatly resented the use of public money, in the form of rates to which they contributed, for the support of Church of England schools. Some Nonconformists went as far as to undertake passive resistance to the Government's policy by refusing to pay their rates. Though not particularly effective, the tactic helped to undermine middle-class support for the Conservatives and it certainly contributed to the Liberal landslide victory in 1906. At the 1901 ILP conference a proposal was made to support forms of passive resistance in protest against the 1902 Bill, including the withdrawal of pupils and teachers from schools. As the result of an intervention by Keir Hardie, Christabel gained an unexpected opportunity to speak in the debate on this question. She used the occasion to oppose resistance to the legislation, urging the critics instead to rely upon normal propaganda and the ballot box to achieve their aims.[10] Even at the age of twenty Christabel remained, on balance, more of a conformist than a natural rebel. The clarity of speech and the decisiveness which became the hallmarks of her political leadership during the Edwardian period were already very evident, but few could have anticipated at this stage the role she was eventually to play.

In fact, until 1901 Christabel continued to drift languidly through life. Before she left Geneva she had written to Emmeline: 'Have you any ideas about me yet? Madame Dufaux [Noemi] thinks I ought to go in for dressmaking too.'[11] This aimlessness evidently lasted for a period of three to four years. At the age of seventeen Christabel had been overheard by Sylvia, who was quite shocked, telling some friends that all she wanted was to find an easy job which would occupy her from ten in the morning until four each day. Many middle-class Victorian girls of her age filled their lives with eager contemplation of marriage and poured their energies into the rituals of courtship. But there is no indication from any source that Christabel took any interest in boys or ever had a romantic male attachment either then or later in life. According to Adela, the young men of the ILP 'adored her', but she ignored them because they came from a different social class and had no education.[12] But nor did she show any interest in pursuing her education with a view to establishing herself in a career. In this situation Emmeline, who may well have suggested dressmaking with the shop in mind, lost no time in finding ways of occupying her daughter. On returning from Geneva Christabel was detailed to help at Emerson's; after all, according to her mother the chief purpose of the shop was to provide for her. Consequently, a thoroughly unappreciative Christabel would contrive to arrive at Emerson's as late as possible each morning. She spent a little time sitting resentfully among the piles of cushions, silks and ornaments with her nose fixed in the latest novel, before disappearing for a two-hour lunch break. She then left for home as early in the afternoon as possible. In fairness, there was so little business that her presence was hardly necessary.

It was not until 1901 that the great gap in Christabel's life began to be filled through her acquaintance with two remarkable and talented women, Esther Roper and Eva Gore-Booth. They were to be so influential in Christabel Pankhurst's personal and political development that some explanation of their role in the Radical politics of late-Victorian Lancashire is necessary.[13]

Esther Roper, who was thirty-two when Christabel met her, was the daughter of a missionary, the Reverend Edward Roper, who died in 1877 when she was only nine. Her mother received a pension of just £50 a year until she too died, aged forty-three, in 1889. Esther was fully aware that her mother's death had been brought on by anaemia, the result of becoming pregnant far too frequently. Her own rather grim childhood had been spent either at her grandparents' home in Manchester or in the Church Missionary Society's Home. As a result Esther grew up to be a self-sufficient and well-organized but unemotional person. When her mother died the twenty-year-old Esther was two years into her course at Owen's College. She took a degree in history in 1891 at a time when women commonly attended the classes but frequently failed to present themselves for the examinations; it was still widely considered that the pursuit of higher education for girls was, at best, unnecessary and, at worst, likely to lead to psychological illness and immoral behaviour. Esther was, in fact, one of the first group of women to obtain formal degrees from what became the Victoria University of Manchester. Such a woman naturally offered Christabel a much more positive perspective on education by comparison with the rather jaundiced view taken by her mother. While a student Esther, like most of the women, had kept a low profile so as to avoid antagonizing the men. But she had participated in a private debating society for women, and from 1894 onwards she gained employment as an organizing secretary for the North of England Society for Women's Suffrage.

Eva Gore-Booth came from a very different background. Born in

1870, she was one of five children of Sir Henry Gore-Booth, a land-owner in County Sligo in the north-west of Ireland. The Gore-Booths were among the more progressive members of the Anglo-Irish gentry, willing to sell their estates to small farmers and keen to improve agriculture by means of co-operative dairies. By the 1890s many of Eva's generation of Gore-Booths had become Socialists and National-ists. Her elder sister, Constance, later became famous as the wife of Count Markievicz and as the Sinn Fein leader who became elected as an MP for Dublin in 1918, though she never took her seat at West-minster. Eva herself grew up to be a poet, a tall, slender, delicate woman with a mass of beautiful golden hair. Although attractive to men and friendly enough towards them, Eva felt alienated by mascu-linity which for her meant possessiveness, domination, materialism and pride. A gentle, nature-loving person, her ideas seem to prefigure the blend of pacifism, environmentalism and feminism that charac-terized the women's movement in Britain later in the twentieth century. Though not obviously assertive, Eva adopted a determinedly noncon-formist approach to life, refusing to become trapped either by marriage or by the role of the maiden aunt of the family. She had few inhibitions about quitting the comfort of the family home for the comparative poverty of life as a companion to Esther Roper in Manchester. From 1896 Eva worked in the University Settlement set up in the Ancoats district in 1895 of which Esther had been a founder. In 1900 she became a joint secretary of the Manchester and Salford Women's Trade Union Council whose objectives were to organize female workers and to improve their wages and conditions of employment.

Eva Gore-Booth and Esther Roper thus came to occupy a strategic position in Radical politics in the north-west around the turn of the century. Their footing both in the women's suffrage movement and in the male-dominated trades council in Manchester enabled them to overcome to some extent the barriers of social class and gender. Their steady work on behalf of working-class communities gave the two women a credibility in the Socialist and Labour organizations which few middle-class feminists could command. They also made women's suffrage more appealing by arguing that the vote would enable women to achieve higher pay.

The potential of Eva and Esther's brand of radical politics only becomes clear when one puts their work in the context of the suffrage movement that had developed since 1867. Under the leadership of Lydia Becker and later of Millicent Fawcett, the National Society for Women's Suffrage, or National Union of Women's Suffrage Societies as it became from 1897 onwards, had painstakingly built up support amongst members of Parliament by respectable constitutional means. They relied heavily on raising petitions to give momentum to Parliamentary bills and on debates initiated by sympathetic MPs. Through innumerable speeches, pamphlets and articles they tackled one by one the multitude of prejudices entertained by men about the consequences of enfranchising women. For most of the period this campaign was waged by a very small army. In 1900 the NUWSS boasted only seventeen societies and a few thousand members. Yet almost imperceptibly these constitutional suffragists won the argument for giving women the vote by converting a majority of MPs.

As a result, in 1897 the House of Commons began to vote in favour of bills introduced by backbenchers to give women the vote; from that point until the First World War the pro-suffragists could invariably command a majority in the division lobbies. This represented a massive achievement for the women's cause which has traditionally been overlooked amid the notoriety attracted by the militant suffragette campaign after 1905. Yet it did not actually resolve the question. As was well-known to the many pressure groups of late-Victorian Britain, politics was above all a matter of priorities. That the sympathies of many politicians had been aroused did not mean that they regarded female enfranchisement as a matter requiring urgent legislative remedy. Indeed, many MPs continued to associate the claim for the vote with middle-class women whom they thought did not especially need it, and with unmarried women who appeared to them to be rather untypical of their sex. They were far from persuaded that the mass of ordinary women really regarded their exclusion from the electorate as a burning grievance – an assumption which the small size of the organized suffrage movement tended to corroborate. This is why the role of *working-class* women was potentially so important. Politicians showed themselves much more responsive towards the demands expressed by such organizations as the Women's Co-operative Guild, which they took to be representative of ordinary housewives, than towards middle-class pressure groups, partly because by the turn of the century they believed the future of the Empire rested upon the birth rate and the health and skills of the married women of Britain. By and large, however, the suffrage movement had based its claim on the case for enfranchising single women, and its membership was strongly middle-class. This did not mean that working-class women did not want the vote, only that this was not very apparent as yet.

In her capacity as secretary of the North of England Society for Women's Suffrage, based in Manchester, Esther Roper brought her organizing skills to bear on this question. She targeted the factory and mill women of the Lancashire towns and involved working women such as Selina Cooper and Annie Heaton in factory-gate meetings rather than in the drawing room functions that were the traditional method adopted by women's suffragists. It was in the course of this work that she had met Eva Gore-Booth. By the spring of 1901 Esther's organizers had collected almost 30,000 signatures for their suffrage petition which was taken to London for a meeting with Millicent Fawcett and presentation to MPs. But a better opportunity soon arose in the shape of a by-election in the Lancashire constituency of Clitheroe, an area with large numbers of female cotton textile workers. Although hitherto a Liberal seat, the candidacy was conceded to David Shackleton, a trade union official who stood on behalf of the newly formed Labour Representation Committee, better known after 1906 as the Labour Party. Pledging himself to work for the enfranchisement of women if elected, Shackleton enjoyed the active backing of Esther and Eva, as well as Emmeline and Christabel Pankhurst in his campaign. His election in 1902 – he became only the third Labour MP at the time – was a triumph and raised expectations amongst the suffragists. Inevitably some disillusionment set in subsequently, for as a backbencher there was not much Shackleton could do especially in a Parliament still dominated by Conservative members who were by now absorbed in an internal struggle between tariff reform and free trade. However, Esther Roper rightly believed that Shackleton and the LRC might have treated the women's demands more seriously especially as over 60 per cent of the members of the union which funded him were women. 'I wish every man in this room could be a woman for five minutes', she said on one occasion, 'and then they would understand the question.'[14] In spite of this Esther and Eva lost none of their conviction in the efficacy of constitutional and Parliamentary tactics. They proceeded to launch a new candidate, a trade unionist called Thorley Smith, who stood at Wigan at the general election in 1906. But at the same time they also made a point of establishing a separate organization, the Lancashire and Cheshire Women Textile and Other Workers' Representation Committee, to press the claim to the vote.

This was the movement with which Christabel became accidentally involved in 1901. With a view to relieving her boredom Emmeline had suggested that she attend some lectures at the University. At one of these lectures on 'Poets and Politics', given by the Vice-Chancellor, Sir Alfred Hopkinson, Christabel got up to ask a question which evidently impressed several of those present. At the end Esther Roper, who sat beside the Vice-Chancellor on the platform, came down to speak to her. She then took her back to her home in Heald Place to meet Eva. This attention proved highly flattering and suddenly opened up an exciting new world to the bored, 21-year-old Christabel. Soon she had joined the poetry circle which Eva ran at the University Settlement. More importantly Esther, who had recognized that Christabel possessed a quick mind and an apt turn of phrase, suggested that she ought to study law at the University. The interest now shown by these sophisticated and worldly women clearly persuaded her to apply herself at last. Emmeline inevitably took more convincing, for her prejudice against the professions remained undimmed. However, she probably regarded the law lectures as no more than a useful way of developing Christabel's histrionic talents. In any case until the passage of the Sex Disqualification (Removal) Act in 1919 it was impossible for a woman to practise as a solicitor or barrister, and so the question of a legal career did not really arise. None the less, Emmeline secured the help of Richard Haldane, the MP and barrister, to sponsor Christabel's application to enter Lincoln's Inn, as her father had done, with a view to admission to the Bar. The application was naturally refused.

The decision to enrol as a law student in 1901 offers a striking indication of the influence her new friends now exercised with Christabel. Until Eva and Esther came into her life there had been no indication that she would devote herself to the cause of women's suffrage. More immediately, the friendship seemed to reveal unsuspected depths in Christabel. Before long her mother began to complain that she was never at home because of Eva and Esther and her work for the suffrage society. In 1902 they invited her to accompany them on a holiday to Venice. According to Sylvia's account, Christabel positively adored Eva who was beautiful, charming and slightly vulnerable. When she suffered from neuralgia Christabel was prepared to sit for hours at a time massaging her head. As Sylvia wrote later:

To all of us at home, this seemed remarkable indeed, for Christabel had never been willing to act the nurse to any other human being. She detested sickness, and had even left home when Adela had scarlet fever and Harry had chicken-pox.[15]

Though Sylvia offered no further comment on this relationship except to emphasize how much it irritated her mother, its significance demands consideration particularly since Christabel's private life has always been rather obscure. In her own autobiography she passed over this formative phase in a surprisingly perfunctory fashion, referring to 'Miss Roper' and 'Miss Gore-Booth' in a way that seems almost calculated to misrepresent the depth of feeling that had once existed between them. This may have been the result of the later political disagreements between them which left Christabel uncomfortable and reluctant to acknowledge her debt to the two women. Additionally, by the inter-war period Christabel may well have felt a little embarrassed by the possibility that Eva and Esther were themselves not simply close colleagues but were in love with one another, and that in befriending the 21-year-old Christabel they were drawing her into the relationship. However, one should resist the temptation to project the late twentieth-century's perceptions back to the late Victorian era. The path of a nineteenth-century woman who wished to live an independent life was fraught with difficulties, including the educational and legal obstacles to a career, and the prejudices she encountered at all levels of society. But by the 1890s and 1900s women of the middle classes commonly paired off for a mixture of motives, material and emotional. Living together enabled them to share their expenses at a time when they were attempting to establish themselves in careers which were often poorly-paid and precarious. Instead of facing the relentless and demoralizing pressure to marry exerted by their families or the long dreary years at home looking after elderly parents, they could pursue satisfying work during the day before coming home to a supportive and understanding companion. Such relationships enabled many talented women to combine a loving private life with successful careers and a campaigning role in the women's movement. Eleanor Rathbone and Elizabeth Macadam, Ada Nield Chew and Mary Macarthur, Cicely Hamilton and Bessie Hatton were just a few examples of the women who adopted this strategy; even after 1918 the young Vera Brittain and Winifred Holtby set up home together in order to enable them to pursue their careers in writing and journalism, though marriage for Brittain brought it to an early end.

It would be wrong to assume that such relationships were necessarily lesbian ones. In many cases sex was not a particularly important element in lives that were filled with a full range of interests, political causes and friendships. On the other hand, the very fact that late Victorian society tended to regard same-sex love as essentially a matter for *men* enabled women to live together without attracting much comment or suspicion – making it comparatively easy for those who did desire a lesbian relationship. In the case of Eva Gore-Booth and Esther Roper, their biographer concludes that there was nothing physical in their friendship.[16] Their lives were filled with a huge circle of friends and acquaintances of both sexes and the satisfaction of pursuing a series of worthwhile causes.

In Christabel's case it would be profitless to spend too much time speculating about the possibility of a love that may never have existed. What we can say is that the friendship with Eva and Esther helps to throw light on the enigma of Christabel Pankhurst. As Sylvia's comments suggest, contemporaries regarded close, emotional bonds as quite untypical of her. During her lifetime people often described her as cold and distant. The suffragist Helena Swanwick recalled: 'She seemed to me a lonely person with all her capacity for winning adorers . . . she was, unlike her sisters, cynical and cold at heart.'[17] It has even been claimed that Christabel *never* enjoyed a close friendship. Yet this is clearly not true. The later relationships with Annie Kenney and Grace Roe in particular showed a capacity for sustained and genuine friendship. Moreover, during the period from the 1930s until her death in 1958, when she had, in effect, escaped from the pressures of a controversial public life, Christabel emerged as a much more gentle, relaxed and sympathetic personality. Yet from an early age she was a somewhat detached figure, a reflection partly of temperament and partly of her position as the eldest child. 'Christabel is not like other women,' Emmeline once remarked. 'She will never be led away by her affections.'[18] Subsequently the natural detachment was compounded because like all politicians Christabel found that the pressure of events placed enormous strain on personal relationships. One writer has commented: 'It is painful to admit that to the jaundiced eye [Christabel and Emmeline] could seem opportunistic charmers who instantly dropped people no longer of any use to them.'[19] In fairness it must be recognized that few successful public figures manage to avoid entirely the charge of using colleagues and friends to promote their causes. Later in life Christabel claimed that she had remained single 'because of my great and quite special responsibility of leadership in the women's cause', overlooking the fact that she was twenty-five when the suffragette campaign began and still only thirty-four when it ended in 1914.[20] Marriage was a feasible option had she wanted it, but she had never been strongly tempted. In her adolescence Christabel had been the kind of girl who was pretty enough to attract young men, but also sufficiently mature and self-possessed to intimidate them. She enjoyed being a leader and professed to consider her male contemporaries as rather foolish. Yet her dominant personality also made it difficult for her to defer to an older man as Emmeline had done and as Adela was later to do. To this extent Christabel was no doubt correct in thinking that there were not many men who would have suited her as lifelong partners. As a result she was, as several of her contemporaries noted, a lonely and even vulnerable personality behind the outward self-confidence and commanding presence. The absence of men in Christabel's life naturally made the need for close female friendships all the greater. Indeed she herself seemed to recognize this when she commented that the young suffragettes were investing in the cause much of the energy they would otherwise have devoted to boyfriends.[21] In effect, her friendship with Eva Gore-Booth, and later with Annie Kenney and Grace Roe, brought Christabel some of the benefits of a love affair without the disadvantages, notably the opportunity to talk freely, to share personal feelings and to gain the support and reassurance needed to cope with the huge pressures of leading a controversial political campaign; it was intimate without the need for secrecy and without the complications of physicality. Though in some ways very mature and sophisticated, Christabel was much less developed emotionally. The friendship with Eva and Esther was almost certainly the first serious and close relationship she had enjoyed, but after 1906 the more she experienced the extreme pressures and stresses entailed in leading the suffragette campaign, the greater her need for such supportive partnerships would become.

What is certain is that during 1901 and 1902 Christabel gained a valuable apprenticeship in public speaking on behalf of women's suffrage and women's employment in the towns of Lancashire and Yorkshire. Lacking ideas of her own, she largely adopted Esther Roper's line of argument to the effect that the best way of winning the Parliamentary vote was by exploiting the influence the female cotton textile workers exercised over the Labour MPs, especially those who were paid directly by their members. This of course was a very cogent argument during the early years of the Labour Representation Committee because it had such scant resources that it could not afford to pay salaries to members elected under its auspices. By 1903, however, many more unions had affiliated and as a result the LRC became able to pay its MPs and consequently exercise greater authority over them. For the time being, however, Christabel held to the view that the political and industrial grievances of working women went closely together and could be resolved by a common strategy. Within a few years Christabel was to repudiate this view, but around 1901–2 she appears to have been as positive as Emmeline and Sylvia about the necessity for a working-class base for the women's cause.

At this time Sylvia appeared much more likely to pursue a career in the world of art rather than politics. In 1902 she won a National Silver Medal for mosaic designs, the Primrose Medal and the Proctor Travelling Studentship, which enabled her to spend a vacation abroad in a country of her choice. She opted to visit Venice to study its mosaics and Florence for the frescoes. Emmeline quickly decided to join her on the journey as this would give her the chance of a holiday with Noemi in Geneva. They crossed to Ostend and made a first stop at Bruges. For Sylvia, who had hitherto seen nothing outside Lancashire and London, the Continent came as a revelation. Even Bruges and Brussels charmed so much that she felt loath to continue to Geneva. The lakes and mountains of Switzerland were a fresh delight, and the hospitality and comfort of the Dufaux household a new pleasure. Emmeline, too, began to relax, and before long she and Noemi had decided to accompany Sylvia to Venice for a short visit. There the two older women amused themselves seeing the sights and visiting a glass factory where Emmeline indulged herself, buying quantities of beads, ornaments, copper and brassware, ostensibly for resale in Emerson's.

Meanwhile Sylvia fell in love with the daily delights of Venice, the bright early-morning light, the sinking of the sun, the brief twilight, the swirling canal waters and the pale palaces: 'the promised land of my sad young heart, craving for beauty, fleeing from the sorrowful ugliness of factory-ridden Lancashire, and the dull, aching poverty of its slums; Venice, O city of dreaming magic!'[22] After a week Emmeline and Noemi bade a tearful farewell to Sylvia who soon settled into a routine. Rising at five she painted until breakfast at eight, spent the mornings in St Mark's Cathedral to copy mosaics and the afternoons in the Rialto painting the crowds, and ending with yet more work by moonlight on the balcony of her lodgings in the Calle dell'Arco. Sometimes people crowded around to watch her working and cried 'Brava! Brava!' when she hastily produced portraits for them. In the winter she joined the life class at the Academia delle Belli Arti, unconcerned at being the only woman there, as well as the landscape class which was more mixed. She greatly enjoyed listening to the conversations of the male students who assumed she understood no Italian.

Life was so delightful and the work so rewarding that Sylvia never moved on to Florence. She felt tempted to stay in Venice indefinitely. But by the spring of 1903 she had begun to receive carping letters from Christabel urging her to return to Manchester. By this time Christabel had decided to take up the law course at the University and, as a result, she needed someone to take her place in the dreaded Emerson's! Emmeline took advantage of the situation to announce that she and Adela would meet Sylvia in Paris at Easter. The return to Manchester was not too much of an anti-climax for Emmeline had hired an attic above the shop where she could have her own studio. But there was no avoiding the need to help with housekeeping and share the drudgery at Emerson's. At least she now enjoyed an opportunity to sell her paintings and to design cotton prints for the shop. In her papers she kept one of the posters she drew presumably for the window display: 'Emerson and Co. Xmas Crackers 5/11'.[23]

By now Sylvia's talent had been recognized outside the family, too. After Richard's death Emmeline suggested that the memorial fund raised by the ILP should be used to build a Socialist hall. By the summer of 1903 the hall had been erected at Hightown in Salford and Sylvia was invited to decorate it, an ambitious undertaking especially as the whole work from design to execution had to be completed in three months. The commission was to have major political implications for Sylvia and the entire Pankhurst family.

6

'He Ought to be a Woman for a While' (1903–4)

'Any class which is denied the vote is branded as an inferior class. Women's disenfranchisement is to them a perpetual lesson in servility, and to men it teaches arrogance and injustice where their dealings with women are concerned.'

Christabel Pankhurst, quoted in Dale Spender, *Feminist Theorists* (1983), p. 269

The campaigns of the militant suffragettes before 1914 are so well known that we tend to regard them as an inevitable element, or even the only significant element, in the struggle for the women's vote. Yet the development of militancy within the British movement was, if not unique, certainly very unusual in the wider context of female emancipation. Even in Britain, militancy appeared relatively late, nearly forty years after the start of the campaign, and even at its height it remained a small part of the movement for women's suffrage. What happened was far from inevitable. After the turn of the century the constitutional campaign for women's suffrage appeared to be on the brink of a fresh phase of expansion, stimulated by a return to domestic issues and rising expectations amongst reformers of all kinds. But in 1903 none of the suffragists possessed a dramatically new blueprint for success. In fact, as Emmeline Pankhurst's appetite for politics returned, she seemed likely to return to the existing pattern of constitutional activity with which she was, of course, familiar, rather than become the pioneer of any radical departure from it. Emmeline always maintained that she was essentially a law-abiding person. Nor did the Pankhursts introduce new ideas or arguments into the debate; their contribution was to force the issue up the political agenda by devising fresh tactics and attracting new resources into the campaign. According to Teresa Billington, one of her early collaborators who met her in 1903, Emmeline was 'of the opinion that the new combined Labour Party would be the instrument of enfranchisement for women'.[1] This underlines that at this stage she still thought in terms of working through political parties using conventional propaganda techniques. Indeed, Emmeline actually intensified her involvement with the Independent Labour Party by attending its annual conferences from 1901 onwards where she spoke on educational questions as well as votes for women. She evidently became a popular and prominent figure at these gatherings. At the Leicester conference in 1901, for example, John Bruce Glasier observed her entertaining the delegates at the piano during the evenings; and she maintained her work for the party at least until 1905.[2]

However, the links between the ILP and women's suffrage proved to be much less securely based than this suggests. At the 1902 conference Emmeline introduced a resolution to the effect that 'in order to improve the economic and social condition of women, it is necessary to take immediate steps to secure the granting of the suffrage to women on the same terms as it is, or may be, granted to men'.[3] Although Emmeline's resolution was unanimously adopted by the conference, it was immediately followed by another resolution proposing *adult* suffrage, which used the same language as Emmeline's and requested the National Administrative Council to draft a bill to be introduced as soon as possible by Keir Hardie. This resolution was also carried. The two resolutions were far from complementary for the second reflected the conviction among many male politicians that adult suffrage deserved priority over any measure confined to women. Men who themselves lacked a vote – as many as four in every ten in the Edwardian period – resented the prospect of some women acquiring it before them. Consequently, behind the scenes the rivalry between women's suffrage and adult suffrage generated increasing friction. When John Bruce Glasier stayed at Nelson Street in October 1902 he complained bitterly:

A weary ordeal of chatter about woman's suffrage from 10.00 p.m. to 1.30 p.m. [sic] – Mrs and Christabel Pankhurst belabouring me as Chairman of the Party for its neglect of the question. At last get roused and speak with something like scorn of their miserable individualist sexism: and virtually tell them that the ILP will not stir a finger more than it has done for all the woman suffragists in creation.[4]

In his refusal to treat votes for women as a priority Glasier was typical of a large number of Socialists who believed it more important to eliminate the *class* bias from the electoral system than to tackle the numerically greater bias against the female gender. Philip Snowden, another leading ILP-er and *bête noire* for the Pankhursts, suspected that a limited extension of the franchise to women would disadvantage Socialists by exacerbating the existing over-representation of propertied people and thus delivering additional votes to the Conservatives. 'He ought to be a woman for a while', commented Christabel, 'as Miss Snowden he would never have been either a councillor or a Parliamentary Candidate.'[5]

Unfortunately the tactical issue was complicated by personal antagonism which seriously hampered the Pankhursts' ability to capitalize fully on their influence in the Labour Movement. This emerges from Glasier's snort of disgust after his argumentative evening with Emmeline and Christabel: 'Really the pair are not seeking democratic freedom, but self-importance.' As ILP Chairman Glasier usually posed as a spokesman for the oppressed masses and therefore did not take kindly when the tables were turned by feminists who derided him as part of the privileged section of society. On the other hand, it was a mistake to alienate him by their overbearing manner; to be accused of seeking self-importance was almost the worst insult within the Labour Movement. The question arises *why* Glasier became so easily antagonized and so suspicious about the Pankhursts' motives. After sleeping on the argument he reflected:

Pankhursts somewhat contrite for last night's harpyism: but I feel tired of them. Christabel paints her eyebrows grossly and looks selfish, lazy and wilful. They want to be ladies not workers and lack the humility of real heroism.[6]

Rightly or wrongly Glasier had discerned a fondness for the limelight in the two women; and this combined with a puritanical dislike for elaborate dress and cosmetics that was not uncommon on the left, led him to see them as middle-class opportunists latching on to the working-class movement. Conversely, Emmeline's deliberate policy of accentuating her conventional femininity by taking enormous trouble over her appearance in public clearly had its advantages, not least in disarming those men who assumed that a suffragist was automatically an aggressive and masculine sort of woman. However, the prejudice all this inspired in men like Glasier became a very real factor in the relations between suffragism and the Labour Movement which time did nothing to erase. Towards the end of 1906 Glasier noted:

Mrs P. and I got into a fierce discussion re women. Her idea is that women should be relieved of all *work* and have rest and intellectual delights! I told her that work was good and that under Socialism she would likely have to do more than she now does seeing she has other people's daughters acting as *her* private servants.[7]

Though we do not have Emmeline's side of this, it is not difficult to conjecture that she had argued that working women were entitled to a fairer share of the opportunities for leisure and self-improvement which were invariably monopolized by men. Again, in Glasier's ill-tempered reactions the element of puritanism surfaces in his belief in the merits of work; and once again his distaste for the Pankhursts' bourgeois penchant for servants left him sceptical about their claim to be Socialists.

Against this background it may seem surprising not that the Pankhursts broke with Labour, but that they maintained their links for as long as they did. Part of the explanation lay in the devoted support they received from certain individuals within the movement, notably Keir Hardie and George Lansbury. Moreover, during the early years of the century there seemed good reason for investing their efforts in labour organizations which were being co-ordinated under the new Labour Representation Committee, formed in 1900, which became known as the Labour Party after 1906. The ILP was a key constituent of the new party and Keir Hardie a prominent figure in it. Admittedly during the first few years of its life the LRC suffered acutely from lack of money and had only a handful of MPs. However, after the Taff Vale Judgement trade-union affiliations multiplied rapidly and, as a result, by 1903 the LRC was much better funded. It engaged in what turned out to be a highly successful deal with the Liberals for fighting the next general election. Consequently, by 1903 it made far more sense for the suffrage movement to cultivate Labour as it now appeared to be the coming force in British politics. On the other hand, as the stakes rose, the LRC became increasingly focussed on its one unambiguous objective: to get more working men elected to Parliament. It was far from clear that the campaign for female enfranchisement would promote that in the short term. At best it represented a diversion and at worst exposed the fledgling party to the danger of being hi-jacked by external organizations whose aims only partly coincided with its own. For many Labour leaders the way in which Keir Hardie allowed himself to be taken over by the Pankhursts and their middle-class supporters proved the point.

None of this made an alliance between women's suffrage and Labour impossible; a formal pact was eventually concluded in 1912. But it required tactful handling and a lot of goodwill on both sides. In 1903 Emmeline, Sylvia and Adela still shared Esther Roper's view that the best chance of winning the vote for women lay in mobilizing female industrial workers in the north of England.[8] Though inclined to be impatient with male Socialists, as her contretemps with Glasier showed, Emmeline continued to feel loyalty towards Keir Hardie and no doubt towards the memory of Richard's role in the early ILP. By 1903 Adela, now seventeen, had grown out of her youthful reaction to enforced socialising with working-class children and developed pronounced left-wing opinions. The experience of long, gruelling days devoted to teaching ragged children in a school at Urmston in Manchester at an annual salary of £30 had awoken her compassion for the poor and her anger with the existing social system. At seventeen she had paid her first visit to the Chorlton Workhouse, to which Emmeline had refused to take her, with a young Russian girl, a revolutionary who was staying with the family. There Adela saw some grim sights – the paupers' coffins awaiting burial, dead babies and, in the 'lock ward', babies suffering from disease who had nothing to do but cry their lives away. As a result she learned about the 'Social Evil' that resulted from capitalism, compelling some poor women to sell themselves to men in order to live. The workhouse – 'indescribably dreadful' – left her shocked and angry. This experience inspired Adela to accompany her mother to ILP meetings in and around Manchester and, in due course, to undertake speaking engagements when Emmeline felt too tired. Although the youngest of the sisters, Adela made as great an impression not least because of her greater originality and intelligence.[9] Above all, she possessed a talent to amuse her audiences, a skill not shown by the better-known members of the family.

Yet despite the Pankhursts' pronounced leftward bias, the link between their campaign for the vote and the Labour Party was effectively severed by Christabel. Still only twenty-two years old in the spring of 1903, she was ostensibly still working under the aegis of the older and far more experienced Esther Roper and Eva Gore-Booth. However, Christabel was no mere acolyte. It is indicative of her self-possession and strategic grasp that after a comparatively short apprenticeship she had diagnosed the main flaws in their approach and had begun to envisage an independent course of action. Christabel's misgivings centred round Eva and Esther's dedication to constitutional methods, their belief in mobilizing working-class women, and, most immediately, their loyalty to the Labour Movement. During the course of 1903 Christabel fought a running battle both in private and in newspaper columns with Snowden, Glasier and other Labour leaders over their treatment of women. In March she complained in a letter to Keir Hardie's paper, *The Labour Leader*, that the recent LRC conference at Newcastle had neglected women's interests, and briskly discounted the claim that they could rely on the additional Labour MPs to look after them: 'Never in the history of the world have the interests of those without power to defend themselves been properly served by others.'[10] Mindful, no doubt, of Esther's difficulties with David Shackleton, she turned her fire on another Labour candidate, John Hodge. When Hodge objected to being heckled on the grounds that he was a pro-suffragist facing an anti-suffragist and that Christabel was damaging his campaign, she replied, unabashed, that there was 'nothing to choose between an enemy and a friend who does nothing'.[11] In August 1903 she returned to the point in a sarcastic attack:

One gathers that some day, when the Socialists are in power, and have nothing better to do, they will give women votes as a finishing touch to their arrangements . . . Why are we expected to have such confidence in the men of the Labour Party? Working-men are as unjust to women as are those of other classes.[12]

Emmeline, perhaps hearing echoes of her own criticisms of Liberal politicians in the 1880s and sharing her daughter's frustration over the condescension shown by the men, looked indulgently on these presumptuous remarks by the 22-year-old. Though she did not appreciate how far Christabel was prepared to go in breaking with the left, Emmeline had already shown a surprising readiness to defer to her daughter's judgement.

However, in 1903 Christabel was still feeling her way towards a new strategy, and it was Emmeline who took the initiative by establishing a new organization to promote women's suffrage. Earlier biographers, largely following Sylvia's account, have usually suggested that Emmeline set up the Women's Social and Political Union chiefly out of jealousy towards Eva Gore-Booth, the object being to drag Christabel away from the all-consuming friendship.[13] Although she undoubtedly felt the need for Christabel's company, this explanation is, at the least, an exaggeration, and, at the worst, a trivialization of her initiative. As far back as 1889 Emmeline had participated in founding the Women's Franchise League. Admittedly, in the years following Richard's death her interest had dwindled, and when she turned to Socialism and the ILP Adela remembered her saying that 'the whole thing had appeared unreal to her'.[14] Yet her experience in the ILP had rekindled her earlier interest in the grievances of women. It was, in any case, scarcely necessary for Emmeline to go to this trouble to drive a wedge between her daughter and the two older women, for Christabel had already become disenchanted with them. Moreover, if Emmeline really planned to draw her away, it seems odd that Christabel did not even attend the inaugural meeting of the WSPU, and it was some time before she devoted herself fully to her mother's new organization. This is not surprising since the methods of the two groups were very similar at first. However, the establishment of a separate body naturally helped to crystallize the differences between the Pankhursts and Esther Roper and facilitated a departure from her thinking and her methods in 1905–6.

The proximate explanation for the founding of the WSPU in October 1903 lay elsewhere. During the summer months Sylvia had been planning and executing her designs for the new Pankhurst Hall which the ILP was building in St James Road in Salford. This involved constructing huge panels painted with carefully chosen symbols: roses (for love), apple trees (for knowledge), doves (for peace), corn (for plenty), lilies (for purity), lunaria (for honesty), bees (for industry), and sunflowers and butterflies (for hope). For a 21-year-old this was a major undertaking and Sylvia was very nervous especially as she was called upon to give a speech explaining her ideas at a ceremony on 3 October when Walter Crane officially declared the hall open. Emmeline reportedly complained that 'there were very few Socialists there – so that she felt almost ashamed to have brought Crane all the way from London'.[15] She had already become disgruntled because while Sylvia had been at work the hall was already partly in use by a local ILP branch which did not admit female members. Evidently the intention was to operate a social club on the premises catering to men regardless of whether they were ILP members. This had become a common practice among political parties who found that they could best sustain their local organizations by operating drinking clubs boosted by the attraction of cheap beer. But in view of the fact that the hall had originated as a memorial to Richard who had devoted so much effort to female emancipation, and, moreover, had been decorated without charge by his daughter, Emmeline's anger about the ban on women was surely justified. When John Bruce Glasier and Philip Snowden arrived to participate in the opening ceremony Christabel refused to speak to them. Emmeline herself decided to withhold her usual contribution to the wages fund which the ILP raised to pay Keir Hardie's salary. 'We must have an independent women's movement', she reportedly exclaimed to her friends. 'Come to my house tomorrow and we will arrange it!'[16]

While these words make the decision appear a characteristically impulsive one, it did not come out of the blue. Even Esther Roper was herself in the process of creating a new women's society to press for the vote at this time. Initially Emmeline regarded her new group as complementary to the ILP which, unlike the older political parties, lacked a separate women's organization. Indeed even the Labour Party neglected to create one until 1906 in the form of the Women's Labour League.

A mere half dozen women, most of whom were already involved with the Manchester ILP, responded to Emmeline's call by gathering at Nelson Street on Saturday, 10 October 1903. Comparatively little is known about the formation and the early months of the life of the WSPU. For once even Sylvia's account is perfunctory, suggesting that, like Christabel, she may not have been present at the first meeting. Teresa Billington who joined soon after the foundation, did leave copious notes, written several years later, though in view of her bitterness towards the Pankhursts following the split of 1907 her account has to be treated with some caution. The original group seems to have included a Mrs Rachel Scott, who agreed to act as secretary, Mrs Pattie Hall, wife of Leonard Hall, an ILP activist who had been imprisoned during the Boggart Hole Clough controversy, and a Mrs Harker who had also been defended by Richard for speaking at the Clough in 1896. These women remained fairly obscure, though Mrs Hall's daughter, Nellie, then a schoolgirl, later became a WSPU organizer and served as Emmeline's secretary in the mid-1920s until her death.[17]

Initially Emmeline intended to call the new group the Women's Labour Representation Committee, a move which would undoubtedly have been interpreted as provocative by the LRC. However, Christabel advised that this would be confused with Esther Roper's new organization, the Lancashire and Cheshire Women Textile and Other Workers' Representation Committee. Consequently she settled on Women's Social and Political Union, though her reasons are unclear. Sylvia suggested that her mother intended to focus on social issues as well as on the vote, which seems plausible especially if she envisaged a continuing relationship with the ILP. On the other hand, in her official report to *The Labour Leader* at the end of October Rachel Scott defined its objectives quite narrowly in terms of securing complete political equality with men. The title 'Political Union' was a traditional one much used by Parliamentary reformers ever since the 1830s, and this may well have been in Emmeline's mind.

Although Emmeline did not use the word feminist to describe herself at this time, she was undoubtedly a feminist in the sense that she aspired to secure equal treatment for women especially in political rights and in pay. Admittedly Adela drew a distinction between her mother and the original married working-class members of the WSPU on the one hand and the middle-class women who joined later; the latter, she felt, were closer to the popular stereotype of aggressive spinsters and man-haters beloved by anti-suffragist propaganda. Emmeline herself was by no means hostile to men. However, Christabel always held reservations about male involvement in the cause, which is why she insisted, later, on an entirely separate organization – the Men's Political Union – for male suffragists. Not only did Christabel see a danger of men usurping women's role, she also believed it essential to keep an all-female WSPU in order to enhance the appeal of its heroism to the mass of apathetic women.[18]

During the initial months of its existence the WSPU operated on a shoestring. Around twenty women met once a week, usually at Nelson Street but occasionally in a room above a warehouse in Portland Street. It had the character of a women's collective rather than a formal pressure group. 'Mrs Pankhurst or Adela would arrive with three or four favourable replies [to offers to address meetings] . . . and the speakers would be allotted.' There was no membership list, or minutes of the meetings, and, apart from those who acted as secretary and treasurer, no officers. Teresa Billington, who observed the Pankhursts at close quarters, described Nelson Street at this time as 'a home of love and unity and confusion'. This, she believed, was because all four were dedicated missionaries – everything else was subordinate: 'To work alongside of [Emmeline] day by day was to run the risk of losing yourself. She was ruthless in using the followers she gathered around her as she was ruthless to herself.' This is corroborated by Adela who felt that family relations were at their best during this period.[19] During the meetings members contributed their loose change, but otherwise Emmeline made the necessary payments from her own resources and secured an occasional donation from friends. There was no attempt to keep the books or present a statement of accounts. This tendency to confuse the family's money with the funds of the organization did not matter much at this stage when expenditure was so low and straightforward, but it was to become the cause of controversy and ill-feeling later when the WSPU's resources had expanded. A little more formality would have been wise. In her account Teresa Billington noted that 'at a very early meeting I was asked to draw up a Draft Constitution to serve as the basis on which at some later date a conference of members would shape the rules and regulations which the movement desired'.[20] From time to time this constitution came up for discussion 'but it was always willingly postponed'. Since the reluctance of the Pankhursts to abide by a democratic constitution was the cause of much subsequent controversy, Billington may well have been using this account to establish the justification for her break-away in 1907. On the other hand her account does seem plausible in that the handful of members probably felt more inclined to focus on getting their message across than to devoting hours to detailed consideration of a constitution. What is beyond dispute is that four years after its foundation the WSPU still functioned without any formal rules, nor were the books audited until the year beginning in March 1906.

No constitution could have conveyed the spirit of the WSPU at this stage in its life. Its only real assets were the energy and enthusiasm of the Pankhursts themselves. We get a glimpse of the exuberant mood of those early days in some of Teresa Billington's description of the leading personalities:

The young Pankhurst enthusiasts saw the fight as a short and sharp one to be succeeded by careers in public life for the leaders ... naïve young Pankhursts prophecised [sic] a Premiership for mother or Christabel on the Woolsack, and though we grave elder ones laughed [,] we were in no sense incredulous ... Contact with their uninhibited younger minds revealed more than crude family megalomania.[21]

Though they come from a biassed source these recollections do capture part of the truth about the Pankhursts. In 1903-4 the WSPU was so small an organization that expectations that it would succeed in winning the vote where others had failed seemed absurd. But Emmeline and Christabel grasped instinctively the necessity to escape the 'realism' that inhibited action by lifting their sights and creating a sense of *inevitability* about their ultimate success. Herein lay their genius as leaders. Inevitably there was another side to this as Billington's reference to 'megalomania' suggests. But it is significant that even she conceded that she had been happy to be swept along by their infectious enthusiasm at least for a time.

At twenty-six Teresa Billington was a confident and argumentative woman who had become a Socialist and a feminist partly as a result of her early life in Blackburn. Her parents' unhappy marriage, her father's selfishness and her mother's thwarted ambitions had all left a deep impression. She quit her home, became a schoolteacher and joined the ILP in Manchester where she met Emmeline. When she joined the WSPU towards the end of 1903 Teresa was a great asset largely because of her impressive platform skills. On the other hand her rebellious and overbearing personality always threatened trouble as Sylvia noted: 'Her lips curled perhaps rather too much, and, like many other bright young people, she pushed her arguments rather too crudely.'[22] Nevertheless, she was an essential member, for according to the traditional accounts at this stage the WSPU relied on no more than five speakers to propagate its message: Emmeline, Christabel, Sylvia, Adela and Teresa. Even this seems to overstate the position, however, for Sylvia recorded that she did not make her first suffrage speech until the autumn of 1904 in London. She had already declined an invitation to debate with Margaret Bondfield, a formidable Labour opponent of the women's suffrage bill.[23] At all events it was no more than a stage army that spread itself across the north of England in the summer of 1904 addressing meetings mostly held by branches of the ILP, Clarion Clubs, Labour Churches, trade unions and trades councils. In the absence of any real organization of its own the WSPU depended heavily on the co-operation of the ILP members to provide it with audiences and publicity.

This is presumably why Emmeline took care to maintain her position in the party. At the annual conference at Easter in 1904 she managed to gain re-election after an absence of several years to the National Administrative Council, though her modest vote put her only eighth out of the thirteen candidates – an indication of her dwindling popularity. In this capacity, however, she secured the reintroduction of her 1902 resolution on women's suffrage which now included an instruction to the NAC to draft a bill on the subject.[24] However, her relations with most of the party's leaders were deteriorating. At an NAC meeting in May Glasier noted: 'Snowden and Mrs Pankhurst fraternize fairly well considering their real hostility.'[25] This was an inevitable result not simply of the formation of the WSPU but of its particular policy on women's suffrage. It demanded what was known as an 'equal terms' bill which sounded democratic but actually meant a limited franchise for women who could qualify as heads of household – that is, single women and widows. This represented a retreat from the days of the Women's Franchise League when Richard and Emmeline had argued for a much more democratic measure of reform to be achieved by the inclusion of married women. There is no evidence that the WSPU had given specific consideration to this important point in 1903. Subsequently its propaganda claimed that *any* measure of women's suffrage was acceptable, however limited, in order to establish the principle, and that, in any case, the 'equal terms' formula would produce a representative female electorate. But in adopting this position the new organization had committed a major tactical error which greatly complicated the WSPU's relations with Labour and the Liberals and arguably set back the progress of the cause during the Edwardian period. On the other hand, the Pankhursts were far from being alone in this, for virtually all the women's groups pressed for the limited measure of women's suffrage up to 1914.

Despite the increasing friction between them, the break between the Pankhursts and Labour was delayed until 1906. Much of the explanation for this lay in the remarkable personal and political links between the family and Keir Hardie. Their friendship went back to 1888 when Richard and Emmeline had encountered him at a conference in London. Hardie, who was two years older than Emmeline, had a genuine and lifelong sympathy for women. Though not really a feminist, his sense of fair play aroused in him enormous compassion for the plight of ordinary women as it did for all underprivileged members of society. This perception may have originated in his appreciation for his own mother's struggle against the odds to sustain a home without adequate male support.[26] Moreover, like George Lansbury, another dedicated working-class suffragist, Hardie seems never to have felt patronized or threatened by self-confident middle-class women. On the contrary, he rather liked them. Emmeline, with her femininity and graciousness, almost certainly aroused protective feelings in him and he enjoyed her company enormously even when her zeal for the vote caused difficulties for him. Though always loyal to his roots, Hardie never regarded social class as a barrier to co-operation or to friendship. By contrast other Socialists of humble origins, such as Ramsay MacDonald and Philip Snowden, suffered from too strong a sense of personal insecurity to be able to cope with what they saw as aggressive and patronizing lady suffragists.

In addition, several aspects of his political make-up predisposed Keir Hardie to the Pankhursts. He shared Richard's rather puritanical outlook, expressed in his religiosity and his lifelong dedication to temperance. But above all, like Emmeline and Richard, he was by temperament a rebel, as ready to dissent from the Trade Union Con-gress establishment in the 1890s as Richard had been to antagonize the Liberal Party in the 1880s. More orthodox Labour politicians found it genuinely difficult to understand why Hardie, who had done more than any other individual to found the Labour Party, was so willing to put the Party's unity and his own standing within it at risk in order to promote votes for women. In fact, though a Socialist, Hardie remained fundamentally a Victorian Radical, always attracted by good causes, however hopeless they appeared to be. In any case his Socialism was not strongly rooted in economics and he never adopted a Marxist analysis of society. As a result Hardie felt less inhibited than many of his colleagues about collaborating with middle-class Radicals and he saw women in Liberal-individualist terms as people justly seeking to establish their rights.

This combination of personal and political characteristics enabled Hardie to bear good naturedly the pressure placed upon him by female suffragists during the Edwardian period. He saw nothing objectionable in their decision to set up a new pressure group and was prepared to use what influence he had with the ILP and in Parliament to advance their cause. Aware of how vulnerable the WSPU was to the charge that the limited suffrage bill would enfranchise propertied women and thus increase the middle-class bias in the electorate, he initiated moves to find evidence likely to discredit the fears of his colleagues. At Hardie's suggestion, the ILP agreed to ask its branches to ascertain the class composition of the existing female local government elector-ate since they were the women most likely to gain the Parliamentary vote. This necessitated laborious house-to-house canvasses, but over forty local branches managed to visit almost 60,000 women. They reported that no fewer than 82 per cent of them were 'working women'. This, of course, was an ambiguous definition that included not just working-class women but those working in middle-class occupations. Also, since the ILP branches scarcely existed in middle-class residential districts, their returns could hardly be seen as representative of the country as a whole. None the less, the evidence was welcome and provided the suffragists with something solid to counter the scare-mongering of their opponents. For Sylvia and Emmeline, Hardie's backing was more than sufficient to justify retaining their links with Labour for several years. Their own resources were so meagre in 1903–4 that it would have been rash to cut adrift so soon. In any case it was tempting to believe that as Labour was now on the verge of an electoral breakthrough, the Party would carry the women's cause forward with it. Though only two LRC members had been elected in 1900, the new party gained three more seats at by-elections in Clitheroe, Barnard Castle and Woolwich during 1902 and 1903.

Christabel alone remained unconvinced. In fact, she continued to be characteristically detached from all the organizations with which she was involved. Though she took her part in speaking for the WSPU, she did not go out of her way to promote the new organization at this stage, possibly because she could not entirely see the point of yet another suffrage group. And far from being prised away from Esther and Eva's suffragists, she continued to belong to their group, and was thus a member of the North of England Society for Women's Suffrage, to which it was affiliated, until 1905. This reflected not only her scepticism about Labour's sympathy for women's suffrage but also her doubts about the new party's influence in Parliament, though there was no point in forcing the issue just yet. Christabel's position in this respect was strengthened by Teresa Billington who took a distinctly condescending view of the working men she encountered in the ILP. Despite the rivalry that later developed between them, Billington con-ceded that Christabel 'was responsible for the decision to break away from the Labour Party. And I think she was right. Not one per cent of its advocates were interested in winning women's suffrage ... Our bellicose emergence was an unwelcome complication.'[27]

Christabel perceived that the WSPU was in danger of becoming just another struggling pressure group exhausting itself by a gruelling programme of public meetings for audiences in small northern townships.[28] By now she had had enough experience of working with Esther Roper to be doubtful whether this was going to work. It is important to remember that during 1903 and 1904 the methods used by the WSPU continued to be *constitutional* and thus not essentially different to the longer-established suffrage societies except in so far as it deliberately courted working-class audiences. Significantly the chief source of novel ideas at this stage was Teresa Billington who suggested that they nominate Emmeline as a candidate at the next general election. There were excellent precedents for this tactic in British Radical history. John Wilkes in the eighteenth century and Charles Bradlaugh in the nineteenth had achieved enormous publicity by repeatedly seeking election to Parliaments from which they had been banned. Billington also proposed sending women into polling booths to slip ballots into the box or conducting separate polls for women with a view to presenting their 'votes' for inclusion at the official count.[29] The idea of a mock election conducted by those not officially eligible to vote had been used by Chartist men during the 1830s and 1840s. However, neither Emmeline nor Christabel had yet begun to think in these terms and so nothing came of these ideas. Although Christabel could not yet see her way out of the tactical dilemma, she was ready to experiment. Since the handful of Labour MPs occupied a marginal position in Parliament, she felt tempted to go over their heads to the politicians who really wielded power. Strictly speaking this meant the Conservatives whose leader, Arthur Balfour, actually sat for a Manchester constituency until 1905. But by 1904 his government appeared to be disintegrating rapidly over its internal divisions, and a fresh general election was increasingly anticipated. Much wiser, then, to focus on the Liberals with a view to extracting pledges from an incoming government. A convenient target came to hand in the shape of North West Manchester, a marginal city-centre seat likely to swing from Conservative to Liberal where, in the spring of 1904, the Liberals were in the process of adopting Winston Churchill, currently Tory member for Oldham but now abandoning his party in protest against tariff reform. Though a young politician, Churchill had already emerged as a major personality as a result of his escape from a Boer gaol from which he had returned to fight the 1900 election. With his instinct for self-promotion Churchill forced himself into the centre of the political debate by recasting himself as a Liberal champion of free trade, and consequently his appearances in Manchester attracted huge crowds and extensive newspaper attention. It is thus easy to see why Christabel identified Churchill as a prime target not only in 1904 but right up to 1914. She shared his penchant for publicity, his boundless self-confidence and his impatience with more cautious minds.

Rather surprisingly Christabel managed to acquire a ticket to sit on the platform in Manchester's Free Trade Hall on 19 February 1904 when Churchill delivered an oration for an hour and a half. He was just proposing the formal adoption of a resolution reaffirming the meeting's 'unshaken belief in the principles of Free Trade', when Christabel interrupted to seek the addition of women's suffrage to his proposal.[30] Since the whole object of the meeting was to propagate the case for free trade, the Chairman quite reasonably pointed out that the organizers wanted the resolution to be adopted unanimously; to import a divisive issue like votes for women at the last minute would make that impossible. They argued over this for several minutes, but amid cries of 'Chair' Christabel eventually backed down and the meeting resumed its course. Writing later she thought this 'first militant step . . . was the most difficult thing I (had) ever done'.[31] Her interruption was not part of a plan, nor even an official WSPU action; for the time being no departure from constitutional methods was in contemplation. But in the shocked faces of the dignitaries on the platform in the Free Trade Hall Christabel had seen an entrancing vision of the future. The hapless Churchill was to become a regular target during his meteoric ascent of the ministerial ladder.

In the aftermath of the Churchill meeting Christabel regretted that she had not made more of a fuss. Yet within the WSPU she continued her swift rise to prominence by getting a series of letters published in the national newspapers. In effect, she had raised her perspective from the purely local campaign run by Esther Roper and diverted her efforts into her mother's organization, simply because as a much smaller and newer society it offered far more scope for her original and decisive mind. As yet, however, Christabel did not give the WSPU her undivided attention, for she was supposed to be studying for the Bar.

Even this could be turned to good effect. After her application to Lincoln's Inn had met with rejection, Christabel and a Miss Ivy Williams received an invitation to make their case in a debate in January 1904 at the Union Society. Her eloquence in the debate gained the support of a majority of those present for women's admission to the legal profession. Christabel followed up this triumph by writing to a barrister, Wallis Grain, who had taken her side in the debate. She claimed that she really wished to be able to practise as a lawyer because it was the profession 'for which I am most fitted', and she acted as secretary for a 'Committee to Secure the Admission of Women to the Legal Profession'.[32] Quite how serious this was remains unclear; her family certainly thought she had little interest in the law to judge from the time she devoted to her studies.

During 1904 Sylvia became equally distracted from the WSPU, at least in the autumn when she took up a two-year scholarship at the Royal College of Art in South Kensington. After completing her work on the ILP Hall she had been faced with returning to the tedium of Emerson's. The scholarship offered a welcome chance to escape, but it involved a gruelling succession of examinations in such subjects as geometry that left her feeling thoroughly demoralized. Consequently the news of the award came as a great surprise to her. In many ways Sylvia's experience in London repeated her three years in Manchester. From the start she found that she simply did not fit in.[33] She disliked the course because of the requirement to study architecture during the first six months, but when she tackled the Principal about this she found herself 'ordered furiously from the room'. Nothing daunted, she quickly became involved in another controversy with the Principal whom she suspected of discriminating against female students in the award of internal scholarships. By enlisting the help of Keir Hardie she even managed to get a question asked about this in the House of Commons which revealed that only three of sixteen internal awards had gone to women. However, this embarrassing publicity produced no change in policy.

Even among the students Sylvia remained a rather aloof and withdrawn figure. She admitted that she left it entirely to others to make the first advances to her. A few of the girls did so, but she made no special friends. The men, regarding her as a 'haughty female with her head in the air', left her strictly alone. Before long Sylvia realized that the College was depressingly full of able art students most of whom faced the prospect of irregular or ill-paid employment and a lifetime spent as teachers for lack of any alternative means of support. Also, like most students fresh to London, she found accommodation a problem. Initially she rented a grim room off the Fulham Road at ten shillings a week, but later moved to Park Cottage at Number 4 Park Walk in Chelsea where she had two rooms and a friendly landlady, Mrs Florence Roe. Sylvia's nearest approach to a social life was a regular invitation to some female students to join her at Park Walk to do some sketching on Saturday afternoons. Saturday mornings were spent in the City selling her designs for cotton prints, and Sundays meeting up with Harry who was now at school in Hampstead.

According to her son Sylvia was in poor financial circumstances during this period. However, this impression may be a little exaggerated for her scholarship was worth fifty pounds a year plus travelling expenses. Though hardly a fortune, a pound a week was sufficient to support an entire family in the Edwardian period. Sylvia refused to economize as most students did by sharing accommodation. She also earned a few guineas by selling some of her work, though she apparently sent much of this money to Emmeline in Manchester. Since her mother still retained her job as Registrar one wonders whether this was necessary, though it was, of course, common practice for sons and daughters to hand over most of their wages at this time. Her contributions may well have been required to help subsidize the WSPU.

What seems beyond doubt is that Sylvia suffered greatly from loneliness for much of her time in London. This was only partly relieved by weekend visits to both her brother and her aunt Mary who had returned to her husband – only temporarily, as it turned out. But Sylvia soon joined the Fulham branch of the ILP and received occasional invitations from Margaret and Ramsay MacDonald to 'At Homes' at their flat in Lincoln's Inn Fields. She also came into contact with Dora Montefiore who had campaigned for the women's vote in New South Wales in the early 1890s, and, since her return to Britain, had been working through the Women's Liberal Federation to pressure Liberal candidates on the issue. On one occasion Mrs Montefiore experimented by holding an open-air suffrage meeting at Ravenscourt Park on a Sunday. As it rained the other speakers failed to turn up and so she asked Sylvia to act as her chairman and to raise a crowd.[34]

Sylvia's reluctance to form relationships with people of her own age goes some way to explaining the rapid development of her friendship with Keir Hardie. At first she and Harry spent Sundays with him, but before long Sylvia began to visit him alone and more frequently. She left a vivid picture of his life in these years. Hardie subsisted on a salary of £150 a year raised by the ILP, but his debts and his expenses as an MP forced him into a more frugal existence than such an income usually entailed. He lived at Number 14 Nevill's Court, an Elizabethan building in a narrow ally off Fetter Lane. A dark winding stair led up to what was basically one room divided by curtains and partitions into a bedroom, living room and kitchen. An old-fashioned fireplace with hobs on either side provided warmth and cooking facilities. The painted wooden walls bore pictures of Robert Owen, Robert Burns and William Morris. Though he possessed a lamp Hardie preferred to work by candlelight.

For the lonely Sylvia this room became a comforting haven in her rather bleak London life. In her eyes Keir Hardie was an idealist, a man full of compassion for the poor and underprivileged, and transparently ready to sacrifice his own material interests for the sake of his principles. In short he was Sylvia's beloved father restored to life, filling the gap that his death had left. Hardie also gave her a window on to working-class life which she had previously seen only from a distance. Since cooking remained a lifelong mystery to Sylvia, she marvelled at his skill in lighting fires, blacking his own shoes, and feeding himself on a diet consisting largely of bread, Scotch scones and butter; she detailed his method of making tea by spooning the leaves directly into a saucepan of cold water and waiting for it to boil. Sylvia spent happy evenings there by the fire while Hardie puffed away on his pipe, answered letters, wrote articles for *The Labour Leader*, and read aloud to her from his favourite authors: Keats, Scott, Burns, Byron, Shelley and Morris.

This friendship with Sylvia clearly helped to fill a gap in Hardie's life too. In spite of his popularity with mass audiences, he was in some ways a rather isolated figure, sheltered by his puritanical attitudes from the more frivolous aspects of the working man's life. He regarded the theatre and the public house as degenerate. But in Sylvia's company he now made occasional visits to restaurants where he sampled black coffee for the first time, and to the Court Theatre where they saw Shaw's play *John Bull's Other Island*. Beyond this Hardie probably enjoyed little social life; his human contacts were confined to a succession of political associates and visitors to Nevill's Court, a Mrs Maggie Symons who worked as his secretary for little or no payment, and the audiences he addressed up and down the country.[35]

Yet for all his puritanism Hardie was flirtatious and enjoyed female company. He unavoidably spent a great deal of time away from his wife, Lillie, and, though fond of his home in Ayrshire, he visited it infrequently. Nor did he encourage Lillie to join him in London.[36] Before long the paternal relationship between Sylvia and Hardie changed. Though usually reticent over personal matters he found it easy to relax and talk with her, perhaps because she sympathized but refrained from criticism. In the portrait she drew of him in charcoal and crayon Sylvia lovingly captured the mixture of sadness, wisdom and integrity she found so appealing in him. Politics, ostensibly the rationale for their relationship, kept them close during the next few years both because Hardie repeatedly demonstrated the sincerity of his support for the women's cause, and because Emmeline and Christabel moved steadily to the right, leaving Sylvia feeling angry at what she saw as the betrayal of her father's principles. Consequently she looked increasingly to Hardie as a political champion as well as a friend. She described her state of mind on one occasion when suffering from rheumatism and neuralgia, generally depressed, irritated with her family and very short of money in her new rooms in Chelsea. Her gloom was suddenly disturbed by the arrival of Hardie who immediately sorted out her boxes and then took her off to an Italian restaurant to cheer her up.[37]

Despite this growing intimacy they probably did not become lovers for some time. In 1903 Sylvia was twenty-one to his forty-seven. She had had no close male friendships and Emmeline had found the subject of sex too embarrassing to offer her daughters any advice on the subject. Sylvia had only one or two unpleasant encounters with men to guide her; in Venice an elderly Count had attempted to seduce her, and on the train home to London a ticket inspector had tried to kiss her.[38] On the other hand, though inexperienced and understandably doubtful about men, Sylvia was not hostile towards them, nor, as is clear from her relationship with Silvio Corio during the 1920s, was she deterred by the idea of sex outside marriage. Consequently the development of her relationship with Hardie from a friendship with someone who shared her interests and opinions and suffered the same loneliness into a love affair was an entirely natural one. But neither of them was ready for it yet.

7

Militancy Begins (1905–6)

'We cannot make any orderly protest because we have not the means
whereby citizens may do such a thing.'
> Christabel Pankhurst, in court at Manchester, 14 October 1905

For the Pankhursts and the fledgling Women's Social and Political
Union 1905 proved to be the crucial year when they leapt unexpectedly
into national prominence and veered sharply away from constitutional
methods to the militant tactics for which they were to become famous.
In national politics the mood was dominated by a growing conviction
that the long period of Conservative dominance which had lasted since
1886 was rapidly disintegrating. Lord Salisbury wisely resigned as
prime minister in 1902, leaving A. J. Balfour to cope with the huge
costs of the South African war. Problems of taxation aggravated a
long-growing split in the cabinet which burst into the open in 1903
when Joseph Chamberlain launched a campaign to impose protection-
ist tariffs on imports into Britain. Before long ministers on both sides
of the argument had left the cabinet, and the Conservative Party
became consumed in a civil war between free traders and tariff
reformers. As the credibility of Balfour's Government dwindled, expectations of an early general election and a Liberal victory steadily
mounted.

In one way these developments created ideal conditions for the
WSPU, for excitement about an election helped it to attract the audiences and members it urgently needed. On the other hand, the competition presented by so many other national issues threatened to cast
women's suffrage into the shade. Consequently 1905 brought as much

disappointment as achievement for the Pankhursts and their little band of followers. The rest of the women's movement was equally galvanized by the prospect of a change of government. In November 1904 Christabel had attended a conference held by the National Union of Women's Suffrage Societies in London at which she urged the women who were members of political parties to be a thorn in the side of the politicians, rather overlooking the fact that they were already. In March 1905 Sylvia also took part in a NUWSS meeting at the Queen's Hall in London and reported: 'It was all very polite and very tame; different indeed from the rousing Socialist meetings of the North to which I was accustomed.'[1] Yet the Pankhursts' disparaging attitude was scarcely justified. By 1905 the Women's Liberal Federation was subjecting all Liberal candidates to two test issues – on female enfranchisement and the equal moral standard – and imposing sanctions by refusing to undertake the canvassing and organizational work on which candidates had grown to rely since the late 1880s. To this extent militant tactics were already underway several years before the WSPU adopted them, a development which goes some way to explaining why Liberal politicians reacted so severely to the Pankhursts; in a sense the Liberals visited upon the Pankhursts the anger which they had felt unable to vent on women working within their own party organization.

The difficulty lay in the fact that although all three main political parties contained staunch supporters of votes for women, none had an official policy on the subject. It was therefore very difficult to translate the pro-suffragist majority that now existed in the House of Commons into backing for any specific women's bill. Even the ILP's sympathy for the women's cause carried less weight now that it had become effectively part of the Labour Representation Committee. On 26 January Emmeline made a final attempt to persuade the LRC itself to take up the cause. This was a formidable task because, unlike the ILP, the LRC was dominated by trade union representatives who harboured deep prejudice against women as workers because they believed that their presence in the labour force enabled employers to hold down wages. The resolution introduced by John Husband for the Amalgamated Society of Engineers and Selina Cooper of the ILP in 1905 was shrewdly worded so as to avoid antagonizing supporters of adult suffrage. It endorsed the women's suffrage bill 'believing it to be a step towards adult suffrage'. However, Harry Quelch, opposing it on behalf of the London Trades Council, moved an amendment urging that 'any Women's Enfranchisement Bill which seeks merely to abolish sex disqualification would increase the political power of the propertied classes . . . Adult Suffrage . . . is the only Franchise Reform which merits any support from the Labour Members of Parliament'. This was the most explicit repudiation the women had yet faced. Denying that any sex antagonism was involved, Quelch attempted to discredit the women's cause by exploiting class hostility:

They had to put Labour first in every case . . . When a strike was on, who suffered most? . . . Did they find that the sympathy of the wife and children of the employers was with the striker and his family? They knew quite as well as he did that the middle-class woman was the worst employer they had. Who was the worst employer of the domestic servant? . . . Let those who were Labour Guardians testify as to whether the middle-class women and the parsons were not the most reactionary elements upon their Boards of Guardians.[2]

Emmeline, probably stung by Quelch's tirade about middle-class women, sarcastically suggested that he was 'probably able to speak for the women of property because he mixed with those of the highest aristocratic circles'. She also claimed that the ILP's canvass showed that 90 per cent of the female voters would be working class. However, this carried little credibility with the conference which eventually carried the adult suffrage amendment by 483 votes to 270 and adopted it as the substantive motion.

This setback played into the hands of Christabel, though for the time being she was content to allow the existing strategy to discredit itself. The explanation for the subsequent adoption of militant tactics lies to a large extent in the Pankhursts' frustration with the Labour Party, even though their immediate target was the new Liberal Government. Following the LRC conference Keir Hardie reassured Emmeline that he would introduce a bill himself, briefly restoring her optimism. 'Now we must get to work to get pressure brought to bear on members by petitions, deputations, lobbying etc. in support of the Bill', she wrote, 'the old-fashioned and official gang will never do it. I have no confidence in them.'[3] Perhaps she chose to forget that the older suffragists had been doing this for some time. As recently as March 1904 they had secured a vote of 182 to 70 in favour of women's suffrage in the House of Commons. Emmeline was now to re-discover what they had been up against for so many years.

The House met on 13 February and the ballot of MPs for places to introduce backbench bills took place on the twenty-first. Emmeline travelled down to London to spend a week lobbying members to pledge themselves to adopt the women's bill. It was disheartening to find so many of them ready to express sympathy but giving priority to other causes.[4] Though Hardie proved unsuccessful in the ballot, eventually they secured the co-operation of a Liberal member, Bamford Slack, who had won the fourteenth place. Unfortunately this was too low down to offer a realistic chance of success and Emmeline asked the prime minister, A. J. Balfour, for facilities for the bill even to the extent of threatening to oppose his party at the general election, but without success.[5] When the bill came up for the second reading debate on 12 May, the anti-suffragist members adopted their usual tactics by extending discussion of the previous measure from twelve until four o'clock. Then the veteran Anti, Henry Labouchere, delivered a lengthy speech, rehearsing all the old arguments until 5.30 when the debate was adjourned without a division.

However, as a result of the efforts made to arouse interest in Slack's Bill, the Strangers' Lobby was crowded with three hundred suffragists, some of whom were from the Women's Co-operative Guild. For many of them the antique procedures and public-school boisterousness of the House of Commons were a novel experience, and reactions varied from anger to tearful dismay. Emerging from the Lobby, Emmeline decided to mark their disgust by holding an impromptu protest meeting. But as Mrs Wolstenholme Elmy, a frail 72-year-old, began to make a speech, the police intervened to break up the gathering. A second attempt was made when Mrs Elmy got on to the plinth of the statue of King Richard I near the entrance to the House of Lords with the same result. Eventually the police agreed to allow a meeting in Broad Sanctuary near the gates of Westminster Abbey; the women marched there under the leadership of Keir Hardie and Nellie Martel, a suffragist who had returned from Australia in November 1904 after standing for the Senate in New South Wales.[6] There they condemned the procedure of the House of Commons and demanded government intervention over the women's suffrage bill before dispersing. For Emmeline this had been her first direct brush with militancy.

On the face of it, however, the episode had ended in anticlimax. Despite the high expectations apparently entertained by some of the delegation, it had been unrealistic to think that so controversial a measure would be enacted during the fading months of Parliament, especially since, had the Bill passed the Commons, it would have been rejected by the Lords on the basis that there was no mandate for such a reform. Nor could the WSPU expect to be taken very seriously. By the summer of 1905, according to Mrs Martel, its total membership stood at barely thirty. One lesson did, however, emerge from the experience. Emmeline rapidly concluded that attempts to gain the vote via backbenchers' bills were futile. From this point on it became a cardinal point of the WSPU's policy that nothing less than *government* legislation would do. She noticed that even in this phase of its life the Balfour Government found the energy and time to introduce bills dealing with unemployment and the Scottish Churches simply because it considered these topics urgent. This was another crucial step in the transition from constitutional to militant methods.

Meanwhile May brought the summer weather and with it the start of the season for open-air meetings throughout Lancashire and Yorkshire. By addressing up to ten meetings each a week, the band of W.SP.U. speakers, even though small, managed to spread the message extensively. In her vacations Adela joined her sisters in this work. Even when standing on a soap box she was so short that it was difficult to see her in a crowd and she was easily knocked off balance; she often had to hold on to another suffragist in order to stay upright. The women targeted the traditional wakes' fairs which still flourished in many northern towns, for the wide variety of entertainments and exhibits virtually guaranteed large audiences for political speakers. Otherwise the WSPU relied on the co-operation of ILP branches, sometimes supported by choirs and brass bands, or simply set up boxes on village greens, at street corners and outside factory gates. The campaign gathered momentum particularly through the recruitment of several women who were to become key figures in the militant phase after 1906. In the spring of 1905 when Christabel held a meeting at Oldham her audience included Annie Kenney who immediately came up to offer her services to the cause. The fifth child in a family of eleven, Annie Kenney had grown up in poverty supported by her father's meagre wages as a textile worker. At ten years she herself had begun work as a half-timer and abandoned her education altogether at thirteen. Though she was not the only working-class figure in the WSPU, she was enough of a novelty to be introduced to her audiences as 'a factory girl and Trade Unionist'.[7] But Annie Kenney's importance lay as much in her personal relations with the Pankhursts as in her political contribution. Her family life had been dominated by her mother who had died in January 1905; subsequently 'the cement of love that kept the home life together disappeared', and Annie quickly adopted the Pankhursts as her substitute family.[8] Aged twenty-six and unmarried – which was unusual for a working-class girl – she remained immature and naïve, a daydreamer looking for the security that a tightly knit cause could give her. Soon Annie, 'the most irresistible blue-eyed beggar' as Ethel Smyth described her, became a favourite with the suffragettes for her charm, enthusiasm and childlike ways.[9] She was to develop many passionate friendships within the movement, but above all she gave uncritical devotion and boundless admiration to Christabel, who, though almost the same age, seemed a worldly-wise and confident figure in Annie's eyes. For Christabel she was exactly the kind of loyal subordinate a leader required.

In some ways Hannah Mitchell was a similar recruit. She came from a poor farming family in Derbyshire's High Peak district and her home life, dominated by a mother who felt very dissatisfied with her lot, had been an unhappy one. After being apprenticed as a dressmaker at thirteen Hannah left home in 1885 to work as a maid and seamstress before marrying in 1895. She admitted that she had married largely to escape living in other people's homes, and she soon became disillusioned with married life in general and her husband in particular.[10] For a time Hannah found some hope in Socialism but, like Christabel, quickly became sceptical about the attitude of the average Socialist towards female emancipation. She began to give lectures for the Labour Church and the ILP, and stood for the Board of Guardians in Ashton in 1904 when she first met Emmeline. In May 1905, aged thirty-three,

Hannah decided to transfer her efforts to the WSPU. She embarked upon an intensive speaking tour of the Colne Valley constituency which stretched from Huddersfield across the Pennines towards Oldham, thereby preparing the ground for a famous by-election victory by Victor Grayson, a pro-suffrage Socialist, in 1907.

The summer of 1905 was a heady time for Radicals of all kinds. In most regional centres protest meetings by unemployed workers took place, and marches and deputations waited on the prime minister and the Opposition Leader, Sir Henry Campbell-Bannerman; meanwhile emergency legislation to create employment schemes was rushed through Parliament. Even Christabel gave lectures on the unemployment question. As late as August ILP members and Labour city councillors in Manchester met at Nelson Street to co-ordinate their campaign on this issue. So far, then, the WSPU had not quite extricated itself from its constitutional methods, nor, despite the friction, had it severed links with Labour. However, by September Christabel, perhaps irritated at having to resume her law studies after a summer of political activity, had concluded that the WSPU was 'making no headway ... our work was not counting'.[11] But an alternative strategy had already begun to take shape in her mind. First, the WSPU must demand nothing short of a government measure to give women the vote; second, the cause must be made *newsworthy*. Christabel fully appreciated that as the excitement generated by the prospective general election mounted, women's suffrage was likely to be marginalized. Teresa Billington also noticed that as the general election approached 'our work became depressingly difficult', largely because Labour lost interest in women's suffrage. She therefore hoped to contrive something similar to the Boggart Hole Clough controversy which would highlight the cause by getting her arrested. A suitable means of attaining these ends presented itself in the shape of a big Liberal demonstration to be held in Manchester on 13 October. As it was to be addressed by Sir Edward Grey, who was expected to become a senior minister in a new government, it would be appropriate to use the occasion to seek pledges about suffrage legislation.[12] Though carefully planned, this scheme was known only to a small group within the WSPU. Christabel and Annie Kenney were to court arrest at the Free Trade Hall meeting while Teresa Billington organized protests in their support and briefed the newspapers. Shortly before the meeting Billington asked Grey to meet a deputation but she received no reply. Meanwhile Annie and Christabel prepared a banner to be unfurled in case their voices were not heard. They were about to paint 'Women's Suffrage' on the white calico cloth when Christabel hesitated. 'Suffrage' was the traditional Victorian term but it invited critics to mock by turning it into 'Suffer-age'. Instead she adopted the bolder slogan 'Votes for Women' which had not generally been used previously.[13]

On Friday, 13 October, the two women managed to secure seats towards the rear of the Free Trade Hall, and after a while Annie interrupted Grey to ask 'Will the Liberal Government give women the vote?' Christabel repeated the question. According to evidence subsequently given in court, they both 'mounted the seats they had occupied and yelled and shrieked to the utmost of their ability'.[14] However, the chief constable of Manchester, William Peacock, came up and persuaded them to send up a written question to be answered at the end of the speeches. This they did, but although Grey saw the question he offered no reply and towards the end of the meeting Annie and Christabel began to shout again and unfurled their banner. The stewards, assisted by plain clothes police, removed Annie and Christabel with a struggle and took them to an ante-room. There Superintendent Watson asked them to behave like ladies and indicated that they were at liberty to leave. It was then that Christabel, anxious not to allow the episode to end without an arrest, spat in his face and in the face of Inspector Mather whom she also struck in the mouth. They were then taken down the stairs into the street and again asked to leave. Christabel repeated her actions – since she had obviously failed to achieve her object – by striking Mather again. The women then shouted to attract a crowd which quickly filled the street. It was only at this point that the police seized Christabel. With Annie clinging to her side they made their way to the Town Hall to be charged. On the way there Annie reportedly said: 'Never mind, we have got what we wanted', to which Christabel replied, 'Yes, I wanted to assault a policeman.'[15]

When they appeared before a full bench of magistrates at Manchester Police Court on the Saturday morning Annie and Christabel were charged with disorderly behaviour, causing an obstruction and assaulting the police. Asked whether she accepted the evidence given by the Inspector, Christabel told the court: 'The main points he has put forward are perfectly correct. There are details I could deny, but I do not wish to trouble to do so.' She proceeded to argue that their actions were justified by Grey's response and as a protest against the legal position of women: 'We cannot make any orderly protest because we have not the means whereby citizens may do such a thing.'[16] Eventually the magistrates curtailed her speech for straying from the charges. While they withdrew the 'Votes for Women' banner was hung over the dock rail. On returning the magistrates imposed a fine of 10s 6d or seven days in gaol on Christabel and 5s or three days on Annie. Emmeline pleaded with them: 'You have done everything you could be expected to do in this matter. I think you should let me pay your fines and take you home.' But a furious Christabel insisted: 'Mother, if you pay my fine I will never go home.'[17] Emmeline promptly backed down and, having refused to pay, they were put in a cab and taken to Strangeways.

Within a few days it was apparent that the interventions at the Free Trade Hall had succeeded in creating a new momentum for the WSPU by giving a novel twist to women's suffrage. Even before the long reports appeared in the *Manchester Guardian* nearly a thousand people had gathered in Stevenson Square on Saturday 14 October where Emmeline, Teresa Billington and Hannah Mitchell made speeches protesting against the treatment of the two women. Annie's release from Strangeways on the sixteenth was celebrated by a crowd of two thousand that evening, and when Christabel came out on the twentieth she returned to the Free Trade Hall to find it gratifyingly filled to capacity in her honour. Bouquets were presented to the prisoners, donations received and Keir Hardie delivered a speech. In effect, the WSPU was repeating the strategy successfully used in the Boggart Hole Clough by provoking the authorities into creating martyrs of its members. 'Twenty years of peaceful propaganda had not produced such an effect', wrote Hannah Mitchell.[18] The best corroboration for this claim lay not in Manchester but in London where *The Times*, an inveterate opponent of women's suffrage which preferred to ignore the issue altogether, felt obliged to report the events in Manchester.

Even so, the famous incident at the Free Trade Hall did not lead immediately to a sustained campaign of militancy. Faced with a threat of expulsion from her course, Christabel promised to abstain from causing any further trouble while she remained at Owen's College. Moreover, as her offer to pay the fines indicated, Emmeline herself felt far from enthusiastic about the sudden plunge into lawlessness. According to Christabel, her face had been drawn and cold when they said goodbye on the night of Grey's meeting.[19] In addition Christabel was somewhat taken aback to find that her action had not been universally welcomed even by pro-suffragists. She herself felt a little uncomfortable about the way in which she had secured her arrest. Although suffragette propaganda presented the women as victims crushed by the heavy-handed forces of law and order, it was noticeable that it had actually been difficult to get themselves arrested; only repeated attempts had secured the result they desired. Christabel claimed that she had not really spat at all, giving only 'a pout, a perfectly dry purse of the mouth'.[20] Her inconsistency had been mocked in court where she was described as demanding first 'Treat us like men' and then complaining 'How can you treat women in this way' on being ejected from the hall. Even Teresa Billington felt some misgivings about the morality of making the Liberals the scapegoats for Christabel's imprisonment when she herself had been completely determined to get herself arrested.[21] Billington recorded that Christabel and Annie made several 'defensive speeches' after their release from gaol:

Eva Gore-Booth was at one of these and one evening [she] seized me dramatically as we left the platform and urged upon me that I should tell Christabel not to vary her defence from one meeting to another. Now she is out in the open, she said, she cannot fit her explanation to her audience. She either spat at the policeman or she did not. She can't tell one tale in Manchester and another in Oldham.[22]

In spite of this, Eva was less hostile than other Lancashire suffragists such as Margaret Ashton of the North of England Society for Women's Suffrage who alleged that they had damaged the cause. She also disputed their account of the meeting itself, claiming for example, that they had been removed more gently than men would have been.[23] One must allow for the fact that Ashton's reaction may have been coloured by her Liberal loyalties, but there is no doubt that Christabel's initiative split the suffrage movement in Lancashire. Some women left the NESWS to become militants, but Eva and Esther declined to do so, on the grounds that working-class women in general disliked this type of activity:

There is no class in the community who has such good reasons for objecting and does so strongly object to shrieking and throwing yourself on the floor and struggling and kicking as the average working woman, whose dignity is very real to them . . . our members in all parts of the country are so outraged at the idea of taking part in such proceedings that everywhere for the first time they are shrinking from public demonstrations.[24]

It is difficult to know how much credence to give such criticisms. Some allowance must be made for the personal element in the reactions of Eva and Esther who could no longer ignore the fact that their protégée had decisively spurned them and their ideas. On the other hand, it is significant that the Pankhursts soon abandoned Lancashire, hitherto the seat of their reputation, and that the strength of their movement thereafter was to be very much in London and the surrounding counties.

Another factor delayed the onset of the militant campaign. The Pankhursts could not help being caught up in the greater turmoil of the general election following the surprise resignation of Balfour on 4 December and the immediate assumption of office by the Liberals. This proved to be a colourful affair even by the standards of the day. The Liberals dramatized the debate over tariff reform by displaying the 'big loaf' which people would be able to afford under free trade and the 'little loaf' to which the higher prices resulting from protectionism would condemn them. The Tories' South African policy was further discredited following the revelation that Chinese indentured labourers had been imported to work in the mines rather than British miners; Chinese 'coolies' in pigtails were paraded through the streets to the horror and fascination of the crowds. Amid these controversies it was difficult for the women's suffragists to make themselves heard. The WSPU turned out to heckle the candidates, which was a traditional activity though a novelty for ladies. But whether they were entirely wise to target the Liberals who were clearly *en route* to victory is doubtful. Annie Kenney and Teresa Billington made the biggest splash with an intervention at the Albert Hall on 21 December where Sir Henry Campbell-Bannerman addressed a huge rally. Sylvia who had twice applied to the organizers in a vain attempt to obtain tickets, eventually prevailed upon Keir Hardie to get them for her. Annie and Teresa, heavily disguised, found their way to balconies on opposite sides of the hall where they unfurled banners, upside down in Annie's case, and shouted questions to the platform party. A quick-thinking organist struck up a loud tune thereby suppressing the noise of the two women's cries as they were grabbed and ejected from the hall.[25]

However, as the WSPU lacked the resources to sustain a campaign in London, its efforts were focussed largely on the north-west. Home for the Christmas holidays, Sylvia joined the band of hecklers along with a new recruit, Flora Drummond, a stout, genial Scots woman and skilled typist who was regarded by some suffragettes as a comic turn. But Mrs Drummond proved to be a fine organizer and rousing speaker; her nickname 'Precocious Piglet' soon gave way to 'The General' as she enjoyed dressing up in military uniform and wielding a baton. When the boys at Manchester Grammar School organized a mock election, Harry upheld the family's honour by standing as a women's suffrage candidate. He was reported as saying that 'if women could win high honours at college, they were surely qualified to vote at elections'.[26] At the close of the hustings the candidates and officials were entertained to tea by the High Master before the declaration of the poll:

A. E. Jalland (Lib)	262 elected
H. L. Hart (Lib)	232 elected
H. Nichols (Con)	222
R. H. M. Harvey (Con)	218
H. Pankhurst (W. S.)	36
G. Benson (Soc)	34
J. H. Doughty (Soc)	28

'We trust the Government will feel strengthened by this addition to their ranks', commented the editor of the school magazine archly, 'and that they will promptly pass a Bill to allow schoolboys to sleep as long as they please in a morning.' We have no indication what Harry's sisters thought of his efforts but at the least he managed to push himself into the mainstream of the family's activities. He was growing into a dreamy, idealistic boy, qualities which Sylvia found appealing, but which tended to exasperate his mother. During the early hours of the morning Harry used to venture out with two friends to paste 'Votes for Women' stickers across the huge red-and-white posters erected by Winston Churchill's Liberal supporters. The prospect of defeating Churchill in the marginal North-West Manchester constituency loomed largest in the Pankhursts' campaign in 1906. It mattered not that Churchill had a reputation as a pro-suffragist up to this point; since Campbell-Bannerman had appointed him a junior minister in the new administration he was the only government member within easy reach. Christabel drafted a special manifesto emphasizing the duplicity and inconsistency of the Liberal Party:

If the Liberal leaders could not promise before the General Election to give votes to women, they will not do it after the Election. Although Liberals profess to believe in political freedom, the Liberal Leaders have always been opposed to Women's Franchise. It was a Liberal Government in 1884 which refused to give votes to women when the male agricultural labourer was being enfranchised.[27]

To this end Sylvia, Adela, Annie Kenney and Flora Drummond turned up regularly at Churchill's meetings to heckle him. Even without their presence he was a huge draw partly because he had recently quit the Tory Party. His meetings were so crowded that he often had to address overflows before he could get in to his main platform; on one occasion the weight of the audience was so great that that the wooden floor began to give way beneath it.[28] The nightly pandemonium that broke out when the suffragettes made their presence known simply added to the entertainment and spectacle. At one of his meetings an exasperated Churchill invited the heckler up on to his platform to put her question. He replied that after the disruption they had caused, nothing would induce him to vote for women's enfranchisement. Amid cheers the heckler was ejected, whereupon Churchill told the audience that he 'was not so hostile to the proposal as he thought it right to say just now (he had voted for the women's bill) but that he was not going to be henpecked'.[29] His subsequent progress around Manchester resounded to shouts of 'Don't be henpecked, Winston!'

Churchill gained the seat from the Conservatives and returned to Westminster amid a triumphant phalanx of 401 Liberal members. This result proved to be doubly unfortunate for the WSPU. With their huge overall majority the Liberals saw no special need to pander to the demands of the suffragists, and, in any case, after being out of office for many years they had their own priorities in terms of legislation dealing with education, land reform and temperance. The dramatic breakthrough by the Labour Party, which returned twenty-nine members, might have offered a lifeline for the women's cause, but since most of these MPs had been elected by courtesy of an unofficial pact with the Liberals, who had refrained from opposing them, Christabel felt at liberty to deride them as government poodles. In addition, Keir Hardie's standing, which had been very high when only two or three Labour members sat in Parliament, was much diminished by this outcome. Now that Labour had become a *Parliamentary* force for the first time he inevitably seemed more marginal and was shortly displaced by Ramsay MacDonald who shared neither his sentimental sympathy for suffragism in general nor his high regard for the Pankhurst family in particular.

In the anti-climax of early 1906 Christabel shrewdly saw that the best policy for the WSPU lay in concentrating its fire on the new government – this meant following it to London. To stay in Manchester would have condemned the Pankhursts to a dog-fight with the other local suffragists who knew them too well and refused to take them at their own valuation. Emmeline, however, felt rather torn. On the one hand, she too saw the attractions of London and was in any case inclined to defer to Christabel's judgement. But on the other hand, she protested: 'We can't afford it.'[30] This was perfectly true, but Christabel blithely insisted that the money would somehow be found.

Until the end of June 1906 Christabel was still tied to her law course, and even Emmeline could spend only a limited amount of time away from Manchester in view of her commitments as Registrar. It was decided, therefore, to dispatch the faithful Annie Kenney at the end of

January to spearhead the organization in London. According to the traditional account she arrived in London with two pounds in her pocket, no resources and little knowledge of the place. Emmeline warned her not to speak with any man in public except a policeman. By way of explanation for this one writer commented that Emmeline was 'disturbed by the subject of sex'.[31] She had good reason to be concerned – the innocent and vulnerable Annie stood in need of some advice and Emmeline probably felt responsible for her. In fact, Annie was by no means alone in London, though there is disagreement about her movements. Sylvia claimed that Annie lodged at her cramped rooms in Cheyne Walk because Emmeline had no compunction about appropriating Sylvia's flat as WSPU headquarters regardless of the disruption to her academic work. But it seems Annie actually went to Dora Montefiore who arranged for her to live with Mrs Minnie Baldock in Canning Town.

Even before Annie's arrival Sylvia had begun to organize the campaign with the help of Dora Montefiore, Minnie Baldock and Keir Hardie who were holding successful meetings in the East End. To them it seemed natural to draw upon the East End women to launch the WSPU, partly because they had done the same in Lancashire and also because during 1905 large numbers of these women had been involved in marches from the East End to Westminster in protest over unemployment. Indeed, it seems probable that Christabel's motive for dispatching Annie so suddenly to the south was an attempt to retain some influence over the policy there. It is unlikely that Sylvia and Hardie would have adopted the East End strategy if Christabel had been present.

It was decided to organize a march to Trafalgar Square on 19 February when the King's Speech would be read to the new Parliament. On being refused permission to use Trafalgar Square by the police, the women hired Caxton Hall, which was within half a mile of the House of Commons. Emmeline reacted to this with dismay. The 700-seat hall was expensive and difficult to fill; the march, she feared, would be a fiasco. In the event, Hardie secured a loan of fifty pounds to cover the rent, and extra money was found to provide bus fares from the East End as well as tea and buns for three hundred women. By this time the Manchester militants had become sufficiently well known to appeal to the curiosity of many prominent women including the Countess of Carlisle, a staunch suffragist who turned up despite being President of the Women's Liberal Federation. A number of respectable ladies reportedly borrowed clothes from their maids so as to get into Caxton Hall without being recognized! This was the first sign of a rich vein of support that the WSPU was soon to exploit most effectively. Consequently Emmeline travelled down from Manchester to find a full hall. After she, Annie and Mrs Montefiore had delivered speeches they received the news that the King's Speech had contained no mention of votes for women. In order to evade the ban on meetings at Westminster the women then divided themselves into groups of twenty who were admitted at the Strangers' Entrance to lobby the MPs. This of course meant that large numbers had to wait outside in the rain for hours. The day's events certainly generated favourable publicity in the London press. In fact, the WSPU had carefully arranged a procession from St James's Park tube station to Caxton Hall for the benefit of the *Daily Mirror*'s photographer. Founded in 1903 by Lord Northcliffe, the *Mirror* proved to be a valuable asset for the cause, not because it backed women's suffrage, but because as a 'picture paper' for ladies it regarded the suffragists as ideal material for its front and back pages which were filled with photographs rather than the columns of advertisements which usually adorned the more sober newspapers at this time.

For several months WSPU strategy continued to be in the hands of a small Central London Committee comprising Sylvia as secretary, Annie Kenney, who was paid two pounds a week as an organizer, Emmeline, Flora Drummond, Mary Clarke (Emmeline's sister), Mrs Roe (Sylvia's landlady), Mary Neal, Nellie Martel, Irene Fenwick Miller and Emmeline Pethick-Lawrence who became Treasurer.[32] However, both Emmeline and Mrs Drummond had to spend much of their time in Manchester. The Committee decided to follow up the protest over the King's Speech by seeking an interview with the prime minister. When their request was refused they marched up Downing Street on 2 March and camped on his doorstep. As Downing Street had no gates in this period protestors could wander up to Number 10 unless the police had already barred the way. On 9 March Annie Kenney and Flora Drummond led another expedition to Downing

Street and waited outside for an hour. The leaders were not sure what to do next when Mrs Drummond inadvertently pressed a button which opened the door. She and another woman rushed inside only to be promptly arrested. Annie then jumped on to the prime minister's motor car and began to deliver a speech before also being arrested. By refusing to be provoked both the police and the politicians were clearly making things difficult. After the incident Campbell-Bannerman asked the police to release the three women because they were 'only seeking notoriety which would be successful if they appeared before a magistrate'.[33] In spite of this, Kenney and Drummond achieved their objective – they featured on the front page of the *Daily Mirror* and secured an offer from the prime minister to receive a deputation of all the women's suffrage societies. It was at this stage that the *Mirror* emulated the *Daily Mail* whose reporter, Charles Hands, had recently coined the term 'suffragette' to distinguish the militants from the 'suffragists' of the National Union of Suffrage Societies who continued to use constitutional methods.

It seems fairly clear that neither Emmeline nor Christabel were effectively guiding the strategy at this stage. Emmeline did, however, return early in April full of determination to deliver a speech from the Ladies' Gallery in the House of Commons. She was persuaded to wait until 25 April when Keir Hardie was to present a resolution on votes for women. Twelve suffragettes duly took their places in the Gallery and as the end of the debate approached without a division, they shouted down at the members in the chamber. Even Hardie felt embarrassed by this outburst which effectively sabotaged the plan which he and Sylvia had devised. The explanation may have been that Emmeline and Christabel had become frustrated at being out of the limelight up in Manchester and were now anxious to make their presence felt.

Yet they found themselves thwarted again when Campbell-Bannerman met the suffrage deputation on 19 May. It was an impressive occasion with 350 delegates representing a wide range of women's organizations including the non-militant suffragists, trades councils and temperance workers. But the Pankhursts formed only a minor contingent. The deputation was introduced by Charles MacLaren, a distinguished Liberal MP related to the famous John Bright; he had earlier presented a memorial signed by two hundred MPs. After Mac-Laren came seven women speakers: Emily Davies, a campaigner since 1866, Eva McLaren, Margaret Ashton, Eva Gore-Booth, Mrs Pankhurst, Sarah Dickenson and Mary Bateson. In her remarks Emmeline tried to exploit the current alliance between the Government and Labour, but she also hinted at a new phase:

The members of the union I represent . . . have worked to create the Labour Party in The House of Commons. They realized that working men needed Labour Representation to protect their interests, and they feel that they, too, as working women, must also have their Labour Representation in the House of Commons . . . What kind of abuse is it that permits no woman to have a vote? . . . A growing number of us feel this question so deeply that we have made up our minds that we are prepared, if necessary, to sacrifice even life itself in getting this question settled . . . We appeal to you, Sir, to make this sacrifice unnecessary by doing in the present year of Parliament this long-deferred justice to women.[34]

Campbell-Bannerman's response has been described as 'odiously patronizing' by one writer.[35] This, however, is to misunderstand the formal language used by Edwardian politicians on such occasions. In fact, the prime minister adopted a very conciliatory approach; he emphasized that he was impressed by the testimony from co-operative societies and trade unions, and accepted that 'you have made out before the country a conclusive and irrefutable case'. This was the most supportive speech by any prime minister since Disraeli. However, Campbell-Bannerman urged patience because 'I am obliged in my position to be careful not to give anything in the nature of a promise or pledge', which was a delphic way of admitting that his cabinet was bitterly divided on votes for women. In view of the crowded legislative timetable, legislation on a suffrage bill remained unlikely in the near future. Though all this was obvious, some of the delegates had clearly hoped for more. Keir Hardie told the prime minister that 'patience, like many other virtues, can be carried to excess'. Annie Kenney jumped up angrily and cried out 'Sir, we are not satisfied and the agitation will go on.'[36] The women then left for Trafalgar Square where 7,000 people had gathered to hear the outcome of the meeting.

The failure of the 1906 deputation inevitably accelerated the fragmentation of the suffrage movement. Many Liberal women wanted to follow the prime minister's friendly advice to keep pestering without antagonizing the politicians. But the Pankhursts interpreted his remarks as a justification for an intensive campaign of heckling ministers throughout 1906 and 1907; after all, Campbell-Bannerman had admitted there were too many Antis in his cabinet. Christabel offered a shrewd rationalization for this form of militancy:

The only way for either men or women to get what they want is to interfere with the peace of mind of the Government. Men can do this by means of their Parliamentary vote. Women, because they have no vote, must adopt some other means of making their wishes felt. Cabinet ministers are very fond of making an impressive public appearance and delivering a brilliant speech which is approved by the public and reported at length in the newspapers. Therefore, nothing is a greater disappointment to them than to find that the attention of their audience is distracted, that their speeches cannot be properly delivered, and that the newspaper reports contain more about the suffragettes than about themselves.[37]

Christabel also grabbed the moral high ground by pointing out that whereas men were allowed to heckle at political meetings, the suffragettes were seized and forcibly ejected by the stewards: 'The reason why women are treated with less ceremony than men is that, since men have votes, it is thought unwise to offend them.' H. H. Asquith, the Chancellor of the Exchequer and an unwavering anti-suffragist, offered an obvious target. His house in Cavendish Square was besieged on 19 and 21 June by a group of suffragettes led by Teresa Billington and Annie Kenney. The police were fairly indulgent on these occasions, allowing the women to spend hours making protests and banging on the door.[38] But eventually Billington brought the confrontation to a head by slapping a policeman's face and kicking him on the leg. For this she was convicted of assault and given a two-month sentence, later reduced to one month, while Kenney and two others also received six weeks. These attempts to bait the politicians at home and on the platform attracted considerable sympathy, even from Liberal newspapers, largely on the grounds that they were traditional methods used by English Radicals throughout the nineteenth century. 'Parliament has never granted any important reform without being bullied', commented the *Daily Mirror*.[39] However, the effect was somewhat spoilt because the Pankhursts insisted on attacking their supporters, such as Lloyd George, as vigorously as their opponents, and because they left the Conservative anti-suffragists alone, thus enabling Liberal critics to paint them as stooges of the Tories. When Lloyd George and Churchill appeared together at Manchester's Belle Vue on 17 June they presented an irresistible target. On this occasion strict precautions were taken to exclude suffragettes, but Adela, prettily dressed in white muslin, a silk coat, and a hat brimming with roses – a Pankhurst favourite – managed to get in. She took her seat in the front row and duly popped her question, only to be grabbed instantly by two ladies beside her and hit from behind by an elderly gentleman with his umbrella. After being ejected, she became embroiled in an argument with a policeman. She slapped his hand – this was becoming standard practice – was charged with assault and received seven days in custody along with Hannah Mitchell. In this way Adela gained her first experience of prison. She coped with the diet of stale bread and porridge, the nights spent under dirty blankets on a wooden plank bed, and the noxious smell of the slop bucket.[40] Indeed, far from being depressed by prison, Adela relished the novelty and drama of the experience. She emerged to a hero's welcome, made the more gratifying because her mother returned from London to join in the celebration.

The end of June 1906 also found Christabel in an optimistic mood. She had completed her studies, gained her LLB with first class honours, and was at last free to come to London to take charge of the campaign. However, her arrival accentuated the dilemma facing Sylvia, who had reached the end of her scholarship but, despite the encouragement of her teachers, declined to apply for an extension to complete the five-year course. Now aged twenty-four, Sylvia suffered a multitude of worries and distractions. She described herself as penniless; she suffered generally poor health, especially from recurring neuralgia; above all she felt very uncertain about her future. Although Emmeline had insisted that she continue as honorary secretary to the WSPU until Christabel had completed her studies, she refused to let her have a paid position, according to Sylvia, because both Adela and Christabel were to be employed by the organization. Adela had abandoned her teaching job without any encouragement from Christabel or Emmeline, though they accepted her decision with good grace.[41] However, in her own notes Sylvia contradicted this when she wrote that, though offered paid work, she declined it partly because she had not yet decided whether to abandon her artistic career, and also because she felt increasingly unhappy about Christabel's 'incipient Toryism'.[42] With the benefit of hindsight it is easy to see that Sylvia would have been better advised to follow her instincts and talents by cultivating her career as an artist and retaining her independence. But as Sylvia still longed for praise and attention from her family, she shrank from making a clean break at this stage in her life. In retrospect Adela also believed she would have been wiser to have avoided the suffragette movement, but she had been brought up to believe that the cause was supreme.

Consequently, Sylvia endeavoured to keep both options open for several years. She maintained her lodgings in Cheyne Walk, surrounded by her books, her easel, her paints, her camp bed and a bag of clothes. Unlike Emmeline and Christabel she never found it worthwhile to devote hours to dress and appearance. Finding commercial work proved a struggle, but not impossible. In addition, Sylvia now began to supplement her earnings from her art by using her other talent as a writer. Keir Hardie helped by encouraging her to sell sketches to the *Pall Mall Gazette*, and subsequently the paper paid her ten pounds a time for articles, much to her delight. In 1911 she wrote the first of a number of books about the suffragette movement. For the rest of her life Sylvia managed to keep herself just clear of real poverty by writing, and although she continued to devote a great deal of time and effort to the Women's Social and Political Union, from 1906 onwards she took courage from the knowledge that she had a strategy for independence should it become necessary.

No doubt Sylvia's problems would not have weighed so heavily had she not felt so lonely. Her state of mind is strikingly revealed by the self-portrait she produced (now in the National Portrait Gallery). Her work demonstrates her enormous skill in sketching and painting other people, yet her self-portrait is unrecognizable as Sylvia Pankhurst. In it she made herself look upwards so as to eliminate the long, lugubrious face that stares out of every photograph of her. Instead she fashioned a youthful, light-hearted Sylvia in contrast to the photographs taken around 1906 that emphasize a heavier, more mature face, the serious eyes and the large mouth. Sadly, at twenty-four Sylvia could not face herself. She wanted to be pretty, poised and popular – like Christabel.

In this mood Sylvia naturally coveted more and more the affection and praise that Keir Hardie was prepared to lavish upon her. Previous biographers have disagreed as to how far their relationship was a physical one and when it actually began.[43] For a time Sylvia and Hardie saw so much of each other that letters were often superfluous, and since the love letters written during Sylvia's spells in gaol were not dated there is certainly some difficulty in knowing whether they became lovers as early as 1906. Hardie's own references to her as 'Little Sweetheart' are consistent with an affectionate but paternal love. But the letters he wrote when she was in America clearly indicate a sexual relationship.[44] And Sylvia's expressions of her longing 'to feel your dear length pressing on me until my breath comes short' leave no room for doubt.[45] Her love for Hardie must be accounted a crucial phase in Sylvia's life. Until this time she appears to have had no sexual experience; the affair lasted until 1912, and they remained good friends until his death in 1915. It is significant that the two love affairs in Sylvia's life arose out of political compatibility – indeed, perhaps largely as a by-product of it. Like the other members of her family, Sylvia found her absorption with public causes so all-consuming that she had little room for intense personal relationships. It is not clear whether the rest of the family became aware just how close she and Keir Hardie had become, though it seems probable that their love remained a secret. On the other hand, her affair with Keir Hardie may well have altered Sylvia's perception of her family by accentuating her sense of the differences between them. Though she never married, Sylvia took a more positive view of the male sex than either Christabel or Emmeline, and she grew to disparage what she regarded as the narrow feminism adopted by her sister and her mother. Thus, while they believed strongly in working through an all-female organization, Sylvia eventually rejected this approach in favour of collaboration across gender lines within the working-class movement.

By the summer of 1906 the WSPU had put itself on a slightly more formal footing as a result of the extra resources it was now attracting. Though Emmeline felt irritated at Sylvia's insistence on resigning as honorary secretary, there was simply too much correspondence for an unpaid part-timer to handle. Charlotte Despard and Edith How Martyn became joint secretaries in her place. Meanwhile Teresa Billington, Nellie Martel and Mary Gawthorpe, a teacher from Leeds who had worked in the Women's Labour League, were appointed as paid organizers while Christabel became Chief organizer on a weekly salary of £2 10s. She took up residence in the apartment of Fred and Emmeline Pethick-Lawrence in Clement's Inn which effectively became the new headquarters of the WSPU.

Christabel soon made her presence felt by spearheading the anti-government campaign at a by-election that took place at Cockermouth in Cumberland during August in which the voters were invited to reject the Liberal candidate. This tactic operated at two levels. Ostensibly it aimed simply to demonstrate the popularity of votes for women and thereby expose the vulnerability of the new government, which faced by-elections in scores of vulnerable seats won in the special circumstances of 1906. But the election also enabled Christabel to engineer a break with Labour and thus to emancipate the WSPU from its reliance upon working-class women, though until 1907 it was far from clear that she would succeed in this. Since the Liberals had won Cockermouth with only a small majority when faced with a Conservative candidate, the intervention of Labour at the by-election threatened to cost them the seat by splitting their vote. Christabel seems to have been guilty of some deception, for she asked the ILP secretary what arrangements had been made for her arrival in Cockermouth, and she stayed with an ILP member. In view of the WSPU's previous record, many people assumed Christabel had come to support the Labour cause. But she had no intention of backing the Labour candidate, Bob Smillie. This made things a little awkward for her three colleagues, Teresa Billington, Mary Gawthorpe and Marion Coates Hansen, who were all members of the ILP. Gawthorpe in fact, defied her by speaking in support of Smillie, for which she was immediately banned from WSPU meetings.[46] Here was the first indication of the internal opposition which led to the split in the organization in 1907. Relations deteriorated sharply when the Conservatives narrowly won the seat, while Labour did unexpectedly poorly. John Bruce Glasier noted: 'Great indignation at the conduct of Miss Pankhurst and Miss Billington who are ILP members, running their suffrage campaign almost avowedly in the interests of the Tory.'[47] Soon afterwards the Manchester and Salford ILP voted overwhelmingly to expel Christabel and Teresa, but they were apparently retained by the Central Manchester branch. Even Keir Hardie disapproved of their actions at Cockermouth, though he tried to defend them to his ILP colleagues.[48]

Significantly the by-election aroused less immediate controversy in the WSPU itself. This was partly because Christabel had avoided giving a frank endorsement of the Conservatives. But it also reflected the fact that the Union still represented no more than a small central coterie which took little notice of its members' opinions. Teresa Billington alone had the assertiveness to challenge Christabel, but she largely shared her attitude towards the Labour Party. In any case Christabel now enjoyed the advantage of living at the headquarters in Clement's Inn where she had an office. When she travelled to Cockermouth she effectively made policy on the wing. Emmeline, who, perhaps significantly, did not go to the by-election, felt uncomfortable about relations with Labour, but shrank from a dispute with Christabel. The issue remained unresolved until the next important by-election at Huddersfield in November. As this was already a tight three-way marginal held by the Liberals, the WSPU felt confident about inflicting a defeat on the government. The Pankhursts' own accounts of their by-election campaigns both at the time and later were thoroughly disingenuous; they invariably claimed credit whatever the result and portrayed public opinion as wholly on their side.[49] Huddersfield demonstrated the extent of their self-delusion. Large crowds eagerly turned up in expectation of entertainment and perhaps some violence. Local press reports indicated, however, that suffragette speakers aroused as much hostility as sympathy. In any case, as in all pre-1918 elections, a large proportion of the people who appeared at meetings were not actually entitled to vote and could not therefore be seen as a reliable guide to the outcome, however much enthusiasm they showed. In Huddersfield, despite the enormous attention attracted by Christabel and Emmeline, and the vulnerability of the seat, very few votes changed hands and the Liberal emerged the victor. The fiasco threatened to discredit Christabel's policy, especially as there had been some confusion as to what advice the suffragettes were giving the voters. Local opinion mocked the Pankhursts for trying so hard to defeat a Liberal who was a consistent supporter of votes for women. In her dismay Christabel gave way to her frustration: 'When we do get [the vote] we shall show you Huddersfield people how to win elections (derisive laughter).'[50] There was an unpalatable lesson to be learned here. Though an inspiration to many women, and to some men, for her eloquence, courage and spirit, Christabel often failed to convince those who started with different assumptions from her own.

In London, meanwhile, the WSPU had raised the stakes by organizing a demonstration for the opening of Parliament on 23 October. At 3.00 p.m., thirty suffragettes were allowed into the Lobby. When Mary Gawthorpe began to make a speech she was arrested along with Adela, Sylvia, Annie Kenney, Emmeline Pethick-Lawrence, Teresa Billington, Dora Montefiore, Edith How Martyn, Minnie Baldock, Mrs Fenwick Miller and Anne Cobden Sanderson. The following day they were charged with intent to create a breach of the peace and ordered to keep the peace for six months or go to prison for two months. This made a bigger impact than previous cases largely because, apart from Mrs Baldock, Annie Kenney and Mary Gawthorpe, all the women were very respectable middle-class ladies who were now committed to the second division in prison, which meant grim conditions in terms of food, clothing and restrictions on their liberty. Political circles registered a particular shock because of the inclusion of Mrs Cobden Sanderson, the daughter of Richard Cobden who, as the author of the repeal of the Corn Laws, was still an object of veneration among Liberals. Amid much embarrassment the Home Secretary, Herbert Gladstone, backed down to the extent of putting the women in the first division, which meant they could wear their own clothes, have food and writing materials sent in and even pursue their professional work. Sylvia, for example, used the opportunity to sketch some prison scenes.

The prisoners were released early and at different times. The worst affected by her experience was Emmeline Pethick-Lawrence, who almost suffered a nervous breakdown brought on by claustrophobia. She was released on 6 November. Whereas Christabel consistently took the view that suffragettes should not make a fuss about prison conditions as this would risk diverting them to the issue of prison reform, Sylvia, characteristically, reacted quite differently. In her 1911 book she included a lengthy account of her experience in Holloway in which she emphasized how deeply she had been affected by the plight of the ordinary prisoners:

Can they really be criminals, all these poor, sad-faced women? How soft their hearts are! . . . If there is a word in the [religious] services which touches the experience of their lives, they are in tears at once . . . Many of them are old, with shrunken cheeks and scant white hair. Few seem young. All are anxious and careworn. They are broken down by poverty, sorrow and overwork . . . How can these women bear the slow-going, lonely hours? Now go back to your cell with their faces in your eyes.[51]

After her release Sylvia accepted an invitation from Fred and Emmeline Pethick-Lawrence to join them on a recuperative trip to Italy. There she gratefully resumed her painting in Venice; but she also made a point of visiting the women's prison in Milan which seemed 'bright and homely' by comparison with the grim fortress at Holloway.[52]

For Adela, who was not released until 25 November, this spell in prison marked her emergence as a major figure among the suffragettes. After maintaining her work for the WSPU during the summer of 1906, she had found the return to schoolteaching increasingly frustrating. Longing to be in the thick of the action, she eventually obtained some leave and was consequently among those arrested on 23 October. By the time of Adela's release the non-militants had decided to pay tribute to the courage of the militants in the shape of a dinner at the Savoy Hotel hosted by Millicent Fawcett, President of the NUWSS, and attended by such celebrities as George Bernard Shaw, the novelist Israel Zangwill, Lady Frances Balfour, Philip Snowden and Mrs Bertrand Russell. Adela was the only Pankhurst to attend this function. Neither Emmeline nor Christabel had been imprisoned and they probably scorned these efforts by 'the old gang' as they called the moderates. But Adela had emerged as a personality in her own right. She seized the opportunity to abandon schoolteaching and became a WSPU organizer on a salary of £2 per week. For several years she shuttled across the country, working in Lancashire and Yorkshire early in 1907, in Cardiff a few months later, in the West Country and Yorkshire in 1908, in Scotland at the by-elections in 1909, and in Sheffield and Scarborough in 1910. Looking back on this phase from the 1930s she recalled: 'I worked my way through England, a lonely girl but happy in my way.'[53]

By November it had become apparent that the WSPU had scored a tactical triumph over the events of 23 October and the repercussions. The Government had been embarrassed and forced on to the defensive. Polite society had become aroused and several large donations began to arrive at headquarters. It was therefore imperative to maintain the momentum by making further attempts to enter Parliament during November and December. On 20 December Flora Drummond almost succeeded in running into the chamber of the House of Commons. Each such escapade was now celebrated with a breakfast or a dinner for the released prisoners which served to keep the cause in the public eye and the contributions flowing freely. At last Emmeline's fears about finding the money to sustain the cause were melting away.

8

Democracy Versus Dictatorship
(1907–8)

'If [Emmeline] had been tolerant and broadminded, she could not
have been the leader of the suffragettes.'
Adela Pankhurst, 'My Mother: An Explanation and A Vindication',
Pankhurst-Walsh Papers, 16/50

Christmas 1906 found the twenty-one suffragettes who had taken part
in Flora Drummond's raid on the House of Commons on 20 December
in Holloway. On their release early in January they were treated to a
late Christmas dinner at the Holborn Restaurant by Fred and Emmeline Pethick-Lawrence. By this time such celebrations were becoming a
standard method for extracting the maximum publicity and sympathy
from suffragette actions. Moreover, lavish dinners at prominent
London hotels indicated that the Pankhursts had at last begun to
attract serious money to the cause. For Emmeline this heralded the
relief of the financial worries which had dogged so much of her adult
life and which obliged her to cling to her modest income as Registrar
in Manchester despite the inconvenience of the job. In traditional
accounts of the suffragette campaign it has not generally been recognized that Emmeline, Sylvia and Christabel enjoyed a talent as fund-
raisers amounting almost to genius. Without their skills the movement
could never have made the impact that it did on Edwardian politics.
The only flaw lay in their inability to *manage* their money efficiently
without expert assistance, an omission that was rectified when Keir
Hardie recruited a brilliant new Treasurer for the Union in the autumn
of 1906.

Emmeline Pethick had been born in 1867, in a middle-class Nonconformist family in Weston-super-Mare. Growing up with a pronounced sense of social justice and a desire to improve the world, she did charitable work with working-class girls in the West London Mission with Mary Neal, who also became a suffragette. Emmeline never concealed the fact that as a girl she had been very troubled by her sexuality and the 'tangle of emotions' it caused. As a result she had rejected the whole idea of marriage and suffered from 'a vague feeling that I was not the kind of girl to attract a mate'.[1] In 1895 she and Mary Neal left the Mission to live together in a workman's flat over-looking the Euston Road. Among other things they ran a dress-making business where employees worked only eight hours a day and received twice the usual wage rates. Despite her reservations Emmeline did get married in 1901, aged thirty-four, to a wealthy and brilliant law graduate, Fred Lawrence. But her marriage was far from typical. They had no children, and Fred proved his readiness to respect his wife's independence by linking his surname with hers and by giving her a separate flat in their apartment in Clement's Inn just off Fleet Street.

Women's suffrage first aroused the Pethick-Lawrences' attention in the autumn of 1905 when they were on a cruise to South Africa. In February 1906 Keir Hardie introduced Emmeline to Mrs Pankhurst, correctly sensing that the Union could benefit greatly from Fred's wealth and her organizational skills. Though initially reluctant, Emmeline quickly succumbed to the pressure of the cause, and also to the charms of Annie Kenny. Annie had a habit of sitting, literally, at the feet of women she admired and pouring out her feelings in a very uninhibited and sentimental fashion. Emmeline clearly responded to this. 'The attraction between them was so emotional and so openly paraded that it frightened me,' wrote Teresa Billington. 'I saw in it something unbalanced and primitive and possibly dangerous to the movement.'[2] However, though embarrassing to some members, their relationship was not so unusual as to arouse great comment, and Emmeline Pethick-Lawrence rapidly became a crucial element in the success of the Union. Until 1912 she and her husband were part of the small coterie which effectively ran the organization. They gave the Union a headquarters at Clement's Inn and also took Christabel into their home there for a period of five years. Their country house, 'The Mascot', at Holmwood near Dorking, became an important refuge for suffragette prisoners who were recuperating or on the run from the authorities. But above all Emmeline organized the office, put the Union's hitherto disorganized finances on to an orderly footing and ensured a steady flow of contributions. Her aim was 'to free the leaders from all unnecessary work and responsibility, and give them the opportunity to move about amongst women everywhere'.[3] In short she was the perfect foil for the more mercurial and impulsive talents of Christabel and Emmeline.

On the other hand, once Christabel and Emmeline had teamed up with the Pethick-Lawrences in the autumn of 1906, the whole atmosphere of the WSPU changed. Sylvia, Teresa Billington and Annie Kenney, who had created the original London organization of the Union, lost their position either by becoming regional organizers or, in Sylvia's case, because she wanted to be detached. Annie, unquestioningly loyal to Christabel, did not mind this, but Billington began to resent being excluded from the limelight by the tightly knit coterie in Clement's Inn: 'We were heard no more in the London halls, parks and street corners', she wrote. This certainly reflects her later bitterness towards the Pankhursts, but other contemporaries believed that she had been marginalized despite being a better orator than Christabel – or *because* of it. She won such favourable publicity in the Hexham by-election in March 1907 that she was thereafter excluded from sharing a platform with Christabel and was not used in any English by-election again.[4] No one was to challenge Christabel as de facto leader and the star figure of the movement.

At the beginning of 1907 the Clement's Inn premises comprised a small room which Christabel, evidently determined to elevate herself above the others, occupied, and a larger room used for 'At Homes' on Mondays from four to six and on Thursday evenings. At first these were informal gatherings of volunteers. A Mrs Sparborough brought the tea round while Christabel mounted a chair to report the week's events flourishing a sheaf of press cuttings in her hand. Before long the room, which held 150 people, became too small. In February 1908 the Monday 'At Homes' were transferred to the Portman Rooms in Dorset Street which held four hundred, and then to the larger Portman Rooms in Baker Street where six hundred people could be accommodated.[5] In the process the Women's Social and Political Union was not merely growing larger: it was advancing up the social scale. Teresa Billington, who had been dispatched to Scotland to spread the organization there, recorded her surprise on returning to Clement's Inn where she 'found the place full of fashionable ladies in rustling silks and satins'.[6] Although Mrs Pethick-Lawrence appealed to 'women of every class and creed' to participate, she strongly endorsed Christabel's deliberate policy of tapping the resources of upper-class ladies and their husbands; before long a battalion of wealthy women were subscribing to the funds including Muriel, Countess de la Warr; Janie Allan, the daughter of the Scottish ship-owner; Lady Weetman Pearson, the wife of a rich contractor who became Lord Cowdray; Princess Sophia Dhuleep Singh, whose father was the Maharaja Dhuleep Singh, former ruler of the Punjab; Mrs Saul Soloman, whose husband had been a distinguished Cape Colony politician and governor-general; Mrs D. A. Thomas, the wife of the wealthy South Wales coal-owner and Liberal MP; the Honourable Evelina Haverfield, daughter of Baron Abinger; and Mrs Joseph Fels, whose husband was a soap manufacturer. Sympathizers who were themselves too elderly or infirm to take part in militancy often derived a vicarious pleasure from subsidizing the escapades of other women. Mrs Pethick-Lawrence was adept at appealing to these leisured women to help the Union.

These connections with middle- and upper-class society put the Pankhursts' campaign into a different perspective. Though in one sense an attack upon the social and political Establishment of Britain, after 1906 it was consciously based *within* that Establishment and drew much of its strength and character from its members. Despite the notoriety associated with the suffragettes, at the time many highly respectable families saw no great embarrassment or loss of status in becoming involved. 'It was almost the done thing in our family to go to prison', wrote Margaret Haig, who later became Lady Rhondda.[7] The involvement of women such as Lady Constance Lytton, the sister of the Earl of Lytton, a leading Tory politician, made suffragette activity fashionable in certain circles for a time. Lady Ricardo observed that police officers were often influenced by the fact that so many titled ladies got themselves arrested and became suffrage supporters as a result![8] That the Union's leaders were fully alive to the social cachet enjoyed by militancy is evident from the techniques they used especially in London where the Union's main strength lay in areas such as Kensington and Chelsea. At Mrs Pethick-Lawrence's suggestion they canvassed residential districts in order to compile lists of wealthy ladies who were then invited to an 'At Home', and later inveigled into making donations.[9] They also made a practice of contacting any woman who had achieved a distinction or official honour. In this way Ethel Smyth, the composer, who was awarded an honorary doctorate by Durham University, first came into contact with the WSPU.[10] Her experience shows how relentlessly the Union exploited social status. Smyth received a letter from Lady Lytton and was subsequently accompanied by Muriel, Countess de la Warr, to her first 'At Home' at the house of Lady Brassey. There she was introduced to Emmeline Pankhurst who made an immediate impression on her: 'A graceful woman rather under middle height; one would have said a delicate-looking woman, but the well-knit figure, the quick deft movements, the clear complexion, the soft bright eyes that on occasion could emit lambent flame, betokened excellent health.'[11]

During 1907 the results of these extensive contacts began to make a dramatic impression on the Union's finances. In the year from March 1906 to February 1907 the WSPU's income had been £2,959 of which £2,700 derived from subscriptions. This in itself represented a considerable increase. But from March 1907 to February 1908 income leapt to £7,545, of which £5,187 came from subscriptions.[12] In the following year to 1909 it rose to no less than £21,213. This enabled the Union to develop a machine capable of taking on the major political parties. It is sobering to reflect, for example, that the Labour Party's income in 1908 was under £10,000. Consequently the Clement's Inn offices soon became crowded not just with enthusiastic volunteers but with paid staff. A Miss Kerr became office manager and Beatrice Sanders the book-keeper, while Mary Home maintained the newspaper cuttings and research material. Mabel Tuke, a widow who was taken up by the Pethick-Lawrences who named her 'Pansy', acted as honorary Treasurer in Mrs Pethick-Lawrence's absence. In May 1908 when a wealthy supporter donated the money to buy a WSPU motor car in order to enable Emmeline to travel more comfortably, a separate fund was raised to cover the upkeep of the vehicle.[13] This necessitated the employment of a chauffeur, a post filled by several women including Charlotte Marsh, who had trained as a sanitary inspector, and Vera Holme, an exuberant young girl who sang in Gilbert and Sullivan operettas. It is probable that Vera Holme had learnt to drive as a result of touring the provinces with a theatrical company; since driving tests had not been invented the chief requirement was a capacity to cope with the frequent mechanical breakdowns and to deal with horse traffic with which Vera was already familiar.[14] Known as 'Jack' or 'Jacko', Vera Holme was an outstanding example of the high-spirited young recruits attracted into the WSPU. She earned her own living, enjoyed an unchaperoned social life, smoked cigarettes and rode her bicycle around London. She was also a lesbian, and developed a close relationship with Evelina Haverfield, which lasted until her death in 1920. In total the Union employed eleven staff during 1906-7 at a cost of £560, but in the next year no fewer than thirty-two were employed, including eighteen at headquarters and fourteen as regional organizers, at a cost of £1,472 in salaries.

This healthy situation at last allowed Emmeline to resign her post as Registrar in March 1907. She had already received a warning letter from the Registrar General pointing out that a complaint had been made on the grounds that her political activities had become detrimental to her duties.[15] Hitherto Emmeline had been reluctant to jeopardize her sole source of income and the pension that went with it, especially as Harry was still at school. She had relied on her sister Mary to deputize during absences and had often taken night trains back to Manchester so as to be in the office the following morning. According to Sylvia, the Pethick-Lawrences agreed to guarantee Emmeline's expenses after she gave up the registrarship, though Rebecca West said she was paid a £200 salary – it may well have amounted to the same thing. Mary also became an employee of the Union, while Harry was apprenticed to a builder in Glasgow.[16] This, however, resolved financial matters only up to a point. From March 1907 onwards Emmeline had no fixed home of her own and was consequently reduced to living either in the homes of suffragette supporters or, since she was constantly on the move, in hotels.

In order to sustain this higher level of expenditure and organization it was essential to keep the WSPU constantly in the public eye. This meant that over the next eight years the Pankhursts felt obliged to employ new and more dramatic forms of militancy in order to retain the impact and novelty value of their campaign. In fact, Christabel showed more subtlety and flexibility than she has traditionally been given credit for. She recognized, for example, that by 1909 the first phase of militancy had passed its peak, and consequently agreed to suspend it during most of 1910 and 1911.

To coincide with the opening of Parliament on 13 February 1907 the WSPU organized the first Women's Parliament at Caxton Hall. At the close a succession of deputations departed for the House of Commons and were surprised to find themselves confronted on the green outside Westminster Abbey by mounted police, who were promptly denounced in the press as 'Cossacks'. Emmeline declared she would not 'shrink from death if necessary for the success of the Movement . . . If the Government brings out the Horse Guards and fires on us, we will not flinch.'[17] This language carried immense political significance amongst Edwardian Liberals who felt outraged at the brutal methods routinely adopted by the Russian Tsarist governments to suppress democratic movements. After the revolution of 1905 the dispersal of the Duma had been condemned by Campbell-Bannerman himself. It was thus severely embarrassing over the next few years for the Liberal Government to be accused of importing 'Tsarist' methods for handling suffragettes who were also seeking political rights. Such heavy-handedness by the authorities enabled the women to gain the moral high ground in their struggle.

Fifty-eight women appeared in court as a result of the clashes of 13 February. The first deputation had been led by Charlotte Despard, who was the sister of General Sir John French, later Britain's Commander-in-Chief on the western front; but according to Sylvia's account, Christabel slipped into one of the later deputations at the last minute, having calculated that a second prison sentence was now appropriate. Next morning she demanded to be tried first on the grounds that she had been the organizer of the march. Most of those arrested received seven to fourteen days in Holloway, though Sylvia and Mrs Despard got three weeks. At least they were put in the first division and were thus able to write and receive letters. Keir Hardie wrote to her, though in cautious terms, probably because he feared that if the correspondence were to be opened a scandal would result.

Sylvia's own letters to him from prison were never dated but she was far less inhibited. She penned a number of love poems, the first of which recalled: 'Dear face so fond to me, Dear sturdy neck that my arms have to twine.' One of Hardie's biographers suggests that such words could have been written by a child to a parent rather than by a mistress to a lover; however, Sylvia was no child but a 25-year-old woman.[18]

For Christabel this second spell in prison carried a different significance. Though she had taken the opportunity to deliver a defiant speech from the dock before being sentenced, she did not see herself as cannon fodder. In fact, after 1907 she endured only one further period in prison, admittedly a lengthy one. Christabel took a characteristically clear and unsentimental view about the roles to be played by the various members of the Union. In 1909, for example, she advised Mary Phillips, one of the organizers, to restrain her natural zeal to join the prisoners:

You speak of getting arrested. Nothing would be more mistaken at the present time. On no account run the risk of it, as the work you have been doing recently would all go to pieces. It will be necessary to get your voluntary workers to make the protest, which of course you will organize.[19]

Here Christabel showed a leader's strategic sense: indiscriminate arrests had to be avoided if possible for fear of undermining the wider campaign. While spontaneous actions by young and idealistic women could never be entirely prevented, the key workers had to remain at liberty. By 1907 Christabel had cast herself as the movement's thinker and strategist. Emmeline, whose willingness to subordinate herself to Christabel's judgement grew stronger with time, evidently accepted her role without question and expected others to follow suit: 'If I can obey, so must you', she liked to say.[20] For a 49-year-old woman of otherwise strong convictions to defer to her 26-year-old daughter in this way struck a number of contemporaries as odd and even unhealthy. 'Emmeline was silly about Christabel, she idolized her', commented Helen Fraser who worked as an organizer in Scotland. According to Mrs Cobden Sanderson, Emmeline would 'walk over the dead bodies of all her children except Christabel and say "look what

I have done for the cause".'[21] During 1907 such criticism became increasingly common, for the effect of marginalizing rivals within the organization was to leave Christabel surrounded by an admiring coterie of women including Annie Kenney, Mabel Tuke, Grace Roe, Flora Drummond and the Pethick-Lawrences who fully endorsed Emmeline's view.

From the outside Christabel's dominance was by no means apparent because of the prominence enjoyed by Emmeline at public gatherings of the WSPU. But, in effect, she acted more as the figurehead than as the leader of the movement. From the start of 1907 onwards her life became a wearying round of excursions all over the country to carry Christabel's message into every by-election. Unfortunately, when back in London she usually lived at the Inns of Court Hotel where her state of mind was not improved by the knowledge that Christabel was living in the pockets of the Pethick-Lawrences at Clement's Inn. Lonely and resentful, she sometimes gave way to tears.[22]

The by-election campaign of 1907 was very much Christabel's inspiration; and like many of her ideas it showed great shrewdness, even though it was ultimately flawed. Among the four hundred Liberal victories won in 1906 the new government naturally had scores of highly vulnerable seats to defend. It could not avoid having to confront its electorate far more frequently than later twentieth-century governments because at this time any member of Parliament who received a ministerial appointment, or who simply moved from one post to another, was technically obliged to resign his seat and seek re-election. This offered countless opportunities to pressure groups to prove that the government lacked a popular mandate by intervening at by-elections. To expose its vulnerability over women's suffrage, Emmeline set off early in 1907 to spearhead the Union's campaign in South Aberdeen. Unhappily Scotland was very staunchly Liberal and the government retained its seat. But Christabel placed great importance on activity north of the Border largely because many leading Liberals represented Scottish constituencies including the prime minister, Campbell-Bannerman, at Stirling, H. H. Asquith in East Fife, John Morley at Montrose, and, later, even that unlikely Scotsman, Winston Churchill, in Dundee.[23]

Emmeline returned to London for the second Women's Parliament on 20 March. This time Lady Harberton, famous as the President of the Rational Dress Society and the divided skirt to which she gave her name, volunteered to lead the deputations from Caxton Hall to present the petition to Parliament. Facing five hundred policemen, the suffragettes pressed on throughout the afternoon until darkness fell, but without success. However, a group of mill girls from Lancashire dressed in shawls and clogs, who had been organized by Adela and Annie during their campaign in the North, managed to get past the Strangers' Entrance, largely because they were mistaken for sightseers – an interesting comment on perceptions about the social class of the suffragettes.[24] Charged with disorderly conduct and resisting the police in the execution of their duty, they received sentences varying from two weeks to a month. Altogether the two attempts to gain entry to Parliament had left 130 women in prison in the space of two weeks. Emmeline was not among them as she had hurried away from the Caxton Hall meeting, taking the night train to Newcastle in order to speak at the by-election at Hexham where the Liberals again retained their seat. Meanwhile Emmeline Pethick-Lawrence carried Christabel, Annie Kenney and Mary Gawthorpe off for a holiday at Bordighera on the Côte D'Azur.

By the summer of 1907 Christabel's by-election strategy stood in need of some dramatic successes. About thirty speakers were ready to take the field including all four Pankhursts. However, Emmeline found Sylvia increasingly reluctant to be dragged into this work. In fact, after her three-week spell in Holloway in February, Sylvia felt tempted to quit the Union and to accept an invitation from a woman artist, Emilia Cemino Folliero, to return to Italy and spend her time painting up in the mountains. Though she declined this offer, she decided to escape from the suffragette campaign for a time by embarking in the early summer for a tour of the north of England with a view to observing and painting the working conditions of women. There may have been another reason for this move. London had lost some of its attraction for her. After the ILP's Easter conference Keir Hardie had suffered a slight stroke and subsequently became ill with intestinal pain. He entered St Thomas's Hospital where Sylvia managed to visit him before his wife, Lillie, arrived. As things did not improve he decided to return to his home in Old Cumnock in Ayrshire. When he boarded the train for Scotland Emmeline and Sylvia gave him a tearful farewell, fearful that he might not recover and, perhaps, recalling the similar illness which had killed Richard nine years earlier. Evidently in need of a long rest, Hardie had hydropathic treatment in Scotland, but in July he departed for a prolonged trip which took him to Canada, India and South Africa from which he did not return until March 1908.

Sylvia meanwhile journeyed to the Black Country, stopping first at Cradley Heath which was notorious as a centre of chain- and nail-making in which women worked for appallingly low rates of pay. Sylvia was too sensitive to be anything other than shocked by the grim desolation of life at Cradley Heath: 'The air smells and tastes of soot', she noted, 'and from the low hills on every side rises the smoke of mill chimneys.' She spent a good deal of time talking to the workers about their lives. 'The women crowded round me, many of them eagerly telling me that they liked working at the chain.'[25] For labouring up to ten hours a day the women earned four or five shillings a week and even the trade unions, seeing no hope of improvement, concentrated on trying to help the male employees. Mothers were obliged to keep babies beside them while working at the anvils with sparks flying dangerously around them. They lived in jerry-built houses which lacked sanitation and were deprived of any form of entertainment or hope of improvement apart from evenings in the public house.[26] Such scenes served to strengthen Sylvia's Socialism and confirmed her conviction that her sister's pursuit of feminism was both narrow and inadequate. However, the misery she witnessed also aroused the artist in her and she produced many sketches executed quickly in gouache in the open air as she had done in Italy.

Before long Sylvia's work was interrupted by a telegram from her mother summoning her to a by-election at Rutland. But since this was another Conservative constituency there seemed relatively little for the WSPU to gain. Although the appearance of suffragettes in small villages was enough to bring the inhabitants running out to see them, they also attracted increasingly hostile treatment from young men. At indoor meetings youths often turned up armed with handbells and cans of dried peas which they rattled noisily, or with boxes of live mice which they released in the hope of creating panic amongst the ladies present. For open-air meetings the Union hired wagons or lorries as platforms for its speakers. However, in the hands of a gang of youths these could be pushed around town squares and village greens and even tipped into ponds to the consternation of the occupants and the delight of the crowds.

Before Rutland polled Emmeline had moved on to a more promising campaign at Jarrow on Tyneside in July. This seat had been won comfortably by the Liberals in a straight contest with Labour in 1906. But the sudden appearance of both a Conservative and a United Irish League candidate split the Liberal vote three ways resulting in a narrow win for Pete Curran, the Labour candidate. In a sense such an outcome was awkward for the Pankhursts. Since the January conference of the Labour Party had rejected the women's suffrage bill by nearly three to one, pushing Keir Hardie to the brink of resignation in the process, the Union could hardly endorse its candidates. But though Emmeline and Christabel opposed Curran at Jarrow, they evidently had no compunction about claiming credit for his success. Emmeline complained that the non-militant suffragists in the north-east had endorsed Curran, whereas she believed that by withholding support from him they would have extracted a commitment from the Labour Party before the end of the election. 'They are dying to have our support, for they see the men are with us', she wrote. 'It won't be long before they, and the Tories too, will be forced to take up the question in a practical way.'[27] No doubt she had been caught up in the excitement of the election, but her reading of the situation was hopelessly unrealistic. None the less, her optimism grew further as the result of a second by-election which overlapped with Jarrow, at Colne Valley in the West Riding of Yorkshire. Emmeline was very taken with Victor Grayson, the eloquent young Socialist candidate in Colne Valley, who advocated votes for women and enjoyed the backing of Keir Hardie, though not of the Labour Party itself. A severe critic of the Liberal–Labour pact, Grayson no doubt seemed congenial as a fellow rebel. Of course, Emmeline and Christabel refused to endorse Grayson's Socialism, but they were shrewd enough to keep on good terms with him. When he squeezed in by a margin of 163 votes they had no difficulty in claiming the result as another victory for women's suffrage. For once some national newspapers endorsed this, at least to the extent of claiming that the charismatic Grayson had aroused great enthusiasm among the local mill girls, whose influence on the result, however, could only have been indirect.[28]

The outcome at Jarrow and Colne Valley gave Christabel's by-election strategy the momentum it needed, though it also raised questions about the wisdom of being so hostile to Labour. Sylvia certainly saw no reason to abandon her own semi-detached relationship with the Union. After her work in Rutland she addressed some suffrage meetings in Leicester where she produced more gouache and water-colour pictures of women in the boot and shoe factories. Then she turned northwards again to Wigan, famous for its 'pit-brow lassies' in the local coal mines. Dressed in clogs, bonnets, shawls and short corduroy knickerbockers, the girls made a picturesque sight. But their labour involved dragging tubs laden with coal when they reached the surface and rolling them on to railway lines, or picking stones and wood from moving belts from which clouds of black dust constantly arose. For this they received only half the wages of the men engaged in similar work. Despite this they seemed to Sylvia to be fit and healthy by comparison with the pale women labouring in the textile mills.[29] She spent much of the summer in Wigan though Emmeline again summoned her to Bury St Edmunds for another by-election. This contest only deepened Sylvia's political misgivings, for Bury was another Tory constituency with no Labour candidate. As a result the suffragettes appeared to her to be a mere adjunct of the Tory campaign and she felt very uncomfortable at being associated with them.[30] On their return to London some of the other speakers reported to Christabel that Sylvia had declared herself a Socialist on the platform and had taken no pleasure in the Conservative victory.

However, Sylvia quickly moved on to the Staffordshire potteries to observe the women working in the famous Wedgwood factory there. In the dipping shed she almost fainted in the heat and felt sick from the sweet taste of the lead which got into her mouth. This was danger-ous work, for contact with lead infected the wombs of many of the women who subsequently gave birth to stillborn babies or to children afflicted with convulsions. All this for seven shillings a week.[31] But in spite of herself Sylvia loved the beautiful products of the women's labours and she produced many 'pot bank' paintings of them crouching intently over their benches. By way of contrast she next travelled north to Scarborough, where she found the itinerant Scots fisherwomen packing and gutting the North Sea herring catch. Her next stop was Berwickshire in the Border country, one of the areas in which women still worked in agriculture, largely in gangs following the plough to pick potatoes or cutting the corn by hand and stacking it in the traditional manner. 'Going down the lanes there some still and misty autumn morning you may often hear the sound of soft and almost whispering voices with now and then, perhaps, a gentle laugh.'[32] She found these outdoor scenes grim but rewarding; she produced many sketches, invariably only half-finished as the women moved so fast across the bleak fields. The periodical arrival of a telegram continued to remind Sylvia of how detached she was becoming from the WSPU and its concerns. But the poverty she had observed among the female workers strengthened her conviction that the roots of their condition lay not simply in their gender but in the economic system. She published her observations in 'Women Workers of England' in the *London Magazine* in November 1908 as well as her paintings of 'The Chainmaker', 'Pit-Brow Lassies' and 'Inside a Cotton Spinning Mill'. At length the approach of winter brought Sylvia to Glasgow and thus to more textile mills. It also enabled her to pick up the threads of what was becoming an increasingly scattered family.

In March 1907, Harry, now aged eighteen, had been sent as an apprentice to a small builder on Clydeside. This seems a bizarre choice of occupation for a rather frail and gentle boy whose inclinations were scholarly rather than physical or practical. In fact, he had a good deal in common with his father. Yet whereas Emmeline had doted on Richard, she evidently failed to appreciate similar qualities in her son. It was as though she found signs of weakness in any of her children distressing, which helps to explain her invariable lack of sympathy with Sylvia whose ability to show her emotions was much criticized, though it actually made her in some sense a stronger personality than Christabel or Emmeline. Not surprisingly Harry suffered greatly from the outdoor work in the hard northern winter. Brother and sister enjoyed each other's company at weekends until, shortly before Christmas, Sylvia returned to London. She then spent several weeks with her mother and Christabel, though it is not clear whether Adela, who was campaigning with Nellie Martel, Annie Kenney and Mary Gawthorpe in the north until February, joined them. Just before Christmas Sylvia received an upsetting message from Keir Hardie who was still abroad: 'It roused in me a sudden storm of misery which seemed to be killing my inner life', she wrote.[33] In a rather obscure but agonized letter Hardie had written: 'I feel as though I had passed through fire and water and a long valley of bitterness.' Though his meaning remains unclear, the implication seems to be that he had suffered severe guilt over his relationship with Sylvia and was trying to bring it to an end; the foreign tour offered a means of doing that. This left Sylvia alone with her shattered emotions, for neither her mother nor Christabel was aware of her anguish. When, on Christmas Eve, they asked her to accompany them down to Devon for another by-election, she reluctantly joined them despite 'feeling that I must be alone with my grief'. But soon she returned, 'unable to control my restless misery in face of their cheerful chatter'.[34] In the event Sylvia did resume her relationship with Hardie after his return to England.

Early in the New Year Harry returned to the south because the builder for whom he worked had gone bankrupt. For a time he joined Sylvia in her lodgings as there was nowhere else for him to go. Harry had felt acutely his isolation from the rest of the family and, as always, he sought to work his passage back into their affections by throwing himself into work for women's suffrage. It was at the Manchester by-election in 1908 that he met Helen Craggs, a teacher from Roedean, and fell in love.[35] But the question remained unanswered: what was Harry to do? Christabel suggested he should become a secretary. Before long he was enrolled for classes in shorthand and typing at the Polytechnic, he acquired a reader's ticket at the British Museum and Emmeline offered him a pound a week for his lodgings. When she rushed away to the next by-election Sylvia and Christabel seized the opportunity to have Harry's eyes tested, as a result of which he acquired glasses and thus began to read easily for the first time in his life.[36] Sadly this new course lasted only briefly. Harry, who had become interested in the back-to-the-land movement, gave a lecture to the ILP on the subject. Unfortunately for him, this gave Emmeline the idea of finding some practical rural experience for her son; for some reason she regarded open-air work as a cure for all kinds of physical weakness. She spoke to Joseph Fels, a wealthy WSPU supporter who owned some smallholdings at Mayland in Essex, to which the unfortunate Harry was dispatched. Though he suffered greatly from the hard work and poor living conditions in Essex he refused to complain. In the absence of documentary evidence Emmeline's treatment of her son seems heartless and inexplicable except in terms of her dislike of physical weakness. Perhaps her understandable desire to demonstrate the competence and independence of women may have led her to regard Harry's presence as an unwelcome complication. Alternatively, she may simply have found herself too preoccupied with the campaign to be able to devote much thought to Harry and his future. Emmeline and Christabel strongly believed that militancy ought to be confined to women in order to enhance the appeal of their heroism to the female sex in general, and that too much male involvement would lead to indiscriminate violence. Though the Union enjoyed the support of a number of men, it rigidly excluded men, with the special exception of Fred Pethick-Lawrence, from its deliberations and organization. As a result a separate Men's Political Union was established for male suffragists who supported militancy, though it eventually broke down because its members found it impossible to co-operate with the Pankhursts effectively.

Following their triumphs at Jarrow and Colne Valley, Emmeline and Christabel became embroiled in a major internal crisis within the WSPU. This had been festering beneath the surface since Christabel's arrival in London in June 1906, but had been kept at bay by the sheer pace and excitement generated by the militant campaign. The first symptom of dissatisfaction surfaced in January 1907 when Dora Montefiore complained about Emmeline's action in expelling a branch of the Union because it had appointed as its secretary a Mrs J. M. Robertson who was the wife of a Liberal MP. This high-handedness crystallized her opposition to the election policy and her concern about the absence of detailed statements of Union funds which culminated in a row at Clement's Inn. Since Mrs Montefiore was not prepared to defer to the triumvirate as the others were she was effectively dismissed from the organization.

In fact, many of the Union's supporters had still not grasped, or had not accepted, the implications of Christabel's control of strategy. By October 1907 the Union had established 69 local branches, including

21 in London, 10 in Scotland and 19 in Lancashire and Yorkshire. Although some of these were guided by the official organizers, much of the expansion reflected a *spontaneous* growth which Christabel feared with good reason. She knew that the East End women who had turned up at the original Caxton Hall meeting in 1906 had sung the 'Red Flag', and subsequently voted to constitute themselves the Camden Town branch of the WSPU. In the north of England women who were already involved with the ILP often set up branches of the WSPU in the belief that they were, in effect, the female wing of the party. As a result, during the early years the WSPU was really *two* organizations with different political views and a different social ambience. However, Christabel had concluded that success could not be achieved simply by extending the original Lancashire pattern to other regions; she believed that politicians would be 'more impressed by the demonstrations of the feminine bourgeoisie than of the feminine proletariat'. In effect, she intended to undermine the resistance of the political Establishment to women's suffrage from within by tapping the resources and influence of upper-class families. The political and geographical heartland of such a campaign was not Lancashire or the East End but Chelsea, Kensington, Holland Park and, increasingly, the Home Counties. No amount of eloquence would extract donations from these areas for an organization which spoke the language of Socialism.

Inevitably there was a price to be paid for this strategy. The social and political implications of enfranchising women – notably the idea that it would promote higher wages for women – had to be played down. In the process the Pankhursts' feminism lost much of its original radical character and began to reflect the outlook of middle- and upper-class women. Christabel herself admitted as much in a private letter to Henry Harben, a wealthy, left-wing supporter, in 1913: 'Another mistake people make', she wrote, 'is to suppose that we want the vote only or chiefly because of its political value. We want [it] far more because of its symbolic value – the recognition of our human equality that it would involve.'[37] This approach obviously had important long-term implications for Emmeline and Christabel. They neglected to develop a broader feminist agenda on which to campaign after the vote had been won, which helps to explain why the WSPU failed to survive the First World War and why, in spite of their great reputation, neither woman saw her future in the women's movement after 1918.

In the short term Christabel's strategy provoked the first major split in the Union. Although her anti-Labour policy had not been challenged within the organization, it rankled with many left-wing members. Charlotte Despard, who was a Socialist, announced at the 1907 ILP conference that she would never again participate in an election 'unless we go to help the Labour Party'. Emmeline, who was present, angrily interjected that she was not going to wait for the Labour Party to give her the vote, and she dramatically offered to resign from the ILP.[38] Rather belatedly both she and Christabel now did so. However, the expansion in the number of WSPU branches made it increasingly doubtful whether the two self-appointed leadersaccurately reflected rank-and-file opinion. Teresa Billington, who had been active in creating new branches in Scotland, quickly saw the opportunity to cut the Pankhursts down to size and to introduce an element of democracy. As a result, the ten Scottish branches established a Council of their own and some decided to defy the anti-Labour policy. Other branches wrote in to headquarters proposing a reduction in the number of paid organizers who sat on the central committee and were, in effect, Pankhurst nominees. 'T.B. is a wrecker,' declared an angry Christabel. But Emmeline, calmer in a crisis, simply suggested: 'We just have to face her and put her in her place. She has gone too far this time.'[39]

It was abundantly clear that when the Union's conference took place on 12 October the control exercised by Emmeline and Christabel would be challenged and possibly overthrown by the election of a new committee and the adoption of a more democratic constitution.[40] 'Don't you trust the members?' Christabel was asked. The honest answer was 'No'. Their patronizing view of the rank and file is evident in the remarks of Mrs Pethick-Lawrence who described the new members as quite ill-informed as far as the realities of the political situation were concerned:

Christabel, who possessed in a high degree a flair for the intricacies of a complex political situation, had conceived the militant campaign as a whole ... she could not trust her mental offspring to the mercies of politically untrained minds.[41]

This of course was highly disingenuous, for opponents like Billington and Despard were politically aware and experienced women who simply refused to take Christabel at her own valuation. Sylvia, who took no direct part in the controversy, seems to have been regarded by Christabel as one of her supporters because she wrote urging her to attend a WSPU meeting at this time. In view of Sylvia's subsequent criticism of her mother, it is worth noting the sympathy expressed in the letter she wrote to Emmeline from Wigan: 'Do not fear the democratic constitution. You can carry the conference with you. There is no doubt of it.'[42]

But the triumvirate was not so sure. They moved ruthlessly to preserve their faltering control by cancelling the October conference and announcing that a meeting to discuss 'important business' would be held at the Exeter Hall on 10 September. However, only London members were informed of this – a clear indication that Christabel had no confidence in the support of the provincial members of the Union. When the committee met on the afternoon of 10 September, Emmeline, in Billington's words, 'tore up the constitution'. A new committee was elected on the spot by the existing committee members. Emmeline simply proceeded to read out the names: she and Mabel Tuke would be joint secretaries, Mrs Pethick-Lawrence the Treasurer, Christabel the organizing secretary along with Annie Kenney, Mary Gawthorpe, Mary Neal, Mrs Wolstenholme Elmy and Elizabeth Robins. When Mrs Despard demanded to know what authority she had for all this, Emmeline simply insisted she could have no one who did not agree with her on the committee. Subsequently she explained: 'The WSPU is simply a suffrage army in the field. It is purely a volunteer army, and no one is obliged to remain in it.'[43] Later that day Emmeline presented this *fait accompli* to the Exeter Hall gathering. Yet she declined to take the risk of offering a vote. Significantly it was Emmeline, not Christabel, who bore the brunt of all this controversy, perhaps because she was much more likely to retain rank-and-file loyalty than her daughter.

As a result of the Pankhursts' coup some seventy members, led by Teresa Billington, Charlotte Despard, Edith How Martyn and Irene Fenwick Miller, met on 14 September to organize a conference and to claim the name 'Women's Social and Political Union' on the grounds that the committee had broken away to create a new organization. But as so often, the autocrats moved faster than the democrats. By 17 September the branches had received copies of a pledge to be signed by all members of the 'National WSPU': 'I endorse the objects and methods of the NWSPU, and I hereby undertake not to support the candidate of any political party at Parliamentary elections until women have obtained the vote.' This at least clarified the split and left no room for compromise or negotiation. 'I am resolutely refusing to reply to any "personal" statements made by the seceders', wrote Emmeline.[44] Though historians have usually accepted the Pankhursts' claim that most members followed them, the evidence suggests a more even split. When delegates from the branches met on 13 October, those representing voted twelve to join the Billington-Despard group and nineteen to stay with the Pankhursts.[45] By 1913 the rebel organization had 61 branches compared with 90 for the NWSPU. The rebels eventually abandoned their claim to the original title and called their new organization the Women's Freedom League. In effect, they attracted suffragettes who preferred to work with the Labour Party and who regarded it as hypocritical for a movement for women's democracy to deny democracy to its own members. They also attempted to develop forms of militancy which were non-violent. Nor did everyone who stayed with the Pankhursts agree with their views. Sylvia, for example, never signed the new pledge, though she failed to join the Women's Freedom League even though its ideas were much closer to her own. The split also accelerated current changes in the Union's composition by removing many of the northern branches and, in the process, many of the working-class members. By 1913 the Union had largely ceased to exist in Scotland where it had only three branches, and in Wales, which also had three; in both countries it was out-numbered by the WFL and dwarfed by the non-militant suffragists.

However, the split made little practical difference to the operation of the WSPU at the national level. While Emmeline, who had no aptitude for the organizational side of its work, continued to act as the chief public face of the movement, Christabel and the two Pethick-Lawrences made appointments, laid plans and raised funds. They saw nothing to apologize for in the coup of September 1907. On the contrary they increasingly justified their control by drawing parallels between the Union and an army: 'Those who cannot follow the general must drop out of the ranks', as Christabel liked to put it. One symptom of this was the formation of the YHB or 'Young Hot Bloods', a group of militants under thirty who were totally devoted to Christabel, including Grace Roe, Jessie Kenney and Elsie Howey. They signed a secret pledge and were available to undertake especially dangerous duties. The YHBs met at a tea shop in the Strand which was rather tame, but the club's members clearly relished the excitement and the sense of belonging to a tightly knit group which offered a substitute for young women who were not romantically involved with men.

Consequently, by 1908 the use of military terminology, regalia and uniforms permeated the whole suffragette movement. In retrospect this led many suffragists to accuse the Pankhursts of being dictators. The actress Cicely Hamilton, herself on the committee for a time, described Emmeline as 'a forerunner of Lenin, Hitler and Mussolini – the leader who could do no wrong'.[46] Quite unabashed by such criticism, Christabel emphasized the advantages of uniforms for members partly as a way of maximizing their impact on public occasions and also as an aid to identifying comrades in crowd situations.The use of purple, white and green as the official colours was inspired by Emmeline Pethick-Lawrence. Before long the major West End stores began to co-operate by marketing coats, dresses, hats and shoes in these colours which they advertised for wear during suffragette demonstrations. In return the WSPU urged its members: 'These firms are helping us to fight the battle, and you are helping by patronizing them.'[47] Allowing for an element of bravado in the self-styled militarism of Christabel and Emmeline, there was, in fact, much to be said for their insistence on having autocratic control of the movement. Militancy led the campaign to evolve into something very like a guerrilla war with the authorities who eventually attempted to suppress the organization. Having acquired unquestioning support from their members the leaders were in a position to make swift decisions and changes of tactics so as to take advantage of new turns in the political situation, whereas their rivals were handicapped by the need for democratic deliberation. On the other hand, by alienating so many able women, they eventually undermined the Union, though this did not become completely clear until 1913 when the leaders were *hors de combat* and there was no one capable of filling their places.

However, in the short term the purge gave Christabel the freedom to pursue tactics which would have caused consternation amongst many of her former colleagues. During October, for example, she began a private correspondence with the former Conservative prime minister, Arthur Balfour, with the object of persuading him to receive a deputation and issue a statement of intent to introduce suffrage legislation when he returned to office. As a consistent, if rather qualified, supporter of votes for women, Balfour felt tempted, though he was ultimately deterred by the knowledge that his leading colleagues, Austen Chamberlain, Walter Long and Lord Curzon, remained violently opposed to the idea. When Curzon became a leading figure in the League for Opposing Women's Suffrage in 1908, the dangers of a split in the party became even more serious. From Christabel's point of view, to elicit any formal commitment from the Tory leader would have been invaluable as a way of outflanking the Liberals. To this end she treated Balfour with consideration, offering to postpone any formal meeting until he felt able to make a definite statement. She also tried to appeal to him as a Conservative by suggesting that a pledge from him 'would prevent the threatened alliance of a large section of the women's suffrage party with the Labour Party', and she claimed it 'would greatly strengthen us in our attempt to make the Liberal campaign against the House of Lords a means of promoting our movement'.[48] This showed some insight. By this time the Liberals had discovered that despite their huge majority, the peers remained defiant about rejecting government legislation. The suffragettes intended to discredit Liberal attacks on the peers by arguing that the government itself had no true popular mandate so long as it refused to admit women to the electorate. Christabel calculated that this fitted neatly with traditional Conservative propaganda which held the House of Lords' power to be justified in so far as elected governments often lacked specific mandates for their legislation. However, Balfour was not to be hooked so easily. Though treating Christabel to a very full, but equivocal, analysis of his opinions, he expressed doubt as to whether women as a whole felt a strong grievance about being excluded from the electorate; and he declined to express his support for women's suffrage in his capacity as leader without consulting his colleagues.[49] This was a little disappointing if not unexpected. But Christabel took good care to keep her avenues to the Tory leadership open and friendly with a view to exploiting them later as the Liberal government discredited itself in its confrontation with the suffragettes.

Another spin-off from the split was the publication of a new journal, *Votes for Women*, by the Pethick-Lawrences. Fred possessed not only the money but also the experience as a former editor of the *Labour Record* and other left-wing journals. Since the demise of Lydia Becker's *Women's Suffrage Journal* in 1890, the movement had been without a newspaper of its own, and *Votes for Women* gave the Union a distinct edge over its rivals as well as an excellent means of keeping members in touch with the campaign and maintaining their morale. Circulation growth offers some indication of the high profile enjoyed by the Union over the next few years. *Votes for Women* began as a monthly publication priced at three pence in October 1907, but became weekly at one penny from May 1908. It sold 5,000 copies at that point, but by May 1909 circulation had soared to 22,000.

During the autumn of 1907, *Votes for Women* gleefully held cabinet ministers up to ridicule as their meetings suffered regular disruption by suffragettes; and it recorded Emmeline's regal progress around the by-election circuit. In December she turned up in Aberdeen at a meeting addressed by the prime minister. Though she was ejected, the President of the local Women's Liberal Federation forced Asquith to answer her question on votes for women. When the stewards tried to throw out several of the men the meeting deteriorated into chaos. As the local press commented, the issue was 'not to be solved by Russian methods of conducting public meetings'.[50] Christabel opened the New Year by announcing that the Union had taken over an extra six rooms at Clement's Inn, bringing the total to thirteen, and would launch a programme of events beginning with the third Women's Parliament on 11–13 February, a suffrage rally at the Albert Hall and a massive demonstration in Hyde Park in June. On 17 January 1908 Flora Drummond led a party of suffragettes into Downing Street where she padlocked herself to the railings while a cabinet meeting was in progress, thereby earning three weeks in prison. Meanwhile, Emmeline had had her most frightening experience in the Mid-Devon by-election where she had been campaigning since before Christmas. In the small towns and villages south and east of Dartmoor Victorian traditions of election violence remained very lively, so much so that all the candidates expected to be howled down from time to time. The local roughs particularly enjoyed seizing suffragette lorries and pushing them around town. But after the declaration of the poll in Newton Abbott and the shock Liberal defeat, things turned really nasty. The new Conservative MP was quickly escorted from the scene by the police who advised Emmeline and Mrs Martell, who accompanied her, to leave Newton Abbott as soon as possible. They simply laughed at this. Emmeline declared she had never been afraid to trust herself to a crowd. However, as she was now the only target left in town, she was soon spotted by groups of young men returning from the clay pits. Shouting 'those women have done it', they pelted Emmeline and Nellie with rotten eggs and chased them into a grocer's shop.[51] As she did not want to become responsible for the breaking of the shopkeeper's windows Emmeline eventually escaped via the back yard only to be caught, flung on to the muddy ground and surrounded by the angry crowd. Someone suggested stuffing her into an empty barrel, but before this happened the police returned and carried her back into the shop where she and Nellie waited for two hours until a car arrived to take them to safety.

In the fracas her ankle had been injured, which made walking difficult for the next year. Her injury did not prevent Emmeline turning up to speak at the next by-election at Leeds South where the suffragettes organized a huge torchlight procession on Hunslett Moor. Although the campaign failed to dislodge the Liberals from their seat, several newspapers, including the *Daily News* and the *Daily Mail*, praised the suffragettes' efforts on the grounds that they had persuaded people to take the issue more seriously than in other recent by-elections.[52] Certainly Emmeline returned from Leeds in a very buoyant mood to attend the third Women's Parliament in session at Caxton Hall. On the first day, 11 February, the Union had hired two furniture vans which they drove to the House of Commons; dozens of women rushed out and managed to enter the lobby, resulting in 54 arrests. Meanwhile Christabel and Annie led a further march from Caxton Hall, proclaiming: 'We want rich women and middle-class women to go out and help.' This led to newspaper headlines announcing 'Suffragette Smart Set to the Fore', which were almost calculated to promote militancy as a fashionable pastime. According to the *Daily Mirror*'s report:

Miss Annie Kenney, a striking figure in electric blue and without a hat, surveyed the troops from a hansom cab. Miss Christabel Pankhurst sought to direct operations from another. Her cab was nearly overturned at one point in the proceedings when their passage was barred.[53]

On the thirteenth Emmeline surprised the Caxton Hall meeting by insisting that she should carry the women's suffrage resolution to Parliament herself. She was clearly contemplating the prospect of higher sentences and seems to have decided to court arrest from this stage onwards. Though some women protested at using her in this way, Christabel approved the idea. Thereupon Emmeline and Annie marched off at the head of a thirteen-strong deputation, though as Emmeline had difficulty walking Flora Drummond produced a dog-cart to carry her. In Victoria Street their way was barred by police, but the women managed to get through in groups of two and three, closely followed. Eventually Emmeline was arrested and taken to Cannon Row Station. The next morning the Westminster Police Court was crowded with suffragettes' supporters and relations. Harry had to sit outside where the ladies fed him buns and chocolate. But the outcome proved something of an anti-climax when Emmeline received a six-week sentence rather than the more drastic punishment she had contemplated.

These events prepared the ground for Mrs Pethick-Lawrence's latest idea – a Self-Denial Week which ran from 15 February. During this week members were to contribute the costs of small luxuries they had sacrificed such as tea, coffee and cocoa, or to present valuables such as jewellery, lace, china and silver for sale at the Clement's Inn headquarters. Famous authors including John Galsworthy, May Sinclair and Lawrence Housman presented signed copies of their books to promote the scheme.[54] The funds thus raised were to be announced at the Albert Hall on 19 March. On that occasion the Union's talent for theatre was brilliantly demonstrated. Since Emmeline remained in prison, her chair on the platform was left empty. But at two in the afternoon she was unexpectedly released, perhaps because the authorities hoped to spoil the effect at the demonstration. When Christabel dramatically announced her release to the throng at the Albert Hall, Emmeline, pale and tired, walked quietly up to take her seat.[55] The 7,000-strong audience rose to its feet, cheering and waving handkerchiefs in the air. The £2,382 raised during Self-Denial Week was augmented by large donations which brought the total to £7,000 by the end of the evening.

Shortly after this triumph at the Albert Hall, the House of Commons debated a women's suffrage bill introduced by a Liberal member, Henry York Stanger. It was on this occasion that Herbert Gladstone, the Home Secretary, made some foolish and illiberal remarks which were later to be thrown back at him:

On the question of Women's Suffrage experience shows that predominance of argument alone . . . is not enough to win the political day . . . Men have learned this lesson, and know the necessity for demonstrating the greatness of their movements, and for establishing that *force majeure* which actuates and arms a Government for effective work.[56]

The suffragettes interpreted this as virtual incitement to fill the streets with masses of demonstrators as radicals had done in the 1830s and 1860s in order to intimidate the authorities. Meanwhile, the Bill received a second-reading majority of 273 votes to 94. This emphatic victory reflected strong support given by Liberal and Labour members who appreciated the fact that Stanger had included both single and *married* women in his bill. Yet the Pankhursts, in common with other suffragists at the time, remained unwilling to recognize the political importance of this wider form of women's suffrage. The Commons division underlined the perverseness of a strategy which involved antagonizing the Liberal and Labour politicians who were best placed, in the 1906 Parliament, to give women the vote. Moreover, as the health of the ageing Campbell-Bannerman deteriorated during the spring of 1908, the political situation was about to take a new turn for the worse. The succession brought the Pankhursts face to face with their most stubborn opponent yet.

9

Methods of Barbarism (1908–9)

'The British Government is as obstinate now as it was when the American colonists felt that they had no recourse except to take up arms against it.'

Emmeline Pankhurst, New York, 29 October 1909

'By the defeat of the Government at Colne Valley our movement is brought a stage nearer to success', Christabel had optimistically claimed in July 1907. 'The only question now is how long the Government can afford to have the WSPU turning the scale against them.'[1] Yet eight months later the politicians had shown no perceptible sign of movement over votes for women. In fact, with the succession to the premiership of Herbert Henry Asquith in April 1908 the prospects deteriorated sharply. As a young MP in 1885, Asquith had imbibed the Gladstonian view of women's suffrage and since then had shown not the slightest susceptibility to persuasion. To some extent this reflected Asquith's narrow partisanship; part of a generation of Liberals that had been shaken by the Tories' success in recruiting middle- and upper-class women, he felt convinced they would give an advantage to his opponents unless the terms of enfranchisement were very carefully thought out. Yet Asquith's prejudice went deeper than this. Nothing in his upbringing had awakened any sympathy for women's dilemmas or opened his mind to women's abilities. His life at Balliol College, the Bar and the House of Commons – a comforting series of all-male clubs – had consolidated this outlook. His rise from his modest origins in the West Riding to smart Metropolitan society had been accelerated by his second wife, Margot Tennant, a socially ambitious

woman too self-obsessed to be able to sympathize with the less privileged women who had to campaign for their rights. Margot's influence
also compounded her husband's natural anti-suffragism in indirect but
damaging ways. Wildly indiscreet, Margot posed a real danger by her
desire to meddle in high politics. Consequently Asquith got into the
habit of refusing to tell her anything and he almost certainly saw in
Margot proof of his view of women's congenital unsuitability for
politics. Since Asquith was to remain prime minister until December
1916, his accession to the leadership proved to be a major stumbling
block for the women's cause.

Yet Christabel characteristically saw the opportunity presented even
by this unfortunate turn of events. Regardless of his intentions, the
new premier could not avoid exposing his government to attack simply
because his own appointment triggered a cabinet reshuffle and thus a
round of ministerial by-elections. Even before his new appointments
had been announced Christabel had dispatched her lieutenants to
Manchester to book all the available halls in the certain belief that
Winston Churchill would be elevated to Asquith's cabinet. Her judgement was soon vindicated. By the time the new President of the Board
of Trade had arrived in his constituency, the suffragettes had set up
their campaign to secure his rejection.

Christabel exulted when Churchill suffered a narrow defeat, though
in such a marginal seat this was not remarkable especially as several
key sectional groups, notably Jewish and Irish voters, had failed to
turn out as usual. However, all the other ministerial by-elections,
at Dewsbury, East Wolverhampton, Montrose, Stirling and Dundee,
returned Liberals in the face of sustained suffragette campaigns. After
losing at Manchester, Churchill proceeded to another constituency at
Dundee where he arrived to find Emmeline already in possession of
the town's Kinnaird Hall. But he won so emphatic a victory that even
Christabel drew a discreet veil over the result. It was going to take
more than this to intimidate the new prime minister. Though irritated
by WSPU intervention, Liberal candidates saw it as merely part of a
whole range of right-wing pressure groups involved in the by-elections,
and neither they nor the local press usually ascribed their defeats to
the women's issue. All that emerged from the first tussle with Asquith
was a statement on 20 May to the effect that the government would

introduce a reform bill before the end of the Parliament which would not include women's suffrage but would be open to amendment. This, however, was subject to the qualification that any women's clause should be 'on democratic lines' and have 'behind it the overwhelming support of the women of the country, no less than the support of the men'.[2] Some commentators declared this to be a solid enough pledge that Christabel would be naïve to reject. She, however, knew perfectly well that Asquith believed his conditions could not be met. In any case it is important to note that as the life of Parliament at this time was seven years and the last election had taken place in 1906, many years might elapse before Asquith had to redeem his promise to introduce a reform bill. Only a week after his statement the prime minister admitted that such a bill belonged to 'a remote and speculative future'. In private, Christabel's response to Asquith's pledge was to take up her correspondence with Balfour, the Conservative leader. She disparaged Asquith's offer and adopted a conciliatory line with Balfour, even though he had offered nothing of any substance in the event of being returned to office. Presumably she hoped he would take the opportunity to outflank the Liberal leader, but Balfour still believed there were more reliable ways of recovering power.

In public, Christabel and the Pethick-Lawrences insisted that the best way to respond to Asquith was to offer unmistakable proof that he was wrong in assuming women's suffrage still lacked public support. To this end they began to plan a massive demonstration to take place in Hyde Park in June. By this time they possessed the resources to attempt this with some confidence. Emmeline and Christabel were probably at the height of their powers as orators during 1908 and 1909, offering both an inspiration to women and an immensely popular draw for men. The two women differed in style in some ways. Emmeline, essentially an evangelist where Christabel was more professional and lawyerly, had such an aversion for writing that she almost never used notes on the platform. But, as so often with brilliant extempore speakers, she became nervous beforehand; Grace Roe recalled that prior to a meeting Emmeline had always to be looked after and could not be interrupted.[3] But once the speech had begun she invariably enjoyed the experience. On the platform, where she never used a microphone even at the Albert Hall, Emmeline was remarkably restrained, making very little use of gestures or other histrionics beyond occasionally stretching her hands out to the audience. She achieved her effect by the expression on her face, her low, calm and clear voice, and by her underlying passion. 'Her face shows the character she possesses, the courage and endurance. Her smile illuminates her clever but sad face. She speaks ... with a great earnestness and simplicity which arrests the attention and keeps one spellbound until she has finished.'[4] Even at her most aggressive Emmeline had a talent for moving her audiences deeply, perhaps by the contrast between her strong words and her physical frailty. She aroused the protective instincts of many men. Ethel Smyth recalled her at a meeting in Glasgow in 1911 when she delivered an indictment of men for the abuse of children. As the audience became embarrassed she lifted them up by holding out her arms: 'Men! ... I know what shame is in your hearts ... It is enough ... I will say no more.' Afterwards they crowded round the platform to take her hand; with eyes shining with emotion, Emmeline could only say 'What *dears* men are!'[5]

Christabel, on the other hand, was regarded as a more brilliant and daring speaker, though lacking the same moral conviction. As with most great speakers of an earlier era it is almost impossible to capture the appeal exercised by Christabel from the written record. At least one recording of her survives from 1908, though it is a statement rather than a speech and cannot convey the spontaneity and vigour that was vital to her performances.[6] The recording does, however, throw some light on her speaking. She had almost completely lost her Lancashire accent by 1908. She had also developed the measured, rhythmical style typical of the professional orator of the pre-1914 period; that is to say, she delivered her sentences in pairs, one answering the other, rather in the style of the Victorian lay-preacher. But, as with her mother, much of Christabel's impact lay in something less tangible than mere words. Contemporaries noticed that in repose her face looked a little heavy:

But with rising to speak she becomes a different being ... at once she becomes alive, keenly, actively alive. Her whole being seems to be lit up with a fresh fire. She loses any sign of heaviness, and is a person transformed.[7]

In contrast to Emmeline, Christabel swayed and gesticulated on the platform. At the start of a speech she would smile in response to the round of applause: 'Presently she raises one arm, and holding out her slender hand, she motions ever so slightly for the applause to end.' Christabel also offered more entertainment value in that she enjoyed being heckled and sharpening her powers of repartee on the audience. 'Go home and do the washing,' someone would shout. 'Don't you know my good man that Monday is washing day and this is Thursday,' she would reply. Many times she was asked: 'Wouldn't yer like to be a man, Miss?' Christabel would look steadily and sweetly at the heckler before replying: 'Yes, wouldn't *you* like to be man?'[8] Even reporters from hostile newspapers found themselves lost in admiration some-times. At the Peckham by-election in April 1908 the *Daily Mail*'s man wrote:

Shall I speak of her logic? It is inexorable . . . she has a good case and relies on it. She is saturated with facts, and the hecklers find themselves heckled, twitted, tripped, floored. I think they like it. She does, and shows it. She flings herself into the fray, and literally pants for the next question to tear to shreds.[9]

Many observers admitted to being enchanted by Christabel's youth, her slim figure, radiant complexion and general femininity. Much of her appeal to young women lay precisely in her capacity to take on the men who sought to put her down. For them it was fascinating to witness the combination of womanly beauty with masculine aggression. One factory girl at Peckham enthused: 'Oh, ain't she sweet? and fancy 'er been to prison! Carn't she tork – my word? Why, she just shuts up them blokes as arsked the questions just like a man.'[10] Many WSPU activists had originally joined in a sudden fit of enthusiasm on hearing Christabel speak. Grace Roe witnessed a performance in Hyde Park in 1908, when she was actually shouted down by a hostile crowd singing: 'Put Me On An Island Where the Girls Are Few', and was completely captivated by her.[11] As a result Christabel soon became the centre of a devoted and idealistic circle of hero-worshipping young women.

During May 1908 the Union increasingly concentrated on the dem-onstration planned for 21 June in Hyde Park. The location was a deliberate choice made in the light of the Park's historic associations with Parliamentary reform. In 1866–7 thousands of men, led by Edmund Beales of the Reform League, had famously broken down the park railings in defiance of the Home Secretary's ban on its use for public meetings. The suffragettes intended to demonstrate to Asquith that they commanded far wider support. Indeed, later in 1908 Christabel took some trouble to mock the cabinet's readiness to make alterations to the voting system for men:

Now why a reform bill for men? Are men fighting for the franchise? Do they ever speak of it? No my friends! . . . It is our agitation that has prompted the Government to the contemplation of this reform bill. Men do not think it worthwhile even to ask for more votes for themselves . . . Then why is Mr Asquith in hot haste to give more votes to men? The answer is that he hopes, by improving the men's franchise, to raise up a stronger barrier against the enfranchisement of women.[12]

The whole Pankhurst family became drawn into the preparations. Harry ventured out daily to chalk the pavements and fly-post the streets of London. Sylvia helped to train the extra speakers needed to keep twenty platforms continuously manned throughout the afternoon. Emmeline, Christabel, Sylvia and Adela were all to take responsibility for their own platforms in the park. Thirty trains were laid on to convey the marchers into London. With a view to avoiding charges of disorder Flora Drummond suggested to the police that they should remove a quarter of a mile of railings around the park. Decked out in peaked cap, epaulettes and a sash, Mrs Drummond, now known as 'The General', marshalled the processions which formed up at seven different locations in the Euston Road, Trafalgar Square, Victoria Embankment, the Albert Bridge, Kensington High Street, Paddington Station and Marylebone Road. The marchers carried seven hundred banners, each eight feet by three on poles six feet long, and thousands of flags. Emmeline Pethick-Lawrence had stipulated the use of a common colour scheme for the first time: purple (for dignity), white (for purity) and green (for hope).

Sunday 21 May turned out to be a brilliantly sunny day. The 30,000 marchers converged on Hyde Park where twenty platforms had been arranged at hundred-yard intervals around a central furniture van, which Fred Pethick-Lawrence dubbed the conning tower. When the bugles sounded, speeches commenced at each of the twenty platforms. Apart from some rowdyism at those manned by Emmeline, Christabel and Nellie Martel, the crowds were well behaved and good-humoured. Literary figures including H. G. Wells, Thomas Hardy, Israel Zangwill and Bernard Shaw graced the occasion. 'I told my wife that I'd go in the procession on one condition only,' declared Shaw, who supported votes for women but liked to be as awkward as possible, 'that I should sit in a Bath chair and that she should push it all the way!' Mrs Shaw declined, but he waved to her as she passed by.[13] Eye-witness accounts suggested that most people had turned up out of curiosity rather than sympathy, but it could hardly be denied that the Union had achieved an enormously impressive spectacle. Photographs taken that afternoon show Hyde Park completely submerged in a vast sea of humanity. Newspaper estimates put the crowd at anything between 250,000 and 500,000. At the end of the afternoon resolutions calling on the government to give women the vote were carried at every platform; the bugles sounded once again and the crowds shouted 'One, two, three – Votes for Women' before dispersing in a happy holiday mood.

After this triumph came an inevitable anti-climax. When Christabel invited Asquith to respond to the demand voiced at Hyde Park, he brushed her aside, saying that he had nothing to add to his previous statement. She interpreted this as proof that he was deaf to purely constitutional pressure; to organize any bigger public meetings was, after all, inconceivable. All the Union's leaders agreed that further militancy was now both justified and necessary. On 30 June when Emmeline led another deputation to Parliament from Caxton Hall without being able to see the prime minister, many of the women were roughly handled by both the police and men in the crowd when they reached Parliament Square. In their frustration two suffragettes, Mary Leigh and Edith New, took a taxi to Downing Street where they produced a bag full of stones which they proceeded to throw at the windows of Number 10. 'It will be a bomb next time', Mrs Leigh reportedly declared. Though an isolated initiative rather than part of a strategy, their act was symptomatic of the rising tide of anger that was now forcing violence to the forefront.

Emmeline spent August in Aberdeenshire but hurried south when a by-election was announced in Newcastle-upon-Tyne for early September. Her first appearance in Newcastle's Bigge Market drew riotous crowds who overturned her platform and forced her to escape under police protection.[14] However, as the intervention of a Socialist candidate split the Liberal vote, she had the satisfaction of seeing another seat lost to the government, albeit temporarily. However, during August and September the Union's triumvirate was chiefly absorbed with planning its next attempt to get a deputation into Parliament, if possible into the chamber of the Commons. To this end they intended to mobilize much more physical support than usual. On 8 October they printed handbills which invited the public to 'Help the Suffragettes To Rush the House of Commons' on 13 October, and advertised their plan at a mass meeting in Trafalgar Square on Sunday 11 October. As a result of this material a summons was served on Emmeline, Christabel and Flora Drummond the next day for a likely breach of the peace. They were instructed to present themselves at Bow Street Police Station at 3.30, four hours before the rush on Parliament. But when police appeared at the Queen's Hall 'At Home' that afternoon they made no attempt to arrest them. The next day Emmeline and Christabel took refuge in a flat rented by the Pethick-Lawrences at the top of the Clement's Inn building. From its roof garden they sent a message to the effect that they would give themselves up at 6.00 p.m., which they duly did. But on arrival at Bow Street they found the court had risen and they could not be offered bail, which meant spending a night in the cells. Lady Constance Lytton went to find the magistrate who said nothing could be done, although the prisoners could be given more comfortable conditions if the police agreed. Emmeline meanwhile dispatched telegrams to several MPs, one of whom, James Murray, the Liberal member for Aberdeenshire, organized a sumptuous meal complete with three waiters which was sent in from the Savoy Hotel to the police station. Meanwhile the deputation went ahead led by Marion Wallace Dunlop. Since around 60,000 people had gathered and 5,000 police had cordoned off Parliament Square the situation soon became chaotic and violent. According to Grace Roe, Sylvia wept and became hysterical as she often did in such situations.[15] However, although the struggles raged throughout the evening, only thirty-seven people were eventually arrested. Several cabinet ministers, including Lloyd George, Herbert Gladstone, John Burns and Richard Haldane, came out to observe the events.

On 14 October Emmeline, Christabel and Mrs Drummond were put on trial at Bow Street, charged with circulating the handbill inciting people to rush the Commons. Christabel immediately demanded to be tried by jury, but the Magistrate, Mr Curtis Bennett, flatly refused. However, he adjourned the trial until the twenty-first to allow the defence time to gather witnesses and marshal its evidence. They chose to conduct their own defence. Although the Magistrate disallowed many of Christabel's questions because they raised matters of opinion or strayed into areas of government policy, he gave her considerable latitude because her cross-questioning proved to be so entertaining. Christabel certainly turned the occasion into a personal triumph, more by her style and manner than by anything she said. In a vivid sketch of the scene Max Beerbohm commented:

She is a most accomplished comedian . . . She has all the qualities an actress needs . . . Her whole body is alive with her every meaning. As she stood there with a rustling sheaf of notes in one hand, the other hand did the work of twenty average hands . . . With her head merrily inclined to one side, trilling her questions to the Chancellor of the Exchequer, she was like nothing so much as a little singing-bird, born in captivity.[16]

The highlight of the case was certainly her exchanges with Lloyd George and Herbert Gladstone, highly reluctant witnesses whom she had subpoenaed.[17] Lloyd George admitted he had acquired a copy of the handbill at a meeting in Trafalgar Square on 11 October.

CHRISTABEL: How did you interpret the invitation conveyed to you as a member of the audience? What did you think we wanted you to do?
LLOYD GEORGE: I really should not like to place an interpretation on the document.
CHRISTABEL: 'Help the suffragettes to rush the House of Commons' . . . What would you think you were called upon to do?
LLOYD GEORGE: Really I should not like to be called upon to undertake so difficult a task as to interpret that document.

CHRISTABEL: I can refresh your memory. The bill said 'Help the suffragettes to rush the House of Commons'.

LLOYD GEORGE: Yes, that's it.

CHRISTABEL: I want you to define the word 'rush'.

LLOYD GEORGE: I cannot undertake to do that.

His repeated evasions began to leave the Chancellor, normally so eloquent, looking a little foolish. He kept glancing at Mr Bennett, who let matters proceed. As one of Christabel's major aims was to produce witnesses to testify to the peaceful character of the crowd that assembled, she soon turned to this theme:

CHRISTABEL: Now what impression did you form of the demeanor of the crowd in Trafalgar Square as to whether they were likely to respond to this invitation to rush the House of Commons?

LLOYD GEORGE: I thought they were a very unlikely crowd to respond.

CHRISTABEL: Did you hear the speakers threaten any violence to you or to any member of the Government?

LLOYD GEORGE: Oh no, Miss Pankhurst.

CHRISTABEL: You didn't think you would be hurt? [the witness smiled and shook his head]

CHRISTABEL: Then you are able to tell me that the speeches were not inflammatory? They were not likely to incite violence?

LLOYD GEORGE: I should not like to express an opinion as to what the result would be of inciting a crowd of people to force an entrance to the House of Commons.

CHRISTABEL: You did not hear the word 'force'?

LLOYD GEORGE: I have only a very vague impression as to the words used.

Here the Magistrate intervened to tell Christabel: 'You are not entitled to cross-examine your own witness.'

CHRISTABEL: I rather anticipated this difficulty and I looked up *Taylor on Evidence* and I saw words which I thought gave me a good deal of latitude.

The Magistrate was evidently sufficiently impressed with this to allow her to continue getting away with it.

CHRISTABEL: Before you reached the House of Commons you were of necessity in the street and you saw something of what took place?

LLOYD GEORGE: Yes, I saw a little bit.

CHRISTABEL: You were not alone, I think?

LLOYD GEORGE: No. I had my little girl with me. [Megan Lloyd George]

CHRISTABEL: How old is she?

LLOYD GEORGE: She is six.

CHRISTABEL: Did you think it safe to bring her out?

LLOYD GEORGE: Certainly. She was very amused not frightened.

Christabel then proceeded to try to embarrass Lloyd George by suggesting that he and other Liberals had set an example to women by advocating acts of revolt. Although Mr Bennett commented that she must not attack her own witness, the exchanges continued.

LLOYD GEORGE: I certainly never incited a crowd to violence.

CHRISTABEL: Not in the Welsh graveyard case?

LLOYD GEORGE: No.

CHRISTABEL: You did not tell them to break down the wall and disinter a body?

LLOYD GEORGE: I gave advice which was found by the Court of Appeal to be sound legal advice.[18]

Beerbohm summed up the encounter: 'The contrast between the buoyancy of the girl and the depression of the statesman was almost painful. Youth and an ideal on the one hand, and on the other, middle age and no illusions left over!' When the Home Secretary appeared in the witness stand, Christabel demanded to know why she had not been charged with unlawful assembly. When he declined to answer, she suggested it was because the Government feared to put the suffragettes before a jury. She then proceeded to quote Herbert Gladstone's recent remarks about *force majeure*, as well as those of his father, W. E. Gladstone, to the effect that mere argument was insufficient to win the vote for *men*. He admitted to making inflammatory statements, which allowed her to conclude: 'Then you cannot condemn our methods any more.' On the whole the Home Secretary cut a sorry figure in the witness box.

After this the court adjourned again. When it resumed Mr Bennett became less indulgent and indicated that he would allow only two or three more witnesses out of the fifty Christabel threatened to call. Undismayed, she proceeded to her summing up: 'Well Sir, that is all I have to say to you . . . We are here, not because we are law-breakers; we are here in our efforts to become law-makers.' Matters then reached a swift conclusion. All three women were found guilty as charged, Emmeline and Flora receiving three-month sentences and Christabel ten weeks. This, however, was the least important aspect of the affair. By her conduct of the case Christabel had made her reputation, regardless of the immediate outcome. The summoning of the cabinet ministers had been a major coup, and her political points had consequently reached a wider audience through the comprehensive coverage given to the trial by the newspapers.

On the other hand, Christabel was now obliged to begin her third and longest spell in prison. She found the isolation very hard to bear. Marie Lawson, who later assisted her during her exile in Paris, believed that prison upset Christabel psychologically in a way that was not true of most other suffragettes. Emmeline Pethick-Lawrence wrote: 'We knew that imprisonment had a dread effect on all, but especially on Christabel, who seemed to lose vitality in isolation and confinement.'[19] It seems probable, then, that this lengthy period in Holloway from October to December 1908 had long-term effects on her, by influencing her in favour of a suspension of militancy and thus the necessity for prison sentences in 1910 and 1911; it was certainly a factor in her decision to leave the country rather than submit to prolonged incarceration after 1912. By contrast Emmeline responded to the experience in a spirited fashion. On 24 October she announced her refusal to abide by the degrading prison regulations, in particular to be searched, stripped and to wear prison clothes; she also intended to speak to her fellow inmates at every opportunity. Though the Governor conceded the first point, he referred the rest to the Home Secretary who obstinately refused to treat the women as political prisoners. Then on 1 November Emmeline broke the rule of silence in the exercise yard: 'I shall insist on my right to speak to my daughter!' This earned her a spell in solitary confinement. Eventually she and Christabel were permitted to be together for an hour each day, partly as a result of interventions by C. P. Scott, the editor of the *Manchester Guardian*.[20] Both women also felt worried about what would happen to the WSPU during their prolonged absence. The fact that Emmeline Pethick-Lawrence instructed Sylvia to deputize for her sister was hardly calculated to reassure Christabel, though with Fred and Emmeline ensconced at Clement's Inn there was not likely to be any departure from the existing policy. During November and December the Union stepped up its practice of interrupting cabinet ministers, culminating in the total disruption of a speech by Lloyd George at the Albert Hall on 5 December when he was subjected to two hours of heckling. As the purpose of the meeting had been to promote votes for women, the action was criticized as counter-productive. Otherwise preparations were laid for the leaders' release from Holloway. Mabel Tuke set up a special fund which purchased a chain and pendant in amethyst, pearls and green agate for presentation to Emmeline.

During Emmeline's incarceration in Holloway, Harry informed Sylvia that he had left the farm at Mayland in Essex for a job as a 'French gardener' at a sanatorium run by a woman doctor. Though he was not really trained for this new employment Harry apparently proved very popular with the female patients at the sanatorium. But the doctor realized at once that his own health was in need of attention and even offered to take him as a patient for a charge of one pound a week providing he also did some gardening.[21] However, Sylvia felt unable to take any decision, and when Emmeline was free she soon put paid to the idea. Harry duly returned to Essex.

Christabel was due for release on 22 December, but the Home Secretary unexpectedly let all three women out on the nineteenth. As this was a Saturday evening no one was waiting for them and even Clement's Inn had closed down. Emmeline and Christabel therefore took the train to Dorking to stay with the Pethick-Lawrences. Next day Christabel went for a long walk and quickly regained her ebullient spirits. On 22 December they were driven in a carriage drawn by white horses and supported by bands to a public breakfast and then to a celebration at the Queen's Hall. There the suffragettes stood in uniform with flags and banners to greet them. Annie Kenny presented Christabel with a purple, white and green standard bearing a gilt shield on which the main dates in her career had been inscribed. In her speech

Christabel went further than usual in repudiating traditional suffragist methods, perhaps wishing to make the most of her own experience as a prisoner: 'I say to you that any woman here who is content to appeal for the vote instead of demanding and fighting for it is dishonouring herself.'[22] This was by no means the attitude taken by her mother who was invariably reluctant to pressurize young girls into going to prison for the cause; Lady Ricardo recalled her telling them 'My dear, you know your own business best.'[23] However, amid the pageantry and fervour of the occasion Christabel's words passed without comment. But she correctly sensed that many women, hitherto inactive in politics, could be galvanized by the example set by suffragette prisoners. Speaking at the Queen's Hall at the end of December she declared:

Sometimes [women] sacrifice themselves rightly, and sometimes wrongly. When I think of the futile sacrifice which is being made every day we live by countless women, I think how well it would be if all that devotion, all that readiness to give could be directed towards great ends . . . our sex is no excuse for submission, for sloth, and for yielding to injustice. The woman who shelters behind her sex, and says 'I need not come out to fight because I am a woman, and I ought not to', that woman either has not a woman's spirit, or has not the right woman's spirit.[24]

After celebrating their release from Holloway, Emmeline and Christabel returned with Annie to the Pethick-Lawrences' country home near Dorking. Only two days later Emmeline wrote: 'They are all quite well and looking bonny.'[25] They remained at Holmwood over Christmas and the New Year, but after a brief festive truce hostilities were resumed with especial reference to cabinet ministers. In January 1909 the unfortunate Secretary of State for War, Richard Haldane, was heckled three times in a single week despite being a pro-suffragist and enjoying full police protection.[26] Emmeline re-embarked on her travels to the Scottish by-elections now looming at Forfar, Hawick, Glasgow and Edinburgh, a tour of Lancashire, and engagements in the west country at Bristol, Torquay and Plymouth. Privately the leaders felt very buoyant at the start of 1909. 'The political signs are most favourable and all is going well,' wrote Emmeline. 'We are getting influences at work that we have never had before and these must be fully tried.'[27] The explanation for this optimism lay in the expectation of a general election which the Liberals seemed likely to lose. In this, however, the suffragette leaders miscalculated. At this time governments enjoyed a term of office lasting seven years which could have taken the Liberals to 1913. The Pankhursts convinced themselves that in their frustration at losing their legislation in the House of Lords, the Liberals would call an early election and be defeated. However, prime ministers rarely hold elections early without being confident of victory and Asquith was shrewder than most.

On the other hand, Emmeline had some grounds for her talk about influential backing at both ends of the political spectrum. It was in February 1909 that Lady Constance Lytton was arrested for suffragette activity, only to find herself treated most gently by the prison authorities in deference to her class and political connections. Her brother, the Earl of Lytton, was a leading Conservative suffragist and very active in trying to coax his party's leadership into backing a women's bill. Lady Constance evidently suffered from no illusions about her value to the cause. When joining Emmeline on the platform she felt that the 'other speakers are superfluous, but I know there is a social layer who will be drawn by my name who wouldn't be by hers'; she was content to give short speeches and to 'be used socially either before or after the meeting'.[28]

At the same time the Pankhursts successfully exploited the sympathy within the Liberal ranks in the shape of C. P. Scott, a man reputed to have the ear of the party leaders because he and the *Manchester Guardian* were held to reflect the opinions of provincial Liberals. Sylvia had informed Emmeline of Scott's attempt to visit her in prison in December and of the interest he had taken in the treatment of the women prisoners. In February Emmeline persuaded him to intervene on behalf of her sister, Mary, who was so weak and depressed that she had to be moved to the prison hospital. Scott soon became a valuable go-between for the Union.[29] When Emmeline Pethick-Lawrence received a two-month sentence in March for leading a deputation to Parliament, Emmeline promptly complained to Scott about the 'flagrant injustice' of her punishment; but although worried about Emmeline's health, she told him she did not want to secure her release because Mrs Pethick-Lawrence 'would very much object to this being done'.

The chief aim at this stage was to ensure that suffragettes were treated as First Division prisoners and thus entitled to have their own food and contact with the outside world.[30] This triangular correspondence between the Pankhursts, the editor and ministers was revealing of the strengths and the weaknesses of the Union's pressure in 1909. By intervening with the prime minister and the Home Secretary, Scott became a vital ally within the system and offered proof that the politicians were susceptible to pressure at least up to a point. His warnings about the need to 'prevent the damage which is being done to our party' clearly struck a chord in so far as Gladstone, who was always uncomfortable about the treatment of suffragettes, carefully monitored the health of the prisoners with a view to recommending their early release. On the other hand, the politicians were far from being the fools the Pankhursts made them out to be. Through his own correspondence with Mary Clarke's husband, the Home Secretary saw Emmeline's sister from a different perspective. Mr Clarke 'seems singularly hostile to the views of Mrs Pankhurst (and his wife) on Women's Franchise', he told Scott. If Gladstone refused to take WSPU claims about the popularity of their cause at face value this was not merely out of blind prejudice, but because he appreciated the limitations of their support. 'It is the old story', he observed, 'these ladies make a great fuss about going to prison, and as soon as they get there they wish to be relieved of its main inconveniences.'[31]

As the tone of Gladstone's remarks suggests, many of the politicians believed they had weathered the worst that the suffragettes could inflict upon them. By the summer of 1909 militant tactics had begun to lose a little of their novelty value, so much so that during June the Union complained about a press boycott of women's suffrage especially on the part of the London newspapers.[32] Since February most of the Liberals' seats had been retained at by-elections, and even Christabel conceded privately that the Government had regained some of its popularity through the introduction of old age pensions.[33] The WSPU's dilemma lay in the fact that it was attempting to achieve two objects that were not wholly compatible. It aimed to educate public opinion about the merits of enfranchising women, but at the same time it had engaged in a fight to discredit what it regarded as an autocratic and illiberal government. 'There is no doubt that our militant action [,] though thoroughly understood and endorsed by our own members, is misunderstood by a large section of the public which is alienated by it,' Mrs Pethick-Lawrence admitted privately.[34]

In spite of this underlying flaw, the campaign continued to go from strength to strength during 1909. The big West End stores, including Peter Robinson, Derry and Toms, Debenham and Freebody, Marshall and Snelgrove and Swan and Edgar, now began to take half- or whole-page advertisements in *Votes for Women* – an unequivocal recognition of the influential readership commanded by the journal and indirect proof of the resources now being channelled into the movement. During 1909 and 1910 the Union's income increased by over 50 per cent to reach £33,000. Its ability to combine morale-boosting displays with commercial success was again demonstrated by the Women's Exhibition, 13–26 May, held at the Prince's Skating Rink in Knightsbridge. The event brought Sylvia back into the centre of events as she was called upon to decorate the huge hall, which measured 150 by 250 feet. Sylvia spent nearly three months preparing the wall hangings with the help of seven students from the Royal College of Art. She chose as her theme 'They Who Sow in Tears Shall Reap in Joy', and drew freely upon the motifs and style of William Morris and Walter Crane. The designs were initially drawn to a quarter the size and then transferred and painted on to huge canvasses spread out on the floor. The scheme involved a pattern of arches and pilasters interlaced with vines, in between massive figures of a woman sowing grain, flights of doves, almond trees in blossom, angels playing stringed instruments and other symbols of hope and self-sacrifice. Sylvia considered this her major piece of work as an artist. Visitors to the Exhibition also enjoyed performances of suffrage plays by members of the Actresses Franchise League, the first appearance of a 29-strong suffragette drum-and-fife band trained by non-commissioned officers, two replica prison cells and the first ice-cream soda fountain seen in England that was sponsored by a rich American suffragist. Tickets for the event produced £919 and sales at the many stalls raised a further £4,578. During the year the Union purchased another motor car for £466 and paid £286 for a chauffeur and running costs. At a time when the motor car was still a rich man's indulgence this was further proof of the status and resources commanded by the organization.

After the exhibition Sylvia, who was totally exhausted by the anxious nights spent preparing the decorations, fled to Ightham in the Weald of Kent for a recuperative holiday. She returned briefly to London, but retired to Penshurst in Kent where she rented a cottage on Cinder Hill in order to paint and write. Meanwhile Christabel went to Germany in the summer to have treatment for digestive and bowel troubles, paid for by Mrs Pethick-Lawrence. This apart, the leaders maintained their pressure on the politicians, convinced that the embarrassment caused to the Liberal Party by its attempts to exclude women from public meetings was reaping dividends. It had become standard practice by 1909 to issue tickets to women only on production of a guarantee from a male member of their good behaviour. However, at Churchill's meeting at the Free Trade Hall in March 1909 this failed, because two suffragettes had concealed themselves inside the building in advance. The press condemned these precautions as 'quite Russian in their severity'. Margaret Ashton, a leading Manchester Liberal, demanded: 'Is the party really trying to get rid of its women members?'[35] By September the prime minister had been reduced to the indignity of relying on a police escort, not only to get to meetings but whenever he ventured on to the golf course at St Andrews or Lympne.

Thus, by the summer of 1909, the issue appeared to have resolved itself into a clash between the irresistible force of the suffragette campaign and the immovable object of Asquithian opposition to votes for women. The onus lay with the WSPU leaders to break out of the impasse. In spite of the triumvirate's claims that everything was carefully planned at Clement's Inn, the campaign now took a wholly new turn as a result of improvisations by rank-and-file members which Christabel found herself obliged to endorse even when she disapproved of them.[36] The leaders had planned yet another parade to the House of Commons for 29 June, claiming, with a view to lending some novelty to a well-tried technique, an ancient right to petition the King: 'Mr Asquith, as the King's representative, is bound to receive the deputation and hear their petition . . . If he refuses to do so and calls out the police to prevent women from using their right to present a petition, he will be guilty of illegal and unconstitutional action.' The march proceeded in the usual way. With music played by the Union's new fife-and-drum band ringing in their ears, Emmeline and eight women walked to Parliament escorted by the police, where they confronted Chief Inspector Scantlebury at the entrance. He presented a letter from the prime minister's private secretary refusing to receive the deputation which Emmeline simply threw to the ground. As the police then tried to push them away Emmeline struck Inspector Jarvis in order to secure an arrest for assault as quickly as possible. Eventually no fewer than 108 women and 14 men were arrested. But at nine o'clock that evening a group of suffragettes appeared outside the Home Office, the Treasury and the Privy Council with stones, wrapped in brown paper and tied to pieces of string, which they used to break the windows. This action had not been authorized by the WSPU. 'We cannot always control our women', Emmeline admitted afterwards. Indeed, there are grounds for thinking that Christabel wished to restrain the window-breakers.[37] However, she had little option but to endorse the action once it had been taken.

The trial of the thirteen suffragettes involved in window-breaking was overtaken by even more dramatic developments. Five days before the attempt to petition the King, Marion Wallace Dunlop, an artist and suffragette, had been arrested for stencilling a notice advertising the demonstration on the wall of St Stephen's Hall at the House of Commons. For this she received a one-month sentence and her request to be treated as a political prisoner was refused. As a result Miss Dunlop went on hunger strike from 5 July. After ninety-one hours the authorities released her from prison. Though it is not clear how she hit upon this tactic, it may well have been the natural outcome of the diet endured in Holloway. Prisoners agreed that the morning tea tasted as though it had been used to boil potatoes; dinner usually comprised two unpeeled potatoes which were blue-grey inside and a piece of meat the size of a half-crown coin; the only variation was a suet pudding of the texture of India rubber and totally indigestible; tea time brought greasy cocoa with a piece of bread and margarine. 'No wonder we all got thinner', wrote Katherine Marshall, 'and, of course, a hunger strike was comparatively easy, as we could eat so little of such horrid food.'[38] Subsequently the women convicted for stone-throwing in Downing Street received sentences varying between four and six weeks. They refused to wear prison dress but were forcibly stripped; they then smashed the windows in their cells and were placed in solitary confinement. But after adopting the hunger strike on 14 July, they were set free six days later.

Once again the novel tactic had not been sanctioned by Christabel, but within a matter of weeks most suffragettes had begun to follow Marion Wallace Dunlop's initiative. During August, twelve women imprisoned after disrupting Lloyd George's famous budget speech at Limehouse in the East End of London were released after a visit by the magistrates who saw how badly they had been affected by their fast.[39] Despite her reservations Christabel publicly defended them and quickly pronounced the new tactic the key to success: 'We feel that the new policy of the hunger strike has given us the means of entirely baffling the Government. They cannot now imprison us, whatever we may do, for more than a few days, unless, of course, they prefer that we should die in Holloway Prison.'[40] She wrote confidently in this sense to several leading figures including C. P. Scott and A. J. Balfour, presumably on the assumption that they would join in condemning the Government and accelerating the collapse of its resistance to the vote.

However, the actions of June and July had greatly raised the stakes. The adoption of violence, even of a nominal kind, gave Scott pause for thought. He told Christabel it was a mistake from the militants' point of view because 'the public do draw a very broad distinction between technical offences against order and others which are not at all technical'.[41] Although Christabel almost certainly shared his reservations, she could not afford to say so. When the *Manchester Guardian* criticized window-breaking, Emmeline accused Scott of hypocrisy on the grounds that he had condoned the kind of treatment of women in British jails which he would have condemned if used in Russia. She reminded him that when reformers in Turkey used violence to win their constitutional rights they were lauded in the West.

Why, bomb-throwing [,] shooting and stone-throwing are time honoured masculine political arguments. Had these heroic women who have come to the door of death in their fast in Holloway been bomb-throwing Russians you would have been full of indignant horror [,] but as they are women of your own race who have exercised the greatest self-restraint and done the very minimum of violence because they have been forced against their will to the belief that the Government would yield to nothing else [,] you and other men take it all quite calmly. It is this apathy and indifference on the part of men who profess to believe in our cause that is responsible for all that has happened and that may happen in the future.[42]

In fact, Emmeline was misjudging Scott here. In her usual quick-tempered fashion she had overreacted to criticism. He had been quick to seek an interview with the prime minister about the problems generated by hunger strikes, though Emmeline may not have realized what he was doing behind the scenes.[43] It was, however, an error to alienate him too soon.

During August, stone-throwing continued sporadically, and the prime minister suffered the usual ambushes on the golf course. Then on 17 September when Asquith was due to speak at the Bingley Hall in Birmingham, two suffragettes, Mary Leigh and Charlotte Marsh, stationed themselves on the roof of a building adjacent to the hall. Consequently, although the Bingley Hall was surrounded by police and all women were excluded, Leigh and Marsh managed to disrupt proceedings quite effectively by removing slates from the roof with axes and throwing them down on to the police, Asquith and his motor car. For this Mary Leigh received a three-month sentence and Charlotte Marsh two months, both with hard labour. When the prime minister returned to London, other suffragettes threw metal objects at his train, breaking the windows of several passenger compartments. Other local supporters smashed the windows of the Birmingham Liberal Club.

Up to this point thirty-seven suffragettes had succeeded in gaining early release from prison by adopting the hunger strike, making the Government look foolish in the process. But the tough sentences handed down at Birmingham would have been a mockery if this procedure had been repeated. Accordingly, on 24 September Leigh and Marsh were subjected to artificial, or what became known as forcible, feeding at Winson Green Prison. Emmeline and Christabel hurried up to Birmingham, taking a solicitor with them with a view to challenging the legality of the action, but they were not allowed to see the prisoners. It took a week before legal proceedings could be initiated. Christabel was quick to see that the creation of suffragette martyrs by forcible feeding would give the Union the moral high ground. But she pursued a dual approach, involving public propaganda to highlight the suffering of the women and private pressure exerted through the political allies of the Government. Mary Leigh's experiences in Winson Green were graphically recorded. After four days without food she described being taken to a room containing no fewer than eight wardresses and two doctors:

On Saturday afternoon the wardresses forced me on to the bed and the two doctors came in with them, and while I was held down a nasal tube was inserted. It is two yards long with a funnel at the end – there is a glass junction in the middle to see if the liquid is passing . . . Great pain is experienced during the process both mental and physical . . . they must have seen my pain, for the other doctor interfered (the matron and two of the wardresses were in tears) and they stopped and resorted to feeding me by the spoon . . . the sensation is most painful – the drums of the ear seem to be bursting, a horrible pain in the throat and the breast. The tube is pushed down twenty inches . . . about a pint of milk, sometimes egg and milk, are used . . . Before and after they test my heart and make a lot of examination. The after-effects are a feeling of faintness, a sense of great pain in the diaphragm or breast bone, in the nose and the ears . . . I was very sick on the first occasion after the tube was withdrawn.[44]

Although Mrs Leigh was released in October, Charlotte Marsh remained under these conditions at Winson Green until the beginning of November. C. P. Scott complained to Asquith of the 'substantial injustice of punishing a girl like Miss Marsh with two months hard labour *plus* forcible feeding', but he also admitted to Christabel that he was not hopeful of achieving any change unless the violence amongst the suffragettes stopped: 'Meanwhile the suffrage movement is being ruined and there is danger of worse.' To this Christabel angrily replied that as the people like Scott who had influence in the Liberal Party didn't use it sufficiently they had no alternative.[45] Two prominent Liberal journalists, Henry Brailsford and Henry Nevinson, resigned from the *Daily News* in protest against its refusal to condemn forcible feeding. The prime minister also received a memorial condemning the practice by 116 doctors led by Sir Victor Horsley, as well as criticism from political allies such as the leading Nonconformist, the Reverend R. J. Campbell, who wrote: 'There is something extremely repugnant to the feelings of the ordinary Briton in the knowledge that women are being subjected to such violent indignities for what after all is a political offence . . . These women are not criminals; many of them are refined and well educated.'[46] Conversely, the Home Secretary argued that it would be inhuman to allow prisoners to starve and that their deaths would expose the authorities to a charge of manslaughter. Failing a political concession, the only other way of breaking the deadlock lay in a resort to the law. Consequently, on 9 December the WSPU brought an action against the Home Secretary and the prison governor on the grounds that forcible feeding could not be performed without the consent of the prisoner. But the Lord Chief Justice ruled that it was the duty of the prison medical officers to prevent inmates from committing suicide.

Adela was the first member of the family to be at risk of forcible feeding. She had spent six months from March to August in Scotland, initially in Glasgow for a by-election. Subsequently she travelled on to Aberdeen where Helen Fraser, the Scottish organizer, noticed that she had difficulty breathing. A woman doctor diagnosed pneumonia. In spite of this Adela continued a gruelling round of speeches and confrontations. In July she was arrested in Edinburgh when attempting to enter a meeting addressed by Churchill, and again at St Andrews in August, though no custodial sentences were involved. In addition to her deteriorating physical health Adela had to cope with some emotional turmoil at this time. Later she told Helen Fraser that she had developed doubts about militancy by late 1909 because of the violence increasingly involved.[47] However, apart from Fraser's own account in the 1970s there is no contemporary evidence for this. Certainly Adela's actions during the autumn of that year give no indication of a retreat from militancy. Yet her personal feelings were becoming awkwardly intertwined with her political views. Away from London for so long, she increasingly felt that her efforts were not appreciated. Adela could hardly be blind to the fact that a close relationship had grown up between Emmeline and Annie Kenney in recent years: 'My mother loved her as her own child', she wrote rather bitterly.[48] The emotional torment generated by this situation was noticed by several of the doctors who had occasion to examine Adela in the Scottish prisons around this time.

By October Adela had tracked her quarry, in the familiar shape of Winston Churchill, north to Perthshire. In company with Helen Archdale, Laura Evans and Catherine Corbett, she hired a motor car to attend one of his meetings at Abernethy where a marquee had been erected in the grounds of a private house in the village. Subsequently Adela claimed 'we had no intention of wrecking Mr Churchill's meeting', and protested rather implausibly that she merely wished to make a separate protest nearby. As they had no tickets the suffragette party stopped their motor car in the road by the entrance to the Liberal function. Then, according to the local press:

Miss Adela, the vivacious, rose to speak: 'Friends we are here' – but the purpose for which they were 'there' was not divulged for the remainder of the utterance was drowned in a great outburst of shouting and cheers for Winston Churchill.[49]

The vehicle was immediately engulfed by a large group of stewards and young men who proceeded to pelt the four women with mud and sods of turf. Finding difficulty in pushing the motor car any distance away, some of them vented their irritation by slashing its tyres and damaging the hood. Others attempted to drag the suffragettes out of their vehicle. One report described Adela as being gripped around the waist at one stage and at another as being nearly choked by a scarf or veil round her throat. In response she belaboured the youths with a green umbrella: 'It went swinging round at twenty strokes to the minute, and many an intrusive hand was smartly rapped.' Adela appealed to the press photographer to 'take this picture and show the people how these beasts of Liberal stewards are handling us this day'.[50] While chaos raged around the motor car, fifteen policemen stood by without intervening. The driver, increasingly worried about the damage to his vehicle, made several attempts to start the car, and eventually managed to get through the crowd and escape to the suffragettes' headquarters at Lamb's Hotel in Dundee. Afterwards the Dundee ILP lodged complaints with the Secretary of State for Scotland over the failure to prosecute the stewards and the inaction of the local constabulary. However, the Superintendent of Police, a Mr P. Macfarlane, claimed that 'the episode had been exaggerated by the reports. The women had come intending to disturb the meeting and refused to move when told they were blocking the road; they had no one but themselves to blame.'[51]

After licking their wounds in the hotel, the women sallied forth two days later for an indoor meeting addressed by Churchill at the Kinnaird Hall. At eight in the evening Maud Joachim, Helen Archdale and Catherine Corbett arrived in a tramcar, jumped down and rushed the barricades outside the hall. Though arrested, they urged the crowd to follow their example, which led to two baton charges by the police. Meanwhile, Adela and Laura Evans had already hidden themselves in the attic of a building twenty yards from the Kinnaird Hall with two local men. From this vantage point they managed to throw stones on to the glass roof of the hall. As they had boarded up the attic it took some time for the police to break in with the aid of axes and crowbars. They found Adela covered in soot and apparently trying to escape up the chimney.[52]

As a result all five suffragettes were given ten-day sentences and taken to Dundee Prison where they immediately announced their intention of refusing food and of doing as much damage and causing as much annoyance as possible.[53] According to the Governor they were noisy and excited on the first day – 20 October – and refused to dress in the prison clothes. During the next four days they consumed nothing but water and received visits twice daily from the medical officers. On the second day one doctor reported that they had become 'very quiet and appear to be weak and worn out by their long fast'; he recommended that they should be allowed to remain in their beds all day.[54] In fact, Adela and her colleagues were fortunate to find themselves in the hands of the Scottish Prison Commission and thus outside the heavy-handed jurisdiction of the Home Office. Although the instructions issued by the Scottish Office allowed the authorities to forcibly feed if necessary, it was emphasized that 'Lord Pentland's [the Secretary of State] instructions do not prevent your discharging the prisoners if medically unfit'. Pentland had apparently seen Herbert Gladstone and 'adjusted policy with him' – presumably a euphemism for ignoring English practice.[55] Furthermore, though Dr Stalker, one of the prison medical officers, agreed that it would be possible to forcibly feed, he 'anticipates a good deal of difficulty in obtaining the services of nurses to assist'.[56]

In the event the doctors seem to have been influenced by their diagnosis of Adela's physical and mental condition. Their daily reports painted an alarming picture of the 24-year-old. 'She is undersized (five feet in height), slender of build and altogether fragile in appearance. She is outwardly calm and indifferent but her pulse is 112 and the heart's action is violent and laboured.' She weighed just seven stone. Even more worrying was the doctors' assessment of her psychological state: 'Mentally she is peculiar, morbid and twisted . . . Dr Sturrock . . . was impressed with her extraordinary appearance and bearing and did not hesitate to say that she was of a "degenerate" type.'[57] This was reiterated in a later report in which 'both Dr Stalker and Dr Sturrock considered Adela Pankhurst a degenerate, but could not certify her'.[58] Since the doctors did not take the same view of the other prisoners their comments cannot be ascribed simply to generalized prejudice against suffragettes. Their accounts suggest that Adela had reacted to her incarceration differently. For her the physical suffering and isolation did not produce the defiant uplifting of the spirit that it did with other suffragettes, rather it deepened her depression. One doctor felt that though outwardly indifferent 'she is suffering . . .though she does not wish it recognized'. The turmoil was being suppressed. This might have reflected her own lack of conviction about militant methods, but it seems more likely that as she failed to win the recognition she coveted for her actions, she became increasingly embittered and desperate. Under the strain the tendency towards breakdown which had been apparent in Adela's youth had returned.

Fortunately for her the Governor and the prison commissioners chose to exercise the measure of discretion which Lord Pentland had given them.[59] They may also have been influenced by Mary Leigh's account of her prison experiences, a copy of which had reached Dundee. The doctors evidently drew some distinction between their prisoners in that they considered feeding Maud Joachim and Laura Evans but decided it was not urgent enough, whereas on the first day they pronounced Adela not fit for further detention. They resolved matters by releasing all five women on 24 October at three in the afternoon. The women managed to walk unaided to two cabs, which conveyed them to Lamb's Hotel where Flora Drummond awaited them. On arrival Adela collapsed. They were put to bed at once and prescribed a diet of milk, brandy and proprietory food by Doctor Emily Thomson.[60] After recovering they went to Inverkeilor near Arbroath as the guests of a Miss McGregor. The Union's leaders were elated at this outcome because the refusal of the Scottish authorities to use forcible feeding represented a break with Home Office policy.[61] This almost certainly reflected a political judgement that Liberal opinion in Scotland would have been even more antagonized by the adoption of such methods; only in the last few weeks before the outbreak of war in 1914 did the Scottish prisons follow the example of their English counterparts.

While Adela had been embarking on her hunger strike in Dundee, her mother had been far away on the other side of the Atlantic. Emmeline's reasons for deciding to visit the United States in the autumn of 1909 are not clear, but the tour proved so successful that it led to two further visits before 1914. She already enjoyed links with some of the leading American suffragists, notably Harriet Stanton Blatch, and by 1909 she could hardly have been unaware that her notoriety had turned her into a very marketable commodity on the lucrative North American lecture circuit. In addition, the deterioration of the situation at home in the summer and autumn of 1909 added greatly to the attractions of a foreign visit. The forcible feeding of political prisoners gave Emmeline a fine text for the United States, and a compelling motive for placing herself beyond the grasp of the British authorities.

The only complication in this plan lay in the sharply deteriorating health of her son Harry. After developing a bladder complaint at the farm at Mayland in Essex, he had gone to the nursing home in Pembridge Gardens in Notting Hill run by Nurse Catherine Pine, a suffragette supporter who cared for many of the victims of forcible feeding. Dr Mills, who looked after Harry, pronounced him too delicate to return to the farm; by early October Harry lay in the nursing home, effectively paralysed. Sylvia returned from Cinder Hill in Kent to be with him. In fact, he had poliomyelitis, though this was not recognized at the time. In several letters written during October Christabel expressed concern that, although he was well cared for, he was not getting the right treatment: 'but changing doctors is so difficult'. Dr Mills evidently relied upon what Christabel called 'the old-fashioned drugging', but by the end of the month even she admitted that Harry had improved a little: 'He has less pain and he sleeps better.'[62] Emmeline decided to leave Christabel and Sylvia in charge of their brother. She had felt tempted to cancel her American tour, but not very strongly tempted, if Sylvia is to be believed: 'So ruthless was the inner call to action.'[63] Though this sounds harsh, in truth Emmeline was not temperamentally suited to a role as nurse and comforter. By sticking to her tour, according to Sylvia, she would be able to raise the money now required for Harry's care. As so often, it is not clear whether Emmeline was going purely as an individual or as the spokesman for the WSPU. The relevant statement of accounts contains no entry for funds raised in America, so she may well have used the money herself.

For a time Harry seemed to improve. He recovered the use of his toes and managed to raise himself from the bed by means of a pulley. But below the waist he remained largely paralysed. In response to his pathetic questions Sylvia insisted that he would walk again, though it would take time. Though she clearly realized this was impossible, she thought it best to keep the truth from both Harry and her mother.

Emmeline disembarked in New York on 20 October. As she left the dockside the customs men raised a cheer for her and she drove off to the Women's University College where reporters were waiting to fire questions at her. This set the tone for the entire visit. 'I come from the storm centre to tell you what we are doing,' Emmeline announced. By implication she regarded herself as the senior figure not only in British suffragism but in the wider world and was now in America to help the less advanced movement there. On the whole Americans seemed content to take her at her own valuation. Perhaps misled by the deference and politeness with which she was received, Emmeline initially overstepped the mark in her exchanges with reporters by implying that Americans were a little dull and behind the times; British women were more politically advanced and likely to gain the vote sooner.[64] In view of the fact that the American suffrage movement had not developed a significant militant wing it was easy to fall into this trap. Subsequently she realized her error and claimed she had been misquoted.

In an editorial the *New York Times* primly raised its petticoats and issued a warning about the visitor: 'She has come over to stir things.' Readers were informed that Emmeline spent $25,000 each year on baiting the police and the prime minister. The paper assumed that she intended to incite militant suffragettes who 'are still happily few here'.[65] Yet for all its ingrained prejudice the press found itself pleasantly surprised at what it found:

Mrs Pankhurst, a small, gentle-looking woman in a gray checked travelling wrap, wearing a gray fur hat encircled with a mauve veil, looks younger than the pictures which have reached America before her – more like a nice, home-keeping mother than a political leader. She speaks in a low unoratorlike voice.[66]

One senses from these press reports that Emmeline invariably played Americans to perfection. Expecting a tough, aggressive feminist accustomed to wrestling with policemen, they were charmed and bemused to find so fragile and feminine a figure. Within the first few days Emmeline had established her image as a 'real' woman which was to sustain her reputation in the United States and Canada through into the 1920s when it became a key part of her self-support strategy.

Soon after her arrival Emmeline travelled to Boston to be greeted by a cavalcade of motors five hundred strong and decked out in suffragette colours, which escorted her to the headquarters of the Massachussetts suffragists. In the evening of 22 October she addressed 2,000 people at the Tremont Temple in Boston, when she explained militant methods but made no direct attempt to urge Americans to emulate them. On the twenty-fourth she returned to New York for a big reception in her honour by a thousand women including suffragists, trade unionists, women's clubs and settlement workers. This was hosted by the local suffrage leader, Mrs O. H. P. Belmont, who organized all Emmeline's subsequent visits. Flattered by this she proceeded the next day to a major speaking engagement at the Carnegie Hall. The function, which had been sponsored by the League for Self-Supporting Women, was presided over by Mrs Stanton Blatch, President of the Equality League. Long before the doors opened queues had formed four abreast stretching round the corner into Seventh Avenue and eventually to Fifty-Ninth Street. The 3,000 seats were soon filled and people had to be turned away. 'New York has never seen such a gathering of women as that which was brought together last night at the Carnegie Hall', reported the *New York Times*. 'The ladies are behaving as well as possible', quipped the Police Captain, 'and the gentlemen are acting like perfect ladies.'[67] As usual the press described in some detail Emmeline's appearance on this occasion: gowned in a mauve Empire frock of velvet, with green and white in the lining of the loose sleeves. 'She showed that she might have been, as is said, the most beautiful woman in England in her youth.' In spite of this one journalist commented that she was old enough to have earned enough money to send four children to university unaided, remarks unlikely to have gone down well with Adela. In her speech Emmeline continued to exploit Americans' curiosity. 'You have come to see what a militant suffragette looks like', she observed, 'and to see what a hooligan woman is like.'[68] But she concentrated largely on an account of militant tactics and on explaining the rationale that lay behind them. This was to be her standard formula in the United States. Even the *New York Times*, by no means sympathetic to militancy, admitted her speech had won both laughter and applause and the support of the audience, despite some reservations about her political methods.

With this triumph under her belt Emmeline left for speaking engagements in New England at Hartford, Greenwich and New Haven. At New Haven she was interrogated about a recent incident at a by-election in Bermondsey when a suffragette had poured acid into one of the ballot boxes. Declining to justify her action, Emmeline insisted 'in all struggles for reform and freedom many regrettable things are done, but the blame for them should be placed on the unjust and tyrannical Government which drives people to do such things in desperation ... The British Government is as obstinate now as it was when the American colonists felt that they had no recourse except to take up arms against it.'[69] By early November her tour had taken in Baltimore and Washington, and on the twenty-fifth she arrived in Chicago in the Midwest. She returned to New York on the thirtieth where she delivered a two-hour speech to 1,000 people at the Hudson Theatre and answered questions for a further hour. The following day she gave her final speech – essentially the history of her campaign and methods with which she had begun. Reporters described her as being much affected on this occasion and her voice as showing much feeling.

She had maintained her purple-white-and-green theme even down to her necklace of amethysts, emeralds and pearls; she carried a bouquet of violets, white gardenias and foliage. Finally, on 2 December, Emmeline sailed for home aboard the *Teutonic*. Suffragette propaganda rightly portrayed her tour as a triumph. Apart from the pleasure of a recuperative voyage and freedom from the privations endured at home, Emmeline's reception in America as a woman of international stature must have been a most welcome boost to morale. By the same token her popularity diminished the British Government a little further in the eyes of its supporters at home.

During Emmeline's absence, however, the political situation had shifted once again. Since the spring of 1909 Lloyd George's famous 'People's Budget', with its radical redistributive proposals for graduated taxation of incomes and extra levies on landed wealth, had increasingly polarized the political debate. Sensing that out of desperation his opponents might use their majority in the House of Lords to reject the budget, Lloyd George had gone out of his way to antagonize the peers in speeches at Limehouse and Newcastle at the end of the summer. In November when the peers threw out the budget he knew that he had outmanoeuvred them. Their action made an early general election inevitable – but now it was an election which Asquith could expect to win. As a result Parliament was dissolved on 15 December. In view of the major issues generated by the controversy it was bound to be extremely difficult to maintain a high profile for women's suffrage. During 1909 the Government had clearly recovered the initiative with its reforms and reduced the loss of votes at by-elections. Above all, the crisis over the House of Lords strengthened Asquith's hand and led many Liberals to close ranks and swallow their doubts about his prevarication over votes for women. In November Christabel vented her irritation on C. P. Scott by pointing out that people such as himself who had influence in the Liberal Party were simply failing to use it. In fact, Scott continued to urge upon the prime minister the 'extreme impolicy' of forcible feeding.[70] But in the circumstances he was unlikely to be effective. As the year drew to a close, Christabel saw that some change of tactics would soon become appropriate.

Hostilities Are Suspended (1910–11)

'I had not yet learned that it was a crime to have an opinion.'
Adela Pankhurst, 'My Mother: An Explanation And A
Vindication', Pankhurst-Walsh Papers 16/50

During her mother's absence in America Sylvia had spent long hours sitting at Harry's bedside in an attempt to comfort him through his pain, and listening, in dismay, to his account of his hard labour at Fels' farm in Essex. In the course of these conversations she realized that Harry had fallen in love with Helen Craggs, a 21-year-old suffragette now employed as a Union organizer, whom he had met in Manchester in 1908. On hearing about this Sylvia sent for Helen, told her that Harry had perhaps three weeks to live and asked her to tell him how much she loved him. Later she found a poem which Harry had written for her:

> I saw thee, beloved,
> And having seen, shall ever see,
> I as a Greek, and thou,
> O, Helen, within the walls of Troy.
> Tell me, is there no weak spot
> In this great wall by which
> I could come to thee, beloved?

Each day as she sat at the bedside Helen helped Harry create a make-believe world in which the two of them would travel to Venice for his convalescence.[1] During these last weeks Sylvia believed that her shy, reserved and gentle brother grew rapidly into manhood. It was as though, since Harry's whole life must necessarily be crammed into this brief interlude, she wanted him to enjoy his first, and last, love affair.

Emmeline, on the other hand, found this very hard to cope with. She criticized Sylvia for taking it upon herself to involve Helen, and complained that she was losing her son to this girl. Meanwhile, as these tensions swirled around his bed Harry, now increasingly under the influence of the drugs that kept his pain at bay, slipped towards unconsciousness. At last he died on 5 January 1910. Sylvia wrote her farewell tribute in *Votes for Women*: 'Courageous in action, unselfishly devoted to the public good, a fighter in the cause of women.'[2] As in the past, Emmeline's brother, Herbert, stepped in to help the family by paying the costs of the funeral, and on Saturday 8 January Harry was buried at Highgate Cemetery where his brother also lay. Sylvia described her mother at the funeral as 'broken as I had never seen her; huddled together without a care for her appearance, she seemed an old, plain and cheerless woman'. Emmeline asked Sylvia to arrange a headstone for both Harry and Frank and insisted 'remember, when my time comes, I want to be put with my two boys'.[3] Unable, as ever, to handle her grief, she quickly left London to deliver speeches at Nottingham and Bradford. She told Mary Phillips to ensure that those who met her there would 'just behave to me as if no great sorrow had come to me just now. It breaks me down to talk about it although I am very grateful for sympathy.'[4] The tragedy greatly upset Christabel but she, too, continued her speaking programme without interruption. It was thus left to Sylvia to receive what few belongings Harry had possessed. Once again tragedy had brought her back into the centre of the family, if only for a short while. She gathered up her own bits of furniture, her paintings and her books, left her rooms on the Embankment and moved into a studio in Linden Gardens near Catherine Pine's nursing home in Pembridge Gardens.

January 1910 was largely consumed with the general election which was the inevitable consequence of the peers' rejection of Lloyd George's budget. Although Christabel put a brave face on the situation, which she presented as an opportunity for the suffragettes to punish the Government, she knew it would be difficult to prevent women's suffrage from being marginalized as the debate became polarized over the budget and the House of Lords. In fact, about 30 per cent of all candidates mentioned votes for women in their election addresses. In December Asquith had reiterated his earlier promise that when the Government introduced a bill to reform the franchise, it would be open to amendment by women's suffragists; the same would apply in the new Parliament. However, Christabel spurned this as virtually worthless. Unfortunately she failed once again in her attempts to extract something better from the Tory leader who was badgered by Constance Lytton and Annie Kenney to give Christabel an interview. Balfour took refuge in the plea that his colleagues remained divided on votes for women and that it was not a party question. For once Christabel showed him some of her anger and disappointment. 'The same thing is true of every other question until the leader speaks', she wrote. 'You will forgive me, I know, for saying that woman suffrage ought to be viewed from the high ground of public duty and national interest. Your reply to us seems to take account only of party convenience.'[5] But it was to no avail; the Union was forced to go into the election with no solid commitment from either party.

In this situation Christabel's tactics were simply to campaign for the defeat of the Liberals as in the by-elections and to encourage members to abstain from acts of militancy. Yet the election exposed the limitations of the WSPU's resources. Emmeline Pethick-Lawrence had warned her organizer in Bradford: 'We shall not be able to send you London workers and helpers because we shall be widely distributed over the country.'[6] In the event they concentrated on about forty constituencies. It was therefore absurd for Christabel to claim credit for the outcome of the election. The Liberals lost ground, but this was inevitable as they had won so many normally Conservative seats in the 1906 landslide. With 275 members of their own, and supported by 40 Labour and 80 Irish members they remained entrenched in office. As a result Christabel felt uncharacteristically uncertain what to do next; she decided that the ball was now firmly in Asquith's court.[7]

However, on 31 January Emmeline, speaking at the Queen's Hall, announced an abrupt change of tactics. Militancy was to end, at least for the time being. The suffragettes would continue to oppose Liberal candidates at by-elections but using only constitutional methods. Since this 'truce', as it came to be known, lasted with a brief interruption until

November 1911, it requires some explanation. Although Christabel regarded herself as the strategic thinker for the movement, she clearly thought it desirable to allow her mother to make the public announcement and perhaps bear the brunt of what could easily have been a controversial decision. The new policy undoubtedly bristled with risks. After all, in view of the disparaging view Christabel had taken about Asquith's pre-election pledge, the suspension of the militant campaign was a tacit admission of failure. This was embarrassing and threatened to undermine the momentum so successfully built up in the previous four years. Many years later Christabel effectively admitted this when she wrote: 'Mild militancy was more or less played out. The Government had, as far as they could, closed every door to it, especially by excluding suffrage questioners from their meetings ... a pause in militancy would be valuable, for it would give time for familiarity to fade.'[8] Her thinking was undoubtedly shrewd, though she was reluctant to reveal the full picture. Since the adoption of hunger strikes and window-breaking things had begun to slip from the control of Christabel and the Pethick-Lawrences. Moreover, as rank-and-file expectations rose, Christabel would herself have been obliged to undergo forcible feeding before very long. She intended to postpone this distasteful eventuality for as long as possible especially as it seemed unlikely that even extreme forms of militancy would succeed in view of the politicians' preoccupation with other issues. The Government's success in winning by-elections during 1910 underlined how far women's suffrage had been squeezed out of public view by the competition presented by other controversies. It was thus clearly wiser to slow things down with a view to returning to militancy at a later stage when it would be likely to make more impact.

Fortunately for Christabel, the decision that was made out of necessity could be taken without serious loss of face. In March the new Home Secretary, Churchill, conceded that the suffragettes would be treated as political prisoners as the Union had always demanded. More importantly, a new initiative had been taken in January by the journalist, Henry Brailsford who formed what became known as the Conciliation Committee. This body represented MPs of all parties including 25 Liberals, 17 Conservatives, 6 Labour and 6 Irish members, with a view to promoting a compromise bill for women's suffrage. This made the truce look respectable from the militants' side, and even put them in a good light since they were seen to be holding their hand in order to allow MPs to resolve the issue without being put under too much pressure. The only flaw in Brailsford's initiative lay in the nature of the compromise which was felt to lean too far to the Conservative view of women's enfranchisement. The Bill proposed a vote for female heads of household and occupiers of property worth ten pounds annually. To its critics this appeared to allow wealthy men the opportunity to manufacture extra votes by bestowing pieces of property upon their female relations. This would have exacerbated an already controversial situation, for the 7.9 million electors included no fewer than half a million 'plural voters': people who, through their possession of property, were already entitled to more than one vote. Liberal and Labour politicians preferred to abolish plural voting altogether, not run the risk of adding to it. Consequently, when the WSPU claimed that the Conciliation Bill must be fair to the working class because the Labour Party supported it, they were being disingenuous. The Labour members voted for it even though it did not really reflect their views.

As a result of the truce the suffragette leaders were able to devote the spring and summer to conventional propaganda on behalf of the Conciliation Bill and even to take some welcome relief from their exhausting schedule. From late March until early April Christabel went off to the Channel Islands with Annie Kenney, spending the time on Sark and Guernsey. During May Sylvia joined Emmeline Pethick-Lawrence and Annie Kenney for a holiday at Innsbruck where they went to Oberammergau to see the Passion Play.[9] For those who remained at home there was every opportunity to enjoy the facilities generously offered by the Union's benefactors and to draw upon the resources of the suffragette community. All across the south of England gracious houses stood open to campaigners in need of material and moral support. In London itself they enjoyed the hospitality of Mrs Hilda Brackenbury, the widow of General Brackenbury, and her suffragette daughters, Georgina and Mary, at Number 2 Campden Hill Square, a quiet, tree-lined enclave in Holland Park. Prisoners released from Holloway also stayed in the home of Hertha Ayton, the distinguished physicist, in Norfolk Square, while those in need of medical treatment were often taken to the Pembridge Gardens nursing home run by Catherine Pine and Gertrude Townend from 1908 onwards where Dr Herbert Mills and Dr Flora Murray were available to attend them. For periods of relaxation and recuperation in the countryside suffragettes had many alternatives including the Pethick-Lawrences' home, 'The Mascot', at Holmwood near Dorking, Ethel Smyth's 'The Coign' at Hook Heath in Surrey, Newland Park, the 600-acre estate at Chalfont St Giles in Buckinghamshire owned by the rich Liberal-Socialist Henry Harben, and Eagle House near Bath where Colonel Linley Blathwayt, his wife Emily and daughter Mary lived. At 'The Mascot', Mrs Pethick-Lawrence liked to play tennis and organize bowls for her visitors, and in a large tree at the end of the garden she built a platform to allow trainee speakers to practise their arts and develop their lungs.

The extent of this support may be estimated by the position enjoyed by Annie Kenney at Eagle House where she became a regular visitor from May 1908 onwards. The Blathwayts accommodated Annie and two of her sisters, Jessie and Kitty, often for prolonged periods; they loaned her money, gave her clothes, watches and other gifts, and paid for extensive dental treatment and private operations for the sisters. Over four years from 1908 most of the leading suffragettes including Emmeline, Christabel and Adela, as well as non-militants such as Millicent Fawcett and Lady Betty Balfour, stayed at Eagle House. The Blathwayts were typical of provincial suffragists in maintaining a footing in the militant and non-militant camps simultaneously. Colonel Blathwayt chose to link his horticultural and his political interests by designating a piece of his land as the 'Suffragette Field' in which distinguished suffragists marked their visits by planting trees. He constructed a summer house known as the 'Suffragette Rest' in which they could read or prepare speeches. Eventually some fifty-four trees with their accompanying plaques were established there.[10] It was a sign of Annie Kenney's omnipresence that she planted four. In March 1910 Emmeline planted a cedrus deodara, Christabel a cedar of Lebanon in November of that year, and Emmeline Pethick-Lawrence a western red cedar, whereas the constitutionalists, Lady Betty Balfour and Mrs Fawcett, both got holly trees. The Colonel classified suffragists as though they were akin to horticultural specimens. He and his daughter planted Christmas Roses around Lady Constance Lytton's tree and white primroses and yellow pansies around Annie's.

These periods of relaxation in country houses also encouraged the development of many close friendships between suffragettes. In some cases these friendships assumed greater importance than the supportive partnerships already common in the women's movement. The extreme pressures generated by suffragette militancy – the experience of public hostility, clashes with the police, ill-treatment in prison and the general sense of being part of a persecuted minority – inevitably led some women into more intimate relationships than was usual; their situation was not unlike that endured by men in wartime conditions, which foster emotional friendships even among those who prefer to stay at arm's length in normal circumstances.

From a variety of sources it seems clear that Annie Kenney became the centre of a network of fairly intense and emotional relationships during this period. This had begun in 1906 when she first met Emmeline Pethick-Lawrence and they quickly fell for each other. Mary Blathwayt recorded the scene in February 1908 when Annie impetuously declared herself ready to go to prison for three months. At this Emmeline 'who is generally all smiles, nearly broke down'; she leant forward to cover her face with her handkerchief until she had recovered her composure.[11] But Emmeline, who bought dresses for Annie and took her on foreign holidays, was only the first of a succession of generous patrons who befriended the impecunious mill girl and answered her perpetual search for love. Once established as the Union's organizer in the west country, Annie spent long periods with the Blathwayts near Bath and in her own rooms in Alma Road, Clifton, in Bristol, where her female friends stayed with her. One emotional attachment began in March 1908 when Mary Blathwayt gave Annie a rose which she wore at her meeting in the Bath Assembly Rooms. The two women spent much of 1908 in one another's company. Mary mended clothes for Annie, got her shoes repaired, washed her hair and, in her absence, wrote to her every day. At twenty-nine, Mary had a comfortable but rather empty existence, and the suffragette movement clearly brought a badly needed element of purpose and excitement into her life and also the affection she lacked. Of course, close friendships between women cannot be assumed to be lesbian relationships simply because the parties were unmarried. But the physical nature of Annie Kenney's relationships seems clear from the evidence of private diaries. In July 1908 Mary frankly recorded that she had been in bed with Annie. And she felt understandably dismayed as a succession of other young women supplanted her there. In August she noted: 'Miss [Milicent] Browne is sleeping in Annie's room now'; in September when Clara Codd came to stay: 'She is sleeping with Annie.'[12] Adela Pankhurst, who was only an occasional visitor to Eagle House, arrived in July. Evidently in an exuberant mood, she tried out a new fire escape from Colonel Blathwayt's bedroom window, and, Mary duly noted, was accommodated in Annie's room.[13]

The exact meaning of these encounters must remain uncertain. When girls and young women kissed, touched and slept together at this time, their behaviour was commonly recognized as romantic but not sexual and aroused no great comment. Since Mary Blathwayt seems to have been rather innocent, she may well never have appreciated why she enjoyed physical intimacy with other women; but the experience was clearly of great importance. In the case of Annie Kenney, she slept so frequently with her female friends and colleagues that it would be surprising if her feelings were not those of a lesbian. The question arises whether the same was true of Christabel. The Blathwayt diaries shed no direct light on this, partly because Christabel was a relatively infrequent visitor, though Mary particularly noted Annie and Christabel's holiday in Sark, and she almost certainly regarded Christabel as a rival for her affections along with the other visitors. From their first meeting Annie had cast herself as Christabel's devoted servant and her tendency to idolize her was noted by several contemporaries.[14] Christabel undoubtedly liked to be surrounded by a group of loyal acolytes among whom she included Annie and Grace Roe. She once commented that neither woman had any idea how to defend herself in an argument with her.[15] If, as seems probable, Grace and Annie had romantic feelings towards Christabel, this does not mean she reciprocated. Interestingly, Christabel herself recognized that many of the young women in the Union were diverting the energy and emotion which they might otherwise have given to men into the suffrage cause.[16] Politics, in short, was a substitute for love affairs, and hero-worship an alternative to physical passion. As pre-war society failed to recognize the possibility of physical relations between women, many of the suffragettes were able to speak of their friendships without embarrassment. Grace Roe, who had been brought up deprived of female company, recalled that men never became part of her social life. She quickly fell under Christabel's spell, because although in some respects a rebel, Roe was a weak personality who had a need to identify totally with a stronger person almost to the point of self-effacement. Christabel and the suffrage cause met her need perfectly.[17] Roe also appears to have lived with Annie Kenney for a time at the end of the First World War, though when asked about this later in life she gave a rare, unguarded reply: 'Oh no, that was over then', which appeared to imply that they had had a relationship earlier on.[18] The explanation is that Roe lived into the inter-war period when lesbian relationships had become recognized and thus more embarrassing, and as a result she adopted a very defensive approach about her pre-war personal life. Her determination to protect the reputation of Christabel and Emmeline in the context of the suffrage campaign led her to obscure what she knew about their private lives. As a result the evidence about Christabel is inconclusive, though the probability is that her need for companionship did not go as far as physical relationships. Those who were close to her recognized what her mother had noticed years before, that she was not easily led astray by her affections. By comparison with the average person she had little need for close, emotional relationships; it was enough to enjoy the support and admiration of a circle of close collaborators bound together by the pursuit of a common cause.

It was during 1910 that Emmeline herself became the target of one of the most frank lesbians in the suffrage movement: the composer, Ethel Smyth. Invariably dressed in severe battered tweeds and a pork pie hat, Smyth appeared forever poised for an assault on the Matterhorn; she epitomized the caricatures of masculine feminists beloved by the anti-suffragist propagandists of the late-Victorian period. Born in 1858, the same year as Emmeline, she had always been aware of her sexuality. 'I wonder why it is so much easier for me to love my own sex than yours', she wrote to Henry Brewster in 1892.[19] Not surprisingly, Ethel, who was very prone to sudden infatuations, admitted that she was 'swept off my feet at once' on meeting Emmeline in

1910. 'I knew that before long I should become her slave', she wrote.[20] Thereupon she decided to suspend her musical career for two years in order to work for the suffrage campaign. Ethel's florid way of addressing Emmeline as 'My dearest Em' and 'My treasure and my pride' could be seen merely as conventional Edwardian terms of endearance, but an unusual element of hero-worship was clearly involved in their relationship. 'The only living thing in me just now is a passion of gratitude that in this world there is a soul, and a brain, and a heart like yours', she wrote; and on another occasion in 1914:

I lie awake at night sometimes and see you like Atlas, bearing up the world of women on your head. I can't tell you what I think of you. If you were to come to me now all I could do would be to hold you in my arms . . . and be silent.[21]

What had begun as a sudden infatuation developed into an increasingly loving and intense relationship between 1910 and 1914, although this does not necessarily imply that Emmeline fully reciprocated Ethel's feelings towards her. As several contemporaries noticed, Emmeline was, understandably, showing signs of becoming rather hostile towards men at this time, but there is no reason to think that her emotions had been anything other than conventional. However, Ethel rightly understood that there was something missing in her life when she commented: 'From intimate friendship she had hitherto held aloof, her boundless love and admiration for her eldest daughter satisfying all the needs of her heart.'[22] However, now that her life had become dominated by endless travels around the country, punctuated by periods living at the Inns of Court Hotel in London – while Christabel was comfortably ensconced in the Pethick-Lawrences' family home – she felt the need of a close friend and confidant. At the least, Ethel helped to fill the gap. She often shared Emmeline's room at the Inns of Court Hotel and entertained her at her own home in Surrey. The unusual intimacy and honesty of their relationship is suggested in one of Ethel's letters in 1914:

You are the unreachable person because of a particular blend in you which there is in no one else – a sort of humanity that the egoism of the musical (or other artistic) specialist puts out of reach. However clever or 'female' you may be, you cannot recast your nature. It is a thing like short and long sight. Your ordinary vision embraces the mass – that's why you have always shrunk from personal relations . . . I am the glorious exception for you – and I think it is the crowning achievement of my life to have made you love me. And proof of your cleverness to have found me – and found a new gift in yourself – the friendship you give me. Yes, I also am getting more and more 'off' men!'[23]

This could be read as meaning that after her initial reluctance Emmeline gave way to Ethel's approaches. Bearing in mind that Emmeline had to cope with both personal loneliness and the enormous stress caused by her repeated experiences in prison, she may well have felt in need of the comfort and love of another woman. This is corroborated by the hostility shown by Christabel who clearly regarded Ethel as a rival for her mother's affections and the friendship as a reproach to her. Ethel's criticisms of Christabel eventually caused the breakdown of the relationship in the 1920s, and Christabel herself went to great lengths to try to suppress the correspondence between her mother and Ethel during the 1930s when Smyth wished to include it in her memoirs.

Throughout the summer of 1910 the suffragette campaign remained in a state of suspended animation, as its leaders waited to see whether their gamble on the truce would pay off when Parliament got to grips with the Conciliation Bill. Thanks to the Union's talent for pageantry the cause could still fill the newspapers. On 18 June a procession of women, 10,000 strong and organized in 130 contingents, designed to illustrate the theme 'From Prison to Citizenship', marched to the Albert Hall to demand facilities for the Bill. Emmeline led them attired in a flowing white dress and plumed hat, backed by a column of 1,600 ex-prisoners equipped with wands tipped with silver gilt arrows. In her private correspondence Christabel showed herself remarkably optimistic. To Balfour she positively oozed confidence: 'I am so happy in the thought that we have your support for the plan of carrying a suffrage bill this year. It means that our troublous times are over.' She even looked forward to the time when they would be 'able to rejoice in Mr Asquith's friendship and the certainty of victory for the bill!'[24] These soothing words were doubtless part of a carrot-and-stick policy for the benefit of C. P. Scott: 'Do you want militant methods to begin again? . . . if they do . . . the public will support us as never before.

For Mr Asquith himself will have shown how necessary militancy is.'[25]

Christabel also took care to let Scott know about her continuing negotiations with the Conservative Leader. She seemed convinced that Balfour had it within his power to compel the Government to grant the Conciliation Bill the Parliamentary time it required if he spoke out in its favour. 'I should like the world to know that you are our friend', she told him. 'Women ought to know how you are helping and serving them.'[26] As usual her flattery extracted nothing tangible from Balfour. None the less, the correspondence underlines Christabel's belief that victory was now fairly close, though at the same time the resumption of militancy remained in the back of her mind. However, the lingering doubts were borne out by Scott, whose interview with the prime minister left him convinced he would not help the Conciliation Bill into law during the current session. Scott, however, left Asquith in no doubt that a resumption of militancy would be worse than before and would threaten the Liberals' position in the north of England. He argued forcefully that as women's enfranchisement was inevitable in the long run, he had an obligation to ensure that when it came the results would not be 'hostile to the permanent interests of Liberalism'.[27] In the face of this advice the cabinet evidently adopted a short-term perspective on Liberal fortunes. After three agonized debates during June the ministers eventually resolved on the twenty-third to offer no more than time for a second-reading debate and a division on the Conciliation Bill.

Eventually the Bill came up for debate on 11 July in the name of the Labour MP David Shackleton and won a comfortable second-reading division by 298 to 189 votes. The House then voted to refer it to a Committee of the Whole House, which effectively meant that it would not proceed any further for lack of time. Christabel denounced this as 'a wicked move on their part engineered by Mr Lloyd George and Mr Churchill'.[28] During the debate Lloyd George had asked the Speaker whether it would be technically possible to amend the bill so as to include the wives of householders in the new franchise. When the Speaker answered in the negative, Lloyd George and Churchill voted against the bill. Although Churchill had presented the suffragettes with an irresistible target in their earlier campaign, now he made a dangerous enemy because he had the ear of the prime minister. Christabel chose to regard the reservations about the Conciliation Bill expressed by Churchill and others as a betrayal because they knew perfectly well that the enfranchisement of married women was not practical politics. It is fair to say that Churchill had wavered, first apparently indicating support for the measure and then changing his mind. But he and Lloyd George were not simply wreckers; they wanted to ensure that women's suffrage would be sufficiently *democratic* to avoid damage to their party interests. This concern had been enormously strengthened by the general election which, though returning the Liberals to office fairly comfortably in terms of seats, had left the Conservatives with over 46 per cent of the popular vote compared with only 51 per cent for the Liberals and Labour combined. In view of the likelihood of another election, the Liberals felt most reluctant to risk giving any further representation to property by an ill-considered reform. In these circumstances Christabel's refusal to recognize that the enfranchisement of *single* women alone was not practical politics was unrealistic and self-defeating.

However, she resisted the temptation to abandon the truce just yet, as the political situation remained extremely uncertain and it was not clear what facilities the Government would offer for the bill in the next session of Parliament. The most she could do was to give the impression of future belligerence. 'Can you and other Liberals wonder that we have come to the conclusion that we must take up again the weapons we laid down after the General Election?' Emmeline complained to C. P. Scott. 'Unless there is a Governmental change of front in November this is what we mean to do.'[29] No doubt there was a large element of bravado in all this, but her words faithfully reflected that fact that patience with the truce had begun to wear thin. On 23 July the Union organized another show of strength in Hyde Park. Two processions formed up at 3.00 p.m., one on the West Embankment, which proceeded up Northumberland Street, Pall Mall, St James's Street and Piccadilly to enter at Hyde Park Corner, while the other approached from Holland Park along Bayswater Road to enter the park at Marble Arch. No fewer than 150 speakers manned the forty platforms during the afternoon. Christabel had considered making this a joint demonstration with the non-militant National Union of Women's Suffrage Societies, but refused their request to rule out militancy; she wanted to keep her options open as long as Asquith's intentions over the Bill remained unclear. At the end of August Emmeline went north for a month in Scotland partly for a holiday and partly to campaign. By October she was back on her usual travels which included a visit to Bath and a stay with the Blathwayts.

Meanwhile the political situation had begun to crystallize. During the summer the talks between the Liberals and Conservatives designed to find a compromise solution to the dispute over the House of Lords had broken down, thereby making it imperative for the Liberals to press ahead, as their followers wished, with a measure to curtail the veto powers of the peers. This necessitated another general election because the King had insisted that he would not create the additional Liberal peers required to push a reform bill through the upper chamber unless Asquith won a specific mandate. When the WSPU gathered at the Albert Hall on 10 November, talk of resuming militancy was in the air. Two days later Sir Edward Grey exacerbated matters by announcing that there would be no time for the Conciliation Bill in the current session. When Parliament reconvened on the eighteenth, no reference was made to the Bill's prospects in the new Parliament. As a result a deputation of three hundred women immediately marched from Caxton Hall to the House of Commons. Emmeline declared melodramatically: 'All other efforts having failed, you will now press forward, ready to sacrifice yourselves even unto death if need be, in the cause of freedom.' On this occasion the police adopted far rougher tactics than usual. For over six hours the women were subjected to kicks and punches, their arms were twisted and breasts were grabbed. It appeared that the whole intention had been to avoid making arrests and to intimidate them with a view to deterring future deputations. Churchill, who was very sensitive to accusations of having instructed the police to adopt these tactics, remonstrated with the Commissioner of the Metropolitan Police for ignoring or misunderstanding him.[30] The explanation appears to be that the men who usually handled suffragette demonstrations, who had become sympathetic and tactful, had been replaced by police brought in from the East End of London. They treated the suffragettes as they usually handled working-class men and women, confident that they could get away with violence. Significantly, as a result of intervention by the Home Secretary, who presumably wished to avoid police methods being exposed in court, none of 115 women eventually arrested were actually charged. The events of 18 November became known as 'Black Friday'. They strongly influenced the tactics later adopted by Christabel after the resumption of militancy; to avoid subjecting women to the crude violence employed on Black Friday, the suffragettes were to commit offences against property which ensured swift arrest rather than prolonged struggles against superior force.

At last, on 22 November, Asquith announced that the Government would grant facilities for the Conciliation Bill in the next Parliament. Christabel pronounced this as wholly insufficient and by 25 November a formal resumption of militancy had been declared.[31] 'Ladies! The truce was all very well, but there is nothing like militancy', she told a breakfast for former prisoners at the Criterion Hotel. 'Let us make the most of it while we have the opportunity.' The Union had already been campaigning against Liberals in two ministerial by-elections at South Shields and Walthamstow where Sir William Robson and Sir John Simon were comfortably re-elected. Further marches took place in London on 22 and 23 November – known as the 'Battle of Downing Street' during which the prime minister's motor car sustained damage and windows were smashed at the Home Office and Colonial Office. Although 177 suffragettes were arrested, only 75 women, who had been charged with damaging property or with assault, were actually convicted. These events appeared certain to destroy earlier hopes of quiet mediation with the politicians over the fate of the Bill. In fact, the Battle of Downing Street was a brief diversion, probably intended to give the activists the chance to let off steam. By the end of the month politics was once again dominated by the general election campaign. As in the January campaign the Pankhursts worked against the Liberals in about fifty constituencies, but they stuck to constitutional methods. Since the outcome was an almost exact repetition of January's result it offered no improvement for the women's cause, though Christabel claimed to have secured the defeat of thirty or forty Liberals. Despite her misgivings she had little hesitation about extending the truce in the New Year.

Christmas 1910 proved to be a depressing time for the Pankhursts. Emmeline's sister Mary Clarke, who had been imprisoned for assaulting the police, was released shortly before the holiday. She had gone to stay with her brother Herbert at Winchmore Hill and made a speech on 23 December. Mary had Christmas Day dinner with Emmeline as usual, but suddenly left the table. Later Emmeline found her unconscious; she had suffered a brain haemorrhage and died. Coming as it did on top of the deaths earlier in the year of her son in January and her mother in April, this was a severe blow, for Mary had been the strongest link with the Goulden family. Emmeline chose to see Mary as a martyr to the suffrage cause. To Scott she wrote:

We who love her and know the beauty of her selfless life, feel it hard to restrain our human desire for vengeance although we know had she foreseen the consequence of her imprisonment she would have been proud and glad to die for the cause of freedom. She is the first to die. How many must follow before the men of your party realize their responsibility.[32]

Sylvia had not been with the family on Christmas Day, choosing to spend the time alone at Linden Gardens. But on Boxing Day Emmeline arrived to tell her of Mary's death and they spent several days together. Emmeline probably found little comfort in Christabel, whereas by contrast Sylvia was able to show her emotions and help her mother to express her grief.

In spite of this brief rapprochement Sylvia continued to be semi-detached from the family and from the WSPU. She had, in fact, been developing her career as an author by writing *The Suffragette*, a very detailed account of the campaign from the origins of the Union to 1909. Both Emmeline and Christabel, who lacked the patience for writing, had turned down invitations from publishers to write the book. *The Suffragette* sold well both in Britain and in the United States, which may have encouraged Sylvia to follow her mother's example by visiting America. Shortly after Christmas Emmeline accompanied Sylvia to Southampton where she boarded the *St Paul* bound for New York. During the passage she attracted the unwanted attentions of the ship's doctor. Though now a woman of twenty-nine, Sylvia was relatively inexperienced with the male sex. When the doctor invited her to his cabin following a little flirtation, she evidently got a shock to find that he was expecting more from her than polite conversation. 'I was quite lucky that the incident wasn't more unpleasant', she told Keir Hardie.[33]

On arrival at New York on 5 January 1911 Sylvia found a small band of reporters waiting for her. As usual the American press insisted on making the English visitor younger than she really was. When she appeared at the Carnegie Lyceum for the first of two lectures which had been arranged for her by Harriet Stanton Blatch, the *New York Times* professed to see 'a little rosy cheeked slip of an English girl [who] last evening held the attention of a distinguished New York audience for over an hour and a half.' Following her mother's tactics Sylvia reminded her audience of the common ground between the suffragette campaign and the American War of Independence with Britain. Then she concentrated on an account of women's pay, political violence and prison conditions in Britain. 'She told her story as a girl might tell it, with absolute simplicity and freedom from self-consciousness.' When it was over the applause and sympathy shown by the audience left her 'looking very much pleased'.[34]

Sylvia spent three months in the United States, travelling extensively in Pennsylvania, Ohio, Indiana, Michigan, Wisconsin, Illinois, Kansas, Tennessee, Missouri and Arkansas. Though she did her duty by speaking on women's suffrage, she refused to allow her American tour to be confined to the cause. By comparison with Emmeline she experienced a wider slice of American society and thought far more about the lessons it held. For example, she made a point of visiting Milwaukee in Wisconsin because 'I want to see a Socialist city and all that has been done there'.[35] Initially excited by the country and its receptivity to new ideas, she flirted briefly with the idea of emigrating. But before long her letters to Keir Hardie resounded with criticisms of Amercian society. In Pittsburgh she noted the 'squalid poverty of new immigrants', and in Indianapolis she concluded 'I wish I'd never seen this ugly place'. In Chicago she stayed with a Pankhurst uncle whose wife she found intolerable – 'absolutely empty-headed' and 'a dead weight'! Unusually for an English visitor, Sylvia ventured into the South to see the Indian University in Arkansas and she attracted much criticism by agreeing to speak at the Negro University in Tennessee. In Nashville, where she had been invited by the Socialist Society of Cumberland University, the students took her to sawmills and blanket factories. At a packed meeting the president of the university declared that the men of Tennessee liked to keep their women 'up in the gallery away from the turmoil of life'. An old man in the audience asked whether women would go out to mend the roads if they got the vote, thereby maintaining the traditional link between citizenship and roads. Suspecting that the law was defunct, Sylvia asked those men who had mended the roads to put up their hands. When only four did so the students yelled, whistled and roared with laughter.[36] Also in Nashville Sylvia made one of many visits to the county gaol, which she thought foul. There she saw the pitch-dark padded cells in which prisoners were confined when the authorities wanted to extract information or confessions from them. 'Four or five days of it always settles them' she was informed. Everywhere Sylvia was dismayed by the casual abuse shown towards negroes and those of mixed race.[37] The workhouse contained no white people at all. Feeling depressed and miserable she eventually left the South deep in contemplation about all the English people who had come to the United States to build a new life 'and have found here a grave for their hopes – and perhaps their souls!' Such a gloomy perspective on the American dream was far from typical among English visitors, and it would have shocked most white Americans. Few Edwardians felt particularly troubled by man's inhumanity to man when it was based upon colour and race; but in this, as in other respects, Sylvia seems to have been ahead of her time.

To some extent Sylvia's gloom during this tour may have been deepened by her growing loneliness. No doubt the experience of travelling by herself brought home to her the fact that she had no really close friend at home apart from Keir Hardie. She began to write him slightly pathetic letters about extrasensory perception as a means of bringing them together. 'When people have discovered the full power of thought transference', she wrote, 'we shall just sit back and look at each other.' Hardie appears to have encouraged this, perhaps because he himself took an interest in seances and in the idea of life after death, or simply because he understood how lonely she felt: 'Don't you think the satisfaction which comes from the pressure of my arms round you must be the transference of something from the one to the other? And so too with kissing. And if this be so surely the transference could be effected without actual, physical contact. To that extent I agree with you.'[38]

Sylvia returned in March 1911 to find the suffrage campaign in a state of considerable uncertainty. The recent election had done nothing to resolve the Union's dilemma over whether to hold its hand in the hope that the Government would revive the chances of the Conciliation Bill or to risk jeopardizing a concession by a premature return to militancy. But as usual the leaders skilfully maintained a sense of momentum. On 23 January the Union once again took over the Albert Hall for the launch of its official song, 'The March of the Women', which had been composed by Ethel Smyth. Having approached John Masefield, G. K. Chesterton and John Galsworthy to write the words without success, she had persuaded Cicely Hamilton, the actress and suffragette, to help out. Her final verse expressed the buoyant mood of 1910:

> Life, strife – these two are one.
> Naught can ye win but by faith and daring.
> On, on – that ye have done
> But for the work of today preparing.
> Firm in reliance, laugh a defiance –
> Laugh in hope for sure is the end.
> March, march – many as one,
> Shoulder to shoulder and friend to friend.

For weeks Dame Ethel drilled a suffragette choir whose members found that, like most of her works, 'The March' made few concessions to the performers. Her intervals were awkward and the singers found difficulty hitting her E flats.[39] But on the day all went well, though Emmeline was nearly late for the performance. *En route* to the Albert Hall, her motor car pulled up suddenly because a woman bystander had been caught by the mudguard and knocked down. At this the crowd turned very hostile, but Emmeline, with great presence of mind, jumped out, gathered the woman in her arms and summoned an ambulance. 'All this time', wrote Ethel Smyth, 'Mrs Pankhurst's face, soft with pity, radiant with love, was the face of an angel.' Before long the crowd's hostility had turned to sympathy and people urged her to press on to the meeting. But as she settled down in her seat Emmeline 'might have been heard ejaculating in a furious undertone, "Drunken old beast, I wish we'd run her over!" '[40] Safely arrived, Emmeline escorted Ethel in her academic robes up the central aisle to be presented with a baton encircled with a golden collar and the date. With this she then conducted the first public performance backed by the organ and cornet. The whole audience joined in. According to Hertha Ayrton, it was sung at least a tone higher than it was written so that 'it became rather a shriek'.[41] But Christabel and Emmeline pronounced themselves delighted with the result.

Privately, however, they were becoming frustrated at being constantly told by politicians that nothing could be done for women's suffrage until the constitutional crisis had been resolved. 'I know quite well that if we wait there will always be something that must be settled first', Emmeline told C. P. Scott. 'At each stage of our struggle I thought "This will move men" and each time I have been disappointed. Now death the irrevocable has come and even now you are not really moved ... I look forward to this year with the deepest foreboding.'[42] Yet although the King's Speech on 5 February made no mention of the Conciliation Bill, Christabel continued to show herself very conciliatory in her editorials.[43] When Sir George Kemp, a Liberal suffragist, won first place in the members' ballot, a date was set for a second reading debate on the Bill on 5 May. The Women's Liberal Federation attempted to organize a big rally in support of the Bill in Manchester at which Kemp and a minister would speak. But, as C. P. Scott pointed out to Emmeline, it would be impossible to get a cabinet minister unless the Union gave assurances it would not interrupt the meeting. She replied that this would be useful provided he offered Parliamentary facilities in 1911. Otherwise it 'would do more harm than good'.[44] Scott could only say rather lamely that the presence of a minister would be proof of intent, which Christabel, surprisingly, accepted; as long as nothing was said to weaken Asquith's pledge 'we will undertake to call upon our members to refrain from interruption'.[45] Clearly she felt it was still worth playing the game – but only just.

By this time the advantages of the truce were beginning to be outweighed by the drawbacks. Inevitably, as the suffragette campaign lost something of its novelty and excitement, it made fewer headlines. During February Christabel complained of another press boycott, and during March and April several meetings addressed by Christabel at

Bristol and Bath attracted much smaller audiences than usual.[46] Another tangible sign of the Union's lower profile was the check to its hitherto expanding income. Official figures for 1909–10 showed £33,000 income and those for 1910–11 £34,500. However, since the previous year included only £1,300 carried over from the previous year, while the second showed £5,100 carried over, income had actually fallen by about £2,500. Though far from disastrous, this underlined the dangers of a prolonged truce.

As if recognizing the danger, Christabel went out of her way to pour scorn on the methods of the constitutionalists when she spoke at the Albert Hall on 23 March: 'What does count? Militancy alone.' In speaking out she doubtless realized that her own leadership had come under question by several militants, including Mary Gawthorpe and Dora Marsden. Rather unhelpfully Teresa Billington-Greig, now a leading figure in the Women's Freedom League, chose this time to attack her for exaggerating wildly the effects of the militant strategy and for allowing it to degenerate into an anti-Liberal policy. Most damagingly, she accused the Pankhursts of exploiting the idealism of women by promoting a cult of hero-worship. Christabel's sensitivity to criticism at this time is evident from her deteriorating relations with Adela, who had continued her suffragist work in Scotland in 1910 and 1911. The Pankhursts were also in the process of falling out with Helen Fraser, their Scottish organizer, whom they peremptorily sacked. Adela had written to Mrs Tuke, pointing out that militancy was not understood in the provinces where it often antagonized those who sympathized with votes for women; it was therefore annoying to receive orders from London which totally disregarded local conditions. At this Mabel Tuke became angry and Adela hastily apologized: 'I had not yet learned it was a crime to have an opinion.'[47] Subsequently when Adela organized a meeting in Glasgow on her own initiative, she was summoned to London and accused of disloyalty. There was undoubtedly a personal element in this, for Adela resented being treated as a mere provincial employee of the Union while Annie Kenney enjoyed praise and prominence in the London press. But the underlying cause of the friction was much the same as that between Teresa Billington and Christabel in 1907. Not only did Adela share the local organizers' reservations about militancy, but her differences over politics had surfaced at last. Christabel disliked Adela's Socialism, which actually went down well in industrial Scotland but which, from the London perspective, seemed calculated to alienate the Union's wealthy backers.[48] She apparently accused Adela of trying to form a breakaway group in the North. There is no evidence for this, but since Billington-Greig had attempted to use Scotland in this way before the 1907 split, one can readily see the drift of Christabel's mind in 1911. The traditional account of the Pankhursts has seen Sylvia as the cause of internal friction in the family, but for most of this period she was less of a threat because she had become more detached from the movement than Adela and thus less inclined to rock the boat; though ultimately Emmeline and Christabel decided to expel both of them in order to maintain the unity of the organization, it was Adela who really crystallized the divisions between them.

This combination of internal criticism and dwindling resources encouraged Mrs Pethick-Lawrence to put even more pressure than usual on the Union's organizers to show a regular profit in their regions. In many ways this was pressure they were ill equipped to bear. The notoriety of the suffragette leaders obscured for contemporaries, as it has done for later generations, the relatively narrow base on which their campaign rested. Significantly the leaders never revealed full membership figures, but the local branches of the WSPU represented only about one in six of the total number of women's suffrage organizations in the country. From the start the Pankhursts had relied upon youth and enthusiasm, as well as publicity, to create momentum and attract resources. This had the advantage of tapping rank-and-file energies by giving young women positions of responsibility very quickly. But it invariably meant appointing them as organizers with virtually no experience or training. The day after Grace Roe made her first visit to Clement's Inn, Christabel wrote inviting her to work for the Union – a sign of the importance of personal patronage in the organization. Roe became organizer for Hammersmith and Kensington, and then for East Anglia, without having any experience.[49] As long as the Pankhursts occupied the headlines this did not matter much because it was comparatively easy to keep the contributions pouring in. But from 1910 onwards it was more of a struggle. Once doubts had developed about militancy, it proved tempting for many of the women who had always maintained a footing in both camps to drop the WSPU and work in one of the non-militant organizations instead.[50]

This fluid relationship between the rival suffragist organizations came to the fore very fruitfully in April 1911 when the Women's Freedom League, the product of the 1907 split, promoted a boycott of the national census. The essence of the WFL's thinking lay in developing forms of militant protest that did not involve violence, and tactics of this sort evidently appealed to women right across the spectrum. Although initially disparaging about the census boycott, Christabel dropped her opposition once it became clear that her own members were participating. However, the tactic proved to be a shrewd one, for it broke the press boycott by generating plenty of newspaper copy as women took refuge in premises which were not their normal place of residence on census night.[51]

On 5 May the Conciliation Bill at last came up for its second debate when it won a resounding majority of 255 votes to 88. Although the Government provided no further facilities for it in 1911, they offered to grant a week in 1912. Subsequently the Foreign Secretary, Sir Edward Grey, explained that this would be an elastic week, that is, sufficient to put the Bill through all its stages. This was confirmed by Asquith on 16 June. In the face of what appeared an unequivocal promise Christabel now became unusually optimistic. Henry Nevinson met her at a dinner where, he noted, she was 'most lovely to me, smiling, indiscreet and trustful . . .[she and Emmeline] now accept Asquith's letter as an absolute pledge, chiefly because he promises in spirit and not in letter . . . All very sweet and pleasant.'[52] On 17 June the suffragists organized a huge Coronation March, perhaps designed to capitalize on the mood of consensus engendered by the accession of George V, in which 40,000 people stretching for seven miles marched from the Embankment to the Albert Hall. 'With sure and certain steps the cause of women's suffrage is marching to victory', commented the *Daily Chronicle*, 'Saturday's remarkable procession in London served as a prelude to the inevitable triumph.'[53] Christabel herself gave every appearance of believing this. She hailed the prime minister's statement as 'a pledge upon which women can base the expectation of taking part as voters of the next and every future Parliament.' Her motive in reiterating all this was almost certainly to make it the more difficult for Asquith to wriggle out without opening himself to charges of deception. But for the time being she kept up a show of confidence by modifying her by-election policy so that Liberals would not automatically be opposed; only those who voted against the Conciliation Bill would be targeted.[54] As a result the Union opposed the Liberals at Bethnal Green in July and Kilmarnock in September, but abstained from the Keighley by-election in October where the Liberal was a consistent pro-suffragist. But in each case the Government won the seat; triumphant tours by Christabel had no apparent impact on the outcome.[55]

Though still the public symbol of the Union, Emmeline was less involved in these tactical considerations. She had spent much of the spring and summer of 1911 travelling the country, often using a new motor car, a large Wolseley, presented by a wealthy American supporter which was driven by another chauffeur, Aileen Preston, who was the first woman to qualify for the Automobile Association's Certificate in Driving. For this the Union paid her £1 a week. If they were not expected at a meeting, Aileen would take Emmeline to spend an hour or two with Ethel Smyth at Woking where she would sit listening to Ethel playing the piano. As was normal with Edwardian motor cars, punctures occurred regularly. When this happened: 'Mrs Pankhurst never got out of the car, she never moved from her papers, so I used to jack up the car. I took that for granted . . . In my mind all the time was, "Mrs Pankhurst's got to be there." '[56] As the motor car was still a novel and rather risky method of travel, a competent and reliable chauffeur was essential, which may explain why Emmeline expressed doubts about her other chauffeur, Vera Holme: 'Mrs Pankhurst thought I was very giddy and she wasn't at all for having me because I used to act the galoot in the office', Vera later admitted. But when Vera drove her all the way to Scotland without mishap Emmeline revised her opinion.

As was now her habit, Emmeline spent much of August and September in Scotland where she addressed large society gatherings at the homes of Lady Cowdray and Lady Wemyss. By the start of October 1911 she had returned to London where she boarded a train for Southampton decked out in purple white and green. On the fourth she sailed on the White Star liner, *Oceanic*, bound for New York, taking Mary Pethick,

Mrs Pethick-Lawrence's sister, as her companion. The Woman's Political Union had organized a big reception for her on 11 October, but the American customs officials refused to issue more than four passes to board the ship. This may have been intended as a rebuff to the WPU which had been formed by young American women keen to follow the British example by spreading militancy to the United States.

This second visit proved to be more relaxed than the first, perhaps due to the new air of optimism surrounding the women's cause. In 1911 California, which was in the process of balloting on women's enfranchisement, became the sixth state to accept the proposal. When Emmeline appeared the bands played 'See the Conquering Hero Comes', and Mrs Blatch introduced her as 'the woman who in all the world is doing the most for suffrage'.[57] According to the *New York Times* she 'looked a different woman from the one who was here a few years ago, her cheeks rosy and looking very pretty, without the careworn and weary expression which was notable then'.[58] After her first speech in New York on 17 October, Emmeline went west to Cleveland and Cincinnati in Ohio, south for the National Convention of the Women's Suffrage Association of America at Louisville, Kentucky, and thence further west to take in Omaha, Kansas City, Helena and Butte in Montana, and Seattle on the Pacific coast. She also crossed into Canada to visit London, Montreal, and Winnipeg. By 20 December she had arrived in Vancouver and Victoria where, in a two-hour speech, she was reportedly 'never at a loss for a word'. Emmeline never changed her style for these North American tours; one reporter noted she spoke in the 'low-pitched, well-modulated tones of the educated Englishwoman, and uses hardly any gestures, for the greater part of the time standing with her hands behind her back ... generally she is grave-faced and earnest, looking out over her audience with the deep-set, dreaming eyes of the zealot'.[59] The only serious show of opposition came at Harvard where the University Corporation had refused to allow her a hall within its precincts. The chief reason was that she had asked for a collection to be taken – a reminder of the importance she continued to attach to fund-raising – which conflicted with the University's policy on fees.[60] When she addressed the students outside the University her speech was punctuated by jeering and interruptions, so much so that the police were called in.

Emmeline did not return to Britain until January 1912. During her absence things had taken a turn for the worse, for the emphatic vote on the Conciliation Bill, combined with the prime minister's promise, had effectively concentrated the minds of Lloyd George and Churchill. In August the Chancellor hinted that the Government might offer a wider form of franchise reform, but Asquith had reassured the suffragists that his promise would still be honoured. Yet behind the scenes Lloyd George worked hard to convince his colleagues that the Bill would 'on balance add hundreds of thousands of votes to the strength of the Tory Party . . . The Liberal Party ought to make up its mind as a whole whether it will either have an extended franchise which would put the workingmen's wives on to the register as well as the spinsters and widows, or that it will have no female franchise at all.'[61] His diagnosis of the electoral implications of the Conciliation Bill was crucially endorsed by the regional Liberal agents when consulted by the chief whip. To this extent Christabel was correct when she complained about 'a conspiracy of wreckers and reactionaries who are bent on carrying widening amendments in Committee in the hope of destroying the majority for the bill'.[62] Yet her underlying assumption – that it would be easier to pass a bill extending the vote to only a million single women than one to cover about seven million including wives – was dubious. She shared the same lack of realism as all the suffrage organizations in choosing to ignore the fact that the Liberal and Labour members, who had provided 171 of the 255 votes given to the Conciliation Bill in May, really preferred a more democratic measure. She should not, therefore, have been entirely surprised when, on 7 November, Asquith announced the Government's intention of introducing its own bill in the next session which would be designed to streamline the registration of voters so as to enfranchise the four million *men* currently excluded from voting. Christabel rightly observed that there had been no great demand from men for this reform. But this was beside the point; radicals had long felt that with its property qualifications and its plural voting the electoral system leant too far towards the representation of the rich and privileged, and this could be rectified now that the power of the peers had been curtailed. In any case the Government's Bill was to be drafted so as to allow the inclusion of whatever amendment for women's suffrage the Commons favoured. Strictly speaking, this took nothing away from the earlier promise to allow time to debate the Conciliation Bill, but, in effect, it fatally undermined that measure simply because most Liberal and Labour members preferred a bill which would extend the male vote as well as creating a democratic female electorate.

Not surprisingly, when Henry Nevinson visited Clement's Inn shortly after Asquith's announcement, he found Christabel 'livid with rage and deaf to reason'. Referring to Lloyd George, she wrote: 'The whole crooked and discreditable scheme is characteristic of the man.'[63] This reaction involved a large element of personal pique. Since the Pankhursts themselves had consistently demanded *government* legislation on the grounds that it was the only type likely to pass, they ought logically to have welcomed Asquith's proposal as many of the non-militant women did. But by this time Emmeline and Christabel had invested a good deal of capital in the Conciliation Bill and had prepared themselves for the triumph which a women-only bill would entail. A general reform bill would have deprived them of some, at least, of the glory, for even though it seemed likely to give the vote to far more women, this was incidental to its main purpose. Several contemporaries who saw Christabel at close quarters at this time believed that she had begun to personalize the issue too much and risked alienating genuinely friendly politicians by her attitude. She became rather inclined to bluster and pretentiousness. This was evident when the prime minister, again outmanoeuvring his opponents, suddenly agreed to receive a women's suffrage deputation on 17 November, something he had determinedly resisted hitherto. Since the deputation included all varieties of suffragists, militant and constitutional, Liberal and Conservative, disagreements over the details and terms quickly emerged. Now in a benevolent and humorous mood, Asquith blandly told the delegates there was no need for belligerence. Christabel read her speech haltingly but had nothing new to say. When the prime minister observed that as head of government he was not going to be responsible for a measure which he did not believe to be in the interests of the country, she dismissed him portentously with an ineffable wave of her hand: 'Then you can go and we shall get another head!'[64]

However, if Christabel's political touch was a little unsure, she certainly had the sense of the suffragette movement. The feeling of betrayal amongst its members was now so strong that she had no difficulty in taking the step which had been in contemplation for some time – the abandonment of the truce. The Union decided to mark this by swiftly organizing a 400-strong deputation for 21 November. Led by Mrs Pethick-Lawrence, the women were instructed to take little money with them, to wear no furs, jewellery or umbrellas, and to equip themselves with food and a change of clothing for a stay in prison. 'You need not worry, as everything has been foreseen, and fortunately the regulations issued by the Home Office last year with regard to prison treatment of suffragettes still hold good.'[65] This referred to Churchill's decision as Home Secretary to give them the status of political prisoners in March 1910.

Meanwhile, a second group met at the Women's Press Shop in the Charing Cross Road equipped with bags of stones and hammers. These women proceeded to smash the windows at the Home Office, the Treasury, the Local Government Board, Somerset House, the National Liberal Federation, the Guards Club, the *Daily Mail* and the *Daily News*, as well as Swan and Edgar's, Lyons, Dunn's Hat Shop and other commercial premises. Thus was the new strategy revealed – to achieve the maximum impact while securing quick arrests and minimizing the violence meted out to the suffragettes themselves. Two hundred and twenty women were arrested for this night's work. When Asquith spoke at the City Temple on 28 November, suffragettes caused so much noise and chaos that he was driven away without delivering his speech. But as in 1909 things quickly began to get out of control. On 15 December Emily Wilding Davison succeeded in setting three pillar boxes alight by dropping burning linen into them. Unlike the window-breaking this had not been authorized by the WSPU. 'They must be mad', declared Lloyd George when he met C. P. Scott for breakfast. Scott agreed: 'They are mad, Christabel has lost all sense of proportion and of reality.' The Chancellor continued: 'It's just like going into a lunatic asylum and talking to a man who thinks he's God Almighty.'[66] Behind Lloyd George's irritation lay a certain amount of embarrassment about the way in which the suffragettes had exposed the limitations of his own pretensions as the outstanding radical leader of the day. On the other hand, under pressure the Pankhursts had become alarmingly erratic in their attitudes. Emmeline decided that she could not now give any consideration to 'that abominable Conciliation Bill' to which she and Christabel had ostensibly been so committed. She insisted that she would tolerate nothing but a government bill for 'full sex equality' and would try to force the Government to take up adult suffrage.[67] It was rather late in the day to reach this conclusion. In any case, neither she nor Christabel had any inclination to unpick their entire strategy at this stage. They remained determined to use the next year to test the policy of militancy to destruction.

I I

Where Is Christabel? (1912–13)

'If men will not do us justice, they shall do us violence.'
Emmeline Pankhurst, quoted in Ethel Smyth,
Female Pipings in Eden (1933)

Fresh from her morale-boosting American tour, Emmeline claimed that the recent advances made by the women's cause across the Atlantic had been chiefly due to the example set by British suffragettes. At a reception for released prisoners in the New Year she delivered a notorious defence of political violence: 'Why should women go to Parliament Square and be battered about and insulted, and most important of all, produce less effect than when they throw stones? The argument of the broken pane of glass is the most valuable argument in modern politics.'[1] In truth, Emmeline had always hated the truce and now that it had ended she could see her way clear again; by posing the most blatant threat to private property she would defy the Government to do its worst and thus accelerate the resolution of the whole controversy. 'I want to be tried for sedition', she repeatedly told her colleagues in the Union.[2] This aim seemed only too likely to be realized because by this stage all the leaders' public utterances were being carefully monitored by Special Branch officers and reported to the Home Office, where Sir Edward Troup, the Under-Secretary, marked with his thick blue pencil those passages which might form the basis for a prosecution.[3]

Perhaps better attuned to the broader political context, Christabel saw how difficult it was going to be to stop the suffragette movement from being engulfed in a more general pattern of political violence in

234

Britain. During 1912, working men organized an unprecedented wave of over eight hundred strikes which caused the loss of nearly forty-one million working days. On the whole industrial militancy stopped short of violence, though troops had been called out to quell rioting in South Wales in 1910 with the loss of two lives, and some politicians believed society was threatened by a general decline of respect for the law. However, the manifestations of violence that most concerned Christabel were those emanating from Ireland. Home Rule had returned to the top of the agenda by 1912 because the Parliament Act of the previous year now made it feasible to push a Home Rule Bill through Parliament in the face of the opposition of the House of Lords. This meant it must pass three times through the Commons. But as the Bill went on its way in 1912, Ulster and its political allies in England began to mobilize an increasingly violent resistance to the policy of the British Government. Christabel appreciated that Ireland impinged on women's suffrage in three distinct ways. She knew from private sources that the Irish Nationalist MPs were willing to vote down the Conciliation Bill out of gratitude to Asquith who was giving them Home Rule at last. As the Ulstermen and Nationalists began to drill their own private armies, it was inevitable that the problem of sporadic suffragette violence would be marginalized by the greater threat posed by civil war in Ireland. Yet from a propagandist point of view Home Rule gave Christabel plenty of scope to attack the Unionist leaders for lending respectability to violent resistance, and to mock the Government for its reluctance to prosecute political opponents like Bonar Law, F. E. Smith and Walter Long for their inflammatory language while using the law to crush a handful of women. 'Ulster militancy is not hardening the Government's opposition to Ulster's demands', she claimed, 'it is melting that opposition and is moving the Government to offer new concessions . . . Politicians have never, when threatened by militancy strong enough, found any difficulty in eating their words and waiving their prejudices.'[4]

While the WSPU announced another big demonstration for 4 March, it secretly planned a mass attack, to take place three days earlier, on the windows of the West End, which was to be led by Emmeline. Since she had little idea about the art of throwing stones, Emmeline received instruction from Ethel Smyth:

As dusk came on we repaired to a selected part of Hook Heath [near Woking] ... in front of my house. And near the largest fir tree I dumped down a collection of nice round stones ... I imagine Mrs Pankhurst had not played ball games in her youth, and the first stone flew backwards out of her hand, narrowly missing my dog. Once more we began at a distance of about three yards ... When at last a thud proclaimed success, a smile of such beatitude ... stole across her countenance, that much to her mystification and rather to her annoyance, the instructor collapsed on a clump of heather helpless with laughter [Mrs Pankhurst's sense of humour was always rather uncertain].[5]

Thus prepared, Emmeline, Mabel Tuke and Mrs Katharine Marshall took a taxi to Downing Street at 5.30 p.m. on Friday, 1 March, while at Scotland Yard a conference deliberated over ways of protecting shopkeepers' windows from the new attacks now anticipated. On arrival Emmeline took two shots but missed the windows, though her companions had more success. All three were arrested and taken to Vine Street Station where Fred Pethick-Lawrence 'who was ever ready to take root in any police station, his money bag between his feet', arrived at midnight to bail them out.[6] At 5.45 other suffragettes, dressed for shopping expeditions, had appeared in Piccadilly and pulled hammers and stones from their bags. By 6.00 p.m. the air around Regent Street, Bond Street and the Strand resounded to the crash of splintering glass, and at 6.15 the attacks fell upon Oxford Street and the Tottenham Court Road. Frightened shop assistants ran out into the street, traffic stopped, policemen blew whistles and each suffragette was soon surrounded by a crowd before being removed to the nearest police station. Altogether 121 arrests were made, keeping the court in session throughout Saturday. But on Monday the fourth, while 9,000 police waited in Trafalgar Square, further raids were launched, this time in Knightsbridge, Kensington High Street and Brompton Road.

Though all this may appear pointless provocation, it was, in fact, another means of bringing pressure to bear on the authorities to resolve the whole issue by harnessing the power of the protests voiced by the commercial interests. In any case, it is now evident that the relationship between the suffragettes and their immediate victims was more complicated than it appeared on the surface. When WSPU members made purchases from the West End stores, they placed little gummed discs on their receipts so that the proprietors would be in no doubt who their customers were. For their part the shops had every intention of hanging on to their suffragette clientele by advertising coats and hats in Union colours as suitable for wear at demonstrations. Katharine Marshall, whose job was to sell advertising space in *The Suffragette* to the shops, recorded that even at the height of the violence during 1913 and 1914 she never failed to fill the space allocated for advertisements each week. Though ostensibly dismayed over the militants' attacks, she noticed that 'one or two of the shops were rather annoyed at not having their windows broken as they were well insured and they would have been glad to have the notoriety of people looking at their damage'.[7]

The next day detectives raided the Union's headquarters in Clement's Inn where they seized large quantities of documents for use in prosecuting the leaders and a leading article written by Christabel on window-breaking intended for *Votes for Women*; in its absence the journal carried a dramatic blank space which was simply signed 'Christabel Pankhurst'. This raid was the start of what became, in effect, an attempt by the state to suppress the entire organization over the next two and a half years. The detectives also had warrants for the arrest of the leaders, but found only Fred and Emmeline Pethick-Lawrence. Emmeline was already back in prison, while Christabel, who by chance had recently moved to a separate flat, was absent.

On hearing about the police raid from Evelyn Sharp and Jessie Kenney, Christabel fled to the nursing home in Pembridge Gardens where Catharine Pine dressed her in a nurse's uniform. The next day she left a note for Annie Kenney: 'I have decided to escape. If I fail and the Government are able as they think to deprive the Union of all leadership, I give to you *full charge* of the policy of the Union.'[8] She then took a cab to Victoria Station and the boat train to Folkestone, dressed now in a long grey coat and a black cloche hat with £100 in her pocket. She got a fright when a fellow passenger suddenly called out 'Policeman', but the lady only wanted him to post some letters for her – a nice sidelight on the role of the Edwardian police! According to one account, on arrival at Boulogne Christabel spent some time at a small hamlet on the coast, but before long she travelled to Paris where she booked herself into the Hôtel Cité Bergère under the name 'Amy Richards'.[9] To all intents and purposes she had disappeared without trace.

As a public relations exercise Christabel's escape proved to be a brilliant coup. The actress and suffragette Elizabeth Robins pronounced her 'a leader with the power of making herself invisible to all her enemies', thereby building the kind of myth on which all political leaders thrive. Until September Christabel's whereabouts remained a closely kept secret, thereby giving the newspapers the excuse for endless speculation under 'Where is Christabel?' headlines. For the enjoyment of their readers they published photographs of a succession of country houses which seemed to be likely bolt-holes. Amateur sleuths followed women wearing green hats all over London and the police were obliged to follow up reports of suspicious-looking women in green dresses.

For the first three or four days in Paris Christabel felt understandably nervous as to what was happening to the Union at home. But Annie, taking a French-speaking suffragette with her, followed Christabel's instructions to make contact. Travelling via Southampton, Le Havre and Rouen, she arrived at the hotel for a two-day visit.[10] Thereafter Annie crossed the Channel each Friday to keep Christabel in touch with developments, returning on Sunday with instructions and an editorial for *Votes for Women*, which was Christabel's only means of maintaining control and continuity. Significantly Christabel flatly refused to contemplate appointing her sister as a substitute during her absence. When Sylvia returned from the United States she expected, not for the first time, to be trusted to take over. Disguised as a nurse with the help of Miss Pine, she, too, crossed to Paris, only to be treated as though she had nothing of importance to contribute. Christabel simply told her to 'keep out of harm's way' and 'just speak at a few meetings'.[11] She intended to work through women like Annie, who was not known as 'The Blotter' for nothing, and Mabel Tuke, who was equally unlikely to pose a threat to her leadership or challenge her policy.

Though Christabel's flight to Paris had involved an element of luck, it was far from being the sudden flash of insight that she claimed in her autobiography; on the contrary, it was a long-premeditated move. Her legal studies had made her aware that political offenders were not liable to extradition. Years later she wrote: 'One could not have led from prison, in the sense of planning and directing action, as one could lead from exile. Exile simply meant long-distance control.'[12] Though plausible on the face of it, this rationale scarcely stood up to the pressures of the next two years. In spite of the regular communication through Annie Kenney, WSPU headquarters soon began to lose its role as the directing power for the movement. This was partly because, even after a new headquarters was found at Lincoln's Inn House in Kingsway, regular raids by the police hampered operations. In any case, as the public campaign gradually dwindled the movement became increasingly fragmented into scattered initiatives by small groups and even individual suffragettes. Though her name appeared weekly in *Votes for Women* or *The Suffragette*, in practice Christabel lost effective control after a few months. During a short absence she might have kept the organization together, but her exile stretched right up to August 1914 when the First World War broke out. During that period she naturally faced great pressure to return and save the Union from collapse. The fact that she always firmly resisted it suggests that there was more to her action than she cared to admit. In effect, Christabel had rationalized her own desire to avoid the necessity to submit to prolonged prison sentences, hunger strikes and forcible feeding. Even after 1914 she spent relatively little time in Britain, and her decision in March 1912 thus proved to be a fateful one not just for the medium-term fortunes of the WSPU, but for her own long-term career. She never recovered fully the pre-eminent position she had enjoyed previously, and her detachment from British politics led eventually to a more prolonged form of exile during the inter-war period as she struggled to re-establish her failing career.

All this, however, lay in the future. It is easy to see why, in the immediate circumstances, Christabel found Paris a most seductive port in the suffragette storm. For this was no spartan exile in a draughty garret. Over the next two and a half years she acquired apartments at a succession of very smart addresses – the Avenue de la Grande Armée, the Rue du Roy, the Rue la Boétie and the Avenue du Trocadéro. She had a maidservant and generally lived in some style. It is far from clear how she was supported during this period, whether from the Union's funds or by friends in France. Through her mother and Ethel Smyth she already had some contacts in Paris, and quite quickly she began to benefit from the support of several wealthy and influential figures, notably the Princesse de Polignac and the Baronne de Brimont who gave her entry into the salon society of the French capital. She also enjoyed the hospitality of Emmeline's American friend Mrs O. H. P. Belmont who had a residence at Trouville, a fashionable resort on the Normandy coast, which offered a congenial meeting place for visiting suffragettes. The 47-year-old Princesse de Polignac was Winnaretta Singer, the daughter of Isaac Singer who invented the sewing machine, and his French wife. Educated in Paris, Winnaretta married Edmond Prince de Polignac, and played an active role as a philanthropist, artist and musician.

From time to time rumours circulated to the effect that the Home Secretary, Reginald McKenna, who had succeeded Churchill in 1911, wished to have Christabel returned to face trial for conspiracy in Britain. Though French co-operation seemed unlikely in principle, this was a time when relations between the two countries had grown much closer. The entente, signed in 1903, had developed into an undeclared alliance as a result of the naval discussions between the two countries which effectively meant that Britain had undertaken to guard France's northern coasts from Germany while the French would defend Britain's Mediterranean route. However, the question of extradition never seems to have arisen explicitly. In March 1912, when the Government was still uncertain of Christabel's whereabouts, the British Consul General in New York informed the Foreign Office that he had reason to think she was there. However, officials pointed out that hers was not an extraditable crime and even if it had been 'her surrender would doubtless be refused on the grounds of its being of a political character'.[13] In May 1913 the French press claimed that the British were attempting to persuade the French to expel her, which led a Liberal backbencher, Josiah Wedgwood, to ask whether the Foreign Office was taking steps to seek Christabel's extradition from Paris. As a result Monsieur Flurian had an interview at the Foreign Office. According to the official record of this meeting: 'We have not asked France to expel her and Monsieur Flurian said if we did it could be very difficult for them to accede.'[14] In June when the matter was raised in the French Chamber of Deputies, Monsieur Pichon, the Foreign

Minister, said that no request for expulsion had been made and none was contemplated by France.[15] Several notes passed between officials of the Home Office and the Foreign Office in which the former pointed out that only the Foreign Office could approach a foreign government, while the latter argued that it really lay with the Home Office to decide whether extradition was wanted. Failing that, the Foreign Office did not contemplate making a request for this would obviously have introduced an unwanted complication into its dealings with the French.

The question arises why McKenna did not, apparently, attempt to have Christabel extradited. And why were Annie Kenney and others permitted to travel unhindered back and forth to receive instructions from the supposed conspirator-in-chief in Paris? Although the women often disguised themselves, by this time they had become familiar figures and were often followed by detectives; it can scarcely have been beyond the capabilities of the Special Branch, even allowing for the incompetence of the British secret services, to have apprehended Kenney. As the departmental exchanges show, the Home Office considered extradition, but failed to come to any decision. Although the Government maintained the fiction that the Pankhursts had turned Paris into the centre of a dangerous conspiracy, it seems likely that they were tolerably well informed about their activities, for, according to Rachel Barrett, whenever she spoke to Christabel on the telephone she heard a click which indicated that Scotland Yard was listening in.[16] McKenna was almost certainly content for Christabel to remain in France. Although WSPU propaganda promoted the idea that Christabel was masterminding new campaigns, thereby to maintain flagging morale, she actually filled her days with shopping, writing and social engagements. For the authorities she caused far less trouble in Paris than she would have done in Britain. This view is corroborated by several contemporaries. At the end of March Annie was reported as saying: 'I am off to Paris for a few days, half work and half play.'[17] She soon came to love the Saturdays in Paris spent strolling arm in arm through the Bois de Boulogne while Christabel talked unceasingly. When Sylvia arrived at Christabel's apartment she found her 'entirely serene, enjoying the crisis of the WSPU and her new life in Paris, the shops and the Bois ... Paris meant relaxation. Her articles dashed off at great speed she was ready for sight-seeing, for which I had no heart.'[18]

No doubt one has to allow for differences of temperament here. Christabel's supporters depicted Sylvia as a misery who always disapproved of self-indulgence and enjoyment, while Sylvia had an obvious motive for exaggerating the gulf between the sufferings endured at home by other suffragettes, including herself, and the gracious life style of her sister abroad. None the less, it seems undeniable that Christabel possessed both the time and the resources to enjoy her exile. She insisted on taking Sylvia to see some paintings, and then to accompany her to her favourite shop where they both bought dresses. After this Sylvia left by the night boat 'unable to endure another day'.[19]

While Christabel settled into her new life in Paris, Emmeline spent most of March in Holloway with the other window-breakers, including Ethel Smyth who had targeted the house of Lewis Harcourt, the Colonial Secretary and a notorious opponent of votes for women. An entire wing of the prison was now given over to the suffragettes. Accounts vary, but all suggest that the authorities adopted a fairly lax approach. Smyth, who was delighted to find herself in a cell next door to Emmeline's, was permitted by a sympathetic matron to take tea with her each afternoon; cell doors were evidently left open for much of the time. After visiting Ethel Smyth, Sir Thomas Beecham noted:

I arrived in the main courtyard of the prison to find the noble company of martyrs marching round it and singing lustily their war-chants while the composer, beaming approbation from an overlooking upper window, beat time in almost Bacchic frenzy with a tooth brush.[20]

Emmeline, for whom the experience was less of a novelty, refused to be softened by the favours granted by the authorities; she reprimanded the female warders for doing their jobs and urged other prisoners to do their best to make life intolerable for the Governor by making complaints about the food, the rules and the bath water. But the warders turned a blind eye to many of their activities, allowing them to have paper, calico and even hammers and nails with which to decorate the walls with suffragette propaganda.[21]

Emmeline was released on the twenty-eighth, just in time to see the impact the latest phase of militancy had been having on the politicians. MPs were about to debate for the third time the Conciliation Bill introduced by Sir James Agg-Gardner. This time they rejected it by 222 votes to 208, reversing the favourable majorities of 167 in 1911 and 109 in 1910. As Lloyd George had intended, the prospect of a government reform bill incorporating a wider franchise for women had triggered shifts among the Liberals. Only 117 Liberals backed the Conciliation Bill in 1912 by comparison with 145 in 1911; and 73 now opposed it as against only 36 the previous year. To that extent Christabel's claims had been vindicated. However, this was by no means a complete explanation for the dramatic reverse suffered by the Bill. The Conservatives had no reason to prefer the Government's new proposals. But 114 of them now voted against the Conciliation Bill compared with only 43 in 1911. This can only be explained in terms of a backlash against the latest wave of attacks on property. In addition, the Irish members completely reversed their votes from 31–9 in favour of the Bill to 35–3 against it, but this was chiefly due to their determination to remain loyal to Asquith now that he was promoting the Home Rule Bill. Of course, this defeat did nothing to alter the underlying pro-suffrage majority in the House of Commons; the March vote reflected temporary conditions rather than fundamentals. But as an unexpected setback it brought condemnation on the heads of the Pankhursts not only from politicians but from non-militant women, and it put the Union on the defensive for the first time.

Emmeline's sentence for the window-breaking in March had been remitted pending the start of her trial for conspiracy in May. This allowed her an opportunity to recuperate in the country, though her peace of mind was disturbed when she became embroiled with her youngest daughter once again. Though little contemporary evidence survives of Adela's activities for this period, she had continued her work in the provinces, making one of her last by-election appearances in South Manchester in the spring of 1912. Photographs of her around this time reveal a sad, distracted young woman. Too much time spent campaigning in the open had undermined an already weak constitution. But it was the combination of physical strain and mental depression which pushed Adela towards another breakdown. Reportedly suffering from bronchitis and pleurisy, she went to Wemyss Bay, a small resort on the Firth of Forth, to recuperate with her friend

Helen Archdale, a journalist and suffragette who had been in prison with her at Dundee. Emmeline visited her there. According to Sylvia's account, Adela now thought of becoming a gardener. This seems unlikely since she had no previous horticultural interest and, in view of her bronchial weakness, it was an unsuitable occupation. On the contrary, the idea has all the hallmarks of Emmeline's mind. However, writing in the 1930s Adela said that she chose gardening, and as a result her mother offered to send her to the Studley Horticultural College in Warwickshire – but with a condition attached. She was never to speak in public in Britain again.[22]

The explanation for this drastic proposal lay in the increasing irritation felt by Emmeline and Christabel over the left-wing bias Adela had given to the case for women's enfranchisement in her campaigns in the north. Even so, their announcement must have come as a crushing blow for a daughter already depressed because she felt unloved; it was tantamount to expulsion from both the cause and the *family*, and a rejection of all that she had done over the previous six years. Yet their treatment of Adela in 1912 underlines not only how vulnerable Christabel and Emmeline now felt, but also how much greater a threat Adela seemed to pose than Sylvia, whose expulsion in 1914 is much better known. 'I would not care if you were multiplied by a hundred,' Christabel told Sylvia, 'but *one* of Adela is too many!'[23] Whatever the thinking behind the decision, the effect was that at twenty-seven Adela had suddenly lost what little purpose she had in life, and, largely for lack of a clear alternative, she enrolled at Studley College for a year. One fellow student there described her as 'a dear, brave girl' who was inclined to keep her problems to herself.[24] The move into horticulture did no more than delay a resolution of her personal difficulties.

It was not until 15 May that Emmeline and the two Pethick-Lawrences were put on trial at the Central Criminal Court charged with 54 counts of conspiracy to incite WSPU members to commit damage, injury and spoil, to the amount of £5, certain glass windows. The case arose out of the police raid on 4 March. The Attorney-General, Sir Rufus Isaacs, led for the prosecution, while the Pethick-Lawrences employed Tim Healy, a prominent Irish politician, and Emmeline opted to conduct her own defence, though she had the advice of a friendly solicitor, Arthur Marshall. Her confidence may have been boosted by the knowledge that this time she faced a jury. Rufus Isaacs and his assistant, Mr Archibald Bodkin, treated the court to extensive quotations from speeches and circulars regarding the two phases of window-breaking in November 1911 and March 1912.[25] To lend credibility to the picture of the Union as a conspiracy they flourished lists of false names used for those who committed militant actions and the elaborate codes by which suffragettes referred to selected cabinet ministers such as 'Thistle' or 'Rose'. The word 'Fox' allegedly meant 'Are you prepared for arrest?', 'Goose' meant 'Do not get arrested', and 'Duck' meant 'Do not get arrested unless success depends on it'.

Although Emmeline pleaded 'Not Guilty' she scarcely offered a defence, rather an attempt to justify her actions. She argued that as no personal gain had been involved, hers was a political, not a criminal, offence; she then recounted her own experience as a Poor Law Guardian, the historical rationale for forming the WSPU, the inadequacy of constitutional methods, and the incitement to violence given by government ministers who, she said, deserved to be in the dock as much as she did. She ended by rejecting the authority of the court:

I may, as a woman, say one word more. We say in England that every man is tried by his peers. I might have been justified as a woman if at the opening of this case I had said you are not entitled to try me for this offence. What right have you, as men, to judge women? Who gave you that right, women having no voice in deciding the legal system of this country, no voice in saying what is a crime and what is not a crime?[26]

In his summing up, Mr Justice Coleridge said that Emmeline had failed to adopt the defence open to her. It was no answer to those whose property had been damaged to say that the attacks had been made for political reasons, not for private gain; the criminal law dealt with intentions, not motives, and so the fact that the crime was political was irrelevant. The jury took only twenty-five minutes to return a verdict of 'Guilty'; however, they put in a recommendation for clemency in view of the 'undoubtedly pure motives' of the accused. Pointing out that he could have sentenced them to two years, the judge gave them nine months in the second division. As he rose to leave Coleridge was hissed from the gallery. Supporters of the three defendants waved, kissed their hands and called 'goodbye'.[27] Arthur Marshall decided not to appeal against the decision. However, the sentence was widely regarded as harsh, and at least one member of the jury wrote to the Home Secretary to complain and to urge that the prisoners be placed in the first division.[28] In a letter to McKenna, Coleridge justified the sentence on the grounds that the defendants had shown no contrition and were determined to repeat their offences; he refused to allow them the first division unless they agreed not to repeat their actions.[29]

Emmeline remained in Holloway from 22 May until 24 June. Her brother Herbert, Sylvia and Adela all put in requests to visit her, the latter on the grounds that she had to see her mother about her college fees. Other benefactors of the Union, including Muriel, Countess de la Warr, Lady Sybil Smith and the Ranee of Sarawak, also applied but were refused as her visits were rationed to one a fortnight. She did, however, receive several crates of French wine thoughtfully sent in by Ethel Smyth who blandly assured the authorities that the daily consumption of half a pint of Château Lafite was essential to her health![30] When Emmeline refused to be medically examined or to do any work in prison the Governor concluded 'it would be better to let the matter slide and take no action'.[31] Under threat of a hunger strike and the political pressure this would place on the Government, the Home Secretary agreed on 10 June to put the three leaders in the first division, though only when they gave an undertaking that they would refrain from further incitement to attack property while in gaol. Next they demanded that the same privilege be extended to the other 79 women in Holloway. Although Emmeline was not subjected to forcible feeding during this imprisonment, by 17 June concerns about her health began to be raised. Following a visit by Sylvia, Herbert Goulden requested an examination by Dr Agnes Savill, a Harley Street doctor who had been treating her for five or six years for a skin complaint: 'Such disease being attributed to the change of life.' But Emmeline herself complained of a throat irritation. As a result the medical officers reported on her general health which they considered very fair, though they described her as 'a person who is of a somewhat neurotic nature'. Another doctor commented: 'It is obvious that she means to hunger strike and wants to get a tame specialist to certify that her throat is not in a condition to allow of her being tube fed.'[32] From 19 June the other suffragettes refused food and on the twenty-second forcible feeding began. However, Emmeline's violent resistance led the warders to leave her alone. The authorities then called in a Dr Douglas Powell, who was also unable to examine her but who described her as follows:

She was somewhat excited and emotional but looked fairly well ... She is passing through the menopausal time of life and has for some time been treated by Dr Agnes Savill ... Mrs Pankhurst was very rebellious at her confinement but she volunteered that the Governor, the Doctors, the Warders and other prison officials had treated her with kindness and consideration ... I cannot help adding that with a person of her excitable and emotional temperament daily communication with her fellows in trouble is most likely to stimulate and maintain resistance to authority.[33]

Dr Agnes Savill meanwhile requested a visit on the grounds that Emmeline had been 'suffering from debility consequent on the bronchitis she had suffered during her imprisonment in March, and also from a degree of neurasthenia and insomnia, due to hard work and overstrain'.[34] Though she was refused permission, the prison medical officer, W. C. Sullivan, examined Emmeline on 23 June when he detected further problems in the shape of increased sound over the aortic area and intermittency of the pulse which suggested cardiac weakness. He concluded that forcible feeding might have a very serious effect if she resisted. When he tested this by trying to give her Brand's Essence by spoon she 'became so violent and excited that it was necessary to desist'. Sullivan's report put strong pressure on the prison Governor:

She has been taking plenty of water, but nothing else since the 19[th][June] and has been most of the time in bed, so that her strength has been fairly maintained. Last evening, however, her pulse was more frequent and compressible and her breath had a strong odour; and this morning she had a slight attack of faintness. I do not think she can stand further abstinence.[35]

Meanwhile Mrs Pethick-Lawrence, whose doctors had warned her that the prison diet would be disastrous to her health because of her chronic gastric condition, had been forcibly fed. This caused shock, faintness and a weak pulse as well as the gastric pain of which she complained. Though the doctors felt she might be exaggerating, they decided by 24 June that it would be unwise to resume forcible feeding, so both women were released that day.[36] Fred Pethick-Lawrence, who had lost four stones and been fed five times, was discharged three days later.

As soon as she felt strong enough, Emmeline slipped away to Paris to be with Christabel. When the Pethick-Lawrences joined them there, they embarked upon a painful debate about the condition of the Union. The absence of all four leading figures for four months had naturally concentrated their minds about future strategy. On the positive side, the police raid had led them to overestimate the extent of the Home Secretary's plans at this stage. In March when a rumour went round that he was about to seize their funds, Evelyn Sharp, who was one of the headquarters staff, promptly asked Mrs Pethick-Lawrence and Christabel to sign a cheque transferring the Union funds to Hertha Ayrton, who placed it in her own account and then transferred it to a continental bank a few hours later.[37] As the money was now beyond McKenna's reach, his only alternative was to identify wealthy subscribers in an attempt to cut off the source of WSPU funds. But from this point onwards money became a source of worry to the leaders who watched anxiously to see how the Albert Hall demonstration planned for 15 June would go in their absence. In the event Mabel Tuke took the chair and speeches were delivered by Annie Kenney, Elizabeth Robins and Tim Healey MP. A reassuring sum of £6,000 was raised, and the total income for the financial year 1912–13 reached an impressive £35,710; but as some £10,000 of this represented money carried over, the Union had raised only £25,000. Although Mrs Tuke coped at first, by November she was finding the strain too much. Even Christabel admitted: 'A great deal falls to [Emmeline] to do nowadays especially as our dear Mrs Tuke is having to rest a bit.' But she refused to be tempted to assume direct control again: 'As long as one is out of reach the Government will not think they can stamp us out. We can't have it every way in this world.'[38]

These tensions were visible only behind the scenes. To the outside world the Union presented a bold face by sponsoring a series of summer meetings in open spaces all around London at Ealing Common, Wimbledon Common, Regent's Park, Blackheath, Peckham Rye, Clapham Common, Finsbury Park and Streatham Common. They were intended to build up momentum towards the Hyde Park demonstration on Sunday, 14 July, timed to coincide with Emmeline's birthday. It was a colourful spectacle. Sylvia organized the manufacture of some 240 banners supported on poles draped with laurel and surmounted by scarlet caps of liberty, consciously designed to echo the great reform demonstrations of the nineteenth century. In the centre Ethel Smyth, dressed in the white and lilac robes of Durham University, conducted the massed bands playing 'The March'. Twenty platforms were manned by ninety speakers, including George Lansbury MP and Keir Hardie resplendent in a white summer suit and red tie.

Yet behind the scenes opinion was beginning to become dangerously polarized by the new phase of militancy and the repressive measures of the government. Early in August the Pethick-Lawrences paid a visit to Boulogne, where their differences with Christabel emerged for the first time. When they departed for a lengthy trip to Canada, Emmeline remained with Christabel in Paris until October, ostensibly to recover from her imprisonment but also to decide how to maintain control of the Union. A number of the leaders of the Men's Political Union, including Brailsford, Nevinson and Housman, had begun to conclude that militancy had been taken to foolish extremes and was now damaging the cause. Conversely, a vocal minority of Liberal and Labour backbenchers, including Josiah Wedgwood and George Lansbury reacted with outrage to the lengthening prison sentences and regular use of forcible feeding for political prisoners.

Henry Harben, a wealthy and idealistic landowner of Socialistic views who had been adopted as Liberal candidate for Barnstaple in February, condemned Asquith and threw over his candidature in July. For some time Harben acted as a valuable support, both financially and on the platform, though his doubts about Christabel's policy grew steadily stronger. Several wealthy women supporters, including Maud Arncliffe-Sennett, Janie Allan and Mona Taylor, withdrew at this time, as did the Blathwayts in 1913. Under the strain the Pankhurst family was now in process of disintegration. Though Adela had effectively dropped out, Sylvia continued to work as a dogsbody for the Union during the summer, dashing around to speak in the provinces. Suddenly new instructions arrived from Paris: Christabel wanted her sister to burn down Nottingham Castle. This was inspired by recent tactless remarks made by Sir Charles Hobhouse, a notorious anti-suffragist, who had referred to the rioting that had taken place at Nottingham during the Great Reform Act of 1832. But in spite of her involvement with militancy Sylvia recoiled from the prospect: 'The request came as a shock to me. The idea of doing a stealthy deed of destruction was repugnant. I did not think such an act could assist the cause . . . I had the unhappy sense of being asked to do something morally wrong.'[39] She may have been exaggerating her disapproval in retrospect. But it can hardly have escaped Christabel's attention that Sylvia's refusal was symptomatic of a wider reluctance to enforce her policy.

Resistance to the official policy may well have been strengthened by the knowledge that an alternative strategy had taken shape during the spring of 1912. The defeat of the Conciliation Bill in March had so embarrassed the non-militant National Union of Women's Suffrage Societies that it decided to abandon the non-party strategy which it had upheld since the 1860s. Katherine Marshall negotiated an agreement with Arthur Henderson, a leading Labour MP, for an electoral pact under which the NUWSS would give active support to certain Labour candidates and attempt to unseat anti-suffrage Liberal ones. For its part, the Labour Party agreed not just to support women's suffrage, which its MPs already did, but to vote against any franchise bill which failed to include women. This constituted an important advance for the cause, not because Labour commanded much direct influence in the House of Commons, but because in the country the Liberals depended on the maintenance of electoral co-operation with Labour for their majority. If the NUWSS were to succeed in encouraging Labour to run more candidates in Liberal seats, the inevitable outcome would be a split in the Liberal vote and the return of the Conservatives to power. This pact thus became the key *strategic* development in women's suffrage before 1914.

Unfortunately, the new policy flew in the face of Christabel's view of Labour as a party in the pockets of the Government, and she therefore did her best to disrupt the alliance during the autumn of 1912 and the spring of 1913. Conversely, for Sylvia the pact represented, in some sense, the logical expression of her own desire to unite the cause of women with that of the working class as a whole. Despite this she never endorsed it; in fact, she continued to express her contempt for the NUWSS for its timidity; yet the new policy undoubtedly exacerbated her unhappiness about the direction the Union had now taken. She saw more clearly than Christabel the disintegrating impact that extreme militancy was having when she visited Crewe to participate in a by-election in July 1912. There she found the Union's campaign short of personnel, lacking an experienced organizer, and being marginalized by the non-militants who were energetically backing the Labour candidate.[40] Their efforts obviously placed her in an embarrassing position. Since Sylvia evidently communicated her impressions of Crewe to her sister, she can only have deepened Christabel's frustration at being marooned in Paris and made her all the more anxious to eradicate opponents within the organization. It was almost certainly with the intention of giving a boost to flagging morale that Christabel decided to reveal her place of exile on 13 September. A week later the *Daily Sketch* offered exclusive photographs of her, smartly dressed, shopping and strolling through the streets of the French capital. Though this did not go down well with all suffragists, it highlighted once again the very special status Christabel had achieved in the movement.

It was in the autumn of 1912 that the disagreements simmering within the militant camp came to a head in the form of a dramatic split between the Pethick-Lawrences on the one hand and Emmeline and Christabel on the other. The Pankhursts took the view that, as a result of the Government's new repressive policy, Fred was ceasing to be an asset to the Union. During the summer the Home Secretary had made the first moves in his attempt to cut off the sources of the Union's money. Since it was difficult to sue an organization for damages, both McKenna and a number of insurance companies decided to target individuals, starting with the easiest victim – Fred Pethick-Lawrence. During August while he and his wife were away in Canada, the bailiffs entered their house at Holmwood and seized furniture, which was sold for about £300. But this left them owing over £800 for the expense of the conspiracy trial, and about £2,000 claimed by ninety-seven shopkeepers. Eventually the Treasury solicitors sold the

Pethick-Lawrences' house and made Fred bankrupt.[41] 'They see in Mr Lawrence a potent weapon against the militant movement and they mean to use it', Emmeline wrote to his wife in September.[42] However, this is not wholly convincing as an explanation for the split. As Emmeline Pethick-Lawrence pointed out, they had never allowed their personal interests to stand in the way of actions for the sake of the Union. In any case, the expulsion of the Pethick-Lawrences from the Union did nothing to deter the Home Secretary or the Treasury solicitors; and if the same logic were to be extended the militants would eventually have lost all their wealthy subscribers. But in addition there was by now a deep disagreement over the Union's strategy which Christabel's exile had exacerbated. The Pankhursts favoured extending the attacks on private and public property in the belief that this would create an intolerable situation for the Government and that most of the women involved could escape arrest. This was very much Emmeline's view, strengthened by her frustration during the period of the truce, but from the perspective of Paris Christabel increasingly saw its attractions. By contrast the Pethick-Lawrences believed it was 'sheer madness to throw away the immense publicity and propaganda value that the demonstration followed by the state trial [of Emmeline in May] had brought to our cause'.[43] On the assumption that public opinion was on their side they wanted Christabel to return home and risk being put on trial.

It is not clear which of the two women was chiefly responsible for the subsequent split. Emmeline had never particularly liked Fred whom she referred to as 'Godfather'; she disliked having to indulge him because of his money. Moreover, she always resented Christabel's habit of consulting the Pethick-Lawrences, was jealous of their influence and had long harboured a desire to cut them down to size. Christabel's motives are less obvious. Her absence from London put her in greater need of the Pethick-Lawrences to run the headquarters organization. She feared that, however loyal, Annie Kenney would be unable to maintain her control of policy in the face of their opposition. But since the Pethick-Lawrences enjoyed the support of many of the members, Christabel eventually decided on a swift strike, similar to that of 1907, designed to pre-empt internal debate. After returning from Canada on 2 October, Fred and Emmeline found themselves summoned to the new headquarters and informed that Emmeline had decided to sever their connection with the Union. However, they refused to believe that Christabel could possibly have agreed with her mother about this. So determined was Emmeline to get her own way that she took the risk of bringing Christabel home. Accordingly she crossed to France and booked a first-class ticket for her return journey while Christabel, heavily disguised, travelled second class on the same boat. On arrival in London on 14 October she avoided cabs for fear of being recognized and made her way on foot to the confrontation with the Pethick-Lawrences. There, supported by Annie Kenney and Mabel Tuke, she backed her mother's decision. Emmeline herself behaved very badly and tried to prevent Fred speaking at all. However, in the circumstances the split proved comparatively painless, largely due to the remarkably restrained way in which Fred and Emmeline accepted their expulsion. As Fred reminded his wife, since they had themselves made Emmeline an autocrat in the WSPU, it was too late to appeal to the members against her. They took the journal, *Votes for Women*, with them, but were shocked to discover that Christabel had a new newspaper of her own, *The Suffragette*, ready for publication. Later they founded their own pressure group, the United Suffragists, which attracted a number of the more left-wing and democratically inclined members of the Union. Sylvia, for whom these events had come as a shock, maintained friendly relations with the Pethick-Lawrences, but she did not join them. Perhaps the most immediately damaging result was the appointment of Emmeline as Treasurer to succeed Mrs Pethick-Lawrence, a post for which she had neither the time nor the ability. It underlined the extent to which the Union was shrinking into a family group, and exacerbated the inevitable confusion between the funds of the Union and those of the Pankhursts which created controversy for many years to come.

Yet the split enabled the leaders to pursue their strategy without internal resistance. Speaking at the Albert Hall on 17 October, Emmeline sought to divert attention from the expulsions by making a fresh call for militancy with an explicit endorsement of violence:

Be militant each in your own way . . . Those of you who can break windows – break them. Those of you who can still further attack the secret idol of property so as to make the Government realize that property is as greatly endangered by woman suffrage as it was by the Chartists of old – do so. And my last word is to the Government: I incite this meeting to rebellion! I say to the Government: You have not dared to take the leaders of Ulster for their incitement to rebellion. Take me if you dare; but as long as men, rebels and voters are at liberty, you will not keep me in prison![44]

In the circumstances this was a bold effort to retain the initiative. But the demonstration raised only £3,600, well below the usual effort, a sign that some supporters felt the Pankhursts had behaved badly towards the Pethick-Lawrences.

In her editorial the next day, Christabel reinforced the political policy by declaring that in future all Labour candidates would be opposed, not just Liberals as hitherto.[45] No doubt her intention was to destabilize the pact between Labour and the non-militants which was now operating at most by-elections. Since many people remained confused by the distinctions between militant suffragettes and non-militant suffragists, it was not difficult for the Union to draw opprobrium on to their rivals by making attacks on the Labour Party. Christabel simply refused to accept that Labour was sincere about women's suffrage and argued that if the party really wanted to help it could force the Government to legislate by refusing to vote for any of its bills. Although the Labour members largely regarded this as unrealistic and as damaging to the party's interests, a minority including Keir Hardie and George Lansbury, felt the moral force of the complaint that they had not done enough. Lansbury, an idealistic and independent-minded man, had been deeply moved by the physical suffering endured by women in prison; in June he made an emotional attack on Asquith in the House of Commons: 'You will go down to history as the man who tortured innocent women. You ought to be driven from public life.' Though not essentially a feminist, Lansbury was moved by a powerful mixture of compassion and old-fashioned chivalry, so much so that he undertook militant actions himself and was subjected to forcible feeding as a result. None of this endeared him to his party leader, Ramsay MacDonald, who dismissed militancy as 'tomfoolery'. But the Pankhursts took advantage of Lansbury's good nature by encouraging him to maintain his criticism of his own

1. Emmeline Pankhurst, 1896.

2. Richard Marsden Pankhurst, 1879.
3. Emmeline Pankhurst with Harry, 1900.

4. Christabel, Adela and Sylvia Pankhurst, 1890.

5. Annie Kenney, 1908.

AY LENA CONNELL
S JOHNS WOOD NW

6. Sylvia Pankhurst in an Arts
and Crafts Movement Frock,
1910.
7. Adela Pankhurst, 1908.

8. Emmeline with Vera Holme on tour in Scotland, 1909.

9. Adela with Annie Kenney in the Suffragette Field, Batheaston, 1909–1912.

overleaf 11. Emmeline with Nurse Pine after a hunger strike, 1913.

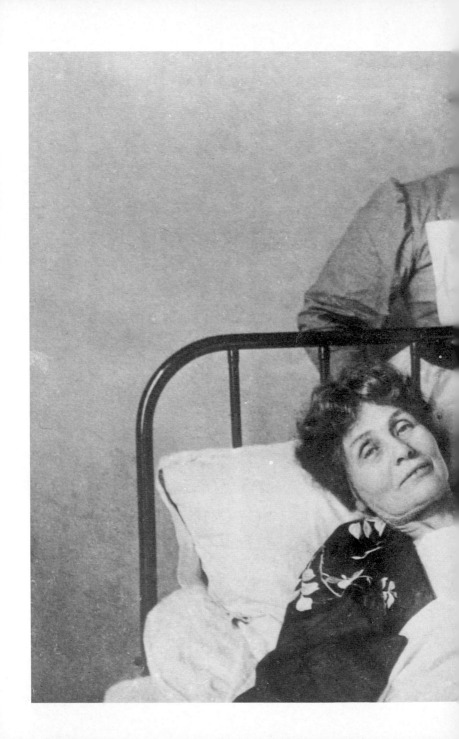

11. A young woman on a bus reading a copy of the newsheet *The Suffragette*.
10. A postcard of a Suffragette commanding her husband, 1913.

13. Suffragettes starting on a tour of London from the WSPU, May 1913.
14. The riot as Emmeline attempted to enter Buckingham Palace to petition the King on suffrage, 1914.

overleaf 15. Christabel at the East Islington election, 20 October 1917.

16. Emmeline with her four adopted girls, 1919.
17. Sylvia with Richard, c.1929.

18. Christabel, Sylvia and Ada Goulden Bach at Emmeline's funeral, Brompton Cemetry, 1928.

19. Sylvia leading her fellow activists outside the House of Commons protesting against proposals to return Eritrea and Somaliland to the Italians, 27 April 1948.
20. Adela Pankhurst-Walsh making a speech from a platform, January 1950.

party leadership. This culminated on 11 November, when he dramatically announced his intention of resigning his seat to fight a by-election
in order to win a specific mandate from his constituents for women's
enfranchisement.

The WSPU leaders contemplated the Bow and Bromley by-election
with undisguised optimism for it seemed likely to kill several birds with
one stone.[46] Since Lansbury's re-election was confidently anticipated, it
would demonstrate to the Government that ordinary men really did
favour votes for women. It would discredit the Labour Party by exposing its timidity. And it would help to regain the initiative from the
NUWSS, especially as its new pact had no victories to show so far.
However, the campaign turned into a total fiasco. The absence of both
Christabel and the Pethick-Lawrences may have hampered the Union's
efforts, and Christabel mistakenly placed the loyal but unsuitable
Grace Roe in charge of the campaign. The situation in Bow and
Bromley bristled with difficulties because the suffragettes were foisting
themselves and their agenda on to a constituency which already had a
Labour organization whose members regarded the contest as, at best,
an unnecessary burden and, at worst, an indulgence for the benefit of
the Pankhursts. Nor did the well-to-do ladies who descended upon the
poverty-stricken East End constituency mesh easily with Lansbury's
existing supporters. The suffragettes simply refused to accept the
Socialism in their candidate's programme. They invited the voters to
ignore Lansbury's Socialism and endorse his feminism.[47] They might
have got away with this had it not been for two other fatal flaws.
In 1910 Lansbury had won his seat in a straight contest with the
Conservatives, which meant that his majority had been achieved with
the votes of Liberals. Although he needed their votes just as much in
1912, the militants stuck obtusely to their usual by-election line by
casting aspersions on the Liberal Government and inviting the voters
to see Lansbury's return as a defeat for Asquith. Inevitably this was
hopelessly counter-productive. Unfortunately for them the Conservative, Reginald Blair, was an unequivocal opponent of women's suffrage
and had no hesitation about saying so. For many working-class men,
the temptation to cut the Pankhursts down to size by voting for him
proved irresistible. As a result Lansbury was comfortably defeated.

It was a measure of Christabel's growing unrealism that she showed herself wholly unwilling to face up to the implications of the setback at Bow and Bromley. Years later she almost eliminated it from her memoirs. From Paris she wrote: 'A great mass of men are still so corrupted and led astray by party politics that to depend simply on the help of the electors to secure the enfranchisement of women is a grave and fatal mistake.'[48] Yet the by-election blew a gaping hole in Pankhurst propaganda by demonstrating that men had not been converted after all. While it had been easy to claim any swing against the Government as proof of pro-suffragism, Lansbury had found, just as other suffragist candidates before him, that it was extremely difficult to win a positive endorsement for female enfranchisement. While some of the non-militants privately accepted this – hence their refusal to put the issue to the test of a referendum – Christabel and Emmeline reacted to the defeat by sweeping public opinion aside. On 28 November they initiated a new assault, this time on pillar boxes, which lasted for five days. This involved not only setting fire to letters by dropping burning objects into the boxes, but also dispatching parcels containing inflammable chemicals which sometimes burst into flames when handled by Post Office staff. A London University scientist with feminist sympathies supplied incendiary materials for this purpose.[49] This represented a dangerous extension of militancy in that members of the public rather than politicians were now being targeted. But the Union adopted an attitude of total defiance. 'What do we care whether we have public opinion with us or not?' asked Annie Kenney. Flora Drummond pronounced letter-box attacks the most effective form of pressure, and Mrs Lamartine Yates reminded members that the approach of Christmas made it an especially appropriate time for them.[50] Each week The Suffragette carried reports and photographs of the damage done and Christabel commented editorially: 'Women will never get the vote except by creating an intolerable situation for all the selfish and apathetic people who stand in their way.'[51]

However, in the aftermath of Bow and Bromley things began to fall apart for the Union. The fiasco finally forced Sylvia to face up to the impossibility of her position in an organization with which she disagreed. In retrospect she claimed to be opposed to the policy of arson as unnecessary and as mistaken in as much as it was making the cause unpopular; instead she advocated the creation of a mass movement for women's suffrage. Yet she admitted 'though I deplored the new policy, I uttered no repudiation. To stop it was impossible; to attack it would but have caused another fissure in the movement.'[52] In fact, even before the by-election she had already begun to edge towards independence by organizing a branch of the Union in Bow. Christabel could not easily prevent this and in any case it had the advantage of keeping Sylvia out of the way. But whereas Emmeline and Christabel dropped the East End once the by-election was over, Sylvia used it to resurrect the original basis of the WSPU. She and Lansbury began to co-operate by promoting universal suffrage for women *and* men. By sharing platforms with Lansbury Sylvia also flouted Christabel's prohibition on appearing with men. She began to publish articles in Lansbury's newspaper, *The Herald*, and his wife, son, Willie, and daughter, Daisy, joined her local branch. In view of Lansbury's prominence both in the East End and nationally, this activity could not be ignored indefinitely by the leaders of the Union.

Autumn brought other signs of strain within the organization when Mabel Tuke suffered a nervous breakdown. In a florid but rather patronizing letter from Paris, Christabel encouraged her to take a rest: 'Even we who are really strong have been a bit under the weather at times and you are not strong.'[53] She must have been feeling lonely for she advised: 'A little course of Paris will do you a great deal of good.' Meanwhile Emmeline was finding her role as treasurer a burden. Concerned that some contributors had been alienated, she composed a series of begging letters: 'I wish you could secure the co-operation of more monied men,' she told Henry Harben. 'I hear privately that there is still a deficit on the Bow and Bromley election.'[54] After this she thankfully took the Channel ferry to spend Christmas in Paris with Christabel.

In January 1913, just when things were looking bad for the WSPU, the politicians offered a new lifeline to the campaign. The Government's Franchise Bill, which had received a second reading in July, was now due to go into committee stage where the pro-suffragists intended to incorporate a clause to extend the vote to wives. But on 23 January the Speaker, James Lowther, ruled that as the original Bill dealt strictly with the registration of voters rather than with franchise qualifications, amendments designed to create a new franchise would alter its nature and thus be out of order. This came as a shock to all concerned and led to the withdrawal of the Bill. Although Christabel claimed this had been a deliberate ploy to wreck women's chances once again, the cabinet papers make it clear that ministers had not expected this procedural hiccough; the anti-suffragists had simply counted on getting all the women's amendments defeated on a vote.[55] Indeed, the fiasco severely discredited Asquith in the eyes of many Liberals who felt he had allowed his obsessive opposition to votes for women to damage the party and the Government.

Whether intentional or not, the loss of the Bill played into Christabel's hands for it embarrassed the constitutionalists, and enabled her to say she had been proved right once again in her view that there was no alternative to continued militancy. Consequently the New Year witnessed a full-scale resumption of arson attacks. On 30 January a package containing sulphuric acid and addressed to Lloyd George burst into flames when opened. At York, letters addressed to the prime minister containing two tubes of liquid ignited on exposure to the air. A postman emptying a letter-box in St Marylebone found his bag on fire due to the phosphorus deposited in one of the envelopes.[56] Five days later Emmeline, speaking at the London Pavilion in Piccadilly Circus, claimed: 'I think we have every reason to be gratified at the progress of the war up-to-date. When you put an army in the field, you want to do as much damage to the enemy as you can, and sustain as little yourself . . . I congratulate our soldiers who have undertaken that particular campaign of destroying golf links.'[57] This relentless use of military terminology exemplified the mood that had settled over the suffragette camp by this time. In effect, the campaign had turned into a series of exploits by small bands of women aiming to strike swiftly at a target and withdraw before the police arrived. They increasingly resorted to disguises and safe houses to evade detection. In many ways the militants now resembled a guerrilla army operating in hostile territory. They hit the headlines on 19 February by exploding a bomb at a house which was being built for Lloyd George at Walton-on-the-Hill in Surrey. In her diary Mary Blathwayt noted matter-of-factly that 'it was not his as he had not quite bought it'. Initial reports of the incident in the suffrage press gave no indication as to who was responsible, though one of the women later wrote to Lloyd George to explain that it had been carefully planned to avoid danger to the workmen.[58] However, at a public meeting in Cardiff Emmeline positively crowed over the episode: 'We have blown up the Chancellor's house!'[59] As a result of her determination to claim personal responsibility, even though she had not been directly involved, she was arrested and brought before Epsom Police Court on 24 February. The trial was set for June. Meanwhile the magistrates offered bail conditional upon her agreement to be law-abiding, but she refused. Back in Holloway Emmeline adopted a 24-hour hunger strike. Sylvia, who had been arrested on a march in the Bow Road, was already there and entering her fifth week of forcible feeding. In a letter smuggled out of prison she described the daily trauma to which she was subjected. In order to use the stomach tube the warders forced her mouth open with a steel gag which left her guns bleeding. Afterwards she invariably vomited much of the liquid. Fortunately, in view of Emmeline's age the doctors advised against forcible feeding: 'Probably unsatisfactory and inexpedient. Not inconsiderable risk in performing the operation owing to condition of heart.'[60] As a result she was promptly released after her brief fast, and her trial was brought forward to April. As Sylvia had been kept isolated from the other prisoners she remained unaware that her mother had joined her in Holloway, and when Sylvia was released shortly afterwards Emmeline was shocked to see her bloodshot eyes and emaciated body; for several days she and Keir Hardie sat at her bedside while she recovered.

Several months previously the police and Home Office officials had reached the conclusion that, although Emmeline had been repeatedly guilty of incitement to commit crimes, it was becoming useless to prosecute her as they could not punish her properly.[61] In fact, since July 1912 dozens of suffragettes had been released before completing their sentences after undertaking hunger strikes, in the process making a mockery of the police and the Government. Matters had come to a head in January when the cabinet discussed the likely reactions of the suffragettes to the controversy over its Franchise Bill. 'Mr McKenna pointed out that in the not improbable event of the rejection of the women amendments, we must be prepared for a recrudescence of what is called "militancy", and after some discussion, it was agreed that it might be necessary early next session to ask Parliament to give the

Home Secretary "in and out" powers in regard to this class of prisoner.'[62] This was the origin of the notorious Prisoners (Temporary Discharge for Ill-Health) Act, or, as it was better known, 'The Cat and Mouse Act'. Since the first three months of 1913 witnessed a succession of attacks on buildings, golf courses, railway trains and the orchid house at Kew Gardens, ministers felt obliged to press ahead with the measure. Introduced on 25 March, it received the royal assent on 25 April. The Act had the advantage of enabling the authorities to resort much less frequently to the forcible feeding that had attracted so much opprobrium. Instead it allowed the authorities to release prisoners who were judged to be seriously weakened by hunger strikes with a special notice or licence which specified the date on which they must return to continue serving their sentence, usually one week later. Offenders were also required to notify the police of their residence after being discharged and not to change it without giving notice in writing. Nor were they to be absent from their residence for more than twelve hours without giving notice. Failure to comply with any of the terms rendered them liable to immediate arrest. This was the trap set for Emmeline as she prepared for her trial at the Old Bailey on 3 April.

12

Prisoner of War (1913–14)

'We are fighting for a time when every little girl born into the world will have an equal chance with her brothers.'
Emmeline Pankhurst, *The Suffragette*, 27 February 1914

On 3 April Emmeline stood trial at the Old Bailey for the explosion at Lloyd George's House. Though not directly involved in the attack she had deliberately claimed responsibility for it; she therefore offered no evidence at the trial and contented herself with making a political speech which was clearly designed to raise the stakes:

I come to stand my trial from the bedside of one of my daughters who has come out of Holloway Prison, sent there for two months' hard labour for participating with four other people in breaking a small pane of glass . . . She is so weak that she cannot get out of her bed. And I say to you, gentlemen, that this is the kind of punishment you are inflicting upon me or on any other woman who may be brought before you. I ask if you are prepared to send an incalculable number of women to prison . . . From the moment I leave this court I shall quite deliberately refuse to eat food . . . I shall come out of prison dead or alive, at the earliest possible moment; and once out again, as soon as I am physically fit I shall enter into this fight again. Life is very dear to us all. I am not seeking, as was said by the Home Secretary, to commit suicide. I want to see the women of this country enfranchised, and I want to live until that is done.

On emphatic instructions from the judge the jury found her guilty, though they made a 'strong recommendation to mercy'. In spite of this

Emmeline was sentenced to three years' penal servitude. 'I have no sense of guilt,' she told the judge. 'I look on myself as a prisoner of war.'[1] As she disappeared once more into the depths of Holloway, suffragettes set up a vigil at the gates; and the following week brought a fresh spate of attacks on private houses, racecourses and railway stations in protest at her punishment.

As the stiff sentence indicated, the stakes had been raised by both sides. Emmeline immediately put herself on a hunger strike, though she took water, and evidently contemplated that the outcome might be her death. A letter to this effect was left with a friendly matron for delivery to Ethel Smyth.[2] For his part the Home Secretary had already considered the political consequences of such a tragedy: 'If Mrs Pankhurst starves herself, the Secretary of State wishes her to be kept constantly supplied with suitable and appetising food.' The Governor of Holloway duly kept a detailed menu.[3] For breakfast each day she was offered 'thin bread and butter, boiled egg, freshmade tea'; the mid-day dinner included filleted plaice, beefsteak, roast chicken and chops; supper comprised buttered toast, bread and tea and, at 7.00 each evening a pint of Bovril was offered. Needless to say, this was vastly superior to the food consumed by the regular inmates of Holloway.

Though Emmeline refused to submit to a medical examination, the prison doctors wrote daily reports on her condition. They described her as 'not robust physically and of a highly strung emotional temperament'. By 10 April her pulse had reached 100 and the first signs of malnutrition were detected. She permitted an examination by Dr Smalley, who reported her as staggering about the cell, having cold hands and pain in the chest, and being very emotional.[4] 'You will smile to hear that during sleepless nights I sang "The March" and "Laggard Dawn" in such a queer cracked voice', Emmeline wrote to Ethel, 'and now that the end is perhaps near I want you to know how happy I am, lifted above these dismal surroundings and feel certain that if I am to die good will come of my going.'[5] On the eleventh, when Dr Craig saw her, he advised that forcible feeding would be ineffective because she had passed too many days without food already. As a result, they released her the next day, put her in a cab and gave her a licence which she promptly tore in half but retained. In issuing a licence for

Emmeline's return the Home Secretary was, in effect, anticipating the enactment of the Prisoners' Temporary Discharge Bill which was still making its way through Parliament. The prison Governor had telephoned Special Branch immediately to let them know of her release.

On being discharged Emmeline went straight to Nurse Pine at Number 3 Pembridge Gardens, where detectives kept watch. Ethel noted: 'She was heart-rending to look at, her skin yellow and so tightly drawn over her face that you wondered the bone structure did not come through; her eyes deep sunken and burning, and a deep dark flush on her cheeks.' She was also dismayed to detect one other symptom: 'The strange, pervasive sweetish odour of corruption that hangs about a room in which a hunger striker is being nursed back to health is unlike any other smell.'[6] According to her licence Emmeline was due to return to Holloway by 4.00 p.m. on 28 April. But on the twenty-second Dr Flora Murray reported to Scotland Yard that it had become necessary to transfer her from the nursing home to the home of Hertha Ayrton at Number 41 Norfolk Square. This was agreed. She travelled by ambulance after dark to avoid the crowds and was carried upstairs to her room. 'I knew nothing about her coming here', wrote Ayrton, 'She was worrying over the harm she was doing the nursing home, through detectives being about and all the excitement of it.'[7] At Norfolk Square Emmeline lay in bed with a white silk handkerchief over her head; whenever she sat up the nurse made her lie down again. But she was reportedly in good spirits and game to return to prison, though too ill to do so yet. When Detective Inspector Hestor and Dr Smalley called with a warrant for her arrest on the expiry of the licence they were at first refused entrance – Ayrton had a chain on the door. Eventually she allowed them in but did not permit them to examine Emmeline. Smalley described her as still very thin and pale, trembling, and on the edge of tears. He concluded that it would be too risky to remove her to Holloway so soon and the two men departed to a chorus of abusive remarks from the crowd at the gate.[8] However, on 5 May Emmeline wrote to Ethel: 'Today I had a glass of champagne and fish ... I'm a different being already ... I begin to realize the glorious fight ahead of me when the fifteen days are over.'[9] Meanwhile, two detectives stood guard at the front of the house, and two at the back, while another was stationed on the roof of an empty house nearby and a taxi waited to give chase should she attempt to escape. It was three weeks later when Emmeline managed to slip away up a side street into a waiting motor car with Catherine Pine. Whether this was a serious attempt to escape or just a gesture of defiance is not clear. Emmeline drove to Ethel Smyth's home near Woking, closely followed by detectives. From the bedroom the two women watched as two plainclothes men squatted beneath a large gorse bush in the pouring rain. Smyth, who claimed that the police secretly adored Emmeline, wanted to lend them an umbrella; but Emmeline would not hear of it: 'Nothing of the sort. Don't make things pleasant for them!'[10] After a while they sent for the WSPU's car, driven by Flora Murray, who took them to Woking police station where she was transferred to a police vehicle and returned to Holloway.

Back in prison on 26 May, Emmeline was reported to be in a fairly good state of health though excitable and irritable. But as she was now nearly fifty-five – though the authorities put her age at fifty-three – her condition deteriorated rapidly from the repeated hunger strikes. The warders carried her into the prison hospital in order to make observation easier. By the twenty-ninth her pulse had risen, she had lost nine pounds and was clearly showing signs of malnutrition. Consequently, the Home Secretary discharged her the next day with a requirement to return to continue the sentence under the Cat and Mouse Act on 7 June.[11] She took some brandy and soda and Brand's Essence before leaving for Number 51 Westminster Mansions in Little Smith Street. There Sylvia found her looking haggard but livelier than expected. Only three days later she wrote a cheerful note to Henry Harben: 'You will be glad to know that I am not too ill and am quite ready for the next move on the part of the Government. Although physically weak I know I can face the ordeal if they decide to take me back to prison next Monday. I shall not ask for any extension of the licence.'[12] In the event she decided not to return on the appointed day. A taxi full of flowers arrived at the flat and Olive Bartels, one of Emmeline's bodyguards, came down with a lady dressed to resemble her. They were promptly seized by detectives, thus allowing Emmeline to slip away for an extra week's freedom.[13] She was eventually re-arrested on 14 June on her way to attend the funeral of Emily Wilding Davison.

A striking figure, tall and slender, with red hair and green eyes,

Emily Davison possessed a first-class degree and had worked as a governess and teacher. But, after 1906, her association with the WSPU had made regular employment impossible. She undertook seven hunger strikes and was forcibly fed forty-nine times. Yet she was never employed by the Union, whose leaders regarded her as too much of a freelance – justifiably, for she was reportedly the first suffragette to set fire to a pillar box in December 1911. Although Emily Davison had written her will as long ago as 1909, there is no real indication that she intended to commit suicide. What is true is that she repeatedly made dramatic challenges to authority designed to draw attention to the treatment of women in prison. On one occasion she had used her plank bed to barricade the door of her cell and was subjected to a drenching from a hose pipe through the window for fifteen minutes. In 1911 while in Holloway she twice threw herself over the railings on a landing and was caught by wire netting designed to prevent suicides. Though it is impossible to be certain about Emily Davison's intentions, for lack of evidence, it seems most probable that she envisaged her fatal excursion to the Epsom races on 4 June 1913 as a similar exploit.[14] By that time many suffragettes had begun to fear that Emmeline herself was close to death. 'Before us stretch the long, intolerable weeks during which they are going to murder Mrs Pankhurst', wrote Rebecca West.[15] Davison's action may well have been designed to prevent this greater tragedy by putting extra pressure on the politicians.

With whatever motive, Emily Wilding Davison arrived at Epsom for the Derby Day races, rushed on to the course at Tattenham Corner and attempted to grab the bridle of 'Anmer' which, by chance, was the King's horse. She fell and was kicked by several other horses. Photographs taken immediately afterwards show her lying on the grass surrounded by policemen who were trying to staunch the loss of blood with newspapers, but to no avail. Since the leaders of the WSPU were all out of action for one reason or another, Grace Roe was deputed to organize Emily Davison's funeral procession through London. She chose a close friend of the dead woman, Charlotte Marsh, to act as standard bearer carrying a large cross at the head of the marchers, a symbol which seems to have deterred rowdy behaviour by the young men in the huge crowds which lined the route.[16] With considerable difficulty Miss Roe also found a church willing to conduct the service

– St George's, in what is now New Oxford Street. From there the coffin was taken to King's Cross station *en route* to Morpeth in Northumberland for burial in the family grave.

Though Davison's death could not be blamed directly on the Government, it forced the treatment of suffragettes under the Cat and Mouse Act into the forefront of public debate. At this time WSPU propaganda skilfully exploited public concern by distributing leaflets which referred to Emmeline in the past tense. As she was not seen in public for some weeks the idea that she had died or was at death's door gained wide currency. Her arrest on 14 June as she was about to enter a carriage taking her to the funeral was also publicized in order to draw attention to the heartlessness of the authorities. Even so, reactions appear to have been mixed. The Labour MP Philip Snowden claimed that most people were unmoved by Emmeline's treatment under the Cat and Mouse Act: 'She is punishing herself because she will not take the punishment which a court of law has imposed upon her for outrages which no community can allow anyone to per-petrate.'[17] Dismissing such views, the leaders of the Union argued that the Government was steadily alienating public opinion by making martyrs of the suffragettes.

Meanwhile the system ground its way through another weary cycle. After her recapture on 14 June Emmeline, who was reportedly bad tempered and excited, was discharged on 16 June under licence to return on the twenty-third of the month. This time she recuperated at Ethel Smyth's home, but broke the terms of her licence by appearing at the weekly 'At Home' held by the Union at the London Pavilion on 21 June. According to a medical report she was not in a critical condition but 'her highly emotional temperament makes her exagger-ate her symptoms'.[18] Nevertheless, as she refused to be weighed the prison staff remained uncertain how rapidly her condition was deter-iorating, and took the precaution of releasing her again on the twenty-fourth. Subsequently Emmeline kept a low profile until 14 July when she and Annie Kenney managed to slip into the 'At Home' at the London Pavilion. Annie, who was also out under a time-expired licence, was seized on leaving the meeting, but in the confusion Emme-line evaded the police. She took refuge with Hertha Ayrton and again surfaced at the London Pavilion on the twenty-first, only to be arrested before reaching the platform. She resisted so vigorously that the police carried her bodily into Holloway. In order to exhaust herself as rapidly as possible Emmeline undertook a food-and-water strike and walked around her cell throughout the night. On 23 July she smashed the utensils in the cell and, according to the report, was in an hysterical condition.[19] Next day they discharged her until 31 July.

Contrary to the claims made by some historians that the Cat and Mouse Act did not work, it seems indisputable that during its first four months the new system had succeeded in allowing the authorities to avoid subjecting Emmeline to forcible feeding while repeatedly recapturing her in order to force her to continue serving her sentence. But at her age she could hardly bear the strain much longer, and she wisely took advantage of the Home Secretary's ruling that he could not prevent suffragettes from going abroad in order to win herself a vital breathing space.[20] To this end Emmeline took the boat to France at the beginning of August, where she remained until early October when she embarked on her third American tour; altogether this gave her over four months out of the clutches of the Cat and Mouse Act.

During the summer Christabel had been staying with Mrs Belmont in her luxurious villa, Les Abeilles, near Deauville. It was at the adjacent resort of Trouville that Emmeline, Christabel and Annie were photographed by the *Daily Sketch* chatting happily in the casino gardens. Though gaunt and haggard on arrival, Emmeline soon recovered her spirits. 'One would imagine that she had never seen the inside of an English prison', commented the reporter. The *Sketch*, which appears to have been favoured by the Pankhursts, printed its usual glowing report on the leader-in-exile: 'Christabel looked as she always does, charming. She had quite a French look about her in her pink frock with a dainty hat to match and a pretty red jacket . . . All three appeared to be in perfect physical health.'[21] It is worth remembering that it suited WSPU propaganda to paint this rosy picture of their leaders as proof to its supporters that, despite the worst the Government and its machinery of repression could do to them, they were sustained by a greater power. Many years later Grace Roe spoke of an external force guiding the movement: 'We were all overshadowed', as she put it.[22] This mystical belief inevitably grew stronger as the struggle grew more desperate during the last year before the outbreak of war.

Meanwhile Emmeline told the reporters that they were enjoying a holiday at Trouville, but, in case this appeared too frivolous, she added that they were having a council of war and had the next plot already mapped out. In view of the deteriorating fortunes of the organization at home, this was the least she could say.

However, neither these periodical visits, nor the regular weekend excursions by Annie Kenney and Grace Roe, could entirely fill Christabel's long days in exile. Emmeline seems to have noticed that something was missing, for she presented her with a Pomeranian dog: 'It keeps one human to have the care of a little helpless creature', she wrote.[23] Christabel called the dog 'Fay' and allowed it to sleep on her bed, much to the disgust of Ethel Smyth. But in her need for company Christabel inevitably became drawn into the circle of artistic sophisticates around the Princesse de Polignac that included Marcel Proust, Claude Debussy, Erik Satie and Igor Stravinsky, as well as a number of active lesbians for whom Christabel must have been an appealing figure. However, it was not the sexual orientation of such people but the political implications of their society that really mattered. Though fashionably feminist, these women regarded votes for women as faintly eccentric and were content to drift along in a comfortable world far removed from the struggles of the women's movement. As long as she contented herself with their company Christabel was unlikely to benefit from the intellectual stimulus that Paris offered to a political exile. To judge from her articles in *The Suffragette*, she became even more obsessed with attacking Socialism and the Labour Party during this phase, which, in view of the rapprochement now taking place between the women's movement and the Labour Movement, only deepened her isolation and complicated her eventual return to British domestic politics. Visitors who attempted to puncture her comfortable cocoon by giving her a candid picture of developments at home got short shrift. Mary Leigh, for example, called at her apartment in the Avenue de la Grande Armée to be met by an exquisitely dressed Christabel carrying the dog under her arm: 'She treated me like some crazy stranger. I didn't stay long and I didn't get anywhere.'[24]

Though Christabel refused to recognize it, the Union's organization fell into a steady decline during 1913 and 1914, partly as a result of deliberate suppression by the Home Secretary, but also due to the repeated changes in personnel and lack of leadership. It became increasingly difficult to hold public meetings both because halls were barred to the suffragettes and because the crowds broke up the gatherings. Emmeline's prolonged absence in prison or abroad only exacerbated matters, while Christabel's efforts to instil purpose into the organization by means of her weekly editorials from Paris were often counter-productive because she had become so autocratic. Even in the early suffragette campaign the leaders had been high-handed in appointing and removing personnel, but under the pressure of her isolation Christabel began to interpret any failings as symptomatic of disloyalty. In July she reprimanded Mary Phillips, an experienced organizer who had undergone forcible feeding, thus: 'Apparently not much progress is being made in your district, but you seem to think that is inevitable ... If local people will provide neither money nor work it is impossible for Headquarters to supply them with an organizer.'[25] Like other organizers, Mary Phillips suffered from the members' reluctance to fund arson and other attacks on property, and a long-standing feeling that too much of the Union's resources was concentrated on London and a handful of leaders. Christabel, however, chose to blame individuals rather than seek the cause, and Miss Phillips found herself peremptorily dismissed with four weeks' salary in lieu of notice. In any case, the obsession with fund-raising seems excessive, for, despite losing some of its backers, the Union actually increased its income to a record £46,000 in the year to February 1914. Admittedly some of this had to be diverted to maintain Christabel in Paris. Not everyone considered this a good investment, but she and Emmeline increasingly looked upon the Union's money as their own.

Any doubts Christabel may have suffered about the soundness of her decision to remain in Paris were allayed by the determination shown by Reginald McKenna to drive the WSPU out of business. The raid in March 1913 proved to be merely the first of a succession of swoops by the police designed to produce evidence of criminal intent on the part of the Union's leaders. Following the abandonment of Clement's Inn the Union shifted its headquarters to Lincoln's Inn House in Kingsway which was also subject to raids and the arrest of the office staff. McKenna also signed warrants to allow the GPO to withhold mail pending examination by the police, and tried to have the telephones cut off.[26] He evidently suffered some qualms as he had consultations as to the legality of police action with the Attorney-General who advised that while they could enter premises and examine documents, it was doubtful whether they had grounds for remaining in possession once this had been accomplished. The Home Secretary, however, preferred to take the risk of remaining in occupation for as long as possible.[27] Meanwhile the Union repeatedly moved its head-quarters to premises in Tothill Street, to Croydon, to the Brackenburys at Campden Hill Square and to Pattie Hall's flat in Maida Vale, where a raid on 22 May 1914 produced a haul of half a hundredweight of pebbles, three hammers and a chopper. Meanwhile a less spectacular but more deadly scheme was in hand to prosecute all the leading benefactors of the Union in order to seek compensation for specific actions such as the slashing of the Rokeby Venus in the National Gallery. By July 1914 the Treasury solicitors had accumulated a mass-ive file of evidence on forty-six individuals against whom proceedings were about to be taken in the name of the Trustees of the National Gallery when war broke out.[28]

McKenna's immediate preoccupation seems to have been with the suppression of *The Suffragette*, no doubt because, in the absence of an effective leadership, it had become the main means of keeping the organization together. In their raid in April 1913 the police had seized a good deal of copy for the paper, and they subsequently extracted undertakings from the printers not to accept material which included incitement to arson. Sydney Granville, the manager of the Victoria Printing House, which handled *The Suffragette*, was prosecuted for failing to abide by this.[29] As a result Christabel sent her agents in a desperate search for alternative printers. The National Labour Press in Manchester accepted the job until Christabel insisted on taking the business away. Marie Lawson received instructions from Christabel to use a small printer in a Whitechapel basement; Lawson obtained his payment from a lady carrying a flower who met her in Sloane Square and handed over a cheque on hearing a password. Finally, Ida Wylie and Rachel Barrett received fresh orders to journey to Edinburgh where they found a printer ready to take on the paper from May 1914 until the war broke out.[30] Meanwhile McKenna calculated that legal proceedings against the printers might lead the editor to produce the paper abroad, probably in Holland. A Special Branch Officer was therefore instructed to make enquiries in Rotterdam, and customs officials were authorized to intercept copies of The Suffragette at Harwich, Hull, Folkestone and other east coast ports. Specimen copies were to be dispatched to Sir Edward Henry at Scotland Yard pending a decision on whether to detain the whole consignment.[31] It transpired subsequently that the Home Secretary lacked the powers to do this, but the parcels were none the less opened and names and addresses of the distributors recorded.

In the face of such sustained efforts at suppression it was a triumph for Christabel's allies to have kept The Suffragette in print each week. It offered a vital means of maintaining morale by presenting the militant campaign as a succession of dramas and moral victories for members whose information was otherwise limited to the reports in an increasingly hostile national press. The paper required a minimal staff since Christabel generated editorials and comment, while the daily newspapers could be culled for a regular two-page summary of the latest suffragette outrages. However, the strenuous efforts made throughout 1913 and 1914 to boost circulation indicate the underlying weakness of the paper. Initially they had printed 30,000 copies but actually sold only 17,000; but by January 1913 circulation had fallen to 10,000 of which only 7,500 were genuine sales.[32] Although the journal made sweeping claims about increased circulation it never published figures, which almost certainly indicates a serious decline.

Since the demise of The Suffragette would undoubtedly have destroyed what claims Christabel still had to be in control of the movement, she devoted much of her time and thought to boosting its appeal. From April 1913 onwards she varied her subject matter by a series of articles dealing with the question of male sexual violence, in particular 'White Slavery' and the role of the government in maintaining the trade; like many feminists before her, she argued that effective protection for women against male behaviour would be one of the consequences to follow from female enfranchisement. During August and September this became a regular subject for Christabel's articles. In particular she warned about the prevalence of venereal diseases such as gonorrhoea which, she suggested, was acquired before marriage by 70 or 80 per cent of men, who subsequently infected their wives, some of whom became sterile as a result: 'Never again must young women enter into marriage blindfolded. From now onwards they must be warned of the fact that marriage is intensely dangerous.' In short, marriage was better avoided 'until such time as men's moral standards are completely changed and they become as chaste and clean living as women'. The articles were subsequently published as a short book entitled *The Great Scourge – And How To End It*.[33]

Christabel's campaign has attracted a good deal of disparaging comment over the years. Yet, if she exaggerated the extent of venereal disease, she undoubtedly highlighted what was widely recognized as a major social problem. Under pressure from doctors the Asquith Government had recently appointed a royal commission to enquire into the whole subject. On the other hand, some contemporaries regarded *The Great Scourge* as a distraction from women's suffrage. Rebecca West, for example, dismissed Christabel's views as 'utterly valueless and likely to discredit the Cause in which we believe'.[34] Dora Marsden, editor of *The Freewoman*, also criticized her negative attitude. It seems likely that some of the older and unmarried suffragists, whose contributions boosted the Union's funds substantially in 1913–14, approved of Christabel's propaganda, while some of the younger women, who were less hostile towards men, felt uncomfortable about the issue. In the long run this may have damaged the Pankhursts' reputation by making them appear old-fashioned to a post-war generation that looked eagerly towards marriage and heterosexual relationships. But in 1913 Christabel spoke convincingly to a generation that had campaigned for decades for an equal moral standard for men and women. Even such constitutional organizations as the Women's Liberal Federation refused to support Liberal candidates if they were not sound on the moral issue as well as on the Parliamentary vote.

There was thus nothing particularly novel or unduly radical in the argument in *The Great Scourge*. What requires explanation is why Christabel and Emmeline chose to highlight the issue in 1913. It certainly offered one means of hitting back at the political system that was persecuting them. At the Old Bailey in April, Emmeline had drawn attention to the way many eminent legal and political figures resorted to prostitutes, much to the irritation of the judge. In July she claimed that the object of police raids on the WSPU had been the seizure of material which exposed the involvement of prominent politicians in the case of 'Queenie Gerald', a notorious brothel-keeper. According to Christabel, the women in another current scandal, the 'Piccadilly Flat Case', had been kept out of court so as to protect politicians connected with the procuring of young girls. But Christabel's calculations had as much to do with the need to raise the profile of *The Suffragette*, which suffered from the competition of the better-established *Votes for Women*. In any case, now that she had disappeared from the public platform, she badly needed some means of keeping her name in the headlines. Sexual scandal offered a welcome variation from the usual diet of suffragist articles and anti-Labour tirades, and could not easily be ignored by the press. *The Great Scourge* therefore offered a way of stamping her authority on a movement in which she was beginning to become marginalized.

Christabel's absorption with moral issues in 1913 also led her to launch attacks on the Church of England which, she claimed, had degraded itself by becoming 'the lackey and hanger-on of the Government'. This was a little unfair as a Church League for Women's Suffrage had been formed with the backing of at least eight bishops and scores of clergymen who petitioned the prime minister to abandon forcible feeding. However, many clergymen resisted suffragette demands for prayers to be said for Emmeline and refused to admit suffragettes to holy communion if they remained impenitent about violent tactics. As a result, some were heckled by their own congregations. The interesting aspect of this dispute is the way it led Christabel to adopt the language of Christianity. She took to peppering her articles with texts such as 'Woe unto you, ye hypocrites' and 'Knock and it shall be opened unto you'. In a famous piece entitled 'The Appeal to God' in August 1913, she claimed: 'Women are offering up their life as the price of other women's redemption from misery and degradation . . . Worldly justice is not as yet given to women, but Divine justice is theirs, and if the recognized ministers of religion will not ask for it for them, the women will ask for it themselves. The appeal they make is from man to God.'[35] Evidently Christabel spent some of her time in Paris studying the Bible, a new development for her that was to make its impact after the war when she adopted Adventism.

Christabel's fears about losing control of the movement explain why she felt increasingly reluctant to tolerate the activities of her sister in London's East End. After Lansbury's defeat in November 1912 the Pankhursts had abandoned the area, leaving Sylvia to develop what she called the East London Federation of the WSPU, effectively an autonomous organization under the aegis of its parent body. It adopted the purple, white and green of the Union but with the addition of red. Though unlike the other members of her family in some ways, Sylvia was just as given to self-promotion, and her description of the East End campaign as a mass movement has to be treated with some scepticism. She faced some daunting obstacles, including a combination of grinding poverty, the lack of trade unions and the shifting immigrant communities which inhibited the establishment of political organizations of all kinds in the East End. Many local people were too absorbed in the daily struggle for survival or simply became cynical about politics. Even the Labour Party emerged much more slowly here than in other working-class communities. But from her headquarters at a shop in the Old Ford Road Sylvia built up a group of eight branches at Bow and Bromley, Poplar, Bethnal Green and Stepney, though the paid membership stood at only sixty. This fragile base was sustained in part by importing a succession of well-to-do treasurers including Lady Sybil Smith, Nora Smythe, whose father had left her some money, the wife of D. A. Thomas, a wealthy South Wales coal owner, and the Honourable Evelina Haverfield. Sylvia saw no irony in her dependence upon capitalists and titled ladies to maintain a Socialist organization. Though she herself attracted hostility initially as a middle-class interloper, she successfully overcame this by her unmistakable sincerity, compassion for the poor, and her readiness to lead from the front when it came to risking prison sentences. In time Sylvia won some devoted supporters from the local working-class community including Annie Barnes. Like many such women, Annie Barnes herself could not afford to get into trouble with the law because she could not spare the time away from her family, but she felt thrilled by Sylvia's campaign: 'I've never known such wonder and excitement in the East End', she recalled years later.[36] In some ways the East End provided Sylvia with the home she had lacked and an alternative family. She became close friends with Nora Smythe and Zellie Emerson, the daughter of a banker from the American Midwest. Two years older than Sylvia, Zellie became a substitute sister for her, sharing her platform, her scrapes with the police and her suffering in prison.

But the East End also gave Sylvia the scope to develop an independent political career that had been denied to her hitherto. Though the East London Federation was small, this made it all the easier for her to dominate its discussions, as the minutes of its meetings show. She also acquired her own platform by launching the *Woman's Dreadnought*, a precarious two-page paper whose libellous copy instilled fear into its unfortunate printers.[37] Though thousands of copies were printed, few were sold, but the paper struggled on until 1924 under a new title, the *Workers' Dreadnought*, from 1917. Throughout the summer of 1913 Sylvia endured a punishing round of arrests, followed by hunger strikes, forcible feeding and release under the Cat and Mouse Act. Though on the face of it an easy target for the police amongst the working women of the East End, she frequently evaded capture by borrowing bonnets and even babies from her collaborators in order to disguise herself.

As Christabel had correctly seen, her campaign was distinguished by the close co-operation with male suffragists which it involved. For example, on 29 June the Men's Federation for Women's Suffrage acquired permission, which had been denied to the women, for a rally in Trafalgar Square. Sylvia marched her contingent from the East End, and addressed the meeting before leading the crowd off to Downing Street to hoot at government ministers. For this she received a summons for disturbing the peace, but she evaded arrest and appeared in disguise at Bromley Public Hall on 7 July. Though surrounded by a bodyguard, she was caught on leaving the meeting, taken to Bow Street and given a three-month sentence. While the warders brought tempting food into her cell she undertook a hunger strike for the next five days until released on a seven-day licence. She then recuperated at the terraced home of a Mr and Mrs Payne in the Old Ford Road where the waiting detectives stood outside enduring the insults of the crowd. This became her home for the rest of 1914. Each day locals called in with gifts of fruit, fresh eggs and flowers, while Flora Murray and a succession of nurses attempted in vain to stop her writing articles and letters from her sickbed. When the licence expired Sylvia disguised herself heavily by applying rouge to her cheeks – a rare thing since she considered cosmetics completely alien to her – and donning a high-collared coat and hat. Thus attired, she made her way to a meeting at Bromley Public Hall for another speech. As Sylvia left, Zellie managed to turn hose pipes on to the waiting detectives, thus enabling her to escape in the ensuing confusion. Later that night Willie Lansbury arrived with a cart laden with sacks of firewood in which Sylvia was concealed. On 27 July when the Men's Federation again organized a Trafalgar Square demonstration attended by 20,000 people, Sylvia was smuggled through the crowd and appeared dramatically on the plinth. Afterwards she jumped down and was surrounded by her bodyguard who escorted her down Whitehall, though they failed to prevent her being arrested and taken to Cannon Row Station. After another five-day hunger strike she was released. However, by September Sylvia accepted the need to recover her health by escaping the attentions of the police for a longer period. She took a boat to Esbjerg and, at the invitation of the Danish Women's Federation, she lectured in Copenhagen, Aarhus and Svendborg; afterwards she travelled to Gothenburg and Oslo for more meetings. This interaction with the wider women's movement marked a contrast with the attitude of Christabel who seems not to have taken advantage of her time in Paris to build connections on the Continent. Like Emmeline, she declined to be diverted from the narrow aim of winning the vote in Britain. By October Sylvia had returned home for a triumphant demonstration in Bromley where she had to be rescued from the clutches of the police by Willie Lansbury and Kosher Hunt, a Jewish ex-prize fighter. But the following night they arrested her at Poplar Town Hall, resulting in another nine-day hunger-and-thirst strike, followed by release on 22 October under licence to return on the twenty-ninth.

During this period Sylvia had followed Emmeline in organizing a bodyguard, though unlike her she had no objection to relying on men. Increasingly influenced by the example of the Irish, Sylvia preferred to describe it as a 'citizens' army'. 'It is no use pretending', she wrote in November 1913, 'we have got to fight. The government is so cowardly that even the appearance of force will make it give way.'[38] Her language underlines how impressed she had been by the way in which the Ulster Volunteer Force had been allowed to arm itself in order to resist the imposition of a Home Rule Parliament on Ireland. How Sylvia reconciled this resort to force with her professed pacifism is unclear. However, she was never particularly bothered about being consistent and took no more than a superficial interest in political ideology, so the question did not greatly trouble her. When challenged she justified her 'People's Army' on the grounds that it was needed to protect working people from the brutality of the police who were simply the servants of the Government. In view of the unpopularity of the police in the East End, this was a perfectly serviceable argument, and the army certainly attracted more recruits than the ELF itself.[39] Of course there was a practical flaw: Sylvia had no notion of how to organize an army. But when she appealed for assistance a former captain in the British Army, Sir Francis Vane, who had already floated the idea of a 'Labour Training Corps', took on the task. From October 1913 onwards the People's Army met each Tuesday to be drilled by Vane and its captain, Nora Smythe. By the winter the initial eighty recruits had risen to seven hundred and Sylvia spoke about marching on Downing Street.[40] However, it is difficult to know how much significance to place on this development. Certainly the newspapers covered the whole scheme in ridicule. The army fought several skirmishes with the police when helping to smuggle Sylvia into meetings after her licence had expired and it guarded her at safe houses where the police were waiting to re-arrest her. There were also several dramatic incidents in December when the Poplar Borough Council had banned the use of its halls by the suffragettes. On one occasion the army marched to a Council meeting but was dispersed by police. In March 1914 it caused pandemonium at another Council meeting by releasing bags of flour and coloured powder in the building.

None of this endeared Sylvia and her movement to the local Labour Representation Committee or the Trades Council, apart from George Lansbury, as she admitted herself. Ironically, Sylvia proved to be no better than Christabel at healing the rift with the mainstream of the Labour Movement. By allying herself with Lansbury she only antagonized the national Party leadership, which was increasingly alarmed by the growth of syndicalism within the trade unions which Lansbury and the Herald League seemed to be promoting. Consequently her efforts to persuade Labour MPs to go further in backing votes for women were firmly rebuffed.[41] Even her relations with Keir Hardie became rather strained at this time, no doubt partly because he strongly favoured the new alliance between Labour and the non-militant suffragists. Sylvia, like Christabel, disparaged this initiative on the grounds that the Liberals could continue to disregard the forty Labour MPs in Parliament. This was true on the assumption that the eighty Irish members remained loyal, which was by no means certain; but in any case it missed the point. Interestingly, Sylvia had more success in her dealings with Lloyd George, who had few inhibitions about negotiating with anyone. In effect, she cast herself as a go-between for him and the women's suffrage movement, a role which he recognized as a necessary one. She urged him to break the deadlock that had been created by the demise of the Government's legislation early in 1913 by championing a bill for adult suffrage, and she took pains to emphasize that she had never favoured the Conciliation Bill of which he had been a severe critic.[42] Their negotiations were beginning to bear fruit in 1914 when the outbreak of war interrupted things. But it is significant that Lloyd George, and even Asquith, regarded Sylvia as someone with whom they could do business; despite her militant activities, they put her in a different category to Christabel, probably because they felt that her working-class connections ought to be treated seriously.

Against this background, it is hardly surprising that by the end of 1913 relations between Sylvia's ELF and the WSPU had deteriorated sharply. The connection only lasted as long as it did because of the prolonged absence of Emmeline and Christabel abroad and in prison. Relations were further exacerbated when Sylvia suggested to Adela, now unhappily adrift from the cause in her role as a student of horticulture, that she should join her in the East End. Nothing could have been more calculated to antagonize Emmeline and Christabel, for it would have meant breaking Adela's promise to abstain from speech-making and set one pair of Pankhursts in competition with another. Christabel, who fervently wished that her sisters would give up the Pankhurst name, commented revealingly on the split in the family when she wrote: 'Sylvia will never be an Amazon. If isn't J[ames] K[eir] H[ardie] it will be someone else.'[43] Adela's later career as a rabble-rouser amongst striking workers suggests that she would have gone down especially well with the working-classes of London's East End. Her involvement threatened to give the ELF an element of charisma which it lacked under Sylvia's leadership and even to eclipse the senior Pankhurst organization.

Quite apart from the possible Adela–Sylvia alliance, the two suffragist organizations were, in effect, in competition. Emmeline and Christabel had become very sensitive about reports in the press during the summer – which they suspected had been inspired by Sylvia – that the Union had lost money and members. Moreover, Sylvia's own organization remained perennially strapped for cash. From time to time she painted pictures to raise money, and usually sold her Cat-and-Mouse licences for £25 a time. She also repeatedly sought donations from Henry Harben to enable the ELF to acquire its own premises.[44] Although Harben's contributions amounted to no more than small change from his fortune, he was simultaneously giving money to the WSPU. To judge from Emmeline's letters to benefactors in this period she was clearly worried about loss of income, and Harben's contributions to Sylvia had more than a financial significance because the connection was accelerating his drift to the far left. He became enormously enthused by Lansbury's attempt to engineer an alliance between militant industrialism and militant suffragism through the Herald League. Christabel regarded this as total anathema for several obvious reasons; she saw Lansbury's alliance as merely a men's movement and as based on class distinction. 'Women', she told Harben 'must grow their own backbone before they are going to be any use to themselves or humanity as a whole.'[45] He accepted that many of the men involved were simply paying lip service to women's grievances. Yet after attending an Albert Hall demonstration addressed by both Sylvia and Lansbury, Harben could not help being impressed by the revolutionary fervour that had been aroused.[46] Now that the suffragettes had largely ceased to hold such demonstrations, Christabel had lost her ability to retain his loyalty. As a result Harben drifted away and by February 1914 he had resigned from the Men's Political Union.

For Christabel, Harben was but a symptom of the wider threat posed by Sylvia when she joined Lansbury at the Albert Hall in November 1913 to protest against the Government's treatment of the syndicalist leaders who had risen to prominence in recent strikes among coal and transport workers. Christabel had consistently regarded such involvement as damaging to the women's cause because it implied an endorsement of Socialism and downgraded the issue of the vote. Yet she could do little more than insist in the pages of *The Suffragette* that Sylvia had attended in a personal capacity and not as a representative of the WSPU. Unfortunately Sylvia rubbed salt into the wound by sending a circular to Union branches in justification of her appearance at the Albert Hall. In this she complained that the Union failed to ask her to speak despite its own shortage of speakers and the headlong decline of its own public propaganda. By contrast the Albert Hall had offered an audience of 10,000 for women's suffrage. An unrepentant Christabel countered: 'The reason for this is that it is essential for the public to understand that you are working independently of us. As you have complete confidence in your own policy and way of doing things, this should suit you perfectly.'[47] Her frustration is understandable. To the general public, already confused about distinctions between militant and non-militant suffragists, and 'Panks' and 'Peths', all the Pankhursts could reasonably be assumed to be in the same camp. They probably exaggerated the damage Sylvia could do, but their inability to control her activities brought relations close to breakdown by Christmas 1913.

While this dispute simmered, Emmeline had decided to spend several months in North America. As the Union was now suffering from a lack of leadership at home this seems unwise, but the decision reflected the need to restore her fragile health and avoid embarking on a further round of hunger strikes. Unhappily, by comparison with her previous visits, this third tour was fraught with complications. A number of American suffragists now showed themselves distinctly unenthusiastic about receiving her; only six of the eight suffragist organizations in New York reportedly supported her visit: 'No one can question Mrs Pankhurst's heroism but her spirit of co-operation is open to serious question. She should have assured herself of the possible harmful effect of her visit on the cause in America before she planned her trip', commented Mary Ware Dennett, secretary of the National American Woman Suffrage Society.[48] This chilly reaction reflected fears among American suffragists about associating themselves with the more extreme forms of militancy currently prevailing in Britain. But another damaging allegation was now levelled against Emmeline: that the chief object of her tour was to make money for the cause in Britain or 'for the tribe of Pankhurst', which would effectively divert resources from the campaign in the United States. Emmeline's organization for the tour gave some grounds for this complaint, for her press agent, Miss Joan Whickham, who arrived two weeks in advance, demanded $1,500 for speaking at the Madison Square Gardens, a liberal share of the gate receipts after expenses, and 60 per cent of the takings over $10,000. 'In other words,' commented the New York Times, 'Mrs Pankhurst regards the American suffragist cause as a fat goose to be plucked for British profit.'[49]

While these allegations were being aired in the American press Emmeline sailed from Le Havre on 10 October in La Provence, watched by two detectives. Attracted by rumours that she would travel in disguise and under a false name, several reporters came on board to question her. However, they received short shrift from Christabel and Flora Drummond who had arrived to see her off: 'Now, mother, this mustn't be an interview,' Christabel insisted with the customary wave of her hand. 'No,' murmured Emmeline, subsiding abruptly into silence.[50] However, once the boat was underway, the reporters returned to tackle her about the other obstacle threatening her visit: would she be allowed to enter the United States as a convicted criminal? Emmeline evidently took this seriously enough to retain an American lawyer, Herbert Reeves, who co-operated with her host, Mrs Belmont, to facilitate her entry. On the trip Emmeline was accompanied by an American author, Mrs Rheta Childs Dorr, who became the ghost-writer for the autobiography of her which was published in 1914.

On her arrival at New York on 19 October the authorities refused Emmeline permission to land. The Immigration Inspector, George W. Moore, boarded the ship to ask her whether she had ever been in prison. 'Yes, many times,' she replied. When she admitted having served only a small part of her three-year sentence, he insisted on detaining her at Ellis Island pending a decision by the Board of Enquiry. However, this did not prevent her going up to the promenade deck to give an interview for some fifty reporters and photographers. Fully aware of the pitfalls facing her, she emphasized that she had not come to teach American women how to win the vote: 'They are too intelligent for that!' She also made full play with the Irish susceptibilities of the Americans. 'My mission to this country is similar to that of men who have come to represent Ireland in this great Republic of the West. I come to appeal for help. Redmond and O'Connor came here to appeal for help for Ireland.' After deliberating for over an hour, the Enquiry Board ordered Emmeline deported as an undesirable alien on the grounds of 'moral turpitude'. She professed herself very surprised at being refused entry 'in what has always been described to me as a free country'.[51] Her lawyer appealed to William B.Wilson, the Secretary of Labour, in Washington, and asked for bail so that she could leave Ellis Island. Emmeline refused to deny a rumour that if refused bail she would put herself on a hunger strike. But her first meeting at the Madison Square Gardens had to be postponed. Miss Mary Hay, the President of the Women's Suffrage Party in New York, condemned the visit as 'merely an exploitation on the part of theatrical promoters in an effort to make money for themselves'.[52] On the other hand a number of telegrams protesting at her detention arrived at the White House, and Jane Adams, the veteran suffrage leader, organized a meeting in her support at Chicago. Fortunately for Emmeline, her fate now lay in the hands of the Democratic President, Woodrow Wilson, a more genuine liberal than many of the politicians she had dealt with in Britain. Wilson convened a meeting with the Secretary of Labour and Anthony Caminetti, the Commissioner General of Immigration. Caminetti admitted he had not made up his mind, but 'I shall not forget that Mrs Pankhurst is a woman of fine character'. They swiftly reversed the deportation order on the understanding that she would leave on 29 November after her lecture tour.[53] The reasons given were that she had property rights in the United States because of her contracts to deliver lectures, and the American immigration laws which provided that political offenders could not be excluded unless their offence involved moral turpitude. In view of America's proud record of admitting rebels from many countries the President would have found it embarrassing to have denied entry to an English suffragette.

When Emmeline's Madison Square meeting eventually took place on 22 October many prominent suffragists reportedly stayed away, and, as the seats proved difficult to fill at $2.50, some people were allowed in free. She faced steady, though good-natured, heckling during the speech. At the end people started to leave early especially when Emmeline asked for a cash collection to be taken. Yet once she had warmed up her face lost its tired and nervous appearance, and when she spoke about Sylvia's experience of forcible feeding her eyes filled with tears. In her speech she relentlessly exploited anti-English sentiment and pride in the revolutionary tradition of modern Americans: 'England', she declared, 'is the most conservative country on earth. Why, your forefathers found that out a great many years ago! . . . Nothing has ever been got out of the British Parliament without something very nearly approaching a revolution.'[54] She reminded her audience that they had helped law-breakers from Ireland who fought for freedom and had extended their sympathies to the people of the Balkans in their struggle for self-determination; they should respond to the women's plea in the same spirit. In the difficult circumstances it was a skilful performance, even though the meeting proved to be one of her less successful ones.

After this, Emmeline's tour took her to Hartford, Providence, Boston, Washington, Philadelphia, Baltimore, Cleveland, Cincinnati, Dayton, Detroit, Chicago, Nashville, Toledo, St Paul and Minneapolis. She devoted large parts of her speeches to the 'White Slave Traffic' which, she argued, would never be suppressed until women had been enfranchised. Emmeline discovered that the moral reform issue played well enough in North America to offer her a valuable means of extending her career after the war when the suffragette campaign had come to an end. In any case, it was tactically shrewd to steer the debate away from militancy, which was now attracting so much criticism. Parcels of *The Suffragette* carrying Christabel's articles on 'The Great Scourge' had been dispatched to each of the cities in which she was due to speak. However, her critics claimed it was an offence to bring 'improper' material into the country and consequently warrants were sought against those responsible for selling the paper.[55] In spite of this, *The Suffragette* continued to be easily available in many places. Press reports give the impression that Emmeline attracted more support as she went further west, perhaps a sign that the political Establishment of the eastern seaboard no longer regarded her as respectable. At Cleveland, Ohio, huge crowds turned out to greet her and men lifted their caps as she passed by; the State's Lieutenant-Governor called to convey her in his motor car to her meeting. There she moved the 4,000 people who had gathered to hear her to laughter and tears with her exposition of women's grievances. It was left to a sceptic from *The Saturday Review* to comment: 'Listening to exciting nonsense about the Ministers of Great Britain is a pastime for which Americans are always ready to pay, and to pay well.'[56]

By mid-November when Emmeline returned to New England for a final round of appearances, the 'social evil' had largely displaced the suffrage question in her speeches. She argued that the origins of the evil lay in men's irresponsible power over women and their ability to dictate to women inside and outside of matrimony. At Hartford she received a public proposal of marriage from a Dr Henry S. Tanner, who claimed to be the world's champion faster. 'It's impudent and most insulting', she replied. 'I'm a politician and not considering such things.'[57] On 24 November she succeeded in filling New York's Carnegie Hall for a final meeting chaired by Charlotte Perkins Gilman. Two days later she sailed for Plymouth on the White Star Liner, *Majestic*, 'with $20,000 [£4,500] in her pockets and a gentle smile on her face'. Totally unabashed, she told reporters of her intention to return for more next year.[58]

Back in England Emmeline's return was eagerly awaited. Hoping to produce her at a big demonstration at the Empress Theatre in Earl's Court, Flora Drummond arranged to meet her with the suffragette bodyguard, armed with India-rubber truncheons, to prevent her falling into the clutches of the police. This time, however, the General was completely outwitted. Before Emmeline's ship docked on 4 December, the Chief Constable and Inspector Riley of Scotland Yard took a tender out to meet her and arrested her without a warrant as she had broken her parole. Leaving the journalists, brass bands and a crowd of 5,000 stranded at the dock gates, they conveyed her to Devonport where she was transferred to a car and driven off to Exeter gaol. The Earl's Court demonstration went ahead without her, but raised an impressive £10,500 all the same.

Accounts of Emmeline's physical condition at this time are contradictory. Joan Whickham told the press she was in excellent health and spirits throughout her journey from New York. But in a letter to Flora

Murray from Exeter, Emmeline said she had been tired by her tour, had endured a bad passage and spent part of the time in bed. On the other hand, Dr Smalley pronounced her to be in perfect health and noted she had put on weight, though Emmeline reported: 'I gave him one of my storms and refused to let him examine me.'[59] Meanwhile her brother Herbert and her sister Ada, now Mrs Goulden Bach, demanded to be informed as to her whereabouts and to be allowed to visit her. At Exeter gaol Emmeline immediately went on hunger strike, though she took some soda water to relieve her nausea. By 7 December her pulse had risen to eighty-two, her breath had become offensive and, according to one report, she was suffering from pleurisy.[60] Consequently, at 10.00 p.m. that day, the prison discharged her. Two officers conveyed her, looking very weak, to the Great Western Hotel and thence by train to London, accompanied by a nurse. With tottering steps she managed to walk from the train to a waiting carriage and was driven off to the nursing home at Pembridge Gardens followed by cabs full of cheering supporters. Before her seven-day licence ran out she decided to get away to Paris, but she was so weak that she had to be taken by ambulance to the station and stretchered on to the train. The police made no attempt to detain her. On arrival she went straight to Christabel's apartment.[61]

When she returned on 15 December with Nurse Pine, just before her licence expired, the police burst into her compartment at Dover, determined to ensure she would not give them the slip. They had cleared the platform at Victoria where they dragged her from the train and threw her into a waiting motor car. Back at Holloway she appeared semi-conscious and lay on the floor for a time before being put to bed.[62] Emmeline had decided to accelerate the breakdown of her health by walking continuously around the cell until she collapsed. As a result of this the prison authorities had concluded by the evening of the seventeenth that it was too dangerous to detain her any longer. She consumed some milk, bread and butter and Brand's Essence, and was discharged at 11.30 until 23 December.

This time, however, Emmeline failed to return. Leaving Pembridge Gardens on the twenty-first with Herbert and Nurse Pine, she managed to give the pursuing detectives the slip. They reached Dover in time to board the 4.00 p.m. boat and arrived at Ostend at six the next morning.

THE PANKHURSTS

This enabled Emmeline to spend Christmas happily tête-à-tête with Christabel and Mabel Tuke and to recover her strength. 'Paris suits me', she told Ethel, 'and Berthe cooks food that agrees with me. I can potter about seeing things, shops included – get up and go to bed when I like.'[63] She remained there throughout January.

It was during this period of recuperation that Emmeline and Christabel discussed the internal threats now facing them and decided to summon both Sylvia *and* Adela for a final confrontation. It is not entirely clear why the long-standing disagreements with Sylvia came to a head at this point, though since the autumn Sylvia had provoked her sister by her growing involvement with George Lansbury and Henry Harben. In a particularly wounding letter whose lack of punctuation underlined her anger, Emmeline told her: 'You are unreasonable [,] always have been [,] and [,] I fear [,] always will be. I suppose you were made so!'[64] Her resolve was evidently strengthened by Ethel Smyth, who accused Sylvia of perversity and of 'constitutional stupidity of a kind only rather gifted people are prone to'. More perceptively, Ethel warned that Sylvia would assume that Emmeline had simply bowed to Christabel's judgement on the issue rather than genuinely sharing the same view.[65] On her arrival in Paris Sylvia agreed to a complete separation of her organization, but she haggled over the title; she wanted to call hers 'The East London Federation of the Suffragettes'. Emmeline, however, resented the use of the word 'Suffragettes' which she felt had become indelibly associated with the WSPU, but Sylvia refused to back down, though later she adopted the name 'Workers' Suffrage Federation'. After a more conciliatory letter to 'My dearest Sylvia', written no doubt because Emmeline wanted as quick a resolution of the dispute as possible, they decided to announce the split on 7 February. The rift between mother and daughter was never healed. At one point Christabel, finding Sylvia alone, apparently suggested that they should continue to meet in spite of the split, 'not as Suffragettes but as sisters'. However, Sylvia spurned the overture: 'To me the words seemed meaningless; we had no life apart from the movement.'[66] This is interesting as the first unmistakable sign that she had grown enough in self-confidence to reject her family.

It is probable that the resolution shown by Emmeline and Christabel in dealing with Sylvia may have been strengthened by the presence of

Adela who, by chance, had been travelling on the Continent. As usual Emmeline seems to have been unreasonably critical of her youngest daughter. She described her travels as 'demoralizing' and determined to put a stop to them: 'I feel it is high time she settled down to real work if ever she is to do any!'[67] This was a little unfair since none of her other children showed much sign of settling down in any conventional sense, and Adela was the only member of the family who had actually tackled a regular job as a teacher. No doubt Emmeline felt provoked by the failure of her latest efforts to 'settle' her as a gardener. After completing her training at Studley College in April 1913, Adela had found employment as head gardener with a suffragette supporter, Mrs Batten Pooll, at Rode Manor, a few miles north of Frome in Somerset. There she received 35 shillings a week and took lodgings in a nearby village. However, she found the work hard and the hours, from 6.00 a.m. to 6.00 p.m. each weekday, very long. The garden was full of peacocks which got her into trouble by eating the cabbages! But above all Adela suffered from loneliness. She had a visit from Maud Joachim, who had been in prison with her in Dundee and was soon to join Sylvia's East London Federation, and she kept in touch with the Blathwayts at Bath who sent her books; but in spite of this she was clearly starved of company in this quiet rural area.[68] Understandably the isolation led her to dwell on what she saw as her rejection by her family and made her long to take up the challenge of the suffragette campaign. The arrival of a letter from Annie Kenney asking her to promise not to speak in England again only twisted the knife. This was unnecessary since Adela had accepted that she could not return to the platform without breaking her promise to Emmeline. She felt too ashamed and demoralized to want to challenge her mother's decision at this time.

To judge from Mary Blathwayt's diary Adela persisted, miserably, with the gardening job during April and May, but made her escape later in the summer when she joined Helen Archdale in Switzerland to act as governess to her two children. All this was doubly irritating to her mother who regarded all teaching jobs as beneath the family's dignity. Moreover, she suspected Adela of trying to work her way back into a political role. Apparently, while in Milan, Adela had been mistaken for Christabel and invited to give a speech. This quickly brought a reprimand from Emmeline and Christabel which was delivered by Annie Kenney, a particularly tactless choice in view of Adela's sensitivity to the role Annie occupied in her mother's affections.[69]

Although Adela, in her unhappiness, doubtless failed to appreciate it, she appeared as a serious threat to her mother and sister who, with some reason, regarded her as more unpredictable and independent-minded than Sylvia. Though Adela did not tell them of Sylvia's invitation to her, they clearly realized that if, as now seemed likely, she returned to England and joined up with her, they would pose a formidable problem. A partnership would have been quite logical since Sylvia and Adela shared left-wing opinions and a common sense of resentment towards the rest of the family. In expelling Sylvia, Christabel had made this outcome more likely, which helps to explain why she and her mother dealt even more ruthlessly with Adela. Attempts to confine her to remote parts of the country and to non-political occupations having failed, they came up with the final solution: she would be sent to Australia. To this end she received her fare, a subsidy of £20 to start her off, and some clothes.

It seems remarkable that at the age of twenty-eight Adela should have allowed herself to be banished in this fashion. That she readily acquiesced is a sign of how crushed in spirit she had become during the previous eight years. When they met in Paris Emmeline 'seemed to think I was a great failure . . . I had not tried to get work'. For her part Emmeline did have some regrets: 'Of course now all is settled I have pangs of maternal weakness', she wrote, 'but I harden my heart.'[70] It is, however, easy to take too severe a view of Emmeline's behaviour. Victorian parents routinely separated themselves from their children for reasons which seem heartless to later generations. The tradition of dispatching young unmarried women to the colonies remained very lively even in the twentieth century. In any case, Adela was not simply exiled to Australia bereft of all friends and contacts. Emmeline equipped her with an introduction to Vida Goldstein, a prominent Australian suffragist who had worked with the WSPU in 1911, and she met up with Jennie Baines, another former hunger-striker recently arrived there. None the less, Sylvia's comment that her sister 'left the country in much grief' was surely something of an understatement. In a transparently autobiographical play entitled *Betrayed*, which she wrote in 1917, Adela depicted a dominating mother figure despatching a rebellious left-wing son to the colonies with the words: 'If you persist in your present attitude I will publicly disown you.'[71]

On 2 February Adela sailed from Southampton on the *Geelong* bound for Melbourne. She never saw her relations again. In the emotion generated by her departure she could scarcely have imagined that this painful rupture was the best thing that had happened to her for a long time; in Australia, Adela's personal and political life was to develop as it could never have done in Britain trapped in the tensions and rivalries of Pankhurst family politics. On board the *Geelong* she helped to look after three hundred children, an occupation which may have helped to stop her dwelling too much on the painful circumstances of her own departure. The ship made leisurely stops at Las Palmas, Cape Town and Fremantle before arriving at Adelaide. There Adela, reinvigorated by the sea voyage and impatient to reach her destination, decided to disembark and took the train from Adelaide to Melbourne. On her arrival there on 27 March she was met by Vida Goldstein and Cecilia John and whisked off to the comfortable Goldstein home in the suburb of South Yarra. The 45-year-old Vida now became a substitute mother for Adela, as well as her political mentor, easing her quickly into the politics of Australia. In some ways Melbourne seemed a warmer and more egalitarian version of Manchester, which suited Adela very well. Australian women had won the vote by stages between 1894 and 1908, partly through collaboration with the Labor Party, and had remained closely linked to working-class politics. Vida Goldstein, who had already stood three times for the Senate and the House of Representatives, saw the vote as just the start of a wider struggle for female equality. Moreover, several Australian feminists who had participated in the suffrage campaign in Britain were well aware of Adela's reputation as a platform performer. Fortunately Vida took the view that the ban on speaking did not extend to Australia, and by May Adela had been invited to speak about the suffragette movement and became a centre of attraction in left-wing circles. Australians appreciated her unassuming approach and admired her doggedness under pressure.

At first Adela saved face by claiming simply to be visiting Australia to improve her health, but this pretence was soon abandoned as she began to enjoy her new freedom and the scope to develop her political reputation without incurring the disapproval of her family. Though Emmeline gave her approval for Adela's return to the platform, there were few communications with home; Christabel ignored her letters and even Sylvia failed to write until Adela joined the Socialist Party in Victoria. One friend from college, Janie Sagar, sent letters via Emmeline, though it is not clear whether Adela received them, and they only established direct contact in 1915.[72]

However, Adela could not rely on her novelty value indefinitely, for there was not much mileage in the suffrage campaign. Under Goldstein's patronage she became an organizer for the Women's Political Association and worked as a reporter for the *Woman Voter*. She also became friends with Robert Ross, the leading figure in the Socialist Party in Victoria State. When Goldstein stood in the state elections in July and August Adela campaigned energetically for her on a programme that included equal divorce, equal access to state employment and retention of their nationality by women who married foreigners. It was an exhilarating experience for Adela; in the space of a few months she had left behind the stale old struggle for the vote and moved on to a fresh agenda, found new friends and established herself as an independent personality at last.

The simultaneous expulsion of Sylvia and Adela in February 1914 was symptomatic of a wider crisis for Christabel and Emmeline. Their treatment of the two sisters becomes more explicable in the light of the beleaguered position in which they now found themselves, not simply through external pressure, but through internal criticism of their leadership. Inevitably Christabel bore the brunt of all this. 'I have often said that [Christabel] goes one better than God, who sacrificed his son', commented Ethel Smyth savagely.[73] Beatrice Harraden, a suffragette author who had written the pro-suffrage play *Lady Geraldine's Speech* (1909), wrote in January demanding to know whether she was really willing to risk her mother's death by persisting with the current tactics. She accused Christabel of having lost her way and of alienating too many old colleagues: 'It must be that ... your exile prevents you from being in real touch with facts as they are over here.'[74] In reply Christabel simply insisted there was no alternative and that in any case public opinion was coming round to their side: 'It is perhaps easier to keep one's vision in exile than when one is at home.'[75] Refusing to be browbeaten, Harraden contradicted everything Christabel said; public opinion had drifted away from the Union because it no longer organized public demonstrations and its local branches had become 'half comatose'; consequently she felt that '[Emmeline's] sacrifice is a vain and useless one'.[76] Christabel had a similarly demoralizing correspondence with Henry Harben, who complained that it had become increasingly difficult to communicate properly with her because she had surrounded herself with a small group of loyalists: 'Your chief officials at Lincoln's Inn are going round the branches turning people out neck and crop . . . People are now saying that from the leader of a great movement you are developing into the ringleader of a little rebel Rump.'[77] Harben almost certainly had Grace Roe and Annie Kenney in mind in making these criticisms of the quality of the headquarters staff. However, Christabel, who continued to heap extravagant praise upon Roe, shut her mind to such views and offered virtually no answer to Harben's complaints. By 1914 she had fallen into the error of all autocratic leaders; her power to manipulate personnel was so complete that it left her increasingly surrounded by sycophants who lacked real ability.

Prolonged exile also exacerbated another of Christabel's weaknesses. Despite producing enough copy to fill several pages of *The Suffragette* each week, she had too much time on her hands and gradually lapsed into the lassitude that had characterized her earlier life. Any arrangement which allowed her to enjoy the leading role while relying on others to do the steady, tedious work suited her admirably; Paris was the culmination of this pattern in her life. As a result, even when the militant campaign came to an end in August 1914, thereby releasing her from exile, Christabel never fully resumed the level of intense activity she had achieved between 1906 and 1912. After this she effectively lived off the reputation she had accumulated in that brief phase.

Despite repeated claims about imminent victory on the part of Christabel and Emmeline, there was no end in sight to the debilitating cycle of arrest, imprisonment and release. As Beatrice Harraden had reminded Christabel, the Home Secretary felt untroubled about the

Cat and Mouse Act largely because he believed, rightly or wrongly, that the general public remained indifferent to the methods being used. The moral-political implications of his policy concerned him less than the purely practical aspect of the Act as a means of controlling hunger-striking prisoners. As early as March 1913, when the Bill was still going through Parliament, Christabel had confidently pronounced that it would be a 'dead letter'.[78] This view has been widely accepted by later writers. However, the evidence points to the effectiveness of McKenna's policy. Whenever Emmeline was released from Holloway, suffragette propaganda claimed another triumph. Yet this simply illustrated the working of the system. Throughout 1913 and 1914 she was repeatedly recaptured, albeit with difficulty on several occasions, and forced to continue serving her sentence, which was, after all, the object of the legislation. But the Cat and Mouse Act made a more fundamental impact on the movement. While in prison a number of suffragettes were offered – and accepted – release without recapture on condition that they gave a signed undertaking to abstain from all militant actions in the future. Others were released because they were judged to be incapable of committing further offences.[79] In effect, the Home Secretary had begun to operate an informal truce designed to whittle down the militant campaign well before the formal truce that he offered after the outbreak of war.

This pattern continued after Emmeline's return from Paris on 10 February when she took up residence at the Brackenburys' home in Campden Hill Square, now known as 'Mouse Castle'. As it had become difficult to hire halls, Emmeline delivered a speech to 1,200 people from an upper window at Mouse Castle. However, she could not afford to remain there surrounded by police for long. To effect her escape she dressed distinctively in a little toque hat with a feather and her mantle. These were then transferred to another lady while Emmeline donned a soft beaver hat and veil which always made it difficult to see who was underneath. When they left suddenly the police went for the white feather, but back at the police station could not make up their minds whether they had arrested Emmeline or not. One said 'It is her', but another insisted 'It isn't.' In the confusion Emmeline managed to slip away with her bodyguard.[80] But she had become almost as much a fugitive as Christabel. A fortnight later she reappeared at Glebe House in Chelsea where she spoke to a large crowd from a balcony for three-quarters of an hour:

We are fighting for a time when every little girl born into the world will have an equal chance with her brothers, when we shall put an end to foul outrages on our sex . . . when every man shall look upon every other woman as his own sisters.[81]

Several days later Katherine Marshall filled several taxis with members of the bodyguard and arrived at Glebe House late at night. When the bodyguard poured out and engaged in a fight with the police and detectives Emmeline emerged to be driven off to Colchester.

A few days after making her escape she was driven up to Glasgow for a big meeting at St Andrews Hall. This involved spending the night in the car so as to avoid attracting attention.[82] On 9 March she managed to make her way into the packed hall by posing as a member of the public and walking in with two other women. The platform had been elaborately fortified with an encircling fringe of flowers and flags which concealed rolls of barbed wire. Accounts of the meeting varied according to the loyalties of the observers. Undoubtedly the police, who had 168 uniformed and plainclothes men stationed in the hall, were desperate to prevent her slipping through their fingers again. According to their account, as they advanced towards the platform they came under attack by members of the bodyguard who threw chairs, bottles, flower pots and buckets of water; Janie Allan, the sister of the wealthy Scots shipowner, fired a revolver containing blank cartridges.[83] In the suffragette version the police simply drew their batons and charged. Several eyewitnesses claimed that they took the law into their own hands, and behaved in a brutal and even hysterical fashion, striking out at anyone who came within reach.[84] In spite of complaints made against the police on grounds of assault, the Chief Constable defended the methods used to arrest Emmeline and the Secretary of State for Scotland refused to institute an enquiry. It was in retaliation for the Glasgow arrest that Mary Richardson made her notorious attack on the Velasquez *Venus* in the National Gallery. Meanwhile Emmeline returned by fast train to Holloway and declared: 'I wish to inform Mr McKenna that when he attempts to arrest me again he will require a regiment of soldiers.'[85]

During these months Emmeline and Sylvia ran parallel campaigns. On several occasions they were in Holloway at the same time, though usually unaware of the other's presence. If anything Sylvia, who earned herself nine sentences between January and June, had begun to eclipse her mother by the sheer spectacle of her clashes with the police. When out on licence from 14 March she was carried on a stretcher by eight men and women all the way from Old Ford Road to Westminster Abbey. As the doors were locked against her she held a meeting on the steps before returning by ambulance. At Easter she left the country to give speeches in Budapest, Vienna and Brussels; she had been invited to Dresden, but was banned by the German authorities. Back in Holloway she deprived herself of food, water and sleep for six days in order to secure release. She then raised the stakes further by threatening that if the prime minister refused to receive a deputation she would fast to death at the Strangers' Entrance to the House of Commons. Lansbury embarrassed the ministers by writing to the King, asking for Sylvia's release on the grounds that she was being treated more severely than he. Whereas he had been released and not subsequently re-arrested, she was repeatedly returned to Holloway. However, McKenna argued that Lansbury had refrained from incitement to further crimes and had signed a petition indicating that he was not likely to commit further offences himself. Had he given a firm promise McKenna would have remitted his entire sentence, and he emphasized that 'in similar circumstances Miss Sylvia Pankhurst would not be re-arrested.'[86] Since he was granting this concession to other suffragettes, there is no reason to doubt McKenna's word. On 12 June Asquith, perhaps judging it impolitic to appear too severe, agreed to meet a deputation from the East End in the course of which he offered to speak with the Home Secretary about the possibility of unconditional release from prison for Sylvia. In an unusually conciliatory response Asquith made it clear that he regarded the working women as more representative than the usual delegations and praised them for avoiding association with 'criminal methods'. In a much-quoted phrase he declared 'if the change [women's suffrage] has got to come we must face it boldly and make it thoroughly democratic in its basis.'[87] Though by no means a capitulation, this response was not without significance. Even Asquith realized that he could not maintain his resistance much longer simply because of the damage the controversy was doing to his party and to his own leadership. During 1914 all the parties had begun to contemplate a general election – indeed one had to take place by the end of 1915. Labour would clearly have entered that election in an alliance with the non-militant suffragists. The Conservative leadership was being carefully primed by the non-militants and by several leading front benchers to make some kind of promise about legislation for women's suffrage. Since Asquith could not risk being outflanked by *both* the other parties, he was trying to find a more constructive policy to offer at the election. There was no question of any legislation before the election or at least not until the bills dealing with Irish Home Rule and the Disestablishment of the Church in Wales had been enacted. But Asquith was prepared to accept that if a majority of Liberals returned at the election wanted to give women the vote this would have to be done. His reference to a democratic reform underlined that he was actually quite close to Sylvia's position in the sense that they both favoured votes for all *men* and women rather than the purely women's bill on which Emmeline and Christabel insisted.

Consequently, after the deputation Lansbury arranged for Sylvia to meet with Lloyd George. She tried to elicit an undertaking from him not to join the next Liberal Government unless it was pledged to a women's bill. Now Lloyd George was an indefatigable negotiator who often contrived to give the impression he was closer to his opponents' views than was actually the case. In this case, however, one can be too cynical. Lloyd George had undoubtedly been irritated by Asquith's endless prevarication on the issue. Behind the scenes he was in fact, using his influence to ensure that all new Liberal candidates adopted for the election were pro-suffragists; and in July he intervened with McKenna to persuade him not to re-arrest Sylvia.[88] When Christabel got to hear of these negotiations she dismissed them at once. But there may have been an element of personal chagrin in this, for against the odds Sylvia had emerged as the suffragette with whom the leading politicians were now keen to deal; but for the intervention of the crisis in Europe she and Lloyd George would almost certainly have announced a deal by the autumn of 1914.

By comparison it was not clear what her mother's tactics were achieving. After her arrest in Glasgow on 9 March, Emmeline had spent just four days in Holloway. She complained of pains over her heart, and during the night her door was kept open so that a watch might be kept on her. On the thirteenth when Dr Smalley found her lying huddled on the cell floor fully dressed, he judged it necessary to set her free that night. In fact, she was discharged on the fourteenth, under licence to return on the twenty-first.[89] At Mouse Castle Dr Murray and Nurse Pine were astonished at the speed of her recovery. Emmeline was now intent on motoring up to East Fife because a by-election was anticipated in the prime minister's constituency. Following the resignation of Colonel Seeley as Secretary of State for War over the so-called 'Curragh Mutiny', Asquith had decided, at some risk, to take over his post temporarily, which legally required him to seek re-election. In the event no candidate opposed him and so no contest took place. Emmeline's journey had been fruitless, and she returned to London to be holed up at Mouse Castle again. In the meantime she found enough energy to reprimand Lord Lytton, a staunch Conservative supporter of votes for women, who had had the temerity to introduce a women's bill into the House of Lords without consulting her. 'I sent for him and gave him a dragooning', she wrote with satisfaction.[90] She considered the bill a waste of time, though it was in fact, another useful way of demonstrating that the peers were rather less opposed to votes for women than had been supposed. Early in May Emmeline disappeared with Annie Kenney to a remote rural location and did not reappear until the twenty-first to take part in a deputation at Buckingham Palace. The object of this was to exercise the right of petitioning the King over the heads of his ministers. This led to her re-arrest and yet another hunger strike. After six days the doctors felt that although she showed no urgent symptoms of malnutrition, in view of her age, pulse rate and temperament, she ought to be released. After she left by cab on 27 May, under licence to return on 3 June, it is not clear where Emmeline stayed. She did, however, send a letter from Number 6 Blenheim Road, London, the home of Ida Wylie, who was then captain of the bodyguard. This house became known as 'Mouse Hole' because suffragettes who recuperated there crossed six garden walls behind the property to re-emerge in the house of a sympathizer and thus make their escape.[91] Somehow

Emmeline managed to slip away and board a ferry to St Malo where she regained some of her strength and even bathed in the sea. On her return on 8 July she was recaptured at Lincoln's Inn House and returned to Holloway where the warders attempted to strip-search her. The reason for this unusual proceeding was that Grace Roe had recently been found attempting to smuggle an emetic into prison. In the struggle Emmeline struck a warder, and afterwards she lay on the floor of her cell with no clothes on until she was lifted on to the bed. For the next three days she was reported to be sullen and abusive, refusing food and declining to be examined. At night she managed to sleep for a couple of hours, but was heard crying in the early hours. Eventually the authorities discharged her on 11 July. She revived herself with some brandy and soda before leaving for Pembridge Gardens.[92] After failing to return, she was recaptured on the sixteenth on her way to attend a Union function in Holland Park. By this time she had become so weak that she had to be discharged two days later.[93] Flora Murray described her as suffering from cardiac discomfort. Fortunately this turned out to be Emmeline's final hunger strike. Though due to return to gaol on 22 July, she managed to slip across the Channel to spend the rest of the month in France. She was at St Malo on 4 August when the First World War broke out.

13

God's Vengeance (1914–16)

'This great war . . . is God's vengeance upon the people who held women in subjection.'

Christabel Pankhurst, *The Suffragette*, 7 August 1914

By July 1914 Paris had sunk into its usual summer torpor as the inhabitants shut up their flats and apartments and dispersed for holidays on the coast. Following their example, Christabel travelled to St Brieuc in Brittany, thence a little eastwards along the coast to St Malo where she joined her mother. It was there on the promenade that they heard the Mayor announce the outbreak of hostilities between France and Germany, followed by the news that Britain had decided to join on 4 August.

At first it was far from clear what implications these events would have either for the women's cause in general or for the Pankhursts in particular, though the rapid advance of the German armies through Belgium threatened to deprive Christabel of her refuge in Paris in a matter of weeks. During those first few days Ethel Smyth and Grace Roe spent hours walking up and down at St Malo with Emmeline discussing what to do.[1] Like almost everyone else they expected a short war similar to the Franco-Prussian conflict of 1870–71. It was widely assumed that Britain would participate chiefly by mobilizing her navy while leaving France and Russia to bear the brunt of the fighting on land. However, the hugely successful appeal for volunteers by the new Secretary of State for War, Lord Kitchener, soon disposed of that notion by leading to the re-creation of a mass British army for the first time since the end of the Napoleonic wars in 1815. Kitchener's policy clearly implied that a protracted struggle involving civilian and military manpower was now in contemplation. Once Paris had been saved and the two sides became bogged down in trench warfare, Britain came under intense pressure to relieve the French by taking over more of the front line. The British Commanders-in-Chief, Sir John French and later Sir Douglas Haig, developed ambitions to score a decisive victory by launching offensives against the German lines, which made them greedy for extra troops and supplies.

This military *bouleversement* had major implications for domestic politics. All the political parties and pressure groups began to devise strategies for weathering a long war during which a general election was to be held. However, the WSPU saw it from a different perspective. 'It was almost with a sense of relief that we heard of the declaration of war', wrote a young suffragette, Elsie Bowerman, 'and we knew that our militancy, which had reached an acute stage, could cease.'[2] In fact, it was by no means clear that militancy could be abandoned until the Government took an initiative by offering a truce. For a cabinet which had lately been absorbed by the alarming prospect of a civil war breaking out in Ireland, the European crisis initially offered a welcome relief. It therefore took the opportunity to lay all the current controversies to rest for the duration of war. The controversial bills for Irish Home Rule and Welsh Church Disestablishment were suspended, and the Home Secretary extended his existing policy to all political prisoners, including several strike leaders as well as suffragettes. On 7 August he announced an amnesty for those 'who undertake not to commit further crimes or outrages', and three days later he waived even this condition: 'His Majesty is confident that the prisoners ... will respond to the feelings of their countrymen and countrywomen in this time of emergency and that they may be trusted not to stain the causes they have at heart by any further crime or disorder.'[3]

In effect, suffragette sentences were being remitted; but the risk was fully justified for the two sides now had a mutual interest in an appeal to national unity. The government could take credit for its magnanimity while maintaining its refusal to back down to force. Equally the truce enabled Emmeline and Christabel to withdraw without loss of face from a confrontation whose only outcome would have been the complete disintegration of the WSPU. This involved a tacit admission that their campaign had been no more successful in winning the vote than that of the non-militants whom they so freely derided. However, they had suspended militancy before, and now they could join the other suffrage organizations in accepting that no domestic reforms were feasible until hostilities had ceased. 'Let us show ourselves worthy of citizenship whether our claim to it be recognized or not', urged Millicent Fawcett.[4]

In the event, this abrupt change of tactics proved much easier for the autocratic WSPU than for the National Union of Women's Suffrage Societies, whose members soon became embroiled in a debate about how far to support the war effort, whether to maintain a watching brief for the suffrage, and whether to seek a negotiated peace settlement. By contrast Emmeline simply announced the suspension of the militant campaign and *The Suffragette* ceased publication until April 1915. When the paper reappeared its pages were filled with articles about France, Russia, Germany and Serbia. She rationalized her decision by arguing that suffragette militancy would be pointless 'by contrast with the infinitely greater violence done in the present war', and in any case, suspension would save the health, energy and funds of the members: 'With that patriotism which has nerved women to endure endless torture in prison cells for the national good, we ardently desire that our country shall be victorious', she wrote.[5] And in an emotional speech at Plymouth she declared: 'One of the mistakes the Kaiser made, one among many, was that he thought under all circumstances the British people would continue their internal dissension. The war,' she continued, 'has made me feel how much there is of nobility in man, in addition to the other thing which we all deplore.'[6] Though it was not apparent at the time, these words marked the end of Emmeline and Christabel's campaign for female enfranchisement, not simply an interruption, and indeed the beginning of the end of their role in the women's movement itself. Whereas the other women's societies more or less maintained their organization during wartime and resumed their campaigns after the war, they rapidly adopted a very different agenda.

Despite this decisive about-turn, Christabel took her time before quitting Paris. Only when convinced that a long war was in prospect did she come home, on 4 September, to take up her residence at Number 69 Cheyne Court in Chelsea.[7] 'The long rest in Paris has restored the beauty that we knew when she first appeared among us', commented the *Star*; but its photographs revealed how much weight Christabel had put on during her absence. Declaring her new mission to inspire patriotism, she told the press: 'I feel that my duty lies in England now, and I have come back. The British citizenship for which we suffragettes have been fighting is now in jeopardy.'[8] Some commentators felt that her autocratic leadership disqualified her from criticizing the lack of democracy in Germany, but in the mood of patriotic euphoria now sweeping the country the press was generally prepared to take her at her own valuation: 'Christabel can reach ears that never heed Mr Asquith and Sir Edward Grey . . . she can arouse the humble women who have been accustomed to listen to her to a sense of their national duty. Christabel has at last found a mission worthy of her powers of reasoning and persuasion.'[9]

Her transition from suffragette to patriot, though brief, inevitably created some friction. On her return to the platform on 8 September at the London Opera House, she disappointed many in her audience by neglecting to refer to votes for women; nor did she write anything on the subject until April 1917, by which time the issue had been resolved. An apparently favourable reference to the prime minister in her speech provoked disbelieving laughter and a little heckling which Christabel brushed aside. Already she had refocussed herself on the new situation and begun to cast herself as an authority on the war; but for some of her supporters this was too neat and abrupt to carry complete conviction. At the Opera House she rather presciently floated the idea of introducing food rationing. As Britain relied on imports for four-fifths of her bread, two-thirds of her sugar and half of her meat supplies, prices had already begun to rise; and heavy losses of merchant shipping greatly exacerbated the problem. Eventually most food items were subject to a rationing scheme. But by advancing the policy so early Christabel demonstrated her remarkable adaptability to the new agenda of wartime. She also received a boost from the decision to distribute her book, *The Great Scourge*, among British troops in France with the approval of Lord Kitchener, who warned the men to safeguard their health and guard against 'any excesses'. The troops themselves may have gained more practical help from the distribution of free condoms than from the study of Christabel's book.

After her re-entry to domestic politics, however, Christabel left it largely to her mother to justify the suspension of the suffragette campaign. Following the conventional line Emmeline argued that 'a war to crush militarism had the approval of [the] women who had fought for political enfranchisement . . . when the time comes we shall renew that fight, but for the present we must all do our best to fight a common foe'.[10] On 24 September she spoke in support of Kitchener's appeal for recruits. No fewer than 450,000 men volunteered during September, but only 137,00 came forward in October and in 1915 the rhetoric on the recruiting platforms became increasingly shrill as the reluctant were winkled out. This created a new role for Emmeline as an unofficial participant in the war effort. Speaking on 'The Country In Danger' at the Kingsway Hall in December 1914, she appealed to young men to join up in the name of women:

In times of war we are compelled to take men at their word. Men say 'leave the fighting to us . . . we fight for you' . . . We take you, gentlemen, at your word . . . During the last few days I have been thanking God I am not a superior person [laughter] . . . It is you enfranchised men. It is the Bernard Shaws and the rest of them [laughter and cheers].[11]

By lightening her patriotism with humour Emmeline showed a surer touch than Christabel, whose speeches verged increasingly towards the portentous. Though she had ceased to ask directly for the vote, Emmeline's platform rhetoric was well calculated to disarm those anti-suffragists who had hitherto taken it for granted that women would be a hindrance to the nation in waging war.

The attitude towards the war adopted by Emmeline and Christabel requires more explanation than it has usually received. In their editorial in The Suffragette on 7 August, they noticeably failed to take a patriotic line; instead Christabel expressed a grim satisfaction in the war as a man-made disaster. 'This great war', she wrote, 'is God's vengeance upon the people who held women in subjection . . . let us in everything strive unceasingly that the world may learn from the tragedy that women must be free', which makes her subsequent view appear a little more calculated.[12] Unfortunately we have little evidence for their opinions on foreign policy during the Edwardian period. Sylvia accused them of abandoning the pacifist views of Richard Pankhurst. Emmeline had certainly opposed the Government's policy in the South African War of 1899–1902, though she had also been impressed by the difficulties such an unpopular line caused for the family. Yet there was nothing remarkable about shifting views between the two wars. Lloyd George had been a famous critic during the Boer War, but staunchly backed British entry into the First World War on the grounds that it was essential to Britain's own security to ensure that France did not suffer another defeat at the hands of Germany. During the previous fifteen years the public had come to regard Germany as a bully towards France, as a threat to the Royal Navy in the North Sea and as ambitious for influence in south-east Europe and the Middle East. One has also to allow for the intangible influence of the company Emmeline and Christabel had kept during the previous decade. Their campaign had become heavily reliant on the support of wealthy and well-connected ladies for whom imperialism and patriotism were instinctive emotions. Since Christabel had consistently tried to suppress any political opinions which threatened to jeopardize their support, she was unlikely to risk association with anti-war views now. Above all, Emmeline's partisanship gained strength from her long-standing love of the French. By 1914 both she and Christabel felt an understandable sense of gratitude to the country that had offered them so congenial a bolt-hole. 'I have enjoyed their friendship and hospitality in times of peace', commented Christabel on her departure from Paris, 'and now at this tragic moment in their history I cannot sufficiently express the admiration I feel for their magnificent spirit.'[13]

However, it was one thing for the Pankhursts to reflect the general upsurge of patriotism in British society in 1914; thousands of women in the suffrage movement devoted themselves to voluntary work for soldiers, sailors and Belgian refugees. But the Pankhursts deliberately went much further in this direction by adopting a high-profile role as unofficial recruiting agents, as lecturers in the manufacturing districts where they attacked strikes as the work of Bolsheviks and traitors, and even as envoys of the British government to several foreign countries. In effect, they completely reinvented themselves; by the end of the war they had transformed themselves from public enemies into ultra-patriots and allies of the political Establishment. However, in the light of their existing connections with the Establishment, this was not as eccentric as it first appeared; the war made explicit what had been obscured by suffragette militancy.

Extreme wartime patriotism also represented another continuity with their pre-war hostility to the Asquith Government. Although the Liberal cabinet had taken Britain into the war with only two resignations, many Liberals loathed the necessity for fighting alongside the Tsarist regime, and believed that Sir Edward Grey, the Foreign Secretary, had embroiled the country in a commitment to France without properly consulting Parliament or the party. Above all the war threatened to disrupt Liberal achievements on the domestic front in social welfare, progressive taxation and constitutional innovation. The Conservatives, already in a dangerously extreme mood after ten years in opposition, now felt extremely frustrated at their exclusion from power and believed that the cabinet lacked the enthusiasm and determination to win the war. While the Tory leaders were constrained in their criticism by the need to appear patriotic, their allies in the press launched an uninhibited campaign to blame the politicians for every setback, even when responsibility would more justly have been laid at the feet of the generals and admirals. In particular, Lord Northcliffe, the proprietor of the *Daily Mail* and *The Times*, who was driven by a dangerous blend of megalomania and commercialism, devoted himself to the destruction of Asquith's Government. In the febrile atmosphere of wartime it was only too easy to attribute every failure on the part of the Allies to either inefficiency among politicians or to the work of spies and traitors ensconced within the civil service. The Pankhursts simply jumped on to this bandwagon. They joined in the persecution of Richard Haldane who, as Secretary of State for War, had brilliantly reorganized the army so as to create the expeditionary force which was instrumental in saving Paris in 1914, on the grounds that he had been an admirer of German philosophy. They repeatedly filled the front page of *The Suffragette* with denunciations of Sir Eyre Crowe, the Permanent Secretary at the Foreign Office, for being a nephew of Admiral von Holtzendorff, who was Chief of the German Naval Staff, and thus presumed to be sabotaging British interests. And they demanded the resignation of Sir Edward Grey for failing to save Serbia from Austria, for allowing the escape of the German battleships the

Breslau and the *Goeben,* and in general for delaying the Allied victory in the war.[14] It was as though they were avenging themselves on the pre-war government under cover of supporting the war effort.

Despite her new role Christabel seems to have suffered considerable unease about her return to Britain, so much so that she spent much of her time abroad throughout the war years. After her reappearance at the Opera House on 8 September, she next surfaced on 14 October in New York. She had travelled incognito as Miss Margaret MacDonald on the Red Star liner, *Finland,* accompanied by Olive Bartels, a former suffragette who went as Miss Mabel Barton. Few people on board knew of her real identity, and even Mrs Belmont, who had entertained Christabel at her villa in France, was unaware of her arrival. She remained in the United States until March 1915 and even then returned to the Continent rather than to Britain.

Christabel seemed reluctant to explain this singular behaviour. 'I always decide what I am going to do and do it immediately', she told the reporters. 'One wastes time otherwise, doesn't one?' She probably got closer to the truth when she admitted: 'I did not wish to stay in England with a suspended jail sentence over me.'[15] But was there any serious prospect of her re-arrest? The original truce applied to those actually in prison, and subsequently the Home Office confirmed that if prisoners at large under the Cat and Mouse Act reported back they could expect remission. But Christabel fell into neither category since she had never begun to serve her sentence. It seems most unlikely that she was not covered by McKenna's truce. Yet so deep-seated was her fear of incarceration that she determined to take no risks.

Wider considerations may have played a part in her decision to go abroad. By casting herself as an unofficial ambassador for Britain in America, she quickly began to build bridges with the politicians and consolidate her new status. At home she would have become involved in distracting arguments with other suffragists. Indeed, the American visit underlined very clearly Christabel's detachment from the women's movement, for she found herself boycotted by the New York State Woman Suffrage Society because of her partisan approach to the war; her denunciations of Germany as a 'male' nation and her habit of dismissing women who took part in peace movements as victims of German propaganda offended many people.[16] At this stage most

Americans regarded the war as a typical product of European imperialism from which they hoped to be able to keep their distance; consequently, at the Presidential election in 1916 both candidates pledged themselves to the preservation of American neutrality.

In this situation Christabel wisely tempered her aggression with flattery. At her first big meeting at the Carnegie Hall on 24 October she dressed up in purple, white and green, entered to an organ prelude and, as the audience rose to applaud, received two large bunches of red roses.[17] Lavishing praise on Americans as champions of democracy, she conceded: 'When you fought us for the principle of freedom, for the right of self-government, you did right . . . we were as much in the wrong as Germany is in the wrong today.'[18] Americans also owed a debt to the French, she suggested, who had given them crucial support in their struggle for independence. Christabel then challenged those who believed it would be safer to stay out of the European conflict by referring to Britain's decision to stand aside when the Germans had previously defeated France and annexed Alsace and Lorraine. 'The seed of this war was sowed in 1870. We are punished now for our neutrality then. Take warning from our fate.' Going even further, she emphasized that America's interests were involved in the European struggle if only because 'she is next in the Kaiser's line of attack'. Germany, she claimed, had so many people that she urgently wanted fresh colonies: 'Undoubtedly the Kaiser would greatly prize territory in South America.'[19] This gave Americans something to think about, but it did not prevent a series of awkward questions being thrown at her. Was it honest to talk about freedom while Britain continued to deny it to Ireland and India? How about the British habit of intercepting neutral shipping? Christabel evaded this like a true professional. 'Oh, I like these interruptions. But I will tell you this, Sir: if you were a suffragette you would have been thrown out.'[20] Then there was the question about Britain's ally, Japan: would Britain come to her assistance if Japan got into a conflict with the United States? Again Christabel offered little answer except to express the hope that the three countries would get together to understand each other better. During her last major speech in New York in January she was subjected to constant interruption especially for claiming that the American peace movement had been inspired by the Germans. One woman commented: 'There was nothing but hatred, hatred, hatred in [Christabel's] talk.'[21] Totally unabashed by the uproar, Christabel described the meeting as magnificent. She doubtless realized that to be reported upholding the Allied cause against American criticism played very well back in Britain. Lord Northcliffe in particular was becoming an admirer of the Pankhursts and was now in the process of reversing his newspapers' opposition to votes for women.

The only flaw in the reinvention of Christabel and Emmeline as ultra-patriots was the attitude of Sylvia and Adela. After attending the Opera House meeting in September 1914, Sylvia had written to her mother to express her sorrow over her views, to which Emmeline replied: 'I am ashamed to know where you and Adela stand.'[22] In a later letter to Adela, Sylvia complained: 'She takes the opposite view in everything. The most extreme jingoism is scarcely enough for her and I only look in wonder and ask "can those two really be sane?" '[23] They had no direct contact except at the end of December when Sylvia and Nora Smythe, who had visited Scarborough, crossed to Paris where Emmeline was spending Christmas with Catherine Pine. 'We were distant from each other as though a thousand leagues had intervened', wrote Sylvia.[24]

While her mother had become totally absorbed in the war effort, Sylvia was now preoccupied by the situation in London where her energies were devoted to tackling the immediate material hardships faced by the inhabitants of the East End. Talking to the mothers who arrived at her headquarters in Old Ford Road, she realized how the war had initially undermined women's employment because of dwindling demand for the products of the clothing and luxury trades on which the East End relied heavily, and the interruption of sugar supplies to confectioners. Sylvia organized a deputation to the Board of Trade to show ministers the evidence of family budgets, and in the pages of the *Woman's Dreadnought* she monitored increases in rents and food prices. Soon the Old Ford Road became the centre of a succession of practical initiatives. Sylvia established an employment exchange for women, a milk distribution centre and four mother-and-baby clinics. She appealed for second-hand clothes and turned her headquarters into a 'Cost Price Restaurant' which served two- course meals for two pence every day from twelve until two. During 1915 no fewer than

70,000 meals were served and 1,000 mothers and babies received treatment at her clinics. She also acquired extra premises in the shape of a former public house which became known as 'The Mothers' Arms'; there three nurses looked after the children, while a Montessori school was opened on an upper floor. Sylvia also turned into something of an entrepreneur in October 1914 when she opened a garment factory paying wages of £1 a week – higher than the local workshops. Taking advantage of the interruption of imports of toys from Germany, she started a toy factory with the assistance of her uncle, Herbert Goulden, who was a businessmen himself. For a time this seems to have made a profit, though Sylvia had to rely on appeals to patriotism to sell the products of the factory. On one occasion she took a taxi full of the toys to Selfridge's, and on another Lady Sybil Smith arranged for her to sell them during a weekend at the Astors' country residence at Cliveden. Though she earned £20, Sylvia found herself offended by the vulgarity and superficiality of Nancy Astor who boasted 'I am going to be austere' while continuing to indulge herself as usual: 'Sadly we set out our toys in the ornate drawing room ... a motley of well-dressed women swept in on us [but] many people enjoy having their hearts touched – then pass to the next sensation quite unchanged.'[25]

When Nancy Astor rather tactlessly enquired: 'I hope you teach the women to be good?' Sylvia replied that it was not her job to do anything more than help them articulate their grievances. As usual all these ventures had to be financed largely by donations from ladies in London's West End and in particular by Nora Smythe who reportedly gave £1,839 between 1915 and 1916. When extra cash was needed Sylvia raised it herself by writing newspaper articles dealing with wartime subjects.

This emphasis on practical strategies for maintaining working-class living and working conditions ought logically to have led Sylvia closer to the mainstream of the Labour Movement during the war. The majority of Labour and Socialist organizations backed the war effort, albeit with reservations, and decided that it was not now appropriate to indulge in recriminations over the pre-war diplomacy and the arms race. This attitude culminated in the entry of the Labour Party into the Coalition Government in May 1915. Labour's chief initiative was to create the War Emergency Workers National Committee to represent all wings of the movement, whether pro-war or anti-war, with a view to bringing pressure to bear on the Government to tackle the economic and social grievances of the workers. Sylvia, however, was not invited to join the WNC and she failed to follow Lansbury in working his passage back into the Party. If anything she became more alienated from Parliamentary politics during the war. To her credit she maintained pressure for an extension of the vote to women, but she steadily lost patience with the Labour Party for its failure to insist on full adult suffrage.

Sylvia's sense of isolation within the Labour Movement was exacerbated by the death of Keir Hardie in 1915. Along with Ramsay MacDonald, Philip Snowden and George Lansbury he had found himself in a minority in adopting a hostile view of the war. After suffering a stroke he entered a nursing home at Caterham early in 1915, but never recovered his health. 'Each time I saw him I knew that he was suffering, that he was tortured by bodily pain and mental anguish', wrote Sylvia. When, towards the end of May he informed her he was preparing to leave London she 'understood that he was announcing to me his imminent death, that he had no hope of recovery'.[26] In a shaky hand he wrote inviting Sylvia to take all her letters to him and the two paintings – 'the products of your genius' – which hung at Nevill's Court.[27] At this last meeting things were a little awkward between them, partly because she regretted not having seen him more often and, no doubt, because she wished to avoid giving way to her emotions. He then left for Scotland to spend his final days in the care of his wife and died there in September. Sylvia had no means of expressing her grief except by writing a eulogy to him.[28] But she retained their letters, the proof of their love and a source of inspiration, for the rest of her life.

To some extent the gulf left by Hardie was filled by rekindled friendships with other former colleagues now active in the anti-war movement, notably Emmeline Pethick-Lawrence, Henry Nevinson, George Lansbury and Fenner Brockway. They were united in a common despair at the politicians' determination to impose military conscription in 1916 and to fight the war to a complete victory over Germany however many casualties this involved. Sylvia joined the

Women's International League for Peace and Freedom, which emerged from a meeting of women from several belligerent countries at the Hague in April 1915. She had planned to attend the inaugural meeting at the Hague but was prevented when the Home Secretary failed to issue permits to cross the Channel. This was the occasion for a public dressing down from her mother: 'I am out of patience with this women's peace conference. English women who go to it are showing themselves strangely thoughtless of the welfare of their country. This is not a time for a move for peace.' Embarrassed at being confronted with Sylvia's involvement, Emmeline insisted: 'She does not realize that she is being influenced by German propagandists who initiated it . . . If I could dissuade my daughter I would do it; but she won't listen.'[29] For her part Sylvia was less concerned about her mother's criticisms than about opinion in the East End. She showed characteristic courage throughout the war not only in advocating a negotiated peace settlement, but in urging tolerance towards the local Jewish and German people whose shops were a tempting target especially when London began to suffer from Zeppelin raids. But when she and her band of speakers set up in Victoria Park they were usually pelted with rotten vegetables and had their platforms overturned by the crowds.[30] Most women believed it would be a betrayal of their sons and husbands to make peace before the Germans had been defeated. The leading London working-class politicians and union leaders – Will Thorne, Will Crooks, Jack Jones and Ben Tillett – adopted belligerently nationalist views, and against them Sylvia carried little weight in spite of Lansbury's support. Consequently, despite her welfare work, the membership of her branches and sales of the *Dreadnought* dwindled during the war. Part of the explanation for this indifference lay in the improvement in material conditions after the initial disruption caused to local employment. The massive expansion of Woolwich Arsenal and other munitions works attracted thousands of younger women into relatively highly paid employment and boosted family incomes in the second half of the war period. As a result Sylvia never managed to politicize the women of the East End and her work was sustained by a small band comprising Norah Smythe, Minnie Lansbury and Charlotte Drake. In the second half of the war she was outflanked by the conventional party organizations in their drive to organize women.

In these circumstance it is hardly surprising that Sylvia eventually became sceptical about the vote and Parliamentary politics in general.

Meanwhile in Australia Adela had shot to prominence as an outspoken opponent of the war. She joined the Women's Peace Alliance and the Australian Peace Alliance and wrote a notable pamphlet entitled *Put Up The Sword*. Her chief role was as a regular speaker at the Bijou Theatre in Melbourne and at Sunday afternoon rallies at the Gaiety Theatre where her self-confidence and courage in the face of howling mobs of soldiers attracted admiration. Adela's opposition to the war appears to have been instinctive rather than ideological, and though she became increasingly anti-imperial in this period, at least one contemporary felt that 'she understood little of basic Socialist theory'.[31] She may also have been influenced by Vida Goldstein, a long-standing pacifist, and by Robert Ross the leading figure in the Socialist party in the state of Victoria, who had befriended her soon after her arrival in Australia.

Australian opinion was evidently more mixed than that in either Britain or the United States. On the one hand, their English origins made many Australians instinctive supporters of the Allies, but in time an element of nationalism began to emerge, especially after the fiasco of the Gallipoli Campaign in 1915 which was widely attributed to the incompetence of English military leaders. By 1915 the demand for troops had forced the issue of conscription on to the agenda in Australia as it had in Britain. The new prime minister, Billy Hughes, who found himself expelled by the Australian Labor Party for advocating conscription, determined to challenge his opponents by holding a referendum. After returning from a speaking tour of New Zealand in June and July 1916, Adela threw herself into the anti-conscription campaign in Queensland and Victoria. Despite her brief time in Australia she now began to show signs of Australian nationalism when she expressed the view that Australia was not simply part of a military empire and ought to remain neutral. She associated herself with the cry for a new political party that would be Socialist and anti-imperial. When the referendum eventually took place in November the opponents of conscription scored a famous victory by a margin of over 70,000 votes. How far this outcome reflected support for pacifism seems doubtful, since the state of Victoria voted in favour of conscription; it was the rural areas, influenced simply by the fear of losing their labour, that tipped the result against the government.[32] But whatever the explanation, the referendum represented the high point of Adela's political career in Australia, for it had given her the kind of national prominence that had eluded her during her years of work in Britain. The triumph was won at a cost, however, for Adela emerged totally exhausted from her campaign and may have been close to another breakdown. She then fell out with Vida Goldstein and was obliged to quit the Women's Political Association because her views were now regarded as too extreme. She had begun to leave her feminism behind and was becoming more of a Socialist.

Although obviously aware of Adela's activities in Australia, Emmeline and Christabel appear to have had no contact with her at this time. She described her mother's reaction to her anti-conscription campaign as ridiculous: 'But it was the family attitude – Cause First and human relations – nowhere. . . if [Emmeline] had been tolerant and broadminded, she would not have been the leader of the suffragettes.'[33] Australia did not impinge on Emmeline and Christabel's work except in so far as they enthusiastically took up Billy Hughes, the Labor premier, whom they regarded as a prime candidate for membership of the War Council in Britain. Hughes's entry on to the British domestic scene exemplified the impact of war in undermining normal party allegiances and promoting the emergence of new political configurations, largely based upon cross-party alliances amongst enthusiasts for the war effort; this gave the Pankhursts a chance to build relationships which were to yield dividends at the end of the war. For a time their vociferous attacks on the Asquith cabinet obscured the remarkable rapprochement taking place between themselves and the Chancellor of the Exchequer, David Lloyd George. Although Christabel had repeatedly denounced him as crooked and devious, the gulf between them was always more apparent than real. Though she refused to recognize the fact, Lloyd George had been consistently pro-suffragist and had never regarded militancy as morally wrong, merely as politically inexpedient. In any case, despite being a favourite victim of suffragette attacks, he bore no lasting resentment towards his opponents. In many ways Lloyd George, Christabel Pankhurst and Winston Churchill shared a common approach to politics; not greatly inhibited by ideology or consistency of thought, they instinctively focussed on immediate problems, often to the exclusion of all other considerations. This was unsettling for their more prosaic colleagues who regarded them as opportunists. Lloyd George had already shown himself Christabel's equal in his speedy adjustment to the conditions of wartime; sloughing off his earlier reputation as a critic of naval expenditure, he championed the view that nothing should be allowed to stand in the way of an outright military victory. While the Government hesitated to state Britain's war aims, all those who opposed the idea of a negotiated or compromise peace settlement found themselves looking to Lloyd George as a potential war leader.

Although he did not have a great deal to do in his capacity as Chancellor, Lloyd George's reputation rose while that of his colleagues wilted under a barrage of criticism over the inability of the generals and admirals to produce any conspicuous victories. This made things awkward for a prime minister due to face an election in 1915.[34] However, Asquith skilfully averted the threat to his government in May 1915 by taking advantage of two crises arising over munitions and the Dardanelles campaign to offer the Conservatives a coalition government, which Bonar Law readily accepted. This sudden demise of the purely Liberal administration met with rejoicing in the right-wing press, especially in the papers of Lord Northcliffe who modestly claimed responsibility. Emmeline met him on the day the Government fell: 'He was quite like a lunatic, bouncing up and down on the leather seat of his arm-chair, crying out: "I did it."' Emmeline, evidently a little embarrassed at this outburst, pointed out that the worst of the old ministers, Grey, remained in his post. At this Northcliffe leapt to his feet crying: 'Don't you worry, my dear girl, I'll get 'em all out.'[35]

Emmeline was correct in so far as Asquith had retained all the key posts except the Admiralty in Liberal hands. But in the process of reorganization he had created an entirely new job, the Minister for Munitions, to which he appointed Lloyd George. One side-effect of this was to accelerate the burgeoning alliance between Lloyd George and the Pankhursts. By 1915 the effect of massive and indiscriminate recruitment had been to create shortages of labour, especially amongst skilled engineering workers upon whom output of munitions depended. Lloyd George had therefore to win the unions' agreement to the substitution of unskilled labour for skilled workers, buy off industrial action by offering wage increases, and achieve more regular work by reducing the incidence of drunkenness which he believed to be hampering production. As a result Lloyd George was understandably prey to all kinds of fears, and consequently on the lookout for new allies and novel ways of achieving his targets. In a speech in March on 'Why Women Should Be Mobilized' Emmeline had argued that Germany was the masculine state which idealized force and upheld the low status of women. She expressed the hope that the new Coalition would declare martial law with a view to imposing universal service for all adults: 'Why have women not been called in to replace workers?' she demanded. 'Germany has 500,000 women in making munitions.' She also claimed that only 2,000 of the 70,000 British women who had registered with the Board of Trade's Labour Exchanges had so far been found employment.[36]

To Lloyd George it seemed obvious that women workers offered a quick – and economical – solution to the shortage of labour. But he had to build up a demand for the change in order to overcome the entrenched resistance of workers fearful of the long-term effects of using low-paid women in hitherto skilled jobs. His unorthodox working methods made him unusually open to the overtures of the Pankhursts. Ever since he first became a minister in 1905 he had bypassed regular channels, especially in the civil service, dealt directly with the interested parties, and used personal contacts and advisers to obtain information and expertise independent of that offered by his official advisers. The Pankhursts fitted perfectly into this approach to government. In addition to Emmeline, other former suffragettes including Grace Roe, Flora Drummond and Charlotte Marsh were invited on an ad hoc basis to undertake work for the Government in a semi-official capacity. This connection proved to be all the easier because of the role of Frances Stevenson at Number 11 Downing Street.[37] Though often portrayed by historians as merely his mistress, Frances Stevenson was in fact, an important figure in her own right. Well educated and as fascinated by politics as Lloyd George himself, she was an emancipated young woman who supported votes for women. If the Chancellor was too busy, she was usually available to act as go-between for him and the suffragette leaders.

In June Lord Stamfordham reported to Lloyd George that the King was 'wondering whether it would be possible to make use of Mrs Pankhurst' in connection with the enlistment of female workers.[38] The Chancellor sent Sir James Murray, a sympathetic Liberal MP, to her to discuss collaboration, and from this emerged the idea for a big demonstration or procession of women demanding employment in munitions.[39] Grace Roe was appointed to organize the event which was to be funded to the tune of £3,500 from the ministry's propaganda fund.[40] The marchers set off from the Embankment to the Ministry of Munitions where Emmeline presented a deputation including Flora Annie Steel, Lady Glanusk, Lady Byron, the Honourable Mrs Freddie Guest, Lady Butlin and Clara Butt. In his response Lloyd George assured them: 'Without women victory will tarry, and the victory that tarries means a victory whose footprints are footprints of blood.'[41] He followed this up by dispatching Grace Roe to France to report on the type of work done by women in munitions, their rates of pay and the provisions made for feeding and housing them.[42] To her credit Emmeline took the opportunity to emphasize that the women should be given *skilled* work, and asked for equal rates of pay. Lloyd George offered equal rates for piece work, but since in practice they were paid by the hour this proved to be a dead letter.[43]

Although these initiatives led to a major influx of women into munitions, Lloyd George continued to worry about the morale and co-operation of the male workers. The number of strikes had greatly diminished during 1915 and 1916 by comparison with the pre-war level, but he remained dissatisfied. 'I want someone to rouse the munitions workers to some sense of their responsibility', he wrote. 'Many of them are working well; others are disgracefully slack, and most of them could do better if they made a real effort.' When he talked with the employers they readily confirmed his view that many men were indifferent, sulky or simply turned up for work drunk.[44] None of them seem to have recognized that the extremely long hours worked may have had something to do with this. A fresh threat to munitions arose in July 1915 when the South Wales coalfield became engulfed in a strike over a demand for a pay rise of 20 per cent. All this convinced Lloyd George of the need to send government missionaries to all the key manufacturing districts to counter anti-war sentiment and rekindle the original patriotic spirit of 1914.[45] He hoped to employ men with front-line experience in this role, but this was easier said than done, for the soldiers generally developed a healthy scepticism about domestic war propaganda. Instead he used a motley collection of lecturers including some bishops, the patriotic union leader, Ben Tillett, and a number of former suffragettes.

As a result Emmeline, Flora Drummond and Mrs Dacre Fox spent much of the autumn of 1915 campaigning in South Wales where meetings were held at Cardiff, Pontypool, Maesteg, Rhondda, Merthyr, Dowlais, Abertillery, Pontypridd and Aberdare. Speaking at Neath, Emmeline was reported as saying she 'did not think the people of Wales adequately realized the stern struggle that was taking place, otherwise the miners would have forgotten their industrial dissensions; a prolonged strike would paralyse the Navy, and if there were an invasion of England the men would be traitors to the women and their country'.[46] The significance of these meetings is questionable, for only workers who were already co-operative and well disposed to the war effort were likely to attend voluntarily. It was therefore easy to be misled by a favourable reception. However, by the end of the war Emmeline and Christabel had convinced themselves, on the basis of their tours in the industrial districts, that they had the ear of the British working class, a delusion which was to have fatal results for Christabel's attempt to enter Parliament in December 1918.

In the short term, however, this missionary work gained them a vital foot in the door whenever they wanted to request urgent consultations with the Chancellor. 'If vigorous action is taken to arouse patriotic and national feeling', Emmeline told him in October, 'much can be done to counteract the pernicious influence of the U[nion] of D[emocratic] C[ontrol]. Strikes and rumours of strikes fill the air. We are working night and day and have huge meetings but we come into the field very late.'[47] There was a self-serving element in this. The more lurid the picture of disaffection she painted, the greater the need for Emmeline and her fellow propagandists to continue their work. In fact, opposition to the war from Socialists and pacifists was very slight in 1915; the industrial discontent was usually motivated by the need to catch up with the rapidly rising cost of living. However, Lloyd George appears to have been at least half-willing to endorse Emmeline's diagnosis of the situation: 'The seditious element has been fostered there by a very well-organized propaganda', he wrote. 'Still, the evil effects are for the present confined to a minority.'[48]

Emmeline's restless patriotism was by no means satiated even by her new role in helping Lloyd George boost the output of munitions. In June she announced a new WSPU initiative for the adoption of 'war babies'. The origins of this idea lay with Kitchener's recruits who had left thousands of young women pregnant but unmarried on their departure for the front. Nine months later when the nation woke up to the deluge of illegitimate births, there was a general feeling that they should be welcomed as 'war babies', a patriotic contribution to the war effort. Emmeline's rash intervention reflected this mood. She appealed for contributions to finance a home for no fewer than fifty babies which she hoped to establish somewhere on the outskirts of London.[49] Accustomed as she was to raising large sums of money almost effortlessly, she was shocked and hurt by the meagre response to this appeal. The reluctance to contribute may partly have reflected the fact that wealthy people had so many other calls on their generosity during the war; but it was also an indication of Emmeline's declining reputation amongst many supporters of the women's movement. As a result her plans were rapidly scaled down. Emmeline visited an orphanage with Katherine Marshall who remonstrated with her for choosing to adopt four three-year-old girls. 'My dear', replied Emmeline, 'I wonder I did not take forty.'[50] Their names were Kathleen King, Mary Gordon, Joan Pembridge and Elizabeth Tudor. According to Emmeline, two of the girls' fathers had been killed at the front and their mothers were unable to look after them.

From every point of view the adoption of the war babies proved to be unwise. Ethel Smyth, who jeopardized their friendship by trying to dissuade her, believed Emmeline's real motive lay in an unconscious longing for a proper home of her own.[51] Since her own interest in young children was extremely limited, in practice the care of the four girls was entrusted to Nurse Pine, though even she was unable to give them a secure long-term relationship. Nor did Emmeline possess the means to support the children, and the responsibility she had so rashly undertaken obliged her to carry on working in her sixties when her health was failing. Even during the war she was reduced to organizing sales of work which raised modest sums of around £30 a time, in the name of the WSPU, in order to maintain her charges.

To the Pankhursts' critics, now growing vociferous, all these initiatives indicated how far they had drifted from their moorings since the outbreak of the war. When Christabel returned from the United States in February 1915, she sailed to Naples before returning to France, where she seems to have divided her time between Paris and Deauville. In May she took part in the ceremonies to celebrate Joan of Arc's *fête* day.[52] But by the autumn rank and file members of the WSPU had begun to organize angry protest meetings over her prolonged absence. Speaking at the London Pavilion in November, Emmeline found herself subject to continual interruptions from women demanding an apology from her for accusing another suffragette of being pro-German. Annie Kenney, in the chair, found it impossible to control the hecklers, and many people walked out when Emmeline refused to back down.[53] Members increasingly felt that she was using the Union's name to promote objects which were outside its remit; in effect, she had disbanded the organization by suspending its work in 1914 but had continued to draw upon its funds for her personal schemes: 'This unwarrantable usurpation has resulted in the removal from the members' list of almost all women who are possessed of influence, capacity or independence of thought', claimed one of the critics.[54] Of course, this was by no means the first time such criticisms had been made, and Emmeline simply swept the complaints aside. She did, however, feel obliged to answer the damaging demand that Christabel should resign from the organization unless she returned from France and took up some war service. 'I'm not nursing soldiers', Christabel reportedly declared, 'there are so many others to do that . . . it is no more to be expected that our organizers should now necessarily take to knitting than that Mr Asquith should set his ministers to making army boots.'[55] Her mother insisted that her war service consisted in putting the Allied case in America, and that by remaining in France she kept in much closer touch with military events and with Allied opinion. But there was no answer to the demand for a proper financial statement for the Union. The accounts had not been rendered since February 1914 when an annual income of £46,000 had been recorded. Moreover, the conviction that this money had been misappropriated for the Pankhursts' own purposes continued to rankle for many years, and it hindered the efforts made to raise money for Emmeline when she was in real difficulties during the immediate post-war period.

In the short term the effect of these controversies was to inflict several more breakaways on the already diminished Union membership. In October 1915 Rose Lamartine Yates founded the Suffragettes of the WSPU as a democratic organization designed to revive the campaign for the vote, and Charlotte Marsh set up the Independent WSPU in March 1916. But by then it hardly mattered, for Emmeline and Christabel had burned their boats with the women's movement; the connection was not likely to be revived even after the war. They may have drawn some comfort from the fact that none of the criticisms made by other suffragists were much reported by the British press. *The Times*, once an eager critic, made no mention of these disputes, presumably because Northcliffe had decided to promote Emmeline in her new role as a war leader.

From her comfortable retreat at the Villa Angele at Deauville – 'a nice quiet little place with such a good climate' – Christabel remained outwardly unperturbed by the criticism, no doubt because she sensed that the political situation was moving in her favour. Regarding the Asquith premiership as a temporary affair, she maintained her contacts with Bonar Law, who seemed likely to become the next prime minister. 'At present', she told him, 'the Government of the country is in the hands of Grey, Asquith and Haldane who have no intention whatever of inflicting a real defeat upon Germany. [It] is a Government which not only cannot but will not win the war.'[56] Christabel had aligned herself with the opponents of the western-front strategy, Lloyd George and Churchill, who argued that Britain ought to use her naval power to avoid the stalemate in France and Belgium by launching attacks elsewhere; by knocking away the 'props' – Austria and Turkey – the Allies would undermine Germany and shorten the war. She especially favoured focussing on the Balkans, believing that the war could be won in the east. Of course, Christabel had very little knowledge of south-east Europe or of military strategy, and so she instructed Annie Kenney and Grace Roe to dig up some information about Serbia for her. She also studied south-east Europe under Professor Seton Watson and the exiled Czech leader Thomas Masaryk. Christabel's thesis was that Germany intended to establish her grip on the Balkans and use this to control the Persian Gulf. From this it followed that Sir Edward Grey's reluctance to rescue the Serbs from Austria was a betrayal of British interests. This, she argued, would isolate Russia from the West and lead the small states to fall under Germany's sway: 'The Balkans simply must be wrested from the German grip. That is for us a question of life and death.'[57] This was perfectly plausible in theory, but Christabel's diagnosis overlooked the facts of the situation. As a landlocked state, Serbia was difficult to help. In any case, when Britain and France landed 400,000 troops at Salonika with a view to advancing north to support the Serbs, they found that, in the absence of good communications, progress was just as slow as on the western front. There were no easy answers except for armchair strategists. To be fair, Christabel was in good company and her criticisms did her no harm with Lloyd George who spent much of the war trying to undermine the policy of Sir Douglas Haig and Sir William Robertson, the Chief of the Imperial General Staff, who were devout 'westerners'.

From Deauville Christabel issued weekly articles calling for the resignation of Asquith and Robertson, demanding that Billy Hughes be brought into the government, and accusing Sir Edward Grey of treason. By 1916 her propaganda had descended to mere absurdity and attracted the attentions of the Special Branch. Police raided the Union's headquarters, Emmeline was briefly arrested in mid-speech in Trafalgar Square, the Albert Hall was banned to the Pankhursts, and printers became reluctant to handle *Britannia*. At the end of December 1915 the paper suddenly appeared in typescript form and was published only at irregular intervals during January and February 1916. But to Emmeline and Christabel all this was proof of the conspiracy in high places which was responsible for Britain's slow progress in the war.

Emmeline herself had spent the first half of 1916 on another visit to the United States. On arrival she was again subjected to the indignity of an examination by the Board of Enquiry at Ellis Island, ordered expelled and granted parole pending her appeal. The Labor Department claimed that if she had notified them of her arrival they would have completed the formalities on board ship and allowed her to land.[58] On this occasion Emmeline travelled in the company of the

Serbian Secretary of State for Foreign Affairs and the Serbian Minister in London with the aim of organizing a relief commission similar to the one for Belgian refugees in London and appealing for financial aid. Although this tour attracted much less attention than her previous ones, it gave her the opportunity to travel to British Columbia where she publicized the Union's work on behalf of the war babies and declared its wider aim of removing the stigma attached to illegitimacy.[59] She received no remuneration for her lectures, but apparently took collections for the War Babies Fund. Emmeline so liked what she saw of the west coast that she returned to Canada after the war with a view to settling there with her four girls permanently. The money she raised helped her to set up a new home for them at Number 50 Clarendon Road, Kensington, in the autumn of 1916, where Catherine Pine assumed responsibility for their upbringing.

When Emmeline eventually sailed for Liverpool at the end of July, she returned to find that, against all expectations, the question of votes for women had returned to the political agenda. The reason had nothing directly to do with women's role in the war effort. The Government found itself obliged to resurrect the general issue of electoral reform simply because, owing to the reduction in the life of Parliament in 1911, a general election was now overdue. Unfortunately, huge numbers of men had left their homes, not only to join the armed forces but to work in munitions factories, in the process interrupting the twelve-month residence qualification which all household voters – who comprised 84 per cent of the total – required in order to register.[60] Some ministers wanted to put off the whole question because it was so politically contentious and because the three-party Coalition made an election unnecessary, but Lloyd George told Asquith: 'I feel [the soldiers] have a right to a voice in choosing the Government that sent them to face peril and death.'[61] He could not be ignored because the Conservatives, many of whom had joined the government with great reluctance, refused to extend Asquith's lease unconditionally; they agreed to extend the life of the old Parliament for only eight or nine months at a time throughout the war, so an election was never very far away. But if an election remained a possibility, then they had somehow to bring the register of voters up to date. It was estimated that by June 1916 the register represented under 60 per cent of those entitled to vote.[62] Yet it was difficult to restore the pre-war voters on the basis of their war service without at the same time introducing a full-scale reform of the voting system by enfranchising the men who had not previously been qualified. Neither Liberals nor Conservatives really wanted to take up women's suffrage during the war, but since they felt obliged to deal with votes for *men* they could not exclude it altogether. In cabinet discussions Arthur Henderson emphasized that if they agreed to extend the vote as a reward for war service to men in the forces it would impossible to rule out those who had been excluded for health reasons or because they had been withheld in vital domestic occupations; the same logic would apply to women. He even suggested, though with what authority if any is not clear, that the women's organizations would be satisfied with a vote for women aged twenty-five and over.[63]

While these arguments continued in the private of the cabinet room, the suffrage organizations worked on the assumption that reform remained unlikely until the end of the war. At the end of 1915 the Labour Party's Workers' National Committee rebuffed Sylvia's demand for action on the vote: 'The public mood is far too much centred on war matters to concern itself very much about suffrage.'[64] However, as some sort of legislation dealing with electoral reform seemed likely, Millicent Fawcett decided to write to Asquith in May 1916. He replied that in the unlikely event of a bill being introduced women's suffrage would be 'fully and impartially weighed without any prejudgement from the controversies of the past'.[65] The non-militants deemed this enough to justify writing further letters to sympathetic politicians, but no public campaign was launched. Emmeline and Christabel took so little interest in the issue that their new ally, Lord Northcliffe, who had now decided to throw his support behind votes for women, badgered non-militants such as Lady Betty Balfour and Millicent Fawcett urging them to organize a public meeting. 'I do not suggest window breaking', he wrote, 'but I do think that some great meeting or united deputation is necessary.'[66] If this were done, he pointed out, it would give the newspapers the opportunity of discussing the issue again. Though amused by Northcliffe's transformation into a suffragist, Fawcett and Balfour ignored him. Meanwhile, in a debate on the updating of the electoral register a Conservative member,

Commander Bellairs, claimed to have been authorized by Mrs Pankhurst to state that the WSPU would never oppose giving votes to the troops even if women were not included.[67] They suspected that Asquith would try to use women to deny a vote to men just as he had used the male franchise to exclude women before the war. This was an indication of how far the Pankhursts' agenda had moved since August 1914. There was now a real risk that Parliament would try to resolve the problem by offering a vote to men on the basis of war service, thereby erecting a further barrier to women after the war.

Eventually the prime minister produced a rather vague proposal to transfer the responsibility for drawing up a comprehensive scheme of reform to be implemented after the war to a committee of backbenchers. This subsequently became the Speaker's Conference when James Lowther, the Speaker of the Commons, was appointed as chairman of the twenty-seven MPs and five peers who were chosen to represent all four parties. At the time no one expected Lowther to succeed, but for Asquith the Speaker's Conference was a timely expedient for shelving the whole issue for the duration of the war. From the point of view of women's suffrage the merit of the scheme was that nothing was ruled out of its terms of reference.[68] The members were supposed to have been selected so as to be evenly balanced on women's suffrage but, as Lowther admitted, it was no longer possible to be certain about their views.[69] Contrary to expectations, the conference met from 12 October and managed to report its conclusions by the New Year. By that time a new Coalition had taken power under the leadership of Lloyd George.

14

Revolution and Reaction (1917–18)

'Our eager hopes are for the speedy success of the Bolsheviks in Russia: may they open the door which leads to freedom for the people of all lands.'

Sylvia Pankhurst, *Workers' Dreadnought*, 17 November 1917

Emmeline and Christabel were far from being alone in their critical view of the way the war was being run. In December 1916 dissatisfaction culminated in a confrontation between a cabal of leading politicians, including Lloyd George and Bonar Law, and Asquith over their demand for a small war cabinet to supersede the talkative and unwieldy pre-war cabinet. After some complex manoeuvres Lloyd George accepted the King's invitation to form a new coalition which saw Britain through to victory in November 1918. These momentous events had important indirect consequences for the Pankhursts. It is an indication of the standing enjoyed by Emmeline with the new prime minister – or perhaps her presumption – that she wrote to Lloyd George asking to see him before he had even composed his cabinet. She argued that as women would not be directly represented they ought to be consulted, and she was anxious, as ever, to see Grey and Robertson excluded from the government.[1] There is, however, no indication that the premier agreed to see her. But Emmeline and Christabel were undoubtedly shrewd in consolidating their links with Lloyd George. His readiness to improvise and experiment with the machinery of government led him to invent new ministries and innumerable ad hoc committees to investigate various aspects of the war effort to which he frequently appointed experts and specialists unconnected with the political parties; in the process he created new opportunities for women to play prominent roles.

One surmises that Lloyd George took some enjoyment from the persistent attacks on Sir William Robertson in the pages of *Britannia* which led the police to raid the Union's headquarters in Portland Street, along with Annie Kenney's flat, in January 1917, and to seize their printing press at Catford. Christabel interpreted all this as proof that the conspiracy which had hampered the prosecution of the war lingered even under the new government. But Lord Derby, the Secretary of State for War, justified the raids on the grounds that the material in *Britannia* was calculated to undermine the authority of an officer and to damage Britain's credibility with her Allies.[2] The author of the offending articles still lay in Paris where she passed her material to Grace Roe, who made the weary and dangerous crossing each week. Christabel simply turned her fire from Robertson to the hapless politicians, including Grey, Haldane and Asquith, who were no longer in office, and also two new Conservative ministers, Balfour and Lord Robert Cecil. *Britannia* also launched a Victory Fund open to everyone who wanted to prevent a compromise peace settlement – which the Pankhursts took to be the main aim of the Foreign Office. This looks suspiciously like a way of tapping patriotic sentiment for the benefit of the WSPU. However, although the various war bonds had attracted huge sums of money, subscribers appear to have been rather hesitant about the new Victory Fund, for only about a third of the modest £10,000 target was collected. After a break of four years Emmeline made an appearance in court in February in connection with a rather bizarre case in which one Alice Wheeldon was accused of plotting to assassinate the prime minister. During cross-examination it was alleged that before the war the suffragettes had spent between £300 and £500 in attempts to kill Lloyd George by smuggling a chamber maid into his hotel equipped with a poisoned nail which was to be driven through the sole of his shoe. It was a sign of the times that the judge decided it would only be fair to allow Emmeline, who was not actually involved in the case, to appear in the witness box to deny these accusations.[3] The affair gave Christabel the opportunity for a lavish application of flattery: 'Our new Prime Minister', she wrote, 'has no more loyal supporters than the suffragettes, who regard his life as one of the most precious necessities, not only for Great Britain, but also for noble France, which is so dear to us.'⁴

Among Lloyd George's innovations Emmeline and Christabel enthusiastically approved the Imperial War Council, whose members included Billy Hughes, the Australian premier, on whose behalf they had run a 'We Want Hughes' campaign during 1916. Hughes, of course, personified the continuing rift between them and Adela. They took the trouble of sending Annie Kenney to Australia to support Hughes in his unsuccessful referendum campaign on conscription, and were immensely irritated at Adela's prominence in the opposite camp. If anything, Adela continued to move leftwards at this time, for the referendum campaign had made her a figure of admiration with many Socialists and trade unionists such as Robert Ross, whose journal, *Ross's Magazine*, published articles by her. It was to Ross that Adela first confessed that she had decided to leave the Women's Political Association. There had always been some friction with Vida Goldstein whom the Socialists regarded as a bourgeois feminist, a rift which made things increasingly awkward for Adela. Contact with Ross had reactivated the intense sympathy she had felt for the working class back in Manchester: 'Socialism is the only thing', as she put it in a letter to Sylvia.⁵ Like Sylvia, Adela had come to regard the women's movement as a little too narrow, and to believe that women's griev-ances would best be resolved in the context of a wider working-class assault on capitalism. There may also have been a personal element. Though grateful to Vida, the mercurial Adela found her cautious and measured approach rather irksome after a while. Consequently she moved into the Ross family home as a paying guest in January 1917 and worked as an organizer for the Victoria Socialist Party.

Full of books, argumentative people and a succession of visiting radicals, Ross's home probably reminded Adela of the Pankhursts' earlier life in Manchester. Among the temporary guests were three girls, Hannah, Bessie and Sallie Walsh, the daughters of Tom Walsh, who stayed there while their father was away at sea. Walsh's wife, Margaret, had died in April 1914. He was an experienced Union leader, associated with the International Workers of the World, who also had a reputation for enjoying his drink and for dealing in contra-band goods. Adela had already met him in the course of the referendum campaign, and one can see why she found him attractive. He was a colourful and straightforward character, who shared her opinions, but was heavily burdened by his three motherless girls. However, few of their friends suspected a romantic connection because Tom spent much of his time away at sea while Adela continued to be in demand as a speaker. February found her at Perth loudly attacking capitalism, militarism and Lloyd George. She also began to encourage window-breaking as part of the protest over the high price of bread. In fact, by 1917 her speeches were considered subversive enough to warrant the attendance of an army intelligence reporter. As a result the police closed down a number of her meetings and the authorities considered prosecuting her for sedition. As in Britain, they felt increasingly worried by the effects of working-class discontent on the war effort; by August the wave of strikes in shipping, railways, trams and the mines threatened to develop into a general strike. Consequently Adela was kept under surveillance and Ross's house was subjected to raids by the police in search of evidence. During the autumn of 1917 Adela even began to change her address in order to avoid the summonses now being issued by the courts. Finally, after leading a torchlight procession to Parliament House in early September, she received a six-month sentence, though she was later released on appeal.

In the course of this hectic activity Tom and Adela fell in love; they were discovered by Ross's son one day holding hands in the sitting room. This came as a surprise to their friends, for although Adela had been an object of admiration among many of the younger men, none had made a move because they felt a little intimidated by her reputation.[6] Tom, who was fourteen years older than Adela, clearly suffered fewer inhibitions. Even so, his appeal for Adela puzzled many people who knew them. Born in County Cork in 1871, Tom had gone to sea at the age of eight and, in his periods of rest, had managed to give himself a rudimentary education largely by reading William Morris, Marx, Engels and other Socialist writers on class. He had arrived in Australia in 1893, aged twenty-two, where he worked on ships sailing the coast and the New Zealand route. From 1908 he was employed by the Seamen's Union, rose to become secretary of the New South Wales branch and thus became acquainted with Robert Ross and the Socialist Party. Though to outsiders Walsh often appeared dour and irritable, Adela found him an exciting and impressive figure. In some ways their relationship resembled that of her mother and father, for they set out with the intention of combining their married life with their political causes. Tom, who had been brought up a Home Ruler, remembered going to hear Richard Pankhurst speak on the subject. Middle-class feminist friends like Vida Goldstein professed to be disappointed; Adela, she said, 'might have chosen a man more of the same mental calibre as herself'.[7] In fact, they were rather similar, and despite his lack of polish Tom Walsh proved himself to be an able lawyer when arguing his union's case in the courts. Goldstein's reactions were probably attributable to snobbery and irritation with Adela for abandoning the women's organization. For her part, the 32-year-old Adela was understandably wondering where life was going to take her. There was probably an element of truth in her remark that she had married Tom for his children and fallen in love with him later! She had always liked young children and seems to have taken on the three girls – Hannah, aged fifteen, Bessie, aged twelve, and Sallie, aged eleven – very successfully. They gave Adela what had hitherto been so elusive in her life – a ready-made family and a real sense of security. She claimed that the marriage was the one really successful thing in her life.

Tom and Adela were married on 30 September 1917 by Frederick Sinclaire of the Free Religious Fellowship; Robert Ross gave her away and Hannah Walsh acted as bridesmaid. From England only Sylvia sent her congratulations, but at least regular contact had been re-established and the three girls began to write to 'Auntie' Sylvia. In any case, Adela was by now impervious to the disapproval of her family. 'This is the life, isn't it,' she wrote to Sylvia two months after the wedding. 'I am happy, more than happy, to carry on our father's work.' Not that things were entirely easy, for from the start money was very short, although according to Adela, Tom planned to start a business 'which ought to make us fairly well to do'.[8] In fact, Adela effectively moved down the social scale by becoming a working-class mother and housewife with no servants and few material comforts or luxuries.

After only six days their married life was interrupted when Adela appeared before the magistrates on an outstanding charge for which she received a four-month sentence. On declaring her intention of giving up politics and concentrating on her family she was released on bail. However, Adela's resolution did not last, and by the end of October she was in Pentridge prison from which she was released early in November pending an appeal. Subsequently the authorities sent her to a women's prison to serve four months. After the brief elation of the wedding this left Adela very depressed, fretting about the children and concerned about missing a second referendum campaign during December:

Tom, I get frightened, sometimes, wondering whether I shall ever get out and find things alright when I do – whether we are ever to have our happy life together. Oh darling, I was so happy for those few weeks. It was a lovely dream. Can it ever be again?[9]

After a visit from Tom she calmed down: 'I don't seem to notice the gaol today because I have the sense that you are still with me.'[10] Fortunately, by January 1918 the government had been deluged with appeals for her release. Hughes, who had won a new term of office in 1917, was prepared to be magnanimous and remitted the remainder of her sentence on 10 January. Tom, meanwhile, had been elected secretary of the New South Wales branch of the Seamen's Union. This meant leaving Melbourne for Sydney where they took a modest flat in the suburb of West Concord. There they created a happy if slightly anarchic home. In November Adela gave birth to her first child, a boy named Richard after her father. But despite previous claims, she had no intention of giving up politics. She now devoted herself to the trade union movement and especially to supporting Tom by editing the *Seamen's Journal*. On one occasion when he was called away to Melbourne she joined him, depositing Richard and his tin of baby food with the Rosses while she dashed off to attend a meeting.[11] By her energy and sheer force of personality Adela succeeded in combining her increasingly onerous domestic role with the public interests which were to sustain her marriage for years to come.

While Adela charted her new course in life, her mother and sister found themselves reluctantly returning to an old concern: votes for women. By January 1917 the Speaker's Conference, somewhat to the general surprise, had put its proposals to the new prime minister. Yet

Christabel remained in France while Emmeline 'held rather aloof from the negotiations that attended the Speaker's Conference', as she euphemistically put it.[12] In fact, neither wanted to be involved, nor was there much scope for them to be. The conference had arrived at a comprehensive scheme of reform covering all aspects of the electoral system of which the central proposal was a vote for all men over twenty-one years based on a simple residence qualification. Towards the end of their deliberations the members tackled women's suffrage, determined not to put the whole compromise in jeopardy over this one issue. They voted 15–6 in favour of enfranchising at least some women, but 12–10 against an equal franchise with men. This allowed Willoughby Dickinson to resurrect his proposal to enfranchise women who already had a local government vote *and* those who were married to local government voters, thereby obviating the long-standing objection to confining the vote to single women. As a safeguard against women becoming a majority of voters the conference recommended imposing an age limit of thirty or thirty-five years.[13]

When Lowther reported these proposals to Lloyd George on 18 January, no one knew for sure how many women were involved. The figure of 6 million was widely quoted, but in fact, no fewer than 8.4 million got the vote, which was far higher than anything proposed by the suffragist organizations before 1914. Partly for this reason the women's leaders made almost no attempt to bargain with the Government over the details; the key thing was the *terms* on which the legislation was to be introduced. On 29 March Millicent Fawcett led a deputation representing twenty-two suffrage societies to see the prime minister in which Emmeline was included in the face of protests by many of the suffragists. Conversely they excluded Sylvia because she, virtually alone, denounced the Speaker's proposals and continued to demand nothing less than full adult suffrage which Lloyd George was not willing to attempt for fear of trying his Conservative allies too far. Though Fawcett disliked the thirty-year age limit, she told him 'we should greatly prefer an imperfect scheme that can pass'. In effect, this meant that the women's clause must be part of the original bill as drafted and should be backed by the government whips. Emmeline adopted exactly the same view, though her remarks were even more conciliatory:

I want to assure you [Lloyd George] that whatever you think can be passed, and can be passed with as little discussion and debate as possible, we are ready to accept [Hear Hear]. We know your democratic feeling and we leave the matter in your hands.[14]

Although the government incorporated the women's vote in the Representation of the People Bill, it left the issue to a free vote of MPs. This, however, was sufficient to satisfy most suffragists who decided to abstain from any agitation for equal suffrage. Their restraint seemed justified when, on 19 June, MPs voted by 387 to 57 in favour of the women's clause including the thirty-year age limit. Celebration was, as yet, premature, for the Bill as a whole would not complete its passage for several months, and had then to face the largely untried hazard of the House of Lords.

In any case Emmeline was far more preoccupied with the Union's 'industrial peace' campaign during the first half of 1917. From March onwards she and Annie Kenney spoke regularly in Trafalgar Square on Saturday afternoons, while Flora Drummond was dispatched to Glasgow where the engineering workers had become discontented over the dilution of skilled labour. Drummond's blunt and cheerful style went down well in Scotland and the north of England. She told the workers that no grievance was great enough to justify putting their fellow workers in the trenches at risk: 'There is some traitor amongst you. For God's sake open your eyes and don't let one or two fellows lead you.'[15] In May Christabel returned to England – not before time – in order to take part in the summer campaign. At first she lived at Clarendon Road with her mother, but she found the domestic ménage with Nurse Pine and the four girls too distracting. Even Emmeline felt slightly oppressed by the situation. 'Sometimes', she told Ethel Smyth, 'I feel appalled at the responsibility I have undertaken in adopting these four young things at my time of life.'[16] Ethel's reaction to this may well be imagined. Since resources were now rather stretched, the Union moved its headquarters from Portland Street to a cheaper and smaller property in William Street in Knightsbridge. There Christabel occupied a small flat on the top floor so as to be separate from the family and strategically placed to run *Britannia* and what remained of the organization. On 22 May she returned to the platform for a meeting at Queen's Hall where even the wartime audience was charged from one shilling to seven and six for tickets.[17] Her speeches in 1917 placed her irretrievably on the right of the political spectrum. She poured scorn on the workers for making a fuss about the dilution of skilled labour: 'We should all like to hear no more of strikes . . . There is too much selfishness even in labour politics.' She also argued that women as a group were opposed to class conflict, which she denounced as essentially a German idea. Looking ahead to peacetime, she suggested with some prescience that even the removal of the Kaiser would not diminish the underlying threat posed by Germany to the west: 'A democratic Germany would be a warlike democracy.'[18] On this assumption Christabel argued that the Allies must ensure that Germany was permanently weakened by the withdrawal of sufficient population, coal and iron resources to inhibit her from taking up arms again.

The Pankhursts' role as unofficial representatives of the Coalition Government was dramatically underlined by Emmeline's mission to Russia during the summer of 1917. Remarkably little is known about this episode despite the full account kept secretly by her travelling companion, Jessie Kenney, which had to be smuggled out of Russia lest it be seized by the Provisional Government. The origins of the mission lay in the British Government's concern over the steady collapse of the social and political system in Russia which brought about the end of the Tsarist regime in the revolution of March 1917. For some months power passed into the hands of a Provisional Government under Prince Lvov and Alexander Kerensky. However, from the start they were threatened by the Bolsheviks, who capitalized effectively on the war weariness of the Russian people. The western powers were desperately afraid that a further revolution would result in Russia's withdrawal from the war, thereby allowing Germany to concentrate her forces on the western front and perhaps make the crucial breakthrough to Paris.

The Russian Revolution also had domestic implications in Britain. British workers were also suffering from war weariness, and during 1917 the number of strikes, which had fallen sharply in the previous two years, began to rise ominously. Although the Labour Party Conference had voted to fight Germany to a finish as recently as January,

Lloyd George feared that pro-war leaders like Arthur Henderson were gradually losing their influence with the rank and file. In May Labour's National Executive Committee proposed that Henderson, who was basically very pro-war, should visit Russia with a view to strengthening the democratic-Socialist government there. Lloyd George's war cabinet happily fell in with this partly because it seemed likely to strengthen Henderson's standing in the party, and also because they were anxious for the Provisional Government to revitalize the war effort in the east. Apparently they decided that Henderson should not only go as an official representative but would also replace the British Ambassador, Sir George Buchanan, who had been too closely associated with the discredited Tsarist regime to carry much influence.[19]

But while Henderson duly departed for Russia, Lloyd George characteristically complicated matters by approving additional British representatives, first Ramsay MacDonald and then Emmeline Pankhurst.[20] According to Jessie Kenney, Emmeline was provoked by the news of MacDonald's visit because she did not regard him as a true representative of British opinion, and therefore asked Lloyd George to issue a passport to her too.[21] Christabel claimed that the anti-war MacDonald had been picked as an envoy of the Foreign Office which really wanted a compromise peace, while Emmeline would be able to counter his defeatism by putting the views of patriotic Englishwomen.[22] But Lloyd George's motives for sending three representatives whose views ranged from far left to far right remain a matter for conjecture. He may have hoped that MacDonald would conciliate pacifist opinion at home by keeping alive hopes of British participation in the conference held at Stockholm to promote a negotiated peace. On the other hand he was anxious not to allow MacDonald to gain too much influence with the general public and Emmeline probably appeared as a useful antidote who could be relied upon to challenge any unwelcome lessons MacDonald drew from the visit.

In fact, nothing turned out as Lloyd George had intended. Emmeline quickly raised funds for her visit through an appeal in *Britannia*, while Jessie, evidently under the impression that she would have to be presentable at diplomatic functions, borrowed some smart clothes from Christabel. They left St Pancras on 9 June on the same train as MacDonald, but on arrival at Aberdeen things turned sinister. A telegram awaited Emmeline from Havelock Wilson, the highly patriotic President of the Seamen's Union, who detested MacDonald's views on the war. Wilson's members were responsible for conveying them on the first stage of the journey to Norway. But under instructions from a Captain Tupper, some of the seamen followed MacDonald to his hotel with a view to preventing him from boarding ship. When the ship sailed on 10 June MacDonald and his two ILP colleagues were left stranded on the quay.[23] Even with Captain Tupper's assistance this was a dangerous voyage, for in 1916 Lord Kitchener, also on a mission to Russia, had gone down when his ship struck a mine off Orkney.

After travelling across Norway and Sweden, the two women eventually reached Petrograd on 18 June in the early hours of the morning. 'The city seemed wrapped in silence and strangely enveloped in that mysterious light of the white nights of Russia,' Jessie wrote in her journal.[24] They were met by the Czech nationalist, Thomas Masaryk, who showed them round. Emmeline busied herself having lunch with Sir George Buchanan and making visits to the French, American and Belgian embassies, and also met Henderson. Yet it was by no means clear what exactly she was to do. She told reporters that she had come to explain British attitudes to the war to the Russian democracy, and pronounced herself delighted that the seamen had refused to allow MacDonald to join the expedition.[25] She proposed to appeal directly to the people even to the point of addressing meetings in the street, though she was advised to concentrate on women's societies and journalists. Communication of any sort was not easy since few people understood English. Henderson, who knew no foreign languages, was rather handicapped, but Emmeline made full use of her fluent French. She had meetings with Prince Lvov, the prime minister, Mr Rodzianko, the President of the Duma, Mr Plekanov, the leader of the Mensheviks, and Prince Yousupov (famous for assassinating Rasputin) whom she found absolutely charming; he had the eyes of a mystic, she said later. However, her talk with Kerensky in the Winter Palace proved rather frosty and not very useful. They chatted in French, but Jessie, who thought him overbearing and rather anti-British, noted that he had high words with the interpreter who was present throughout. After her return Emmeline referred disparagingly to 'the feverish and voluble talk which babbled from Alexander Kerensky', and claimed that he had not turned out to be the inspiring nationalist she had expected. He seemed to her completely obsessed with the counter-revolution and more interested in killing fellow Russians than Germans. Emmeline also blamed Kerensky for inflicting the Committee system on Russia and for starting the demoralization of the Russian army.[26] The Tsar also sent a message asking to see her at Tsarskoe Selo, but Kerensky refused to allow this; such contact would in any case have prejudiced their work with ordinary Russians.

At factory-gate meetings Emmeline presented herself as another revolutionary and explained why, as a revolutionary, she backed the Allied war effort. She was repeatedly asked how Russian women could help. Although the women they met appeared to be supporters of the new Government and to be hostile to the Bolsheviks, it was difficult to mobilize them in a patriotic campaign unless they could be offered effective protection. But before long Emmeline and Jessie began to be denounced by anti-government forces as 'bourgeois women', and it became too dangerous for them to hold outdoor meetings. The two sides were now manoeuvring for a final struggle for power. One night Emmeline and Jessie were woken up in order to go out on to their balcony to watch the Cossack regiments riding into the square below their hotel. Almost as though they were sitting in a box at the theatre they peered down upon these colourful troops, singing and waving their pennants in the strange light of early morning. While the Cossacks backed Kerensky, the Bolshevik forces had become very active in taking control of the telephone service and the Secret Service Department. By mid-July Jessie recorded that the rival forces were fortifying each side of the bridges across the River Neva, and to venture out into the streets was to risk being shot. On 5 August they left for Moscow and did not return to Petrograd until 2 September. They watched a march-past by the Bolshevik troops which seemed designed to intimidate the population. 'We were struck by the mechanical precision of it. The symbols, the music and colours ... everything seemed sinister and destructive. The band was playing Chopin's *Funeral March* at a slow tempo with an extraordinary effect.'[27] According to Jessie, whenever the Bolsheviks appeared to be gaining the upper hand the atmosphere changed and the workers became more sullen. Even the hotel staff went on strike from time to time, thereby forcing the guests to prepare their own food. At the best of times they could scarcely cope with the poor quality of the food. Emmeline suffered from diarrhoea and could not eat the black bread at all. By contrast Jessie always felt ravenous because she obtained so little nourishment from her diet. The arrival of a food parcel from the WSPU in July gave them only a temporary respite.

By the beginning of September they had reached the conclusion that the Provisional Government was failing to retain the allegiance of the people despite the sympathy it enjoyed among women. One day when Emmeline felt too ill to do anything but rest in the hotel, Jessie ventured out, only to get caught up in the clashes between the patriotic crowds and the Bolsheviks. When she returned to the hotel, thoroughly frightened by her experience, she broke down completely. Weakened by sleepless nights and their poor diet, both women were getting to the end of their tether. At this point Emmeline decided: 'The sooner we get away the better.' With tears in her eyes she put her hand on Jessie's shoulder saying, 'My dear child, the world is out of joint!'[28] Both women now realized their helplessness in the face of the frightening forces at work in Russia.

They left by train on 13 September, travelling through Finland to Stockholm and then to Oslo. After a rough North Sea passage, they arrived back at Holland Park where Christabel and Annie awaited them with a bottle of champagne. Shortly after her return Emmeline suffered a serious attack of pleurisy which kept her at home until early November. Jessie complained of nausea every day and her doctor diagnosed kidney trouble. Both badly needed rest and an improved diet. As Jessie was suffering from a lack of fat they sought the help of Frances Stevenson, who arranged for an extra supply of bacon for her.[29]

During their absence in Russia Christabel had taken it upon herself to rearrange the household. The house in Clarendon Road clearly meant a lot to Emmeline. 'I have got to love this home of mine', she had told Ethel in May. 'I pray heaven I shall be able to keep it.'[30] However, the remaining WSPU funds had been used to buy a large property called Tower Cressy in Aubrey Road, Holland Park, an imposing Italianate building on four floors. The windows had to be fitted with wire nets, presumably for the safety of the children. Ethel mischievously observed that it was the best place to commit suicide she had seen.[31] The object was to revive the original plan for a large adoption home and a day nursery. To this end Jessie and Kitty Kenney, who had been trained under Maria Montessori, were installed to help Nurse Pine look after the girls and to cope with the additions which were now expected. However, the move generated a good deal of tension. According to Ethel, Emmeline was horrified at the expense involved in furnishing Tower Cressy, though Christabel claimed later that they had bought second-hand items and used volunteers to make the curtains. At this stage Christabel took over responsibility for one of the girls, Betty Tudor, perhaps in order to relieve the burden on Emmeline, though since Christabel raised no additional money it is not clear how far she really helped. She also insisted on the Montessori system which Pine, who regarded it as too liberal and permissive, seems to have ignored in bringing up the girls. Unhappily the appropriation of Union funds for the purchase of Tower Cressy generated renewed controversy which rumbled on through the post-war period. Christabel disingenuously claimed that the members had raised no objection to the use of the small balance remaining after the women's victory had been achieved, though she consulted no one.[32] In any case the new home proved to be a flop because far too few children joined the original four to justify such a large operation. Tower Cressy thus became another drain on Pankhurst resources, and was abandoned altogether in 1919 when the home was transferred to the National Adoption Association.

In spite of her mother's poor health, Christabel arranged for her to report to Lloyd George two days after her return. Though it is not known what she told him, some years later Christabel recorded that she had advised the prime minister that Kerensky was unlikely to survive and that the Communists would take over.[33] This may, however, have been hindsight. When Emmeline spoke at the Queen's Hall on 7 November – the day the Bolsheviks actually seized power – she argued that Russia was breaking down under the Committee System, that her army was disintegrating and that the Allies should no longer expect her to be of any assistance.

In fact, the various missions to Russia had more impact on British domestic politics than on the situation in Russia itself. Henderson, who returned in August convinced of the urgent need to strengthen the Provisional Government by giving Russians some hope of peace, fell out with Lloyd George who sacked him from the war cabinet. From the opposite perspective Emmeline now interpreted the strikes that were taking place in engineering and munitions in the name of democratic control as proof that the contagion of Bolshevism had spread to the west. She had been shocked, and perhaps frightened, by the brutality of revolutionary politics in Russia. 'You have in Russia', she said 'an object lesson for the democracies of the world.'[34] In particular, her observation of the effects of destroying traditional authority almost certainly accelerated her own growing conservatism. In one factory of 30,000 workers she found no fewer than eight hundred men employed full time in committees in the name of democracy and representation. Such a system seriously hampered the war effort; yet she returned to Britain to find people urging workers to emulate the Russian example. Her fears were by no means baseless. On 3 June a convention took place at Leeds, which became known as the Leeds Soviet, at which Ramsay MacDonald, who was no revolutionary, emphasized the positive significance of the Russian revolution for British Labour. The Leeds convention welcomed the revolution and proposed to establish Workers' and Soldiers' Councils in England.

As so often in the Pankhurst family, these ideological issues became entangled with personal rivalries. From Sylvia's perspective the events in Russia in 1917 were a powerful symbol of hope rather than a cause for concern. Regardless of her mother's efforts, she felt confident that Kerensky's regime would be swept aside leading to Russia's withdrawal from the war; the spirit of revolution would then spread across Europe and accelerate the growth of nationalism in India and other parts of the Empire. Consequently the Home Office kept Sylvia and her journal under surveillance in the belief that she had become an agent of Bolshevik influence in Britain. In July she published a dramatic letter by Siegfried Sassoon denouncing the war, which was a deliberate defiance of the military authorities, made all the more embarrassing by his distinction as a recipient of the Military Cross for his gallantry in the war.[35] The authorities dealt with Sassoon by carrying him off to a mental hospital, and they increasingly invoked their powers under the Defence of the Realm Act to raid the *Dreadnought* offices and prevent publication.

During 1917 there had been a qualitative change in Sylvia's work. The *Dreadnought* gave much less attention to the local, material issues affecting the East End and devoted more space to theoretical and ideological questions. Several of the restaurants in Bow and Poplar closed down, and the toy factory became independent. Sylvia herself accepted that many of those who had been involved in her welfare work in the early stages of the war had been alienated by her growing interest in Russia and in the cause of Marxism. She underlined the change of emphasis by adopting a new title for her journal (the *Workers' Dreadnought*) in 1917, and new names for the organization – Workers' Suffrage Federation in 1916 and Workers' Socialist Federation in 1918. Its objects were now defined as the overthrow of capitalism and the establishment of a Socialist system in which the people owned the means of production and distribution. The *Dreadnought* carried articles on Marxism by John McLean, the Scottish Socialist, and T. Walter Newbold, who later became a Communist MP, as well as translations of Lenin's speeches and pieces on Karl Marx written by an Italian anarchist-Socialist named Silvio Corio.

Was Sylvia any less of a feminist as a result of these connections? Like Adela she seemed reluctant to be confined to working within the women's movement; and as a professed Marxist she had committed herself to the view that the real cause of women's oppression lay in the capitalist system, which many British feminists certainly refused to accept. However, the extent of Sylvia's understanding of Marxism remains unclear.[36] Though obviously attracted by novel forms of political organization such as the workers' soviets, she was less of a revolutionary leader than she sometimes sounded. Her WSF members were not directly involved in the soviets or the shop stewards' movement which was spreading through British industry at this stage. Moreover, at least until the summer of 1917 she continued to involve herself in pressure for the vote, though increasingly this sat awkwardly with her revolutionary Marxist affiliations and her disillusionment with the Parliamentary system. The deterioration of her organization in the East End underlined the growing gulf between her and Labour leaders like Lansbury who stuck to the Parliamentary path. From the summer of 1917 onwards the bulk of the Labour Party and the trade unions began to concentrate on fighting the next general election on a wide front so as to take full advantage of the expanded electorate. Sylvia herself was invited to stand as a Socialist candidate in Sheffield Hallam in November 1918, though she refused. In her view the Labour Party had 'hitherto existed without a programme and discusses only fugitive, partial reforms'; she denounced it at the election, saying that if elected it would 'give us nothing more than a wishy-washy Reformist Government which, when all the big issues that really matter came to be decided, would be swept along in the wake of a capitalist policy'.[37] By that time she considered the extension of the vote merely as part of a conspiracy by the Establishment to con the workers into accepting the discredited Parliamentary system. Though Sylvia always claimed to be the true political heir of her father, it is fair to say that he would have been as dismayed by her left-wing repudiation of Parliamentarianism as by Christabel's retreat to the far right.

Meanwhile, with the encouragement of Frances Stevenson and Lloyd George, Emmeline had resuscitated the 'industrial peace' campaign by taking on two additional organizers. Along with Flora Drummond and Annie Kenney she addressed meetings especially on Tyneside, Clydeside, at Sheffield and at Woolwich Arsenal, the leading centres for the manufacture of munitions. Christabel appears to have confined herself to weekly speeches at the Aeolian in London where she rehearsed her stale attacks on the Asquithians. But she continued to have the overall strategy in her hands. The industrial campaign set the scene for the launch of the 'Women's Party' on 2 November, which was designed to facilitate the Pankhursts' transition from the women's movement to a new long-term role in post-war British politics. November 1917 thus marked the official end of the WSPU.

By this time much of the programme of the Women's Party was already familiar: the subordination of everything to the war effort, the elimination of aliens from government and the civil service, the imposition of a punitive peace on Germany and her allies, and opposition to Irish Home Rule. The new element lay in the development of a social and economic agenda including the now-fashionable demand for house-building organized on a co-operative basis so that water, heating, medical services and even restaurants were to be constructed for the inhabitants of the new housing estates. Nor were women entirely forgotten; the party supported equal pay, equal divorce laws, equal rights for parents, the raising of the age of consent (currently sixteen), and the provision of clinics for mothers and children. But the underlying principle in Women's Party thinking was that the interests of the community must take precedence over all private interests, especially those of workers and employers. Thus, Parliament, acting as the ultimate representative of the nation, would settle all economic issues, notably wages, in the light of the national interest. This was consistent with what Emmeline and Christabel had been saying for some time about the irrelevance of trade unions, class conflict and workers' control. Given co-operation and the absence of industrial conflict, the state would be able to guarantee full employment, a shorter working day and greater freedom for people to pursue their individual interests in their leisure time.

This prospectus clearly contained more than a suggestion of the corporate state, and it is not surprising that a number of leading industrialists including Lord Leverhulme, the soap magnate, looked with approval on Christabel's ideas. The explanation for the interest shown by industrialists in the Pankhursts is not hard to find. The war had had the effect of stimulating British manufacturers and bankers into organizing to defend their interests. They regarded a closer relationship with the state as a means of enabling them to control their labour force and also as a guarantee of secure markets and profit margins. In the longer term they wanted to pressurize the government into reducing wartime taxation and retaining or extending the protective tariffs imposed against German imports. In December 1916 a new pressure group, the British Commonwealth Union, was created by, among others, Dudley Docker and Sir Vincent Caillard, with the aim of influencing the post-war Conservative Party from within; to this end the BCU subsidized twenty-four Tory candidates in 1918 as well as a number of patriotic trade union candidates under the aegis of the Lloyd George Coalition. The Women's Party was another part of this wider strategy.

During 1917 the BCU and the Women's Party began to cultivate each other assiduously. Whenever Christabel visited provincial cities, she obtained letters of introduction from the prime minister to the leading local industrialists. These 'Captains of Industry', as Grace Roe called them, invited her and Annie Kenney to an employers' dinner where they showed their appreciation of the Union's efforts at mobilizing women and supporting the war effort.[38] As a result several major businessmen began to pay subsidies to the Women's Party to help it maintain and extend its campaign against industrial militancy.

This new element of corporatism, combined with her well-established belief in the principle of leadership and discipline, suggests that by 1917 Christabel was on the high road that leads to fascism. This is by no means as improbable as it sounds since several active suffragettes who became disillusioned with Parliamentary politics did end up working for the British Union of Fascists in the inter-war period, notably Mary Richardson, Mary Allen, Mrs Dacre Fox and Mercedes Barrington.[39] Though Christabel showed no sign of going quite that far, her rapid disillusionment with the women's vote and Parliamentary elections after 1918 revealed a very similar mind-set to those women who saw the Fascist movement as a natural successor to militant suffragism. During the 1920s Christabel expressed great admiration for Mussolini and his efforts to resurrect the Roman Empire, though she never gave her endorsement to his Fascist ideology.

This, however, is to look ahead. In 1917 the Women's Party was firmly focussed on Parliamentary politics. Since no proposals for allowing women to become Parliamentary candidates had yet been proposed, there are no grounds for seeing the new party as simply an expedient for getting Christabel into Parliament at this stage. Rather it was envisaged as a device for attracting subsidies now that the original aims of the WSPU were near to success. The only real obstacle to the Representation of the People Bill now lay in the House of Lords whose Leader, Lord Curzon, had been President of the National League for Opposing Women's Suffrage since 1910. However, in the crucial debate on 9 January 1918, Curzon collapsed magnificently by advising the peers to abstain; as a result they accepted the women's vote by 134 to 71. Jessie Kenney was sitting with Christabel in her flat when the news came through. It seemed rather an anti-climax, largely because the victory had been taken for granted since the spring of 1917. Two days later Lloyd George invited Emmeline to breakfast.

'Now we must work harder than ever to keep women out of the clutches of MacDonald and Co.', she told him.[40]

It was widely believed in 1918 that because many women would be hesitant about exercising their new rights they needed to be educated to raise their political awareness. With this aim in mind the Women's Citizens' Association had also been launched by Eleanor Rathbone, and all three political parties created new organizations designed to mobilize women. Above all politicians feared the formation of a political party based solely on gender, though fortunately for the Pankhursts. they recognized that this was not really the object of the Women's Party. The *Daily Mail* and the *Daily Express* regarded the prestige of the Pankhursts as a useful bulwark against the influence of the Labour Party, which was known to be reorganizing with a view to setting up women's sections in every constituency.[41] Despite this endorsement, the Women's Party was a little lucky to be accepted by the Coalition leaders as part of their alliance at the 1918 election, for its industrial campaign was the work of no more than a stage army whose effectiveness remained largely unproven. In fact, the industrial situation continued to deteriorate sharply; after falling to 532 in 1916, the number of strikes rose again to 730 in 1917 and to 1,165 in 1918. On the other hand, the more proof emerged of working-class militancy, the more grateful Lloyd George's ministers felt for the work done by the Women's Party. They were now conscious of the risks they must run at the coming election with a huge new electorate of 21 million voters compared with barely eight million before the war. The revolution in Russia, the expansion of trade union membership and the increase in militancy had frightened politicians into thinking that pacifist or Socialist doctrines were gaining a hold over the susceptible new voters in Britain. Consequently Lloyd George and his Conservative supporters looked for allies likely to extend their appeal. A number of patriotic Labour and trade union candidates joined the Coalition as 'National Labour' candidates, and the Women's Party was seen as filling a similar role even though its own organization was very limited.

Thus the launch of the Women's Party in November 1917 proved very timely. From December onwards even Christabel took a high profile in its campaign, venturing north to Glasgow and other centres. In March 1918 Emmeline returned to Manchester where the engineering workers had threatened to strike. She spoke at the Armstrong Whitworth Works to the women employees who carried a resolution condemning the strike, and later to 1,800 women at the Belize Motor Works. She wound up the visit with a public meeting in Stevenson Square.[42] Apart from the kudos gained by confronting working-class militancy in this way, the Women's Party stood to gain much-needed financial contributions. At an Albert Hall demonstration on 16 March, officially to celebrate winning the vote, an impressive £8,000 was collected. Christabel also took care to consolidate her alliance with the prime minister by printing a 'Black List' naming all the pro-Asquith MPs who had voted against him in a debate on 9 May when he was forced to answer accusations of having withheld troops from the generals on the western front. In this way the Women's Party was well prepared – but for what exactly remained unclear. For all their outward confidence, Emmeline and Christabel were still waiting for something to turn up.

Perhaps for this reason Emmeline left the country early in June 1918 for yet another trip to the United States and Canada. This attracted some hostile questions in the House of Commons from opposition members anxious to know whether she represented the British government, whether she was receiving state funds and why she had been permitted to travel to America when Margaret Bondfield, the union leader, had been refused. For the Foreign Office Balfour replied vaguely that it was in the interests of the Allies for Emmeline to visit the United States.[43] According to *Britannia*, the specific object was to rouse American opinion in favour of Japanese intervention in Siberia, in effect, to give military aid to the anti-Bolshevik forces which were now in retreat.[44] However, the Government itself felt reluctant to admit to such interference in the affairs of another country especially as it would have been very controversial at home. *Britannia*'s version may have been an indiscretion, for Emmeline confined herself to general attacks on Bolshevism, on women's role in the war, and on the need to guard against German propaganda.[45] She also criticized the Irish for their lack of support for the war, thereby attracting condemnation as tactless and mischievous in the British press. 'It is unfortunate', commented the *Daily Chronicle*, 'that this egregious person cannot keep her opinions secret.'[46]

Emmeline returned to Britain in the autumn to find speculation about a general election mounting rapidly. However, the prospective election put Lloyd George on the horns of a dilemma because he was a prime minister with no real party of his own, as the majority of the Liberals remained loyal to Asquith. Consequently, his best chance of retaining the premiership lay in fighting the election in alliance with the Conservatives. To this end the Conservative and Coalition Liberal whips began to allocate the constituencies to candidates who were to be equipped with the 'Coupon' – in effect, a letter of approval signed by Lloyd George and Bonar Law – to indicate that they were the official representatives of the Coalition Government.

However, these arrangements left the Pankhursts floundering in the rear. By the autumn, when most seats had been allocated, no mention had been made of Women's Party candidates or of any specific constituencies they might contest. Nor had Lloyd George made any attempt to introduce a clause into his reform bill to enable women to become Parliamentary candidates, largely because he had no wish to antagonize the Conservatives on whom his coalition heavily relied in the Commons. It is often forgotten that during the entire campaign for votes for women since the 1860s the suffragists had almost wholly avoided advocating women MPs. This was largely for tactical reasons, for they knew how provoking this prospect would be for many of the existing male members. There was, of course, some presumption that any person who was eligible to vote was also eligible to stand for election. However, this had last been tested after the first County Council elections in 1889 when two of the defeated Conservative candidates went to court and successfully challenged the right of women who had topped the poll to sit. Consequently, even if some returning officers had accepted the nomination of female candidates in 1918, their right to be elected would have been doubtful. Finally on 23 October an Opposition Liberal, Herbert Samuel, introduced a motion urging the Government to act.[47] Since no one wanted to be seen to put obstacles in women's way so close to the election, legislation was rapidly enacted a few weeks before the election was due to take place. Shortage of time and the fact that most candidates had already been chosen helps to explain why only seventeen women stood in the Coupon election. The declaration of the Armistice on 11 November accelerated matters because it made Lloyd George anxious to appeal to the country while his prestige as 'The Man Who Won The War' was at its height.

In this situation the Pankhursts acted with characteristic decisiveness. On 19 November Emmeline announced that the Women's Party would contest just one constituency and that Christabel would be its candidate. In its edition on 22 November *Britannia* carried a front-page photograph of Christabel as the candidate for Westbury in Wiltshire. Why they chose Westbury remains a mystery although, as the sitting Asquithian Liberal there had been blacklisted by them, it presented an obvious target. Nor is it entirely clear why they confined themselves to a single candidate. 'Mother is absolutely bent upon my getting elected', Christabel told the prime minister, though even she felt faintly embarrassed by the praise her mother heaped upon her: 'She is the woman of the hour ... I am her most ardent disciple ... had her war policy prevailed in the early years, many thousands of lives would have been saved.'[48] As always Emmeline's readiness to subordinate herself to her daughter was not entirely wise, for she herself would have made a more effective candidate. Over the years Christabel had become rather aloof and pretentious and she antagonized many of the men; though she clearly exercised an appeal to women, who now constituted about 40 per cent of the electorate, it was by no means certain that the new female voters were keen to vote for a woman candidate. By contrast Emmeline had more of the common touch and was admired by men who warmed to her motherly appeal and probably felt a little protective towards her. She and Flora Drummond enjoyed much more experience in addressing crowds of working men and women than Christabel who had restricted herself to big set speeches in large halls. The chaos surrounding the election of 1918 is underlined by the fact that even before Christabel's candidacy at Westbury had been announced, she had changed her mind. 'I want to see you about my candidature', she wrote to Lloyd George. 'Something very much better than Westbury is now available but for one little difficulty which you can clear away for me.'[49] She was alluding to Smethwick where, unfortunately for her, the local Conservatives already had a candidate. She wanted the prime minister to persuade Bonar Law to pressurize his party into withdrawing in her favour.

Lloyd George duly obliged, though, to add to the confusion, his letter referred to another West Midlands seat at Wednesbury. He asked the Tory Leader to see Christabel and claimed that the local Conservatives regarded their candidate as unsuitable, which was manifestly untrue. He also pointed out that Lord Northcliffe was keen to back her by running a special edition of the *Evening News* in the area. Indeed, several days previously Northcliffe had intervened to say that 'the best possible seat should be got for Miss Pankhurst, who has more brains than the rest of the women put together, and is a lady into the bargain – also pleasant to look upon – and will therefore have power over the men in the House'.[50] Since the local situation was clearly awkward Lloyd George emphasized the broader considerations to Bonar Law: 'I am not sure that we have any women candidates, and I think it is highly desirable that we should. The Women's Party ... has been extremely useful, as you know, to the Government especially in the industrial districts where there has been trouble during the last two years. They have fought the Bolshevik and Pacifist element with great skill, tenacity and courage.'[51] But on receipt of this encomium Bonar Law merely expressed his appreciation of Christabel's help: 'For that reason I should personally be glad to see you returned to the House, and hope you will be able to find a suitable Constituency.'[52] Though not quite a rebuff, he clearly implied that she should look further afield than Smethwick. However, as time was running out Emmeline and Christabel decided to force the issue. They travelled to Smethwick to meet Major Thompson, the adopted candidate. After taking tea Christabel sweetly suggested that he should withdraw in her favour. He replied that he could not do so as he had been nursing the seat and she ought to withdraw. She insisted that this was impossible as she was the leader of the Women's Party.[53] When Thompson met his committee later on they decided to allow Bonar Law to make the decision for them. He then advised Thompson to withdraw, which he did.

This left Christabel in an apparently strong position, for she faced only one opponent, J. E. Davison, an experienced union official and currently the national organizer of the Ironfounders Society, who stood for Labour. With anti-German feeling now at its height, opinion generally swung sharply to the right and delivered an overwhelming victory to the supporters of the Coalition Government. Many candidates reported that voters were demanding that Germany should be made to pay the full cost of the war and that the Kaiser should be hung for his crimes. As a result candidates who had favoured a negotiated peace or had been less than enthusiastic about prosecuting the war were soundly beaten. Even in working-class and industrial constituencies Lloyd George and the Conservatives were swept to victory. Christabel's record during the war and her endorsement by the Coalition leaders enabled her to benefit from the xenophobic mood in which the election was fought.

Smethwick was a newly created constituency comprising 33,000 voters of whom 14,789 were men and 12,726 were women; 5,393 of the men were absent voters in the armed forces entitled to a postal vote, though few actually took advantage of this novel arrangement. The town was dominated by heavy industry including Guest Keen and Nettlefold's steel works, as well as glass factories, large breweries and tube works.[54] Christabel and Emmeline had chosen it essentially as a suitable forum in which to defeat the Labour Party. Although the seat had no separate political record, it had been carved out of the old Handsworth division which had been consistently Conservative and Unionist. It stood squarely in the right-wing populist tradition of the West Midlands and to that extent suited Christabel's brand of politics very well.

Even so, Emmeline and Christabel had a good deal of explaining to do when they rushed down to Smethwick on 27 November. They claimed they had chosen the constituency after a careful examination of all 700 seats; as it was a new one no party or candidate could have any special claim upon it.[55] But despite their claims Major Thompson was a local man, prominently identified with the town, whose last-minute ejection inevitably left some Conservatives feeling disgruntled. In this situation Christabel foolishly declined to cultivate the local Conservatives whose votes she needed for victory. The Women's Party set up its committee room in the High Street and proceeded to import its own organization rather as though it were conducting an Edwardian by-election campaign. Elsie Bowerman, who was appointed as agent, admitted to being inexperienced and ignorant of electoral law.[56] Emmeline, Flora Drummond, Annie Kenney and the two party organizers formed an impressive phalanx of speakers, and volunteers flooded in from all over the country. But, as Bowerman pointed out, they all lacked local connections, and compounded the impression that Smethwick was being taken over by outsiders. They had not learned the lessons of Bow and Bromley.

In her campaign Christabel exploited anti-German sentiment, condemned her opponent as anti-patriotic, saying 'the fight today is between the Red Flag and the Union Jack', and advocated that all jobs be reserved for the men serving in the forces. She also suggested that Smethwick had the opportunity to make a name for itself by being the first constituency to elect a woman MP and that it would gain by having a national figure to represent it.[57] Press reports indicated that she attracted sympathetic interest from female audiences especially when she scored off the men who came to interrupt her. Some of the exchanges recalled suffragette days on the platform:

HECKLER: Have you yourself ever worked in a factory?
CHRISTABEL: No, I have not; neither have your friends Ramsay MacDonald and Philip Snowden. [*Cheers.*]
HECKLER: Two blacks don't make a white.
CHRISTABEL: I am glad to hear you think Mr MacDonald and his friends are black.[58]

For his part Davison denounced Christabel's candidature as 'the most diabolical conspiracy ever inflicted on the electorate'. He would have been even more contemptuous had he been aware that the British Commonwealth Union had donated £1,000 for her campaign on the basis that 'the transaction must be treated as a strictly secret one'.[59] Davison also mocked Christabel's lack of local connections and her pretensions by contrasting her with Major Thompson: 'He did not claim to have won the war. [*Laughter.*] Neither did he claim to have given women the vote. [*Laughter.*]'[60] He reminded the voters that before 1914 she had encouraged young women to commit acts of violence from the safety of her luxurious Paris apartment.

The 1918 count was actually delayed for several weeks in order to allow the ballots of the absent voters in France and Flanders to arrive. Even so, the turnout proved to be very low, reaching only 54.7 per cent in Smethwick. The first count put Davison ahead by 915 votes. Nothing daunted, Christabel demanded a recount, saying that she was not sure the men could count properly! Eventually Davison received 9,389 votes and Christabel 8,614, a majority for him of 775. Afterwards Davison said by way of explanation that he felt the women voters had not realized the implications of an election and had not voted very heavily. Since no separate returns were made it is impossible to know whether this was true; but it must have been galling for Christabel to have come so close. Yet she had only herself to blame for the result. The previous four years had convinced Emmeline and Christabel that they enjoyed the sympathy of industrial England; they had averted strikes and maintained the war effort by their persistent attacks on Pacifists and Bolsheviks. It was a flattering analysis, made the more appealing because it had been endorsed by Lloyd George, Lord Northcliffe, Lord Leverhulme and other influential men. But Christabel had become too much the grand lady to carry complete conviction with a working-class electorate and was too aloof to be able to establish personal contact, especially at short notice as was necessary at Smethwick. Self-delusion had led the Pankhursts to insist on contesting a working-class constituency where they hoped to inflict another defeat upon the Labour Party and thus consolidate their new role in British politics. If they had simply accepted the offer of the Westbury constituency, where a Couponed Conservative candidate won comfortably, Christabel would almost certainly have been returned in 1918 as Britain's first female member of Parliament.

15

Available for Work (1919–21)

'Lenin has charged Miss Sylvia Pankhurst with the task of amalgamating all the British Communist parties. He could scarcely have made a worse choice.'

Special Branch report, 30 September 1920

Christabel's defeat at Smethwick struck a blow to her morale from which she never really recovered. For some time afterwards she seemed in danger of relapsing into the lassitude which had characterized her earlier life as an adolescent. But in the belief that she would soon regain her vitality and determination, Emmeline and her little band of followers decided to send her away for a holiday in January 1919. 'Of course, it is certain', wrote Annie Kenney, 'that she will become a member of Parliament.'¹ However, in order to achieve this it was essential to keep the Women's Party in the news and, more immediately, boost its funds. Christabel wrote some articles for the *Daily Sketch* under such headlines as 'If A Woman Were Premier! Famous Suffragist Leader Shows How She Would Solve The Strike Crisis In Britain'. Fortunately for the Women's Party, the industrial situation deteriorated alarmingly during 1919 when no fewer than thirty-five million working days were lost compared with five and a half million in 1918. Writing to Sir Vincent Caillard of Vickers, Annie Kenney shamelessly appealed for subsidies by implying that the party might have to economize by suspending its industrial campaign until Christabel got into Parliament. As a result Caillard told Patrick Hannon of the British Commonwealth Union that the party's work on the Clyde justified continuing subsidies to it.²

Meanwhile Emmeline bustled round and discovered that the member for the Westminster Abbey Division, William Burdett-Coutts, was in poor health and contemplating resignation. She swiftly seized upon his seat as an ideal constituency for Christabel. However, since it had become a very safe Conservative seat it was necessary to persuade the Tory Party Chairman, Sir George Younger, that his local party should step aside for Christabel.[3] As at Smethwick, Emmeline tried to present her candidacy as a *fait accompli* by announcing it and appealing for contributions. In March she went to Paris, hoping to see Lloyd George, ostensibly because she and Christabel were worried about 'the way the peace conference is going', but presumably to badger him about the prospective vacancy in the Abbey division. Christabel, who had taken up residence at the Hotel Westend near the Champs-Élysées, informed the prime minister that she wanted to see him to explain to him the views of those who had voted for him and backed him during the war: 'I hope that you can arrange to spare time today for a good long talk.'[4] In the circumstances it was presumption bordering on arrogance to think that she could command his attention in this way. Emmeline and Christabel were now overplaying their hand. Fresh from their election triumph – the Coalition had won 526 seats – Lloyd George and Bonar Law now saw little reason to pander to their demands. However, Emmeline did manage to see a variety of influential people including Billy Hughes, Thomas Masaryk and Edvard Beneš in Paris.

It was of more immediate concern that some of their business backers had begun to develop doubts because of the alleged misman-agement of funds. 'Our relations with the Women's Party have been unsatisfactory beyond words', complained Patrick Hannon.[5] At the start of 1919 Flora Drummond had applied for £3,130 from the BCU to enable them to discharge debts to their printers. She also required regular weekly contributions to enable the party to maintain its speaking programme. Hannon, who felt the party enjoyed 'a somewhat elaborate central organization', clearly suspected that the BCU's money was really being used to maintain Christabel and her loyalists in the style to which they were accustomed rather than in combating labour unrest.[6] Despite his reservations, however, the BCU contributed £250 a week. Hannon later complained 'we were rushed at a critical moment in the industrial situation'.[7] He attempted to impose conditions on the use of the money; the BCU must be kept informed about what the Women's Party was actually doing, its accountant must inspect the books, proofs of *Britannia* must be examined two days before publication, and it should exercise a veto on what was printed.[8]

Against this background the BCU leaders were naturally sceptical later in March when they interviewed Christabel in connection with her request for financial support for her candidature. Hannon claimed he had been 'totally unable to get any information of any sort or kind from these women and I have told them this morning that unless Mrs Drummond sees me today I shall be obliged, acting with the authority of my Committee, to stop supplies'.[9] In the absence of an efficient, reassuring manager like Emmeline Pethick-Lawrence, the party's organizers were simply unable to satisfy their backers' conditions. In his irritation Hannon also revealed wider doubts about the viability of the Pankhurst project:

Quite honestly between ourselves the pretensions of Miss Pankhurst and the worshippers who surround her are becoming almost unbearable. I don't believe for one moment that Miss Pankhurst stands the ghost of a chance of being adopted as the official Unionist candidate for the Abbey Division, and whatever may be the future of women MPs I most earnestly hope for the sake of the peace and quiet of those who are now in the House that Miss Pankhurst will not be returned.[10]

Unaware of the imminent collapse of the pillars on which *Britannia* and the Women's Party rested, Christabel had begun, in April, to address meetings at the London Pavilion as prospective candidate. While maintaining her attacks on pro-Germans, pacifists, Asquithians, and Socialists, she also urged the government to embark on a social reform programme, which probably did little to enhance her standing with the employers who were now very anxious to see reductions in income tax from wartime levels. In external affairs she put herself firmly with the critics of the League of Nations which she believed would never enjoy the power needed to counter Bolshevik or German pressure. British interests were best protected by maintaining the alliance with France and, if possible, keeping the United States involved in Europe. Failing this, Christabel predicted that Russia and Germany would collaborate to force the West into another war in twenty years' time.

Meanwhile Christabel decided to acquire an expensive new house for herself in South Street, off Park Lane, with views over Hyde Park. To the Baronne de Brimont, she explained that there was no room at party headquarters now, and 'it makes life too hectic to be always under the same roof as our office!'[11] It was not long, however, before all her plans collapsed. No by-election occurred in the Westminster Abbey division until 1921 when Burdett-Coutts died, and in any case there was no indication that the Conservatives were willing to give Christabel such a plum seat. Although the BCU did assist in paying off Women's Party debts, by the end of the summer it had abandoned the organization, thereby effectively killing Christabel's campaign to become an MP. Both the party and *Britannia* now folded and Tower Cressy passed into the hands of the National Adoption Association. As if to symbolize her retreat to the political margins, Christabel took herself off to Looe in Cornwall for the summer 'to celebrate, if you will, this great *Peace*' as she sarcastically put it in a letter to the Baronne. She felt certain that the agreements devised at Versailles were inadequate to resist the Russo-German threat, but 'our Prime Minister knows very well what mother and I think on the subject'.[12] The unmistakable implication was that neither he nor anyone else was now listening.

Christabel had plainly reached a painful turning-point in her career. After brilliantly reinventing herself during the war she had put herself in an excellent position to benefit from the swing of the pendulum to the right in 1918. But the folly of rejecting the seat at Westbury now became apparent. She had been perfectly positioned to become an anti-Soviet figurehead at a time when Conservatives were increasingly fearful of a surge towards the Labour Party among the new voters. With her histrionic talents she would have been much appreciated in the House of Commons where the Conservatives found themselves lacking able orators, especially after 1922 when they broke with Lloyd George who took several leading Tories with him into Opposition. Stanley Baldwin, who became leader in 1923, was fully alive to the need to promote women and be seen to have women's interests in mind; he would almost certainly have found a front-bench role for Christabel. However, in the autumn of 1919 this entrancing prospect suffered an eclipse when Nancy Astor stepped into her husband's seat in a by-election at Plymouth and became at a stroke the most prominent woman in public life. Though Baldwin reluctantly concluded that Astor was not ministerial material, by 1924 he had appointed another woman MP, the Duchess of Atholl, as a junior minister. That neither Astor nor Atholl had done anything to promote votes for women – indeed, Atholl bitterly opposed it – must have made their success all the more galling for the Pankhursts. But Christabel's pride prevented her from making any further attempts to get into Parliament, and she effectively washed her hands of politics at this stage.

Thus, by the end of 1919 both she and her mother stood in urgent need of yet another reincarnation, not just to restore their battered morale, but because they had no visible means of support. Since 'Pankhurst' was still a household name, it should not have been impossible to find another public role. What seems striking is that neither woman envisaged playing any further part in the women's movement in Britain. Not that there was any lack of scope or of causes to fight for. Though many politically active women opted to work through the party political organizations in the 1920s, a high proportion of pre-war feminists believed in the necessity to maintain an independent women's movement. The Women's Freedom League, for example, carried on its campaigns until 1961. The National Union of Women's Suffrage Societies changed its name to the National Union of Societies for Equal Citizenship and developed a broader agenda as well as maintaining the fight for equal voting rights until 1928 when the thirty-year age limit for women was finally abolished. Although the WSPU disappeared, several new organizations sprang up, notably the Six Point Group under Lady Rhondda, many of whose members had previously been suffragettes. Far from folding up, the feminist movement remained very active during the 1920s, especially over issues such as equal guardianship, widows' pensions, the equal moral standard, divorce law reform, equal pay and the provision of birth-control information for married women.

But in this situation the Pankhursts adopted a lofty and detached tone. 'Christabel and I intend to return to the plough like Cincinnatus and see what other women will do with the power we won for them', wrote Emmeline in 1920.[13] The truth was that they had alienated so many feminists that it would have been difficult to put together a new women's organization, especially one run on the usual autocratic lines. None of the Pankhursts settled for long in an organization which they did not dominate; and by this time Christabel did not even feel tempted. Before long she pronounced herself disappointed that women's enfranchisement had not changed the world or even checked the decay of democracy; she concluded that women suffered from much the same political defects as men.[14] It is fair to note that Emmeline never displayed the same degree of disillusionment. There was, however, a further problem. By 1919 Emmeline was sixty-one. To the younger generation of women her mid-Victorian views about women, especially about morality and sexuality, had begun to appear distinctly old-fashioned. Despite – or perhaps because of – their wartime experience employed in hitherto 'male' occupations, many young women had become anxious to marry and have children by the early 1920s, and they looked askance at the pre-war suffragist leaders whom they often regarded as man-hating spinsters. The long-term reaction in favour of marriage had set in.

At the same time many women of the late-Victorian and Edwardian generation felt dismayed at what seemed the frivolous attitude of the young 'flappers' who were apparently determined to enjoy themselves and to dress up for the pleasure of men. When Emmeline told a journalist: 'We wanted to preserve as enfranchised women that modesty and delicacy which have been held to be our adornment', she betrayed the wide gulf now opening up between herself and the post-war generation. Always particular about clothes, she objected to the 'modern abbreviated styles in women's gowns . . . and too much rouge and lip paint . . . So many of these younger and older women would be attractive in gowns of the right length; so many would be charming if they were not so heavily rouged.'[15] Even Christabel, still only thirty-nine in 1919, remained noticeably loyal to her flowing Edwardian dresses and broad-brimmed hats for much of the remainder of her life. Dress was but a symbol of deeper attitudes and divisions. Many women of Emmeline's generation felt dismayed at the liberal approach to sex after the war, and in particular at the growing interest in birth control which appeared calculated to relieve women of the need for self-restraint and thus to lower them to the level of men. It is no accident that she eventually found a comfortable new role campaigning against sexual liberalism, though significantly not in Britain itself.

Once the Women's Party had disintegrated, the rest of the circle around Emmeline and Christabel also dispersed, though its members remained in contact for many years. Flora Drummond put her talents to good use by founding another right-wing pressure group, the Women's Guild of Empire, with Elsie Bowerman. Annie Kenney studied theosophy at St Leonard's where she lived with Grace Roe until 1920, then she married James Taylor and had a son; she played no further role in public affairs. Grace Roe subsequently accompanied Christabel to the United States and then stayed on for many years, acting as a personal assistant and companion to a number of wealthy American women.

With the unanswered questions about the future hanging over her head, Emmeline took the children off to spend the summer of 1919 at Peaslake in Surrey where she rented a cottage. Ethel Smyth recorded with disapproval that the girls 'flitted about like fairies, offered you scones with a courtesy, and kissed their hands to you when they left the room'.[16] When she criticized their behaviour Emmeline got annoyed and called Ethel an old maid. Dressed in white kid boots and fancy bonnets, the girls clearly attracted attention. Once when in a restaurant a woman angrily came up to them and proposed to take them away because she believed them to be the 'lost princesses of Russia'![17] Though Christabel adopted a far more relaxed approach with the children, she was absent too often at this time to have much influence over their upbringing. Emmeline by contrast still followed a strict Victorian view of child-rearing. At home she usually 'received' the children formally at tea time when they had been carefully brushed and combed. She continued to take little interest in education beyond insisting that they learned French, to which end several governesses were employed.[18] But they were never given toys except at Christmas and on birthdays; one of them remembered that when taken to a toy shop in about 1924 she had no idea what she wanted as she had never seen one before.[19]

Catherine Pine, who looked after them on a day-to-day basis, appeared to outsiders as a real martinet, though this was disputed by Catherine who claimed she was much more lenient with them than she appeared to be.[20] The girls undoubtedly appreciated Nurse Pine for her sheer efficiency and for the element of stability and order that she brought into their young lives. Responsible for cooking and caring for them, she appeared to have no life of her own; she never went out or had visitors, nor was she usually included when Emmeline entertained her own guests.[21] In effect, Pine occupied a role somewhere between companion and servant for Emmeline until the mid-1920s.

Despite the vital support of Catherine Pine, Emmeline grew rather bitter over being 'forced to work summer and winter to support these children'. Reading between the lines, one surmises that she felt that Christabel ought to have taken more responsibility for them.[22] But Christabel was fast relapsing into her natural torpor. In the summer she employed a Miss Muriel Cook as a secretary and chauffeur to drive her between her country retreats and her London flat, and also a nurse to look after Betty. However, Cook soon found that Christabel was not actually doing enough to justify her position and seemed to be increasingly vague and detached; her costs were apparently met by 'the cause', though what exactly that meant at this stage is unclear.[23] As money ran short she began to resort increasingly to lengthy visits to the homes of well-off friends, beginning with her aunt, Ada Goulden Bach, an expedient which she employed for the rest of her life. For some time Christabel seemed quite unable to devise a means of supporting herself. With her legal training and her reputation for court appearances she might well have embarked on a career in the law; the Sex Disqualification (Removal) Act of 1919 had opened up the professions to women and, by 1935, 116 women practised as solicitors and 79 as barristers.

It was, however, Emmeline who took the initiative in resolving the dilemma in September 1919 when she embarked upon her fifth tour of the United States and Canada to earn some badly needed cash by lecturing on the threat of Bolshevism. She was irritated to find that though separated from her second daughter by the Atlantic Ocean, Sylvia's politics continued to introduce unwanted complications into her life. It was pointed out to her that her publicity material suffered because some people were confused as to whether Emmeline was anti-Bolshevik or pro-Bolshevik! 'If you forgive the suggestion', wrote Dr Gordon Bates, 'I believe this is due to a misreporting of some of the work which Miss Sylvia Pankhurst has undertaken in recent years.'[24]

There was, however, no ambiguity so far as Sylvia's attitude towards the Revolution was concerned. While her mother and sister cast about for a new role, Sylvia was sustained by the conviction that events had moved decisively her way. Throughout 1919 and 1920 she became enthused with the notion that the revolution was spreading inexorably from Russia to the West. In a private letter which fell into the hands of Special Branch she told a friend in Glasgow: 'I expect the Revolution soon, don't you?' She simply dismissed the conventional political system: 'Parliament is a decaying institution: it will pass away with the capitalist system.'[25] As a result one of her biographers describes Sylvia at this time as 'living in a world devoid of political reality'.[26] Yet this seems excessively harsh and written with the benefit of hindsight. In 1919 much of the British political Establishment shared this belief in revolutionary contamination from Russia, and with some reason. That year produced an unprecedented wave of strikes which almost merged into a de facto general strike and had to be bought off with major wage concessions. In May Sylvia appeared at a Trafalgar Square demonstration with Tom Mann, Walter Ponder and Guy Aldred when British soldiers were openly urged to refuse orders to go to Russia to help the counter-revolutionary forces. She herself advocated a general strike and the creation not only of workers' soviets in industry but of household soviets of mothers and wives who would meet weekly to determine rules for repairs, furnishings, food supplies and nurseries.[27] For a time the continued expansion of trade union membership gave extra credibility to the advocates of direct action by working men and convinced them that their goals could be attained by ignoring the Coalition Government. The chief focus for direct action arose out of the intervention by western Governments in Russia designed to aid the anti-Bolshevik forces in the civil war. Special Branch reported that every section of the working class appeared hostile to this military intervention, though it noted that this did not reflect sympathy for the Bolsheviks so much as the fear that it might lead to the permanent imposition of conscription in Britain.[28] In May the *Workers' Dread-*

nought carried an article by Harry Pollitt appealing to the London dockers to refuse to load ships carrying arms to Russia, and in July even the Labour Party Conference voted in favour of direct action to stop such a policy.[29] At a meeting at Old Ford Road Sylvia raised £200 to employ Tom Mann to assist with an agitation in the docks.[30] These efforts reached their greatest success when one ship, the *Jolly George*, was prevented from embarking with its cargo of arms.

Some light is thrown on Sylvia's professed Marxism after the war by a dispute arising out of an article on Keir Hardie in *The Call*, the journal of the British Socialist Party. In this John Askew contended that Hardie had ignored Marxism and the class struggle. Modern scholars, while acknowledging Hardie's interest in Marx's writing, agree that he rejected the idea of achieving working-class aims by revolution which he considered inappropriate in Britain. But Sylvia, perhaps stung by the reminder of how far she herself had departed from her original views, and offended that someone presumed to understand Keir Hardie better than she did, replied in an article portraying Hardie as an unqualified Marxist.[31] Yet she confined herself to bald assertions and anecdotes about him; though she quoted at length from writing in which Hardie had referred to Marx, she failed to engage in any analysis of his views.

Ideology, however, was the least of Sylvia's worries in 1919. She was now desperately short of money, especially as her former backers in the West End, with the exception of the Countess of Warwick, drew the line at subsidizing the revolution. Fortunately a new source of funds appeared in the shape of a Russian agent, one Theodore Rothstein, who had access to money for the support of newspapers and organizations sympathetic to the Soviet regime. Sylvia certainly benefited from this though she sometimes had to make remarkable efforts to obtain the money.[32] Late in 1919, for example, she accepted an invitation from the German Marxist and feminist, Clara Zetkin, to attend a conference in Stuttgart. Though denied a passport Sylvia managed to travel to Italy where she attended a Socialist Conference at Bologna, and then crossed on foot to Switzerland, eventually making her way to Stuttgart to meet Zetkin. They went on to Frankfurt where the conference actually met, and the Russian agent known as 'the eye of Moscow' paid her £500. Apart from the obvious advantages of cultivating

Bolshevik agents, Sylvia appears to have exploited her Russian connections with a view to raising her standing among the British Marxists. According to Special Branch she claimed in June 1919 to be secretly maintaining an emissary from Lenin in a hotel but refused to allow anyone to have access to him. However, 'careful investigation and enquiry leave little doubt that he is a mythical person'. It was also her practice to seek out seamen returning from eastern Europe and to put into their mouths 'coloured reports [on Russia] that she has received from other sources'.[33] Such bizarre activities remind us that the politics of the far left involved an internal struggle for dominance, not simply a battle with the forces of the British government.

However, by 1920 the hopes of the previous year had begun to subside. The collapse of the economic boom led to a dramatic rise in unemployment, the start of what turned out to be a very protracted fall in trade union membership right up to 1934, and the demise of direct action. If revolution was not going to come quickly, it followed that the forces of the left had now to settle down to building their support. But for this they required a more coherent organization and a strategy. During 1920 and 1921 Sylvia was to play a controversial part in getting the British Communist Party off the ground.

The chief expression of the Marxist tradition in British politics had been the Social Democratic Federation, which had been founded back in 1881 and was dominated by H. M. Hyndman. Though briefly affiliated to the Labour Party in 1900, the SDF remained rather marginal. However, during the Edwardian period the left gained influence among younger working men through the spread of the ideas of the American Socialist, Daniel de Leon, who advocated industrial rather than Parliamentary methods for achieving radical change in society. In 1916 the SDF, which had changed its name to the British Socialist Party, came out in opposition to the war. Prominent Marxists such as John Maclean and Willie Gallagher gave a lead to the discontent with wartime restrictions in the manufacturing districts and urged workers to form soviets on the Russian model after 1917. However, while the Bolshevik Revolution stimulated the far left in Britain, it also put limits on its influence in the sense that it provoked the Labour Party and most union leaders into reaffirming their belief in a Parliamentary strategy and rejecting the Leninist idea of bringing about revolutionary change through the dictatorship of a minority party of disciplined revolutionaries.

The formation of the Communist International at the beginning of 1919 led the Russians to invite sympathetic organizations in other countries to send delegates to a conference in Russia in March, thereby putting the various groups of Marxists in Britain under pressure to constitute themselves as a single Communist Party and so become full members of the International. As a result, from May onwards protracted negotiations took place between the BSP, Sylvia's Workers' Socialist Federation and other left-wing groups with a view to establishing the basis for united action. However, they were fundamentally divided over strategy. Many members of the BSP, which was much the largest of these groups, supported Parliamentary methods and co-operation with the Labour Party. Sylvia herself remained wholly opposed to a Parliamentary strategy and to affiliation with the Labour Party, but as her organization represented only a tiny minority of the movement she could not hope to get her way simply by open debate. Rather naïvely assuming that Lenin would endorse her views, she took the initiative by writing to him in July 1919 and explaining the divisions among the British Marxists. 'I believe you would say: concentrate your forces upon revolutionary action; have nothing to do with the Parliamentary machine. Such is my own view', she wrote.[34] Lenin's reply was replete with contradictions. He indicated that it would be a mistake to renounce Parliamentary participation, but praised revolutionary workers for repudiating 'bourgeois Parliamentarianism'. He wanted above all unity among the fragile and quarrelsome British groups, but he suggested that as a first stage it would be acceptable to have two Communist Parties.

In this situation Sylvia forced the pace by calling a conference of her own in June 1920 and reconstituted her WSF as 'The Communist Party – British Section of the Third International', a characteristic attempt to maximize her influence by presenting a *fait accompli* to her opponents. Sylvia's Communist Party promulgated a programme including the substitution of Soviets for the Parliamentary system, the replacement of capitalism with Communism, the abolition of the wages system, the abolition of social classes, the break-up of the British Empire, no affiliation with Opportunists (i.e. the Labour Party), and industrial organization to displace the reactionary trade union leadership.[35]

The BSP and the other groups responded to this by organizing the first Unity Convention in July and consulting Lenin about Sylvia's initiative. She printed an open letter to the delegates explaining that her CP–BSTI refused to run candidates at elections because this would be to risk lapsing into reformism and also encourage the delusion that leaders could fight the workers' battles for them.[36] When Lenin sent a message to the effect that 'I consider the policy of Comrade Sylvia and the WSF in refusing to collaborate in the amalgamation of the BSP, SLP and others into one Communist Party to be wrong', she proposed to visit Russia and meet him in debate.[37] His pamphlet 'Left Wing Communism, an Infantile Disorder' was influential among the British Marxists and helped to undermine Sylvia's position still further. The delegates at the Unity Convention voted overwhelmingly in favour of Parliamentary action and narrowly in favour of affiliation to the Labour Party.[38] Special Branch commented on the new 'Communist Party – Great Britain': 'It will wage war upon the rival Communist party of Sylvia Pankhurst and though it may succeed in drawing away some of her supporters, it will irretrievably split asunder when the leaders begin unCommunistically to push one another out of the limelight.'[39]

Meanwhile Sylvia's new party was reported by Special Branch to be in serious financial difficulties almost from the start, so much so that the Party urged members to donate their Saturday afternoon wages to the funds.[40] This of course gave Sylvia another motive for making a visit to Russia to attend the congress of the Third International during August 1920. She was accompanied by Willie Gallagher, a Scottish shop steward who shared her views but emerged as a rival in the course of the trip. Sylvia left without a passport, but her travel was arranged by Russian agents.[41] At Harwich she stowed away on a Norwegian freighter assisted by the 'underground line', and arrived in Sweden via Copenhagen. From there she travelled through Norway and boarded a 'Soviet Steamer', which turned out to be a battered old motor boat, at Vardo; in this she spent 'hours of misery' crossing the Arctic Sea to Murmansk where she eventually landed amid a fleet of grey Soviet ships flying the Red Flag, rusty submarines hauled up on shore, and a mass of broken metal left behind by the Allied occupation.[42] Accounts of what passed at the conference in Moscow are rather inconsistent. On the face of it Sylvia considered herself, absurdly, to be Lenin's equal and refused to be browbeaten, saying she had seen during the long fight for women's votes how important it was to be extreme. Though Lenin flattered both Sylvia and Gallagher, he emphasized, on the contrary, that neither had much experience of revolutionary activity. In a private conversation he dismissed the arguments about Parliamentary action and affiliation to the Labour Party as merely tactical not fundamental, and pointed out, quite correctly, that Labour would probably reject the application anyway; in his view the sooner the reformists (i.e. Labour) came to power the sooner they would discredit themselves and thus advance the cause of revolution. He urged them strongly to join with the Communist Party – Great Britain on their return.[43]

Sylvia could not expect to have it both ways; unless she gave some undertaking to promote the unity movement she was not going to get the subsidies her organization so badly needed. Inevitably she succumbed partly to Lenin's pressure and perhaps to the sheer thrill of being at the centre of the Revolution. She and Gallagher had sat round the table with Lenin in the Tsar's bedroom, and one night the two of them were driven in the Tsar's motor car to the opera where they occupied what had been the royal box.[44] The experience also influenced Sylvia in other ways. Anxious to glimpse what she believed to be an ideal society, she visited factories and a 'House of the Mother and Child', which offered support for unmarried women and those not supported by a man. The revolution had abolished the stigma attaching to illegitimacy. She concluded that the ending of capitalism would effectively make the state responsible for motherhood and children, and thereby alter the whole institution of marriage which had hitherto been another expression of property relations.[45] This may well have fortified Sylvia a few years later when she opted for motherhood without marriage.

The return journey proved to be even more hazardous. Between Moscow and Petrograd the train caught fire, and Gallagher had to drag Sylvia half-suffocated from her smoke-filled compartment and carry her off the train. They then had a stormy passage in a small boat from Murmansk during which Gallagher again saved her from being swept overboard. But later in their journey she suddenly abandoned Gallagher by departing in another boat. The explanation probably lies in her anxiety to get home first and proclaim that Lenin had appointed her to unite the warring factions of the Communist Parties. Gallagher made the same claim for himself, and he may well have been correct because Lenin took a dim view of women in general and believed Sylvia in particular to be temperamentally unsuited for revolutionary work.[46]

Whatever the truth of this, the visit had been well worth while, for Sylvia returned with Russian money and expectations of more to come. In fact, the other organizations became jealous because her small party appeared to have acquired an unduly large share of the available funds. She continued to receive money from Rothstein via a Swedish courier and through Nora Smythe, who made trips to Sweden for the purpose. Special Branch reported in some detail how the subsidies were to be spent: £1,500 to settle the debts of the Agenda Press, £500 for the WSF, £300 for Sylvia's People's Russian Information Bureau and £250 towards its debts. In addition weekly payments were to be made: £15 for staff, £20 for a canvasser to boost *Dreadnought* sales, £5 for a sub-editor, £6 for an agitator in the docks, £6 for an agitator in the army, and £10 for the distribution of free literature.[47] Towards the end of November Sylvia was reported to have received another £1,500 and a sum of £750 handed over to Nora Smythe.[48] On the other hand this made it easier to outmanoeuvre her on her return, for she had evidently taken the money on condition that she would help promote Communist unity, and failure to do so would lead Moscow to turn off the tap. In September a further unity convention took place in Manchester on which Special Branch commented: 'this need not disturb us over much for no one has yet ever succeeded in working amicably with Sylvia Pankhurst.'[49]

The inevitable result of all this activity was that Sylvia was watched even more closely than before by the police who routinely opened her mail. She countered by developing a system of 'shadow' secretaries, organizers and committees who passed on parcels of literature to each other without knowing the identity of the recipient in order to forestall police raids. In October the press reported the arrest of a 'Mysterious

Alien' who had failed to register with the authorities, but was believed by the police to be acting as a courier between the Soviet Government and the 'Revolutionary Party' in Britain. They found in his possession a letter from Sylvia to Lenin.'Dear Comrade', she wrote:

The situation here is moving in a revolutionary direction more swiftly, but of course we are far away yet. The prices of necessaries are rising though the cost of living is not totally supposed to have risen this month. Unemployment is now acute, and the unemployed are restive . . . unemployed in various towns march to factories, enter them, make speeches and speak of seizing them. Ex-soldiers arm and drill. Do not exaggerate these things – they are not formidable yet.[50]

Sylvia also took the opportunity to emphasize what a struggle she was having to keep the *Dreadnought* going since one of her creditors had taken legal action and thus inspired the others to follow suit. This was an unmistakable request for subsidies which elicited a positive response.

Shortly before writing to Lenin Sylvia had been arrested, though she was released on bail of £1,000, which Nora Smythe had obtained by mortgaging the Agenda Press. 'I considered a hunger strike', wrote Sylvia, 'but I am afraid that weapon is destroyed now, since the Government is letting the Irish hunger strikers die.'[51] She had been charged with promoting sedition among the troops by encouraging them to mutiny in several articles published in the *Dreadnought*. Her editor was already in gaol on a similar charge. When her case came up at the Mansion House Police court in November, Sylvia offered a rambling and irrelevant defence.[52] In a lengthy autobiographical speech she told the court she had been brought up a Socialist and declared that Marxist ideas were available everywhere. Though the magistrate, Sir Alfred Newton, interrupted to remind her that she had strayed from the charge, she ignored him and claimed that she would be applauded for what she had done in Russia. 'The Soviet Government which you admire so much, Miss Pankhurst, would not have given you such a patient hearing as I have done,' commented Sir Alfred. Reminding her that she was fortunate the Government had not charged her with treason at the Old Bailey, he imposed a six-month sentence in the second division which he described as 'totally inadequate for the offence'. Only three hundred people turned up at a protest meeting in Trafalgar Square against the sentences handed down to Sylvia and three others, and a collection yielded just five pounds.[53] At her appeal in January 1921, Sylvia delivered a melodramatic speech lasting an hour and a half in which she claimed that prison would be a death sentence for her, but would have the effect of spreading her views and thus herald the triumph of her cause. When she sat down she seemed completely drained, her hair falling all over her face. George Bernard Shaw was one of very few who wrote her a sympathetic letter, though even he pointed out that she should never have got herself arrested in the first place.

During her absence in prison a second Unity Convention was held at Leeds that included Nora Smythe and other representatives of Sylvia's party. By this time the Labour Party had removed much of the controversy by firmly rebutting applications for affiliation from the Communists. As a result the two Communist Parties were merged. However, Sylvia remained a thorn in the side of the Party as long as she retained control of the *Workers' Dreadnought*.

Sylvia felt sad and isolated during her imprisonment; she had few visitors, suffered from colitis and had to work as a cleaner. She spent four months in the hospital where she was put on a diet of milk and eggs because she could not cope with the usual prison food. However, after serving five months of her sentence, she was released on 30 May because of good conduct. A large crowd gathered in the rain and sang the 'Red Flag'. On emerging at nine o'clock she looked unwell and had difficulty walking.[54] Unfortunately, she had virtually lost control of her organization while in prison and only retained the *Dreadnought* with difficulty. She was summoned to an interview with the executive of the Communist Party – Great Britain and, in her words, 'the disciplinarians set forth their terms'.[55] Essentially they wanted her to surrender editorial control of the *Dreadnought* or simply hand the paper over to the executive, but since it remained her only real source of influence she refused and had to appear for another confrontation in September. The Party, she explained to her readers, 'is at present passing through a sort of political measles called discipline which makes it fear free expression and circulation of opinion within the Party'.[56] She argued, quite reasonably, that if they found themselves in the throes of a revolution, rigid discipline would be justified, but while the British party remained small it was more likely to benefit from free and open debate. But by this time Sylvia did not even speak for her own organization which was itself a mere fraction of the united party. This time the executive expelled her. Ironically she had informed them that the *Dreadnought* was about to cease publication, a ploy which probably backfired.[57] But her funds were exhausted and in the circumstances she could no longer expect to be bailed out by Moscow. However, once expelled from the Party, Sylvia seems to have changed her mind about winding up the paper. She turned for help to George Bernard Shaw, who dismissed the request: 'Though I am quite as much disposed to make a spoiled child of her as the rest of her friends, I am not really sorry that she should lose a toy so expensive and dangerous as a printing press.'[58] Fortunately, Nora returned from a visit to the Continent with enough money to allow the *Dreadnought* to continue until 1924 when it finally ceased publication. Sylvia's Communist phase still had some time to run, but the Revolution had ceased to be the overriding goal of her public life.

It must have been some comfort to her to know that in Australia Adela's career had been running on parallel lines. Sylvia had even published an article on 'Communism and Social Policy' by her sister in the *Dreadnought*. Adela's consistent belief in Christianity did not prevent her being swept up in a whirlwind affair with Communism between 1919 and 1922 when the pacifism of previous years seemed forgotten as she urged the violent overthrow of the capitalist system. As a result of her enthusiasm for supporting Tom and making a success of his leadership of the Seamen's Union Adela was actually closer than Sylvia to the working-class movement. But she was no mere follower; her friends regarded Adela as the more forceful partner, though this probably reflected her relative youth rather than her views.[59] From early 1919 Tom's major task was the organization of a strike, provoked by a wage award in December 1918 which the seamen felt failed to keep pace with price rises. Speaking at the Socialist Hall in Melbourne in July, he urged the men: 'Do all you can to throw this city into darkness . . . Destroy the Murray River Bridge and scuttle a ship in the Rip.'[60] Not surprisingly he and his supporters soon became derisively

known as 'Walsheviks'. Before long violence broke out between striking seamen and the ex-servicemen who were keen to take their jobs,
and Tom's inflammatory language landed him in court for inciting
industrial conflict. He was fined £200 and put in Pentridge prison for
three months until the end of September. However, during his absence
his members became divided and decided to end the strike. In spite of
this the strike was regarded as a great success and it considerably
enhanced his reputation.

Adela interpreted the events of 1919 as the start of a series of strikes
that would culminate in the downfall of capitalism in Australia. On
the strength of her scant knowledge she wrote a number of articles
extolling life in Russia after the Revolution. This Utopian vision probably helped sustain her in what was by now a wearing daily grind. She
clearly wrote from personal experience – four children and stepchildren, a small income and no servants – when she called upon the
wealthy to compare their comfortable lives and living standards with
those of the working-class housewife trapped in an endless round of
cooking, washing, cleaning and baby care, not to mention shabby
clothes, high rents and cheap furniture that wore out as soon as it had
been paid for. Her second pregnancy doubtless gave an extra edge,
even a touch of despair, to her writing, for at thirty-five she saw long
years of domestic worry and drudgery stretching ahead of her with a
husband much older than herself.

The new baby, who was named Sylvia, arrived in October 1920 in
time to be taken along to the foundation meeting of the Australian
Communist Party with both her parents. Adela sat on the executive
and contributed articles to the *Australian Communist*. In May 1921
she was among the leaders of a 2,000-strong rally of Communist
supporters in Sydney where the Union Jack was burnt and the 'Red
Flag' sung. To Adela the flag had become merely the symbol of the
master class. Her campaign culminated in September, when she led a
march of unemployed people through Sydney to the town hall,
delivered a wild speech outside the Parliament building and advocated
the smashing of windows. As a result of this she was charged and
fined but not imprisoned. Yet for all its belligerence the Australian
Communist Party had been launched into what was still a conservative
society and at a time when a reaction against the left had already set

in. The war had stimulated a new pride in Australia, and, when they chose to, the ex-servicemen and patriots could put far more people on to the streets than the far left.

By 1922 Adela's love affair with the Communist Party had evaporated after little more than a year. Despite her extreme rhetoric, her role in the new party had always been a little incongruous from an ideological point of view as is clear from the articles in which Adela appears to have interpreted Marxism to suit her own attitudes, especially as regards social issues. As she shared with her mother and Christabel a traditional feminist view of birth control and sexual emancipation, Adela found it easy to attack capitalism for promoting sensuality and immorality; conversely she portrayed Communism as a puritanical moral force which would abolish prostitution, develop the mind, encourage virtue and self-restraint, and remove the poverty and drudgery from married life.[61] To the Party loyalists, steeped in the theory of Marxism, this suggested that Adela was ignorant of ideology. Not that she could be blamed for the schismatic nature of the party which, within six weeks of its birth suffered the first breakaways. As in Britain the members, who expended much energy on factional struggles, received guidance from envoys from the Comintern on the correct strategy. But Adela was not sufficiently well informed about ideology to contribute much to this debate, nor was she temperamentally equipped for the intrigue and faction-fighting that plagued the far left. Her forte was the inspiring platform speech and confrontation with the political Establishment. Consequently, like Sylvia, Adela instinctively reacted against dictation from above, and by the end of 1921 she had effectively left the Party. Although Tom claimed to have been influenced by his wife, he remained a party member until 1923. However, in 1922 when Communist Party members were instructed to join the Australian Labor Party in order to use their influence from within, he began to fear a threat to his own control of the Seamen's Union which had elected him President in 1921.

Yet although they severed their links with the Party, neither Tom nor Adela were yet ready to abandon their left-wing opinions; and it was not until 1924 that Adela began to revise her anti-capitalist views. Friendly critics explained her shift away from the left in terms of her mercurial temperament and her middle-class background.[62] It is probably fair to say that she had naïvely expected dramatic and speedy changes to follow from the spread of revolutionary doctrines after 1919, and rapidly lost heart when the left-wing tide receded. Easily moved by suffering and injustice, Adela flourished in the excitement of a physical campaign, but was not designed for the slow and unrewarding work that was necessary for a revolutionary movement. As Australia settled down again after the political and economic tumult generated by the war, she lost her clear sense of direction for a time.

While Adela and Sylvia opted into and out of revolutionary politics, Emmeline was experiencing the very different political climate of North America. In September 1919 when she crossed the Atlantic she found herself in the company of the Earl of Camperdown and the Duke and Duchess of Sutherland, who behaved like aristocractic émigrés. The view on board held that Europe had been turned upside down, and that it was consequently wise to keep away from the place until the unemployed ex-servicemen had found jobs again.[63] On arrival Emmeline told journalists that her object was now the suppression of Bolshevism, and that in order to preserve the peace of the world it would be essential for Britain, France and America to maintain their wartime alliance. Accustomed to the excitable atmosphere in Britain where right-wing pressure had led the government into intervention in support of the counter-revolutionary forces in Russia, she failed to register the return of Americans to their normal mood of isolationism. The country was now in full-scale retreat from its involvement in European conflicts, so much so that the Senate refused even to ratify United States' membership of the League of Nations which President Wilson had worked so hard to establish. In the circumstances Emmeline inevitably attracted criticism for meddling in American politics.[64] When she opened her campaign with a speech at the Cooper Union under the auspices of the American Defence Society, two cordons of police were thrown around the building and more stood on guard inside. Throughout the speech she was interrupted and heckled, though also applauded when she attacked Bolshevism for aiming to abolish marriage and religion.[65] Despite her protests several hecklers were ejected from the meeting.

Whether because of this hostility or from prior intention, Emmeline concentrated more on Canada. Crossing into Ontario in October, she found a more promising political climate, for Canadian women, who had recently won the vote, were being added to the electoral registers in preparation for a referendum on prohibition later that month. In any case Canadians were very pro-British and more receptive to her anti-Bolshevik message. Emmeline soon grew to like Canada and Canadians: 'I am more and more of an Imperialist every day', she wrote to Ethel Smyth.[66] By November she had arrived in Victoria on the Pacific coast to speak at the Women's Canadian Club where she denounced the class war and described Bolshevism as 'the second German offensive against which [we] all must fight.'[67]

At that time Victoria was an attractive town of 38,000 people, very English in character, with gardens and houses running down to the sea. Emmeline saw it as a good place in which to bring up children. She took up residence at the St James Bay Hotel for some time before returning to Britain. But in July 1920 she sailed into New York on the *Aquitania*, accompanied by Mary, Joan, Kathleen, Nurse Pine, a French governess and a Pomeranian dog called 'Tiny'.[68] There Emmeline left the party for a while, presumably to attend to her speaking engagements. They then travelled by train across the Rockies *en route* to British Columbia; Catherine Pine had to arrange for a porter to bring food for Tiny each day. Soon after their arrival they went to live in a rented cottage near the St James Bay Hotel where Pine looked after them.[69] Emmeline told the press that she intended to make Victoria her headquarters for a long, recuperative holiday. 'This is a lovely spot and very cheap', she wrote to Ethel. 'For the sake of money I have been trying to ... write, so far without success. I am really very reluctant to do anything except potter about, sewing for myself and the children, and reading. Also I am getting fatter than I have ever been, and am having massage and "rolling" exercise to reduce my weight.'[70] However, as nothing came of the writing, she took off on a tour of Canada during the autumn, and crossed into the United States to lecture in the Southern states before reaching New York in December 1920. Her message had not changed: 'Mrs Pankhurst To Fight Our Reds', proclaimed the headline in the *New York Times*. She also pronounced herself opposed to the separation of Ireland from England, a reference to the recent agreement to establish the Irish Republic.[71] However, in view of the strength of Irish Nationalist support in the United States, this was extremely tactless. Nothing daunted, Emmeline left New York to tour the Midwest states before returning to Canada. At the end of December her brother Herbert died, though she did not hear of it until January. 'It is a dreadful blow that he, so much younger than I am, should go first', wrote Emmeline. 'Today I feel life and its burdens almost intolerable and yet one must go on to the end.'[72] After Herbert's loyal support during the suffragette campaign she now felt guilty that she had seen so little of him and not shown him more affection.

Meanwhile in England Arthur Marshall, the solicitor, and his wife, Katharine, had formed a committee to raise a testimonial fund for Emmeline and Christabel in December 1919; its members included Lady Constance Lytton, Dr Flora Murray, Lady Rhondda and Elsie Bowerman. According to press reports their aim was to raise £10,000 with which to purchase a house and to fund an annuity. Unfortunately the testimonial fund turned out to be a major embarrassment; by 1922 the subscriptions amounted to only £2,866 of which £1,000 had been given by Lady Fanny Houston, a wealthy eccentric better known for financing Fascist organizations.[73] Explanations are not hard to find. Many of the Pankhursts' Edwardian backers had long since been alienated, and some regarded their wartime jingoism as shameful. In addition, the mention of money inevitably reactivated the ill feeling over the way the Pankhursts were believed to have appropriated WSPU funds for illegitimate purposes during the war. When Sylvia was working on her biography of Emmeline in 1929 she consulted Mrs Pethick-Lawrence, who told her: 'From what I know, I think your Mother's financial affairs would not be easy to explain', and advised her to keep quiet on the subject.[74] To add to these handicaps, the committee clearly erred in including Christabel in their appeal, for many friends who considered it high time she galvanized herself and took over responsibility for looking after her mother had no wish to subsidize her in a life of indulgence and idleness, however anxious they were to help Emmeline. Ethel Smyth characteristically took it upon herself to put this to Emmeline, who promptly took umbrage and returned her letter: 'You may wish to destroy it. I would if I were you.'[75] This spat effectively put an end to another friendship. Eventually the testimonial fund committee spent nearly £1,500 on acquiring a house at Westward

Ho in Devon and sent the other £1,431 to Emmeline in Canada.[76] Some of Christabel's confidantes suggested that she needed a country house as a kind of 'Chequers' for ex-suffragettes, but North Devon seemed a remote location for such a purpose. In fact, Christabel only used the house very briefly and it was sold at a loss in 1922.

Meanwhile, by the start of 1921 Emmeline had decided to settle in Canada. She planned to earn enough money to buy 'one of those little houses in Victoria with 1 to 3 acres of garden and orchard, where I could live happily and comfortably with the babes'.[77] Now in her early sixties, the need for a secure home clearly exercised an ever stronger attraction for her. On the other hand, Emmeline very quickly became bored if confined to a purely domestic environment; she needed either amusement or some definite objective to keep her going. Unfortunately her plans continued to be hampered by Christabel who seemed as incapable as ever of reorganizing her life. Adopting an expedient that smacked of desperation and arrogance in equal measure, she placed an advertisement in the *Daily Express* in January 1921:

Miss Christabel Pankhurst (owing to the victorious termination of her leader-ship in the cause of women's political enfranchisement) seeks remunerative non-political work.

Interviewed by the paper's reporter, she explained that she could not continue as a political leader because she lacked financial indepen-dence: 'I open a new chapter in my life today', she declared.[78] The subsequent lack of response to this must have been humiliating, though the *Weekly Dispatch* invited her to write five articles in April. The first of these promised much: 'Confessions of Christabel: Why I Never Married: First of a Candid Series'. However, she revealed little in the article except a growing tendency to pretentiousness. Claiming to have followed an instinct to keep herself free for her life's work, she declared: 'For its sake I have had to remove not only all ideas of marriage, but many other things less important, such as social pleasures and various intellectual and artistic interests.' She was consciously helping to create the myth of a great political leader's sacrifice for the cause. Christabel did, however, come closer to admitting she had never been strongly tempted by marriage when she wrote: 'I am afraid that such a sum-total of human perfection as I should have required in a husband has seldom, if ever, existed.' She also advanced a limited case for remaining single on the grounds that husbands were now in short supply, and 'besides this, the country would be very much the poorer if it lost all of us unmarried women.'[79] She devoted the second article to 'My War Chest', a defence of the management of suffragette funds. In this Christabel explained that she had received the same 'honorarium' as the other organizers; even when in Paris 'I lived in great seclusion and in a very simple way . . . my own expenses were kept to a minimum'.[80] She attributed the failure to publish financial statements after February 1914 to the fact that the Government was about to prosecute subscribers, though she undermined this by admitting that many gave donations anonymously anyway. She passed over the wartime expenditure and simply claimed that when the organization had been wound up in 1919 'all liabilities were met and nothing remained'. This appears to have been contradicted by Christabel herself when she told her secretary that her expenses were paid by 'the cause' late in 1919 when both the Union and the Women's Party had ceased to exist. The campaign, she concluded, had left her mother poorer than she had been, and neither had made a fortune out of it. There was, of course, some truth in this last claim, though critics felt that they had somehow managed to spend a fortune even if nothing was now left. After this disingenuous and selective account, Christabel moved to safer ground with pieces on 'Politicians I Have Known' and 'What I Think of Lloyd George'. But throughout the series she had focussed on the past as though the present and the future had been relegated to the backwaters of her mind.

Emmeline, meanwhile, had managed to arrange a paid post for herself as an itinerant lecturer with the Canadian National Council for Social Hygiene, a body which originated in 1919 as the Canadian Council for Combating Venereal Diseases. She had met its General Secretary, Dr Gordon Bates, at a dinner party in Victoria and left him deeply impressed with her abilities as a public speaker. Though the Council received some government support, the terms of her employment evidently required some determined negotiations. Emmeline emphasized her credentials as a former member of a Poor Law Board, a School Board and a Registrar of Births and Deaths. Her usual fee, she informed Bates, was $100, though some lecturers charged as much as $300: 'If I were a rich woman I would give you a whole year for nothing and pay my own expenses.'[81] Doctor Bates duly consulted his executive of whom eleven members were in favour of the appointment, two opposed and six uncertain.[82]

After reaching a deal with Dr Bates, Emmeline embarked on a tour of Canada in April 1921, beginning with a succession of meetings in such centres as Toronto, Windsor, Winnipeg, Brandon, Regina, Medicine Hat and Calgary. In the rural districts she would borrow a motor car and persuade local organizations such as the Women's Institutes to arrange meetings for her at a rate of two per day. In the larger cities which were reached by railway she would usually hold a mission lasting a week and involving local doctors and churchmen.[83] Emmeline believed that the Council had not hitherto been very good at whipping up interest. Her tactics were to arrive a few days in advance of a lecture and arrange an interview with the local newspaper. Her press releases billed her as the woman who had kept the munitions factories of England running throughout the war by purging the country of strikes. Her arrival was obviously a major event, especially in the smaller Canadian towns. At Bathurst in New Brunswick the Mayor turned out and proudly showed her round the town. When they came upon an impressive new building Emmeline asked him what it was. Somewhat embarrassed, the Mayor replied, 'Well, as a matter of fact, Mrs Pankhurst, this is a home for fallen women.' At which Emmeline sweetly enquired: 'Where is your home for fallen men?'[84] After travelling for thousands of miles and addressing countless meetings it was some comfort for her to know that her campaign had been judged a great success; in 1922 the provincial Board of Health concluded that the recruitment of Emmeline 'has been the means of arousing the greatest interest in social hygiene among the women of Ontario'.[85] By using her talent as an extempore speaker and drawing on her reputation amongst women, she had found a means of supporting her family in Canada even though, as 1922 was to show, it was a temporary expedient rather than a lasting solution.

16

The Second Coming (1922–5)

'Having now become politically responsible, [women] can more easily realize that we are wholly unable . . . even to form, much less to put into effect, a policy that will regenerate the world.'

Christabel Pankhurst, *The Lord Cometh* (1923)

In August 1921 Christabel arrived in Montreal with Betty and Grace Roe. For once she declined to give the press much information about her intentions, probably because she was now on the brink of a completely new direction in her life and wanted to talk things over with her mother. Leaving Betty with the other three girls, she and Grace travelled on to California where they rented a house in Hollywood. There Christabel surprised her audiences when, towards the end of lectures dealing with the suffragette campaign and issues of international politics, she suddenly switched to the subject of Biblical prophecy, and her latest panacea for the world: Second Adventism.

In a life marked by sudden and dramatic turns, this seems the most eccentric of Christabel's reincarnations, and it is certainly one that her biographers have felt unable to explain satisfactorily. On the face of it, her Adventist phase appears to be a complete discontinuity in her life, for she had been brought up largely without Christian influence owing to her father's agnosticism and her mother's sceptical attitude towards religion. On the other hand, many progressives of Christabel's generation had grown up rejecting religion in favour of a moral rationalism. In her case, the only indication that a change might be in the offing came after her return from America in 1915, when Olive Bartels was surprised to see a Bible with annotations, presumably by

Christabel, in her room in Paris. Yet Christabel herself characteristically offered no explanation other than a brief indication that towards the end of the war she had chanced to pick up a volume in a second-hand bookshop written by the Reverend F. B. Meyer, a prolific writer on Biblical prophecy. When interviewed later in life, Grace Roe loyally repeated this version of the origins of Adventism.[1] However, such a trite and superficial explanation scarcely seems adequate for such a major change in Christabel's life and views, unless it is simply put down to opportunism. This view is certainly corroborated by Christabel's increasingly desperate search for an income and by the calculated, professional manner in which she exploited her new career. Never a particularly introspective person, Christabel showed no interest in the moral or theological aspects of Christianity, and her published writing put only a politician's gloss on her motives; her instinct was to throw her energies into mastering the new brief.

Despite this, the connections between Christabel's earlier life and her later Adventism are not impossible to find. The women's movement had certainly reflected religious influence in several forms, notably Theosophy with which Annie Besant and Charlotte Despard had been closely involved, as, later, were the Brackenburys, Grace Roe and several of the Kenney sisters.[2] During the Edwardian period prominent members of the Church of England and the Nonconformist churches gave public support to women's suffrage, thereby strengthening the traditional links with moral reform in the women's movement. Indeed, the suffragette campaign had increasingly annexed the language and symbolism of Christianity for its propaganda. Joan of Arc, who was beatified in 1909, figured prominently in suffragette pageants and demonstrations at this time as an archetypal militant. Increasingly suffragettes spoke of their conversion, their sacrifice and their mission, and saw themselves as a persecuted sect that was guided and sustained by a superior force.[3]

Though not explicitly brought up to be a Christian, Christabel had grown to adulthood in an era in which politics and religion were still closely interrelated, both in terms of substance and style. She liked to compare the suffragettes with the self-sacrifice of Christ and his readiness to face the censure of the world, and argued that only those who had been involved with the women's campaign could truly understand the meaning of Christ's life and death. In her 'Appeal to

God' in 1913 she attacked those churchmen who forgot that 'its own seed was the blood of the martyrs; [they have] no pity for the martyrs of the present day'. By this time a number of suffragettes had taken to praying aloud in church for the life of Emmeline Pankhurst, much to the irritation of the clergy. Moreover, during its climax between 1912 and 1914, the suffragette agitation had acquired an almost millenarian quality in that its leaders viewed their campaign as a struggle between the forces of good and the forces of evil, as represented by men in general and the Asquith Government in particular, which was leading inexorably to an apocalyptic conclusion. After 1914 Christabel continued in this mode, though she now identified the source of evil as Germany, thereby, in effect, preparing the ground for her post-war movement to save humanity through the Second Coming. In short she had come increasingly to see the campaign for the vote as a holy war, referring to it as 'simply the dim reflection of a far struggle on some celestial battle front where greater hosts than ours clash in the eternal struggle for light'.[4] Against this background her post-war stance was much less of a discontinuity than it appears at first.

In fact, the post-war world offered a good deal of scope for the kind of role in which Christabel now cast herself. During the war most of the churches had lost members, and the advocates of liberal theology or 'Modernism' had been particularly undermined. The reaction against Modernism was led by men like Dr Reinhold Niebuhr, the author of *Europe's Catastrophe and the Christian Faith*, who argued that history was moving towards the revelation of the Anti-Christ and then Christ himself. Perhaps because it had been so badly demoralized by its unprecedented losses during the war, British and American society seemed especially susceptible to apocalyptic predictions of this kind. With the collapse of traditional political institutions across Europe, the undermining of social values and behaviour, and the disruption of the world economy, many people lost confidence in temporal expressions of authority. The mood was articulated by W. B. Yeats in his 1921 poem 'The Second Coming', and in the 1930s by the publication of the famous book by George Dangerfield, *The Strange Death of Liberal England*. A classic attempt to find the origins of present ills in an earlier era, his book was poor history, but symptomatic of the fears current in inter-war society.

As conventional Christianity retreated, some of the lost ground was recovered after 1918 by the more marginal groups including Seventh Day Adventists and Jehovah's Witnesses. This pattern suited Christabel's practical needs and her own psychology particularly well, for in the aftermath of 1918 she had suffered an unusual degree of personal uncertainty and even demoralization. Adventism offered a means of restoring her sense of purpose and personal worth. In some ways it resembled the suffrage cause with its air of moral superiority, its sense of inevitability and its faith in a great leader. It must have been flattering for Christabel to believe that just as she had earlier been singled out to lead the women's movement, so she had been saved for a special purpose once again. In addition, the absence of a regular clergy in Adventism made it relatively easy for a personality like Christabel to rise quickly in the movement despite her lack of formal qualifications. The Reverend Mr Meyer, who was chairman of the Adventist Preparation Movement, recognized the momentum which a national celebrity like Christabel would generate for the cause, and the publishers, Scott Morgan, of which he was a director, took two of her early books on Adventism. She produced no fewer than five volumes: *The Lord Cometh: the World Crisis Explained* (1923), *Pressing Problems of a Closing Age* (1924), *The World's Unrest: Visions of the Dawn* (1926), *Seeing the Future* (1929) and *The Uncurtained Future* (1940).

There was little that was original in the case Christabel advanced in her books and lectures in the inter-war period. In all her publications she relied heavily on the standard textual references on Biblical prophecy and followed the usual Adventist practice of treating the Bible as a work of history. She devoted a good deal of her writing to interpretations of current manifestations as proof of the imminence of the Second Coming. 'Even Nature shares the unrest of the times', she wrote, referring to the incidence of storms, earthquakes and other natural phenomena in unexpected places. Much weight was also placed upon developments in the political sphere, notably the recent ejection of the Turks from the Middle East, the return of the Jews to Palestine and the prospective restoration of a Jewish national homeland.[5] According to Biblical prophecy, all this was a precondition for the return of Christ. Similarly she interpreted the revival of the Roman Empire in the shape of Italian expansion in northern Africa as an indication of the imminence of the last and universal kingdom. As Mussolini's ambitions and status expanded during the 1920s, this theme loomed larger in her writing.[6]

Christabel showed some shrewdness in exploiting the mood of pessimism that gradually developed during the 1920s. Starting from a gloomy view of the Treaty of Versailles, she found it natural to put the next war squarely on to the agenda. Dismissing the League of Nations and the Disarmament Convention at Geneva, she argued that peace was simply a hopeless cause. She drew on military-scientific authority to lend credibility to her thesis that humanity now faced unspeakable disasters: 'Bombs cast from noiseless aeroplanes whose successful test has been announced, the deathly gas, the long guns and other resources, will fully empower an army for the massacre of the most modern kind!'[7] On the political front she suggested that the effect of the war had been to hasten the downfall of democracy, even in states such as France and Britain, and to usher in an age of autocrats and dictators which was another important precondition for the Return of Christ. This allowed Christabel to offer an explanation for the evolution of her own thinking. She claimed to have realized after 1918 that the problem of politics lay not in military victory nor in political machinery, but in human nature. The world needed a sure and stable policy to guide it, but 'there is nothing more unknowable than the result of popular elections . . . and there is nothing more changeable than the popular will'.[8] In short, democracy was inherently unstable. Christabel now admitted to having been wrong about women because: 'We women too are human . . . having now become politically responsible, we can more easily realize that we are wholly unable, just as men are unable, even to form, much less to put into effect, a policy that will regenerate the world.' And so the franchise, once so highly valued, was dismissed as a devalued currency. Christabel insisted that since women suffered from the same divisions as men they were just as likely to indulge in warmongering. Consequently, she felt there could be no *women's* solution to the problems afflicting the world.[9] Interestingly this diagnosis seems not to have been endorsed by Emmeline, who gave every indication of retaining her faith in both female influence and in the Parliamentary system generally. But Christabel's expressions of lack of confidence in political values and institutions rang bells with many of those who looked back to what now appeared a more secure pre-war world. This was part of the outlook that fostered fascism in western societies. Though Christabel's thinking clearly encompassed the rise of fascism, she concluded that it did not lie within the capacities of any statesman or system to cope with the world's problems. As the crisis grew worse, she argued, a Caesar would indeed emerge but only to lead the final resistance to the Kingdom of Christ.

The success of Christabel's new role as an Adventist is not easy to assess. Like all the Pankhurst campaigns, Adventism proved to be more than just a cause – it was a job creation scheme. The books and lectures went some way to alleviating the acute financial crisis that faced her in the early 1920s. For example, *The Lord Cometh* went into six editions between 1923 and 1927 and *Pressing Problems of a Closing Age* into three. Christabel attracted large crowds to her lectures in England, Ireland, Canada and the United States, and even critics freely acknowledged that she had not lost her ability to hold an audience. On the other hand, she allowed her role as prophet of doom to take her to exaggerated depths to which few people could follow. Many Christians found the bleak assumption that no progress was possible rather offensive, and some contemporaries were quick to attribute her pessimism about the world's prospects to her personal disappointment in 1918 and 1919.[10]

By February 1922 Emmeline had decided to move her headquarters to Toronto because so many of the requests to speak came from Ontario where the bulk of the Candian population lived; she hoped thereby to reduce her travelling and limit herself to one speech a day. Consequently, Catherine Pine and the girls packed up their possessions for the journey along with Tiny the dog, who was installed in a bird cage so that he could be fed in the railway cabin *en route*.[11] Toronto was to be their home until early in 1924. Emmeline was also keen to persuade Christabel to join them, to which she agreed after some encouragement from Grace Roe.

This coincided with the launch of Christabel's American Adventist campaign. Grace Roe helped to arrange her meetings before eventually going into social work, which kept her in the United States for the next nine years. As a result, both Christabel and Emmeline spent a good deal of time away from home delivering their lectures. In April Emmeline turned up unexpectedly at Baltimore for the Pan-American Women's Conference where she spoke on behalf of the Canadian moral hygiene movement. 'Closing a few houses will not cure the situation, though it may alleviate it', she insisted. 'We must go to the cause that underlies the traffic in human bodies, and men and women must cease to make concessions to the human nature of man . . . there must be one moral law for men and women alike. When they cease to sell themselves the union of the sexes will produce a race physically and mentally perfect.'[12] Although Christabel spoke in churches and at Bible meetings rather than to women's organizations, her message had much in common with her mother's. Like Emmeline, she found the stricter and less sophisticated audiences in Canada and in the rural areas more receptive to her moral line than those on the west coast of the United States. When she preached at the John Knox Presbyterian Church in Toronto in November 1922 the building overflowed and the doors had to be closed. There she attacked the younger generation for snatching at pleasure and for undermining Christian moral standards by self-indulgence. Throughout 1922 and 1923 she travelled across North America, addressing Bible conferences and congregations on personal religion, but she refused to classify herself with any particular body of Adventists. In the process she appears to have modified her platform style in favour of a quieter approach. 'There is nothing of the sur-fervid evangelist about Miss Pankhurst', commented one journalist. 'Her manner in conversation is one of strong conviction.'[13] At the Old Tent Evangelical in New York she preached every evening for a week and twice on Sunday in August 1923, holding the rapt attention of large audiences according to the press. Adopting a confessional stance, she pointed to her own experience on both sides of politics during the women's campaign and since the enfranchisement of women. 'Some of us have been in a fool's paradise and we thank God that our eyes are opened.'[14] Working a now-familiar routine, she debunked all the alternatives which gave people hope. No sooner had women obtained the vote than they had been confronted with questions that could not be answered either by voting or by war. Those who looked to working-class participation in government discovered that it made little or no difference after all. Going even further to the left was equally futile: 'We know that Communism in Russia has not made people kind.'[15] As a result, Christabel claimed that people were losing their superficial optimism about solving the problems faced by the world and recognizing their need for the guidance of some superior power. She closed the year with an especially pessimistic message delivered to 5,000 people at the Moody Tabernacle in New York where she declared Britain and America to be in great moral danger and 'deeper in the mire than the people of ancient Rome ... The darkest chapter in human history is open ... That was a happy, foolish phrase "A war to end wars". The sun has never shone since that war.'[16]

While travelling, Christabel left Betty in Toronto in the company of Nurse Pine and the other girls who were now aged seven. During her spells at home Emmeline sometimes took them on outings to Niagara Falls, to the circus and to the theatre where they saw Pavlova dance, but otherwise her life was rather separate from theirs.[17] When visitors arrived they found the girls smartly dressed and handing round cakes just as Sylvia and Christabel had once done in Russell Square. But on the whole their lives centred around Catherine Pine. They had no visitors and rarely went shopping, they played in the nursery and the garden and took occasional walks with Pine. As Emmeline's views on education had not changed, they attended school only very briefly when Pine fell ill, and usually relied on a succession of governesses.[18] The girls remembered the occasional drama when the dog died after being bitten by a collie in the park, or the time when Joan and Kathleen had to have their tonsils removed and the formidably competent Pine carried out the operation on the kitchen table with no complications.[19] Otherwise their life was very uneventful.

Unfortunately, the arrival of Christabel in April 1922 introduced an element of instability into a household accustomed to a strict and regular regime. Christabel herself was disorganized and very lax towards Betty, which inevitably caused some awkwardness for the other girls and eventually led to friction with Pine, a strong personality who resented the disruption of her routine. She refused to conceal her contempt for Christabel's Adventist preaching, which now permeated her domestic life and her personal correspondence to an alarming degree. Pine sometimes observed that, if Christabel happened to be right about the Second Coming, it hardly seemed worth cooking the dinner![20] During 1923 she evidently decided she had had enough, and one day the girls awoke to find that she had gone, presumably to avoid the need to explain her reasons to them. She left a Bible and a hymn book for Kathleen, who was her favourite, a fact she had hitherto managed to conceal.[21] This was a serious blow for the girls since no one took Catherine Pine's place in the family. She had also been the pivot of Emmeline's life for several years and her departure almost certainly loosened Emmeline's ties with Canada where she had hoped to settle permanently. The two women corresponded but never saw each other again. Not for the first time Emmeline had paid a heavy price for the priority she allowed to Christabel in her life.

While Emmeline and Christabel concentrated on rebuilding their careers in North America, Sylvia's public role had been quietly subsiding after the dramas of her involvement with the revolutionary left. In fact, she was now moving into the most domestic phase of her life largely through her friendship with Silvio Corio, an Italian seven years her senior who shared her political outlook and literary talent. Born in Turin in 1875 to Luigi and Chiara Domenica, Corio had enjoyed an eventful but insecure life before he met Sylvia. His training as a printer nicely complemented his political interests first as a Socialist and later as an anarchist. After being conscripted into the Italian Army, he was discharged for misconduct after a year. In 1900 he left for France, got arrested in connection with a bomb plot and was banished from the country. After this, Corio took refuge in England where he occupied himself with anarchist propaganda, taking on printing jobs and working as a waiter in hotels and restaurants. After the outbreak of war he appears to have supported the Allied cause at least until 1916 when he came out in opposition, influenced by the Italian Socialist, Errico Malatesta, whose speeches he translated into English.

It seems probable that Silvio and Sylvia met during the war. He was forty by 1915, bald and stocky but in some ways a natural partner for her. As he travelled freely around Europe, even during the war, Corio managed to gather news for publication in the *Dreadnought*. The two were also in Paris during the Peace Conference and in Italy in 1919 when Sylvia attended the Socialist Conference at Bologna. By this time Corio had come under surveillance by the Italian police, who assumed he received some external funding as he had no resources of his own. By 1920 he had taken up residence in London where he worked closely with Sylvia as manager of the Agenda Press and as printer for the *Dreadnought* at £5 per week. He also arranged the translation of a number of works from Italian into English in which 'Signorina Pankhurst' assisted him.[22] However, his anarchist views made him suspect on the left and may have been a further factor complicating Sylvia's relations with the Communist Party.

Corio's personal life before he met Sylvia had been complicated. He had a son by an unknown Italian woman, and a daughter named Roxanne by his Socialist mistress, Clelia Alignaris. Relations between Corio and Clelia were punctuated by repeated quarrels, splits and reconciliations, and they had spent most of the period from 1907 to 1920 apart. Though an affectionate person, Corio did not support his children to any great extent. At one point in the early 1920s Roxanne wrote to Sylvia, asking for money to help her buy winter clothes as 'I seldom see my father now and the money he gives is less than negligible'.[23] It is not clear when Silvio and Sylvia became lovers, but it was probably during the mid-1920s. The foundation for the partnership was no doubt their working relationship and their common political sympathies; they felt drawn together by the oppressive power of the state. Corio also introduced a little humour and domesticity into Sylvia's rather serious life. They enjoyed a joke about the similarity of their names, and he offered her a little flattery, which was an unusual experience for her. With a string of affairs and liaisons behind him Corio was clearly not the marrying type, though this scarcely mattered to Sylvia. Now in his mid-forties, he showed some inclination to settle down, and Sylvia, in spite of her poverty and insecurity, probably offered a more stable relationship than he had been used to throughout his adult life. Together they planned to launch a new literary, left-wing journal called *Germinal*. It appeared in 1923 under Corio's editorship and contained poems and reviews by Sylvia, but swiftly collapsed.

Sylvia's relationship with Corio coincided with a complete re-arrangement of her political life. In 1924 the *Dreadnought* ceased publication, and the previous autumn she had sold her headquarters in the Old Ford Road, in the process leaving the unfortunate Norah Smythe with a large bill for rates to be paid on behalf of the WSF.[24] Sylvia was obliged to appeal to George Lansbury to get the council's threat to distrain Nora's property lifted; meanwhile, a testimonial fund was raised to help her out. On quitting the East End Sylvia had acquired a four-room, 300-year-old property at Woodford Wells, on the London–Essex border, situated in a lane just off the High Road in a large, wild garden full of roses and screened by trees and shrubs. It is not clear whether Corio lived there or just visited regularly at this stage. 'You've got a gardener, Sylvia,' commented Annie Barnes on seeing him there for the first time, obviously unaware of their relationship.[25] Apparently their original intention was to use 'Red Cottage', as they named the house, as a meeting place for left-wing discussion groups, but it was an obscure location for such a purpose. Before long it transpired that Sylvia regarded Red Cottage as a means of easing her perennial financial problems now that she had lost the subsidies which had kept her going in the East End. As the property stood opposite a public house which attracted large numbers of summer visitors going to and from nearby Epping Forest, she decided to open a tea room to cater to families and children. Although the tea room succeeded in drawing customers, the scheme suffered from an obvious flaw. Sylvia lacked even the most basic notion about cooking and service; she had never been taught and throughout her life her meals had somehow arrived through the efforts of others. On one occasion she was discovered attempting to deal with a rasher of bacon by boiling it. Wisely she decided to supply her customers at Red Cottage by simply buying cakes in town.[26] Fortunately Corio was more practical and domesticated, if equally haphazard about money; he cooked, grew vegetables in the garden, built a wooden cabin and a greenhouse and set up tables and sunshades for the customers. The wooden cabin, for which they apparently borrowed money from the Pethick-Lawrences and Henry Harben, caused some ill feeling as Corio appears to have overspent.[27]

In addition to Corio, Sylvia also relied heavily upon a number of unpaid assistants including Nora Smythe, Annie Barnes and her sister Rose, as well as other friends from the East End. 'Oh Mrs Barnes,' Sylvia would say,' when I see you get off the bus I breathe freely.' On these occasions Sylvia seized the opportunity to retreat into her study to write, leaving Annie with instructions to cook the supper and to see that she was not disturbed.[28] Annie and Rose appear to have accepted this treatment as they regarded Sylvia as a very special person and Corio as an intellectual. Despite being close friends, it is significant that Sylvia called her 'Annie' on some occasions and 'Mrs Barnes' on others.[29] In effect, she was exploiting their loyalty by treating them as unpaid domestics. When she did employ a servant the woman soon ran off taking the saucepans with her, but Sylvia, who scarcely noticed the chaotic state of the household, simply commented that she probably had greater need of them.[30] In view of Sylvia's lack of any business sense the Red Cottage was never likely to make much money – in Annie's opinion, she never charged enough for her teas. But it proved viable as a supplement to her earnings from journalism and books, and she remained there until 1929.

Whereas for Sylvia domesticity clearly went against the grain, Adela, alone among the Pankhursts, possessed a natural flair as a 'home-maker', to use the language of the 1920s. Not that she was ever conventionally domestic. Largely uninterested in food, Adela smoked a lot, fed herself largely on bread and butter, and relegated housework to the bottom of the list. But she and Tom complemented each other very well; he cooked and cheerfully tolerated the domestic chaos presided over by Adela who was described by one of her daughters as 'supremely untidy'.[31] Tidiness, however, was probably an unattainable ideal because when the family moved back to Melbourne in April 1923 they lived in a small and crowded cottage in the suburb of Hampton. By 1923 Adela had three children of her own – Richard, now four, Sylvia two, and the baby Christian – while a fourth, Nancy Ursula, was born the following year. While the children found Tom a little severe, Adela was a warm, affectionate mother, and in spite of her continued activities outside the home, the children never felt neglected. On the contrary, she aroused in them love, respect and what Ursula called 'a strange desire to protect her', perhaps because of her diminutive size and the burden she had to carry in Tom's declining years.[32] Above all Adela's close relationship with the three daughters from Tom's first marriage was a triumph. After their mother's death the girls had had a disrupted home life and been forced to move repeatedly; it would not have been surprising if they had resented their father's new wife, especially as he was so obviously devoted to her. Fortunately Adela possessed more awareness of other people's feelings than any other Pankhurst; indeed she once remarked that she had to be nicer towards her stepchildren than to her own.[33] As the girls grew older they helped more in running the cash-strapped household and in looking after the toddlers when Adela was out at meetings. That they kept in touch with their stepmother later in life was further proof of the successful relationship they had established in the 1920s.

Nor do the older Walshes seem to have been antagonized by their parents' political activities, for they grew up to be Socialists and were keen to help them in their campaigns. In these years Adela managed somehow to combine her demanding family life with her wider interests. She continued her writing for the *Seamen's Journal* as well as acting as sub-editor and proof-reader on occasion. In 1923 she rejoined the Victoria Socialist Party as an unpaid organizer and became active in the Women's Socialist League. She also returned to her early love for history by reading classic works on the French Revolution as well as biographies of Robespierre and Danton. This may have accelerated her failing sympathy for the revolutionary cause in Russia, for though she continued to see capitalism as a system beyond repair, she abandoned any idea of overthrowing it by revolutionary means. On the contrary, she argued that revolutions often made the lives of ordinary people worse rather than better. Instead she adopted a more mainstream Labour belief that the workers should use their collective influence in order to curtail the worst features of the system and extract the maximum benefit from it.

On the other hand, Adela was enough of a Pankhurst to find the middle ground an uncomfortable place. To be fair, her migration away from the left was greatly accelerated by Tom and his increasing difficulties with his union. During 1924 he found himself in the unusual position of being outflanked on the left by a younger man, Jacob Johnson, who promoted a number of wildcat strikes in the shipping industry thereby making Tom's policy of arbitration appear a little tame. Their relations became even more fraught as a result of allegations about the disappearance of union funds in the Victoria branch. Perhaps as a way of refurbishing his own radical credentials, Tom backed a number of strikes by Australian and British seamen in Fremantle in Western Australia in November 1924, which resulted in his being arrested and fined £150 for inciting strikes. In January the following year, the state's Labor Government deported him back to Melbourne. However, he continued to urge the men to disrupt the ports and by May the Seamen's Union had been de-registered and forced to move its headquarters to Sydney. By this time the situation had become so desperate for the ship-owners that the new Nationalist prime minister, Stanley Bruce, who had come to power in July, introduced legislation to allow the Government to deport 'alien agitators'. Both Walsh and Johnson were the targets of this policy. Tom attempted to force the authorities to back down by fomenting a general strike, but outside the ranks of the seamen there was by now insufficient sympathy, partly because the disruption of Australia's exports had exposed many workers to unemployment or short-time working. This enabled Bruce to win an election on the law-and-order ticket in November. Within a few days of his victory police conducted a dawn raid on the Walshes' home in Sydney in which Tom was dragged off to prison on Garden Island while the Government prepared its case for his deportation from the country. Meanwhile the strike collapsed, partly as a result of hostile intervention by the British union leader Havelock Wilson. Stuck in a suburb without her own transport, Adela was obliged to take her toddlers by taxi to visit Tom in prison, and meanwhile keep the family going on irregular wages. She dreaded the prospect that Tom, now aged fifty-four, would be deported to England where he would have found it very hard to find work. But as the authorities advised her to start raising the money to take herself and the children to England, she arranged for the sale of their cottage and furniture to pay off the mortgages.[34] Fortunately in December 1925 the High Court ruled that Parliament had exceeded its powers in the new legislation; the Immigration Act was thus invalid, and in any case Tom could not be classified as an immigrant because he had resided in Australia before the formation of the Federation.

For a brief period Tom and Adela became heroes for successfully defying the authorities. But the deportation case had only diverted attention from the underlying power struggle being waged within the Seamen's Union. Johnson, who had also been imprisoned and thus enjoyed as much kudos as Tom, continued to undermine his older rival with accusations of financial malpractice and vowed to destroy his career. The strain of these events left the Walshes depressed and ill. On Christmas Day Adela felt so weak that she called the doctor and was taken into hospital where, in the New Year 1926, she gave birth prematurely to a fifth child, a girl named Faith Hope, who died in her arms after only three days.[35] This was her worst period in Australia, and for a time Adela allowed her political work to lapse in order to concentrate on recovering her strength and spirits and keeping the shattered family together.

Though her life in the early 1920s lacked the drama of Adela's, Emmeline eventually found the strain of her work as an itinerant lecturer more than she could bear. Now sixty-five, she complained of the intense cold of the Canadian winters and the suffocating heat of the summers. By chance she visited the annual exhibition in Toronto in September 1923, where her interest was engaged by a stand on Bermuda which gave her the idea for her next move. Unhappily the departure for Bermuda in the summer of 1924 caused a further break-up in the family, or perhaps provided the occasion for reducing a burden which Emmeline now found insupportable. She decided to take her favourite child, Mary, who was a lively, red-haired, blue-eyed girl, with her to Bermuda. The fact that Mary had some money in the shape of a trust fund founded by an unknown lady (who was believed to be her mother) was no doubt another factor in her decision.[36] However, the two other girls were sent back to Britain into the temporary care of a Miss Andrews, who was in charge of Tower Cressy, until permanent homes could be found for them. While to a later generation this action appears callous, Emmeline simply reflected Victorian practice; large numbers of British children continued to be separated from their parents and shipped around the empire throughout the inter-war years. Joan subsequently went to a wealthy couple who lived in Scotland, and Kathleen was adopted by John Coleridge Taylor, a journalist on the *Evening Standard* who lived at Wallington in Surrey. The traumatic effect of this separation and disruption in the lives of the girls can only be imagined; subsequently they appear to have lost contact with each other, though Kathleen once met Nurse Pine.

Emmeline spent a year on Bermuda with Mary and Christabel's Betty from the summer of 1924 to 1925. Though she told everyone that she was there on holiday, it proved impossible to avoid some public speaking because her arrival inevitably resurrected the long-running campaign for the enfranchisement of the women of Bermuda. In April 1925 the island's House of Assembly debated a suffrage bill which was overwhelmingly rejected, much to Emmeline's displeasure.[37] This aside, she and the two girls enjoyed something approaching a normal family life on Bermuda; they rented a house called Roche Terre on a hill overlooking the Sound near Buena Vista, and Emmeline joined the children in regular bathing in the sea. She even managed to persuade Christabel to spend some time with them, though she remained largely absorbed with drafting her next volume on the Second Coming, surrounded by piles of newspaper cuttings on the latest natural disasters and international crises. Whenever a new idea occurred to Christabel she would jump up and disappear into her room. To the girls she seemed eccentric, but they had by now grown accustomed to the idea that she and her mother were great personalities who behaved strangely, even if they were not quite sure why. From Bermuda Christabel wrote to Lloyd George, asking whether he had read her latest book.[38] As he was himself in the process of engineering a second coming as Leader of the Liberal Party he may have been too preoccupied to reply, though they remained on friendly terms in this period. She made it a practice to send her publications to most leading politicians. However, these contacts only exacerbated Christabel's feeling of isolation on Bermuda and she remained chiefly concerned about maintaining her profile as an Adventist in Britain as well as in America.

As Christabel continued to spend much of her time on trips to the American mainland, Emmeline soon grew bored with life on Bermuda. Although she had resumed her correspondence with Ethel Smyth she felt the absence of close friends there. Moreover, after a while the money presumably began to run out. Yet if she could not afford to stay indefinitely on Bermuda, nor could she face a return to Canada and the rigours that her life there had entailed. In these circumstances Emmeline's thoughts turned once again to England. However, it remained uncertain whether she could support herself without relying on the generosity of her sister Ada.

With a sad inevitability Emmeline searched the pages of her life and came up with a proposal to start yet another business. She believed that if she could involve Christabel this would have the double advantage of drawing her away from her campaign and recreating the family home for which she longed, as well as giving them all some financial security.

Rather fortuitously, Christabel, who had been preaching in America from January to May 1925, suddenly announced her own intention of returning to England. At this Emmeline quickly made up her mind to join her. She contacted an old friend from suffragette days, Mabel Tuke, and they hatched a scheme to go to the south of France to open an English teashop; they all loved France, the benign climate of the Riviera would suit them well, and the numerous English expatriates who wintered there would provide plenty of custom. It is a mark of the uncomfortable symmetry of Pankhurst family affairs that Emmeline and Christabel should have embarked on this enterprise while Sylvia was engaged in the same activity in the more bracing climate of Essex. Even though Sylvia was not in touch with her mother at this time, Emmeline may well have gained the inspiration for a teashop from her knowledge of her daughter's activities at the Red Cottage.

In the event Mrs Tuke put up most of the money required, though Emmeline also drew upon her slender savings. Inevitably Christabel felt less than enthusiastic about this new venture, but, perhaps feeling a little guilty about her mother, she agreed to indulge her. However, when writing to her friend the Baronne de Brimont she said nothing about a teashop, merely that her mother wanted to find a suitable house on the coast in which to spend the winter.[39] By August the three women had arrived in Paris with Mary and Betty where they took an apartment in the Avenue Victor Hugo. But they left, all too soon for Christabel, in order to acquire something suitable in the south before too many people arrived. The end of August found them ensconced in the Pavillon Rivoli in Nice. The girls enjoyed themselves on the beach while Christabel was pleased to discover a bookshop stocked with Adventist literature opposite the hotel. By this time she had begun to sound like a public meeting even in her private correspondence. 'My poor England is face to face with serious economic difficulties and perhaps with some sort of uprising,' she wrote to the Baronne. 'I should be in despair but for the certainty that behind, above the clouds, the Son of Righteousness is shining and in due course and very soon (will) make Himself visible in all the power of His majesty.'[40] She punctuated her letters with Biblical references, Adventist predictions and observations on the great men she had met.

Eventually Emmeline and Mabel Tuke settled on Juan-les-Pins

where they opened the 'English Tea-Shop of Good Hope'. But the enterprise was doomed from the start. None of the three had any business sense, and only Mrs Tuke possessed the ability to make the necessary scones and cakes. Christabel, who could be forgiven for regarding the role of waitress as an embarrassment for one who had lately been preaching to thousands on the Second Coming, did her best to pretend that the whole thing had nothing to do with her. A *Sunday Express* journalist reported in January that while Mrs Tuke took the orders Christabel sat talking politics at a nearby table. She came across 'as though entertaining in her own drawing room [and] told me how she had come out to write a new book, and out of the kindness of her heart had been helping an old comrade of militant days.'[41] Sensing, no doubt, that another fiasco loomed, Christabel had probably decided to pander to her mother's wishes for the sake of a quiet life and a few months in France. However, the customers failed to materialize, and as winter came on Emmeline realized that the south of France was not quite as warm as she had imagined it to be. By Christmas she had returned to England with Mary to stay with her sister, Ada, in London, leaving Mrs Tuke to struggle on for a while.

The failure of the teashop proved to be a serious blow because it carried away the last of Emmeline's savings. According to Ethel Smyth a few faithful friends such as the Marshalls continued to help her and Christabel, but Emmeline declined to discuss the subject.[42] By 1926 she was sixty-seven; she had no regular income and few prospects. Her plight had recently attracted an offer from Lady Rhondda, on behalf of the Six Point Group, of a salaried post at £400 a year. The work would have been similar to her lecturing in Canada but much less exhausting; yet she refused Rhondda's offer, probably out of pride. During the mid-1920s the women's organizations who were trying to put pressure on the prime minister, Stanley Baldwin, to extend the 1918 Reform Act by giving women the vote at the age of twenty-one rather than thirty, calculated that Emmeline's involvement would help to build the momentum behind their campaign. But she dismissed the whole idea, saying that it would be 'undesirable to re-open the franchise agitation in such a world crisis as this, especially as women have already enough voting powers if effectively employed'.[43] In short, she chose to regard the issue as settled and refused to admit that the WSPU campaign had been anything other than 100 per cent successful. In a way she was right, for it would have seemed a tame anticlimax to have returned to the old cause without the drama and publicity generated by the militant campaign. As a result the offer passed and she received no others.

17

Unmarried Mother (1926–8)

'I wanted a baby . . . I suppose you think I am awfully silly, don't you!'
Sylvia Pankhurst, *News of the World*, 8 April 1928

'England is the freest country in the world – freer than the United States,' Emmeline told the London press in January 1926 soon after her return. 'My stay in Canada has made me more of an Imperialist than ever,' she continued. 'I believe in the British Empire and its mission for the world. It stands for just government and for fair play for everyone.'[1] At this stage the reporters had no idea what, if anything, Emmeline's declaration portended, and she merely fended off their suggestions about taking up women's suffrage once again, saying she would leave it to others. Asked whether she was satisfied with the use women had made of their votes since 1918, she replied: 'I don't think they have done badly', which was a tacit confession of her disappointment or perhaps lack of interest. Meanwhile she took up residence with her sister Ada in Gloucester Street. Christabel soon followed her back to London, consigning the teashop to the catalogue of business failures, in order to embark on an extensive programme of Adventist meetings in the autumn which took her to Bristol, Cardiff, Portsmouth, Birmingham, Liverpool, Manchester, Ipswich, Edinburgh and Dublin. She filled the Albert Hall's ten thousand seats with ease. Two further volumes on the Second Coming followed in 1926 and 1929. At a meeting in the Queen's Hall, the scene of many a suffragette speech, she made a characteristically late entry and sat slightly slumped in her seat, half-hidden beneath the huge Edwardian hat which was now her trademark. When the time came to speak the audience, half old suffragette and half new Adventist, stood to welcome her. At this the Reverend Mr Meyer bridled and reminded them to remember the purpose of the gathering; but even he made a graceful personal tribute: 'If she were a little older I might call her Deborah, a real Mother in Israel.' In her addresses Christabel took grim satisfaction in what appeared to be the steady retreat of democracy in favour of dictatorship in Italy, Spain, Greece, Bulgaria, Hungary and Turkey, and even suggested that France was likely to succumb to the trend. She dwelt especially on the revival of the Roman Empire which 'is about to become the dominant factor in international affairs . . . Dictatorship as a mode of government is clearly indicated in prophecy to be characteristic of the closing years of this Age'.[2] With apparent approval she pointed to Mussolini's recent visit to Tripoli as a step towards fulfilling Italy's destiny by the recovery of her empire in Africa, and suggested that the expansion of her population by half a million a year made it unreasonable to confine her to the Italian peninsula. She envisaged the restoration of Italy's relations with all the countries that had formerly belonged to the Roman Empire and their reorganization into a new imperial group stretching across south and central Europe.[3] With the benefit of hindsight it is natural to see this confidence in Mussolini as hopelessly misplaced. But this is to overlook the mood of the mid-1920s. While Italy appeared to be a buoyant, expanding society, the British reacted to their declining birth rate with dire predictions about a fall in the population. To many western statesmen the Italian regime undoubtedly appeared formidable, in view of her strategic position across the Mediterranean shipping routes, and potentially a force for good in international affairs. It is also worth remembering that when Christabel cast aspersions on the League of Nations she reflected the prejudices of the leading politicians. Though they paid lip-service to the League so as not to offend public opinion, they preferred to rely on more traditional methods for maintaining their security and the peace settlement. Even at this early stage Christabel frankly warned that the League would be superseded by some other force for maintaining western security, and urged the necessity for France and Britain to become Italy's partners in the Mediterranean area. This appeared feasible since neither France nor Britain had any objection in principle to Italian colonization in North Africa.[4]

These expressions of sympathy with Italian expansionism put Christabel once more at odds with Sylvia who had begun to take an increasing interest in Mussolini's regime, partly through the influence of Silvio Corio. She filled the pages of her notebooks with material for a book to be entitled 'The Red Twilight' about the Fascist seizure of power in 1922. She also took up the cause of the widow of Giacomo Matteoti, the Italian Socialist murdered by the Fascists in 1923. On behalf of the Women's International Matteoti Committee Sylvia wrote to the American President to bring to his attention the plight of Matteoti's widow with a view to sending a delegation to Italy to negotiate better treatment for her.[5] During the later 1920s the threat of Fascism gradually displaced her earlier involvement with Communism until, by the time of the invasion of Abyssinia in 1935, it became the chief cause in her life.

Despite being so immersed in Adventism, Christabel showed some signs of being diverted by a return to politics in March 1926. At a dinner organized by the Six Point Group at which she was the guest of honour, she received public invitations from Lady Rhondda and Nancy Astor to stand for Parliament again. Though four general elections had taken place since the enfranchisement of women, only eight women MPs had been returned in 1923 and a mere four in 1924; the dinner was intended as part of a campaign to achieve greater political equality for women. Astor impetuously declared that as Christabel's place was in the House of Commons, she would gladly give up her own seat at Plymouth for her. This was ridiculous as Astor had been elected as a Conservative and could not, therefore, hand it over to anyone on her own authority. In any case she enjoyed being an MP far too much to relinquish the role. Christabel declined the offer, saying 'I must win my own seat'; but she gave some indication of being ready to do so: 'I will go [to Parliament] if I am sent there and if you want me.'[6] Her only real chance lay in becoming an official Conservative candidate, but to embark on that route in 1926 would have involved recanting much of her recent writing about the futility of democracy and party politics.

However, Lady Rhondda's efforts were not entirely wasted, for Nancy Astor was also reported as offering her seat to Emmeline on the grounds that she herself was only in Parliament 'as a sort of preliminary canter waiting for a real horse to come along'.[7] Whether it was this that put the idea into Emmeline's head is not clear, but during 1926 she took a renewed interest in party politics, so much so that by June she had publicly aligned herself with the Conservative Party, an action described by Sylvia as 'utterly amazing, infinitely sad', and as a further betrayal of Richard Pankhurst. In a wounding letter published in *Forward*, she suggested that her mother's lapse was attributable to 'that sad pessimism which sometimes comes with advancing years, and may result from too strenuous effort'.[8] Yet Emmeline's announcement only extended a pre-existing trend in her views, for the war and her experience in Canada had accelerated her move to the right. She said herself that she had lost the advanced views of her youth: 'I can no longer support the view that state ownership of the means of distribution, production and exchange would be of any benefit to the community.'[9]

However, the proximate explanation for Emmeline's new initiative lay in the political crisis looming in Britain when she returned from France. During 1925 the Conservative Government under Stanley Baldwin had become embroiled in the problems of the coal industry caused by overproduction, inefficiency and the loss of export markets since the war, recently exacerbated by the Government's decision to return to the Gold Standard. The coal owners proposed drastic cuts in wages, a move which was regarded, correctly, by the other unions as the start of a general policy of lowering wages in order to maintain the pound at its new level. As a result, for the first time in its history Britain faced the prospect of a general strike in 1925; but the Baldwin Government bought time by offering subsidies to the industry while a Royal Commission investigated its problems. This delayed the crisis for nine months until May 1926 when talks finally broke down and a nine-day strike took place. The prospect of a general strike galvanized many people on the far right of politics into action designed to keep essential services going. The best-known response was the Organization for the Maintenance of Supplies which attracted about 80,000 volunteers, but several former suffragettes also participated in anti-strike activities including Flora Drummond, whose Guild of Empire waged propaganda campaigns in the coalfields. Mary Allen, another ex-suffragette, who joined the British Union of Fascists in the 1930s, expressed the fashionable view that there was a distinct women's angle on the strike: 'When the mothers of the strikers' children are convinced that the strike is wrong, it will end.'[10] Emmeline herself believed that if the miners' wives had been consulted in a secret ballot, the strike would never have taken place at all.[11] Allen formed a Women's Auxiliary Service, with shades of patriotic wartime work, to disseminate counter-strike propaganda and to arrange relief entertainments for women in the East End with a view to keeping them off the streets and away from strike meetings.

Inevitably the events of May 1926 deepened the gulf separating the various members of the Pankhurst family. When the miners stayed out on strike for six months, risking terrible hardship in the process, Sylvia took in children from South Wales mining families and farmed out others to sympathizers in the East End. As they helped her at the Red Cottage in return for board and lodging, this was not wholly philanthropic, but it put her squarely on the opposite side of the barricades to her mother once again.

The unexpected decision by the Trades Union Congress leaders to call off the general strike after only nine days turned the crisis into a great triumph for Baldwin, at least in the short term. Participation in anti-strike activity had had the effect of accelerating Emmeline's general political awareness, and in particular it left her with a very high opinion of the prime minister whose eloquent appeals for class concili-ation coincided with her own views. When challenged subsequently on why she had become a Conservative, she resorted to a little chicanery, saying that she had always been a *Constitutionalist* and it was because she valued the British Constitution so highly that she had wanted to bring women within it.[12] Barely a month later came the announcement that she was to become a Conservative candidate and hoped to stand somewhere in London. Emmeline was subsequently adopted for Whitechapel, one of the poorest working-class constituencies in the East End. This choice appears distinctly odd; to become a Conservative was one thing, but to stand in a hopeless seat at Emmeline's age was quite another. The Conservatives had not even bothered to run a candidate in Whitechapel in 1923 or 1924 and the seat had been held fairly comfortably for the Labour Party by Harry Gosling in a straight fight with the Liberals. Since a general election was not due until 1929

Emmeline could almost certainly have waited for a better prospect to come up. However, Commander Lindsay Venn, who was currently the Conservatives' London County Council candidate in Whitechapel, felt that Emmeline herself had insisted on taking on a tough seat, rather than being forced into it by an ungracious party organization.[13] The national leadership of the Conservative Party was naturally pleased at its coup in recruiting her, which seemed likely to strengthen its appeal to the women who already comprised over 40 per cent of the electorate. Emmeline's recruitment to the Tory Party must have accelerated the fulfilment of the promise which Baldwin had made several years previously to introduce equal suffrage for women. In April 1927 he finally announced a bill which had the effect of adding another five and a half million female voters to the existing nine million, thereby making them a majority of the electorate for the first time.

On the other hand, Nellie Hall, who became Emmeline's personal secretary towards the end of 1926 and remained close to her until her death, believed that the officials of the Conservative Central Office treated her badly; they regarded Emmeline as 'a poor and unwanted step-relation'. She noticed that even the staff in the local party headquarters in Cable Street felt no great devotion to her, though the rank-and-file members liked her.[14] Yet this was understandable since, for those whose chief loyalty was to the Party, the sudden arrival of a major personality with her own coterie of followers and assistants made them feel they were being used. What Nellie Hall described as 'the tragedy of those last two or three years' was undoubtedly coloured by the fact that, at sixty-eight, Emmeline struggled against poor health while continuing to be plagued by her perennial financial worries.

In fact, Emmeline's chances of election were so poor that one wonders whether she had other motives for undertaking the campaign in Whitechapel. Since each of the Pankhursts' previous campaigns had brought financial subsidies in its wake, she may well have anticipated more backing from Conservative sources than actually materialized. Or was she simply drawn irresistibly by the thrill of the platform? Emmeline had, after all, tried domesticity in recent years and knew that it did not suit her, especially as her family had dwindled, and Christabel continued to be absorbed by her Adventist work. She needed the challenge of a cause to keep her going and the love and admiration of the crowds to assuage the loneliness in her life.

One further factor probably contributed to her decision. After suffering the embarrassment caused by Sylvia's association with pacifism, Communism and syndicalism for the last twelve years, Emmeline almost certainly felt stung by the accusation that she had betrayed her husband's political principles. Now she deliberately raised the standard of the right in that part of London which Sylvia had treated as her own stamping ground since 1912. If the working-class women voted Conservative, what would this say for Sylvia's efforts in the East End? In this way the long-running battle between mother and daughter moved inexorably towards its tragic conclusion during 1927 and 1928.

During the autumn of 1926 Emmeline gathered her little organization, comprising the former suffragettes Barbara Wylie, Edith Fitzgerald and Nellie Hall, around her. They evidently avoided dealing with the party officials unless absolutely necessary. Nellie would arrive at Ada Goulden Bach's house each morning to find Emmeline sitting in front of the fire in her dressing gown having her breakfast. They would go through her post before setting off to arrange meetings, though this was difficult as neither woman had the use of a motor car. By the spring of 1927 Emmeline had decided to move into the constituency in order to make the work easier. But the most she could afford was a spartan set of lodgings above a barber's shop in the Ratcliffe Highway in Wapping, which she found noisy from the roar of traffic and rather claustrophobic. 'I hate small rooms,' Emmeline complained.[15] None the less, she laid a new black carpet on the floor to offset the garish wallpaper and moved in with her desk and a few other personal possessions; the barber and his wife looked after her while Dr May Williams attended her regularly.

Emmeline officially launched her Whitechapel campaign on 3 March at a demonstration in the Town Hall in Cable Street supported by Sir William Bull, MP, and Dame Caroline Bridgeman, the chairman of the National Union of Conservative Associations. Her speech on the need to defend the Empire from the revolutionary forces threatening it, and to save British industry by eliminating class hatred and restoring co-operation between employers and workers, demonstrated how easily she had mastered the orthodox Conservative case.[16] But if the

Party was to achieve its aim of reviving its fortunes in the East End, Emmeline had to inject more of her distinctive personality into the campaign. Following Edwardian practice, she refused to use a microphone, an increasingly common aid for inter-war politicians. She organized large numbers of daytime meetings for women, especially on half-closing days when it was easy for them to attend. At these functions, which effectively became tea parties with some politics thrown in, Emmeline's ability to put across a point without talking down to ordinary people quickly made her a popular figure. None the less, she faced an uphill task, not least because the political tide was now flowing against the Conservatives owing to the inability of Baldwin's Government to reduce unemployment significantly. By Easter 1927 she had so exhausted herself that the Marshalls carried her off for a cruise to Gibraltar in the hope of restoring her health and spirits.

Despite this, the candidature steadily took its toll on Emmeline's fragile health and on her state of mind. She was obliged to spend more time resting in bed and sometimes cancelled meetings while Nellie and Dr Williams made sure that she took her medicines. On one occasion Nellie found her in tears because a toy dog given to her by Christabel, which was 'very highly bred with ancestors a mile long and a constitution resembling a snowflake', had fallen ill.[17] The cause of her upset lay in the fear that Christabel would suspect her of neglecting the dog. Unfortunately she still saw very little of Christabel, who continued to be occupied with her Adventist lectures. The combination of overstrain, deteriorating health and sheer loneliness was gradually wearing her down. She took some comfort from the overwhelming vote in the House of Commons for equal franchise for women on 29 March 1928. Though Emmeline had gone to hear the debate with Nellie Hall, she found herself too weak even to get up to the Gallery; a young policeman wept when he saw her.[18]

Sadly, even at this stage Emmeline's life continued on its collision course with that of her second daughter. Sylvia, now forty-five, had for some time wanted to become a mother. However, neither she nor Corio had much respect for the institution of marriage. When he moved into Red Cottage in 1926, Annie Barnes asked Sylvia why she did not marry him, but she replied: 'My dear, if I were to marry Silvio [,] he is a refugee from fascism and I'm a Socialist, the government would deport us both to his country and we'd be shot.'[19] Though this sounds rather melodramatic, Sylvia was correct about the danger of forfeiting her rights as a British citizen. During the 1930s it became a major objective of feminists to enable British women who married foreigners to retain their nationality as did men who married foreign women; but as no legislation was enacted, Sylvia would certainly have been at risk in becoming Corio's wife.

During 1926 when she was trying to become pregnant Sylvia enjoyed a good deal of moral support from Charlotte Drake, an old friend and colleague from her campaigning days in the East End. At one point Charlotte took her to be examined by a midwife at Custom House, thoughtfully equipping her with a wedding ring so as to avoid any embarrassment. However, it emerged that Sylvia's intense yearning for a baby had given her a phantom pregnancy. She began to fear that she was now too old to become a mother. In February 1927 she once again rang Charlotte to tell her she was pregnant, but she must have been wrong because it was not until April that her pregnancy was finally confirmed.[20] Conscious that Sylvia was unlikely to enjoy much support from her mother, Mrs Drake offered to let Sylvia have the baby at her house. However, by the inter-war period the practice was changing in favour of hospitalization during childbirth. Anticipating the need for medical assistance at the birth and aftercare, Sylvia gladly accepted offers from Lady Sybil Smith, who arranged for her to enter a nursing home in Hampstead, and from Emmeline Pethick-Lawrence, who contributed to her expenses after the birth. On 4 December Sylvia gave birth to a baby boy whom she named Richard Keir Pethick Pankhurst after the three most influential people in her life.

Unfortunately the prospect of becoming a grandmother in these circumstances filled Emmeline with dread. Since her return from France the two women had met only once and the distance between them remained as wide as ever. According to Nellie Hall, Ada Goulden Bach had made sure Emmeline did not receive Sylvia's letters while staying at Gloucester Road, and when Sylvia called at the house during her pregnancy Emmeline fled to her room 'like a sulky girl', refusing to see 'that Scarlet Woman'.[21] In the circumstances it was hardly surprising that Sylvia turned to Mrs Pethick-Lawrence for support rather than her mother, but the rejection, surely the most wounding possible for a mother towards her daughter, engendered further unpleasantness a few months later. No doubt Emmeline had some reason to feel upset. In the 1920s unmarried motherhood was a considerable embarrassment, more especially for a political figure like Emmeline whose recent career had been spent advocating the need for higher standards in sexual morality. Moreover, Emmeline evidently believed that Sylvia had got pregnant largely with a view to causing the maximum humiliation for her. This sounds like the kind of exaggerated accusation made in the heat of the moment in family arguments. However, Sylvia gave some grounds for her mother's belief by her subsequent behaviour. News of Richard's birth had not been reported in the British press apart from an advertisement which appeared in the *Daily Herald*. But Sylvia was not content to return quietly to Red Cottage after leaving the nursing home. Four months later on 8 April the *News of the World* boasted a front page headline: 'Eugenic Baby Sensation. Sylvia's Amazing Confessions. Soul Mate of 53'. The paper's report continued: 'From the obscurity in which she has lived since the memorable days of the militant suffragettes, Miss Sylvia Pankhurst springs a new sensation upon the world today.'[22] Nor was Sylvia a reluctant victim of press intrusion, for she had cabled an article to the North American newspapers two days before the *News of the World*'s scoop. The *New York Times* reported her as saying that she was leaving it to the father to disclose his name if he wished, but she would describe him only as a foreigner and as being interested in politics; she emphasized her view that marriage was a purely personal matter between independent people who loved each other. As for Richard: 'I hope he will be a great man, and if he enters politics carry on the family tradition'; by agreement with his father he would take the Pankhurst name.[23] Speaking to a journalist in the garden of Red Cottage, Sylvia explained that she had postponed motherhood until after the women's campaign and the war were over, and referred to the father as 'an old and dear friend I have loved for years' but who was unable to contribute much to the baby's support. 'I suppose you think I am awfully silly don't you?' she remarked. Apparently unable to resist twisting the knife deeper, she said she could not understand why the Pankhurst family had had nothing to do with her since Richard's birth or why her mother had failed to reply to her letter on the subject.

Meanwhile Katharine and Arthur Marshall had taken Emmeline to stay with them at Chipping Ongar early in April. She looked desperately ill and 'when the news came through she wept all day without ceasing . . . I shall never be able to speak in public again', she kept repeating.[24] This is why some of her friends subsequently accused Sylvia of responsibility for accelerating her mother's death. When the Marshalls returned her to her lodgings in Wapping on 11 April, Emmeline took to her bed suffering from the gastric complaint that had recurred ever since her hunger strikes before the war. She was in pain and unable to keep her food down, but neither Dr Williams nor Dr Abrahams from the Westminster Hospital could determine exactly what was wrong with her. She managed to maintain her spirits by seeing visitors, looking forward to another cruise with the Marshalls and reading letters from Christabel and Adela. The one bright spot in this period was the news that Adela and Tom had espoused the same view of class conciliation as Emmeline herself, which made for a belated reconciliation in the weeks before her death. However, at the end of May, Christabel, who had never approved of her mother's decision to live in the slums of Wapping, had her transferred to a nursing home at Number 43 Wimpole Street. At this stage she and Ada took control and called in a specialist, Dr Chetham Strode, who had treated her previously. May Williams was now excluded for several days, as was Nellie Hall, even though Emmeline kept asking for her.[25] On 13 June she suffered a relapse and died the following day, just one month short of her seventieth birthday and a month after the final passage of the legislation which gave women the vote on equal terms with men.

The public comment on Emmeline's death was, perhaps predictably, not all sympathetic. In the course of a largely hostile editorial the *Daily Mail* described her as 'the spiritual descendant of all the martyrs and fanatics who have ever worn themselves out in pursuit of an ideal'.[26] The *New York Times*, never a friend, suggested rather absurdly that as 'a practitioner of direct action [she] was rivaled only by the terrorist activities of the Russian revolutionists of a generation ago.'[27] Writing privately to Sylvia, Emmeline Pethick-Lawrence offered a candid verdict: 'I regard your mother dispassionately (as you do) as a most interesting human problem. She was undoubtedly a *great force* rather like Napoleon.' She went on to say that her object obsessed her like a passion . . . she threw scruple, affection, honour, loyalty and her own principles to the winds. The movement developed her powers – all her powers for good and for evil . . . She was capable of beautiful tenderness and [a] magnificent sense of justice and self-sacrifice. These things in the course of the struggle became damaged. We all sacrificed many things – she sacrificed her very soul.[28]

But amid all the tributes to her qualities it was the suffragist journalist Henry Brailsford, writing two years later, who best captured the essence of her life:

There are literal minds which suppose that Mrs Pankhurst faced obloquy and prison to win votes for women. She did a greater thing than that. She suffered to remove from the mind of every young girl the sense that she is born to a predestined inferiority. The strength of this woman was in her torrential emotions . . . For me it was Mrs Pankhurst's voice that revealed her. She spoke very quietly and simply, but her voice could give to the plainest statement an almost intolerable power to move . . . it was when she spoke that all the bitterness that came from powerlessness, all the thwarted moments of pity and sympathy which women had felt for centuries in vain, were audible at last.[29]

Emmeline's funeral service took place on 18 June at St John's Church in Smith Square, a stone's throw from the House of Commons where she had endured so many rebuffs at the hands of the authorities. Through the night Katharine Marshall, Rosamund Massey, Olive Walton and Dorothy Bowker had kept vigil. During the morning a crowd gathered opposite the church, a few hawkers tried to sell memorial souvenir cards and two mounted policemen waited for the procession, which had been organized by Flora Drummond and Vera Laughton Matthews, to emerge. The sight of the police and the purple, white and green banner draped across the door of the church evoked poignant memories of suffragette days at Westminster.[30] Inside the church many members of the congregation wore WSPU buttons or the silver grating badges which symbolized prison sentences. In the front pew sat Mrs Lucy Baldwin and Nancy Astor representing Emmeline's recent political affiliations. Behind them were old colleagues including Annie Kenney, Charlotte Despard, the Pethick-Lawrences, Henry Nevinson, Arthur and Katherine Marshall, Lady Sybil Smith, Lady Rhondda and George Lansbury. Family members included Christabel, Sylvia, Ada, her younger brother, Robert Goulden, her nephew, Edward Goulden Bach, and three nieces, Enid, Lorna and Sybil Goulden Bach. The coffin, draped in purple, stood before the high altar beneath a great wreath of white lilies and more flowers – purple irises, white lilies and green foliage – massed on either side. The congregation sang Emmeline's favourite hymn, 'Thou Saviour Dear', heard an address by the Reverend W. F. Geikie and brought the service to a close with 'Abide With Me'.

To the strains of Chopin's *Funeral March* the coffin emerged from the church and was carried down the steps to the waiting hearse by ten suffragette pall bearers: Marion Wallace Dunlop, Ada Wright, Katherine Marshall, Barbara Wylie, Marie and Georgina Brackenbury, Rosamund Massey, Harriet Kerr, Mildred Mansel and Marie Naylor. Flags were lowered and the policemen saluted, some reportedly weeping as the cortège moved off to Brompton Cemetery. A large crowd of over a thousand people were waiting at the Fulham Road entrance and others lined the long central avenue of lime trees. Headed by a Union Jack draped in black and a WSPU banner carried by Minnie Baldock, the procession passed down the avenue to the open grave which was lined with laurel, ivy and privet. At the foot stood Christabel, Sylvia and Ada; this was the only occasion after the end of the war when the two sisters were to meet. Sylvia reportedly wept and almost fainted. Knowing that she could now never win her battle for her mother's love and approval, she felt overwhelmed as the regrets over their exchange of personal insults crowded in upon her. The Reverend Hugh Chapman described Emmeline as a truly holy woman whose patience and piety revealed 'the mark of a saint'. Already she was being sanctified. This was too much for Ethel Smyth, who wrote later that she had expected Emmeline to get up from the grave to protest at his remarks. When the service concluded, friends came up to throw flowers into the grave.

In the immediate aftermath of the funeral there were a few dismal arrangements to be made. During Emmeline's final illness Mary had stayed with Kathleen and after her death she was briefly looked after by Marion Wallace Dunlop, famous as the first suffragette hunger striker back in 1909. Mary attended the funeral which she found bewildering and was later introduced to a Miss Bevis who lived in Brighton and became her guardian.[31] Nellie Hall applied for a post at Conservative Central Office on the strength of her work with Emmeline, but was rejected on the grounds that, as her methods were not those of the Party, the experience was not a great advantage. July brought the saddest epitaph on Emmeline's life in the shape of her will; it transpired that she had left a gross estate of just £86.[32] Meanwhile Sylvia returned to an increasingly desperate struggle to earn her living by writing while coping with baby Richard at the same time. Christabel remained in England for some time completing her book, *Seeing the Future*, which was published in 1929. She reportedly made a visit to Woodford in order to persuade Sylvia to give Richard his father's surname.[33] This could be true, since after her mother's death Christabel became very protective about the Pankhurst name and reputation; but if she did she made no impression on her sister. In December she accepted an invitation to attend a suffragette reunion in London before returning to the United States the following year.

Many years previously, when she and Emmeline had been strolling round the yard in Holloway together, Katherine Marshall had cheered her up by reminding her that one day statues would be erected in her memory. In the aftermath of Emmeline's death she and Rosamund Massey became joint secretaries of a Pankhurst Memorial Fund whose objects were to arrange a headstone for her grave, to purchase the portrait by Georgina Brackenbury which was subsequently hung in the National Gallery, and to commission a statue. Some considered this last aim premature. 'While the transition from martyrdom to sculptured memorials is familiar', editorialized the *New York Times*, 'the process in Mrs Pankhurst's case has been unusually brief.'[34] Despite her public effusions of admiration for Emmeline, Nancy Astor also did her best to throw cold water on the idea which she described as 'quite impractical . . . everyone is so particularly hard up just now . . . Also to be quite frank, I do not think from my personal knowledge of Mrs Pankhurst that she would have approved of such a memorial. She would have realized that she was not statuesque.'[35] Undeterred, Mrs Marshall pressed ahead with the arrangements. In fact, the chief obstacle was not money but finding a site near to Westminster for the statue. The sympathetic Chief Commissioner of Works, Sir Lionel Earle, told her it was out of the question as they were still searching for somewhere to put Lord Kitchener! Mrs Marshall suggested a space beside Oliver Cromwell, which made him laugh, or making room at the top end of Downing Street.[36] But eventually her persistence paid off. She received permission to use a corner of Victoria Tower Gardens, just along from the Houses of Parliament, though this required the passage of a special bill which Sir William Bull agreed to escort through the House. Finally, after three attempts to interview Stanley Baldwin, she secured his agreement to unveil the statue. A. G. Walker was commissioned to execute the sculpture and Sir Herbert Baker to supply the pedestal. They came up with a life-sized statue of Emmeline standing with her hands outstretched as though addressing a meeting. The Committee paid the Ministry of Works the sum of £160 to have the statue cleaned in perpetuity and £330 to keep a plant for ever in the vase.[37]

The ceremony took place on 6 April 1930. Rosamund Massey's prison badge and hunger striker's medal had been placed in a casket in the plinth of the statue. Mrs Marshall had arranged two facing platforms draped in WSPU colours, one for the speakers and one for the band. Loudspeakers enabled people to hear the ceremony for up to half a mile away. Dressed in cap and gown, Ethel Smyth conducted the Metropolitan Police Band in several of her own compositions including 'The March of the Women' and extracts from 'The Wreckers'. Political leaders of all varieties had been invited to attend, including Emmeline's worst opponents. At 11.45 the traffic was stopped and at twelve the three speakers, Lady Rhondda, Fred Pethick-Lawrence and Stanley Baldwin, mounted the platform, and Flora Drummond opened the ceremony. Always a master of such occasions, Baldwin treated the audience to a fine example of his style:

I say with no fear of contradiction that whatever view posterity may take, Mrs Pankhurst has won for herself a niche in the temple of fame which will last for all time . . . if Mrs Pankhurst did not make the movement [for women's suffrage] it was she who set the heather on fire . . . [Women's] rights have been vindicated. The harder part of life is before them; and that is to perform and discharge their duties; and in the attempt to discharge those duties no woman in the years to come, as she passes by this place, will fail to draw inspiration from the example and the courage of the heroic woman whose statue we today unveil and whose memory we are here to honour.[38]

But even as a statue Emmeline could not entirely escape controversy. Although the memorial committee had pointedly excluded Sylvia from their arrangements, she none the less turned up with baby Richard in tow and sat in the audience, not on the platform. Flora Drummond read out a telegram from Christabel who was by now in the United States, but ignored Sylvia altogether. Subsequently Sylvia vented her anger in letters of complaint to those she blamed for the insult. Moreover, the raising of Emmeline's statue following upon the conclusion of the suffrage campaign in 1928 signified the start of the next battle over the historical reputation of militant suffragism and of the Pankhursts themselves. A Suffragette Fellowship had recently been formed which held regular dinners and reunions for ex-suffragettes, but Sylvia was not informed of its functions. She retaliated by publishing articles about her mother in the *Evening Standard* and the *Star* which upset the loyalists by emphasizing the role and opinions of Dr Richard Pankhurst and bringing the Pethick-Lawrences and others who had been forced out of the organization fully into the picture. These were the first shots in a long-running struggle in which Sylvia was to have full revenge over her sister and on those who had marginalized her own role in the suffrage movement.

18

Passing Into History (1929–34)

'The emancipation of today displays itself mainly in cigarettes and shorts.'

Sylvia Pankhurst, 'Women's Citizenship', 1934

For all three daughters, their mother's death proved to be a turning point, for it decisively relegated the whole struggle for the women's vote to the pages of history, provoking, in the process, a fresh round of controversy amongst the participants. In the short term, however, Emmeline's passing could not deflect them from what was now a daily struggle to make ends meet. Although there were still welcome spin-offs from suffragette days, at least for Christabel and Sylvia, in the form of legacies from supporters, to a large extent all three sisters now found a lifeline in their writing.

According to her friend and helper from the East End, Annie Barnes, Sylvia was left some land at Bradwell-on-Sea which she presumably sold.[1] This enabled her to move from the Red Cottage in 1929 to 'West Dene', a large, three-storeyed property in nearby Woodford. The local estate agent, evidently aware of her reputation, political and personal, showed himself reluctant to let her have it, and so she rented initially but bought the house later. West Dene offered plenty of scope for Sylvia's study, spare rooms for guests and a top floor, which was let to tenants as a flat. Sylvia and Corio also installed printing machinery, thereby enabling themselves to run their extensive publishing ventures efficiently from home.

In spite of this, Sylvia's life during the late 1920s and 1930s was dominated by a desperate need to earn cash by her writing. Her son recalled entering her room each morning 'to find her still at her desk where she had been writing since dinner the previous night.'[2] She filled dozens of notebooks with her increasingly erratic handwriting in thick pencil – the basis of a remarkable succession of substantial books over the next six years. Some of these, such as her massive volume on India, remain largely unknown, while others, like her work on the suffragette movement, became classics. However, in her late forties and in indifferent health, Sylvia found it a struggle to maintain her research and writing while also coping with her baby son. In a letter to Nora Walshe, probably written early in 1929, she admitted to her despair over her inability to write regularly despite being under contract for a book:

Richard wakes early and keeps me on the go till eleven or so . . . I find myself so irritated and jaded that when I sit down to write I am often unable to produce a sentence for some time. Yet in the old days the words used to come out without difficulty at any odd moments in 'bus, train or anywhere.[3]

This was a plea for help. Although Corio appears to have lived at West Dene and played a supportive role in the family, his own health was not good. 'Richard's father [significantly she did not refer to him by name] has been ill with sciatica so I can't count on him to help me with the boy. Indeed when he is at home I get less done than when he is out!'[4] Mrs Walshe evidently came to look after Richard while Sylvia concentrated on her work.

The household in Charteris Road was a strange one in some ways. 'My parents' life centred almost entirely on their work and political activity', wrote Richard, 'there were few relaxations or recreations, only the basic necessary minimum.[5] Sympathetic visitors invariably described the house as a mess, especially Sylvia's study which was 'of almost incredible untidiness, with books, papers piled everywhere'.[6] Now rather stout and untidy as ever, Sylvia adopted a vaguely fashionable hair style at the suggestion of her friend, Mrs Drake, who showed her how to put a basin over her head and simply cut around it. She would hand visitors a cup of tea with no saucer and with the spoon standing up in it. The pram looked shabby and several of the chairs had only three legs.[7] Corio, described by friends as a small, grey, crop-haired man, made a favourable impression on all who met him for his charm and intelligence. 'He seemed kind and anxious to please', remembered Nora Walshe. Yet Sylvia's attitude towards Corio seemed rather equivocal in that she never introduced him to friends and visitors, one of whom assumed he was actually the gardener while another thought of him as an ordinary working man, not an educated person.[8] Instead of joining in socially with Sylvia's friends, he was more likely to undertake the cooking and to serve the food. It was Sylvia, relentlessly talking and organizing, who dominated the household. Corio loyally followed her vegetarian diet, heavy in lentils, though he took the opportunity to go to London once a week to eat steak with his Italian friends. In spite of this they seem to have been very happy together during this period, enjoying a genuine partnership in their publishing ventures and more domestic stability than either had previously known.[9] Sylvia started a Montessori school at Charteris Road that catered to Richard and three other children. Later he attended The Bancroft, a good day school in Woodford. Since she made no secret of her attitude towards marriage, the circumstances of Richard's birth became widely known in the neighbourhood, which must have caused some embarrassment for him. Just like her father, Sylvia remained quite oblivious to the trials imposed upon children by their parents' principles.[10] Yet although Richard grew up in an intensely political household as his mother had done, as an only child he had the advantage of taking an accelerated route to adulthood free from the tensions and rivalries of her home. Fortunately the tone was tempered by Corio, a more indulgent parent who invariably brought a present for Richard from his weekly trips into town. In this house bulging with books and throbbing with good causes Richard learnt his letters at an early age and soon began to play chess with his father. He emerged with the better qualities of each of his parents. A gentle, rather self-effacing person, he combined a well-developed social conscience with a capacity for hard work and skill in research and writing.[11]

Sylvia was too determined and courageous to succumb to the depression caused by the pressures of her work for long; once she had abandoned the *Workers' Dreadnought*, she was able to concentrate her formidable energies on writing books. It is not generally appreciated that much of her attention in the mid-1920s was attracted by the question of India. Her son remembered how books about India filled the study at Woodford where Sylvia spent long hours drafting a 600-page volume entitled *India and the Earthly Paradise*, which was published in Bombay in 1926, though not in Britain. This interest is by no means surprising in view of Sylvia's hostility towards British imperialism, her expectations about the spread of revolution, and her liberal attitudes towards race. Since Keir Hardie's controversial visit to Bengal during the agitation over the partition of the province in 1909 she had been aware of the growing challenge posed by nationalists to the Raj. In view of her sceptical attitude towards electoral reform in Britain it was inevitable that Sylvia would regard concessions to Indian self-government in 1919 as a mere ploy designed to prop up British control by dividing nationalist opinion. By 1922 Gandhi had effectively countered British strategy by transforming the Indian National Congress into a genuine mass movement by means of his Non-Cooperation campaigns.

Against this background Indian independence might easily have become the great passion of Sylvia's later life rather than Ethiopia and anti-Fascism. However, India was a distinctly over-crowded field in which Sylvia would have had difficulty making an impression. Though Congress had always welcomed English allies, nationalists were apt to be antagonized by foreigners who expressed independent opinions about India, and Sylvia, whose sceptical attitude towards religion prevented her from sympathizing with either Hinduism or Islam, inevitably adopted a critical view of the treatment of women and untouchables in Indian society. But the fundamental explanation for Sylvia's lack of impact lay in the political tactics and ideology of the national movement. Ever since the foundation of the Congress in 1885, the British had worked on the basis that India was too divided by social, cultural and religious communities to be able to unite against imperial rule. The key to Gandhi's success lay in his appreciation of the need to stop playing into the hands of the British by accepting this logic; to be distracted by the divisions in Indian society would be to slow down progress towards self-government, if not to postpone it indefinitely. Consequently he developed a national movement which embraced almost the whole social range from landless labourers to small farmers and big landowners, and the political spectrum from Socialism to Indian business and commerce. But the inevitable consequence of adopting this route to independence was that the social revolution had to be relegated to a distant time *after* the freedom struggle, not before it. In the mid-1920s Sylvia was still enough of a Marxist in her thinking to regard this as a flawed approach. For her the premature expulsion of the British would simply substitute one form of exploitation for another, this time by Indians themselves. She saw visions of a Communistic village society in a country still wedded to the virtues of individual ownership of the land. However, the success of the campaigns conducted by Gandhi made this a minority view during the inter-war period. As a result, not only did *India and the Earthly Paradise* remain unknown in Britain, it was hardly distributed in India either, and where it was known it attracted criticism.

After this setback Sylvia found several surprising and novel subjects for her pen. During the mid-1920s she became interested in the idea of an international language, partly because she felt that Communists all over the world needed some means of communication. She discounted Esperanto but favoured Interlingua, which Corio had learnt, and in 1929 she put the case for it in *Delphos: The Future International Language*. Rather optimistically she suggested it would become familiar within thirty years and in the process help to unite the peoples of the world. In the following year she published a translation of the work of Mihail Eminescu, a nineteenth-century romantic nationalist who wrote epic poems. This ambitious undertaking won praise from G. B. Shaw, who usually enjoyed taking the Pankhursts down a peg or two; 'Sylvia', he wrote, 'you are the queerest idiot-genius of this age . . . the translation is astonishing and outrageous; it carried me away.'[12] Just to be awkward, Shaw refused her request to write a preface for the poems, but Sylvia simply printed his letter at the start of the book in the hope of attracting attention to what was a fairly esoteric subject.

Although these books did not make her much money, Sylvia was also developing an entirely new and more topical theme. Richard's birth in 1927 inspired her to set herself up as an authority on motherhood and to cast herself as a progressive mother. 'Richard is never told "You must not do that"', she wrote. 'He works when he wants to and plays when he wants to. He is a free baby; he should be a free man.'[13] Whether consciously or not Sylvia had made a timely move, for the long-standing public concern about motherhood and the birth rate was reaching new heights during the inter-war period, fuelled by the fear, erroneous as it turned out, that the wartime casualties would condemn thousands of women to lives as spinsters and lead to a fall in the British population.

When interviewed by the *News of the World* reporter in 1928, Sylvia had made some surprising references to her 'eugenic baby'. Of course, eugenics had been a respectable cult in intellectual circles since the late-Victorian period, especially among those who feared that the practice of birth control among the middle classes would lead to a deterioration in the quality of the national stock. But the relevance of eugenics for the women's movement was rather dubious, though some of its advocates developed a feminist rationale, arguing that independent, educated women would actually fulfil their mission as nature's mothers all the better. This line of thinking gained national prominence in 1918 with the publication of Marie Stopes's work on birth control which she presented as a means of strengthening the national stock by the deliberate spacing of babies who would grown into healthier children. Stopes's books, *Married Love* and *Wise Parenthood*, enjoyed such a wide circulation that it is unlikely that Sylvia was unaware of her arguments, though she was hardly keen to see women as breeding machines serving the interests of the state or the race. Yet in 1928 she had told reporters: 'It is good eugenics, I believe, if one desires parenthood, to consider if one is of sufficient general intelligence, bodily health and strength and freedom from hereditary diseases to produce.'[14] Annie Barnes remembered Sylvia telling her that she wanted a child because she needed to know what the experience of motherhood was like when she wrote about it.[15] Later a rumour circulated to the effect that she had become pregnant by artificial insemination, though in the absence of any corroboration this should probably be discounted.[16]

However, by the later 1920s eugenic ideas had, in fact, ceased to be fashionable, and Sylvia approached the topic from a different angle. In *Save the Mothers*, published in 1930, she advanced a powerful and well-supported plea to reduce the annual total of deaths arising out of childbirth which currently ran at around 3,000. While death rates generally had continued to diminish, the maternal mortality rate noticeably increased from 4.83 per thousand births in 1923 to 5.94

by 1933. In *Save the Mothers* she identified a number of causes for this trend including poverty, overwork, lack of nourishment and poor pre-natal care. She also waded into the medical aspects of the issue, pointing out that England and Wales had enough maternity beds to cope with only 50,000 of the 750,000 women who gave birth each year. She dwelt at length on the neglect of obstetrics in the training of doctors, which was crammed into a brief period at the end of their courses and allowed many of them little practical experience in delivering babies. Doctors, she argued, also carried much of the responsibility for the transmission of septic infection which remained the chief medical cause of death among women in childbirth and was wholly preventable. She proposed the introduction of a £10 maternity bounty for each woman and a National Maternity Service to cover all mothers, married or not, because single women received the very worst treatment, if any at all. At a time when the birth rate in Britain had fallen from around 24 per thousand population just before the war to 16 in 1930, this could not be ignored. By comparison with many inter-war feminists Sylvia's proposals seem unusually mild; she did not, for example, demand the provision of advice on birth control which had been widely advocated during the 1920s. But her book helped to create a climate in which action would be taken.

Sylvia seems to have worked on *Save the Mothers* while also preparing her most celebrated volume, *The Suffragette Movement*, published by Longman in 1931. As long ago as June 1928 she had been endeavouring to interest publishers in what she billed as the 'inner history of the suffragette movement'. She told Richard she had put everything she had to say on the subject into the book, which was self-evidently true for it became a huge, unwieldy volume in need of some revision. However, the ill-assorted mixture of history and autobiography exaggerated the role of the Pankhurst family at the expense of the earlier suffragists, and anyone who had fallen out with the Pankhursts was practically written out of the story – not least Adela. In this way the book distorted perceptions of the movement which were not corrected until comparatively recently. Contemporary reactions were dominated by what seemed the unfair treatment of Christabel and Emmeline. Sylvia had set the cause in the context of her father's politics, as a Radical and Socialist movement that had been hi-jacked by Christabel, distorted by autocratic leadership and had finally been betrayed amid the jingoism of the First World War. In view of the divisions aroused by the campaign, any account was likely to be controversial, but Emmeline's death had raised the stakes by transforming votes for women into history, thereby making the interested parties keenly aware of the need to defend their reputations and their ideas. In 1927 when Ray Strachey published *The Cause*, a sober and balanced account of the women's movement since the 1860s, Sylvia herself took exception. She objected to a section referring to Emmeline's mismanagement of the WSPU funds which led to the temporary withdrawal of the book. Sylvia was chancing her arm here because she knew perfectly well that the financial side of the Union would not stand close examination, but she was determined to protect the reputation of the Pankhurst family, or at least to ensure that any criticisms of it were her own. She can hardly have been surprised when her own book infuriated those suffragettes who had been loyal to Emmeline and Christabel, and provoked demands for the latter to write an 'official' version of the movement as well as a biography of her mother. However, though she had apparently advertised for material about her mother soon after her death, Christabel found writing a burden and may have been exhausted by her four volumes of Adventist literature. None the less, energized by her anger, she did start drafting her own autobiography – it is not clear exactly when – though the book was not published until after her death. Why did Christabel fail to rise to the challenge during her lifetime? The explanation is probably that she realized that her own account would look inadequate by comparison with her sister's rich and detailed narrative. *Unshackled* was not only much shorter, but strangely formal, even stilted; it lacked the vitality and commitment of Sylvia's writing, which no doubt reflected the detachment Christabel now felt from the old suffragette days. By 1930 she had withdrawn into a narrower world of certainties in which she knew her lines backwards and where her views, like her clothes, could be preserved in Edwardian aspic.

Significantly, Sylvia showed no more interest than her sister in playing a part in the current women's movement. In 1934, on the twenty-first anniversary of the death of Emily Wilding Davison, she admitted her predictions about the impact of enfranchising women had been misplaced and that she was far from satisfied with the results. She disparaged the women MPs who 'have sponsored no epoch making causes' and complained about women's apathy: 'The torrential Women's Movement has dwindled to a mere streak. The average woman, who, by the hundred thousand, was enthused twenty years ago with the sense of a social mission, is today concerned merely with her own or her husband's financial prospects.'[17] In this Sylvia revealed the same political weakness as her father – a tendency to self-righteousness. This naturally offended the younger generation of feminists who felt that, in the absence of the subsidies that had enabled the Edwardian suffragists to be full-time campaigners, they were obliged to work for feminism by pursuing their careers.

After her mother's death Christabel had remained in Britain for some time awaiting the publication of her next Adventist volume, *Seeing the Future*. She continued to make great play with the evidence for the increasing instability of the world, pointing to physical upheavals including earthquakes, floods, hurricanes, typhoons and tornadoes all over the world. She also derived grim satisfaction from the Wall Street Crash of 1929, which not only led to economic ruin for thousands of individuals, but also destabilized Britain's second Labour Government under Ramsay MacDonald, which had the misfortune to be elected in May of that year. On 27 September Christabel sailed for New York to begin a six-month tour of the USA and Canada. In December she travelled to Washington, where the National Women's Party was holding its convention, to attend a memorial service held in the Crypt of the Capitol to honour the memory of Emmeline. There she addressed representatives of some forty women's organizations as well as congressmen and members of the diplomatic corps on her mother's affectionate interest in the women's movement in America: 'It is one of the beautiful things we have in common to remember how the suffragists of our two countries with never a cloud between them worked together for equal suffrage and equal rights for women.'[18] From Baltimore she told the Baronne de Brimont: 'This was a wonderful occasion and a very moving ceremony. Mother was really loved in America and everywhere I go people tell me that they heard her speak and remember her.' Even the attendant on the Pullman train told her: 'She was a mighty sweet lady.'[19] She planned to spend

Christmas in Montreal with Mrs T. C. Thomson at 'The Chateau', then travel to Pasadena, near Los Angeles, in January 1930 before returning to Paris in March.

Meanwhile Christabel had had to make arrangements for her adopted daughter, Betty. They had stayed together after Emmeline's death but, as Christabel's constant travelling made any settled home life impossible, Betty was placed in a boarding house at Eastbourne run by an Adventist couple. After her time with the other girls this must have come as a shock to her, and Betty reacted by retreating into a world of her own. In 1929 Christabel decided to send her to a girls' boarding school at Headington near Oxford where she stayed until 1932. During this time Betty made it clear that she wanted to change her names. In January 1930 she added 'Aurea' to the 'Elizabeth Pankhurst', though subsequently she also substituted 'Clifford' as her new surname.[20] These decisions no doubt reflected the turmoil facing the vulnerable adolescent whose confusion about her identity had been exacerbated by her arrival at a new school. The four adopted girls had always been told that if they were good they might take the Pankhurst name. However, they clearly had no wish to do so. Kathleen also changed both her first and surnames. After 1932 Aurea received some coaching to prepare her for entry to one of the Oxford women's colleges, and in 1934 she was admitted to St Hugh's to read PPE. But despite her connections with the Pankhursts and the world of politics, she seems to have been an unworldly and unsophisticated girl, whose arrival at university made her anxious to achieve adulthood as quickly as possible. Unfortunately her route to adulthood involved running up debts, abandoning her academic work for boyfriends, becoming pregnant and having an abortion, apparently unknown to Christabel.[21] Aurea left Oxford without a degree, took a secretarial course and spent some time in the United States, whether with Christabel is not clear. Unable to cope with life, she had lost contact with the other adopted girls and apparently died in America before Christabel.

Christabel continued to divide her life between Britain and the United States during the 1930s, but she showed little interest in maintaining her English connections. She received invitations from Edith How Martyn, who had founded the Suffragette Fellowship in 1926 and was now attempting to retrieve the flags, banners and other property seized by the police in 1913–14. Although Christabel agreed to attend a Suffragette Fellowship presentation to Mrs Marshall in 1930 and to donate £1 to the fund, she responded in rather formal terms to the approaches made by How Martyn and kept her role to the minimum.[22] In the autumn of 1930 she returned to America; the New Year found her once more in Los Angeles, by now her favourite part of the country, for a series of lectures on international affairs and their relation to Biblical Prophecy. In April she delivered several speeches to the Women's League for Palestine in New York, urging continued support for the pioneer workers in Palestine and promising the backing of the British people. At the Congregation Rodelph Sholom she even ventured to criticize the Jews for not going to Palestine in greater numbers: 'You have the divine right to that land,' she insisted. 'You have also a historical right . . . Governments may come and fall but the Balfour Declaration will stand . . . It is the word of God.'[23] After addressing the annual convention of the World's Christian Fundamentals Association in May, she returned to Britain where she joined Lloyd George as a double bill at the Welsh Baptist Chapel near Oxford Circus in July. Christabel made the most of the occasion: 'We two veterans of the pulpit today have each won a war', she remarked affably to her former antagonist who was in an equally benign mood.[24] They exchanged platitudes about the need to secure world peace by a change of heart rather than through the machinery of the League of Nations, their reliance on moral uplift being a sign that both had become detached from real influence. In fact, both Christabel and Lloyd George were about to be further marginalized by the establishment of the National Government, following the collapse of the Labour Government in August 1931, which lasted until 1940. By leading the country out of the economic depression, albeit slowly, the National Governments went some way to restoring faith in the Parliamentary process and reducing the sense of impending crisis, in the process undermining Christabel's message about the disasters supposedly enveloping the world. Yet it was good for her morale to find that leading statesmen were still prepared to treat her as indulgently as Lloyd George had done. September found Christabel at Chartwell in Kent visiting another apostle of doom currently down on his luck, Winston Churchill, on whom she bestowed the usual copy of *The*

World's Unrest. Their old antagonism had evidently been put behind them, especially as they shared a common hostility to Bolshevism and a conviction that disarmament and the League of Nations would inevitably fail. By November 1931 Christabel had returned to Los Angeles, where, in the following year, she resumed her round of lectures, still fervently pointing to the signs that the Second Coming was now at hand.[25]

If Christabel's life during the 1930s had become one long and gradual diminuendo, at least her continuing ability to attract respectful audiences sustained the comforting illusion that she remained a figure of international standing. The only flaw was her sister's irritating habit of publishing embarrassing books dealing with her earlier career which, frankly, she preferred to forget. Even worse, Sylvia's work had begun to inspire others to dredge up their memories and to put their own interpretation on the events of Edwardian England. One unpleasant controversy blew up in 1933 when Dame Ethel Smyth published the first version of *Female Pipings in Eden* in which she quoted from letters – whose return had been demanded in vain – written to her by Emmeline, without obtaining the consent of Christabel as her mother's literary executor. For once Sylvia sympathized with her sister's angry reaction to Smyth's book. This led to a confrontation between the two women in the office of the publisher, Peter Davis, early in 1934 when Christabel returned to England. In the ensuing row when Ethel Smyth became aggressive and raised her umbrella, Davis intervened physically between them.[26] Rather surprisingly, however, Christabel subsequently agreed to allow publication in a revised form and gave Smyth copyright of the letters. No doubt she realized that legal action would only give greater publicity to things she wished to remain private. Christabel almost certainly resented her mother's intimacy with Dame Ethel which had, after all, been in part a reflection of Emmeline's loneliness and her neglect by her daughter during the suffragette campaign. Coming on top of Sylvia's book, the new volume must have made her realize she was losing the battle over the history of the suffragette movement. Her reaction may have also reflected an additional worry about the nature of Emmeline's friendship with Ethel. Ethel certainly gave the impression that they had been in love for a time, and Christabel undoubtedly found it embarrassing to publicize

Emmeline's friendship with a woman known to be a lesbian. By this time the publication, and banning, of the lesbian novel, *The Well of Loneliness*, by Radclyffe Hall in 1928 had raised awareness of the possibility of love between women to a level unknown before 1914. Whenever subsequent authors took up the subject of Ethel Smyth, Christabel tried to insist that they should write only about her musical career and omit the suffragette phase altogether.

Faraway in Australia Adela also reacted with some anger to the publication of Sylvia's verdict on Emmeline and the suffragette campaign. Eventually she drafted a lengthy response for the Suffragette Fellowship in Britain entitled 'My Mother', and followed up with 'The Philosophy of the Suffragette Movement' and 'The Story of My Life'.[27] However, Adela offered only a limited defence of Emmeline in these manuscripts. While recognizing her neglect of the family as a necessary price to pay for winning the vote, she also endeavoured to settle old scores by transferring some of the blame to her father, which was of course calculated to antagonize Sylvia, whom she portrayed as narrow-minded, domineering and neurotic. Since she managed to publish some of her recollections in Australian journals, Adela must have been well satisfied with the chance to earn some cash while setting history to rights at the same time. Even allowing for the fact that her account bore the impression of her current personal and political views, Adela's perspective on the women's campaign merits attention. In 'The Philosophy of the Women's Movement' she opened up a fresh line of dispute by arguing that the original WSPU should not be interpreted as a revolt by women against men. She drew a distinction between those who joined the movement later, and those like herself and her mother who, she believed, shared a similar outlook as a result of their common experience as wives and mothers. 'The fact that our menfolk depend on us gives women a satisfaction and pride in themselves that nothing else can ever do', she wrote. 'My mother certainly knew nothing about "male domination".'[28] As a result, according to Adela, Emmeline 'had no wish to alter the relationships between men and women, marriage or parents, except to make their mutual interests stronger ... It was far from her thoughts to deny fathers' rights and duties in the family, or to destroy women's interest in the home for a career in professions or industry.'[29] There was surely some validity in the comparison she had drawn with her mother, for they had both chosen to marry older men, to have large families and to attain a partnership with much-loved husbands. On the other hand, Adela, from her perspective as an inter-war Socialist, surely underestimated Emmeline's feminism, partly out of a desire to revenge herself on other suffragettes whom she regarded as man-haters. It is also fair to say that Emmeline's own attitude towards men changed somewhat during her lifetime, becoming more hostile after Richard's death partly because of her growing awareness of her own abilities and also from her sense of the oppressiveness of the male-dominated political and legal system.

Adela had taken up her pen again out of sheer necessity as well as from a desire to vindicate herself. During the later 1920s she had maintained a much lower profile than previously and become more fully absorbed by domestic life and the management of the Walshes' meagre resources. When receiving his full salary Tom earned £360 a year, which was more than an average working man's pay but scarcely enough for a family comprising seven children and two adults. They sought compensation over the Government's attempt to deport him, but the settlement in March 1927 brought a mere £25. Meanwhile Tom's bitter struggle for control of the Seamen's Union with his rival Johnson continued; though he managed to be reinstated as General Secretary his opponents prevented him receiving his salary for some time. In his disillusionment Tom began to float the idea of a new union dedicated to arbitration rather than to industrial action, though this failed to get off the ground and only encouraged his opponents to accuse him of being a scab. In her anger and dismay over the lack of support from his union after his years of self-sacrifice, Adela, too, began to lose faith in strike action. But their reaction was more than a personal one, for it reflected the broader political climate in Australia during the later 1920s, characterized as it was by a sense of anti-climax after the revolutionary phase and a return towards reformism and conciliation in industrial affairs. As a result Adela began to argue that reformist strategies were compatible with revolutionary ideas, and she found herself increasingly attracted by the idea of collaboration between the classes in pursuit of the national good, something she would have scorned a few years earlier. By the end of the decade both she and Tom had effectively abandoned their radical politics, but, lacking paid employment with the Seamen's Union, they had no means of support other than an erratic income derived from journalism.

Not that this prospect deterred Adela from following her new opinions to their logical conclusion. Tom Walsh was, after all, by no means the first trade unionist to find himself at war with the left. For many years British seamen had been organized by the autocratic, right-wing leader, Havelock Wilson, who by 1928 faced stiff competition for membership from the Transport and General Workers Union led by Ernest Bevin. As part of his war with the left Wilson had established an Industrial Peace Association, with backing from employers and union leaders, and he now agreed to engage Adela to build new branches of the organization amongst women in Australia. In August 1928 Wilson sent £2,200 to the Walshes, of which £250 was intended for Adela's pay and expenses. He also promised that if Tom failed to obtain further paid employment with his own union, he would be appointed as the New South Wales representative for the National Union of Seamen.[30] The launch of the IPA in Sydney in October 1928 brought Adela back to the platform in fine style. So dramatic a shift of allegiance inevitably provoked charges of treachery and opportunism from erstwhile colleagues on the left, but Adela brushed these aside, claiming to have been consistent in her fight on behalf of the poor. Eventually the violence within the union convinced Tom of the need to sever his connections, and as a result he spent much of the next decade writing bitter articles attacking Communism at home and abroad. At fifty-seven Tom suddenly found himself bereft of most of his friends as well as deprived of a regular income. Adela apparently told her friend Robert Ross that she had received a legacy from her mother in 1928.[31] However, as Emmeline clearly had almost no money to leave her daughter, even had she wished to, it seems likely that Adela invented this story to avoid admitting that she was receiving subsidies from Havelock Wilson who was a detested figure on the left. Unfortunately, Wilson's death in 1929 put an end even to this. As a result the family quit their brick bungalow in the suburb of Wollstonecraft for a smaller house in Greenwich which, in turn, was abandoned in 1930 for something even cheaper. Adela scraped a basic income by writing a monthly article at £10 a time for *Stead's Review*, usually on women's questions or her earlier life in England, and also contributed to *Pioneers*, a women's magazine. Tom also wrote for *Stead's*, typically pieces on 'Christianity and Communism', attacking the Bolsheviks for taking God away from man and using class hatred to hold their society together.[32] But it was a precarious life style, relieved only when Tom's eldest daughter gained paid employment.

But before long Adela had discovered another lifeline in the shape of the Australian Women's Guild of Empire, a right-wing pressure group which had been founded by the former suffragette, Flora Drummond, just after the war. The Women's Guild of Empire aspired to combat Communism, to secure industrial peace, to uphold Christian ideals, to promote awareness of the value of British citizenship, and to develop Australia as part of the Empire. It was especially vociferous in condemning strikers for imposing hardship on women and children.[33] Mrs Drummond readily agreed to employ Adela to build up new branches in Australia. As a result, in 1930 Adela embarked on an exhausting round of speeches and radio broadcasts on behalf of the Guild whose membership rose from around 1,000 to 6,000 by 1938. Wherever a strike broke out, or even where one threatened, Adela would turn up in the Guild's ramshackle motor, set up her soap box and harangue the locals about the need to promote the national economy. This required considerable courage; as she was regarded as a cat's-paw of the employers, she attracted stiff heckling. But at forty-five she enjoyed enough experience to be able to brush off the insults and even an occasional drenching with buckets of water.

Despite her success, Adela enjoyed very little security in her role as lecturer, for the Guild experienced some difficulty in paying her salary owing to the reluctance of Australian businessmen to finance the organization.[34] However, her salary of £4 a week represented a distinct improvement on her previous situation, and as Tom's daughters were now able to work, the financial pressures on the family were greatly relieved. Now that her own children were of school age Adela found it easier to combine her political work with her domestic role, especially as Tom was often at home writing and ready to help around the house. As a result the family moved to more attractive houses in 1931 and in 1934, though their lifestyle remained modest. Adela herself continued to get through the day happily enough by rolling a cigarette or two and consuming a frugal diet largely comprising tea, bread and butter.

Yet although Adela's links with the Guild of Empire lasted through-out the 1930s, her position in such company was never wholly comfort-able, for she had made herself dependent upon the goodwill of an organization dominated by middle-class women whose views only partly coincided with her own. Though middle class herself, Adela never felt entirely comfortable with the well-to-do whom she regarded as ignorant of the lives of ordinary women. Nor did her own brand of feminism, which centred around her belief in the virtues of domesticity, endear her to most feminists, especially as she opposed demands for equal pay and equal rights in guardianship. Radical in some ways but conservative in others, Adela had left herself a little exposed; by the end of the decade she and Tom had alienated so many people on both left and right of the spectrum that they had come to be regarded as eccentrics and opportunists ready to turn their rhetoric and their pens to catch any prevailing wind.

One unavoidable price to be paid for Adela's lurch to the right was a rupture in her relations with Sylvia. Though she, too, had abandoned the Communist Party after a brief period, she remained consistent in her political beliefs; and, as the threat of Fascism loomed larger, the gulf between her and Adela widened still further. As yet, however, Sylvia remained focussed on her writing rather than on active cam-paigning. Hot on the heels of *The Suffragette Movement* came *The Home Front* (1932), a study of life in Britain during the Great War. Once again she showed astute timing, for several writers including Vera Brittain, Robert Graves and Siegfried Sassoon, were currently enjoying huge success with books based on their own experience of the war. Unfortunately Sylvia's lacked the emotional appeal of their works, being a lengthy, sober and detailed account of living and working conditions in the East End rather than a story. Though enlivened with critical passages dealing with politicians, conscientious objectors, the Defence of the Realm Act and the reintroduction of the state regulation of vice, *The Home Front* read too much like a report to become really popular. Sylvia was disappointed when the publisher's advance for which she had hoped while finishing the book failed to materialize. Financial pressures were also compounded by poor health during the early 1930s. 'Nose generally to the grindstone', she complained. 'Days are so short! So many days this year were wasted with headache.'[35] She was also distracted by her teeth; first the back ones had to be extracted, followed a fortnight later by all the front ones. This was expected to cost £52, which was money she did not have, but fortunately a dentist friend agreed to do the job more cheaply. Friends conjectured that Sylvia continued to receive financial help from the Pethick-Lawrences and from Henry Harben, who paid Richard's school fees. In spite of her efforts, however, by March 1933 a number of tradesmen were urgently demanding the settlement of her bills. In July, when her water rates were £1 13s 7d in arrears, the board threatened to withdraw supply.[36] Annie Barnes recalled opening the door to a representative of the telephone company who proposed to disconnect West Dene on account of the unpaid bills. Sylvia rose magnificently to the occasion by pushing the startled man out of the door, shouting, 'You'll get your money!'[37] Occasionally litigation proved worthwhile. When a former Scotland Yard detective referred in his memoirs to a 1914 plot by East End suffragettes to kidnap the Prince of Wales and hold him hostage, Sylvia seized her opportunity. Apart from forcing him to amend the book, she won £300 in damages, which was tantamount to a year's income for her.

Such windfalls were especially welcome since not all of Sylvia's projects came to fruition. She gathered copious notes for a book to be called 'In the Red Twilight', another autobiographical work which combined her own Communist phase with the waning of the revolution and Mussolini's seizure of power, but it was never published. By 1935 she had returned to familiar territory with *The Life of Emmeline Pankhurst*, in which she treated her mother less harshly than before. However, by this time there was little mileage to be gained from exploiting the triumphs of the past. Despite its failure to find a publisher, 'In the Red Twilight' betrayed the drift of Sylvia's mind as she became increasingly absorbed by the threat posed by the spread of Fascism. In 1932 she had revived the Women's International Matteotti Committee which took up the case of the widow of Giacomo Matteotti, who was still subject to persecution by the Fascist regime.[38] In 1934 she also joined the British Organizing Committee of the Paris-based International Congress Against War and Fascism. Unfortunately, her prominence in these causes made Continental travel increasingly dangerous. In 1934 she, Corio and the six-year-old Richard visited Romania for the unveiling of a statue of Mihail Eminescu. Fearful that Corio might be arrested if they entered Italy, they travelled via Berlin which they found decked out in Nazi flags for the funeral of von Hindenburg, the former German President. Romania itself was the home of a virulently anti-Semitic form of Fascism led by Corneliu Codreanu and the Iron Guard, a terrorist organization. Though King Carol's regime supposedly imposed rigorous controls over the Fascists, Sylvia was dismayed to see how far Fascist sympathies had actually subverted the system when, at a lunch for the National Council of Romanian Women, she heard Princess Alexandrina praise the idea of the corporate state as a way of getting things done. With her usual frankness Sylvia told the princess she was helping to bring about Fascist dictatorship whether she knew it or not. Despite this, Sylvia loved the Romanian countryside, especially the medieval churches and Byzantine paintings, so much so that on her return home she began to write a book about the country which was never completed. But the chief result of the Romanian visit was to push the cause of anti-Fascism into the forefront of Sylvia's agenda where it was to remain for most of the remainder of her life.

19

Fascism and Anti-Fascism (1935–9)

'The great betrayal of today is excused by the thought that liberty and justice for an African people do not matter.'

Sylvia Pankhurst, *New Times and Ethiopia News*, 11 July 1936

Ever since seizing power in October 1922, Benito Mussolini had been preoccupied with foreign affairs, largely because, although Italy had been among the victors in the First World War, she had missed out on the territorial gains enjoyed by Britain and France. Moreover, since the national sense of inferiority threatened the stability of the Fascist state, a succession of triumphs abroad became an essential prop to Mussolini's regime. As a result the Italians launched a series of aggressive actions against Greece, Yugoslavia and Albania during the 1920s. In this situation both the British and French governments showed themselves anxious to conciliate Mussolini and to overlook the brutality of his regime with a view to obtaining his support against Germany. Despite this, however, Mussolini saw no way of resolving his two worst grievances: the presence of the Royal Navy in the Mediterranean, which rendered his claims to 'Italy's Sea' rather hollow, and the check to his influence in the Tyrol, which left Austria perpetually vulnerable to a takeover by Germany. He therefore looked to the softer targets which presented themselves in Africa where the Italians already held Somaliland (1889), Eritrea (1890) and Libya (1912). As Christabel's Adventist writing had shown, many people in the west accepted at face value the pretensions of the Fascist state as a dynamic, modernizing force and regarded Italian aspirations to recreate a 'Greater Italy' by colonizing sparsely populated African territory as perfectly legitimate.

Consequently, Mussolini focussed his ambitions on the independent state of Abyssinia, which Africans preferred to call Ethiopia. The prospect of avenging the defeat suffered by Italian forces at Ethiopian hands in the Battle of Adowa back in 1896 made the country an attractive target. Yet Ethiopia, which had never been part of the Roman Empire, was ruled by Ras Tafari, the former regent and Crown Prince, who had ascended the throne as the Emperor Hailie Selassie I in 1930. It could not be acquired by Italy without the most flagrant act of aggression, especially as the country had been a member of the League of Nations since 1923. However, from September 1933 Mussolini began making plans for an invasion of the country which was largely surrounded by European territory, in particular Italian Somaliland along the coast to the south, British Somaliland on the Gulf of Aden, French Somaliland around Djibouti, and Italian Eritrea bordering the Red Sea. As the boundaries between these territories had been indistinctly drawn, there was ample scope for disputes of the kind that occurred at Wal Wal in the south in December 1934 when Italian troops clashed with Ethiopians after crossing into their territory. Athough Mussolini's propaganda machine portrayed the Italian armed forces as perpetually ready for battle, his preparations had been far from adequate.[1] However, the invasion was accelerated by events elsewhere, notably the failure of the Disarmament Convention at Geneva in 1934 and the announcement of conscription by Germany in March 1935. Since this implied that Hitler would soon be ready to push ahead with his designs on Austria, Mussolini concluded that Ethiopia ought to be dealt with quickly so that by 1936 he would be able to focus on curbing German influence in central Europe.

Even so, Mussolini made haste cautiously by seeking an agreement with the French on the basis of their common fear of Hitler. In January 1935 the French prime minister, Pierre Laval, had visited Rome for discussions which Mussolini interpreted as an indication of France's readiness to concede Italy a 'free hand' against Ethiopia, something later denied by Laval.[2] In the hope of ensuring there would be no interference from other European powers Mussolini also met British and French representatives at Stresa in April, where the three states agreed to oppose any unilateral repudiation of the peace treaties which might 'endanger the peace of Europe'. Though Ethiopia was not formally discussed at Stresa, the British and French understood what the Italians wanted; by inserting the reference to 'Europe' in the agreement the British appeared to be giving Mussolini the encouragement he wanted to proceed with his invasion in Africa.

This assumption was borne out when Mussolini launched his invasion from Eritrea on 3 October 1935, for the British and French Governments united chiefly in their desire to find ways of allowing him to get away with it. To this end the newly appointed Minister to the League of Nations, Anthony Eden, was dispatched to Rome to offer Italy territory in the Ogaden while Britain compensated Ethiopia with part of British Somaliland around the port of Zeila in the Gulf of Aden. If Mussolini had wanted proof of British weakness he now had it. In essence the British Government took the view that no significant British interest was at stake in Ethiopia; indeed, she had traditionally supported Italian expansion in the region. On the contrary, Britain's priority in 1935 lay in maintaining the Stresa Front as the best means of keeping Germany isolated and thus checking further attempts to revise the peace settlement. The Government therefore chose to present Ethiopia as a barbarous country where slavery still existed, and Haile Selassie as a medieval autocrat engaged in wars with his own provincial chieftains for control of the country; it was questionable, in this view, whether Ethiopia could be defined as a state in the European sense rather than as a loose federation of tribes.

Unfortunately this policy was complicated by Ethiopia's membership of the League and by Britain's commitment to uphold the League by invoking collective action to stop unprovoked aggression by one state on another. In fact, however, the leading British politicians had, from the start, disapproved of the League, those on the left because they saw it as a means for upholding the punitive Treaty of Versailles, and those on the right because it represented a potential threat to British colonialism and it involved 'open' discussion of matters that ought to be kept secret. Privately the leader of the National Government, Stanley Baldwin, and his ministers shared these reservations, but in view of the popularity of the League with the public they had appointed Eden as Minister for League Affairs; the idea was to keep on the right side of public opinion by avoiding being seen to be responsible for undermining its authority. Sir Samuel Hoare, the

Foreign Secretary, professed to believe that sanctions against Italy would not receive the backing of France and the other powers, and that, even if they did, sanctions would be ineffective; but 'it must be the League and not the British Government that declares that sanctions are impracticable'.[3] In this Hoare was supported by the military advisers who exaggerated Italy's strength, and especially by the First Sea Lord, Sir Ernle Chatfield, who pleaded that the Royal Navy was not ready to do anything in the Mediterranean despite the fact that Italy's intentions had been perfectly well known for a long time.[4]

Rather inconveniently the Government had decided to hold a general election in November 1935 which made it imperative to keep on the right side of the League for the time being. In the famous – and misleadingly titled – 'Peace Ballot' of June 1935, no fewer than 94 per cent of 10.2 million respondents voted in favour of economic sanctions against an aggressor power, and 74 per cent of 8.7 million voted even for military sanctions. Since Hoare and Baldwin understood that the public were overwhelmingly hostile to Mussolini's invasion and in favour of upholding the League of Nations, they got through the election dishonestly by professing their loyalty to the League. Four days later on 18 November economic sanctions were imposed on Italy. But early in December the Government sent Hoare to Paris where he and Laval negotiated the notorious pact designed to get Italy off the hook by ceding two-thirds of Ethiopian territory to her and granting Ethiopia access to the sea by a narrow strip of land which was famously denounced in *The Times* as a 'corridor for camels'. The public outrage when this deal became known forced Baldwin to extricate himself by sacking the Foreign Secretary; but he still did nothing to put real pressure on Mussolini. No attempt was made to close the Suez Canal or to impose the oil sanctions to which Italy was extremely vulnerable. In the event, though even limited sanctions caused serious distress in Italy, they did not hinder supplies to the invading forces which had succeeded in overrunning Ethiopia by May 1936.

In the immediate aftermath of Mussolini's invasion a dozen pressure groups devoted to the independence of Ethiopia sprang up in Britain. However, much to the relief of the Government, most of them proved to be ephemeral and attracted remarkably little support from the political parties. It was to be Sylvia Pankhurst's achievement to keep the issue alive until 1941 when the Italians were finally expelled. She proved to be much quicker than others on the left to take up the Ethiopian question and she remained the leading figure throughout the campaign. Part of the explanation for this lay in the influence of Corio, whose contacts with Italian opponents of Mussolini during the 1920s made him unusually well-informed and alive to the spread of Fascist ideas and organization abroad. In the 1920s Mussolini was regarded, even on the left, as a constructive modernizing statesman; perhaps because of his origins as a Socialist it was believed by some that his coup would forestall a Communist revolution of the sort that had occurred in Russia. But before he came to be seen as a major threat Sylvia and Corio had concluded that Mussolini's march on Rome signalled the end of the post-war revolutionary advance and they interpreted Bolshevism and Fascism as expressions of the growth of dictatorship in Europe.[5] Though the Bolshevik Revolution was in the line of progress, Sylvia believed it had degenerated as the original selfless idealists were replaced by office-holders and businessmen; it had diverged from socialism, abandoned its aim of extending the revolution, compromised with capitalism and suppressed workers' movements. Fascism she saw as a form of violence designed to prevent capitalist society being superseded by a more advanced form of social organization. Financed by capitalist interests, it was aiming to reverse the tide of progress by destroying the institutions on which the workers relied to defend themselves. However, the relative weakness of the British Fascisti, the Imperial Fascist League and even Sir Oswald Mosley's British Union of Fascists made the mainstream of the Labour Movement slow to see Fascism as a major international threat. It was not until 1936 that the civil war in Spain ignited widespread fears, accelerated the Labour Party's acceptance of rearmament, and stimulated the idea of a Popular Front. With some reason Sylvia believed that without her efforts to keep Ethiopia in the public eye the issue would simply have been marginalized. 'People stood by while Ethiopia was vanquished', she wrote; 'this is Africa; this is not a white man's country. They listened to Italian propaganda; these are the primitives, their customs are barbarous.'[6]

The other distinctive feature of Sylvia's whole approach to the issue was her fundamental opposition to the *racist* element in Fascism at home and abroad. Dismayed by the evidence of Fascist support in London's East End in 1936, she noted:

It plays on the racial prejudice which is found among the least intelligent sections of a poor and overcrowded population and the jealousy of the women of the paid labourers and unemployed men who contrast the sturdy well-clothed children of the Jewish shopkeepers with their own ragged, ricketty little ones.[7]

It is her awareness of racial discrimination, in addition to the issues of gender and social class, which makes Sylvia so much more modern a figure than many left-wingers of her generation. Yet she had grown up in a period in which the rapid expansion of the British Empire was widely assumed to be a great moral good because of the superiority of the Anglo-Saxon people and their duty to guide the less enlightened races of the world. Most of her colleagues in the pre-war women's movement reflected this conventional thinking, which sometimes coloured their arguments for female suffrage. They regarded Parliamentary democracy as the peculiar genius of the white people of north-west Europe and North America, and expressed doubts about its suitability for southern Europeans, let alone for Asians and Africans. They also capitalized upon conventional prejudices by linking the backwardness of Egypt and Turkey to the low status enjoyed by women in those countries.[8] The origins of Sylvia's liberalism remain obscure, though she may well have learned from her father to be sceptical towards crude ideas about white superiority and black inferiority. It is also possible that her sympathy for all underprivileged people originated in her sense that her own worth was insufficiently recognized by those around her. Sylvia had little direct experience of black people before the First World War, though when visiting the United States she had been shocked by the crudity of racial prejudice and the derogatory way in which most Americans referred to negroes. In 1920 she published several articles by the Jamaican poet, Claude McKay, on the work of the National Association for the Advancement of Coloured People, and she attacked the use of pass laws and other forms of racial discrimination in South Africa at this time.[9] From McKay she learnt that racism extended to the left of politics as well as the right. In 1920 he attacked the prominent Radical, E. D. Morel, for publishing an inflammatory article in the *Daily Herald* about the employment of black troops by the French in parts of Germany which he pronounced a threat to white women because of the sexual morals and appetite of Africans.[10] When the newspaper refused to print McKay's protest Sylvia printed it in the *Dreadnought*. Subsequently she invited McKay to contribute regular articles on political events seen from the perspective of black people.[11]

After crossing the Eritrean border in October 1935 the invading forces enjoyed a comparatively easy passage to the capital, Addis Ababa, by May 1936. Just before their arrival Haile Selassie fled to Djibouti where he boarded a British ship, leaving Mussolini to proclaim Victor Emmanuel as Emperor in his place. Although the Italian troops performed poorly, the lack of artillery and aeroplanes on the Ethiopian side gave them an overwhelming advantage. In this situation Sylvia bombarded the newspapers and politicians with letters urging that the enforcement of sanctions would expose the weakness of the Italians, and that if they were allowed to get away with their aggression they would inevitably join with Hitler and turn against the western democracies. In March she spoke at a 'Stop the War in Abyssinia' rally in Trafalgar Square to demand the immediate imposition of oil sanctions. As a result of these interventions Sylvia became a friend and colleague of Dr Charles Martin, the Ethiopian Ambassador, who introduced her to the Emperor when he arrived in Britain in June. She accompanied Haile Selassie to Geneva where he put his case before the Assembly of the League of Nations. For several years Sylvia and Dr Martin organized fund-raising activities for Ethiopia independently of the Emperor who had undertaken not to engage in political activity during his exile. For a time she joined the Abyssinia Association under Professor Stanley Jevons and Francis Beaufort-Palmer, one of a multitude of organizations involved with propaganda and fund-raising. Those who worked with Sylvia at this time recognized her single-mindedness and total integrity, but found her impatience and her disrespect towards the Foreign Office irritating. According to one contemporary, her habit of bombarding the Emperor and his private secretary with advice nearly drove them mad.[12] As always, Sylvia never felt comfortable in an organization which she could not dominate. The natural outcome was that she made her chief contribution to the Ethiopian cause by starting another newspaper. The *New Times and Ethiopia News*, whose title was presumably intended to embarrass the pro-appeasement 'old' *Times*, appeared in May 1936 when the cause stood at a low point. Corio did much of the editing and wrote articles under the pseudonym 'Crastinus' and 'Luce'. The paper, which eventually ran to eight pages each week, sold around 10,000 copies, but reached 40,000 at its height, an indication of growing support for a Popular Front strategy, not simply sympathy for the plight of Ethiopia itself. It seems to have been sustained by fêtes, bazaars and other appeals backed by Haile Selassie and Dr Martin, as well as donations from Henry Harben and Nancy Cunard and subsidies from the Bank of Ethiopia.

Sylvia's first biographer, Patricia Romero, gave a fairly disparaging account of her campaign, perhaps reflecting the feelings of Jevons and others in the Abyssinia Association who found her relentless exposures of Italian atrocities and her poster-parades around Whitehall crude and embarrassing. However, this seems unfair, for she was, after all, essentially a *propagandist* dealing with a slippery and weak-willed Foreign Secretary who was happy to prevaricate endlessly on the issue. To be conciliatory and patient was only to play the Foreign Office's own game; only by sheer persistence and by over-simplifying the issues could she hope to embarrass the authorities sufficiently to make any impact on them. Later Sylvia told Teresa Billington-Greig that her campaign fell into two parts: first to seek effective sanctions against Italy, and, when that had failed, to keep alive Ethiopia's claims to independence by exposing the evils perpetrated by the Italian invaders.[13] Her tactical difficulty lay in the fact that by May 1936 the military struggle appeared to be over; consequently the authorities became susceptible to Italian pressure to abandon sanctions and forget the whole issue. In this situation Sylvia was justified in feeling there was nothing to be gained by being polite towards the Foreign Office. To this end the *New Times and Ethiopia News* carried reports about Ethiopian refugees hiding in caves and mountain passes to escape the fighting and in particular about the mustard gas used by the Italians. Sylvia demanded that the British create enclaves under their control to offer some protection to civilians against gas and bombing.[14] Reporting proved difficult because Marshal Badoglio imposed such strict censorship that many journalists gave up and left the country, and when the victims of gas attack were produced, the Italians claimed they were suffering from leprosy. While Dr Martin supplied her with much information, Sylvia also benefited from a number of informers in Ethiopia and in neighbouring British and French territory, notably the Ethiopian consul at Djibouti who passed information to an Indian, Wazir Ali Baig. This enabled the *New Times* to itemize the use of gas and to ask why 259 tons of gas had been allowed to pass unchallenged through the Suez Canal. It also printed photographs of Red Cross lorries and tents bombed by Italian planes and of civilians suffering the effects of gas burns.[15]

Sylvia quickly realized that the British Government's professions of neutrality obscured an increasingly pro-Italian policy. For example, the ban on arms to both sides only damaged the Ethiopians who had a greater need of them. Moreover, though the authorities allowed Haile Selassie safe passage out of Ethiopia, they tried to insist that he avoided anything that might prolong resistance to the occupation of his country. At Gorë in the west of the country, in which the exiled Ethiopian Government took refuge, the British consul advised people to submit to the occupation.[16] When the Emperor arrived in Britain in June, Sylvia endeavoured to maximize the Government's embarrassment by organizing a big welcome at Waterloo Station attended by the Dean of Westminster, Norman Angel and a bevy of MPs, including Eleanor Rathbone, Philip Noel-Baker and a Conservative, Vyvian Adams.[17] The Government altered his route in order to avoid the cheering crowds. Subsequently the Foreign Office did its best to ignore Haile Selassie's presence, the King refused to invite him to Buckingham Palace, and when he took tea at the House of Commons Baldwin scuttled away to avoid a meeting. For his part the Emperor made things easier by spending his five-year exile largely in Bath where Sylvia visited him regularly.

It was, of course, easy for Sylvia's critics to ridicule her position as a democrat and republican acting as spokesman for the imperial ruler of a feudal state which still tolerated slavery. One of her biographers attributed her infatuation with 'her new idol' to the need to find another father figure in her life.[18] However, such remarks seem over the top. It is true that Sylvia's tendency to see issues in black-and-white terms led her to depict Haile Selassie as a heroic figure working selflessly for his people and oblivious to personal danger and discomfort. Yet her propaganda was not entirely baseless, for the Emperor had gone into battle with his men and operated a machine gun against the enemy. Moreover, though autocratic and surrounded by the trappings of medievalism, he was also a reformer and innovator already responsible for a new constitution and Parliament, school building and the first criminal code in Ethiopia's history; he had taken the country into the League of Nations and officially abolished slavery in 1924. And although Sylvia relied on the Emperor to help sustain her propaganda effort, they never became particularly close, not least because of his imperfect English. Sylvia became more friendly with his youngest daughter, Princess Tsahai, who learned English, moved freely in English society and trained as a nurse at the Great Ormond Street Children's Hospital. In any case, as she had taken up the cause of Ethiopian freedom well before meeting him, it is hardly necessary to explain her devotion in personal terms.

While granting Haile Selassie refuge in Britain, Sir Anthony Eden, the Foreign Secretary, took advantage of his exile to claim in the House of Commons that no Ethiopian government now survived, and that in any case the guerrilla fighters were hostile to the Emperor's rule as much as to the Italians. For several years Sylvia countered the Government line by issuing regular reports on the progress made by the Ethiopian resistance, but her most effective reposte to official complacency was to place the invasion in the wider context of Italian ambitions to recreate an empire covering the Balkans, Turkey, Palestine, Trans-Jordan, Yemen, Tunis, Egypt and the Sudan. Mussolini, she suggested, was already softening up the Egyptians by promoting anti-British agitations and subsidizing Egyptian newspapers while building up his forces in adjacent territory.[19] However, though damaging, none of this deflected the Government from its determination to extricate itself as soon as it decently could from the whole affair. As early as May 1936 Eden had accepted in principle the need to abandon sanctions, but he wished to delay, partly in order to bargain with the Italians and also for fear of the embarrassment this would cause for one who was supposedly tougher towards Mussolini than his predecessor. However, in June Neville Chamberlain, then Chancellor of the Exchequer, forced the issue by publicly describing sanctions as 'the very midsummer of madness', and on 17 June the cabinet agreed to give a lead in proposing to lift sanctions at Geneva. Secure behind their large Parliamentary majority, the National Government could afford to brush aside the handful of backbenchers, including Josiah Wedgwood, Eleanor Rathbone, Arthur Creech-Jones, Reginald Sorensen and Philip Noel Baker, who persistently questioned Eden about British policy in Ethiopia. By chance, the most vociferous critic of appeasement was Sylvia's own MP in Woodford – Winston Churchill. But when she took him to task in the local newspaper for the inconsistency between his conciliatory view of Mussolini and his alarmist attitude to Hitler, he failed to answer her directly. In fact, Churchill approached the question on the assumption that Britain's interests lay in maintaining the isolation of Germany by keeping on the right side of the Italians: morality did not really come into it. He was therefore not prepared to support sanctions as a gesture against Italy unless convinced that this would really help Ethiopia as distinct from merely causing inconvenience to the Italians.[20]

Churchill's defects as a popular leader were unfortunate because the outbreak of the civil war in Spain in July 1936 created the potential for a much wider anti-Fascist movement. In the *New Times*, Sylvia began to carry regular reports on developments there, including dramatic photographs of Spanish children killed by Fascist forces. Though she felt understandably dismayed that the loss of European lives made a greater impact than the loss of African ones, she accepted that the civil war had triggered a powerful emotional response in the western democracies and accelerated the trend away from pacifism in the British Labour Movement. On the other hand, though the Spanish Civil War loomed large at the time, it proved to be of far less significance than contemporaries expected, largely because General Franco kept Spain out of the Second World War. By contrast, the invasion of Ethiopia was the decisive event in precipitating Europe on the downward path to war by destroying the western strategy for resistance to Hitler. The adoption of sanctions, however ineffective, shattered the Stresa Front, thereby pushing Mussolini into collusion with Hitler. Moreover, it left the British feeling let down by the French whom they blamed, quite unfairly, for the failure to take a firm line with Italy. The effect of this diplomatic disruption was to encourage Hitler to take the enormous risk of marching his troops into the demilitarized Rhineland zone in March 1936, calculating that the estrangement of the three other powers would prevent them co-operating to check him which, from a military point of view, they could quite well have done. Consequently, by the end of the year the strategic situation in Europe had altered to the immense disadvantage of France, which had lost its safeguard against a future German attack in the Rhineland and faced hostile Fascist powers on two fronts, or three including Spain; her pacts with the states of Eastern Europe now appeared worthless as the Munich Settlement was to demonstrate. The British Government had managed to get the worst of all worlds over Ethiopia, by antagonizing the French, alienating the Italians and convincing the dictators that they would always give way under pressure.

While Sylvia spent 1936 making herself a thorn in the side of the National Government, Christabel began the year basking in its favour. January brought the news that she was to become a Dame of the British Empire 'for public and social services' in the New Year's Honours List. Edward VIII held the investiture, the first of his brief reign, on 18 February. 'I shall feel that with me at Buckingham Palace are Mother and all who helped her and me and devoted members of the Women's cause', she wrote.[21] The honour appears to have come as a complete surprise, and can only be attributed to the prime minister, Baldwin, who as Christabel noted, 'has been a good friend to the Women's cause'. For Christabel, who was living with Ada Wright, an elderly former suffragette, at her Bayswater flat at this time, the DBE offered welcome proof that she had not been completely forgotten. Her surviving correspondence with Ada Flatman and others around 1936 suggests that, though in touch with ex-suffragettes, she remained a little distant; her letters were rather formal and the occasional meetings were fitted in around her Adventist activities.

In view of Christabel's confident prediction of General Franco's victory on the grounds that Spain was destined to become part of the restored Roman Empire, she must have been tempted to rebut Sylvia's views on the dictators and the League of Nations. However, she kept clear of controversy. The *New York Times* described her, significantly, as living in semi-retirement, though aged only fifty-six.[22] Christabel can hardly have been unaware that her occasional appearances on behalf of the Bible Testimony Friendship in 1937 and 1938 were attracting far less public attention than her sister's anti-Fascist campaign. When she met a Mrs Grant, the editor of *Life of Faith*, at the offices of Marshall, Scott and Morgan, her Adventist publishers, she paced up and down lecturing her: 'Young woman, do you realize that you would not be sitting where you are if it had not been for me and my friends?' She demanded to know whether the hapless Mrs Grant used her vote: 'Do you vote for the most good-looking candidate? Most women seem to,' she snorted.[23] The bitterness, usually concealed by an outward show of self-confidence, betrayed Christabel's inner resentment of the success now enjoyed by women, many of whom had not been involved in the struggle for the vote. Nowhere was this more evident than in the opportunities created by the inter-war women's magazines for women such as Mary Grieve who edited *Woman* after its foundation in 1937 and Alice Head, the editor of *Good Housekeeping* from 1924 onwards, who was reputedly Britain's most highly paid woman. Neither accepted any responsibility for promoting the further extension of women's rights. In the first edition of *Woman*, Mary Lane, in a comment that might have been aimed at Christabel, wrote: 'The fierce feminist is an old-fashioned figure unsympathetically remembered by all but a few.'[24] In her views on the younger generation Christabel, for once, found herself in complete agreement with Sylvia, who feared that women were slipping back into a world of domestic trivia and trying to make themselves attractive to men. She disparaged 'the emancipation of today [which] displays itself mainly in cigarettes and shorts . . . in painted lips and nails, and [the] return of trailing skirts and other absurdities of dress which betoken the slave-woman's sex appeal rather than the free-woman's intelligent companionship.'[25]

After the dramatic developments in Spain and Ethiopia, 1937 proved to be a quieter year in international affairs, making Sylvia's task in preventing people from forgetting about the invasion all the more difficult. In this situation she sought to demonstrate, week in week out, that resistance to the Italians still continued. This was essential since, by April, Eden had privately concluded that Britain ought to recognize the Italian conquest, and he and Chamberlain, who succeeded Baldwin as prime minister in May 1937, believed that

Ethiopia should not be allowed to stand in the way of closer relations with Mussolini any longer. However, the regular revelations about the atrocities committed by Italian troops made it too awkward to say so publicly. Sylvia's reputation as a troublemaker in official circles was exacerbated by the extensive circulation of the *New Times and Ethiopia News* throughout West Africa, the West Indies and Kenya where she became a respected figure amongst nationalists. She became acquainted with the young Jomo Kenyatta, who stayed at Charteris Road, Harold Moody of Sierra Leone who founded the League of Coloured Peoples, and the West Indian, George Padmore, who was later a close associate of Kwame Nkrumah of Ghana. For them the Ethiopian war became a key event in the emergence of Pan-Africanism. The extensions of European imperialism in the late nineteenth century had left only Liberia and Ethiopia as independent states in the entire African continent; consequently the restoration of Haile Selassie became of enormous symbolic importance as the major expression of African culture and politics. This is why the war stimulated so much interest in the West Indies where the growth of nationalism and racial tension added to the long-term costs of the British Government's determination to sweep the Ethiopian question under the carpet. Although the authorities banned the *New Times* in some colonies in the hope of dampening down the unrest, they acted too late to check its influence.

In February 1938 the domestic implications of the policy of conciliating Mussolini also came home to roost, when Chamberlain, who was anxious to start negotiations with Mussolini in the hope of detaching him once again from Germany, encountered opposition from Eden. Unfortunately, the resignation of the Foreign Secretary failed to discredit the policy of appeasement as it might have done because Eden delivered a weak and cautious resignation speech failing to define clearly the issues that had provoked this rupture. For her part Sylvia embarrassed the government by reporting that Jubaland, a strip of desert territory in the west of Italian Somaliland, had been given to Germany, thereby restoring to her a foothold in East Africa, access to the port of Mogadishu and the opportunity to use submarine and air bases to threaten British shipping in the Indian Ocean.[26] By the start of 1939 it had become increasingly difficult to conceal the difficulties facing the occupying forces in Ethiopia. Though Italian troop numbers were put officially at 90,000, Sylvia claimed the total stood at 360,000. After heavy fighting in January, about three-quarters of Tigre, the province in the far north of the country, was reported to be in the hands of rebels who were well supplied with rifles and machine guns captured from the Italians. Every two or three days, according to Sylvia's informants, ten to fifteen lorries arrived at Massawa carrying Italian dead and wounded; the latter went on to hospital at Asmara in Eritrea and the former were buried in great secrecy.[27] These reports led to denunciations of Sylvia as a 'prurient old spinster' in the Italian press and to fresh pressure on the British authorities to suppress the *New Times*. In fact, the conflict in Ethiopia had by this time evolved into a classic guerrilla war. The rebels occupied provincial towns, withdrew when the Italians appeared in strength, but then retook them later. Since the invasion had to be sustained from Italy by importing food supplies, not just military equipment, the invaders were forced to rely on the railway from Djibouti to Addis Ababa for which they had to pay the French in scarce foreign currency.[28] They therefore resorted to the much longer routes by road which increased the cost of living. In any case, without heavy troop escorts transport by road was too dangerous. As a result, many Italians who had been brought out to settle the country began to return home. During February Ethiopian forces took Gondar and Babbat to the north-west of Addis Ababa, and fighting broke out in Wallo province north of the capital. Increasingly the Italian forces were concentrated either in garrisons or on the borders with French and British territory, waiting for the position in Europe to move in their favour. By April Sylvia's informants claimed that much of Tigre, Amhara and Gojjam, the provinces in the north and west of Ethiopia, had been cleared of Italian troops; the main aim of the invaders now was to control the road from Addis Ababa to Asmara and to withdraw from the remoter districts.[29] No doubt this picture exaggerated the rebels' strength, for the Italians were not finally ejected from the country until 1941 following the entry of British troops, but the vulnerability of an occupation that depended on such long supply lines had become obvious by 1939.

Whatever the effect of Sylvia's propaganda in London, it had no impact in Sydney where Adela had become increasingly alarmed by the drift of events. 'What do we in Australia know of Abyssinia, its Emperor or its people?' she demanded in one of a number of articles which criticized the League of Nations for dragging Europe towards another conflict. Even Adela's biographer accused her of losing the thread 'somewhere in her ideological wanderings' during the 1930s.[30] This, however, seems a little unfair, for her ideas grew as much from her perception of national interest as from ideology. As with the majority of Australians, Adela's view of foreign affairs started from a staunchly pro-British position, but during 1936 and 1937 she developed profound doubts about the value of the traditional reliance on the mother country which were quite soundly based.

Paradoxically, in view of the charges of Englishness that were levelled at her, this was in part a natural reflection of Adela's growing identification with Australia. It was this that led to her questioning the wisdom of Britain's commitment to the Treaty of Versailles and to condemn her readiness to risk war for the League; these entanglements led Britain into forgetting the Australians, beleaguered as they were on the edge of Asia whose teeming millions threatened to overwhelm them. Adela's sense that Britain was now losing its will to retain influence in the far-flung areas of the world was strikingly reflected in an article in which she criticized Britain for conceding too much power to a small minority of voters in India. Democracy in such a society, she insisted, was a farce; the British were, in effect, abdicating power and leaving the people to their fate.[31]

This pessimistic conclusion inevitably led her to consider carefully Australia's relations with Japan. There had, in fact, always been an element of deception in Britain's role as the protector of Australia, for as early as 1902 the Government had signalled its unwillingness to maintain sufficient naval strength in the Far East by making an alliance with Japan. This enabled her to concentrate on Europe. However, after the First World War the Anglo-Japanese Alliance had been allowed to lapse, and in the absence of American co-operation, which offered the only realistic alternative, successive British governments had no credible policy to put in its place. The surrender of Singapore and the rapid unravelling of the Empire during the Second World War offered dramatic proof of the dangerous vacuum in Britain's Far Eastern strategy. To this extent Adela's concern seems fully justified, and the connection she made between Britain's European policy and Australia's predicament was entirely rational. However ineffective Britain's support for the League of Nations appeared to Sylvia, from Adela's perspective it was steadily leading her into entanglements which put her dangerously at odds with Germany, Italy and especially with Japan, who had alienated the western democracies by her aggression in China. Adela simply regarded Japanese expansion as a price worth paying:

Are the Japanese to be bottled up, perpetually, in their cold, quaky islands, three thousand to the arable mile, because Britain's army and navy are pledged to the League and the other nations in the League demand that they shall be used to confirm them in their present possession, however much they have neglected their resources and abuse and enslave the human beings under their control?[32]

In effect, she argued, since the turn of the century Japan had loyally supported Britain in the Far East and guaranteed that Australia would not be inundated with the Asian multitudes; consequently, there was no good reason to deny them expansion on the mainland for the sake of the United States or the League.[33] As things stood, however, the approach of war over Abyssinia threatened to involve Australians in a conflict in which Japan would inevitably be Britain's enemy along with Germany and Italy. 'If the people of Europe fear an invasion and conquest by foreign states ... how much more must we, here in Australia, dread the possibility of being overwhelmed by our Asiatic neighbours ... nothing would remain of the European economic standards and culture which have been built up in Australia, should this country be invaded from Asia and the national resistance of Australians broken down.'[34]

Eventually this combination of nationalism and isolationism led Tom and Adela into an injudicious defence of the Fascist and neo-Fascist powers. Still pursuing his vendetta with the Communists, Tom wrote in 1936: 'It is sheer nonsense to pretend that the workers' position in both Italy and Germany has not improved since the class war ceased.'[35] To some extent they both succumbed to the picture of Mussolini as a dynamic modernizer, which complemented their view of Britain as an ineffectual and antiquated power. 'If there is no liberty', declared Adela in reference to Hitler's Germany, 'at least there are jobs.'[36]

In this way, between the spring and autumn of 1936, Adela revised her views from those of a classic Empire enthusiast to an advocate of an accommodation with Fascism. Her growing sense of an impending war strengthened her conviction in the correctness of her diagnosis. Inevitably she and Tom attracted a deluge of criticism and the scorn of the intellectuals, to which they responded with a succession of speeches, articles and interminable, unpublishable letters to the newspapers. As regular critics of Bolshevism they found it tempting to argue that Britain and Germany were being manoeuvred into a war by the Soviet Union in defiance of their real interest which lay in treating the Fascist regimes as the natural barrier to the spread of Communism across Europe. As the debate continued Adela adopted ever wilder language and more extreme opinions, thereby causing offence to members of the Guild. As one friend put it, the Guild was composed of 'middle-aged, better-class suburban patriots' who were happy to use Adela's help but drew the line at her pro-German and pro-Japanese views.[37] By 1938 it was tempting to blame her extremism for the failure to recruit new members, though the decline of industrial militancy made the Guild's decline unavoidable. For her part Adela believed she was simply being consistent in arguing for peace just as she had done during the previous war; she welcomed National Socialism because it seemed the more effective means of responding to the collapse of capitalism and the hardship it had inflicted on working people.

As appeasement reached its peak in 1938 Adela found it easier to show her appreciation of British efforts to reach an accommodation with Germany. While Sylvia condemned the Munich Settlement in September and demanded Chamberlain's resignation, Adela went out of her way to commend it in a radio broadcast as 'decent and humane', saying that it would be futile to go to war with Germany again. She claimed that the Czech state, whose frontiers were built on hatred for Germany, had never been a realistic proposition; neither France nor Russia could offer it practical assistance because of the territory intervening between it and them.[38] But as usual her enthusiasm carried her too far. 'Why should anyone think that Mr Chamberlain or Herr

Hitler wish to plunge their own people to death and disaster?' She insisted the two men could be trusted to ensure there would be no war. The optimism engendered by Munich emboldened Adela to advocate friendship between Australia and Japan, much to the irritation of her colleagues in the Guild, some of whom sought to discredit her by circulating malicious gossip about her contacts with Nazi supporters and claims that she received money from them. When business funding for the Guild began to dwindle she inevitably bore the blame, and by May 1939 her radio broadcasts had been discontinued. Increasingly distraught as war became imminent, Adela drafted a huge personal manifesto in the form of a letter of resignation from the Guild in which she protested that she represented the working-class women not the rich ladies who felt so bothered about her attacks on Communism. She declared her total opposition to another war between Britain and Germany on the grounds that it would merely allow the United States to penetrate British markets in the Far East and kill off the economic recovery in Europe.[39] Although it was not until October that the executive finally asked for her resignation, it was already obvious that she had been miscast amongst the patriotic, pro-British ladies of the Guild. As Australia went to war, Adela and Tom faced not only the massive rejection of their views, but the prospective loss of their only reliable source of income.

20

For War and Peace (1939–45)

'Remember – everywhere, always, fascism means war.'
Sylvia Pankhurst, *New Times and Ethiopia News*, 9 May 1936

As the German tanks rolled into Poland on 1 September 1939, all Sylvia's predictions about the menace of fascism seemed to have been confirmed. Two days later Britain issued an ultimatum, albeit with great reluctance, and for the first time since 1917 Sylvia had grounds for believing that she was working with the grain of history. The only awkward aspect of all this from the perspective of her Ethiopian campaign was that Mussolini had warned Hitler that Italy would not be ready to fight for four years; consequently it was not until May 1940, when the German armies were overrunning France, that she entered the war. Following the declaration of war three and a half million people fled from London in anticipation of a bombing offensive by the Luftwaffe, though the Germans were too preoccupied with Poland at this stage.

The threat led Sylvia to consider dispatching the twelve-year-old Richard to safety in Canada as many middle-class families were now doing. Fortunately, Emmeline Pethick-Lawrence sensibly cautioned her against this on the grounds that neither would be happy if separated for long. In the event Richard remained at home where he joined Sylvia and Corio in the two Anderson shelters dug into the garden at Charteris Road.

After the initial panic the country settled into a period dubbed the 'Phoney War'. For some time the advocates of appeasement, who remained influential within the government, continued to hope that

Germany would content herself with a war in eastern Europe or that shortages of resources would force her to contract her war effort. By contrast Sylvia spent the Phoney War period in a whirlwind of activity. She immediately added a subtitle – 'The National Anti-Fascist Weekly' – to the *New Times and Ethiopia News* on the grounds that hers was the only weekly to have warned consistently that Fascism would unleash another war on Europe. From the start she advocated total military victory: Fascism must be utterly destroyed so that it would never rise again.[1]

This involved dissociating herself from her former pacifist colleagues in the London Federation of Peace Councils, of which she was vice-president, who supported Moscow and denounced the war as merely a conflict between two forms of imperialism: 'Britain must go to war soon or late. Better let it come now, in defence of international justice, than finally for ourselves alone, with every pledge broken, every friend betrayed and vanquished.'[2] Sylvia also made a point of linking feminism with the war in her attacks on the Fascist regimes for treating women as breeding machines. In Italy, she noted, women had lost their personal liberty, the laws protecting women and children from rape and abduction had been weakened, and their role in municipal affairs had been abolished.[3] To those who remembered Sylvia's First World War pacifism all this seemed a remarkable transformation, though many on the left shared her belief that this was a just war. She revived her previous role by becoming honorary secretary of the Women's War Emergency Council, an organization founded by Mary Corigan in October to protect the living standards of working-class families during the war. Using its links with sympathetic MPs such as Eleanor Rathbone, the Council pressed the Government over a multitude of issues including price controls on all basic foods, profiteering, separation allowances for wives, the need for uniform payments for the billeting of soldiers, widows' pensions, allowances to mothers of single men in the forces and compensation for unpaid domestics injured in air raids.[4] In fact, the council was pushing at an open door. When Sylvia led a deputation to the Ministry of Food in November she was surprised to be told that the officials had read *The Home Front* and were contemplating starting cost-price restaurants of the sort she had opened in the East End. In this war there were to be no arguments about the need for food rationing or for subsidies on the essential items needed by pregnant women and young children. The Labour member, Reginald Sorensen, organized a meeting at the Commons where Sylvia received a sympathetic hearing for her demand for the end of the family means test and the substitution of a single rate system, which was conceded in 1941.

Sylvia also devoted a great deal of time to her work with the Friends of Free Italy to secure the release of anti-Fascist Italians from internment and with the Jewish Refugees Committee which regularly approached her for help. This involved a huge detailed correspondence on individual cases with Herbert Morrison, who became Home Secretary after May 1940 when the Churchill Coalition replaced Neville Chamberlain's Government. By November she had presented Morrison with a full list of both Fascists and anti-Fascists.[5] At the outset of war the authorities had rounded up about a thousand known supporters of the British Union of Fascists including Sir Oswald and Lady Mosley. However, Sylvia believed that some of the officers in charge of the internment camps, notably Peel Camp on the Isle of Man, were allowing the Fascists to gain the upper hand and even permitting them to enjoy radio contact with their leaders in Italy. During his time in Brixton Mosley was treated as a political prisoner, allowed to bring in food and drink, wear his own clothes and associate with fellow prisoners during meals, work and recreation periods. Although the press exaggerated the comforts of prison life, its suspicions about the pro-Fascist sympathies of many people within government were well founded. Sylvia joined in the condemnation when the Mosleys were released following medical advice in November 1943. However, by the start of 1941 she had become increasingly frustrated because her applications for the release of the opponents of Fascism were now being rejected, perhaps because the most deserving cases had been dealt with by then. By the autumn she had decided to withdraw from this work and concentrate on Ethiopia.

Wartime conditions obliged Sylvia to incorporate much more material about the European situation into the *New Times*, and to reduce it to four pages as a result of the shortage of paper. In March 1940 she claimed that Italian troops were deserting and that only one province, Harrar, remained fully under their control.[6] However, the reliability of such reports is questionable because during wartime Sylvia became dependent for news on Emmanuel Abraham, a student sent to the Ethiopian legation in London. Her repeated telephone calls for information alerted Abraham to the fact that anything he told her immediately went into print, and he consequently rationed the news with a view to avoiding material which would cause friction between Britain and the Emperor. Sensitive information such as the Emperor's return to Ethiopia was withheld from her for a time. However, Sylvia gained an invaluable new and sympathetic source of information in the shape of Major Orde Wingate, who accompanied the Ethiopian forces which entered the country from the Sudan and was one of the first to enter Addis Ababa in 1941.[7]

In June 1940 Sylvia greeted the news that Mussolini had at last entered the war with jubilation: 'The freedom of Abyssinia is now assured.'[8] With the Italians occupying British Somaliland and small parts of the Sudan, the Horn of Africa now became a theatre of war for Britain. Yet if Italy had become an enemy, it remained uncertain how far the Government regarded Ethiopia as a friend. Nagging doubts about its attitude led Sylvia to inundate the new prime minister with letters throughout 1940, 1941 and 1942 seeking assurances that Britain had retracted her original recognition of the Italian occupation and that Ethiopia would be restored to its former independence. She demanded the expulsion of all Italians as soon as possible, and reminded Churchill that in deference to the wishes of its people, the country should be known officially as Ethiopia not Abyssinia.[9]

However, when Geoffrey Mander raised the issue of Ethiopia's independence in the Commons on 19 June, the Under-Secretary, R. A. Butler, offered an evasive reply, though eventually the government did recognize the country as an ally and the Emperor as its lawful ruler. Although Sylvia believed that this implied the full territorial restoration of Ethiopia after the war, the Government clearly had no intention of giving such an unequivocal undertaking.

Meanwhile Sylvia's prominence had attracted hostile attention from Fascist sympathizers in Britain who sent her several threatening letters: 'Unless the publication of the *New Times and Ethiopia News* ceases by the end of this month, this weekly journal will find itself without an Editor.' Another warned that after the German invasion of Britain:

We shall punish you by order of our Leader as you well deserve for the article in your filthy paper against the Italian Fascists. Your house in Woodford will be bombed and burned to the ground. Hitler knows your address. You will pay with your life . . . Do not dare to go out in the dark or you will be murdered.[10]

Amateurish as these threats appeared to be, they brought Sylvia the novel experience of police protection during wartime. In a BBC broadcast Corio made an even more provocative call to Italian workers in which he reminded them that England had been their loyal ally in the struggle for independence in the nineteenth century and urged them to lay down their arms, sabotage the regime and refuse to work in the factories of Germany.[11]

By comparison Christabel's war proved to be quiet and uneventful. In 1939 she had been staying at Bickley near Bromley in Kent where she was finishing her last Adventist volume, *The Uncurtained Future*. Largely a *réchauffé* of the earlier books, it retraced her early life and explained how her illusions had been shattered by the outbreak of the Great War and her lack of confidence in the League of Nations. Fortunately the war gave a topical edge to this rather stale volume. How, Christabel demanded, were conventional theologians to explain why, if there was a God, He had allowed another World War to occur? For her the only way of reconciling Christianity with war was by accepting the return of Christ.[12]

Shortly before the declaration of war Christabel had returned to the United States, and, despite requests from Annie Kenney to return home, she spent the remainder of her life there, mostly in the vicinity of Los Angeles. Exactly how she supported herself in this period remains unclear, for though she gave the occasional lecture and participated in television discussions and interviews, according to Grace Roe, she did not make much money from this work.[13] Whether from habit or lack of money, Christabel continued to dress in classic Edwardian style during the 1940s, appearing for tea in long flowing dresses and huge picture-hats with roses perched on the brim. However, Christabel is known to have been the beneficiary of three wills between 1929 and 1940 alone. Ada Wright left her £1,600 in 1939, and she received an annuity of £250 from a Mrs Olivia Durand-Deacon. But when asked after Christabel's death whether her friends had paid her expenses,

Grace Roe failed to give an answer.[14] However, her life was comfortable and enjoyable because – and this was what made America so much more appealing than Britain – Christabel's celebrity status gave her easy access to the homes of wealthy people, often as a long-term house-guest. Her chief companion from pre-war days was Grace Roe, who had spent nine years in America as a social worker until the mid-1930s before taking employment with a wealthy Theosophist, Mrs Roland Grey. When Mrs Grey died in the 1950s Roe stayed on at Ventura a few miles north of Los Angeles and thus remained in close contact with Christabel.

For three months in 1941 Christabel was ensconced at the palatial home of Mrs Frances de Lacy Hyde, a noted hostess, in Plainfield, New Jersey. Dr Marjorie Greenlie who knew her there found Christabel a gentle and courteous conversationalist, 'but utterly impervious'.[15] She retained her total certainty that nothing would save the world except the return of Christ, a subject about which she spoke at length. Nor had her turn-of-the-century English views changed at all; she found it impossible, for example, to understand why Indians and Africans were not simply grateful to be ruled indefinitely by the British. In 1942 Christabel returned to Hollywood where she lived in the Vista Del Mar Avenue with a Mrs Shirley Carson Jenny, the author of some fifty novelettes, who was active in the Writers' Club of Hollywood. Mrs Jenny had also become a noted psychic who claimed to be in contact with the English poet, Percy Bysshe Shelley, whose communications she wrote down and published.[16] Christabel flourished in this literary atmosphere. Friends believed that she and Mrs Jenny were not particularly close and that the arrangement was primarily a matter of convenience for both.[17] Although Christabel became a familiar figure in the British colony in Hollywood she had no particularly close friends; she impressed everyone as charming and kind but was too reserved to invite confidences. However, most Americans, who saw this as quite natural and authentically English, loved to hear her flawless English, her melodic delivery and the Biblical allegories with which she laced her conversation. It was all the more flattering that, unlike many British people, Christabel made no secret of her love for America and its people. She never criticized America because, as she put it, 'I am not a citizen but a guest of this great country.'[18] Apart from being ready to discuss any topic under the sun, Christabel also took a great interest in classical music, opera and young writers. Fortunately, as her health remained good she was able to do a lot of walking, though she never learned to drive. Even in her sixties her appearance impressed acquaintances as much as it had in her youth; one friend recalled that she 'had a flower-like quality, with a clear white skin and a soft Madonna face'.[19]

In this happy situation Christabel felt understandably reluctant to respond to a heartfelt letter from Annie Kenney in 1942, urging her to come home and to write her own account of the suffragette movement. Annie herself had published a very thin volume of memoirs in 1924, of which she was inordinately proud, but, deferential as ever, felt that 'none can ever make the great appeal as [sic] the book sent forth to the world from *you*, the heart of the whole transformation – it would give a wonderful finish to a great life'.[20] According to Grace Roe, Christabel had, in fact, written her autobiography in England in the 1930s, but she obviously had no intention of publishing it. In America the one topic she never talked about was the suffragette campaign. Rather than raking up old controversies she preferred to spend these happy American years growing old gracefully and enjoying the relaxed social life she had largely missed during her youth. To play a well-defined role as the English lady abroad naturally appealed to an essentially detached personality like Christabel, because it enabled everyone to know exactly where they stood; in the comfortable community on America's Pacific coast it attracted friends and a full social life, but involved nothing too close or complicated.

After Italy's entry into the war Sylvia felt increasingly aggrieved by the obvious reluctance of the Foreign Office to supply arms to the Ethiopian guerrillas or to allow the return of the Emperor to his homeland. Eventually, however, the RAF flew him to the Sudan and by early 1941 he had crossed into Ethiopia with a small force comprising about two thousand Ethiopian refugees and Sudanese soldiers. Meanwhile, British forces advanced on three fronts, from the Sudan into Eritrea and thence south towards Addis Ababa, from Kenya north and west to Mogadishu, and from the Gulf of Aden west to Harrar and Addis Ababa. On 6 April they entered the capital, followed by Haile Selassie himself a month later.

This dramatic reversal of the Italian occupation might well have rendered Sylvia's campaign suddenly redundant, but she quickly redirected her fire towards the British authorities who, rather perversely, insisted on treating Ethiopia as Enemy Occupied Territory on the basis that the war dated from 1939, not from 1935. She mobilized her Parliamentary allies to press Sir Anthony Eden, once again Foreign Secretary, to declare full Ethiopian independence as an essential British war aim. However, Churchill refused to accept this, choosing to ignore Ethiopia's history as a separate country and its membership of the League of Nations. Sylvia suspected with some reason that the Government preferred to keep the country as enemy occupied territory so as to facilitate the annexation of certain regions such as the Ogaden. She demanded not only the restoration of the pre-1935 territory, but the return of Eritrea and Somaliland which the Italians had acquired in the nineteenth century. In her view the country also needed access to the sea as an alternative to the French railway to Djibouti.[21] To this end Sylvia bombarded the Foreign Office, the Ministry of Information and the prime minister with interminable letters and turned up to harangue officials from time to time. Reactions to this varied. One of the civil servants at the Ministry of Information was surprised to find, not the cantankerous idealist he had expected, but a rather gentle, slightly scatty and overworked old lady. By contrast the Minister, Brendan Bracken, damned the *New Times* as 'a poisonous rag' and claimed it had insulted British troops.[22] In 1942 Sylvia took Churchill and Eden to task for treating Ethiopia as a subordinate territory. Why, she demanded to know, did the BBC, which played the national anthems of all the Allied countries in the closing minutes of its daily broadcasts, decline to include that of Ethiopia? Why did Churchill omit Ethiopia from the list of countries to be included in the United Nations? Subsequently the BBC backed down, but this was a minor victory.

Sylvia's fears about government intentions may seem paranoid. Why, after all, should Britain have wanted to take on new responsibilities by partitioning Ethiopia? Yet several official actions did give substance to her claims. By refusing to treat the country as Allied territory, the British effectively undermined Haile Selassie's control and made it difficult for him to collect revenue. The British also disarmed Ethiopian troops and remained in occupation of the Ogaden for many years after the war.[23] However, in the House of Commons Eden blandly reiterated the official line that negotiations between Britain and Ethiopia were proceeding amicably, though the very fact that they lasted until February 1942 gave grounds for doubt. Sylvia's suspicions were increased by the intervention, apparently with official sanction, of Margery Perham, a Reader in Colonial Administration at Oxford, in November 1941. Though posing as sympathetic to Ethiopia, Miss Perham added a certain academic respectability to the Government's imperialism. Describing the country as too backward and disunited to be fully independent, she argued that the Italians had been badly treated after 1918, and she advocated the annexation of territory to the neighbouring powers. In effect, Miss Perham shared the paternalistic mind-set of British administrators and politicians who found it inconceivable that an African state, even one with as long a history of self-rule as Ethiopia, could simply be left to its own devices. Sylvia briskly rejected Miss Perham's enthusiasm for Italian modernization as too high a price to pay for the brutal enslavement of the African people, though it was more difficult to rebut her claim that Haile Selassie would not be able to control his country effectively because some Ethiopians had opposed his rule while others had collaborated with the Italian occupation. Whether that justified the establishment of a British protectorate was another matter. Perham's intervention prompted Sylvia to accuse Churchill of using the possibility of revolts against the Emperor as an excuse for maintaining British troops in the country and of seeking to deny independence by partitioning Ethiopia.[24] She felt that to remain in occupation of the Ogaden was almost calculated to encourage separatism and undermine the Emperor.

Churchill often passed her complaints to the Foreign Office which kept a file labelled 'How To Answer Letters From Miss Sylvia Pankhurst'! However, it would be wrong to disparage Sylvia's methods. There was no easy way to put pressure on the Foreign Office except by keeping its actions and motives constantly in the spotlight. It is a measure of her success that the authorities considered closing down the *New Times*, though this was rejected on the grounds that it would only draw more attention to Sylvia's campaign. In any case Sylvia was no fool where government departments were concerned. Appreciating exactly where the Coalition's weakness lay in terms of external relations she took care to keep the American Secretary of State, Sumner Welles, and Eleanor Roosevelt, the wife of the President, fully informed about British ambitions in the Horn of Africa. Franklin D. Roosevelt needed no reminding that it was not America's function to assist the British in extending their Empire or even in maintaining it, and in view of the dependence of the Government on material support from the United States, even Churchill pledged himself to uphold the principle of self-determination.

Significantly, Sumner Welles endorsed Sylvia's charge that the British appeared to aspire to establish a protectorate in Ethiopia, and as a result the President decided to send a letter of support to Ethiopia and to remind Eden of the United States commitment to independence for the country as a victim of Fascist aggression.

Even so, when the Anglo-Ethiopian agreement was finally reached in February 1942 it bore out Sylvia's fears about Eden and Churchill. The Ethiopians agreed to accept a British representative in Addis Ababa who would have precedence over any other accredited foreign emissary – a classic example of nineteenth-century practice as used by the British in Afghanistan, for example.[25] Britain also restricted the Emperor's right to appoint advisers other than those approved by the British. His government was required to consult Britain on currency matters and to act only with its agreement. British troops also remained in the Ogaden and a narrow strip of territory encircling the port of Djibouti, effectively cutting the country off from the sea. Although this amounted to something less than a protectorate over Ethiopia, it was obviously less than full independence and thus justified Sylvia's continual harrying of the authorities since 1941.

While Sylvia at least had the satisfaction of knowing that she was now pulling with the tide of political events, Adela found herself isolated as never before during the Second World War. By September 1939 she had committed herself too firmly to peace to be able to retract or even compromise her position. But as so often with people who are on the losing side of the argument, her views gain a measure of credibility from a longer perspective. She insisted that the conflict would be disastrous for Britain, whether she won or lost, a view nowadays endorsed by some academic opinion. As for Australia, tied to Japan by her exports of wool and wheat, she considered it vital to avoid being dragged in. Nor did Adela see anything to apologize for in the spread of Japanese control over much of China; indeed, the recent clashes between Japanese and Russian troops only underlined their role as the only check on Soviet expansion in the event of a German defeat in the west. Carrying this to its logical conclusion, Adela advocated an Australian alliance with Japan as her best defence against Communism. Inevitably such views put Tom and Adela in a highly vulnerable position once the patriotic emotions of Australians had been engaged. Even by their standards it was rash to accept an invitation sponsored by the Japanese Tourist Bureau to visit Japan in the autumn of 1939. None the less, in November Tom, now aged sixty-eight, and Adela, fifty-four, sailed happily off, evidently unaware of the deep waters into which they had blundered. To be fair, it should be remembered that, with the attack on Pearl Harbour two years away, it still seemed possible to limit the spread of the war. When asked why she had accepted the Japanese invitation, Adela replied, honestly but naïvely, that it was such a wonderful offer to be able to travel in comfort and to see something of life abroad which she had never been able to afford before.[26] Their enjoyment of the voyage was marred only when some of the British passengers attempted to have them put off the ship at Hong Kong.

On arrival in Japan they were accommodated in good hotels and flattered to find how attentively their hosts listened to their views. But the visit was no holiday. The Walshes embarked on a whirlwind tour of private homes, factories, schools, shrines and theatres from which they emerged full of praise for the strength of Japanese family life, the survival of the small farmer, and the sense of community which they felt contrasted favourably with the excessive individualism of Australian society. In December Tom caused a sensation when he denounced the embargo Australia had imposed on exports of iron ore to Japan; if persisted in, he said, this policy would present a justification for the forcible opening of Australia's vast resources to the teeming millions of Asia.[27] After their return in February 1940 the Walshes delivered lectures and published articles designed to put Japan in as favourable light as possible, and they inundated the Government with letters urging better relations. In these they took pains to praise the beauty, cleanliness, dress, manners and culture of the country; even the position of women was represented as being very similar to that prevailing in the west during the Victorian era. In general they sought to play down the undemocratic character of Japanese politics and portray it as a force for stability and progress in Asia. Somewhat implausibly in view of their aggression in China, Adela strongly rebutted claims that the Japanese aspired to settle Australia's empty spaces as 'quite fantastic', on the grounds that they lacked the huge amounts of capital this would require. 'People who glibly say that Japan could conquer the Philippine Islands and then come and conquer Australia can only be speaking of some remote possibility a thousand years hence, but not of present day politics or possibilities.'[28]

With more courage than sense Adela decided to stand for election to the Senate in New South Wales in September 1940. Unfortunately this coincided with Japan's entry into the Tripartite Axis Pact with Germany and Italy, which of course meant that Australian troops could be involved in fighting them at any time. Inevitably her treatment of her adopted country seemed not just unpatriotic but positively traitorous to many Australians. Her son, Richard, was now serving in the forces, though his relations with his parents continued to be friendly judging from his letters. Although their controversial opinions got him into arguments with his mates, he showed more concern for Tom and Adela than for his own welfare. In the election, in which her expenses amounted to eight pence for a train ticket, Adela polled only 1,700 votes, hardly unexpected, but a blow to her morale none the less. In November the Government intervened to stop publication of *The Voice of the People*, a journal she had started in May, on the grounds that it had become necessary to restrict the import of paper.[29]

It was at this point that Adela, in a last-ditch attempt to keep the country out of war, joined the Australia First Movement, an organization which attracted an eccentric collection of anti-British and anti-American individuals, ex-Communists, pro-Fascists and anti-Semites. To top it all, most of the leaders also disliked Adela, in some cases from sheer misogyny. They considered her dangerously pro-British and completely repudiated her positive view of the Japanese. But as Adela's platform skills still made her an asset, Australia

First employed her at a salary of £5, money she desperately needed, though it seems she only ever received one month's pay. The Movement attracted few members and Adela's meetings often deteriorated into brawls; on one occasion the pianist saved the day by striking up 'God Save the King', which diverted the rowdies and brought proceedings to an early close. Unfortunately her prominence in Australia First quickly exposed Adela to charges of being a security risk, especially as she was now associated with several former Communists. Although she soon withdrew from the organization the damage was done.

When Hitler launched his invasion of Russia in July 1941 and the Japanese attacked the American fleet at Pearl Harbour in December, Adela's world was suddenly turned upside down. Not only were the despised Russians and Americans now allies, but the prospects of a Japanese invasion began to materialize with alarming speed. In a mood of rising panic the new prime minister, John Curtin, an old opponent of Adela in the conscription campaign, prepared to evacuate the country north of Brisbane. Already in July and December the Walsh home in Sydney had been searched, and in March 1942 security police returned in the middle of the night, though again they found little except some pro-Japanese literature.[30] Though understandable in the circum-stances, these raids were essentially sops to public opinion. The Walshes had been completely open about their opinions and they enjoyed insignificant support in the country; they could not seriously be represented as clandestine or subversive elements within Australian society. However, as Adela had been in the pay of Australia First, however briefly, she was bound to be regarded as a security risk. On 20 March, along with a dozen members of Australia First, she was taken into precautionary detention, though Tom, who had been ill with cancer for some time, escaped internment. When her appeal was heard, Adela treated the Supreme Court to an unconvincing rehearsal of the Pankhurst family's patriotic credentials, their friendship with Stanley Baldwin, and Christabel's DBE. However, her appeal was dismissed and she returned to an internment camp. Eventually on October 12, aged fifty-seven, she secured her transfer to the Concord Military Hospital by embarking on a hunger strike. As the doctors refused to subject her to forcible feeding she was released the next day.

In these years Adela had to exist with no income apart from Tom's old age pension and the money Richard sent from his pay. Her family felt aggrieved that no compensation was ever paid for what they regarded as her unlawful detention. During the five months following her release she devoted herself to nursing Tom, who eventually died on 5 April 1943. After this Adela withdrew finally from public life and looked around for employment, though in view of her notoriety, this proved hard to find. She worked in the canteen of a munitions factory but was dismissed, then as a companion to an elderly lady, and finally as a nurse in a hospital for retarded children which she found the most satisfying. It was only when her own health failed that Adela left this job and went to spend her declining years with her daughters and their families.[31]

Even in the later years of the war Sylvia maintained her defence of Ethiopian interests as vigilantly as ever. To her critics this now seemed a fixation, but to her supporters her single-mindedness was justified by the pro-Italian bias which still ran strongly through the British Establishment. When, for example, the BBC invited her to report on Ethiopia, it warned her to say 'nothing that would upset the Italians'. But Sylvia's steadfast refusal to take the easy road only added to her credibility among African nationalists in general and Ethiopians in particular who decided to name a street in Addis Ababa after her in 1942. Sylvia began to embarrass the Government again in March 1944 by levelling charges to the effect that Britain was intriguing to dismember Ethiopia by sponsoring a referendum in Tigre, the province bordering on Eritrea. When invited by Eleanor Rathbone to deny this in Parliament, Brendan Bracken lost his temper and accused Sylvia of propaganda 'worthy of Goebbels'; but he failed to answer the charge. Rathbone rebuked the minister for insulting the *New Times and Ethiopia News* by reminding him that it had been 'a very useful watchdog in the interests of Ethiopia.'[32] Much to the irritation of the British legation in Addis Ababa, copies of the paper attacking British policy were now circulating in the country. The diplomats complained to the Foreign Office, where an official replied with the usual superciliousness: 'Miss Pankhurst is quite incorrigible on the subject and I don't think any communication to her would do any good.'[33] The sensitivity shown by the British at this time may have been due to a further recent settlement with Ethiopia which effectively restored self-government except for the Ogaden which remained under British occupation on the grounds that it had never been securely under Ethiopian control. This left open the question of the ultimate fate of the territories when a comprehensive decolonization of the Horn of Africa took place.

It was in 1944 that Haile Selassie invited Sylvia to pay a visit to his country. However, as this required a visa from the British Government, which believed she had caused enough mischief already, her chances looked doubtful. Fortunately the Emperor provided a suitable pretext. She was to come as his personal guest to advise about a policy for women and in particular to discuss a site for a hospital to be built in memory of his daughter, Princess Tsahai, who had died in 1942; it was intended as the country's first modern hospital and as a medical school to train doctors. Although the British officials in Ethiopia opposed her visit, the Foreign Office and the Ministry of Information evidently decided to get her out of their hair for a while; they issued a visa, though not for Richard who was now seventeen.[34] In October Sylvia sailed from Liverpool to Alexandria, and thence by aeroplane from Cairo to Asmara, her first flight which left her somewhat breathless. Her presence in Asmara proved awkward since Sylvia did not hide her belief that Eritrea ought to be amalgamated with Ethiopia; but the British officials escorted her round and answered her many questions with good grace, though they felt that she had arrived with a closed mind and listened only to those who agreed with her over unification. For her part Sylvia, newly arrived from a European war ostensibly fought to eradicate Fascism, was shocked at finding the British happy to maintain Italian judges in Eritrea and to continue the colour bar operated by the former rulers. As usual she refused to suppress her misgivings; in British company she was heard to remark of one reactionary official: 'He was born half dead and now his age is telling against him!'[35] The officials were doubtless relieved when she boarded the next flight for Addis Ababa.

On arrival Sylvia was greeted by the Emperor's private secretary and equipped with a motor car, a chauffeur, two servants, a major to escort her, and a villa in what had been the Italian compound. Deputations of both Christians and Muslims turned up with bouquets of flowers to welcome her and offer thanks for her support over unification. At the palace she had an audience with Haile Selassie and private dinners with members of the royal family. The Emperor conferred the Order of Sheba and the Order of the Patriots with five palms on her. Since the recent agreement with Ethiopia had forced the British to back away from the control to which they had aspired, the thought of Sylvia up at the palace criticizing British policy left officials seething with indignation; one complained: 'Miss Pankhurst's sense of her own importance . . . shelters inadequately behind an affectation of modesty.'[36] In a rather petty reprisal, the Foreign Office objected that as the Emperor had breached protocol when awarding the medals, she should not keep them. However, as Sylvia promptly informed the press of the honours, it wisely backed down. Now sixty-two, Sylvia would have been less than human had she not succumbed to the attention and appreciation shown to her after her years of struggle to keep the Ethiopian cause alive. She described her experience as like entering a dreamland or a fairyland. The artistic sensibilities that had sparked her enthusiasm as a young woman in Italy burst into life again as she admired the splendour of the imperial household and toured the countryside luxuriant with eucalyptus trees and exotic flowers. At eight thousand feet above sea level Addis was exhausting, but Sylvia refused to be content with ceremonies and congratulations. She demanded a daily programme of tours to see farms, schools, orphanages and factories. Already she was gathering ideas and material for the further work on Ethiopia which was to sustain her for the next sixteen years of her life. More immediately there were battles still to be fought, and the Emperor seemed keen that Sylvia should continue propagating the case for giving Ethiopia an outlet to the sea and unification with Eritrea. Though impervious to the hostility shown to her from British quarters, Sylvia was gradually worn down by illness while in Ethiopia and she became somewhat frustrated by the unreliability of her chauffeur and the motor car which kept breaking down. Despite this, she did not return to Britain until early in 1945 at a time when the wartime Coalition was about to give way to a new and promising political era.

21

Corners of a Foreign Field (1945–61)

'It is enough to say that she worked and died fighting for peace, happiness, fair-play and humanity for others. Could any life have been better lived?'

His Excellency Ras Andargue Massai, Addis Ababa,
28 September 1960

After the German surrender in May 1945 Winston Churchill formed a caretaker Conservative Government prior to the general election which took place in July. In Woodford Sylvia made it known that she intended to vote for the Independent who was standing against the prime minister. Although the opinion polls had pointed to a Labour victory since 1943, it was still a shock when the party swept into power with 393 members, its first clear majority. In these circumstances Sylvia might have moved closer to the political Establishment. Labour, after all, was fully committed to eradicating the Nazi and Fascist regimes and bringing the leaders to trial for their crimes, and was pledged to a precise and extensive programme of Socialist innovations. However, there is no indication of a rapprochement between them. Despite the inclusion of her old friend, Fred Pethick-Lawrence, in the cabinet as Secretary of State for India, and of Arthur Creech Jones, who shared her views on African and Asian nationalism, at the Colonial Office, Sylvia continued to be a thorn in the side of the government. It could hardly have been otherwise in view of the dominance of the new Foreign Secretary, Ernest Bevin, an old-fashioned patriot and militant anti-Communist, much admired by the Conservatives, who was determined that Britain should retain her status as a Great Power and back the Americans in the Cold War. As a result of Bevin's policies, Britain maintained conscription in peacetime and entered the 1950s with an army 900,000 strong. This became a personal as well as a political issue in 1952 because Richard was due to be called up for service. As a conscientious objector he refused to register: 'He would not have minded fighting the Nazis,' Sylvia was reported as saying, 'but he would not want to fight in Kenya.'[1]

Initially, however, Sylvia had assumed that Labour would be more sympathetic to her views. On her return from Ethiopia in 1945 she sent Bevin reports of her tour, and after the election she suggested he should send a delegation comprising herself and three Labour MPs to investigate her charges against the British administration in the Horn of Africa. However, the Foreign Office simply filed her letters and decided not to encourage any further visits. Her criticisms of the British in Eritrea were by no means entirely fair, for she overlooked the reductions in taxation and expansion of school building since the defeat of the Italians. On the other hand the British were guilty of flagrant attempts at stripping the country of its limited assets by dismantling and selling off Italian railways and disposing of Italian property including oil installations. As a permanent critic of all British governments Sylvia found plenty to occupy her during the next decade. In 1950 she was a prominent supporter of Seretse Khama who found himself exiled from Bechuanaland (now Botswana) for daring to marry a white woman; she correctly claimed that the British were deferring to South African racial prejudice on this issue. She also attacked the white settlers for their treatment of the Kikuyu which led to the 'Mau-Mau' wars in the early 1950s.

But Sylvia's chief cause continued to be Ethiopia, in particular her campaign to restore Eritrea and Somaliland to Ethiopian control. In 1946 she turned up in Paris to press her case at the peace negotiations, and over the next few years she lobbied MPs, sent poster parades around Westminster, and issued propaganda in pamphlets and the *New Times* in an attempt to ensure that the United Nations would take up Ethiopia's case. Sylvia's argument that Ethiopia, Eritrea and Somaliland constituted a natural economic and geographical unit was valid only up to a point, for in the absence of road and rail links Somaliland and Ethiopia remained separated by vast areas of semidesert roamed by nomadic tribes to whom political boundaries seemed irrelevant. Moreover, Ethiopia wholly lacked the resources required to develop the two other territories, and enforced unity was likely to provoke border warfare which would divert the country from its internal needs – a view borne out by subsequent conflicts in the Horn of Africa. Whether the area formed a cultural and political unit was in fact, highly questionable, for the existing borders were the artificial product of imperialism during the 'Scramble for Africa'. No doubt, before the sixty-year Italian occupation Eritrea had been, for a time, under Ethiopian control. But Ethiopia itself was largely a product of the conquests of King Menelik in the nineteenth century, when it had expanded from its origins as a Christian power in the highlands of the north-west. Sylvia referred to the Muslims in areas such as the Ogaden and in Somaliland as 'ethnic Ethiopians' and, by implication, natural members of one state. However, this seemed implausible both to local people and to western observers. She persistently interpreted expressions of anti-British sentiment by Somalis and Eritreans as evidence of pro-Ethiopian views, which was simply unrealistic. In fact, there was a stronger case – supported by Bevin – for uniting the Somalis in French, British and Italian Somaliland with the Somalis of north-west Kenya and the Ogaden in a Greater Somalia, rather than leaving them divided by the artificial boundaries which were very uncertain on the ground. Unfortunately Sylvia had a completely closed mind on the subject. Choosing to act as a mouthpiece for Haile Selassie, she refused to accept that the Somalis might have genuine aspirations to self-determination.

In the short term nothing happened because the West was in no hurry to eliminate Italian influence from the Horn of Africa. Though treating the Nazi leaders with severity, they chose to ignore Marshal Graziani's atrocities in Ethiopia and were willing to allow Italy to control Eritrea and Somalia, in the hope that she would remain pro-western and resist the temptation to succumb to Communist influence. In 1949 the United Nations voted to award Italy trusteeship of Somaliland for ten years – in effect, a step towards eventual independence and a clear defeat for Sylvia. During the summer of 1950 a UN commission assessed opinion in Eritrea and concluded that it should become a separate state. However, in December, the General Assembly voted to institute a federation of Ethiopia and Eritrea which Sylvia treated as a victory; it led to an Ethiopian takeover in 1962 which eventually broke down. Finally, in 1955 the British and Italian parts of Somaliland were united with one another. In the face of all the evidence Sylvia never ceased to regard the failure to bring Ethiopia, Eritrea and Somaliland into a single state as 'one of the great injustices of history'.

Beyond the major political issues, however, she remained an indefatigable fund-raiser for Ethiopia in the post-war period. In particular she laboured to raise £100,000 for the hospital in Addis Ababa, founded in memory of Haile Selassie's daughter, which involved radio appeals, organizing bazaars and garden parties and obtaining the services of prominent actors and actresses including Dame Sybil Thorndike, Wendy Hiller and Donald Wolfit. She made the cause respectable by enlisting the Liberal peer, Lord Amulree, to act as chairman for the fund committee. Sylvia's propensity for spending money before it had been raised gave her colleagues many moments of alarm, but Amulree usually bailed them out in the end. Their efforts produced over £90,000 for the hospital.

To those who worked with her in this period Sylvia seemed a curious mixture: on the one hand domineering and ruthless, on the other charming and confused. Her neighbour in Woodford, Vera Klein, knew her as a mildly spoken little old lady who betrayed no trace of political extremism. But when at work she could be impatient and imperious; a telephone caller would be greeted with: 'Who is it? What do you want? Please be brief. I am a busy woman.'[2] But the strain often seemed too much for her; Lord Amulree remembered her arriving at meetings 'particularly untidy, wisps of hair floating, papers awry, flustered'.[3] A journalist who interviewed her, aged seventy, in 1952, felt she had an Edwardian look about her; her grey hair was scooped back, she wore an ancient black corded coat, no jewellery and no make-up, especially lipstick, of which she strongly disapproved.[4] Her household and work were supported by a surprisingly large staff, including one full-time and four part-time assistants, not to mention Corio and Richard and a 'daily' who usually did the cooking, though, as Sylvia said, 'food is not important to us'.[5]

Sylvia could not have maintained this organization from her modest earnings from journalism and book royalties. However, she received legacies from former suffragettes including Maud Joachim and Emmeline Pethick-Lawrence who left small annuities for both Sylvia and Richard on her death in 1954. Sylvia also admitted to having several thousand pounds from her American tours in 1910.[6] But much the largest element in her finances was the regular subsidy which she and one of her assistants, Mrs Ivy Tims, collected from the Ethiopian Embassy. According to Mrs Tims, this amounted to £1,000 a month for her personal and household expenses and another £1,000 to cover staff wages, publications and the costs of the *New Times*. At a time when £10 a week was a working man's wage this was clearly generous and may well have been an exaggeration. Yet on top of this Sylvia asked the Emperor for extra contributions for special purposes, though these were not always granted. As Mrs Tims discovered, Sylvia had still not learned to keep proper financial records or to spend money prudently.[7] The money also generated friction between Sylvia and Corio, who spent unwisely and asked her for further subsidies. Corio's position in the household remained an uncomfortable one in that, while he got on well with Richard, his relations with Sylvia became increasingly fraught. The many Ethiopian students who stayed at Charteris Road were puzzled by the domestic situation there and noticed that, although Corio was friendly towards them, he became rather subdued whenever Sylvia appeared; he often retreated to his room to read, leaving Sylvia as the dominant figure in the household.

To some extent Corio became less important to Sylvia as Richard took on a larger share of her work. Throughout the late 1940s and 1950s she waged war with assorted critics of Ethiopia, including her old adversary Margery Perham, whose 1948 book, *The Government of Ethiopia*, was subjected to reviews in two editions of the *New Times*. Like most academics writing on Asian and African countries, Perham almost inevitably offended nationalist opinion by presenting what it saw as a united movement as rather complex and fragmented. Without mentioning Sylvia, she emphasized her intention of correcting the distorted picture of Ethiopia recently circulated in Britain. Other western writers also dwelt heavily on the less attractive features of Ethiopia, notably its poverty, ill health, the lack of democracy and the bribery of the officials. John Gunther, author of *Inside Africa* in 1956, though by no means wholly hostile, offended Sylvia by ignoring her and praising Perham. Sylvia considered herself a leading expert on the country especially now that she had spent some time there, which Perham had not. But, as usual, she found it difficult to reach a balanced view of the subject. She emphasized that the constitution of 1955 granted a vote to all men and women, and that women were entitled to half their husband's property, which was not the case in Britain. But to portray Ethiopia as comparable to a western liberal system was scarcely credible as long as the Emperor appointed members of the upper house and retained effective power over finance. He wanted the system to appear as a constitutional monarchy and thus enjoy the approval of the West, while leaving imperial control substantially intact. Jointly with Richard, Sylvia published several works, *Ethiopia and Eritrea* (1952), an account of the 'reunion', and *Ethiopia: A Cultural History* (1955), which was dedicated to Haile Selassie and ran to over seven hundred pages. These unwieldy volumes were essentially a labour of love and suffered from insufficient editing. Despite her impressive knowledge of the subject, Sylvia had not managed to make the transition from propagandist to academic. She made her second visit to Ethiopia from October 1951 to May 1952 for the opening of the Princess Tsahai Hospital. Though pleased to find that the British had virtually withdrawn from the Ogaden, she continued to voice her hopes for the unification with Somaliland, infuriating the Italians and leading to the banning of both her book and the *New Times*, which had already been banned in British Somaliland.

Under the strain of her work Sylvia's health began to deteriorate during the 1950s. Hoping to forestall a complete nervous breakdown, she spent some weeks at the Royal Forest Hotel not far from her home, but kept up with her correspondence through Mrs Tims who visited her each day. But in April 1953 she suffered her first heart attack. As a result Richard took over some of her writing, and by May she was getting back to normal. Unhappily Sylvia suffered a fresh blow when Corio died, aged eighty, in January 1954. In a generous, if rather formal, tribute the *New Times* gave him full credit for spurring Sylvia to found the paper, and for his technical help in launching the paper by the time the Italians marched into Addis Ababa in 1935. Reports of Sylvia's reactions to his death vary. Some suggest she took it calmly, though this would certainly have been out of character; others suggest she wept for days afterwards, and it was thought that her second heart attack was caused by grief over Corio.[8] Later that year the passing of Mrs Pethick-Lawrence struck an even greater blow, for in some ways Emmeline had been a substitute mother for her. As with Corio, Sylvia paid full tributes to her in the *New Times*, even though Emmeline had not been much involved with Ethiopia. However, Sylvia's spirits were lifted by the visit of Haile Selassie to Britain in October 1954 when she attended the presentation of his honorary degree at Oxford, a banquet at the Guildhall given by the City of London Corporation, a luncheon at the Mansion House and a reception at the Ethiopian Embassy to thank the hospital committee for all its work. Coming after Corio's death, these celebrations doubtless suggested both to Sylvia and to Haile Selassie that a turning-point had been reached in her work for Ethiopia. A new ambassador showed greater reluctance to continue the subsidies on the same scale, understandably, for there was little now to be achieved in Britain. However, as it would have been ungracious after all her efforts to have withdrawn support too abruptly, Haile Selassie bided his time before offering a way out of the situation.

On America's west coast Christabel wisely showed no inclination to return home when the war came to an end. She would not have found post-war austerity and Socialism under the Attlee Government much to her liking. By this time the English colony in California included the actresses May Whitty and Mary Pickford with whom Christabel became acquainted. She also met Helen Craggs occasionally and kept in touch with Grace Roe, who lived at Santa Barbara further up the coast where she ran a bookshop and a metaphysical library. Though close to Christabel, whose executor she eventually became, Roe gave little away about this phase of her life, when interviewed many years later, beyond emphasizing that she had an enjoyable social life and was in great demand. Another ex-suffragette, Olive Bartels, described Roe as being silent about these years, and speculated that her reason might have been that Christabel had become eccentrically religious or 'batty'.[9] However, there is no corroboration for Bartels's view from the Americans who socialized with Christabel in Los Angeles, though they may have interpreted her eccentricities as quintessentially English.

Christabel's life during the late 1940s and 1950s seems to have centred around a succession of social and literary functions. She was an honoured guest at the large dinners organized by Mrs Eunice Griffiths for the 'John O' London Society', as well as at smaller parties she gave for members of the English colony. Christabel and her host, Mrs Shirley Jenny, participated in the functions of the Writers Round Table, which were organized by their close friend Miss Jaime Palmer. On Sunday afternoons Christabel was an essential ingredient in the gatherings of a world-affairs discussion group at which she, along with Mrs Jenny and the Vicomtesse Vivian de Berard-Alais, acted as hostess. On these occasions Christabel charmed everyone, but also impressed by the 'remarkable qualities of an English gentlewoman who had the very special talent of analytical thought expressed with crystal clarity'.[10] She was invariably asked to deliver the 'wind-up' talk at the end which she did brilliantly according to observers, though she had a habit of bringing everything round to the Second Coming and would 'start showing an increasing emotion'.[11] Then the guests departed to have tea and more lively discussion about the problems of the world. Douglas Field, who managed an outdoor concert area, the Hollywood Bowl, during the summertime and organized recitals by young artistes in the winter, regularly invited her to his events. She also attended musical evenings to hear Doris Székely sing, and in return got invitations for her to functions patronized by the British Consul in Los Angeles.[12] Christabel's friendship with Mrs Jenny was tragically ended when the two had a motoring accident when driving to Ojai in the hills about fifty miles north-west of Los Angeles. Mrs Jenny died as a result, while Christabel herself endured her injuries, including a broken hip and other fractures, philosophically. She told Doris Székely: 'You know, I am the one who should have died in this accident because I am not afraid of death. I believe in Heaven – but she was afraid.'[13] After this Christabel lived for a time with a Mr Bernard Hambledon, a composer, and his wife, who got on very well with her owing to her interest in astrology. But after their return to England she seems to have lived alone. Although Christabel enjoyed her life in Hollywood, she wanted to move to Santa Monica a few miles away on the coast. In 1951 Grace Roe, who now lived at Ventura further up the coast, found her an apartment in Ocean Avenue on the seafront at Santa

Monica where she was to spend the last seven years of her life. Roe sent her gardener and acquired some furniture for her as Christabel had not previously had to furnish her own home.[14]

Happily ensconced in Santa Monica, Christabel remained obdurate in her decision to put the past behind her, though she made an exception in 1948 by giving an address to commemorate the birth of the American suffragist leader Susan B. Anthony. But towards the end of 1956 Teresa Billington-Greig got short shrift when she wrote asking for information about Christabel's activities since the 1920s to help her with some lectures she was giving on the Pankhurst family. In a long and rather pompous reply Christabel offered no assistance and even tried to discourage her. Observing that men never wrote about their struggle for the vote, she loftily advised Billington-Greig to do something useful for women instead.[15] Her uncooperative response may have had something to do with the revival of interest in the history of women among writers and academics. News had reached America that Billington-Greig, an enemy of the Pankhursts in the 1907 split, had been assisting Roger Fulford to write his account of the women's suffrage campaign. Published in 1957 and widely read in Britain, *Votes for Women* did nothing to improve Christabel's state of mind. Though the book was narrative and anecdotal in character rather than analytical, it is not difficult to see why it offended Christabel and her loyal followers. Fulford treated Emmeline Pankhurst as *the* leader of the movement and made remarkably little reference to Christabel, implicitly casting her as a marginal figure rather than the directing brain she believed herself to be. It is possible that Fulford, appreciating her litigious bent, simply wanted to avoid offering her a target, for he included no footnotes and few quotations. In the same year the detested Ethel Smyth, who had died in 1944, reappeared to trouble her old age when Herbert Van Thal, who proposed to write her biography, injudiciously wrote to the *Sunday Times*, asking for material on the subject. Declaring herself shocked by Smyth's treatment of her mother in her own book, Christabel insisted she did not want any of her letters republished: 'I regret that I ever agreed to the publication of any of them.'[16] In an effort to discredit Smyth's own account in *Female Pipings in Eden*, she pointed out the first edition had been withdrawn and reissued because of the libellous and false material it contained. She also drew up a massive ten-page memorandum of errors still included in the book, including a defence of the expenditure of WSPU funds during the war. Speaking on behalf of 'the family' by which she presumably meant Emmeline's sister, Ada Goulden Bach, she tried to insist that the biography should deal with Smyth only as a composer, not as a suffragette, and that Emmeline should be entirely excluded from it.[17] She even wanted to know whether Mr Van Thal was a gentleman, what was his record and which political party he belonged to. But the pressure had its effect. Van Thal abandoned his book and the next biography of Dame Ethel by Christopher St John had to wait until 1959 – after Christabel's death. This incident was chiefly revealing of Christabel's state of mind towards the end of her life. Beneath her outward calm and self-control Christabel still seethed with resentment not just on her mother's behalf, but because she felt her own role had been misrepresented by Sylvia and other writers. Yet in spite of this she continued to allow her own manuscript to gather dust in a trunk in her apartment.

As Christabel was generally thought to be in good health, her death on 13 February 1958 came as a shock. She was reportedly discovered sitting upright in her chair in her flat, looking towards the sea. Although Grace Roe said later that she had been with her when she died, this does not appear to be the case as she was not found until the following day. The *Santa Monica Outlook* reported that no reason for death had been discovered, which may have started the unsubstantiated rumour that she had committed suicide.[18] Christabel was buried at the Woodlawn Cemetery, Santa Monica, and in Britain a memorial service took place at St Martin-in-the-Fields where Lord Pethick-Lawrence, now eighty-six, delivered a fitting tribute, more political than personal, which emphasized her brilliance as a tactician and her sacrifice for the cause: 'There are few people of whom it can be said that they changed the course of history and that they changed it for the better. But this can with confidence be said of Christabel Pankhurst. May her memory inspire us to lives of high and noble endeavour for the upliftment of mankind.'[19] The Suffragette Fellowship established a memorial committee, including Lady Astor, Vera Laughton-Matthews, Fred Pethick-Lawrence, Enid Goulden Bach, Grace Roe and Sybil Thorndike, which raised money to pay for additions to

Emmeline's statue and add a plaque to the Free Trade Hall in Manchester. A crowd of 250 people gathered on 13 July 1959 to hear Lord Kilmuir, the Lord Chancellor, unveil the memorial and hear the WRAF band play 'The March' once again.[20] Christabel had designated Grace Roe as her executor and it was she who discovered her unpublished account of the women's campaign, which she passed on to Fred Pethick-Lawrence. He did a little editing before arranging for it to be published as *Unshackled: The Story of How We Won the Vote*, in 1959. No one had so far written her biography, and remarkably no one was to attempt it for nearly twenty years.

Although the Pankhurst sisters shared Christabel's reservations about the suffragette books which had begun to emerge, they do not appear to have had any contact with one another during the last phase of their lives. Adela resisted the temptation to give public voice to her feelings about the dropping of the atomic bomb on Japan, the Communist takeover of China and the Korean War about which she presumably felt strongly. Having dropped out of politics in 1943, she found it easier to cultivate her earlier connections with former suffragettes, a number of whom had arrived in Australia by this time. Helen Fraser, who had known Adela well in her capacity as Scottish organizer for the WSPU, had stood three times for Parliament in the 1920s, become Mrs Moyes, and eventually emigrated in 1939. They had a good deal in common, for Helen had resigned in opposition to stone-throwing, and she lost no time in contacting Adela on arrival in Sydney.[21] Another Scottish friend, Helen Archdale, remained active in the women's movement as editor of *Time and Tide* from 1922 to 1926, as international secretary of the Six Point Group to 1933 and as a member of the Open Door Council. After the Second World War she spent two years in Australia visiting her daughter, Betty, to whom Adela had been a nanny, who had become Principal of the Women's College in the University of Sydney. Edith How Martyn, who had been one of the first to break with Christabel in 1907, had also stood for Parliament after 1918 and emerged as the first woman leader of Middlesex County Council in the 1920s. In 1939 she and her husband emigrated to Australia where she continued her work for the Suffragette Fellowship by founding a branch which attracted a hundred members. In July 1948 Mrs How Martyn invited Adela and other suffragists to a tea party to mark the ninetieth anniversary of the birth of Mrs Pankhurst. After listening to a succession of speeches in praise of Emmeline in which no one delved into old controversies, Adela moved a vote of thanks, repeating what she had already said in print: 'I suppose my mother belonged more to the world than to her family.' She enjoyed the occasion enough to take part in a 'Prisoners' Day' in October that year to celebrate the arrest of Edith and herself in 1906. As all the women were now elderly it proved impossible to maintain such meetings, though Adela kept in touch with Helen Moyes until her own death. Helen Archdale returned to England and died in 1950, and Mrs How Martyn, whose health was already poor, died in 1954. But much the worst tragedy to face Adela was the death of her own daughter Sylvia, who had contracted tuberculosis in New Guinea, in her mid-twenties. After this she 'just put the shutters down' according to her grand-daughter.[22]

Adela herself suffered from a heart condition and eventually gave up her work in the hospital for retarded children. Her declining years were spent living with her daughters Christian and Nancy (Ursula). Though as undomesticated as ever, she clearly played a key part in Christian's household by looking after the children. Her granddaughter, Sue, recalled that Adela would go to infinite trouble to please children; she was on their wavelength, took them seriously, and always believed what they told her.[23] In the mornings her grandchildren would take advantage by jumping into bed with her, keen to hear one of her stories in which they themselves were allowed to suggest the main ingredients. Otherwise Adela occupied her time with voluminous reading and chain-smoking, in the process filling soup bowls with her ash. The children watched in fascination as she inexpertly rolled her own cigarettes, waiting for them to flare up alarmingly when set alight. They also delighted in her favourite diet – sugar sandwiches and tea. In complete contrast to Christabel, Adela remained to the end of her life quite indifferent to her appearance, though she was relaxed about taking advice from friends and family. When they took her out to buy a new dress to celebrate Sue's birthday, they found that Adela had no idea what size she required or what suited her.[24] Not that any of this mattered. Her needs were simple, fortunately, because she had nothing to live on except her old age pension. Although the Australian

Government had established a commission to consider the wartime internments, its report in 1946 offered no compensation to Adela. Eventually her heart condition worsened so much that, in May 1961, she entered a nursing home at Wahroonga where, after ten days, she died from a coronary arrest on the twenty-third, aged seventy-five. After a Requiem Mass at St Patrick's Church – she had been received into the Roman Catholic Church shortly before her death – she was buried next to Tom in the Northern Suburbs Cemetery. In its obituary the London *Times* did full justice to her career as a leading suffragette and rebel. Despite this, Adela died the least known of the Pankhursts, but perhaps the best-loved member of the family.

For Sylvia, by contrast, old age brought no perceptible relaxation of her public work. In July 1956, at the age of seventy-four, she and Richard left for Ethiopia where she was to spend the remainder of her life. Corio's death may have had something to do with this, for Charteris Road could never be the same without him.[25] On reaching old age most people feel inclined to go home, but Sylvia lacked any strong sense of home or place – the pull was always her work. She remained too absorbed with her writing about Ethiopia to pine for England. In any case, by the 1950s she had become an increasingly marginal figure, even on the left, in British politics. Nor was there much she could do to promote the Ethiopian cause in Britain now that the British had vacated the Ogaden and the territorial settlement of the Horn of Africa had been accomplished, a consideration which may have prompted the Emperor to make his invitation to her. In any case, like most survivors from the Edwardian period, Sylvia felt uncomfortable in 1950s Britain, even if less alienated than Christabel. 'I am a little disappointed with what women have done with the vote,' she told one reporter. 'Women's great work today is peace. And they are not doing it.' She also complained about the importation of American culture into Britain, especially in the shape of deplorable popular films and the crime she thought they caused. When Richard was younger she had often found herself leaving the cinema early to avoid 'those insipid blondes and all those people being murdered'.[26]

Thus, after twenty years, the *New Times* printed its last edition on 5 May 1956, though its place was to be taken by a new monthly, the *Ethiopian Observer*. During the 1950s the political content of the paper had already diminished in favour of articles on the economy, culture, history and even wild life of Ethiopia. By dwelling on economic development Sylvia clearly intended to promote the country to the rest of the world. Richard assisted her in this. Having gained his PhD at the London School of Economics, he succeeded in obtaining an appointment as lecturer at the University College of Addis Ababa and later became Director of the Institute of Ethiopian Studies. Sylvia sold West Dene shortly before leaving, taking her white Persian cat with her but not much else. Apart from two drawings of Keir Hardie, which were presented to the National Gallery, the rest of the contents of the house went up for auction, purchased out of curiosity by the residents of Woodford Green.

Haile Selassie's invitation to Sylvia had included not just a grace-and-favour residence, but two maids, a gardener, a cook who spoke French, and a chauffeur who spoke Italian. As she did not speak the local language, Amharic, Sylvia had little communication with the servants; but as long as the household ran efficiently it did not greatly interest her. She adapted easily to life in Ethiopia: 'It is like a perpetual English summer', she wrote. She lived in a slightly dilapidated Italian-built bungalow with a big veranda in which much of her work was done. Her own room was spartan, embellished only by a portrait of her father hanging over the bed. All around stretched a large and unfenced garden filled with lemon, orange and eucalyptus trees. With her nearly white hair and her white cotton dress, Sylvia became a familiar figure as she drove round Addis Ababa, sometimes heading for the palace. She enjoyed long drives in the countryside where she would sit silently observing the valleys and mountains whose wild beauty almost inspired her to resume painting after an interval of fifty years; but she decided she was too busy.[27]

The household in Addis Ababa was still not quite complete. A year before leaving England Richard, whom one acquaintance described as 'a nice gentle person with a rather high voice and a self-effacing personality', had met Rita Eldon when they both taught evening classes at Toynbee Hall and in the Extra-Mural Department of London University. Her family had emigrated from Romania some years earlier. Rita joined him in Ethiopia in November 1956 and they were married there the following September.[28] The conjunction of work and domestic life in the household might have made for friction between the two women, but in fact things seem to have passed off smoothly, largely because Sylvia was totally focussed on her work and Rita did nothing to threaten that; she worked as a librarian and also managed the household which Sylvia had no desire to control. Though not especially motherly, Sylvia simply accepted Rita as part of the household; in the same way her relationship with Richard was more akin to that of a collaborator than a conventional mother.[29] As a family, their absorption in research and writing left little time for a social life, so much so that Saturdays, Sundays and holidays followed much the same pattern as weekdays. After breakfast Richard and Rita would usually go off to the National Library, returning for lunch in the garden, and again for the evening meal after which the household dispersed to do more work.[30] Throughout the day and often late into the night Sylvia laboriously drafted material for the *Ethiopian Observer* in longhand; her work was her only relaxation, though she did read and write poetry and contemplated a book about her father. She and Richard functioned as a team to produce the paper, driven by the monthly cycle it imposed on their lives. Once the copy for the next edition had gone to England they could relax a little, but on the arrival of the proofs the pressure mounted again.

Despite suffering heart attacks in England, Sylvia continued to be very active in her last four years, though troubled by her digestion, probably as a result of her prolonged hunger strikes before 1914. She coped best with eggs and milk puddings. On one occasion when Richard and Rita suggested that an eight-hour drive in a bumpy Land Rover would not be a good idea, she merely replied, 'Do you think I have come to the end of my active life?'[31] Not content with presenting Ethiopia to the outside world, Sylvia threw herself into an unofficial programme of internal improvement that involved visits of inspection, often at short notice. Her style had not changed over the years. On one occasion she rang up the Governor of the Ogaden, whom she did not know, and plunged abruptly into business: 'I am Miss Pankhurst. I want to see the Ogaden again. Tell me what there is new to see there.'[32] She took a hand in innumerable innovations including a blood donor service, a centre for the manufacture of artificial limbs, a maternity wing for the hospital, a centre to rehabilitate the mentally ill and the first employment exchanges in the country. However, Rita put Sylvia's position in Ethiopia into perspective by pointing out that her personal relationship with the Emperor had been exaggerated. Though she had audiences and sometimes sought his help for individuals, theirs was not a real friendship. Though greatly respected in Ethiopia, Sylvia did not have influence; her chief role lay in cultivating the image of the country abroad.[33] She was also untiring in offering assistance to Ethiopian students going to Britain and to anyone in difficulty. Orphans would turn up on her doorstep to be found clothes and schooling, and she was known to stop her car on the street, on seeing crippled children, and carry them off to hospital for an operation. It was as though, knowing that she could not have many years left, Sylvia had determined to follow her father's injunction by cramming the last moments of her life with useful causes for the benefit of others.

Thus the explanation for the happiness of the last four years of Sylvia's life is not hard to find. Like her mother, she could not endure a purely domestic life for long, but Ethiopia supplied the necessary sense of purpose admirably. It is no exaggeration to see Ethiopia as by far her most satisfying cause. The women's suffrage campaign had been a very mixed triumph, partly because it had exacerbated relations with Emmeline and Christabel, and also because of the limited nature of the success achieved in 1918. Sylvia herself had clearly drifted away from the women's movement by the early 1920s and resigned herself to the fact that any improvements resulting from the vote would be very gradual. She considered her role in the emergence of the Communist Party after the war as less than a success, so much so that she actually tried to suppress that phase of her career. After her death Richard corrected the *Times* obituary on his mother by insisting that she had never been a member of the Party and thus could not have been expelled from it.[34] But Ethiopia had been different. It was very much *her* cause and the victory had been complete, or very nearly so, by 1945. This is certainly how Sylvia herself saw it from the perspective of the later 1950s.[35]

Despite her age and health problems Sylvia must have seemed indestructible as she battled on through the late 1950s, working as long a day as she had done in her youth. It was on 27 September 1960

that Richard and Rita returned home from a long drive to find the
cook waiting for them at the top of the drive with the news that she
had died in their absence. She was seventy-eight and still in the midst
of fund-raising for the maternity wing of the hospital in Addis Ababa.
Her friends in Britain decided to make this her memorial at a meeting
in December led by Clement Davies MP, Lord Amulree, Lord Pethick-
Lawrence, Eirene White MP and the Ethiopian Ambassador.[36] In
Britain and the United States the newspapers recorded Sylvia's passing
with dutiful tributes, and a memorial service took place at Caxton
Hall, the scene of many suffragette demonstrations. But in Addis
Ababa Sylvia's passing was an event of national importance. Her
funeral on 28 September at the Holy Trinity Cathedral attracted 3,000
mourners and thousands of others who lined the streets. Not only
Haile Selassie and the imperial family, but the entire cabinet and the
diplomatic corps turned out for the occasion. Since the Ethiopian
Church did not recognize the name 'Sylvia', she was posthumously
awarded an appropriate one – Walata Kristos, meaning 'Daughter of
Christ'. The Minister of the Interior, His Excellency Ras Andargue
Massai, delivered a moving funeral oration:

As we have walked this last mile of the road with her in an attempt to pay our
respects as relatives and friends, we cannot but recall the life she lived and the
blessing that her sojourn here with us has meant to so many ... The noble
deeds of this great woman are so many and so varied that it is impossible to
recount them. It is enough to say that she worked and died fighting for peace,
happiness, fair-play and humanity for others. Could any life have been better
lived? ... As it is His Imperial Majesty's good pleasure that you rest in peace
on Ethiopian soil may God take note of all the good deeds you have done on
earth and grant you a place of Honour in heaven.[37]

The coffin, draped in gold cloth and surrounded by a vivid host of
Coptic priests, was carried by the Imperial Guard to be buried in
ground reserved for Ethiopia's patriots. It was inevitably an occasion
full of paradox. The Emperor himself led the mourners by laying a
wreath on the grave of the staunch Republican. Sylvia's life, lived as
an agnostic, culminated in a burial conducted according to the rites of
the Church. With this exotic ceremony in the invigorating air of Addis

Ababa, scented with the eucalyptus of which she had become so fond, Sylvia had travelled a long way from late-Victorian Manchester. But, as she would doubtless have insisted, to the end she had remained in all fundamentals as close as ever to the ideals and values of her beloved father.

Sources

Papers of Individuals

Janie Allan Papers, National Library of Scotland
Maud Arncliffe-Sennett Papers, British Library
A. J. Balfour Papers, British Library
Eveline Bennett Correspondence, in the author's possession
Teresa Billington-Greig Papers, Fawcett Library
Mary Blathwayt Diaries, Dyrham Park
Helen Craggs ms., Fawcett Library
Helen Crawfurd ms., Marx Memorial Library
Master of Elibank, Elibank Papers, National Library of Scotland
Ada Flatman Papers, Museum of London
Millicent Garrett Fawcett Papers, Manchester Central Library and Fawcett
   Library
David Lloyd George Papers, House of Lords Record Office
John Bruce Glasier Diary, Sydney Jones Library, Liverpool University
Patrick Hannon Papers, House of Lords Record Office
Henry Harben Papers, British Library
Vera Holme Papers, in the possession of John D. Holme
Jessie Kenney ms., Fawcett Library
Andrew Bonar Law Papers, House of Lords Record Office
E. Katherine Marshall ms., Museum of London
David Mitchell Papers, Museum of London
Hannah Mitchell Papers, Manchester Central Library
Roland Muirhead Papers, Mitchell Library Glasgow, and National Library
   of Scotland
Henry Nevinson Diary, Bodleian Library, Oxford
E. Sylvia Pankhurst Papers, International Institute for Social History,
   Amsterdam
Pankhurst-Walsh Papers, National Library of Australia, Canberra

Mary Phillips Papers, Camellia plc
C. P. Scott Papers (*Manchester Guardian*), John Rylands Library
Ethel Smyth Papers, Dr Piers Brendon Notes

Brian Harrison tapes: recorded interviews, Fawcett Library

Annie Barnes; Olive Bartels; Fiona Billington-Greig; Mrs Blackman; George Dugdale; Mrs Lyndal Evans; Helen Fraser (Moyes); Sue Hogan; Marie Lawson; Rita Pankhurst; Lady Ricardo; Grace Roe; Jessie Stephen

Papers of Organizations and Institutions

Chorlton Union Manual, Manchester Central Library
Communist Party of Great Britain, Unity Convention, Marx Memorial Library
Fawcett Library Autograph Collection
Glasgow and West of Scotland Association for Women's Suffrage
ILP Annual Conference Reports
Labour Party Archives
Labour Representation Committee Annual Reports
Manchester League for Opposing Women's Suffrage Papers
Manchester Men's League for Women's Suffrage Papers
Manchester Society for Women's Suffrage Papers
National Liberal Federation Annual Reports
National Union of Women's Suffrage Society Papers
North of England Society for Women's Suffrage Reports
PRO (Public Record Office, Kew) – CAB, HO, MEPOL, PCOM, TS
Scottish Prison Commission Papers
Scottish Women's Liberal Federation Papers
Suffrage Fellowship Collection
Women's Franchise League Papers
Women's Freedom League (WFL) papers
Women's Liberal Federation Papers
Women's Social and Political Union (WSPU) – Annual Reports, Cash Statements, Self-Denial Week Reports, Pamphlets

Journals and Newspapers

Anti-Suffrage Review
Britannia
Cambrian Daily Leader
Church of Ireland Gazette
Clarion
Common Cause
Communist International
Conservative and Unionist Women's
 Franchise Review
Contemporary Review
Daily Chronicle
Daily Citizen
Daily Herald
Daily Mail
Daily Mirror
Daily Sketch
Dundee Advertiser
Dundee Courier
East London Observer
Ethiopian Observer
Evening Standard
Fortnightly Review
Glasgow Herald
Globe
Gorton and Openshaw Reporter
Hansard
Huddersfield Daily Examiner
ILP News
The Labour Leader
Labour Record
Macmillan's Magazine
Manchester City News
Manchester Examiner and Times
Manchester Guardian

Morning Advertiser
National Review
New Times and Ethiopia News
New York Herald Tribune
New York Times
Newcastle Evening Chronicle
News of the World
The Nineteenth Century
Santa Monica Outlook
Saturday Review
The Scotsman
Smethwick Telephone
South London Press
South Wales Daily News
The Star
The Suffragette
Sunday Express
Sunday Telegraph
The Sunday Times
Sydney Morning Herald
The Times
Toronto Daily Star
Toronto Globe and Mail
Toronto Star Weekly
Victoria Colonist
Victoria Times
Votes for Women
Weekly Dispatch
Western Daily Mercury
Westminster Review
Woman's Dreadnought
Women's Franchise
Women's Suffrage Journal
Workers' Dreadnought

Pankhurst publications

Christabel Pankhurst, *The Great Scourge – And How To End It* (1913)
— *The Lord Cometh: The World Crisis Explained* (1923)
— *Pressing Problems of a Closing Age* (1924)
— *The World's Unrest: Visions of the Dawn* (1926)
— *The Uncurtained Future* (1940)
— *Unshackled: The Story of How We Won the Vote* (1959)
Emmeline Pankhurst, *My Own Story* (1914)
E. Sylvia Pankhurst, *The Suffragette* (1911)
— *Soviet Russia As I Saw It* (1921)
— *Save the Mothers* (1930)
— *The Suffragette Movement* (1931)
— *The Home Front* (1932)
— *The Life of Emmeline Pankhurst* (1935)
Richard Pankhurst, 'The Right of Women to Vote Under the Reform Act, 1867', *Fortnightly Review*, IV, 1868

Notes

1 Radical Manchester (1858–78)

1. Winston Churchill to the President of the North West Manchester Liberal Association, 18 April 1904.
2. See the vivid description in Chapter 2 of Asa Briggs, *Victorian Cities* (1963).
3. The phrase 'The Manchester School' was coined by Disraeli in a speech on 27 February 1846.
4. The Great Reform Act of 1832 introduced the vote for all owners and occupiers of property worth £10 per annum, but left the complex range of traditional qualifications in place. Even so, the total electorate numbered only 717,000, approximately one in five adult males. The Act had specified 'male persons' for the first time.
5. See E. Sylvia Pankhurst, *The Suffragette Movement* (1931) and *The Life of Emmeline Pankhurst* (1935), and Christabel Pankhurst, *Unshackled: The Story of How We Won the Vote* (1959).
6. In E. Sylvia Pankhurst Papers.
7. Richard Pankhurst, *E. Sylvia Pankhurst* (1979).
8. Rebecca West, 'A Reed of Steel', p. 248, in Jane Marcus, ed., *Rebecca West, 1982* (first published in *The Post-Victorians* (1933) – her essay on Emmeline whom she knew in the WSPU.
9. Adela Pankhurst, 'Philosophy of the Suffragette Movement', p. 6, Pankhurst-Walsh Papers, 22/66.
10. According to E. Sylvia Pankhurst, *The Life of Emmeline Pankhurst*, p. 7.
11. See Olive Banks, *Becoming A Feminist: the Social Origins of First Wave Feminism* (1986), pp. 26–9.
12. E. Sylvia Pankhurst, *The Life of Emmeline Pankhurst*, pp. 9–10. Lydia Becker (1827–90) also came from Manchester. She served as honorary secretary of the Manchester Committee for Women's Suffrage in 1867 and remained a key figure in the non-militant movement, especially as editor of the *Women's Suffrage Journal* from 1870 to 1890.

13. Grace Roe, interview with Brian Harrison, 4 October 1974.
14. E. Sylvia Pankhurst, *The Suffragette Movement*, p. 55.
15. Ibid.
16. West, 'Reed of Steel,' p. 248, in Jane Marcus, ed., *Rebecca West*.
17. E. Sylvia Pankhurst, *The Life of Emmeline Pankhurst*, p. 13; Adela Pankhurst, 'My Mother: An Explanation and a Vindication', 24 January 1933, p. 5, Pankhurst-Walsh Papers, 16/50.

2 'Every Struggling Cause' (1879–84)

1. Surviving evidence of Richard's early life is limited. The best source is the E. Sylvia Pankhurst Papers; see also Andrew Rosen in *The Biographical Dictionary of Modern British Radicals*, edited by J. O. Baylen, and Olive Banks and J. O. Baylen, *Biographical Dictionary of British Feminists*.
2. Richard Pankhurst, 'The Right of Women to Vote Under the Reform Act, 1867', *Fortnightly Review*, IV, 1868. The early suffragists pointed to legislation introduced by Lord Brougham in 1850 and by Lord Romilly in 1854 which established that acts purporting the masculine gender should be deemed to include females unless the contrary was explicitly stated.
3. *Manchester Guardian*, 24 May 1873.
4. *Manchester Examiner and Times*, January 1874, cuttings collection in E. Sylvia Pankhurst Papers, 33/329.
5. E. Sylvia Pankhurst, *The Suffragette Movement*, p. 55.
6. Christabel Pankhurst, *Unshackled*, p. 21.
7. Ibid, p. 22.
8. E. Sylvia Pankhurst, *The Suffragette Movement*, p. 57.
9. Ibid.
10. Adela Pankhurst, 'My Mother', Pankhurst-Walsh Papers, p. 7.
11. *Manchester Guardian*, 24 and 27 September, 1883.
12. E. Sylvia Pankhurst, *The Life of Emmeline Pankhurst*, p. 19.
13. *Manchester Guardian*, 5 October 1883.

3 Upwardly Mobile (1885–92)

1. West, 'Reed of Steel', p. 248, in *Rebecca West*, edited by Jane Marcus; Adela Pankhurst, 'My Mother', Pankhurst-Walsh Papers, p. 5.
2. Adela Pankhurst, 'My Mother', Pankhurst-Walsh Papers, p. 4.

3. Verna Coleman, *Adela*, p. 12.

4. E. Sylvia Pankhurst, *The Suffragette Movement*, p. 108.

5. Adela Pankhurst, 'My Mother', Pankhurst-Walsh Papers, p. 4.

6. E. Sylvia Pankhurst, *The Suffragette Movement*, p. 4; Verna Coleman, *Adela*, p. 15.

7. E. Sylvia Pankhurst, *The Suffragette Movement*, p. 99.

8. Ibid, p. 136.

9. Mrs Nellie Hall-Humpherson to David Mitchell, 12 June 1964, David Mitchell Papers, 73.83/36.

10. E. Sylvia Pankhurst, *The Suffragette Movement*, pp. 109–10.

11. Verna Coleman, *Adela*, pp. 15, 17; Adela Pankhurst, 'My Mother', Pankhurst-Walsh Papers, p. 31.

12. Emmeline Pankhurst to Miss Briggs, August 1885 and to Florence Balgarnie, 17 September 1885, E. Sylvia Pankhurst Papers, 33/348.

13. *South London Press*, 31 October 1885.

14. *South London Press*, 14 November 1885.

15. *South London Press*, 28 November 1885.

16. E. Sylvia Pankhurst, *The Suffragette Movement*, pp. 74–6.

17. This is borne out by the record of Rotherhithe in returning Conservative members at each election from 1885 to 1900.

18. See E. Sylvia Pankhurst Papers, 33/348–51.

19. E. Sylvia Pankhurst, *The Suffragette Movement*, p. 22.

20. Christabel Pankhurst, *Unshackled*, p. 25.

21. E. Sylvia Pankhurst, *The Suffragette Movement*, p. 84.

22. Ibid, p. 88; Verna Coleman, *Adela*, p. 8.

23. E. Sylvia Pankhurst, *The Suffragette Movement*, p. 103.

24. Christabel Pankhurst, *Unshackled*, p. 30.

25. West, 'Reed of Steel', p. 248, in Jane Marcus, ed., *Rebecca West*.

26. E. Sylvia Pankhurst, *The Suffragette Movement*, p. 97.

27. Ibid, pp. 90, 111.

28. *Annual Report*, Women's Liberal Federation, 1892.

29. *Hansard*, House of Commons Debates, 3rd Series, CCXXIII, 7 April 1875, c.449.

30. The Women's Franchise League left few papers; some are in the E. Sylvia Pankhurst Papers, 33/329; see also the discussion in Sandra Stanley Holton, *Suffrage Days* (1996), pp. 76–82.

31. Sir Charles Dilke (1843–1911), a Radical and enthusiast for empire, had been President of the Local Government Board under Gladstone and was widely regarded as a future Liberal Leader, but was ruined when cited in a

divorce case involving Mrs Donald Crawford in 1885–6; he lost his seat in 1886, but returned as member for the Forest of Dean.
32. E. Sylvia Pankhurst, *The Suffragette Movement*, p. 97.

4 The Making of a Political Leader (1893–8)

1. See Sylvia's report in E. Sylvia Pankhurst Papers, 1/1–6.
2. E. Sylvia Pankhurst, *The Suffragette Movement*, p. 124.
3. Ibid, p. 121.
4. Ibid, p. 124.
5. Ibid, p. 120.
6. Verna Coleman, *Adela*, p. 20; Adela Pankhurst, 'My Mother', Pankhurst-Walsh Papers, pp. 15, 23–4.
7. E. Sylvia Pankhurst, *The Suffragette Movement*, p. 126.
8. The Address is in E. Sylvia Pankhurst Papers, 33/347.
9. Beatrice Webb (1858–1943) joined the signatories to an anti-suffrage petition launched by the novelist Mrs Humphry Ward and published in *The Nineteenth Century*, largely because she felt no personal disadvantage as a woman; by 1906 she had changed her view.
10. *Gorton and Openshaw Reporter*, 24 November 1894.
11. *Manchester City News*, 10 November 1894.
12. *Chorlton Union Manual*, 1895–6.
13. E. Sylvia Pankhurst, *The Life of Emmeline Pankhurst*, p. 37.
14. *Gorton and Openshaw Reporter*, 22 December 1894.
15. *Manchester City News*, 21 December 1895; E. Sylvia Pankhurst, *The Life of Emmeline Pankhurst*, pp. 36–7.
16. Miss Enid Goulden Bach, 'Aunt Emmeline', press cutting, 7 July 1958, David Mitchell Papers.
17. *Manchester City News*, 31 August 1895.
18. *Manchester City News*, 21 September 1895.
19. *Manchester City News*, 26 January 1895.
20. *Manchester City News*, 9 February 1895.
21. *Manchester City News*, 9 March 1895.
22. Ibid.
23. Henry Pelling, *A Social Geography of British Elections 1885–1910*, p. 246.
24. *Gorton and Openshaw Reporter*, 6 July 1895.
25. *Gorton and Openshaw Reporter*, 13 July 1895.
26. E. Sylvia Pankhurst, *The Suffragette Movement*, p. 136.

27. John Bruce Glasier Diary, 21 June 1896.

28. Ibid, 3 July 1896.

29. Ibid, 12 July 1896.

30. K. O. Morgan, *Keir Hardie*, p. 96.

31. *Hansard*, House of Commons Debates, 4th Series, XLI, 22 June 1896, c.1967–8; XLII, 2 July 1896, c.535.

32. John Bruce Glasier Diary, 24 October 1896.

33. Ibid, 30 November 1896.

34. E. Sylvia Pankhurst, *The Suffragette Movement*, pp. 144–5.

35. Verna Coleman, *Adela*, p. 21.

36. E. Sylvia Pankhurst, *The Suffragette Movement*, p. 165.

37. Ibid, p. 123.

38. Christabel Pankhurst, *Unshackled*, p. 35.

39. Ibid.

40. John Bruce Glasier Diary, 17 July 1896.

5 The Emergence of Christabel (1898–1903)

1. *Toronto Daily Star*, 24 October 1921.

2. E. Sylvia Pankhurst, *The Suffragette Movement*, p. 152; Adela Pankhurst, 'My Mother', p. 25, and 'Philosophy of the Suffragette Movement', p. 16, Pankhurst-Walsh Papers.

3. For details of his share certificates, see E. Sylvia Pankhurst Papers, 3/329.

4. Today it is preserved as the Pankhurst Centre by the Pankhurst Society.

5. Adela Pankhurst, 'My Mother', Pankhurst-Walsh Papers, p. 24.

6. E. Sylvia Pankhurst, *The Suffragette Movement*, p. 154.

7. Adela Pankhurst, 'My Mother', Pankhurst-Walsh Papers, p. 27; Verna Coleman, *Adela*, pp. 25–7.

8. Teresa Billington-Greig, 'Autobiographical Fragments', n.d., Billington-Greig Papers, 397 A/6.

9. E. Sylvia Pankhurst, *The Suffragette Movement*, p. 158.

10. ILP Annual Conference Report (1901).

11. Christabel Pankhurst, *Unshackled*, p. 37; E. Sylvia Pankhurst, *The Suffragette Movement*, p. 147.

12. Adela Pankhurst, 'Philosophy of the Suffragette Movement', Pankhurst-Walsh Papers, p. 17.

13. Gifford Lewis, *Eva Gore-Booth and Esther Roper: A Biography* (1988); Adela Pankhurst, 'Philosophy of the Suffragette Movement', Pankhurst-Walsh Papers, p. 17.

14. Gifford Lewis, *Eva Gore-Booth and Esther Roper: A Biography* (1988), p. 89.

15. E. Sylvia Pankhurst, *The Suffragette Movement*, pp. 164–5.

16. Gifford Lewis, *Eva Gore-Booth and Esther Roper: A Biography* (1988), pp. 6–8.

17. Helena Swanwick, *I Have Been Young* (1935), p. 188.

18. E. Sylvia Pankhurst, *The Life of Emmeline Pankhurst*, p. 47.

19. Gifford Lewis, *Eva Gore-Booth and Esther Roper: A Biography* (1988), p. 9.

20. *Weekly Dispatch*, 3 April 1921.

21. In a comment by Olive Bartels, interview with Brian Harrison, 27 March 1976.

22. E. Sylvia Pankhurst, *The Suffragette Movement*, p. 160.

23. Five shillings and eleven pence is about thirty pence in today's terms; in 1903 these were expensive crackers.

6 'He Ought to be a Woman for a While' (1903–4)

1. Undated notes, Billington-Greig Papers, 397 A/6.

2. John Bruce Glasier Diary, 5 April 1901.

3. ILP Annual Conference Report, 1902, p. 27.

4. John Bruce Glasier Diary, 18 October 1902.

5. *Clarion*, 6 May 1904.

6. John Bruce Glasier Diary, 19 October 1902.

7. Ibid, 16 December 1906.

8. Roper in the North of England Society for Women's Suffrage Report, 1902, pp. 13–14.

9. Adela Pankhurst, 'The Story of My Life', pp. 3–4, 26/83, and 'My Mother', pp. 32–3, Pankhurst-Walsh Papers; Verna Coleman, *Adela*, p. 29.

10. *The Labour Leader*, 14 March 1903.

11. *The Labour Leader*, 30 May 1903.

12. *ILP News*, August 1903, p. 1.

13. E. Sylvia Pankhurst, *The Suffragette Movement*, pp. 164–5.

14. Adela Pankhurst, 'Philosophy of the Suffragette Movement', Pankhurst-Walsh Papers, p. 11.

15. John Bruce Glasier Diary, 3 October 1903.

16. E. Sylvia Pankhurst, *The Suffragette Movement*, pp. 168–70; Andrew Rosen, 'Rise Up Women', pp. 30–32.

17. See Mrs Nellie Hall-Humpherson to David Mitchell, 12 June 1964, David Mitchell Papers, 73.83/36.

18. The Men's Political Union was founded in 1909 as a militant organization for male suffragists. Forty men were imprisoned up to 1914. The key members were Lawrence Housman, Victor Duval, Charles Gray and Henry Nevinson.

19. Undated notes, Billington-Greig Papers, 397 A/6; Adela Pankhurst, 'My Mother', Pankhurst-Walsh Papers, p. 34.

20. Ibid.

21. Ibid.

22. E. Sylvia Pankhurst, *The Suffragette Movement*, pp. 177–8.

23. Ibid, pp. 187–8. Margaret Bondfield (1873–1953) left school at thirteen, rose to become Assistant Secretary of the National Union of Shop Assistants in 1898, was elected to parliament in 1923 and became the first female cabinet minister in the 1929–31 Labour Government.

24. ILP Annual Conference Report, 1904, p. 30.

25. John Bruce Glasier Diary, 13 May 1904.

26. See Caroline Benn, *Keir Hardie* (1997), pp. 4–12. James Keir Hardie (1856–1915) was born the illegitimate son of a Scottish farm servant in Lanarkshire, grew up in great poverty and worked underground from the age of ten. He became secretary of the Scottish Miners' Federation in 1886 and chairman of the Scottish Labour Party in 1887, and was first elected to parliament for South West Ham in 1892.

27. Undated notes, Billington-Greig Papers, 397 A/6.

28. Christabel Pankhurst, *Unshackled*, p. 44.

29. Undated notes, Billington-Greig Papers, 397 A/6.

30. *Manchester Guardian*, 20 February 1904.

31. Christabel Pankhurst, *Unshackled*, p. 46.

32. See David Mitchell, *Queen Christabel* (1977), pp. 55–6.

33. See the account in Richard Pankhurst, *E. Sylvia Pankhurst*, Chapter 4; and E. Sylvia Pankhurst, *The Suffragette Movement*, pp. 171–3.

34. E. Sylvia Pankhurst, *The Suffragette Movement*, p. 178.

35. Caroline Benn, *Keir Hardie*, p. 177.

36. Ibid, pp. 177–9.

37. E. Sylvia Pankhurst, *The Suffragette Movement*, p. 217.

38. Patricia Romero, *E. Sylvia Pankhurst*, p. 28.

7 Militancy Begins (1905–6)

1. E. Sylvia Pankhurst, *The Suffragette Movement*, p. 182.

2. See 5th Annual Report, Labour Representation Committee, 26 January 1905.

3. Emmeline Pankhurst to Dora Montefiore, 19 February 1905, in D. B. Montefiore, *From a Victorian to a Modern*, pp. 117–18.

4. E. Sylvia Pankhurst, *The Suffragette*, pp. 11–12.

5. Ibid, p. 15.

6. Accounts by Isabella Ford, *The Labour Leader*, 19 May 1906; and E. Sylvia Pankhurst, *The Suffragette*, pp. 16–17. New South Wales gave all women the vote in 1902, following South Australia (1894), West Australia (1896), and before Tasmania (1903), Queensland (1904) and Victoria (1908).

7. Annie Kenney, *Memories of a Militant* (1924), p. 30; E. Sylvia Pankhurst, *The Suffragette Movement*, pp. 19–20.

8. Annie Kenney, *Memories of a Militant*, p. 26.

9. Ethel Smyth, *Female Pipings in Eden*, p. 199.

10. Hannah Mitchell, manuscript autobiography, pp. 49–50.

11. The *Sunday Times*, 8 March 1908, quoted in Andrew Rosen, 'Rise Up Women', p. 49.

12. *Manchester Guardian*, 16 and 25 October 1905.

13. Christabel Pankhurst, *Unshackled*, p. 49.

14. *Manchester Guardian*, 16 October 1905.

15. Ibid.

16. Ibid.

17. Emmeline Pankhurst, *My Own Story* (1914), pp. 48–9.

18. Hannah Mitchell, autobiography, pp. 90–1.

19. Christabel Pankhurst, *Unshackled*, p. 50.

20. Ibid, p. 52.

21. *Manchester Guardian*, 16 October 1905.

22. Undated notes, Billington-Greig Papers, 397 A/6.

23. Gifford Lewis, *Eva Gore-Booth and Esther Roper*, pp. 112–13.

24. Eva and Esther to Millicent Fawcett, quoted in Gifford Lewis, *Eva Gore-Booth and Esther Roper*, p. 114.

25. E. Sylvia Pankhurst, *The Suffragette*, pp. 41–2.

26. Anon., *Ulula* (1906), p. 10.

27. Christabel Pankhurst, *Unshackled*, pp. 57–8.

28. Violet Bonham-Carter, *Winston Churchill as I Knew Him* (1965), p. 127.

29. Ibid, p. 129; E. Sylvia Pankhurst, *The Suffragette*, pp. 43–7.

30. Christabel Pankhurst, *Unshackled*, p. 61.

31. Piers Brendon in the *Sunday Telegraph*, 5 August 1979.

32. E. Sylvia Pankhurst, *The Suffragette*, p. 61.

33. PRO MEPOL 2/1016, 9 March 1906.

34. Gifford Lewis, *Eva Gore-Booth and Esther Roper*, p. 121.

35. Ibid, p. 116.

36. Ibid, pp. 124–5.
37. Christabel Pankhurst, 'Why We Protest At Cabinet Ministers' Meetings', not dated, WSPU.
38. PRO MEPOL 2/1016, 21 June 1906.
39. *Votes for Women*, 10 November 1907; *Daily Mirror*, 2 March 1907.
40. *Labour Record*, November 1906, p. 235.
41. Richard Pankhurst, *E. Sylvia Pankhurst* (1979), p. 60; Adela Pankhurst, 'My Mother', Pankhurst-Walsh Papers, 34.
42. Autobiographical Notes, E. Sylvia Pankhurst Papers, 1/7–15.
43. Caroline Benn, *Keir Hardie*, p. 223; Patricia Romero, *E. Sylvia Pankhurst*, p. 37.
44. Keir Hardie to E. Sylvia Pankhurst, 10 March 1911, E. Sylvia Pankhurst Papers, 1/7–15.
45. E. Sylvia Pankhurst to Keir Hardie, undated, *c*. 1906, E. Sylvia Pankhurst Papers, 1/7–15.
46. Andrew Rosen, 'Rise Up Women', pp. 69–71.
47. John Bruce Glasier Diary, 2 August 1906.
48. Ibid, 8 August 1906.
49. Christabel Pankhurst, *Unshackled*, pp. 68–9, 72; for a corrective see Martin Pugh, *The March of the Women*, pp. 231–47.
50. *Huddersfield Daily Examiner*, 21, 22, 23 and 29 November 1906.
51. E. Sylvia Pankhurst, *The Suffragette*, pp. 119–20.
52. Richard Pankhurst, *E. Sylvia Pankhurst*, p. 49.
53. Adela Pankhurst, 'The Story of My Life', Pankhurst-Walsh Papers, p. 5.

8 Democracy Versus Dictatorship (1907–8)

1. Emmeline Pethick-Lawrence, *My Part in a Changing World*, pp. 58, 67.
2. Teresa Billington-Greig to J. Kenney, not dated, Autograph Collection, XX; see also Grace Roe, interview with Brian Harrison, 23 September 1974.
3. Emmeline Pethick-Lawrence to Mary Phillips, 14 January 1908, Mary Phillips Papers.
4. Teresa Billington-Greig, 'Autobiographical Fragments', in Carol McPhee and Ann Fitzgerald, eds., *The Non-Violent Militant*, p. 105; Helen Fraser (Moyes), interview with Brian Harrison, 19 August 1975.
5. WSPU, Second Annual Report, 1908.
6. Undated notes, Teresa Billington-Greig Papers, 397 A/6.
7. Lady Rhondda, *This Was My World*, p. 161.
8. Lady Ricardo, interview with Brian Harrison, 29 November 1974.

9. Emmeline Pethick-Lawrence to Maud Arncliffe-Sennett, 11 July 1907, Maud Arncliffe-Sennett Papers.

10. Christopher St John, *Ethel Smyth*, p. 145.

11. Ethel Smyth, *Female Pipings in Eden*, p. 191.

12. See WSPU Annual Reports and Cash Statements, 1906–9.

13. Muriel Thompson, circular letter, 14 May 1908, Suffragette Fellowship Collection 50.82/1116.

14. Vera Louise Holme (1881–1969) was an accomplished violinist and sang in the chorus of the D'Oyly Carte Company; she joined the Actresses Franchise League in 1908. From 1911 she lived with Evelina Haverfield, and served in the Women's Volunteer Reserve and the Scottish Women's Hospital Transport Unit in the Balkans during the war.

15. Christabel Pankhurst, *Unshackled*, pp. 79–80.

16. E. Sylvia Pankhurst, *The Life of Emmeline Pankhurst*, p. 68; Rebecca West, 'A Reed of Steel', p. 257.

17. *Daily Chronicle*, 14 February 1907.

18. Caroline Benn, *Keir Hardie*, p. 223.

19. Christabel Pankhurst to Mary Phillips, 26 November 1909, Mary Phillips Papers.

20. E. Sylvia Pankhurst, *The Life of Emmeline Pankhurst*, p. 71.

21. Helen Fraser (Moyes), interview with Brian Harrison, 19 August 1975.

22. E. Sylvia Pankhurst, *The Suffragette Movement*, pp. 266–7.

23. Christabel Pankhurst to Mary Phillips, 12 November 1907, Mary Phillips Papers.

24. E. Sylvia Pankhurst, *The Suffragette Movement*, p. 154.

25. Undated notes, E. Sylvia Pankhurst Papers, 2/27.

26. Ibid; E. Sylvia Pankhurst, *The Suffragette Movement*, pp. 261–2.

27. E. Sylvia Pankhurst, *The Life of Emmeline Pankhurst*, p. 69.

28. *Daily Mirror*, 20 July 1907; *The Times*, 20 July 1907.

29. Undated notes, E. Sylvia Pankhurst Papers, 2/27.

30. E. Sylvia Pankhurst, *The Suffragette Movement*, pp. 269–70.

31. Undated notes, E. Sylvia Pankhurst Papers, 2/27.

32. Ibid

33. E. Sylvia Pankhurst, *The Suffragette Movement*, p. 272.

34. Ibid.

35. Grace Roe, interview with Brian Harrison, 23 September 1974.

36. E. Sylvia Pankhurst, *The Suffragette Movement*, p. 273.

37. Christabel Pankhurst to Henry Harben, 1 August 1913, Henry Harben Papers, Add. Mss 58226.

38. ILP, Annual Conference Report, 1907, p. 48.

39. Emmeline Pankhurst to E. Sylvia Pankhurst, 23 June 1907, E. Sylvia Pankhurst Papers, 23/193; E. Sylvia Pankhurst, *The Suffragette Movement*, p. 263.

40. Teresa Billington-Greig, 'The Militant Suffrage Movement', in Carol McPhee and Ann Fitzgerald, eds., *Non-Violent Militant*, p. 82.

41. Emmeline Pethick-Lawerence, *My Part in a Changing World*, pp. 175–6.

42. E. Sylvia Pankhurst, *The Suffragette Movement*, p. 264.

43. Teresa Billington-Greig, 'Autobiographical Fragments' and 'The Militant Suffrage Movement' in Carol McPhee and Ann Fitzgerald, *Non-Violent Militant*, pp. 106, 168; Emmeline Pankhurst, *My Own Story*, p. 59.

44. Emmeline Pankhurst to Mary Phillips, 21 September 1907, Mary Phillips Papers.

45. Claire Eustance, 'Daring to be free: the evolution of women's political identities in the Women's Freedom League, 1907–1930', Ph.D. thesis, York University, 1993, p. 54.

46. Cicely Hamilton, *Life Errant*, p. 68; see also comments in Helena Swanwick, *I Have Been Young*, p. 188, and Mary Stocks, *My Commonplace Book*, p. 70.

47. *Votes for Women*, 26 March, 30 April, 7 and 14 May 1909.

48. Christabel Pankhurst to A. J. Balfour, 6 October 1907, A. J. Balfour Papers, Add. Mss 49793.

49. A. J. Balfour to Christabel Pankhurst (copy), 23 October 1907, A. J. Balfour Papers, Add. Mss 49793.

50. Quoted in *Votes for Women*, January 1908, p. 59.

51. E. Sylvia Pankhurst, *The Suffragette*, pp. 185–7.

52. *Votes for Women*, March 1908, p. 85.

53. Antonia Raeburn, *The Militant Suffragettes* (1973), p. 50.

54. See WSPU Self-Denial Week Report, 1908.

55. E. Sylvia Pankhurst, *The Suffragette*, p. 210.

56. House of Commons Debates, 28 Febuary 1908, c.244.

9 Methods of Barbarism (1908–9)

1. *Women's Franchise*, 25 July 1907.

2. *The Times*, 21 May 1908.

3. Ethel Smyth, *Female Pipings in Eden*, pp. 194–6; Grace Roe, interview with Brian Harrison, 4 October 1974.

4. Lady Ricardo, interview with Brian Harrison, 29 November 1974; Ethel Smyth, *Female Pipings in Eden*, p. 194; undated notes, Mary Phillips Papers.

5. Ethel Smyth, *Female Pipings in Eden*, pp. 195–6.

6. See *The Blaze of Day*, Pavilion Records CD; *The Century in Sound*, The British Library CD, 1999.

7. Undated notes, Mary Phillips Papers.

8. Lady Ricardo, interview with Brian Harrison, 29 November 1974; Mrs P. E. Hosgood to David Mitchell, July 1975, David Mitchell Papers.

9. *Daily Mail* report quoted in E. Sylvia Pankhurst, *The Suffragette*, pp. 214–15.

10. Ibid.

11. Grace Roe, interview with Brian Harrison, 23 September 1974.

12. Christabel Pankhurst, speech at St James's Hall, London, 15 October 1908.

13. E. Sylvia Pankhurst, *The Suffragette*, p. 237.

14. *Newcastle Evening Chronicle*, 8 September 1908.

15. Grace Roe, interview with Brian Harrison, 23 September 1974.

16. In *The Saturday Review*, quoted in Christopher St John, *Ethel Smyth*, p. 147.

17. See 'The Trial of the Suffragette Leaders', WSPU, 1908; press cuttings in David Mitchell Papers; E. Sylvia Pankhurst, *The Suffragette*.

18. As a young solicitor, David Lloyd George had made his name in the Llanfrothen Burial Case in 1888 by advising the family of a Nonconformist who had been banned from burial in an Anglican churchyard to break open the gates and go ahead.

19. Marie Lawson, interview with Brian Harrison, 20 November 1974; Emmeline Pethick-Lawrence, *My Part in a Changing World*, p. 205.

20. Emmeline Pankhurst to C. P. Scott, 7 January 1909, C. P. Scott Papers (*Manchester Guardian*), 128/121.

21. E. Sylvia Pankhurst, *The Suffragette Movement*, pp. 298–9.

22. E. Sylvia Pankhurst, *The Suffragette*, p. 357.

23. Lady Ricardo, interview with Brian Harrison, 29 November 1974.

24. Christabel Pankhurst, speech at the Queen's Hall, 31 December 1908.

25. Emmeline Pethick-Lawrence to Mary Phillips, 21 December 1908, Mary Phillips Papers; Mary Blathwayt Diaries, 21 December 1908.

26. *Votes for Women*, 28 January 1909.

27. Emmeline Pankhurst to Mary Phillips, 8 March 1909, Mary Phillips Papers.

28. Lady Constance Lytton to Mary Phillips, 3 July 1910, Mary Phillips Papers.

29. Emmeline Pankhurst to C. P. Scott, 7 January, 7 February and 12 February 1909, C. P. Scott Papers (*Manchester Guardian*), 128/66, 128/121, 122.

30. Emmeline Pankhurst to C. P. Scott, 8 March 1909 and 11 March 1909, C. P. Scott Papers (*Manchester Guardian*), 128/124, 125.

31. C. P. Scott to H. H. Asquith, 8 February 1909, and Herbert Gladstone to C. P. Scott, 9 February 1909, C. P. Scott Papers (*Manchester Guardian*), 128/67, 68.

32. Emmeline Pethick-Lawrence in *Votes for Women*, 25 June 1909.

33. Christabel Pankhurst to C. P. Scott, 21 May 1909, C. P. Scott Papers (*Manchester Guardian*), 128/80.

34. Emmeline Pethick-Lawrence to Mary Phillips, 16 September 1909, Mary Phillips Papers.

35. *Votes for Women*, 4 June 1909.

36. Emmeline Pethick-Lawrence to Mary Phillips, 21 September 1909, Mary Phillips Papers.

37. Sandra Stanley Holton, *Suffrage Days*, p. 146.

38. Katherine Marshall, 'Suffragette Escapes and Adventures', ms., 50.82/1132.

39. *Votes for Women*, 13 August 1909.

40. Christabel Pankhurst to C. P. Scott, 22 July 1909, C. P. Scott Papers (*Manchester Guardian*), 128/86.

41. C. P. Scott to Christabel Pankhurst (copy), 26 July 1909, C. P. Scott Papers (*Manchester Guardian*), 128/87.

42. Emmeline Pankhurst to C. P. Scott, 17 July and 21 July 1909, C. P. Scott Papers (*Manchester Guardian*), 128/130, 85.

43. C. P. Scott to H. H. Asquith (copy), 31 July 1909, C. P. Scott Papers (*Manchester Guardian*), 128/101.

44. 'Fed By Force: How the Government Treats Political Opponents', WSPU, not dated.

45. C. P. Scott to Christabel Pankhurst (draft), 31 October 1909; Christabel Pankhurst to C. P. Scott, 1 November 1909; C. P. Scott to H. H. Asquith (copy), 7 November 1909, C. P. Scott Papers (*Manchester Guardian*), 128/102, 103, 105.

46. R. J. Campbell to H. H. Asquith, 30 September 1909, Mary Phillips Papers.

47. Helen Fraser (Moyes), interview with Brian Harrison, 19 August 1975.

48. Verna Coleman, *Adela*, p. 47.

49. *Dundee Courier*, 18 October 1909.

50. *Dundee Advertiser*, 18 October 1909.

51. *Dundee Courier*, 18 October 1909.

52. *The Scotsman*, 20 October 1909.

53. Governor's Report, 20 October 1909, Scottish Prison Commission, HH/55/323.

54. Dated 21 October 1909, Scottish Prison Commission HH/16/619.

55. D. Crombie, 22 October 1909, Scottish Prison Commission HH/16/619.

56. D. Crombie to the Commissioners, 23 October 1909, Scottish Prison Commission HH/16/619.

57. Doctor Stalker's Report to the Governor, 22 October 1909, Scottish Prison Commission HH/16/619.

58. D. Crombie to the Commissioners, 23 October 1909, Scottish Prison Commission HH/16/619.

59. Telegram from the Under Secretary, 23 October 1909, Scottish Prison Commission HH/16/619.

60. *Dundee Advertiser*, 25 October 1909.

61. *Glasgow Herald*, 25 October 1909.

62. Christabel Pankhurst to Mrs Badley, 21 and 28 October 1909, Autograph Collection Vol. XX.

63. E. Sylvia Pankhurst, *The Suffragette Movement*, p. 320.

64. *New York Times*, 24 October 1909.

65. *New York Times*, 22 October 1909.

66. *New York Times*, 21 October 1909.

67. *New York Times*, 25 and 26 October 1909.

68. *New York Times*, 26 October 1909.

69. *New York Times*, 29 October 1909.

70. Christabel Pankhurst to C. P. Scott, 1 November 1909; C. P. Scott to H. H. Asquith (copy), 7 November 1909, C. P. Scott Papers (*Manchester Guardian*), 128/103, 105.

10 Hostilities are Suspended (1910–11)

1. Sally Walker, Helen Craggs ms, p. 22; E. Sylvia Pankhurst, *The Suffragette Movement*, p. 323.

2. *Votes for Women*, 7 January 1910.

3. E. Sylvia Pankhurst, *The Suffragette Movement*, p. 324.

4. Emmeline Pankhurst to Mary Phillips, 9 January 1910, Mary Phillips Papers.

5. Christabel Pankhurst to A. J. Balfour, 1 January 1910, A. J. Balfour Papers, Add. Mss. 49793.

6. Emmeline Pethick-Lawrence to Mary Phillips, 7 December 1909, Mary Phillips Papers.

7. *Votes for Women*, 14 January and 18 February 1910.

8. Christabel Pankhurst, *Unshackled*, pp. 153–4.

9. Mary Blathwayt Diaries, 19 March, 30 March and 7 May 1910.

10. Leslie Hilliard, 1 February 1976, in David Mitchell Papers, 82/719.

11. Mary Blathwayt Diaries, 12 February 1908.

12. Ibid, 5 July, 18 August and 7 September 1908.

13. Ibid, 1 and 3 July 1910.

14. James Taylor, interview with Brian Harrison, not dated.

15. Grace Roe, interview with Brian Harrison, 4 October 1974.

16. Olive Bartels, interview with Brian Harrison, 27 March 1976.

17. Grace Roe, interviews with Brian Harrison, 23 September and 4 October 1974.

18. Grace Roe, interview with Brian Harrison, 4 October 1974.

19. Christopher St John, *Ethel Smyth*, p. 9.

20. Ibid, p. 146.

21. Ethel Smyth to Emmeline Pankhurst, 16 December 1913 and 3 April 1914.

22. Ethel Smyth, *Female Pipings in Eden*, p. 192.

23. Ethel Smyth to Emmeline Pankhurst, 9 April 1914.

24. Christabel Pankhurst to C. P. Scott, an undated note and 6 June 1910, C. P. Scott Papers (*Manchester Guardian*), 128/171, 172; Christabel Pankhurst to A. J. Balfour, 12 June 1910, A. J. Balfour Papers, Add. Mss 49793.

25. Christabel Pankhurst to C. P. Scott, 8 June 1910, C. P. Scott Papers (*Manchester Guardian*), 128/173.

26. Christabel Pankhurst to A. J. Balfour, 14 June 1910, A. J. Balfour Papers, Add. Mss 49793.

27. C. P. Scott to H. H. Asquith (draft), 10 June 1910; C. P. Scott to Grey (draft), 10 June 1910, C. P. Scott Papers (*Manchester Guardian*), 128/174, 175.

28. Christabel Pankhurst to C. P. Scott, 14 July 1910, C. P. Scott Papers (*Manchester Guardian*), 128/190.

29. Emmeline Pankhurst to C. P. Scott, 16 August 1910, C. P. Scott Papers (*Manchester Guardian*), 128/195; *Votes for Women*, 19 August 1910.

30. Winston Churchill to Sir Edward Henry, 22 November 1910, Randolph Churchill, *Winston Churchill*, Vol. 2, Companion Vol. III, p. 1457.

31. *Votes for Women*, 25 November 1910.

32. Emmeline Pankhurst to C. P. Scott, 27 December 1910, C. P. Scott Papers (*Manchester Guardian*), 128/224.

33. Quoted in Patricia Romero, *E. Sylvia Pankhurst*, p. 57.

34. *New York Times*, 7 January 1911.

35. Undated notes, E. Sylvia Pankhurst Papers, 1/7–15.

36. Undated notes, E. Sylvia Pankhurst Papers, 2/29.

37. Ibid.

38. E. Sylvia Pankhurst to Keir Hardie, 26 February 1911; Keir Hardie to E. Sylvia Pankhurst, 10 March 1911, E. Sylvia Pankhurst Papers, 1/7–15.

39. Christopher St John, *Ethel Smyth*, pp. 151–2.

40. Ethel Smyth, *Female Pipings in Eden*, pp. 199–200.

41. Evelyn Sharp, *Hertha Ayrton*, pp. 232–3.

42. Emmeline Pankhurst to C. P. Scott, 9 January 1911, C. P. Scott Papers (*Manchester Guardian*), 332/3.

43. *Votes for Women*, 3 February 1911.

44. C. P. Scott to Emmeline Pankhurst (copy), 5 March 1911; Christabel Pankhurst to C. P. Scott, 6 March 1911, C. P. Scott Papers (*Manchester Guardian*), 332/14, 15.

45. Christabel Pankhurst to C. P. Scott, 8 March 1911, C. P. Scott Papers (*Manchester Guardian*), 332/18.

46. Editorial in *Votes for Women*, 3 February 1911; Mary Blathwayt Diaries, 2 March and 15 April 1910.

47. Adela Pankhurst, 'My Mother', Pankhurst-Walsh Papers, p. 36.

48. Verna Coleman, *Adela*, p. 48; E. Sylvia Pankhurst, *The Suffragette Movement*, p. 367.

49. Grace Roe, interview with Brian Harrison, 23 September 1974.

50. Martin Pugh, *The March of the Women*, pp. 183–7.

51. *Votes for Women*, 24 March, 31 March and 7 April 1911.

52. Henry Nevinson Diary, 2 June 1911, C 72/3.

53. *Daily Chronicle*, 16 June 1911.

54. *Votes for Women*, 14 July 1911.

55. *Votes for Women*, 29 September 1911.

56. Quoted in Antonia Raeburn, *The Militant Suffragettes*, pp. 94–5, 163.

57. *New York Times*, 18 October 1911.

58. *New York Times*, 12 October 1911.

59. *Victoria Times*, 21 December 1911.

60. *New York Times*, 29 November and 7 December 1911.

61. David Lloyd George to the Master of Elibank, 5 September 1911, Elibank Papers, 8803.

62. *Votes for Women*, 6 October 1911.

63. Henry Nevinson Diary, 8 November 1911, e. 73/1; *Votes for Women*, 10 November 1911.

64. H. M. Swanwick, *I Have Been Young*, p. 214.

65. WSPU circular, not dated, Arncliffe-Sennett Papers.

66. C. P. Scott Diary, 2 December 1911, in Trevor Wilson, ed., *The Political Diaries of C. P. Scott*, p. 58.

67. H. N. Brailsford to M. G. Fawcett, 22 January 1912, Millicent Garrett Fawcett Papers, M50.

11 Where is Christabel? (1912–13)

1. *Votes for Women*, 23 February 1912.
2. Emmeline Pethick-Lawrence, *My Part in a Changing World*, p. 278.
3. See PRO HO45/10678/219337.
4. Christabel Pankhurst in *The Suffragette*, 2 January 1914.
5. Ethel Smyth, *Female Pipings in Eden*, pp. 208–9.
6. Ibid, p. 209.
7. E. Katherine Marshall, 'Suffragette Escapes', pp. 82–3.
8. E. Sylvia Pankhurst, *The Suffragette Movement*, p. 374.
9. *Votes for Women*, 20 September 1912.
10. Annie Kenney, *Memories of a Militant*, p. 177.
11. Quoted in Patricia Romero, *E. Sylvia Pankhurst*, p. 62; E. Sylvia Pankhurst, *The Suffragette Movement*, p. 384.
12. Christabel Pankhurst, *Unshackled*, p. 76.
13. PRO FO372/405/1192, dated 20 March 1912.
14. PRO FO372/432/25380, dated 2 June 1913.
15. *The Suffragette*, 13 June 1913.
16. Elizabeth Crawfurd, *The Women's Suffrage Movement*, p. 36.
17. Mary Blathwayt Diaries, 22 March 1913.
18. E. Sylvia Pankhurst, *The Suffragette Movement*, pp. 383–4.
19. Ibid.
20. Christopher St John, *Ethel Smyth*, p. 155.
21. Ethel Smyth, *Female Pipings in Eden*, pp. 209–10; E. Sylvia Pankhurst, *The Suffragette Movement*, p. 376.
22. Adela Pankhurst, 'My Mother', Pankhurst-Walsh Papers, p. 39; E. Sylvia Pankhurst, *The Suffragette Movement*, p. 406.
23. E. Sylvia Pankhurst, *The Suffragette Movement*, p. 384.
24. Janie Sagar to Adela, 11 May 1915, Pankhurst-Walsh Papers, 20/61; E. Sylvia Pankhurst, *The Suffragette Movement*, p. 384.
25. *The Times*, 16 May 1912.
26. Speech in court, 21 May 1912.
27. Ibid.
28. See PRO HO45/24630/223849.
29. Ibid, 22 May 1912.
30. PRO PCOM 8/175.

31. Ibid, 23 May 1912.

32. PRO HO45/24630/223849, dated 17 June 1912; PCOM 8/175, dated 18 June 1912.

33. PRO PCOM 8/175, dated 21 June 1912.

34. Agnes Savill to R. McKenna, 21 June 1912, PRO HO45/24630/223849.

35. Agnes Savill to R. McKenna, 21 June 1912 and DMO report, 24 June 1912, PRO HO45/24630/223849.

36. Ibid, DMO report, 24 June 1912.

37. Evelyn Sharp, *Hertha Ayrton*, pp. 234–5.

38. Christabel Pankhurst to Mary Phillips, 17 November 1912, Mary Phillips Papers.

39. E. Sylvia Pankhurst, *The Suffragette Movement*, p. 396.

40. Ibid, pp. 396–8.

41. See the massive documentation in PRO TS27/19; and E. Sylvia Pankhurst, *The Suffragette Movement*, p. 415.

42. On 8 September 1912, quoted in June Balshaw, 'Sharing the Burden: the Pethick-Lawrences and Women's Suffrage', p. 147, in Angela V. John and Claire Eustance, eds., *The Men's Share*.

43. Emmeline Pethick-Lawrence, *My Part in a Changing World*, pp. 277–8.

44. *The Suffragette*, 18 October 1912.

45. Ibid.

46. *The Suffragette*, 15 and 22 November 1912.

47. Grace Roe, interview with Brian Harrison, 23 September 1974; Pugh, *The March of the Women*, pp. 244–5.

48. *The Suffragette*, 29 November 1912.

49. Marie Lawson, interview with Brian Harrison, 20 November 1974.

50. See PRO HO45/10695/231366.

51. *The Suffragette*, 6 and 12 December 1912.

52. E. Sylvia Pankhurst, *The Suffragette Movement*, pp. 401–2.

53. Christabel Pankhurst to Mrs Tuke, 19 December 1912, Henry Harben Papers, Add. Mss. 58226.

54. Emmeline Pankhurst to Henry Harben, 20 December 1912, Henry Harben Papers, Add. Mss 58226.

55. See Martin Pugh, *Electoral Reform in War and Peace 1906–1918*, pp. 41–2.

56. See the *Times* reports, 30 and 31 January 1913.

57. Dated 4 February 1913, PRO HO45/10695/231366.

58. Mary Blathwayt Diaries, 3 April 1913; *The Suffragette*, 21 February 1913; anonymous letter in David Lloyd George Papers, dated 12 November 1913, C/10/2/25.

59. *The Suffragette*, 28 February 1913.
60. Dated 27 February 1913, PRO PCOM 8/175.
61. Cover notes, PRO HO45/10695/231366.
62. H. H. Asquith to King George V, 22 January 1913.

12 Prisoner of War (1913–14)

1. *The Suffragette*, 11 April 1913.
2. Ethel Smyth, *Female Pipings in Eden*, p. 212.
3. Memoranda, 4 and 9 April 1913, PRO PCOM 8/175.
4. Reports in PRO PCOM 8/175.
5. Ethel Smyth, *Female Pipings in Eden*, p. 213.
6. Ibid, p. 214.
7. Evelyn Sharp, *Hertha Ayrton*, p. 239.
8. Report, 29 April 1913, PRO PCOM 8/175.
9. Ethel Smyth, *Female Pipings in Eden*, p. 214.
10. Ibid, p. 214.
11. Reports 26, 28, 29 and 30 May 1913, PRO PCOM 8/175.
12. Emmeline Pankhurst to Henry Harben, 2 June 1913, Henry Harben Papers, Add. Mss. 58226.
13. Olive Bartels, interview with Brian Harrison, 27 March 1976.
14. Though in 'The Price of Liberty', published in the *Daily Sketch*, 28 May 1914, she clearly contemplated sacrificing her life for the cause.
15. 'The Life of Emily Wilding Davison', *Clarion*, 20 June 1913.
16. Grace Roe, interview with Brian Harrison, 23 September 1974.
17. 'The Case of Mrs Pankhurst: A Victim of the Cat and Mouse Act', WSPU, not dated, 1913.
18. Report, 24 June 1913, PRO PCOM 8/175.
19. Reports 22 and 23 July 1913, PRP PCOM 8/175.
20. Notes, 6 May 1913, PRO HO144/1254/234646.
21. *Daily Sketch*, 22 August 1913.
22. Grace Roe, interview with Brian Harrison, 23 September 1974.
23. Ethel Smyth, *Female Pipings in Eden*, p. 219.
24. David Mitchell, *Queen Christabel*, p. 218.
25. Christabel Pankhurst to Mary Phillips, 9 July and 1 August 1913, Mary Phillips Papers.
26. Notes, 2 May 1913, PRO HO45/10700/236973.
27. PRO HO144/1318/252288.
28. PRO HO45/10725/252949 and TS27/51.

29. PRO HO144/1268/238215.

30. Marie Lawson, interview with Brian Harrison, 20 November 1974.

31. Notes, 8 and 13 May 1913, PRO TS/1/11541/9882.

32. E. Sylvia Pankhurst, *The Suffragette Movement*, p. 462.

33. *The Suffragette*, 18 April; 25 July; 15, 22 and 29 August; 5, 12, 19 and 26 September 1913.

34. *Clarion*, 26 September 1913.

35. 'The Appeal to God', *The Suffragette*, 8 August 1913.

36. Annie Barnes, interview with Brian Harrison, 27 November 1974.

37. J. E. Francis to E. Sylvia Pankhurst, 13 February 1914, E. Sylvia Pankhurst Papers, 26/225.

38. Barbara Winslow, *Sylvia Pankhurst*, pp. 56–7.

39. Letter (copy) to the editor of the *Daily Citizen*, 24 November 1913, E. Sylvia Pankhurst Papers, 23/180.

40. Barbara Winslow, *Sylvia Pankhurst*, p. 58.

41. Charles Duncan to E. Sylvia Pankhurst, 12 February 1914, E. Sylvia Pankhurst Papers, 26/225.

42. E. Sylvia Pankhurst to David Lloyd George (draft), 21 July 1913, E. Sylvia Pankhurst Papers, 26/227.

43. Christabel Pankhurst to Emmeline Pankhurst, 12 December 1913, Ethel Smyth Papers.

44. E. Sylvia Pankhurst to Henry Harben, 1 February and 20 March 1913, Henry Harben Papers, Add. Mss. 58226.

45. Christabel Pankhurst to Henry Harben, 7 August 1913, Henry Harben Papers, Add. Mss. 58226.

46. Henry Harben to Christabel Pankhurst (copy), 5 November 1913, Henry Harben Papers, B. M. Add. Mss. 58226.

47. Circular by E. Sylvia Pankhurst, 19 November 1913; Annie Kenney, 25 November 1913; Christabel Pankhurst to E. Sylvia Pankhurst, 27 November 1913, E. Sylvia Pankhurst Papers, 23/188, 189.

48. *New York Times*, 4 October 1913.

49. Ibid.

50. *New York Times*, 12 October 1913.

51. *New York Times*, 19 October 1913.

52. Ibid.

53. *New York Times*, 20 and 21 October 1913.

54. *New York Times*, 22 October 1913.

55. *New York Times*, 23, 24 and 25 October 1913.

56. *New York Times*, 26 October and 11 November 1913.

57. *New York Times*, 13, 16, 18, 25 and 26 November 1913.

58. *New York Times*, 27 November 1913.

59. *New York Times*, 5 December 1913; Emmeline Pankhurst to Flora Murray, 4 and 7 December 1913, PRO PCOM 8/175; Emmeline Pankhurst to Ethel Smyth, 10 December 1913, in Ethel Smyth, *Female Pipings in Eden*, p. 216.

60. *New York Times*, 10 December 1913.

61. Ibid.

62. Emmeline Pankhurst to Ethel Smyth, 19 December 1913, in Ethel Smyth, *Female Pipings in Eden*, p. 217.

63. Ethel Smyth, *Female Pipings in Eden*, p. 219.

64. Emmeline Pankhurst to E. Sylvia Pankhurst, 19 and 29 January 1914, E. Sylvia Pankhurst Papers, 26/227.

65. Ethel Smyth to Emmeline Pankhurst, 15 and 16 January 1914, Ethel Smyth Papers.

66. E. Sylvia Pankhurst, *The Suffragette Movement*, p. 518.

67. Ethel Smyth, *Female Pipings in Eden*, p. 221.

68. Mary Blathwayt Diaries, 4 April, 16 April and 3 May 1913; Adela Pankhurst, 'My Mother', Pankhurst-Walsh Papers, p. 40.

69. Verna Coleman, *Adela*, pp. 53–4.

70. Ethel Smyth, *Female Pipings in Eden*, p. 221; Adela Pankhurst, 'My Mother', Pankhurst-Walsh Papers, p. 42.

71. Verna Coleman, *Adela*, p. 55; E. Sylvia Pankhurst, *The Suffragette Movement*, p. 406.

72. Adela Pankhurst, 'My Mother', Pankhurst-Walsh Papers, p. 44; Janie Sagar to Adela Pankhurst, 11 May 1915, Pankhurst-Walsh Papers, 20/61.

73. Ethel Smyth to Emmeline Pankhurst, 6 May 1914, in David Mitchell, *Queen Christabel*, p. 196.

74. Beatrice Harraden to Christabel Pankhurst (copy), 13 January 1914, Janie Allan Papers, Acc. 4498.

75. Christabel Pankhurst to Beatrice Harraden, 16 January 1914, Janie Allan Papers, Acc. 4498.

76. Beatrice Harraden to Christabel Pankhurst (copy), not dated, Janie Allan Papers, Acc. 4498.

77. Henry Harben to Christabel Pankhurst (copy), February 1914, Henry Harben Papers, Add. Mss. 58226.

78. *The Suffragette*, 28 March and 18 April 1913.

79. See PRO HO144/1275/23958; 1274/239318; 1261/236533.

80. *The Suffragette*, 13 February 1914; E. Katherine Marshall, 'Suffragette Escapes', p. 74.

81. *The Suffragette*, 27 February 1914.

82. Ethel Smyth, *Female Pipings in Eden*, p. 226.

83. See memoranda, 11 and 26 March 1913, PRO HO144/1254/234646.

84. See papers and questionnaires in Janie Allan Papers, Acc. 4498.

85. Memorandum, 11 March 1913, PRO HO144/1254/234646.

86. PRO HO144/1264/237169.

87. *Manchester Guardian*, 13 June 1914.

88. David Lloyd George to Reginald McKenna (copy), 6 July 1914, David Lloyd George Papers, C/5/12/9.

89. Reports 12 and 13 March 1914, PRO PCOM 8/175.

90. Ethel Smyth, *Female Pipings in Eden*, p. 228.

91. I. A. R. Wylie, *My Life with George*, p. 180.

92. Reports, 9 and 10 July 1914, PRO PCOM 8/175.

93. *The Suffragette*, 24 July 1914.

13 God's Vengeance (1914–16)

1. Grace Roe, interview with Brian Harrison, 23 September 1974.

2. Elsie Bowerman, 11 October 1964, David Mitchell Papers 73–83/42.

3. *Hansard*, House of Commons Debates, 10 August 1914, c.2265; *Votes for Women*, 336, 14 August 1914.

4. *Common Cause*, 278, 7 August 1914.

5. *Votes for Women*, 7 August 1914.

6. *Western Daily Mercury*, 17 November 1914.

7. Grace Roe, interview with Brian Harrison, 23 September 1974.

8. *Weekly Dispatch*, 6 September 1914; *Star*, 4 September 1914.

9. *New York Times*, 6 September 1914.

10. *New York Times*, 25 September 1914.

11. *The Times*, 1 December 1914. Shaw had published a book entitled *Commonsense About the War*.

12. *The Suffragette*, 7 August 1914.

13. *Weekly Dispatch*, 6 September 1914.

14. *The Suffragette*, 10 September 1915; *Britannia*, 15, 22, 29 October and 12 November 1915; 7 January 1916.

15. *New York Times*, 15 October 1914; E. Blackwell to WSPU, 26 August 1914, Suffragette Fellowship Collection 60/15/1106.

16. *New York Times*, 12 January 1915.

17. *New York Times*, 25 October 1914.

18. Speech at the Carnegie Hall, 24 October 1914.

19. Speech in Washington, 24 January 1915.

20. 'International Militancy', speech at the Carnegie Hall, 13 January 1915.

21. *New York Times*, 15 January 1915.

22. E. Sylvia Pankhurst, *The Life of Emmeline Pankhurst*, p. 153.

23. E. Sylvia Pankhurst to Adela Pankhurst, 11 July 1918, Pankhurst-Walsh Papers, 20/61.

24. E. Sylvia Pankhurst, *The Home Front*, p. 124.

25. Ibid., pp. 143–6.

26. Ibid, 6/66.

27. Dated 27 May 1915, E. Sylvia Pankhurst Papers, 1/7–15.

28. *Woman's Dreadnought*, 2 October 1915.

29. *New York Times*, 25 April 1915.

30. Julia Bush, *Behind the Lines*, pp. 72–8.

31. Edgar Ross to David Mitchell, 4 August 1966, David Mitchell Papers.

32. Verna Coleman, *Adela*, p. 74.

33. Adela Pankhurst, 'My Mother', Pankhurst-Walsh Papers, p. 45.

34. See Martin Pugh, *Electoral Reform in War and Peace*, pp. 49–50 on party preparations for a wartime general election.

35. Christopher St John, *Ethel Smyth*, p. 221.

36. *Daily Sketch*, 23 March 1915; *New York Times*, 21 May 1915; *The Times*, 25 June 1915.

37. Grace Roe, interview with Brian Harrison, 23 September 1974.

38. Lord Stamfordham to David Lloyd George, 28 June 1915, David Lloyd George Papers, D/19/5/2.

39. Christabel Pankhurst, *Unshackled*, pp. 289–90.

40. PRO MUN5/70/324/26.

41. *The Suffragette*, 23 July 1915.

42. David Lloyd George to Albert Thomas, 28 July 1915, David Lloyd George Papers, D/19/6/5.

43. PRO MUN 5/70/324/1.

44. David Lloyd George to Geoffrey Robinson (copy), 4 and 13 August 1915, David Lloyd George Papers, D/18/1/22 and 25.

45. David Lloyd George Papers, D/18/1/21–25.

46. *Cambrian Daily Leader*, 21 October 1915; *South Wales Daily News*, 25 October 1915.

47. Emmeline Pankhurst to David Lloyd George, 14 October 1915, David Lloyd George Papers, D/11/2/24.

48. David Lloyd George to Emmeline Pankhurst (copy), 15 October 1915, David Lloyd George Papers, D/11/2/25.

49. *New York Times*, 4 May 1915.

50. Katherine Marshall, 'Suffragette Escapes', p. 95.

51. Ethel Smyth, *Female Pipings in Eden*, p. 238.

52. *New York Times*, 17 May 1915.

53. *Morning Advertiser*, 5 November 1915.

54. *New York Times*, 27 November 1915.

55. *Daily Sketch*, 27 January 1915.

56. Christabel Pankhurst to Andrew Bonar Law, 18 December 1915, Andrew Bonar Law Papers, 52/1/56.

57. Ibid.

58. *New York Times*, 16 January 1916.

59. *Victoria Colonist*, 7 and 8 June 1916.

60. Martin Pugh, *Electoral Reform*, pp. 49–51.

61. David Lloyd George to H. H. Asquith (copy), 17 June 1916, David Lloyd George Papers, D/18/2/18.

62. Arthur Steel-Maitland to Andrew Bonar Law, 13 June 1916, Andrew Bonar Law Papers, 64/G/8.

63. PRO CAB 37/147/31.

64. 13 December 1915, Labour Party Archives, WNC 29/5.

65. H. H. Asquith to Millicent Fawcett, 7 May 1916, Autograph Collection, Vol. XX.

66. Northcliffe to Millicent Fawcett, 25 December 1916; Northcliffe to Betty Balfour, 20 December 1916, Autograph Collection, Vol. XX.

67. *Hansard*, House of Commons Debates, 14 August 1916, c.1451–2; *Britannia*, 18 August 1916.

68. See Martin Pugh, *Electoral Reform*, pp. 70–75.

69. Letter from the Speaker to the Prime Minister, Cd. 8463(1917).

14 Revolution and Reaction (1917–18)

1. Emmeline Pankhurst to David Lloyd George, 10 December 1916, David Lloyd George Papers, F/94/1/27.

2. *Britannia*, 12 February 1917.

3. *Britannia*, 19 February 1917; 12 and 19 March 1917.

4. David Mitchell, *Queen Christabel*, p. 261.

5. Verna Coleman, *Adela*, p. 75.

6. Edgar Ross to David Mitchell, 4 August 1966, David Mitchell Papers.

7. Verna Coleman, *Adela*, p. 80.

8. Adela Pankhurst to E. Sylvia Pankhurst, 23 November 1917, E. Sylvia Pankhurst Papers, 1/7–15.

9. Adela Pankhurst to Tom Walsh, not dated, Pankhurst-Walsh Papers, 20/61.

10. Ibid.
11. Edgar Ross to David Mitchell, 4 August 1966, David Mitchell Papers.
12. Christabel Pankhurst, *Unshackled*, p. 293.
13. Martin Pugh, *Electoral Reform*, pp. 84–5.
14. *Britannia*, 9 April 1917.
15. *Britannia*, 2 April 1917.
16. Ethel Smyth, *Female Pipings in Eden*, p. 238.
17. *The Times*, 10 May 1917.
18. 'No Peace Without Victory', speech at the Queen's Hall, 23 June 1917.
19. Chris Wrigley, *Arthur Henderson*, pp. 112–14.
20. PRO CAB 144/23/2/187.
21. Jessie Kenney, 'The Price of Liberty', ms., 7/YYY5; *The Times*, 13 June 1917.
22. *Britannia*, 6 and 13 June 1917.
23. *Britannia*, 13 June 1917.
24. Jessie Kenney, 'Liberty'.
25. *New York Times*, 21 June 1917.
26. *Britannia*, 5 July 1918.
27. Jessie Kenney, 'Liberty'.
28. Jessie Kenney, 'Liberty', 8 September 1917.
29. Jessie Kenney, 'Liberty'.
30. Ethel Smyth, *Female Pipings in Eden*, p. 238.
31. Ibid, pp. 243–4.
32. Typescript by Christabel Pankhurst on Ethel Smyth's *Female Pipings in Eden*, p. 6, David Mitchell Papers, 82–719.
33. Ibid.
34. Jessie Kenney, 'Liberty'; *Britannia*, 16 November 1917.
35. *Workers' Dreadnought*, 28 July 1917.
36. Mary Davis, *E. Sylvia Pankhurst*, pp. 58–62.
37. *Workers' Dreadnought*, 17 November 1917 and 14 December 1918.
38. Grace Roe, interview with Brian Harrison, 23 September 1973.
39. Julie Gottlieb, *Feminine Fascism*, pp. 148–61, 164–7.
40. Ethel Smyth, *Female Pipings in Eden*, p. 245.
41. See press comment in *Britannia*, 2 November 1918.
42. *Britannia*, 5 April 1918.
43. *Britannia*, 21 June 1918.
44. *Britannia*, 28 June 1918.
45. *Britannia*, 27 July 1918.
46. *Britannia*, 19 July 1918.
47. *Hansard*, House of Commons Debates, 23 October 1918, c.813–22.

48. Christabel Pankhurst to David Lloyd George, 21 November 1918, David Lloyd George Papers, D/30/2/55A; *Britannia*, 20 November 1918; *The Times*, 20 November 1918.

49. Christabel Pankhurst to David Lloyd George, 21 November 1918, David Lloyd George Papers, D/30/2/55A.

50. Lord Northcliffe to William Sutherland, 31 October 1918, David Lloyd George Papers, F/41/8/23.

51. David Lloyd George to Andrew Bonar Law (copy), 21 November 1918, David Lloyd George Papers, F/30/2/55.

52. Andrew Bonar Law to Christabel Pankhurst (copy), 23 November 1918, David Lloyd George Papers, F/30/2/55B.

53. Mrs P. G. Hosgood to David Mitchell, July 1975, David Mitchell Papers.

54. *The Times*, 28 November 1918.

55. Ibid.

56. Elsie Bowerman, 11 October 1964, David Mitchell Papers, 73–83-42.

57. *Smethwick Telephone*, 14 December 1918.

58. *Britannia*, 6 December 1918.

59. General Secretary to Annie Kenney (copy), 29 November 1918, Patrick Hannon Papers, Box 11/5.

60. *Smethwick Telephone*, 7 December 1918.

15 Available for Work (1919–21)

1. Annie Kenney to Sir Vincent Caillard, 27 January 1919, Patrick Hannon Papers, Box 11/5.

2. Sir Vincent Caillard to Patrick Hannon, 11 February 1919, Patrick Hannon Papers, Box 11/5.

3. C. Wilbraham Ford to E. Manville, 18 March 1919, Patrick Hannon Papers, Box 11/5.

4. Christabel Pankhurst to David Lloyd George, 5 April 1919, David Lloyd George Papers, F/95/1/19.

5. Patrick Hannon to E. Manville, 21 March 1919, Patrick Hannon Papers, Box 11/5.

6. Undated memorandum, 'Women's Party', Patrick Hannon Papers, Box 11/5.

7. Patrick Hannon to E. Manville, 21 March 1919, Patrick Hannon Papers, Box 11/5.

8. Memorandum, 23 January 1919, 'Relations with the Women's Party', Patrick Hannon Papers, Box 11/5.

9. Patrick Hannon to E. Manville, 21 March 1919, Patrick Hannon Papers, Box 11/5.

10. Ibid.

11. David Mitchell, *Queen Christabel*, p. 278.

12. Ibid.

13. Ethel Smyth, *Female Pipings in Eden*, p. 250.

14. Christabel Pankhurst, *The Lord Cometh*, p. 6.

15. *The Globe*, April 1921; *Toronto Star Weekly*, 16 October 1926.

16. Ethel Smyth, *Female Pipings in Eden*, p. 248.

17. Article on Mary Gordon by David Mitchell in *The Times*, 25 July 1975.

18. Ibid.

19. Miss Eveline Bennett to the author, 13 April 2000.

20. Ibid.

21. Ibid.

22. Ethel Smyth, *Female Pipings in Eden*, p. 252.

23. David Mitchell, *Queen Christabel*, pp. 280–81.

24. Dr G. Bates to Emmeline Pankhurst (copy), 10 October 1921, David Mitchell Papers.

25. PRO CAB24/71/6425; *Workers' Dreadnought*, 15 September 1923.

26. Patricia Romero, *E. Sylvia Pankhurst*, p. 135.

27. 'Report on Revolutionary Organizations in the United Kingdom', 28 May 1919, PRO CAB24/24/80/7367; *Workers' Dreadnought*, 19 June 1920.

28. Report, 30 April 1919, PRO CAB24/78/7128.

29. *Workers' Dreadnought*, 10 May 1919.

30. Report, 4 June 1919, PRO CAB24/81/7417.

31. *Workers' Dreadnought*, 6 March 1920.

32. Notes in E. Sylvia Pankhurst Papers, 10/88, confirm that she received Rothstein's money.

33. Report, 26 June 1919, PRO CAB24/82/7566.

34. E. Sylvia Pankhurst, *The Communist International*, p. 51.

35. *Workers' Dreadnought*, 3 July 1920.

36. *Workers' Dreadnought*, 31 July 1920.

37. *Official Report*, Unity Convention, 8 July 1920, Appendix B.

38. *Official Report*, Unity Convention, 8 July 1920, p. 33.

39. Report, 5 August 1920, PRO CAB24/110/1743.

40. Report, 15 July 1920, PRO CAB24/109/1634.

41. Notes in E. Sylvia Pankhurst Papers, 10/88.

42. E. Sylvia Pankhurst, *Soviet Russia As I Saw It*, p. 7; Notes, E. Sylvia Pankhurst Papers, 10/88.

43. E. Sylvia Pankhurst, *Soviet Russia As I Saw It*, pp. 45–8.

44. Report, 11 November 1920, PRP CAB24/114/2089.
45. E. Sylvia Pankhurst, *Soviet Russia As I Saw It*, pp. 126–8.
46. Report, 30 September 1920, PRO CAB24/112/1908.
47. PRO CAB24/111/1885 and CAB24/112/1908.
48. Report, 25 November 1920, PRO CAB24/115/2169.
49. PRO CAB24/112/1908.
50. *The Times*, 27 October 1920.
51. Ibid.
52. *Workers' Dreadnought*, 6 November 1920.
53. PRO CAB24/207/2316.
54. *The Times*, 31 May 1921.
55. *Workers' Dreadnought*, 17 September 1921.
56. Ibid.
57. Report, 22 September 1921, PRO CAB24/128/3333.
58. G. B. Shaw to Silvio Corio, 14 September 1921; Patricia Romero, *E. Sylvia Pankhurst*, p. 154.
59. Norman Jeffrey to David Mitchell, not dated, David Mitchell Papers, 73:83, 27.
60. Verna Coleman, *Adela*, p. 87.
61. *Workers' Dreadnought*, 26 February 1921.
62. Norman Jeffreys to David Mitchell, 25 November 1965, David Mitchell Papers, 73:83, 27.
63. *New York Times*, 14 September 1919.
64. *New York Times*, 8 October 1919.
65. *Toronto Globe and Mail*, 6 October 1919; *New York Times*, 5 October 1919.
66. Ethel Smyth, *Female Pipings in Eden*, p. 25.
67. *Victoria Times*, 28 November 1919.
68. Miss Eveline Bennett to the author, 13 April 2000.
69. Ibid.
70. Ethel Smyth, *Female Pipings in Eden*, p. 252; *Victoria Colonist*, 19 August 1920.
71. *New York Times*, 29 December 1920.
72. Ethel Smyth, *Female Pipings in Eden*, p. 253.
73. Ibid, p. 266.
74. Emmeline Pethick-Lawrence to E. Sylvia Pankhurst, 17 December 1929, E. Sylvia Pankhurst Papers, 1/7–15.
75. Ethel Smyth, *Female Pipings in Eden*, p. 245.
76. Ibid, p. 266.
77. Ibid, p. 253.

78. *Daily Express*, 20 January 1921.

79. *Weekly Dispatch*, 3, 10, 17, 24 and 29 April 1921.

80. Ibid, 10 April 1921.

81. Emmeline Pankhurst to Gordon Bates (copy), 25 March 1921, David Mitchell Papers, 73:83, 37.

82. Gordon Bates to Catherine Pine (copy), 24 March 1921, David Mitchell Papers, 73:83, 38.

83. Emmeline Pankhurst to Dr Bates, 14 August 1921, David Mitchell Papers, 73:83, 38.

84. Gordon Bates to David Mitchell, 29 April 1965, David Mitchell Papers, 73:83, 37.

85. Report of the provincial Board of Health, 1922, p. 104.

16 The Second Coming (1922–5)

1. Christabel Pankhurst, *The Lord Cometh*, p. 11; Grace Roe, interview with Brian Harrison, 23 September 1974.

2. Charotte Despard, *Theosophy and the Woman's Movement*.

3. Grace Roe, interview with Brian Harrison, 23 September 1974.

4. *Weekly Dispatch*, 3 April 1921.

5. Christabel Pankhurst, *The Lord Cometh*, p. 90, and *Pressing Problems of a Closing Age*, pp. 73–6.

6. Christabel Pankhurst, *Pressing Problems of a Closing Age*, pp. 100–103.

7. Ibid, pp. 14–17.

8. Ibid, pp. 29–30.

9. Christabel Pankhurst, *The Lord Cometh*, pp. 6–8, and *Pressing Problems of a Closing Age*, pp. 38–41.

10. *Church of Ireland Gazette*, 5 November 1926.

11. Miss Eveline Bennett to the author, 13 April 2000.

12. *New York Times*, 22 April 1922.

13. *New York Times*, 19 August 1923.

14. *New York Times*, 16 August 1923.

15. Ibid.

16. *New York Times*, 3 December 1923.

17. Miss Eveline Bennett to the author, 13 April 2000.

18. Ibid.

19. Ibid.

20. Ethel Smyth, *Female Pipings in Eden*, p. 257.

21. Miss Eveline Bennett to the author, 13 April 2000.

22. Francesca Bernadini to Silvio Corio, 26 August 1925, E. Sylvia Pankhurst Papers, 32/315.

23. Roxanne Corio to E. Sylvia Pankhurst, undated, E. Sylvia Pankhurst Papers, 32/315.

24. E. Sylvia Pankhurst to G. Lansbury, 28 November 1923, Suffragette Fellowship Collection, 50.82/1118.

25. Annie Barnes, interview with Brian Harrison, 18 December 1974.

26. Ibid.

27. Notes by E. Sylvia Pankhurst, not dated, E. Sylvia Pankhurst Papers 1/16–21.

28. Annie Barnes, interviews with Brian Harrison, 27 November and 18 December 1974.

29. Annie Barnes, interview with Brian Harrison, 18 December 1974.

30. Ibid.

31. Ursula Young to David Mitchell, 12 April 1966, David Mitchell Papers, 73:83, 28.

32. Ibid.

33. Verna Coleman, *Adela*, p. 94.

34. Notes, Pankhurst-Walsh Papers, 26/83.

35. Ibid.

36. *The Times*, 25 July 1975.

37. *New York Times*, 19 April 1925; Terry Tucker to David Mitchell, 10 February 1965, David Mitchell Papers, 78:83, 38.

38. Christabel Pankhurst to David Lloyd George, 8 December 1924, David Lloyd George Papers, G/30/3/45.

39. Christabel Pankhurst to the Baronne de Brimont, 26 August 1925, David Mitchell Papers, under file 'Christabel in Paris'.

40. Christabel Pankhurst to the Baronne de Brimont, 4 August 1925 and 8 September 1925, David Mitchell Papers, under file 'Christabel in Paris'.

41. *Sunday Express*, 24 January 1926.

42. Ethel Smyth, *Female Pipings in Eden*, p. 266.

43. Ibid, p. 260.

17 Unmarried Mother (1926–8)

1. *New York Times*, 29 January 1926.

2. Christabel Pankhurst, *The World's Unrest*, pp. 17–21.

3. Ibid, pp. 26, 42–3.

4. Ibid, pp. 42–3.

5. Notes, E. Sylvia Pankhurst Papers, 10/89 and 29/277.

6. *New York Times*, 5 March 1926.

7. *Toronto Daily Star*, 4 March 1926.

8. E. Sylvia Pankhurst, *The Life of Emmeline Pankhurst*, p. 172; Richard Pankhurst, *E. Sylvia Pankhurst*, p. 191.

9. *New York Herald Tribune*, 3 June 1926.

10. *New York Herald Tribune*, 11 May 1926.

11. *New York Times*, 24 May 1926.

12. Dorothy Spencer to David Mitchell, 4 January 1965, David Mitchell Papers, 78:83, 36.

13. Interview with Commander Venn, 13 July 1965, David Mitchell Papers, 78:83, 36.

14. Mrs N. Hall-Humpherson to David Mitchell, 12 June 1964, David Mitchell Papers, 78:83, 36.

15. Ibid.

16. *East London Observer*, 5 March, 8 and 29 October 1927.

17. Mrs N. Hall-Humpherson to David Mitchell, 12 June 1964, David Mitchell Papers, 78:83, 36.

18. Ibid.

19. Annie Barnes, interview with Brian Harrison, 27 November 1974.

20. Annie Barnes, interviews with Brian Harrison, 27 November 1974 and 18 December 1974.

21. *The Times*, 25 July 1975.

22. *News of the World*, 8 April 1928.

23. *New York Times*, 6 April 1928.

24. Ethel Smyth, *Female Pipings in Eden*, p. 269.

25. Mrs N. Hall-Humpherson to David Mitchell, 12 June 1964, David Mitchell Papers, 78:83, 36.

26. *Daily Mail*, 15 June 1928.

27. *New York Times*, 15 June 1928.

28. Emmeline Pethick-Lawrence to E. Sylvia Pankhurst, 17 December 1929, E. Sylvia Pankhurst Papers, 1/16–21.

29. *Daily Herald*, 5 June 1930.

30. *Manchester Guardian*, 19 June 1928; *New York Times*, 19 June 1928.

31. *The Times*, 25 July 1975.

32. *The Times*, 31 July 1928.

33. David Mitchell, *The Fighting Pankhursts*, p. 236.

34. *New York Times*, 8 March 1930.

35. Christopher St. John, *Ethel Smyth*, p. 277.

36. Ethel Smyth, *Female Pipings in Eden*, pp. 272–3; E. Katherine Marshall, 'Suffragette Escapes', p. 100.

37. E. Katherine Marshall, 'Suffragette Escapes', p. 102.

38. Ethel Smyth, *Female Pipings in Eden*, p. 273.

18 Passing into History (1929–34)

1. Annie Barnes, interview with Brian Harrison, 18 February 1974.

2. See Introduction to the 1977 Virago reprint of *The Suffragette Movement*.

3. E. Sylvia Pankhurst to N. E. Walshe, not dated, Autograph Collection, Vol. XX.

4. Ibid.

5. Richard Pankhurst to David Mitchell, 31 March 1965, David Mitchell Papers, 73:83/11.

6. Yevonde Middleton to David Mitchell, not dated, David Mitchell Papers, 73:83/17.

7. Mrs Walshe to David Mitchell, 3 December 1964; Vera Klein, conversation with David Mitchell, 23 August 1965, David Mitchell Papers, 73:83/21.

8. Mrs Walshe to David Mitchell, 2 and 6 November 1964, David Mitchell Papers, 73:83/21.

9. F. Beaufort Palmer, interview 20 August 1965, David Mitchell Papers, 73:83/17.

10. Mrs Walshe to David Mitchell, 19 July 1965, David Mitchell Papers, 73:83/21.

11. Yevonde Middleton to David Mitchell, not dated, David Mitchell Papers, 73:83/17.

12. David Mitchell, *The Fighting Pankhursts*, pp. 243–4.

13. Ibid, p. 241.

14. *News of the World*, 8 April 1928.

15. Annie Barnes, interview with Brian Harrison, 27 November 1974.

16. Stephen Wright to David Mitchell, 24 December 1965, David Mitchell Papers, 73:83/17.

17. E. Sylvia Pankhurst, 'Women's Citizenship', E. Sylvia Pankhurst Papers, 18/131.

18. *New York Times*, 9 December 1929.

19. Christabel Pankhurst to the Baronne de Brimont, 9 December 1929, David Mitchell Papers, under 'Christabel in Paris' file.

20. David Mitchell, *The Fighting Pankhursts*, p. 309.

21. Ibid, p. 310.

22. Christabel Pankhurst to Edith How Martyn, 19 July 1930, Suffragette Fellowship Collection, 60/15/3.
23. *New York Times*, 16 and 20 April, 1931.
24. David Mitchell, *Queen Christabel*, p. 299.
25. *New York Times*, 11 April 1933.
26. Notes by Herbert van Thal, David Mitchell Papers, 73:83/34.
27. Adela Pankhurst, 'My Mother', 25 January 1933, Pankhurst-Walsh Papers, 16/50.
28. Adela Pankhurst, 'The Philosophy of the Suffragette Movement', p. 5, Pankhurst-Walsh Papers, 22/66.
29. Ibid., p. 25.
30. Havelock Wilson to Tom Walsh, 18 August 1928 and 7 March 1929, Pankhurst-Walsh Papers, 21/64.
31. Verna Coleman, *Adela*, pp. 108, 113.
32. Pankhurst-Walsh Papers, 9/30.
33. 'The Women's Guild of Empire', Pankhurst-Walsh Papers, 9/31.
34. Verna Coleman, *Adela*, p. 118.
35. Notes, E. Sylvia Pankhurst Papers, 10/87.
36. Notes, E. Sylvia Pankhurst Papers, 1/1–6.
37. Annie Barnes, interview with Brian Harrison, 27 November 1974.
38. *New York Times*, 24 August 1932.

19 Fascism and Anti-Fascism (1935–9)

1. Benito Mussolini to Marshall Badoglio, 30 December 1934.
2. Pierre Laval to Benito Mussolini, 22 December 1935, and Benito Mussolini to Pierre Laval, 25 December 1935.
3. Sir Samuel Hoare to Sir George Clark, 24 August 1935.
4. Sir E. Chatfield to Sir Robert Vansittart, 8 August 1935.
5. Notes for a meeting about dictatorships, E. Sylvia Pankhurst Papers, 29/270.
6. *New Times and Ethiopia News*, 1 August 1936.
7. E. Sylvia Pankhurst to the *Manchester Guardian*, 31 August 1936, E. Sylvia Pankhurst Papers, 28/267.
8. See Martin Pugh, *The March of the Women*, pp. 53–4.
9. *Workers' Dreadnought*, 21 January 1920.
10. *Workers' Dreadnought*, 24 April 1920.
11. Mary Davis, *E. Sylvia Pankhurst*, p. 105.
12. H. D. Molesworth, interview, 3 February 1965; John H. Lodge to David Mitchell, 26 September 1965, David Mitchell Papers, 73.83/17.

13. E. Sylvia Pankhurst to Teresa Billington-Greig, 5 June 1956, David Mitchell Papers, 78.83/21.

14. *New Times and Ethiopia News*, 9 May 1936.

15. *New Times and Ethiopia News*, 16 May and 13 June 1936.

16. E. Sylvia Pankhurst to the *Manchester Guardian* (copy), 31 August 1936, E. Sylvia Pankhurst Papers, 28/267.

17. *New Times and Ethiopia News*, 13 June 1936.

18. Patricia Romero, *E. Sylvia Pankhurst*, p. 226.

19. *New Times and Ethiopia News*, 16 May 1936 and 18 July 1936.

20. David A. Thomas, *Churchill: The Member for Woodford*, pp. 82–3.

21. Christabel Pankhurst to Mrs Sadd Brown, 22 January 1936, Autograph Collection, Vol. XX.

22. *New York Times*, 1 January 1936.

23. David Mitchell, *Queen Christabel*, pp. 303–4.

24. *Woman*, 5 June 1937.

25. Brian Harrison, *Prudent Revolutionaries*, p. 197.

26. *New Times and Ethiopia News*, 21 January 1939.

27. *New Times and Ethiopia News*, 7 and 14 January 1939.

28. *New Times and Ethiopia News*, 11 February 1939.

29. *New Times and Ethiopia News*, 18 March 1939, 15 April 1939.

30. Adela Pankhurst, 'Collective Responsibility', 10 March 1936, Pankhurst-Walsh Papers, 9/30; Verna Coleman, *Adela*, p. 137.

31. Adela Pankhurst, 'Are Empires Wrong?', 18 October 1937, Pankhurst-Walsh Papers, 13/41.

32. Adela Pankhurst, 'The British Empire and the League of Nations', 27 June 1937, Pankhurst-Walsh Papers, 9/32.

33. Tom and Adela Pankhurst to the *Sydney Morning Herald*, 1 September 1938, Pankhurst-Walsh Papers, 9/33.

34. Adela Pankhurst to *The Times*, 30 August 1937, and 'Australia's Future', 4 July 1937, Pankhurst-Walsh Papers, 13/41.

35. Tom Walsh to the *Sydney Morning Herald*, 5 October 1936, Pankhurst-Walsh Papers, 9/30.

36. Verna Coleman, *Adela*, p. 144.

37. Mrs M. Jessop to David Mitchell, 13 October 1964, David Mitchell Papers, 73.83/29.

38. Adela Pankhurst, 'The Munich Agreement', 23 October 1938, Pankhurst-Walsh Papers, 13/42.

39. Adela Pankhurst to the Guild of Women, 7 August 1939, Pankhurst-Walsh Papers, 13/41.

20 For War and Peace (1939–45)

1. *New Times and Ethiopia News*, 30 September 1939.
2. Ibid.
3. E. Sylvia Pankhurst, draft letter, 11 December 1940, E. Sylvia Pankhurst Papers, 28/277.
4. Minutes, Women's War Emergency Committee, 5 October 1939, E. Sylvia Pankhurst Papers, 30/294; *New Times and Ethiopia News*, 14 October 1939 and 20 January 1940.
5. Sylvia to Paolo Treves, 12 October 1940, E. Sylvia Pankhurst Papers, 30/296.
6. *New Times and Ethiopia News*, 27 January and 23 March 1940.
7. Christopher Sykes, *Orde Wingate* (1959), pp. 350–51; Patricia Romero, *E. Sylvia Pankhurst*, p. 231.
8. *New Times and Ethiopia News*, 15 June 1940.
9. E. Sylvia Pankhurst to Winston Churchill (copy), 25 June and 12 July 1940, E. Sylvia Pankhurst Papers, 28/277.
10. *New Times and Ethiopia News*, 24 August 1940.
11. David Mitchell, *The Fighting Pankhursts*, pp. 285–6.
12. Christabel Pankhurst, *The Uncurtained Future*, p. 104.
13. Grace Roe, interview with Brian Harrison, 23 September 1974.
14. Ibid.
15. Marjory Greenlie to David Mitchell, 19 March 1965, David Mitchell Papers, 73.83/30.
16. Jay Trevor Weiss to David Mitchell, 21 August 1965; Douglas Field to David Mitchell, 21 July 1965, David Mitchell Papers, 73.83/30.
17. Jaime Palmer to David Mitchell, 8 July 1965, David Mitchell Papers, 73.83/30.
18. Jay Trevor Weiss to David Mitchell, 21 August 1965; Jaime Palmer to David Mitchell, 8 July 1965; Douglas Field to David Mitchell, 21 July 1965, David Mitchell Papers, 73.83/30.
19. Jaime Palmer to David Mitchell, 8 July 1965, David Mitchell Papers, 73.83/30.
20. Annie Kenney to Christabel Pankhurst, not dated, David Mitchell Papers, 73.83/33.
21. *New Times and Ethiopia News*, 26 July 1941.
22. H. D. Molesworth, interview, not dated, 1966, David Mitchell Papers, 73.83/17; *New Times and Ethiopia News*, 25 March 1944.
23. *New Times and Ethiopia News*, 27 September 1941.

24. *The Times*, 14 March 1942; E. Sylvia Pankhurst to Winston Churchill, 3 December 1941, E. Sylvia Pankhurst Papers, 29/277.

25. *New Times and Ethiopia News*, 7 February 1942.

26. Mrs G. M. Christie to David Mitchell, 22 June 1964, David Mitchell Papers, 73.83/28.

27. See press cuttings from *Sydney Morning Herald*, 7 December 1939, David Mitchell Papers, 73.83/28.

28. 'My Impressions of Japan', Pankhurst-Walsh Papers, 9/32; 'What We Should Know About the Orient', 'Observations on Japan as Viewed by Foreigners', 'Conditions in Japan', David Mitchell Papers, 72.83/22.

29. Pankhurst-Walsh Papers, 24/72.

30. Ursula Young to David Mitchell, 12 April 1966, David Mitchell Papers, 73.83/28.

31. Sue Hogan, interview with Brian Harrison.

32. *New Times and Ethiopia News*, 25 March 1944.

33. Patricia Romero, *E. Sylvia Pankhurst*, p. 237.

34. H. D. Molesworth, interview, 3 February 1965, David Mitchell Papers, 73.83/17.

35. Ibid.

36. Patricia Romero, *E. Sylvia Pankhurst*, p. 247.

21 Corners of a Foreign Field (1945–61)

1. *Evening Standard* cutting in David Mitchell Papers, 78.83/21.

2. Vera Klein, interview, 23 August 1965, David Mitchell Papers, 78.83/21.

3. David Mitchell, *The Fighting Pankhursts*, pp. 310–11.

4. *Evening Standard*, cutting in David Mitchell Papers, 78.83/21.

5. Ibid.

6. Ibid.

7. Patricia Romero, *E. Sylvia Pankhurst*, pp. 261–2, based on an interview with Mrs Tims; this is disputed by Rita Pankhurst in 'Sylvia Pankhurst in Perspective', *Women's Studies International Forum*, 11, 3, 1988, p. 258, in which she admits to 'some modest contributions towards the printing of some of Sylvia's publications', but offers little explanation for her income in this period.

8. *New Times and Ethiopia News*, 23 January 1954; *Daily Mail*, 29 September 1960.

9. Olive Bartels, interview with Brian Harrison, 27 March 1976.

10. Jay Trevor Weiss to David Mitchell, 30 May 1965, David Mitchell Papers, 73.83/30.

11. Ibid., 21 August 1965, David Mitchell Papers, 73.83/30.

12. Doris Székely to David Mitchell, 5 October 1964, David Mitchell Papers, 73.83/32.

13. Ibid; Douglas Field to David Mitchell, 6 October 1964, David Mitchell Papers, 73.83/32.

14. Grace Roe, interview with Brian Harrison, 4 October 1974.

15. Christabel Pankhurst to Teresa Billington-Greig, 13 November 1956, David Mitchell Papers, 73.83/30.

16. Christabel Pankhurst, 1 November 1957, David Mitchell Papers, 82/719.

17. Christabel Pankhurst to H. Van Thal, 5 November 1957, David Mitchell Papers, 82/719.

18. *New York Times*, 15 February 1958; *Santa Monica Outlook*, 14 February 1958.

19. Speech, 14 March 1958, Mary Phillips Papers.

20. Sally Walker, Helen Craggs ms, pp. 70–71.

21. Helen Fraser (Moyes), interview with Brian Harrison, 19 August 1975.

22. Sue Hogan, interview with Brian Harrison.

23. Ibid.

24. Ibid.

25. Lord Amulree notes, 27 January 1975, David Mitchell Papers, 73.83/17.

26. *Evening Standard* cutting, David Mitchell Papers, 78.83/21.

27. Richard Pankhurst, *E. Sylvia Pankhurst*, p. 218.

28. Yevonde Middleton to David Mitchell, not dated, David Mitchell Papers, 73.83/17.

29. Rita Pankhurst, interview with Brian Harrison, 1975.

30. Ibid.

31. Ibid.

32. *Ethiopian Observer*, Vol. V, No. 1.

33. Rita Pankhurst, interview with Brian Harrison, 1975.

34. *The Times*, 27 October 1960.

35. E. Sylvia Pankhurst to Teresa Billington-Greig, 5 June 1956, David Mitchell Papers, 78.83/21.

36. Dated 20 January 1961, E. Sylvia Pankhurst Papers, 32/325.

37. Dated 28 September 1960, E. Sylvia Pankhurst Papers, 32/325.

Index

Pankhurst, Emmeline – *cont.*
dispute with father 12–13, 30;
disapproves of schools 10, 34,
59–60; unable to handle death
47, 80, 205–6; early political
influences 9–10; and feminism
8–9, 13, 107–8, 355–7, 424–5;
and marriage 12–13, 15, 22,
24; influenced by France 8,
10–15, 303; and sex 25, 135,
375–6; marries Richard 22–3,
24; as mother 25–6, 32–3,
58–9, 357; married life 24–5,
33, 424; political
apprenticeship 40–41, 44, 49;
attacks judge 43; opens shops
44–5, 48–51, 82; becomes
political hostess 45, 48–51;
becomes a Socialist 50, 56,
61–2; as a constitutional
suffragist 52, 100, 103,
110–11, 123–4; loses
confidence in constitutional
suffragism 28, 55; views on
married women's vote 52,
53–4, 55; criticizes Liberals 55,
61; defers to Christabel 60,
155–6, 281, 346; returns to
Manchester politics 60–61, 63,
70, 75; works in ILP 61, 63, 64,
75, 186–7, 98, 100, 103,
110–11, 165; disillusioned with
Labour 102, 106, 123;
candidate for school board
64–5, 86; elected a Poor Law
Guardian 65–70; promotes
Richard's career 40–44, 48–51,
70; in Boggart Hole Clough
72–5; as a speaker 73, 176–7,
229, 283; suffers financial

problems 44–5, 81–2, 201,
317–19, 372–3; seeks home life
81, 374; in Boer War 85;
resents Chirstabel's friendships
93; visits Venice 96; dispute
with Glasier 100–102;
employed as Registrar 82, 134,
153; founds WSPU 105–8; and
militancy 124–5, 129–30,
253–4; suffers from loneliness
156, 214, 401–2; campaigns in
by-elections 156, 157, 159,
162, 170–71, 181, 187; sees
WSPU as army 166, 258; courts
arrest 172–3, 185–6, 234; tried
for rushing House of Commons
181–5; attacks C. P. Scott
193–4, 217, 220, 224; tours
United States (1909) 200–204;
(1911) 228–9; (1913) 280–84;
(1916) 320–21; (1918) 344;
(1919) 358, 371; suspends
militancy 207; friendship with
Ethel Smyth 213–15; and
martyrdom 220, 261; practises
stone-throwing 235–6; in
Holloway 242, 246–8, 259,
262–3, 264, 266–7, 285, 296,
297; tried for conspiracy
243–6; dispute with the
Pethick-Lawrences 248, 249,
251–3; endorses attacks on
property 256, 258, 259; tried at
the Old Bailey 260–62, 272–3;
sustains hunger strikes 262–3,
264, 267, 284–5, 297;
contemplates death 265–6;
detained at Ellis Island 281–2;
arrested at Devonport 284;
expels Sylvia 286–7; expels

www.vintage-books.co.uk